A History of the Later Roman Empire, AD 284–641

Blackwell History of the Ancient World

This series provides a new narrative history of the ancient world, from the beginnings of civilization in the ancient Near East and Egypt to the fall of Constantinople. Written by experts in their fields, the books in the series offer authoritative, accessible surveys for students and general readers alike.

Published

A History of the Ancient Near East, second edition
Marc Van De Mieroop

A History of the Archaic Greek World
Jonathan M. Hall

A History of the Classical Greek World
P. J. Rhodes

A History of the Later Roman Empire, AD 284–641
Stephen Mitchell

A History of Byzantium
Timothy E. Gregory

In Preparation

A History of the Persian Empire
Christopher Tuplin

A History of the Hellenistic World
Malcolm Errington

A History of the Roman Republic
John Rich

A History of the Roman Empire
Michael Peachin

A History of the Later Roman Empire

AD 284–641

The Transformation of the Ancient World

Stephen Mitchell

Blackwell
Publishing

© 2007 by Stephen Mitchell

BLACKWELL PUBLISHING

350 Main Street, Malden, MA 02148-5020, USA
9600 Garsington Road, Oxford OX4 2DQ, UK
550 Swanston Street, Carlton, Victoria 3053, Australia

The right of Stephen Mitchell to be identified as the Author of this Work has been asserted in accordance with the UK Copyright, Designs, and Patents Act 1988.

First published 2007 by Blackwell Publishing Ltd

3   2008

Library of Congress Cataloging-in-Publication Data

Mitchell, Stephen.
    A history of the later Roman Empire, AD 284–641 : the transformation
of the ancient world / Stephen Mitchell.
      p.   cm. — (Blackwell history of the ancient world)
  Includes bibliographical references and index.
  ISBN 978-1-4051-0857-7 (hardcover : alk. paper)
  ISBN 978-1-4051-0856-0 (pbk. : alk. paper)
    1. Rome — History — Empire, 284–476.   2. Rome — History — Germanic
Invasions, 3rd–6th centuries.   3. Byzantine Empire — History — To 527.
  4. Europe — History — 392–814.   I. Title.   II. Series.

  DG311.M66 2006
  937'.09 — dc22   2005037149

A catalogue record for this title is available from the British Library.

Set in 10.5/12.5pt Plantin
by Graphicraft Limited, Hong Kong
Printed and bound in Singapore
by Utopia Press Pte Ltd

The publisher's policy is to use permanent paper from mills that operate a sustainable forestry policy, and which has been manufactured from pulp processed using acid-free and elementary chlorine-free practices. Furthermore, the publisher ensures that the text paper and cover board used have met acceptable environmental accreditation standards.

For further information on
Blackwell Publishing, visit our website:
www.blackwellpublishing.com

For Lawrence, Daniel, and Samuel Mitchell, and Polat Aydal,
students of science, law, history, and business,
shapers of an uncertain future

Contents

Illustrations

Maps

Maps 3.1, 3.3, 4.1, and 4.3 are adapted from *Grosser Historischer Weltatlas I. Vorgeschichte und Altertum* (Munich, 1963), 40–3. Map 3.2 is based on N. McLynn, *Ambrose of Milan. Church and Court in a Christian Capital* (Berkeley, 1994), 89. Map 4.2 is based on M. Meier, *Justinian. Reich, Religion und Herrschaft* (Munich, 2004), endpaper. Map 11.1 is based on G. Fowden, *Empire to Commonwealth. Consequences of Monotheism in Late Antiquity* (Princeton, 1993), endpaper.

Diagrams

Abbreviations

REFERENCE WORKS AND JOURNALS

AJA	*American Journal of Archaeology*
Ant. Tard.	*Antiquité Tardive*
Byz. Zeitschr.	*Byzantinische Zeitschrift*
CAH	*Cambridge Ancient History*
CQ	*Classical Quarterly*
EHR	*English Historical Review*
GRBS	*Greek, Roman and Byzantine Studies*
HSCP	*Harvard Studies in Classical Philology*
JHS	*Journal of Hellenic Studies*
JRA	*Journal of Roman Archaeology*
JRS	*Journal of Roman Studies*
JTS	*Journal of Theological Studies*
PBA	*Proceedings of the British Academy*
PBSR	*Papers of the British School at Rome*
PCPS	*Proceedings of the Cambridge Philological Society*
REA	*Revue des études anciennes*
ZPE	*Zeitschrift für Papyrologie und Epigraphik*

ANCIENT AUTHORS, WORKS, AND DOCUMENTS (DETAILS OF TRANSLATIONS CAN BE FOUND IN THE BIBLIOGRAPHY)

HE = *Historia Ecclesiastica* (*Ecclesiastical History*)

AÉ	*L'Année épigraphique*, published in *Revue Archéologique* and separately. 1888–
Anon. Val.	*Anonymus Valesianus*
Anth. Pal.	*Anthologia Palatina*
Aur. Victor, *Caes.*	Aurelius Victor, *de Caesaribus* (*On the Emperors*)
Cassiodorus, *Var.*	Cassiodorus, *Variae*
Chron. Gall.	*Chronica Gallica* (*Chronicles of Gaul*)
Chron. Min.	*Chronica Minora* (*Monumenta Germanicae Historiae*)
Chron. Pasch.	*Chronicon Paschale* (*Easter Chronicle*)
CIL	*Corpus Inscriptionum Latinarum.* 1863–
CJust.	*Codex Iustinianus* (*Code of Justinian*)
Claudian, *de bello Gothico*	On the Gothic War
Claudian, *In Eutrop.*	Claudian, *In Eutropium* (*Against Eutropius*)
Constantine Porphyrogennitos, *De Caer.*	Constantine Porphyrogennitos, *De Caerimoniis* (*On Ceremonies*)
CTh.	*Codex Theodosianus* (*Code of Theodosius II*)
De Caer.	Constantine Porphyrogennitos, *De Caerimoniis* (*On Ceremonies*)
Epiphanios, *Pan.*	Epiphanius, *Panarion* (*Medicine Chest Against Heresies*)
Eusebius, *VC*	Eusebius, *Vita Constantini* (*Life of Constantine*)
Eutropius, *Brev.*	Eutropius, *Breviarium* (*Abbreviated History of Rome*)
Festus, *Brev.*	Festus, *Breviarium* (*Abbreviated History of Rome*)
FHG	C. Müller. *Fragmenta Historicorum Graecorum.* 1841–70
Greg. Tur., *Hist.*	Gregory of Tours, *Historiae* (*History of the Franks*)
Hieron. *Chron.*	Hieronymus (Jerome), *Chronica*
ILS	H. Dessau. *Inscriptiones Latinae Selectae.* Berlin. 1892–1916
John Lydus, *de mag.*	John Lydus, *de magistratibus* (*On Magistrates*)
Jordanes, *Get.*	Jordanes, *Getica* (*Getic* [*Gothic*] *History*)
Julian, *Caes.*	Julian, *Caesares* (*The Emperors*)
Justinian, *Nov.*	Justinian, *Novellae* (*New Laws*)

Lactantius, *DMP*	*de mortibus persecutorum* (*On the Deaths of the Persecutors*)
Libanius, *Or.*	Libanius, *Oratio*
MAMA	Monumenta Asia Minoris Antiqua
Marcellinus, *Chron.*	Marcellinus, *Chronicle*
Optatus, app.	Optatus, *Against the Donatists, appendix of documentary evidence*
Pan. Lat.	*Panegyrici Latini* (*Latin Panegyrics*)
Photius, *Bibl. cod.*	Photius, *Bibliotheke codicum* (*Library of Manuscript Books*)
Procopius, *Bell. Goth.* (*Pers., Vand.*)	Procopius, *Bella Gothica, Persica, Vandalica* (*Gothic [Persian, Vandal] Wars*)
Ps-Joshua, *Chron.*	Pseudo-Joshua, *Chronicle* (The *Chronicle* of Ps-Joshua the Stylite)
SEG	*Supplementum Epigraphicum Graecum*
SHA [Carus]	Scriptores Historiae Augustae (*Vita Cari* [*Life of Carus*])
Sidonius, *Carm.*	Sidonius Apollinarius, *Carmina* (poems)
Sulpicius Severus, *Martin*	Sulpicius Severus, *Life of Martin*
Symmachus *Rel.*	Symmachus, *Relationes*
Theophanes, *Chron.*	Theophanes, *Chronographia*

Preface

There have been many historical accounts of the later Roman Empire. Edward Gibbon's *The Decline and Fall of the Roman Empire* has stimulated rather than deterred a host of followers, although none has matched the scale and eloquence of that masterpiece. My attempt to find a way through the immense complexities and sheer bulk of the evidence has been guided by four principles. Firstly, my aim throughout has been to focus on the evolution of the Roman Empire from the late third to the early seventh centuries. This book is therefore written, for the most part, from a top-down perspective. In this respect it is much closer to the tradition of scholarship that extends from Gibbon to A. H. M. Jones than to the revolutionary approach to the study of late antiquity, which has been created, with captivating effect, by Peter Brown and his many followers, especially since the publication of Jones' *The Later Roman Empire* in 1964. However, this work on late antiquity has changed our perceptions of the later Roman Empire ineradicably, and to a large extent supplanted the paradigm of decline and fall, established by Gibbon, that had set a conscious or unconscious framework of interpretation for historians of the nineteenth and twentieth centuries studying this period. Approaching the period from a background of study in the Hellenistic world and the early Roman Empire, I have attempted, as my second principle, to explain historical developments as transformations in response to circumstances, rather than to interpret them for signs of decadence and collapse.

The third of my primary aims in writing this book has been to create as precise a picture as I could of major events and historical processes. This has meant including a good deal of detailed information about dates and geography, to fix those events in time and place. There is a greater emphasis on a historical narrative than has been the case with most recent studies of the period. I have been sparing in developing lengthy and complex explanations of cultural developments and have preferred, as a fourth principle, to let the primary evidence and contemporary witnesses speak for themselves. The numerous quotations from the primary source material, principally from contemporary observers, are included precisely for this purpose. My greatest debt in this respect has been to the small army of scholars, in particular in recent years, who have produced scholarly translations of the literature of late antiquity. These translations, particularly in the series of Liverpool Translated Texts and those from Oxford University Press, contain much of the finest scholarly work on the period, and have made it immeasurably easier to write works of history such as this one. At the same time as trying to do justice to the primary source material, I have aimed to absorb as much as possible of the secondary literature. Much superb work in ancient history has been written about the later Roman period. I have drawn on this bibliography for ideas and information with grateful enthusiasm, and incorporated as much as I could into my notes and bibliographies.

There are specific debts to acknowledge. I am grateful to the University of Exeter, which granted me a year of study leave in 2003/4 during which most of the book was written. Several of the illustrations have been provided by courtesy of the German Archaeological Institute's branches in Berlin, Istanbul, and Rome, with the particular assistance of Dr Richard Posamentir (Istanbul) and Dr Michael Wörrle, as well as my own colleague Professor Barbara Borg. Fergus Millar has encouraged me by advice and example, and channeled a stream of insights emerging from his own work on the Roman Empire of the fifth century. I have benefited from many observations from Wolf Liebeschuetz. Mark Whittow provided invaluable guidance on recent archaeological literature, and Geoffrey Greatrex was an inspirational tutor on Procopius. Al Bertrand commissioned the volume for the Blackwell series in May 2002. I should also like to thank the team that has turned my manuscript into a finished book: Angela Cohen and Louise Spencely (editorial), and Bill MacKeith (index). As I was working on the final chapter I came across a passage from the great Persian *Book of Kings* by the epic poet Ferdowsi, which seemed curiously apt to the relationship of editor and author.

> At Shushtar there was a river so wide that even the fish could not traverse it, and the Sassanian king said to the Roman emperor Valerian, "If you are an engineer, you will build me a bridge as continuous as a cable, such a one as will remain everlastingly in position as a pattern to the wise when we have turned to dust. The length of this bridge, reckoned in cubits, shall be one thousand; you may demand from my treasury all that is required. In this land and region apply all the science of the philosophers of Rum, and when the bridge is completed, you may depart to your home or else remain my guest as long as you live." In gallant fashion the emperor undertook the task and brought the bridge to completion in three years. (Ferdowsi, *Shahnameh*, abbreviated translation by R. Levy, London 1967, 143)

Three years later, having completed a survey of the history of *Rum*, not a thousand cubits but 357 years long from the accession of Diocletian to the death of Heraclius, I shall be glad, like Valerian, to accept the offered respite from a task that has been as satisfying as it has been demanding.

Stephen Mitchell
Exeter, April 2006

1

An Introduction to Late Roman History

250	300	350	400	450	500	550	600	650

The evolution of the classical world in late antiquity
The later Roman Empire or late antiquity?
Change and development in late antiquity
Summary of this book

This book is concerned with the final three and a half centuries of classical antiquity. This lengthy period in the history of the ancient world was characterized by profound transformations in its character, and led to the emergence in the west of medieval European civilization, and, in the east, of a world dominated by a new religion, Islam.

The ancient classical world was formed from the interlocked civilizations of the Greeks and the Romans. Greek culture was based on a closely integrated community of city-states, which first took shape in the Aegean region around 1000 BC. These city-states, called *poleis*, evolved a style of self government that was designed to preserve and promote their collective and community interests, which we still designate by the word politics. Over a period of some 1,500 years, these small- and medium-scale communities explored and developed amid myriad variations a pattern of social organization and collective action which has inspired all western democracies today. Although Greek city-states were a highly localized form of political organization, each making its own political decisions, they were bound together by strong cultural and social ties. Except to a very limited degree the homogeneity and unity of the Greeks was not based on ethnicity, however that be defined, but on a shared language and a common religious outlook. While individual city-states aspired to run their own business and restricted membership to their own citizens, there were virtually no limits to the spread of Greek culture, which proved overwhelmingly attractive to the other peoples of the Mediterranean and the Near East. The outcome was a process which we call Hellenism. Innumerable communities beyond the core region of the Aegean adopted the language, religious notions, and political ideas of the Greeks. They thus created the foundations of a common culture whose features could be identified among peoples extending from Spain to Afghanistan.

As this culture spread more widely, especially in the eastern Mediterranean and the Near East, it adapted to other forms of political organization, in particular the creation of large territorial kingdoms and empires. The emergence of such large scale territorial political units had been an eastern development, exemplified by the ancient civilizations of Egypt, Mesopotamia, and, especially during the seventh to fourth centuries BC, which were a critical period for the history of the Greek city-states, of Persia. This model of the large hegemonic empire was fused with the Greek city-state system after the fall of the Persian Empire to Alexander the Great between 334 and 323 BC. During the following three hundred years most of the east Mediterranean and the Near East was controlled by the Graeco-Macedonian kingdoms that succeeded Alexander. Increasing numbers of the inhabitants of this region began to speak the Greek language, modified their religious beliefs and institutions in conformity with Greek models, and adopted the city-state as the basis for local community politics. The whole era is consequently known as the Hellenistic period.

From the third century BC the Romans exercised a fundamental and dramatic influence on the Hellenistic world. Rome itself was in origin a city-state, which broadly resembled the Greek political pattern. However, like the other city-states of central Italy it belonged to a different cultural tradition, with its own language and religious system. During the fourth and third centuries BC Rome succeeded in conquering much of Italy. The growth of Roman power led in the third century BC to a hegemonic clash with Carthage, the other major power of the western Mediterranean, which resulted in Roman dominion extending beyond the Italian peninsula to Spain, north Africa, and Sicily. After the defeat of Hannibal, the Carthaginian leader, Rome became embroiled in the affairs of the east Mediterranean. Two further centuries of expansion and conquest extended the limits of the Roman Empire to the river Euphrates during the first century AD.

Along this eastern frontier the Romans confronted Persian power in a new guise: the successive empires of the Parthians and Sassanians, based in Lower Mesopotamia and the Iranian plateau, which had regained control over the eastern parts of the Hellenistic world. Throughout the remaining centuries of antiquity the Roman and Persian empires faced each other across a line which extended from the east end of the Black Sea to the Persian Gulf. Territory on either side of this frontier was disputed between the opposed great powers, and regularly became a theater for war and campaigning.

The Romans thus incorporated within their empire almost the entire Hellenized world. They made no efforts to suppress or replace the system of city-states, or Greek culture as a whole, but rather incorporated both of these into their empire. The Romans were successful from the outset as conquerors, but more important than this was their ability to evolve a style of imperial rule which was sustained for almost a thousand years. One of the crucial strengths of the Roman Empire was its capacity to incorporate newcomers and outsiders. Thus, so far from being defined by ethnic or even broader cultural boundaries, the Roman state was continually replenished and revitalized by new blood drawn from its subject provinces. As early as 200 BC the granting of Roman citizenship to outsiders was a recognized source of political resilience, and the strategy of inclusivity was particularly critical when a succession of imperial dynasties, which began with Augustus, took over from the earlier republican system of government. Although the privileges of citizenship became less significant in the late empire, the habit of absorbing new human resources from marginal areas was ingrained, and was exemplified throughout late antiquity in the relationships between the Roman Empire and its barbarian neighbors. Moreover regional differentiation within and between provinces was overridden by the emergence of hierarchies throughout the empire that conformed to one another and to a Roman archetype. Provincial societies, both in the eastern and in the western empire, were highly stratified, with a massive and growing gulf between the rich and the poor. The richest property owners, who controlled most of the empire's resources, were those most closely aligned with the ideals and objectives of the Roman state.

Equally important for the longevity of the Roman Empire was an evolving mastery of the arts of hegemonic rule. In the initial phases of conquest there was a greater emphasis on outright military power. This was achieved not simply by the courage and commitment of citizen soldiers and by ambitious and talented military leaders, but by a much higher degree of military organization than was achieved by other ancient states. After the creation of the monarchic system by Augustus this experience and talent for organization was transferred to the mechanisms which were devised for ruling provinces, assessing and collecting taxation, and developing a universal legal system. The empire combined Greek political ideas, including theories about just rulership, with a practical attention, based on experience, to the crafts of administration.

The emperors also adapted techniques, which had been honed in the eastern monarchies, for projecting an ideal image of the rulers, which embodied their imperial might. These conveyed a fundamental message that the earthly empire was sustained as part of an overall structure of cosmic order, and that harmony and stability was guaranteed by a religious compact between the rulers of men and the divine world. As the Roman polity developed into an worldwide empire increasing emphasis was placed on the state religion. It was an article of faith that Rome's success was due to the support of the gods. Roman emperors were seen as controlling all religious activity in their territories, and were regarded as custodians of a pact with the gods, the *pax deorum*. This central feature of the ideology of Roman rule was projected in all the available media of imperial propaganda: panegyric speeches, the designs of buildings and sculptures, commemorative inscriptions, the legends and designs used on Roman coinage.

These structural features are clearly identifiable in the history of late antiquity. Rome's empire and the opposing eastern empire of the Sassanians in Persia continued to be the dominant powers, and they set the framework within which large scale interstate activity took place. Rome continued to control her subjects by deploying organized military power, by employing the sophisticated machinery of government and administration, and above all by maintaining an ideology of empire that was rarely called into question. During late antiquity, when the Roman world, and especially the Roman state, became Christian, the substance and form of this ideology inevitably changed, but the significance of religion in maintaining the Roman Empire increased. The city-states of the earlier classical periods were still the most important settlements and communities of most of the ancient world, especially in the eastern parts of the Roman Empire, but they too underwent radical changes. They lost most of their political independence and the right to self-determination. But they remained for most people the most important fora of social, economic, and religious activity and retained their overall importance within the wider scheme of ancient civilization.

Historical circumstances brought about a major geo-political split between the western and eastern parts of the Roman Empire. Between the fourth and the seventh centuries, German-speaking tribes such as the Alemanni, Franks, Vandals, and Goths, the Huns, Alans, and Avars, who had moved west from central Asia, and the Slavs and Turks, broke through the old frontiers of the Rhine and Danube rivers. As the northern boundary of the empire collapsed, much of the Balkan region slipped from Roman control, and regular overland communications between east and west were seriously threatened. While the former eastern provinces of Asia Minor, the Near East, and Egypt remained relatively unscathed, the western empire proved unable to defend itself militarily from the barbarian newcomers. Accordingly, Rome devised new strategies of accommodation, by which the barbarian peoples were integrated into the western classical world. The major Germanic tribes divided up large parts of Roman territory into kingdoms, although they continued in most cases to acknowledge the sovereignty of the emperors. Roman military and political weakness in the west thus led to the abandonment of the former Roman provinces in Britain, Gaul, Spain, and the Danubian region. Even Italy itself was relinquished after the fall of the last western emperor in 476. But the idea of a unified empire, including these territories, was never abandoned, and during the sixth century the emperor Justinian made a partially successful attempt to reunite eastern and western territories under a revived system of direct imperial rule.

The Roman state during this period was anything but weak and degenerate. The empire was resilient and highly effective. Emperors, whatever their individual qualities, generally had long reigns. Internal conflict and civil war between rival contenders for power extended through the third and fourth centuries, but the imperial system as such was not called into question. Remarkably, the same situation can be observed both in Sassanian Persia, Rome's eastern counterpart, and in the major Germanic kingdoms which were established in north Africa and western Europe. Their rulers too evolved ideological and administrative systems which provided long periods of stability.

The Later Roman Empire, Late Antiquity, and the Contemporary World

Historical approaches to the final centuries of classical antiquity have been very varied. The differences between them are implicit in the various names that have been applied to the period in modern scholarship: the later Roman Empire; the early Byzantine Age, late antiquity. These variations reveal divergent perspectives. Historians who have identified their subject as the later Roman Empire, have generally focused their attention on the history of the Roman state and its institutions, usually from an empire-wide perspective. Studies of Byzantium or the Byzantine Age, whatever chronological limits are adopted, necessarily deal with the eastern part of the empire, which was ruled from Constantinople. Histories of the west naturally have a very different emphasis, on the rise of the Germanic kingdoms and the origins of medieval western Europe.

Late antiquity is at first sight a less slanted term, embracing the entire geographical range of the Roman and post-Roman world. However, in practice, the study of late antiquity has acquired much more specific connotations. It has mostly been concerned with the eastern Mediterranean region and the Near East, concentrating on social, cultural, and religious themes, at the expense of political or institutional history. Histories of late antiquity have looked beyond the Roman state or the Roman Empire and drawn attention to other underlying conditions which gave unity to the period. Inevitably they place most stress on religious history, above all on the change from the polymorphous paganism of the ancient classical world to the predominantly monotheistic systems of early medieval Europe and the Near East: Judaism, Christianity, and Islam.

This change of focus also tends to involve displacing the chronological boundaries of the period. While most studies of the later Roman Empire cover the period from c.300–600, limits which are explicable principally in terms of political developments, writing on late antiquity usually favors a longer span from around 200 to 800, sometimes referred to as the "long late antiquity." This period covered two great religious transformations and their social consequences: the conversion of the Roman world to Christianity and the emergence and rapid spread of Islam in the Near East in the seventh and eighth centuries. The educated classes of the Greek-speaking East and their less numerous western counterparts also preserved large elements of the classical culture of the Greco-Roman world. Students of late antiquity are as much concerned with the survival of this culture as they are with the impact of Christian and Islamic monotheism.

There are, therefore, radically different ways of approaching the last centuries of antiquity. The greatest historian of the period, Gibbon, pre-empted the choice for most of his successors by writing *History of the Decline and Fall of the Roman Empire*. The famous title not only placed the Roman state in the foreground of his study, but also set a historical agenda which has dominated the thinking of most historians since his time. The challenge is to analyze and explain Rome's decline. The Roman Empire remains the central point of focus for most major studies of the period written since Gibbon. This is explicitly acknowledged in the titles of J. B. Bury, *The Later Roman Empire from the Death of Theodosius I to the Death of Justinian (395–565)*, E. Stein, *Geschichte des spätrömischen Reiches I (284–476)* (1928) and *Histoire du Bas-Empire II. De la disparition de l'empire de l'occident à la mort de Justinien (476–565)* (1949), and A. H. M. Jones, *The Later Roman Empire 284–602. A Social, Economic and Administrative Survey* (1964). These major studies, together with A. Demandt, *Die Spätantike. Römische Geschichte von Diocletian bis Justinian 284–565 n. Chr.* (1989), still today offer the most ambitious and comprehensive surveys of later Roman history.

The inspiration for the alternative approach can be attributed to the influence of a single scholar, Peter Brown. His short book, *The World of Late Antiquity*, which was loosely defined chronologically as covering the period from Marcus Aurelius to Mohammed, effectively tore up the late Roman agenda and redefined the period as an object of study. Brown's own large output, and that of a generation of scholars inspired by him, has explored areas and aspects of the history of late antiquity which were hardly noticed in the mainstream tradition of later Roman history. From the prodigious abundance of early Christian literature Brown and his followers have teased out and expounded an extraordinarily variegated picture of society and culture in all its regional diversity. Underlying this project is a pervading concern to explore the effects of religious change on individual and collective mentalities.[1]

The impact of this new approach to late antiquity has been enormous but uneven. Without question it has brought new impetus and vitality to the study of the period, especially in the English-speaking world. It has shifted attention away from the traditional objects of historical attention – emperors, generals, empires, states and armies – to religious figures, above all Christian writers, to communities united by faith, and to the role of common men and women living in uncommon or remarkable times. It is, of course, far harder to elicit generalized patterns of meaning from studies of this sort. Individual episodes and individual lives stand out from the crowded texture of events, sometimes with dazzling immediacy and vividness, but it is not easy to locate them within a larger context, and harder still to transform these contexts into an accurate representation of a social and cultural *zeitgeist*. Classical and medieval historians alike have been captivated by these studies, but not always convinced by them.[2]

No one studying late antiquity today can fail to be influenced by the work of Peter Brown and his school, and much contemporary scholarship on the period, at least by English-speaking historians, tends to be eclectic. Thus the *Cambridge Ancient History* volumes XIII and XIV, which between them cover the period from 337 to c.600, combine a core of narrative history, emphasizing political, military, and broad institutional themes, with discussions of family and social life, religious phenomena, and approaches to the *mentalité* of the period. Brown himself has contributed important sections to both volumes. The titles of Averil Cameron's two books written in the early 1990s illustrate the same dichotomy of approach. *The Later Roman Empire AD 284–430* (1993) is a largely traditional history of the late Roman state, while *The Mediterranean World in Late Antiquity* (1993), written for another series, abandons the chronological framework and detailed discussion of the institutions of the empire, in favor of a looser thematic survey, with a greater emphasis on social, economic, and religious issues. David Potter's detailed and challenging survey of Roman history from 180 to 395, *The Roman Empire at Bay*, is an ambitious attempt to represent many facets of social, intellectual, and religious history within the grand sweep of political events.

This book conforms to the older pattern of late Roman history. There are several reasons for this. One is quite simply that it is easier to organize the teeming abundance of historical evidence within the traditional contours than it is to reconfigure the framework into completely new thematic patterns. The point will be obvious to anyone who compares a volume such as *CAH* XIV, or the current standard German history, A. Demandt's *Die Spätantike*, with Bowersock et al.'s *Late Antiquity. A Guide to the Postclassical World* (1999), which is the first attempt to collect the harvest of the Brownian approach into a single handbook. Chronology, emperors, and armies are almost entirely jettisoned to make way for four thematic chapters on religion, two on attitudes to the past and the classical tradition, two on material culture, and one each on barbarians and ethnicity, and on war and violence. Only the last two overlap substantially with the more traditional agenda. The new approach is original, stimulating, and often carries historical conviction, but it also demands a huge sacrifice. The recent volume edited by Simon Swain and Mark Edwards, *Approaching Late Antiquity* (2004) follows a more conservative agenda, in part due to the decision to focus on a much shorter period, from around 200 to 400.

Among the victims of the preference for the late antiquity rather than the late Roman history approach to the period are the historians of the period themselves. Historical writing was a central part of the educated culture of antiquity and it flourished in late antiquity. Between the fourth and sixth centuries writers of extraordinary talent carried on the heritage and tradition of classical historical writing, which began with Herodotus and Thucydides. The histories of Ammianus Marcellinus and Procopius are essential for understanding the Roman Empire in the fourth and sixth centuries respectively. Their fifth-century counterparts, including Olympiodorus, Priscus and Malchus, survive only in fragments, but these are sufficient to demonstrate their quality.

The period was also documented by numerous less ambitious chroniclers, who presented visions of world history from the creation up to the writers' own times, but with a localized, regional focus. Late antiquity also witnessed the birth of an entirely new historical genre, Church history. This was created by Eusebius, whose history of the Church up to Constantine was continued and emulated by four works of the mid-fifth century, the histories of Socrates, Sozomen, Theodoret, and the Arian Philostorgius, and by the sixth-century writers, Evagrius, John of Ephesus, and Zacharias of Mytilene. The work of these figures taken collectively underpins serious history of the later Roman Empire. It contributes only marginally to studies in the modern fashion of late antiquity.

Modern historiographical interests have also inevitably shaped contemporary approaches to the late classical world. Historians of the late twentieth century have widened the definition of their subject dramatically by choosing new themes and approaches. There has been a tendency to study social attitudes rather than social structures, popular activity in preference to high culture, mentalities rather than educational patterns, issues of personal or communal identity rather than questions of national politics. One general feature of these new approaches has been to play down the significance of individuals or specific events and look instead for underlying patterns, unconscious influences on human behavior, and, in social and economic history, to the importance of long-term, slow-moving change, the *longue durée*. The classic modern exposition of *longue durée* history, F. Braudel's *The Mediterranean in the Age of Philip*, has been a huge influence on historians of late antiquity.

This approach, however, suggests a distinct detachment from the world that we experience. Modern media and the dissemination of news and information make it easier for us to appreciate the impact of historical developments as they unfold, and we should not too readily underestimate the significance of these changes simply because they have occurred in a short space of time. The extraordinarily rapid breakdown of the Soviet empire in 1989/90 not only revealed how fragile imperial structures may be, but has also led to major shifts in the balance of world power. Within the same few years one of the world's great religions, Islam, has also undergone a drastic transformation. Radical movements have become prominent, religious belief has crystallized into violent political action, secular statecraft has lost ground to the charisma of religious leadership. Similar developments can easily be identified within Christianity and Judaism. The significance of the Islamic terrorist attack on the twin towers in New York has been colossal. Events of this magnitude lead to huge shifts in the world's historical alignments. The nations of the world have been presented with stark choices about the nature of their relationship to the remaining imperial power, the USA. The nations of Europe after the collapse of the Russian empire have been reconfigured into the European Union, the world's most powerful economic bloc. Its members confront the implications of this for their own nationhood, and debate whether religious identity should be a prime criterion for membership. Population transfers and large scale migration, especially within Europe, have had profound social and economic implications, and have contributed to the formation of new communal identities. The viability of nation-states themselves, the foundation of the modern world order, faces serious challenges both from transnational economic corporations and from religious ideologies.

Within our own immediate recollection we can appreciate the impact of imperial power and the entanglement of religion and secular politics. We have not only observed but undergone changes in national character and communal identity, and our recent experience enables us to document the vulnerability of national sovereignty to economic, political, or religious pressures. In addition many of the shifts in our collective perceptions can be traced to specific events and political developments. The world is not immune to the impact of *histoire événementielle*. The events through which we have lived in the last twenty years cast a strong light back on later Roman history. They help to enhance our understanding of the evolution of the Roman and Sassanian empires, the role of Christianity as a defining force within society, the role of smaller civic units, the impact of the barbarian migrations, and the political and social transformations that followed from them. The history of the later Roman Empire holds up a mirror to the world we live in today. Through our contemporary experience we are better able to appreciate and learn from the past.

Change and Development

Since the preponderance of recent studies of late antiquity have been thematically organized, there has been a relative neglect of chronology. But historical change occurred over time and has to be traced sequentially. It is important not to conflate evidence from widely disparate periods. There was an enormous difference between the Roman Empire of the fourth century, which was shaped by the actions of emperors and their officials who were constantly on the move and actively engaged in warfare, and that of the fifth and sixth centuries, when the rulers and their courts were confined to Constantinople. The religious landscape also changed radically. In the fourth century Christianity was still challenged by the numerous forms of pagan polytheism. In the sixth century it faced no serious rivals as a universal religious system. The character of the cities of the ancient world was also transformed. In the fourth century cities were still nominally governed by local landowners, who represented local interests. During the fifth and sixth centuries this form of "constitutional" civic government was replaced by a more patriarchal system, in which power was largely monopolized by imperially nominated officials, estate-owning grandees, or bishops. It is crucial to keep this change in view in studying the evolution of urban life in the later empire.[3]

The time span from the accession of Diocletian in 284 to the death of Heraclius in 641 is a long one and the study of this period covers several concurrent and interlocking histories. It deals with the later Roman Empire, the early history of Christianity, and the barbarian invasions and settlement of western Europe, to say nothing of the newer agendas within the study of late antiquity. The geographical scope of these histories encompasses all of Europe south of the rivers Rhine and Danube, the Mediterranean basin, and the Near East, with consideration given also to the Iranian plateau, the Caucasus region, and the steppes of eastern Europe and western Asia. Each of these histories had its own chronological dynamic and developed with considerable regional variety. The chapters that follow this one provide a variety of approaches to these histories.

Chapter 2 surveys the main sources for the period, with particular emphasis on the historians. These need to be read not merely for the information they contain, but for the views they took of Roman and Christian history, and for their understanding of the world they lived in.

Chapter 3 is a chronological narrative of the history of the empire from the accession of Diocletian in 284 to the beginning of the fifth century, ending in the west with the sack of Rome by the Gothic leader Alaric, and in the east with the accession of Theodosius II. The fourth century was an age of warrior emperors, engaged in unceasing struggles against external enemies and also in civil wars against would-be usurpers. Military history is inevitably the dominant theme.

Chapter 4 takes the narrative forward until the middle years of Justinian and the great plague which swept through virtually the entire inhabited world in 542. The destinies of the eastern and western provinces of the empire parted ways during the fifth century. During this period, the supremacy of the western emperors was challenged and eventually superseded by the Germanic kingdoms, which led to their eclipse in 476. However, the eastern rulers remained closely involved in the immensely complicated political events which encompassed the eclipse of the western emperors in 476. Meanwhile the eastern empire itself enjoyed a long period of relative stability and growing prosperity, which was largely due to peaceful relations with the Sassanian Empire along the eastern frontier. These were interrupted when war broke out with Persia at the beginning of the sixth century, but the early years of Justinian's reign witnessed a major reassertion of Roman dominance. The unforeseeable outbreak of the plague and the other enormous setbacks which Rome encountered during the 540s mark a major caesura.

Chapter 5 is concerned with the Roman state and the nature of Roman rulership. It focuses on the use of ritualized political procedures, the use of visual propaganda, the ideology of the emperors and the ruling class, and the administrative framework of the empire.

Chapter 6 is a corresponding study of the major barbarian powers of the west, including the so-called empire of the Huns, and the kingdoms of the Visigoths, Burgundians, Franks, and Ostrogoths, which assumed political power in western Europe. Within each there were contrasting forms of military organization and mechanisms for asserting state power and projecting an ideology of rulership. The continuing influence of the Roman Empire remained strong in all cases.

Chapter 7 traces the religious development of the Roman world after the third century. It analyses the diversity of religious practice and experience with which the period began and the reasons behind the enormous change that led Christianity to become the dominant religion of the empire by the end of the fourth century. The chapter also examines the position of the state in matters of religious tolerance, both from the perspective of pagan rulers in the face of Christianity, and their Christian counterparts who confronted the survival of paganism.

Chapter 8 looks at the social context of religious conversion by examining the three best documented individual examples from the fourth century, the emperors Constantine and Julian, and the greatest figure in western Christianity, St Augustine. The chapter then turns to the study of Christianity as a political phenomenon in the late empire, and the evolving doctrinal disputes around the central tenets of Christian belief. Discussions were carried on amid bitter controversy at the highest level by leading bishops and theologians, under the eye of the emperors. The political objective was to establish a unified Roman state that was co-extensive with a unified Christian Church. Church politics, therefore are central to the history of the late Roman Empire. Orthodox Catholic Christianity became the central feature of the political ideology of the empire, and thus the main symbolic identifier of the Roman inhabitants of the empire.

Chapter 9 is concerned with the economic basis of the empire, and the political and social institutions by which this was maintained. It draws attention to the importance of distinguishing local economies, patterns of interregional trade, and the development of city life. The survival of the Roman Empire depended on the sustainability of long-distance links, enabling the circulation of people, goods, and ideas. Without these its political unity and common culture would have disintegrated. Particular emphasis is placed on the economic importance of the state *annona* system. The organization of the *annona* is also a major factor explaining the extraordinary growth of the capital cities, Rome and Constantinople, and of the major regional centers at Alexandria, Carthage, and Antioch.

Chapter 10 turns to the regions and provinces, considering the evidence for patterns of rural settlement, the evolution of civic life, and the importance of regional security to economic development, which played a decisive role in the split between the eastern and western parts of the empire.

Chapter 11 resumes the narrative pattern of chapters 3 and 4. The focus is on the enormous challenges that the Roman Empire faced in the middle years of the sixth century. In the forefront were the blows dealt by the plague, which recurred throughout the century, other devastating environmental disasters, and earthquakes. These were compounded by military setbacks arising from the reconquest of Africa and Italy, and by the resurgent power of Sassanian Persia. Although these challenges led to major internal changes to Roman society, and in particular to a much more explicit reliance on religious means to maintain the morale and coherence of communities, they did not impair the

Roman will to maintain the empire, which proved resilient against the growing threats to its existence.

Chapter 12 examines these threats in the final phase which led to the loss of more than half the eastern empire. It traces the impact of new barbarian incursions from central Asia and northern Europe, the arrival of Avars and Turks, Slavs and Lombards; the resurgent militarism of the Sassanian Empire, which culminated in the great struggles of the early seventh century between the Roman Empire of Heraclius and Persian Empire of Khusro II; and finally the transformation of tribal society in the southern areas of the Levant, which heralded the coming of Islam and the Arab conquests. These enormous external forces, rather than internal decadence and decay, provide the main clues to the decline and fall of the Roman Empire. When Heraclius died in 641 his rule extended southeast of Constantinople only as far as the Taurus mountains, retaining Asia Minor, but excluding all territory to the south.

NOTES

1 See Averil Cameron, "The long late antiquity," in T. P. Wiseman (ed.), *Classics in Progress: Essays on Ancient Greece and Rome* (Oxford, 2002), 165–91; W. Liebeschuetz, "The birth of late antiquity," *Antiquité Tardive* 12 (2004), 253–61.
2 See Alexander Murray, "Peter Brown and the shadow of Constantine," *JRS* 73 (1983), 191–203.
3 W. Liebeschuetz, *The Decline and Fall of the Roman City* (Oxford, 2001).

2
The Nature of
the Evidence

The history of the later Roman Empire depends on a copious and diverse range of written and non-written material. It would be futile to try to identify and characterize the entire spectrum of sources for the period. The quantity and variety of the written material alone far exceeds what is available for earlier periods of Graeco-Roman antiquity, such as classical Athens or late republican Rome, and archaeological remains of late antiquity, which of course overlie earlier levels on classical sites, are also extremely prolific, although they remain understudied. The overall extent, especially of the written material, is simply too wide to encompass. More importantly, the sources are not an inert mass of potential information, waiting to be quarried, but yield different answers to

different questions. The approach to the history of the period not only deter-
mines the range of sources that are examined but also the way in which they
are interrogated. The following selective survey is inevitably an individual one.

The Problem of Christian Sources

The written sources in particular are difficult to interpret, not least because the
categories and genres to which they belong are substantially different from those
for earlier periods of Roman history. Most of this new literature is Christian.
This survives in prodigious quantity, including works of hagiography, church history, sermons, and theological discussions, which correspond to little that survives
from the pagan tradition. Much of this Christian literature is transparently and
unabashedly partisan in the way that it portrays the world of late antiquity.
Few Christian writings make allowance for the existence of pagans and their place
in the world, still less for the substance of their beliefs. This poses a problem
for interpreting all Christian sources and relating them to their wider context.
    Pagan writings are much more sparsely represented than Christian ones,
especially because Christians were not interested in copying and reproducing
work in genres that lay outside the Christian tradition. Christians disseminated
their own literature but had an interest in suppressing the products of pagan
culture. We may see this in the preservation of mainstream historical writing.
Three large-scale church histories written in the middle of the fifth century
by Socrates, Sozomen, and Theodoret survive in their entirety, and we even
have extensive fragments of the historical work of the Arian Philostorgius. On
the other hand only highly selective excerpts are preserved from the secular
historians of this period – Eunapius, Olympiodorus, Priscus, and Malchus –
even though the last two of these were certainly themselves Christians. The
one surviving pagan historical narrative from late antiquity, by Zosimus, is
missing its second book, which may have been suppressed by copyists as it
must have contained a strongly anti-Christian view of the persecutions at the
beginning of the fourth century.
    Some pagan writings are preserved, especially from the time of Julian and from
Roman writers of the late fourth century, and the pagan philosophical tradition
is also represented. But these were theoretical treatments that give little indication about the vitality of paganism on the ground. Pagan authors of the later
fourth century were discreet and unassertive in the face of Christian orthodoxy.
Prominent pagans, such as the political orators Themistius and Libanius, and
the leading Roman senator Symmachus, adopted an eirenic approach and wrote
pleas for mutual tolerance between themselves and their Christian counterparts.
Most writers of panegyrics avoid the issue. By the fifth century the game was
almost up, and the only substantial pagan literary products to survive, apart
from works of philosophy, are Eunapius' *Lives of the Sophists*, comprising short
biographies of several leading pagan intellectuals of the fourth century, and
Zosimus' truncated history.

The large discrepancy in the survival rate of Christian and pagan literature from late antiquity makes it difficult to assess the relative importance of the religious cultures throughout the period, and to trace the speed of Christian progress and pagan decline. The problem is compounded by the nature of the literature that does survive. No writers of the period undertook to provide a balanced and non-partisan account of the rise of Christianity in relation to pagan polytheism. The secular historical writers of the fourth century were either, like Aurelius Victor or Eutropius, conventionally indifferent, or, like the militantly pagan Eunapius (in the form preserved for us by Zosimus), scathingly hostile to Christianity. Neither these writers nor Ammianus Marcellinus, whose views on Christianity were more complex, have much if anything to say about the extent and influence of the Christian community as a whole. Subsequent historical writers in the secular tradition up to the sixth century, even though almost all of them were Christians themselves, presented Christianity as an epiphenomenon, rather than as a central feature of their times. Even so, the growing domination of religious ideas and institutions within the fabric of social life as a whole leads it to occupy a larger place in the later narratives.[1]

The problem is even more acute when viewed from a Christian perspective. Eusebius' *Ecclesiastical History* and his *Life of Constantine* relate early fourth-century history exclusively from a Christian viewpoint, and it is almost a matter of accident that these works sometimes provide a glimpse of the wider pagan or secular environment. The same is true to a lesser extent of the church historians of the fifth century, who were embedded in a culture which was almost completely Christian. However, the integration of church and state had advanced so far by the time that they were writing, that their work inevitably contains important information about state affairs in general.

Hagiography

Biographies were in vogue in late antiquity. Whereas the earlier classical tradition of biographical writing, represented above all by Plutarch, used the lives of prominent men to illustrate general truths about human character, the genre was increasingly used after the third century to reflect the aura of charismatic individuals. The subjects are represented as possessing divine or semi-divine status, and this was often demonstrated by their supposed supernatural powers. It is no coincidence that these works began to appear during the most import-ant period of change from pagan polytheism to Christianity, since they served as ammunition in the propaganda war between rival religious and philosophical camps. Philostratus' *Life of Apollonius of Tyana*, Porphyry's *Life of Plotinus*, and Iamblichus' *Life of Pythagoras*, written in praise of philosophical heroes, as well as Eunapius' *Lives of the Sophists*, show that such charismatic biographies could serve the pagan cause.[2] Eusebius' *Life of Constantine*, the most important single source for the first Christian emperor, an extraordinary collage of pan-egyric, documentary history, and hagiography, is a hybrid work that belongs to this period of literary experimentation and intense religious competition. Like his *Church History* (see below) it incorporated many contemporary documents verbatim, notably several letters from the emperor himself. Critical engagement with the *Life* is essential to any modern reappraisal of Constantine's religious views and political achievements. The major problem lies not with the veracity of what Eusebius says, but in appreciating the context of his claims and gaining a good perspective on how much he omits.[3]

Christian hagiography is arguably the most distinctive literary genre of late antiquity. By definition hagiographies were written by Christians about Christian heroes, usually martyrs or ascetics. The era of the persecutions from the mid-third to the early fourth century provided writers with vivid subject matter, and the stories of heroic Christian deaths inspired the early church with extraordinary confidence. As Tertullian had rightly anticipated when persecution was inflicted on the Christian community of Carthage around 200, the blood of martyrs would be the seed of the church. Eusebius' *Martyrs of Palestine*, a record of the impact of the persecution of Maximinus on his home region, was a pioneering work. Some of the earliest saints' lives, however, relate not to martyrs but to heroic figures of the pre-Constantinian church or leading ascetics. The most influential of these was the *Life of Antony*, written around 350 and generally attributed to Athanasius of Alexandria. Antony, inspired by reading the gospels, foreswore a secular career for a life of increasing asceticism and seclusion. Worldly goods were traded for holiness; the comforts of a suburban existence in the Nile valley for a bleak hovel in the eastern desert. By resisting temptations and mortifying the body through fasting Antony acquired talismanic power. The story was rapidly translated, perhaps from a Coptic original, into Greek, Syriac, and at least twice into Latin. Augustine in his *Confessions* famously recalls how two imperial civil servants of the emperor Valentinian II were converted at Trier after a reading of the *Life*. This work was enormously influential and provided a hagiographical template which was replicated many times over in narratives of less famous saints. Hagiography was a popular genre that was produced for the edification of local congregations and communities. Although saints' lives routinely invent or distort much of their material, they often preserve valuable information about local religious practices, topography, and even church politics. The lives of Symeon the Stylite in northern Syria, Daniel the Stylite in fifth-century Constantinople, Nicholas of Sion in Lycia, and Theodore of Sykeon in late sixth-century Anatolia, for instance, have been quarried for detailed local information about the places and regions where holy men exercised their influence.[4] Again a word of caution is in order: the writers' gaze in these works was always firmly fixed on their saintly heroes, and the background may be blurred and distorted.

Panegyrics

Another factor that influences the evidence as a whole is related to the autocratic and authoritarian nature of the late Roman state. We may reasonably suppose that major political and social issues were subject to debate and discussion, as they are in most societies, but open dissent was not encouraged, or even tolerated, by those in power. We thus find the extremes of praise and vituperation, but little between them by way of measured discussion. One of the most important sources for the history of the period are panegyric speeches or poems, which present the character and actions of emperors and high officials in the most flattering terms. It is tempting to dismiss them out of hand as unreliable, but when their context, rhetorical style, and habits of omission and exaggeration are taken into account, they emerge as critical historical sources for many aspects of high politics. Key works in this genre are the twelve Latin panegyrics, which were probably compiled by the Gallic orator Pacatus, and were prefaced by the younger Pliny's lengthy panegyric for the emperor Trajan (I). Apart from Pacatus' own work of 389 in praise of Theodosius I (II), this includes speeches for Maximianus in 289 (X, by the elder Cl. Mamertinus) and 291 (XI), for Constantius the father of Constantine in 296 (VII) and 298 (IX), for the marriage of Constantine and Fausta in 307 (VII), for Constantine in 310 (VI), 312 (V), 314 (XII), and 321 (IV, by Nazarius), and for Julian in 362 (III, by the younger Cl. Mamertinus on his own appointment to the consulship). The earlier works are indispensable for a historical reconstruction of the tetrarchy and the rise of Constantine.[5] The other side of the coin during this period is found in the polemic satire of Lactantius' *On the Deaths of the Persecutors*, probably written around 314. This blatantly partisan and distorted account of the tetrarchic period nevertheless preserves in recognizable form a kernel of historical accuracy in relation to major policies and initiatives of the period.[6]

There is a substantial number of later panegyric works. The speeches of Themistius are critically important for our grasp of the political history of the Roman state in the fourth century. Themistius belonged to the first generation of public men who grew up at Constantinople. He played a key role in building up the status and authority of the Constantinopolitan senate in the late 350s, and rose to become prefect of the city under Theodosius I. Throughout this period he was a close advisor to the emperors from Constantius to Theodosius. Many of the speeches he delivered in their presence offer a subtle exposition of imperial policy on major matters, including pagan-Christian relations, foreign affairs, and taxation policy. It was clearly not the purpose of these speeches to offer the speaker's personal views on these high affairs of state, but to publicize and argue for policies that had essentially been formulated, after consultation, by the emperors themselves. Themistius was thus a spokesman for the regime. The general tone is not dissimilar to that of speeches delivered today at the US party conventions during a presidential campaign, or at party-political congresses. That is, they present a simplified and rhetorically powerful case for controversial policies within a wider framework which praised the emperor and argued or implied that he was the ideal ruler to carry them through. Although Themistius was not a Christian himself, this proved no obstacle to his dealings with Christian emperors, and his entire career suggests that the atmosphere of public life in the eastern capital was much less concerned with religious differences than we would suppose from Christian authors of the period.[7]

Themistius' counterpart and contemporary was the rhetorician and teacher Libanius, who spent most of his career in his native Antioch. His students were mainly from the city-based upper classes of the eastern provinces, and many of them aimed at careers in state service. Libanius' prolific correspondence (over 1,000 letters survive) documents the network of contacts that he maintained, and illuminates the role of this highly educated middle class and its impact on contemporary civic life. His pupils were as likely to be Christians as pagans, but the cultured education (*paideia*) which he offered was entirely rooted in the classical tradition.[8] Libanius' speeches have a more parochial perspective than those of Themistius. They relate to society and politics at Antioch, drawing attention to local and regional issues, rather than high imperial policy. Some of these, including those written after the riot of the statues in 387, when the city faced potentially devastating punishment by Theodosius, were cast as direct appeals to the emperor, but it is not clear that they were actually delivered to him. The young Julian had been prevented from attending Libanius' lectures at Nicomedia in the late 340s, but the two came into close contact when Julian stayed at Antioch as emperor in 362–3, and five of Libanius' works are panegyrics in his honor. The longest and most important of these, a virtual biography from a passionate pagan admirer, is the funeral oration.[9]

It is appropriate at this point to mention the works of the emperor Julian himself, as these are a key to his motives and personality. Julian had acquired both a pagan and a Christian education, and stood squarely between the two traditions. More than any other works of the period, his private letters, longer tracts, such as the *Letters to the Athenians*, the *Letter to Heraclius*, a Cynic philosopher, and occasional pieces in many genres, illuminate the cultural and religious outlook of the eastern provinces in the middle of the fourth century. He alone offers a view of the Roman world, which takes in both the Christian and non-Christian perspectives.

While he was Caesar Julian himself contributed to the panegyric genre, writing speeches in praise of the emperor Constantius and his wife Eusebia. He also made two remarkable contributions to the satirical genre. The *Caesares* was a personal review of the rulers who had preceded him, including his hero Alexander the Great. Constantine's Christianity is mocked and belittled in terms very similar to those found in the pagan historian Zosimus. The *Misopogon* was his parodic and self-mocking defense against the scurrilities and abuse which had been leveled at him by the people of Antioch.[10] Neither was a youthful student work. Both were composed while the emperor was resident in Antioch during the winter of 362–3, preparing for the Persian expedition, the former on the occasion of the Saturnalia, the latter for the New Year festival, both occasions which provided a license to defy social conventions.

The most notable exponent of the panegyric tradition at the end of the fourth century was the Egyptian poet Claudian. Like the historian Ammianus he broke away from his Greek-speaking background to write hexameter poems in praise of the emperor Honorius, the generalissimo Stilicho, and other leading political figures of the western empire; devastating attacks on Rufinus, the

praetorian prefect of the East, and his eunuch successor Eutropius; and verse
accounts of the wars against the usurper Gildo in Africa and Alaric the Goth.[11]
Claudian's work was clearly an inspiration to the versatile and highly talented
Sidonius Apollinaris, whose letters, collected and published in nine books,
illuminate the preoccupations of the cultured landowning society of southern
Gaul between c.460 and 480, poised in their allegiance between the Roman
Empire and the barbarian kingdoms. Sidonius, who ended his career as bishop
of Clermont-Ferrand, was the last Roman poet of the West who wrote with
complete mastery of the high tradition of classical Latin poetry. He wrote
substantial verse panegyrics for the emperors Avitus and Majorian, as well as
occasional poetry, which shows virtuoso mastery of several metrical genres.[12]

Two panegyrics in praise of Anastasius are particularly important, as no substantial historical narrative survives for his reign. Priscian, from Caesarea in
Mauretania, was an active teacher of grammar and rhetoric in Constantinople
and wrote a Latin verse panegyric for the emperor in 503. This celebrated
his victories in the Isaurian wars and his generosity in peacetime, notably the
abolition of the tax known as the *chrysargyron*, when the records of debtors were
burned in the hippodrome. Its prose counterpart is the classicizing work of
Procopius of Gaza, written in Greek, which compared the emperor to great
figures of the Greek past.[13]

The Secular Historians

Our knowledge of the events that gave an overall shape to later Roman history
derives in the first instance from the secular historians of late antiquity. Their
prime object was to preserve a record of the successes and failures of the Roman
Empire and its rulers, including the activities of emperors and senior officials,
of armies and campaigns, of diplomacy and power struggles, and other political
events. We are well served by them. Some of the finest historical writing from
the ancient world comes from late antiquity. These major writers, who were well
aware of the tradition to which they belonged, continued the secular tradition
of historiography that had begun in the fifth century BC. The best historians of
the period, Ammianus Marcellinus, Procopius, and the fragmentarily preserved
Greek writers of the fifth century, bear comparison with their classical predecessors, Herodotus, Thucydides, Polybius, and Tacitus.

Almost all the secular historians of late antiquity share two characteristics.
Firstly, they held office in the Roman government, as lawyers, diplomats, or
military officers, and participated in state affairs at a high level. Secondly, they
wrote not about the distant past but about events that they had lived through
themselves, or that were within the memory of people they talked to. They
were thus men close to the center of Roman power with access to good
information about major events. Like the emperors themselves and other high
officials, they formed a view of what was going on in the empire as a whole. In
view of the pressures and military uncertainties which beset the Roman state

throughout the period, they also devoted much attention to regions and peoples beyond the imperial boundaries. These political historians, as we may reasonably call them, took advantage of the highly privileged positions they occupied. The universal historians of late antiquity exploited their access to the inner circle of power, because this was the only vantage point from which a synoptic overview of the ancient world was possible.

This point is of some importance also for understanding how emperors and their advisors operated. They had access to the same level and quality of information as the historians, and were able to take this into account in devising their own policies and responses to conditions and situations across the empire. The secular histories were critical for contemporaries, as they are for us, in shaping and articulating a reflective view of Rome's place in relation to its neighbors, and of grasping similarities and differences between one region and another, of identifying shifts in policy, and making reasoned judgments about political behavior. News about what was going on in other places in general traveled slowly and fitfully. Unlike in today's global village, very few people had any accurate idea of events taking place beyond the region where they lived. Modern media and news dissemination allow us to form perspectives today which were inconceivable in antiquity. Without the historians of late antiquity it is unlikely that we would be able to make any unified sense of the period.

One of the major problems in reconstructing the political history of the first half of the fourth century is the lack of any large-scale historical narrative from the period. What we do possess are three summaries written in the 360s and 370s by Latin writers who had held positions at court or in the army, and whose purpose was to provide succinct historical information, perhaps for official purposes. Aurelius Victor published a series of short imperial biographies from Augustus to Constantius, called *Caesares*, in 360. Eutropius wrote a *Breviarium*, a history in ten short books from the foundation of Rome to the accession of Valens, which appeared in 369, when he held the post of *a libellis* and was the emperor's *magister memoriae*. Three years later Festus, who also held the post of *a libellis*, produced another *Breviarium* organized on a different principle, thirty chapters devoted to the origins of each of the provinces of the empire. An anonymous *Epitome de Caesaribus* covered similar ground to Aurelius Victor's work, but brought the record up to 395. These short works evidently drew on a now lost common source, which has been dubbed the *Kaisergeschichte*, a history of the emperors, and is thought to have been written c.337. Another source for Constantine, independent of this tradition, is an anonymous Latin account of his reign, probably written around 390, whose one surviving manuscript bears the misleading title *Origo Constantini Imperatoris*. It is brief, but sober.

Ammianus Marcellinus is the most important historical writer of the fourth century, and has a claim to be the finest Latin historian of any period. This is the more remarkable for the fact that he was born in a Greek-speaking milieu of the Near East, perhaps at Syrian Antioch, and acquired Latin as a second language, doubtless partly in the course of service as a senior army officer (a *protector domesticus*) under Constantius and Julian. He was born in the mid-330s, and served in Gaul from 354, during the period when Julian was Caesar, until he was transferred to the East in 359 with Ursicinus, a personal friend and one of the heroes of his narrative. One of the most dramatic sections of his history describes his own escape from the Persian siege of Amida in 359. Subsequently he took part in Julian's Persian expedition, and returned to Antioch in the autumn of 363, where he seems to have resided through the 370s. Ammianus' military service is one of the keys to his historical personality, and explains the scorn in which he held most civilian courtiers and other imperial advisors. His experience reinforced the view he shared with other historians and political commentators, that emperors were often the victims of malicious and partisan advice. Between travels, he spent most of the last phase of his life at Rome, and probably completed his history before the death of Theodosius in 395.

Ammianus provided the clearest pointer as to how his history should be read and understood in the final paragraph of the whole work:

> This is the history of events from the reign of the emperor Nerva to the death of Valens, which I, a former soldier and a Greek, have composed to the best of my ability. It claims to be the truth, which I have never ventured to pervert either by silence or a lie. The rest I leave to be written by better men whose abilities are in their prime. But if they choose to undertake them, I advise them to cast what they have to say in the grand style. (Ammianus 31.16, trans. Hamilton)

Service as a military officer provided Ammianus with the privileged access to information and to high-level informants, who were indispensable for his historical project. At the beginning of book 15, in a passage that deliberately echoes Thucydides, Ammianus makes plain that such sources were invaluable:

> Using my best efforts to find out the truth, I have set out, in the order in which they occurred, events which I was able to observe for myself or discover by thorough questioning of contemporaries who took part in them. The rest, which will occupy the pages that follow, I shall execute to the best of my ability in a more polished style, and I shall pay no heed to the criticism which some make of a work which they think too long. Brevity is only desirable when it cuts short tedious irrelevance without subtracting from our knowledge of the past. (Ammianus 15.1.1, trans. Hamilton)

Active, energetic, and often brutal military service meant that he had little time for the imperial court and its intrigues, which he frequently paints in a lurid light. Unlike Procopius, however, he was not primarily a war historian, and he set Roman warfare and campaigns within the full scope of political and diplomatic activity. Following the example of many of his Greek and Latin predecessors, he interspersed the narrative with large-scale excursuses, on ethnographic matters, natural phenomena, and other matters of major interest. Like all serious historians of antiquity, he saw his task not merely as a matter of record, but also as a matter of judgment. Moralizing appraisals of particular actions or of men's entire lives are a pervasive feature of his writing, and these judgments of course reveal his own personality and prejudices. They do not, however, compromise the seriousness with which he attempted to maintain high standards of accuracy and detail.

His decision to write in Latin, not his native Greek, which continued to influence his style and expression, is readily explicable by the environment in which he worked. His history was begun in the time of Valentinian and Valens, when the leadership of the empire was in the hands of a Latin-speaking dynasty. In later years he was active in the cultivated senatorial circle at Rome.[14] Many of these senators were still pagans, and so was Ammianus at this stage of his life. By describing himself as a *Graecus* he identified himself as a Hellene in the sense that it would be understood in the fourth century, a pagan whose outlook was shaped by Greek culture and religion. While Ammianus' decision to write in the secular tradition of classical historiography precluded any extensive discussion of Christian events and institutions, his work contains much subtle polemic against Christianity.[15] His own religious views were a sophisticated form of pagan monotheism, influenced by Neoplatonic philosophy. They differed in significant ways from those of Julian, who nevertheless was portrayed with enthusiasm that verged on the panegyrical.

The final sentences of his work, quoted above, underlined Ammianus' ambition, and made a programmatic statement that his intention was to write critical history. By choosing the death of Nerva as his starting point he explicitly claimed that he was the successor of Tacitus, whose *Annals* and *Histories*, covering the history of the first century AD, had not been matched by any subsequent historical writing in Latin. Ammianus' surviving books, numbered XIV–XXXI, cover the period from 354 to 378, ending soon after the defeat and death of Valens at Adrianople.[16] The choice of the concluding date was decided not so much by any perception that Adrianople marked an epochal moment in Rome's decline, as by the fact that Theodosius came to power in 379 and was still alive while Ammianus was writing. Ammianus could not hope to maintain the critical stance towards Theodosius that was possible when he was writing about dead emperors. Thus he ironically relinquishes responsibility for writing about the period after 379 to "better men" who would write in a grander style, that is in a suitably panegyrical manner.

Ammianus' claim to be a dispassionate searcher after the historical truth cannot be left uncontested. He famously acknowledged the partisanship in his own account of Julian's career as Caesar and Augustus (Ammianus 16.1). His writing is spiced with satire and personal prejudice. Editorial judgment is barely distinguished from factual reporting, and he can be as biased in his presentation of individuals as Tacitus. Furthermore the excursuses on ethnic groups, for all their vivid rhetorical coloring, tend to be works of the schoolroom, culled from outdated sources, and written with more of an eye for literary effect than for historical accuracy. But the weaknesses of Ammianus' *Res Gestae* are far outweighed by their strengths. The sweep and dynamism of the narrative are conveyed in colorful, pointed prose, and laced with acerbic judgments. Most important of all is that the huge canvas is crammed with detail. In contrast to the anemic Latin chroniclers of the fourth century, or the church historians with their narrower focus, Ammianus offers a panoramic view of the Roman world of the fourth century.[17]

Ammianus' work was continued by Sulpicius Alexander, a Latin writer who began his history at the point where Ammianus left off, but only fragments from the period 387–93 survive, in excerpts quoted by Gregory of Tours (*Histories* 2.9). One other Latin history survives from this period, the *History Against the Pagans*, which was completed in 417 by the Spanish priest Orosius (see below).

We are less well served for the fifth than for the fourth century. An important sequence of Greek writers took up the challenge of writing large-scale histories of the Roman Empire. Their subject matter was not confined to the eastern provinces, but only fragments of their work are preserved and it is very difficult to form an impression of how they interpreted the history of the period as a whole.[18] A large proportion of the fragments were preserved in a tenth-century collection of "Excerpts concerning diplomatic embassies," *Excerpta de legationibus*. These contain important detailed information, and have a bearing on major issues of Roman foreign policy, but of necessity they give a misleading impression of imperial history as a whole, neglecting warfare, internal dynastic affairs, and other matters. A consequence of this uneven survival has been that modern scholarship in turn has concentrated to a considerable degree on diplomacy during this period.[19] In particular it is extremely difficult to form a balanced picture of the processes by which the various Germanic tribes and the Huns increasingly dominated the western part of the empire and brought about its dissolution in the 470s. This was a major theme for any historian, and it is a serious loss that no contemporary presentation survives in full.

The fragmentary classicizing historians of the fifth century AD, as they are labeled in the collected edition with translation and commentary by Blockley, are an indispensable source for the history of the period. The first major figure was Eunapius, a pagan author from Sardis in western Asia Minor, who was born around 349, and died after 404. One of his works, the *Lives of the Sophists*, is preserved, and provides a series of portraits of important pagan intellectuals and philosophers of the fourth century, among them some of the teachers of Julian. His main work was a *Universal History* covering the period 270–404, which is now only preserved in fragments. These are couched in obscure language and display vituperative pagan prejudice. It is clear that this served as a main source for the later pagan historian Zosimus for events from Constantine up to 404.[20] Eunapius' work was continued by another pagan writer, Olympiodorus of Thebes, who wrote a history covering the period from 407 to 425, which was also cited or summarized at length in books 5 and 6 of Zosimus, and extensively used by the church historians, especially Sozomen. The fragments of Olympiodorus are enough to show that his work was of much higher historical quality than Eunapius'.

Priscus, from the Thracian city of Panion, who lived from around 420 to 479, wrote a history in eight books, which seem to have covered most of his own lifetime from 434 to 474. The starting-point was determined by an event not in Roman but in barbarian history, the moment when Attila the Hun assumed power from his father Rua, initially in consort with his brother Bleda. The Huns took center stage at least in the first part of Priscus' history, and Attila emphatically dominates the surviving fragments. The longest of these provides a compelling and memorable account of the Constantinopolitan embassy to Attila of 449, in which Priscus himself participated (discussed below in chapter 6). Priscus' style, like those of the other fifth-century historians, was especially influenced by Thucydides, but the embassy to Attila shows him to have been a writer of perception and imagination, and a keen and alert historical observer.[21] If his work had survived in full there is no doubt that he would be seen as one of the major historians of antiquity.

Malchus of Philadelphia wrote a history in seven books of the period 474–480, which was published around 491. The fragments are the most important source for relations between Zeno and the Goths and also for the emergence of the Isaurian dynasty at Constantinople. He offers a very hostile view of the Isaurians, which doubtless reflected the general opinion of the educated class in Constantinople. The history of the Isaurian dynasty certainly formed the main focus of the work of their compatriot, Candidus, who wrote a history in three books, which began with the accession of Leo in 457 and ended with the death of Zeno in 491. Its contents are known to us from the succinct summary of Photius, made in the tenth century (Blockley fr. 1; *FHG* IV, 135–7). Many more fragments survive of the history written by John of Antioch, but these appear to have been composed at the earliest in the seventh century. They lack the authority of Priscus or Malchus, although they must of necessity be pressed into service to reconstruct a narrative framework for the period.

Zosimus was the only major historian whose works survive who is known to have been active under Anastasius. His *New History*, written in six books around the year 500, covered the period from Augustus to 409, where the manuscripts break off in the middle of book 6, shortly before the sack of Rome by Alaric, which may have formed a melancholy climax to the narrative.[22] Zosimus wrote from an aggressively pagan viewpoint, and it is a matter for ongoing dispute how much of this stance is due to his copying the pagan views of his main sources, especially Eunapius, and how much represents his own convictions. Much of book 2, covering the period of Diocletian and the tetrarchy, is not preserved, and we may reasonably guess that it contained a vehemently anti-Christian account of the period of the Great Persecution, which led later copyists to omit it. The period up to 404 is heavily dependent on Eunapius, and from 406/7 to 409 on Olympiodorus. Zosimus' overall motivation was to offer an explanation for Rome's decline from its former greatness. He contrasts his task with that of Polybius. While Polybius had traced Rome's rise to imperial power in a mere fifty-three years, Zosimus claimed that Rome's power had been ruined in an equally short space of time (Zosimus 1.1 and 57). His explanation for the decline was the conversion of Rome to Christianity, which he held responsible for the corruption of Rome's political virtues. The most militantly Christian emperors of the fourth century, Constantine and Theodosius, are viciously pilloried; the account of Julian is as positive as that of Ammianus, and both authors often drew on the same sources of information. When describing how Theodosius visited Rome, and abolished state support for public sacrifices, in defiance of the wishes of the senators, Zosimus comments that the city had been preserved intact for 1,200 years by observing these traditional rites. It was their abandonment that caused the empire to be reduced and to become a home for barbarians, or to be so depopulated that places which had once been cities could now no longer be recognized (Zosimus 4.59). Zosimus also identified the barbarization of the empire as another cause of its ruin. At the end of his lengthy account of how Diocletian staged the secular games in 305, he quoted the Sibylline oracle which associated Roman success with the conduct of the major public sacrifices on this occasion. "But once this festival was neglected after Diocletian's abdication, the empire gradually collapsed and was imperceptibly barbarised" (Zosimus 2.6, trans. Ridley). The two themes of barbarization and the neglect of the gods surely coalesced in the missing account of the sack of Rome by Alaric. The loss of this section may either be the responsibility of Christian copyists, exercising their form of religious censorship, or be due to the accidental loss of the work's final pages. Although Zosimus is an indispensable source, especially for the period after 378 where Ammianus had stopped, the historical quality of the work is low, marred by careless use of sources leading to doublets in the narrative and other errors, as well as by transparent prejudice. These drawbacks are exposed, but also redeemed, by the splendid detailed edition and commentary by Paschoud.

Almost contemporary with Zosimus is the invaluable Syriac *Chronicle* attributed to Joshua the Stylite, the pseudonym of a monk from Edessa in Mesopotamia, who was commissioned by his abbot to write an account of the afflictions suffered in Mesopotamia in the years around 500, which culminated in war with the Persians. The year 500 aroused millenarian expectations, and the earthquakes, plagues, famine, and pestilence, which were observed at the time, strengthened men's conviction that the end of the world was at hand.[23] The *Chronicle* noted with relief that they had somehow evaded destruction:

> For behold there leaned heavily upon us the calamities of hunger and pestilence in the time of the locusts, so that we were well nigh going to destruction; but God had mercy upon us, though we were unworthy, and gave us little respite from the calamities that pressed upon us. (Ps-Joshua, *Chron.* 5, trans. Wright)

The author described himself as a man of plain speech who recorded the truth about what people in Edessa had experienced, and the work is full of detailed circumstantial information about the conditions in the city at a time when it was beset with natural disasters and warfare. However, it also provides a remarkably well-informed perspective on events on the world stage as they appeared to a community on the border between the Roman and Persian empires. Ps-Joshua traced the origins of the Persian invasion of Roman territory in 502 back to the 480s, and provided many details about the internal condition of both empires at this period.[24] He took trouble to establish the facts:

> I have written down these narratives in brief terms, because I was anxious to avoid prolixity. Some of them I found in old books; others I learned from meeting with men who had acted as ambassadors to both monarchs; and others from those who were present at these occurrences. But now I am going to inform thee of the things that happened with us, because with this year commenced the violent chastisements and the signs that have taken place in our own days. (Ps-Joshua, *Chron.* 25, trans. Wright)

The *Chronicle* is the most remarkable example of a local history to survive from late antiquity, and is all the more valuable for the fact that no contemporary general history survives from the early part of the sixth century.

Much retrospective information about the reigns of Anastasius and Justin is found in the enormous *oeuvre* of Procopius, the last great historian of antiquity and the main chronicler of the age of Justinian. Procopius, who was born around 500 and died c.560, was one of the extraordinarily talented generation that emerged in Constantinople in the late 520s, and contributed to the dynamism of the first half of Justinian's reign. He reveals that he was an *assessor*, or legal advisor, on the staff of Belisarius in 527 (*Bell. Pers.* 1.1.3, 1.12.24) and accompanied the general on campaign in Mesopotamia, in Africa and in Italy until the siege of Ravenna in 540, when Belisarius was recalled to Constantinople. His narrative of the various wars indicates that he took significant responsibilities as a prominent staff officer (*Bell. Vand.* 3.14.7–17, 3.21.6; *Bell. Goth.* 5.4.1–2).

His main work was a history of the wars under Justinian, comprising two books on the Persian Wars (1–2), two books on the Vandal Wars (3–4), three books on the wars with the Ostrogoths in Italy (5–7), with a final book continuing the story on all three fronts (8). This unusual form of organization has its precedent in Appian's account of Roman history, written in the middle of the second century AD, which was arranged according to the various regions where Romans campaigned against major enemies. The work covers the period 527–551. The scheme is remarkably effective, and enables Procopius to provide very coherent accounts of Roman activities in each of the theaters of war, without sacrificing detail. There are inevitable problems of achieving clarity where the chronology of the wars overlapped. The history of the campaigns against the Persians presents no complications up to the "eternal peace" of 532, but later diplomatic and military activities in the East occurred during the period of the wars against the Goths in Italy, which seriously hampered the Roman war effort in the East. The highly successful African campaign against the Vandals of 533–4 is convincingly portrayed in the two books of the Vandal Wars; less effective is Procopius' much less detailed account of later developments in Africa, when the Roman grip was threatened by Moorish and other rebellions. Commentators have drawn a distinction between the positive, even triumphal, tone of the first seven books of the wars, when Roman successes far outweighed their failures, and the subdued note struck by book VIII. In this final book Procopius continued the story on all fronts through the late 540s, recording setbacks, disappointments, and a growing sense of disillusion with the regime. However, a closer reading of *Wars* as a whole shows that Procopius was neither a supporter of Justinian's imperial ambitions nor sympathetic to the tenor of his reign as a whole. On the contrary he used highly sophisticated literary artistry to criticize the regime which he served. His is one of the most extraordinary dissident voices to have made itself heard in a totalitarian state.[25] The aptest parallel to his achievement may be found in a very different context. The compositions, and especially the symphonies, of Dmitri Shostakovich, the most important composer of the twentieth century, provide a mocking, often terrifying, critique of the tyranny of Lenin, Stalin, and later Soviet rulers, while simultaneously presenting a face that was for the most part acceptable to and applauded by the regime.

Procopius left two other works, which have been as influential as *Wars* in shaping modern perceptions of the age of Justinian. *Buildings* is a lengthy, panegyrical account of building undertaken by Justinian throughout the empire, including churches, fortifications, and even new cities. Much effort has been devoted to matching Procopius' descriptions to the archaeological evidence on the ground, with conflicting results. Unsurprisingly Procopius tends to ascribe as much building work as possible to Justinian's efforts, but in particular cases, as for instance his account of the frontier fortress city of Dara in Mesopotamia, it seems that he has effectively withheld credit which is due to Justinian's predecessors.[26] This may have been a deliberate ploy by Procopius to undermine the credibility of his own work. He was an embittered and acerbic critic of Justinian's policies, and writing panegyric will not have been a welcome task. The famous *Secret History* or *Anecdota* (literally "not published") is a pungently critical reappraisal of the workings of the Justinianic state. It unveils the disreputable intrigues and dubious, self-interested motives behind the actions and policies of the leading figures in the regime, in particular Justinian and the empress Theodora, Belisarius and his wife Antonina. The tone adopted for the *Secret History* is not unparalleled in *Wars*. Some short passages are common to both works, and the two analyses present views of the age of Justinian from the inside and the outside, which are carefully designed to complement one another. The criticisms found in the *Secret History* can be paralleled in the work of many earlier historians writing about dead emperors and their associates. Condemnation of court intrigues, for instance, is an essential ingredient of Ammianus' history. Procopius, however, goes far beyond retelling court scandals and immoralities, to deliver a devastating indictment of an emperor whom he came to regard as an incarnate demon. It may have been that Procopius expected to integrate the findings of his *Secret History* into his main work after Justinian's death. As it was the emperor outlived him, and the fusion was never achieved.

Jordanes, the first major chronicler of barbarian history, was also active at the same time as Procopius and wrote two works, the *Getica* and the *Romana*, in 551. The former is of particular importance, as it is the first comprehensive narrative account of Gothic history. The author was himself a Goth, and *notarius* to a noble Gothic family (*Get.* LX, 316). One of the sources which inspired this work was a lost account of Gothic history by the Roman senator Cassiodorus, which is described in a letter written by the Gothic king Athalaric to the Roman Senate in 533:

> Why, honourable sirs, should you suppose that Cassiodorus was content merely to essay the study of living lords, a task of inevitable tedium, although they may be expected to reward it? (4) He extended his labours even to the ancient cradle of our house, learning from his reading what the hoary recollections of our elders scarcely preserved. From the lurking place of antiquity he led out the kings of the Goths, long hidden in oblivion. He restored the Amals, along with the honour of their family, clearly proving me to be of royal stock to the seventeenth generation. (5) From Gothic origins he made a Roman history, gathering, as it were, into one garland, flower buds that had previously been scattered throughout the field of literature. (Cassiodorus, *Var.* 9.25.3–5, trans. Barnish)

Jordanes explained his debt to Cassiodorus in his own preface:

> You urge me to leave the little work I have in hand, that is the abbreviation of the chronicles, and to condense in my own style in this small book the twelve volumes of Senator on the origin and deeds of the Getae from olden times to the present day, descending through generations of the kings. (Jordanes, *Get.* LX, 316)

Jordanes avowed that this was a difficult task:

> But worse than any other burden is the fact that I have no access to his books that I may follow his thought. Still – and let me lie not – I have in times past read the books a second time by his steward's loan for a three-day reading. The words I recall not, but the sense and the deeds related I think I retain entire. To this I have added fitting matters from some Greek and Latin histories. I have also put in an introduction and a conclusion and inserted many things of my own authorship. (Jordanes, *Get.* I.1–2)

The format of the first half of the *Getica* precisely corresponds to the description of Cassiodorus' lost work.[27] Most of this is etiological or genealogical fiction, designed to enhance the dignity and antiquity of the Gothic race and place them on a level with Romans, Greeks, and Jews.[28] As a source of historical information Jordanes is most valuable for his excerpting and use of Priscus, who is cited by name in four passages and is clearly the main source for the account of the mid-fifth century. This includes extended descriptions of the defeat of the Huns at the battle of the Catalaunian Plain, the encounter between

Attila and Pope Leo, and the death of Attila. Mommsen drew attention to the much higher quality of these sections of Jordanes:

> in these pages are found accurate descriptions of the distinguishing traits of various peoples, a life-like and truthful portrayal of men, a keen and careful analysis of the causes and meanings of various events, and the use of apt figures of speech and comparisons.

At the same time as Jordanes was active, an anonymous writer, known to modern scholars as the *anonymus Valesianus*, wrote a short Latin account of events in Italy from 474 to 526, concentrating on the achievements of the Ostrogothic king Theoderic. He had access to well-informed sources, including Maximinus, bishop of Ravenna in the 540s and 550s. He had also read and cited the Life of St Severinus of Noricum (*Anon. Val.* 10.45–46). This short biography, written by Eugippius, one of the inhabitants of the former Roman province who sought refuge around the Bay of Naples at the beginning of the sixth century, is a circumstantial account of conditions along the northern frontier of the empire at the end of the fifth century, when the region was given up definitively to the barbarians.

The next surviving "chronicle of barbarian history" after Jordanes is the work of Gregory of Tours, the founder of early medieval Latin literature. The ten books of his *Histories* (widely referred to today as the *History of the Franks*) are reminiscent not only in their title but also in their content of Herodotus, as they relate the affairs of Gaul under the Frankish kings in astonishing detail up to c.590. The last five books, covering the period from 575 to 591, were effectively a chronicle of his own times, concentrating especially on the activities of the Frankish kings and leading figures in the church, which Gregory brought up to date on a yearly basis until two years before his death. They present a world that has almost lost contact with its classical Roman roots.

Three major historians covered the second half of the sixth century. Agathias of Myrina began where Procopius' *Wars* had left off.[29] He was also the author of a substantial collection of verse epigrams. He conceived his history on a large scale, and the five books that survive cover only the period from 553–9. Agathias shared Procopius' interest in technical matters and practical achievements. It has recently been argued that both writers belonged to the shrinking circle of pagan intellectuals.[30] However, the differences between the two authors were greater than their similarities. While Procopius wrote about Justinian's wars as a participant observer, Agathias compiled his history at the end of his life, probably between 579 and 582, and at a considerable remove from the events he described and the persons who had lived through them. His focus was on the period when Justinian's regime had turned in on itself, and the narrative lacks the dramatic wartime narratives and overall political grasp of Procopius. The work is notable for important digressions on the Sassanians and the Franks, and for events in Lazica, at the east end of the Black Sea, which had become the main theater of war between Rome and Persia.[31] Overall, however, there is a notable emphasis on the unexpected blows of fate which the empire endured, and the natural catastrophes and disasters which afflicted Constantinople in the 550s, to the extent that these become the guiding elements in Agathias' pessimistic reading of Justinian's later years.[32]

The history of Menander Protector ("the Guardsman"), which was written in the 580s, covered the period from the 559 to the death of Tiberius II in 582. It perpetuates the qualities of the best fifth-century historians, and provides a sober and reliable guide to events. Most notably, it preserves the full text of the treaty struck between Rome and Persia in 561/2. As with Priscus, most of the fragments of Menander derive from the tenth-century *Excerpta de legationibus*, thus creating the impression that Roman foreign policy depended disproportionately on diplomacy. In contrast to Agathias and Procopius, Menander makes his personal Christian convictions clear.

Theophylact Simocatta wrote his substantial secular history in eight books in the reign of Heraclius (610–41). It was devoted to the reign of the emperor Maurice. Most of the content of his history concerns the wars fought by Maurice's generals, in the East against the Persians, and in Thrace and Illyricum against the Avars. He creates the impression more of a litterateur than a historian. The style is over-elaborate and often bombastic, and he makes little attempt to reconcile conflicting narratives that he found in his sources. These often contained identifiable biases. Chronology and the topography of campaigns are confusingly reproduced. He is a flawed but indispensable authority for the last quarter of the sixth century, and the value of his work stands out the more for the fact that no large-scale historical narrative of the following reigns of Phocas and Heraclius has survived.[33]

The Church Historians

In addition to the secular histories, late antiquity saw the birth of the new genre of church history, created by Eusebius of Caesarea at the beginning of the fourth century. Eusebius conceived his task as that of chronicling the Christians as a nation. Christianity, he believed, had always been the archetypal and primeval religion, but its truth was obscured until the birth of Christ, God's son. This coincided with the reign of the emperor Augustus, so for Eusebius the Roman Empire had brought about conditions which allowed the full truth of Christianity to be revealed. He outlined the subject-matter of Christian history in his opening paragraph: the achievements of the heirs of the holy apostles since Christ's day, important matters in the history of the church, the doings of its leaders and the preachings and writings of those who had spread God's word, including those who introduced error into doctrine. He was also concerned with the disasters that befell the Jews who had conspired against the Savior, the struggles of Christians against the gentiles, and the trials of martyrdom that Christians suffered in their cause (Eusebius, *HE* I.1.1–2). The closest model for this program came from the Jewish writer Josephus, whose two great works on the *Antiquities* and *Wars of the Jews* adopted a similar approach in presenting the history of a religious movement as a type of national history. Eusebius also took further a very important feature of Josephus' historical writing, which was not part of the secular historical tradition. This was the practice of incorporating verbatim transcripts and citations of relevant documents. The appeal to the *ipsissima verba* of written evidence was a natural one for writers whose faith involved belief in the authority of holy books, and the practice remains characteristic of much Christian and Jewish historical writing today. In a few cases versions of documents quoted by Eusebius have survived independently as papyri or inscriptions, and they confirm the authenticity of the record he preserved.[34] The *Church History* was the subject of revision and expansion as history itself unfolded in the first decades of the fourth century. A major issue is the question of when Eusebius wrote his first version. T. D. Barnes has argued that books 1–7 were completed before 300. This would imply that the church had established a confident foothold in the mainstream of social and religious activity before the Great Persecution and the conversion of Constantine. A later date of composition harmonizes better with the opposing view, that Christianity remained relatively insignificant as a political and social force until 312.[35]

Eusebius' *Church History* was edited and brought up-to-date by Rufinus, who published a Latin translation with two additional books in 402,[36] but his most important successors were the Greek writers Socrates, Sozomen, and Theodoret, who published a trio of surviving church histories between 439 and the early 450s. Socrates' first book replicates some of the ground covered by the last section of Eusebius' work in order to include additional documents and further discussion of the origins of the Arian heresy and the split in the church which followed the Council of Nicaea. These writers share much material in common, but were, to some extent, written from different cultural perspectives. Socrates and Sozomen had received training as lawyers in Constantinople, and wrote as committed laymen, not as clerics. Sozomen preserves information and insights related to his place of origin, Gaza in Palestine. Theodoret, by contrast, was born in Syrian Antioch and became bishop of Cyrrhus in northern Syria. He also published a series of short biographical sketches of Syrian holy men, and an extensive correspondence, much of it devoted to petitioning the imperial authorities on behalf of his community. All these writers, but most of all Socrates, reflected the eirenic ideals of Theodosius II's religious policies. Socrates condemns violent conflicts in the church. While supporting the orthodox theology which was the touchstone of imperial religious policy after the Council of Constantinople in 381, he treats the views of schismatics, notably the Novatian Church, about which he was well informed, and even those of heretics, with sympathy. Socrates' work served as the main, but not the only source for Sozomen, who wrote in a more elaborate rhetorical style and laid greater emphasis on the growth of asceticism and the monastic movement. All three authors incorporated references to secular affairs in their account of church affairs, and Sozomen in particular quoted at length from

Olympiodorus' history of the first quarter of the fifth century. This tendency was not simply a matter of authorial choice, but an inevitable reflection of the increasing fusion of church and secular matters in the Theodosian period.

The universal *History Against the Pagans* of Orosius, written in the 420s and dedicated to St Augustine, represents a different tradition of Christian historiography. Like the compilers of Christian chronicles, Orosius made a major effort to integrate secular classical history with the chronologies of other world empires and with Christian chronology. Unlike the chronicles, however, his work was conceived on a large scale and was designed to demonstrate that disasters, above all the sack of Rome in 410, had not come into the world through the fault of the Christians and due to neglect of the old gods. On the contrary Roman history before Constantine was replete with disaster and oppression. The fall of Rome itself was appropriate punishment for the sins of its leaders, who had espoused paganism too readily, and mitigated by the fact that the city's conqueror, Alaric, was himself a Christian.[37] The seventh book covered the period from the time of Augustus and the life of Christ up to Orosius' own day, and is valuable for his observations on events and episodes in the western provinces, as they were being overrun by the Visigoths and the Vandals.

Three church histories survive from the sixth century. The Monophysite Zacharias followed a legal career in Constantinople before becoming bishop of Mytilene in 527. His history covered the period from c.450 to 491. Only books 3–6 survive in a Syriac translation. John of Ephesus wrote an ecclesiastical history during the reign of Maurice, which also survives in a Syriac version. Evagrius of Antioch began at an earlier date and continued beyond Zacharias up to the twelfth year of the emperor Maurice in 593. After brief preliminaries, which identified the six books as a sequel to the work of Eusebius and the Theodosian trio of writers, Evagrius began in earnest with an account of the Council of Ephesus of 431. This introduced the fundamental controversy concerning the one or two natures of Christ, which was to divide the eastern church throughout the rest of antiquity. The early part of his history is dominated by long summaries of the proceedings of the Church Councils at Ephesus in 431 and 449 and at Chalcedon in 451, where this matter dominated the doctrinal agenda. The first two books contain extensive excerpts from the documents of these Councils, which are also independently preserved. The later books contain a much higher proportion of non-ecclesiastical material. They effectively provide a narrative thread through the political and external history after the mid-fifth century, while paying particular attention to major religious initiatives, such as Zeno's attempt to unify the Monophysite and Chalcedonian branches of the church with his *Henotikon*, and the Monophysite tendencies of Anastasius. Evagrius is also a major source for events in Antioch and in Syria, especially during the Persian invasions of the sixth century. He made extensive use of secular sources, including Procopius' *Wars*, and his work, like that of John of Ephesus, is not only valuable for church history.

On a less ambitious scale there were numerous chronicles and digests of historical events. These took the Creation of the World as their starting point, and began with rapid chronological summaries of Biblical history which were cross referenced, as far as possible, with secular events, and thus served to illustrate the workings of divine providence in human affairs. The seventh-century *Chronicon Pachale* was a summary account of the events of world history told from a Constantinopolitan viewpoint. It contains invaluable, but also limited, information about episodes in the eastern capital, and is especially important for the reign of Heraclius. The *Chronicle* of John Malalas served a similar function for Antioch. Both were written in a terse, non-rhetorical style with few literary pretensions, but it appears that in their original form many of these chronicles were supplied with illustrations, which will have enhanced their popular appeal.[38] These eastern compilations were matched in the West by a group of Latin chronicles, and partly overlap with them. The chronicles are an invaluable source of information for the chronology of events in late antiquity, and often preserve notice of events and episodes for which we have no other information, but they rarely provide a context for their historical interpretation. The *Chronographia* of Theophanes, a Constantinopolitan work in this genre, deserves to be mentioned, even though it was written in the early ninth century, since it probably preserves important detail about the campaigns of Heraclius in the 620s, and is thus one of the critical sources of information about this momentous decade (see below, chapter 12).[39]

The Legal and Administrative Sources

The narrative of Roman history contained in this book depends to a large degree on histories and chronicles, but thematic study of the period draws on other sources. The great compilations of legal texts – the Theodosian and Justinianic Codes; the new regulations, *Novellae*, issued by fifth- and sixth-century emperors, especially Justinian, who was by far the most energetic legislator; as well as smaller compilations of a similar nature – illustrate the workings of the Roman state from the perspective of the rulers. These official collections of material underpin virtually all modern attempts to reconstruct how the empire was governed. The Theodosian Code was a compendium of about 2,500 rescripts and a few edicts, issued by all the Christian emperors since Constantine, organized into sixteen books by topic. It was compiled by a team of jurists who had been commissioned by Theodosius II and was designed as an authoritative handbook of Roman public law, valid for both parts of the empire. The work was published in 437, perhaps in connection with the marriage at Constantinople of Theodosius' daughter Eudoxia to the western ruler Valentinian III, and a copy was formally presented to the Roman Senate in January 438. It thus emphasized the constitutional unity of the eastern and western provinces. The compilers drew their material from various sources, including local provincial archives, and this is reflected in the type of document found in the collection. The general laws and imperial edicts of empire-wide scope, are vastly out-numbered by specific decisions addressed to named Roman officials in specific places and provinces.

The Theodosian Code is admirably systematic in conception. Each entry was listed with the name of the ruling emperor(s), the name and rank of the official who received the decision, the place and date, and details about the receipt and publication of the order. Laws were listed in chronological order and in each case the latest decision on a given issue was held to be legally definitive. In practice inevitable mistakes occurred, and details were sometimes garbled. The rulings themselves were not given in full but in abbreviated form. However, by far the biggest problem that arises from studying the workings of the empire through the Code is the false impression that it creates of the emperor and his advisors acting as a pro-active legislature, in the manner of modern governments. The role of emperors in the early principate was almost entirely a reactive one. Problems that arose in the cities and provinces were brought to the emperor's or his officials' attention by letter or by personal petition, and were then dealt with on a piecemeal basis.[40] In the late empire the monumental presence of the Theodosian Code suggests at first sight that the ruling emperors had initiated countless measures to deal with all manner of problems. In fact, it is obvious in almost every case that the initiative lay with their subjects and officials, who had raised matters of concern which required a decision or some other form of intervention. The pattern of petition and response thus continued to characterize late Roman rule. The imperial replies varied in tone between rulers, and thanks to the work of Tony Honoré it is possible to assign many of them to specific officials, the imperial quaestors, who were responsible for drafting the emperors' responses.[41] In general they were written in an overblown rhetorical style, which denounced illegalities in a highly exaggerated way. Late Roman law was marked by increasing judicial savagery,[42] although on closer inspection the scope of imperial action and the scale of punishments appears to have been less drastic than appears at first sight. The Theodosian Code is an indispensable source of information for social and cultural history, although we may be led to overestimate its historical importance because of the wealth of detail that it contains. Its contents reflect not the activities of society as a whole, but only those areas in which the state intervened.

The Justinianic Code formed one part of the enormous work, which has been known since the sixteenth century as the *Corpus Iuris Civilis*, the Body of Civil Law.[43] The other sections were the *Digest*, a definitive compendium of Roman private law, and a large scale legal manual, the *Institutes*. The Code of Justinian added relevant imperial rulings from the period before Constantine, including many of Diocletianic date. The corpus was one of the most astonishing monuments, some would argue the defining achievement, of the age of Justinian. A first edition of the Code was issued in 528–9, the *Institutes* and the *Digest* appeared in 533, and a second edition of the Code in 534. The driving force behind the enterprise was Tribonian, in charge of an editorial commission of ten lawyers. They submitted their work to the emperor seven years ahead of the planned schedule for completion.[44] Much of the imperial legislation collected in the Theodosian and Justinianic Codes camouflages imperial decisions in a torrent of hostile rhetoric. The imperial rulings give ample evidence for the ideological and moral high ground claimed by the Roman state, but often tell us very little about how such legislation was applied to actual cases.

The law codes map out the scope and range of state activities, from lofty matters of high politics to the dealings and legal competences of the most humble citizens. At one extreme, for instance, the letter of Justinian to Archelaus, the first praetorian prefect of Africa after it was recovered from the Vandals in 533, sets out the entire ideology of the conquest, as well as details of how the whole region, now seven provinces, should be governed, by a staff of 396 persons attached to the prefect, and fifty to each of the three senior, consular, governors. A parallel letter to Belisarius set out the specific military arrangements for troops and the locations of the garrisons (*CJust.* 1.27). In an entirely different sphere, the same emperor wrote three years earlier to Julianus, praetorian prefect at Constantinople, to rule on whether persons suffering from a mental illness could make a valid will:

> We order that a will of this kind, where the testator became insane while in the very act of making it, shall be void. If, however, he should, during a lucid interval, wish to execute a will, or make any final disposition of his estate, and, being of all the time sound mind and without the return of his affliction he began and finished the will, or other final disposition of his estate, we decree that it shall stand, provided that all the formalities required by law in instruments of this kind are observed. (*CJust.* 1.22.9, Sept. 1, 530)

Legal rulings illuminate features of late Roman history, which we might otherwise take for granted. Labeling heretical sects after their leaders was a practice enshrined in a law of Theodosius II:

> Nestor, the founder of a monstrous superstition, having been condemned, remember that it is proper for his followers to be branded with his name, and not abuse the appellation of Christians; but just as Arians are so-called from Arius, on account of similar impiety, by the law of Constantine of divine memory, and Porphyrians from Porphyry, so everywhere the members of the infamous sect of the Nestor shall be styled Nestorians. (*CJust.* 1.5.6, Aug. 1, 435)

This style of referring to outlawed religious groups is, of course, familiar from other evidence. By contrast, if it were not for the wording of another law of Theodosius II, dating to 444, we might not suspect that statues in honor of provincial governors or other office holders in the cities of the empire were to be paid for at the expense of the person honored (*CJust.* 1.24.4).

The barbarian kingdoms of the West issued their own codes in imitation of the great Roman compilations.[45] These too are essentially works of Roman law. From time to time these allow a glimpse of Germanic *Volksjustiz*, but they draw heavily on the rulings and practices of the imperial collections. The most important of these were the *Breviarium* of Alaric the Visigoth (506), and the *Lex Burgundionum* of Gundobad (c.535). Theoderic produced no similar code for Ostrogothic rule, which was in line with the conception that he was ruling Italy in the name of the eastern emperor.

Two other works from the fourth and sixth centuries are particularly valuable for illustrating the role played by senatorial officials in the government of Italy. Quintus Aurelius Symmachus wrote forty-nine reports (*relationes*) to the western emperors while holding the office of Prefect of Italy in 384.[46] In 537 Cassiodorus retired from a public career that had included seven major senatorial positions. This is documented in his *Variae*, a collection in twelve books of the official letters he had written on behalf of the five successive Ostrogothic rulers from Theoderic to Vitigis, and the Senate, as well as those issued in his own right as Prefect of Italy from 533–6.[47]

The production of the legal codes was an attempt on the most ambitious scale to introduce system and order to the process of Roman rule. The same tendency is visible in the lists and catalogues, which described the components of the empire. These included the *Laterculus Veronensis* (the Verona List), which was a catalogue of the provinces around 314;[48] the *Notitia* of the city of Constantinople, which described the districts and buildings of the city in the time of Theodosius II; and the *Notitia urbis regionum XIV*, which was a similar gazetteer of the fourteen districts of the city of Rome in the fourth century. The most important work in this genre to survive is the *Notitia Dignitatum*, the catalogue of ranks, which covered the civilian and military offices both in the East, probably compiled around 401, and in the West, dating to 425. These provided a list of officials and military units, with an indication of their location, and illustrated them with appropriate emblems: magisterial insignia, shield blazons of military regiments, and forts controlled by officers in charge of frontier troops.[49] The *Notitia Dignitatum*, like the law codes, has been a major source for the reconstruction of the late Roman state, and especially for assessing its military strength and the deployment of army units.[50] This approach, however, pays excessive credence to the value of official lists. Even if we allow that the lists are accurate compilations in themselves, it is unlikely that they conformed to reality. Commanders will have overstated the numbers of active men in their units when they put in claims for supplies; bureaucrats will have exaggerated the number and importance of ranks of all sorts, in order to enhance the empire's and their own importance.[51]

One other class of documentation is even more abundant than the legal sources; the records of church councils, notably Constantinople 381, Carthage 411, Ephesus 431, Ephesus 449, and Chalcedon 451. Although bishops were the main players at these ecumenical meetings, dealing with major matters of doctrine and discipline, imperial officials were inevitably involved, and there was much related official correspondence between the leading ecclesiastical politicians and the ruling authorities. The quantity of surviving documentation may be explained by three converging factors: the bureaucratization of the late

Roman state, the importance within Christian culture of the written word, and the obsession with absolute verbal accuracy in recording creeds and doctrinal statements. The records of the councils at Ephesus and Chalcedon reveal the complex networks that linked church and state, and demonstrate in detail how the empire was governed from Constantinople under Theodosius II.[52] The acts of the Council of Carthage in 411 are one of the most extraordinary sets of records to have survived from antiquity. The entire proceedings of the three-day meeting, which was designed to put an end to the Donatist controversy, were recorded by two teams of stenographers, acting for the two sides, and checked word for word against each other. The proceedings of all but half a day have been preserved. We have, in effect, a real-time record of every word and action of the meeting in which the emperor Honorius imposed the will of the Catholic Roman Church on the African schism.[53]

Letter Collections

Law codes and official lists create an idealized view of the Roman Empire, as it was conceived by lawyers, bureaucrats, and perhaps even emperors. The real world was often different, and sources that reflect local conditions throughout the empire are the historian's antidote to a surfeit of legal and administrative rhetoric. Some of the best information for what Roman society was like and how the empire worked in practice comes from contemporary letters. The bias towards preserving Christian texts has meant that most surviving correspondence was written by bishops, who frequently took the role of secular civic leaders. From Gaul we have large collections of letters by Sidonius Apollinaris, from Caesarius bishop of Arles in the early sixth century, his contemporary Avitus of Vienne, and Remigius of Reims.[54] Other western collections in Latin are those of Ambrose, bishop of Milan from the late fourth century, Augustine in Africa in the early fifth century (including a newly discovered collection of previously unpublished letters), and Ennodius of Pavia, the bishop of Milan, relating to Ostrogothic Italy. In the East, Basil, bishop of Caesarea from 370 to 378, wrote numerous letters to officials at all levels from the praetorian prefect of the East to local censors. The majority of these petitions contained requests for tax exemptions.[55] Basil's closest fifth-century counterpart was Theodoret, bishop of Cyrrhus in north Syria from 423 to c.460. His pleas for Cyrrhus and its citizens included a letter to the Augusta Pulcheria herself (*ep.* 43), as well as praetorian prefects, various quaestors of the imperial palace, leading patricians of the time of Theodosius II, and military commanders.[56] The major churchmen of the period were usually prolific correspondents. Most of their letters relate to internal church affairs and doctrinal matters, but supply many vital clues to the wider social context in which the church was embedded. Some were selected and edited for wider circulation, such as the main collection of Ambrose's correspondence, and these were doubtless designed to show the writer in a favorable light.[57]

Inscriptions

Countless inscriptions in Greek, Latin, and other peripheral languages have survived from late antiquity, but they are less numerous than for the early empire and have played a less important role in modern studies of the period. Public inscriptions in particular were not produced in a vacuum, but reflected their institutional and cultural background. So the senatorial aristocracy of Rome continued to be commemorated by honorific inscriptions in the same tradition as their predecessors in the early empire. These documents are extremely important for defining the culture and political outlook of the final generations of pagan society in the West.[58] The thriving urban culture to be found in North Africa up to the fifth century is revealed by the texts of honorific statue-bases set up for members of the local elites.[59] Two monographs have also been written which chart the history of Athens and Attica, and of Carian Aphrodisias, through a study of their inscriptions.[60] The largest body of public epigraphy from this period, however, is to be found at Ephesus in Asia Minor. In Greek cities there was a growing vogue for verse inscriptions set up to honor benefactors. Apart from over two hundred inscribed examples, many more survive in the pages of the Palatine Anthology.[61] However, it is striking that most of the honorific texts of late antiquity in the eastern provinces were set up not to honor local civic dignitaries but imperial officials. They thus clearly reflect the growing centralization of authority and the decline in civic values. Major imperial rulings continued to be published as inscribed documents during the late empire. The most famous example is Diocletian's Price Edict of 301, known from multiple copies found in Greece and western Asia Minor (Plate 2.1). There is also a growing number of other official edicts and rescripts of tetrarchic date from the eastern provinces, all of which, significantly, were inscribed in Latin.[62] Imposing imperial building inscriptions, put up in urban centers and along the military frontiers, were another emphatic hallmark of the new order of Diocletian and his colleagues.[63] Between the fourth and sixth centuries Greek increasingly replaced Latin as the language of choice for such documents in the eastern provinces, although Latin remained the language of law and administration in Constantinople itself.[64] Inscribed acclamations are a genre that is especially characteristic of late Roman public epigraphy. Chants and shouts raised in public meetings to acclaim benefactors, governors, local church leaders, or emperors were now carved in stone on columns, on the exterior walls of buildings, or on statue bases, often in combination with the symbol of the cross.[65]

Epigraphy at a more vernacular level also reflected cultural and social trends. In the western reaches of Britain metrical Latin inscriptions reveal that the inhabitants still retained knowledge of classical culture and could quote and appreciate Vergil, long after the political structures of the empire had been eclipsed.[66] Inscriptions set up in the Burgundian kingdom between the fourth and sixth centuries used Roman consular dating as a mark of cultural and political affiliation to the empire.[67] Above all inscriptions mark the spread of

Plate 2.1 The Price Edict of Diocletian, carved on the parapet wall of the circular meat market at Aezani in Phrygia (S. Mitchell)

Christianity. The heretical and schismatic Christian groups of central Asia Minor – Novatians, Encratites, Montanists – and others, as well as Jews of the diaspora, are readily identifiable from their inscriptions. The diversity of these groups contrasts markedly with the general tone of patristic Christian literature, which asserted the triumph of a dominant orthodoxy.[68] The Christian inscriptions of the Near East, including over a thousand texts relating to church construction, are an enormous resource for understanding the cultural development and social and economic relations in the region.[69] Another vital body of epigraphic material from the Levant are the inscribed texts of the seventh and eighth centuries which covered the era of the first Islamic conquests.[70]

The Material World

Representational art is a particularly important source. As the emperors themselves became more remote from their subjects, the manner in which their images were publicly presented became more contrived, and carried elaborate encoded meanings. This is particularly evident in fourth-century representations of emperors and members of their families, which were subtly designed,

Plate 2.2 The head and other fragments of a colossal marble statue of the emperor Constantine, now on the Capitol at Rome. The emperor's upward gaze is explained by Eusebius, *Life of Constantine* 4.15: "In the imperial quarters of various cities, in the images erected above the entrances, he was portrayed standing up, looking up to heaven, his hands extended in a gesture of prayer" (S. Mitchell)

according to well-understood conventions, to convey essential propaganda messages about the regime. They express ideal relationships between the rulers and their subjects. Free standing sculpture such as the porphyry groups depicting the tetrarchs, figured friezes, like those on the obelisk base of Theodosius I in Constantinople, and decorated silver plate, like the *missorium* of Theodosius from Madrid, are a visual counterpart to the imperial panegyrics. They provide a key to understanding how rulers conceptualized their office.[71] Portrait-sculpture and coinage were also vital media for the presentation of a ruler. During the period of Diocletian and Constantine portraits were used more than at any time since the age of Augustus to project and differentiate the character and regime styles of the emperors, and accentuated the competition between them (Plate 2.2).[72] There was also still room in the fourth and fifth centuries for statues of leading public figures, displayed along the streets and in the main squares of provincial capitals and other large cities.[73] Notable groups have been found at Ephesus and Aphrodisias, and exemplify the tradition of display that remained central to civic life in the eastern empire. The choice of subject reflected cultural developments in late antiquity. A large house that seems to have housed a pagan philosophical school at Aphrodisias was decorated with a series of tondo portraits of famous intellectual figures from the Greek tradition. The hippodrome at Constantinople was adorned with major monuments for successful charioteers.[74] Imperial images on coins at this period were also designed on the same principles. However, a major change is observable after the end of the fourth century. It becomes impossible to distinguish one imperial bust from another on most fifth- and sixth-century coin issues. As the emperors themselves retreated into the seclusion of the palace, their authority derived not from individual charisma and presence, but from the immanent sacral and institutional power of their office. The coinage matched this development. In the later Byzantine period, the imperial image vanished altogether and was replaced exclusively by Christian symbolism.

However, the largest advances in understanding late antiquity from a material perspective have not come from representational art, but from the archaeological study of settlements and settlement patterns. In particular enormous attention has been given to investigating the remains of cities throughout the empire. Civic life from the fourth to the sixth century is now no longer viewed through the lens of Roman legislation, as it was when A. H. M. Jones completed his massive survey of the later Roman Empire,[75] but as the much more complex organism revealed by archaeology. Especially in the East it is now clear that the booming urban development of the early imperial period did not go into recession, but continued through the fourth and fifth centuries.[76] More settlements were described as cities in the *Synekdemos* of Hierokles, compiled in 527, than at any earlier period, and the evidence on the ground suggests that many urban settlements were larger than they had ever been. Of course archaeology demonstrates not only continuity and growth, but also wholesale urban transformation, which accompanied Christianization and other deep-rooted social changes. Meanwhile in the western part of the empire, archaeological survey of rural settlements has been equally important in tracing the end of Roman villas and the steady encroachment of a smaller scale, more localized village society across western Europe at the expense of the earlier imperial structures and networks.

In both halves of the empire archaeologists have paid particular attention to the evidence for trade, commerce, and exchange, especially by sea. Amphorae, which were used for transporting oil, wine, and other foodstuffs, are the trace element for the movement of goods in patterns of long distance maritime trade. They have become the starting point for almost all serious work on the late Roman economy.

NOTES

1 Alan and Averil Cameron, "Christianity and tradition in the historiography of the late empire," *CQ* 14 (1964), 312–28.
2 Patricia Cox, *Biography in Late Antiquity. A Quest for the Holy Man* (Berkeley, 1983); G. Fowden, "The pagan holy man in late antique society," *JHS* 102 (1982), 33–59; Mark Edwards, *Neoplatonic Saints. The Lives of Plotinus and Proclus by their Students* (Liverpool, 2000); G. Clark, *Iamblichus, On the Pythagorean Life* (Liverpool, 1989).
3 The translation and commentary of Averil Cameron and Stuart Hall (Oxford, 1999). For the hybrid nature of the work see T. D. Barnes, "Panegyric, history and hagiography in Eusebius' *Life of Constantine*," in R. Williams (ed.), *The Making of Orthodoxy; Essays in Honour of Henry Chadwick* (Cambridge, 1989), 94–123.
4 R. Doran, *The Lives of Simeon Stylites* (Michigan, 1992); R. Lane Fox, "The Life of Daniel," in M. J. Edwards and S. Swain (eds.), *Portraits: Biographical Representation in the Greek and Latin Literature of the Roman Empire* (Oxford, 1995), 175–225; C. Foss, "Cities and villages of Lycia in the life of St Nicholas of Sion," *Greek Orthodox Theological Review* 36 (1991), 303–37; Theodore: S. Mitchell, *Anatolia* II (Oxford, 1995), 122–50.
5 B. Rodgers and C. E. V. Nixon, *In Praise of Later Roman Emperors. The Panegyrici Latini* (California, 1994). There are translations of II (Theodosius) and III (Julian) by Nixon and S. Lieu respectively in the Liverpool Translated Texts series.
6 Translation and commentary by J. L. Creed (Oxford, 1984).
7 J. Vanderspoel, *Themistius and the Imperial Court. Oratory, Civic Duty and Paideia from Constantius to Theodosius* (Michigan, 1995); P. Heather and D. Moncur, *Politics, Philosophy and Empire in the Fourth Century. Select Orations of Themistius* (Liverpool, 2001); P. Heather and J. Matthews, *The Goths in the Fourth Century* (Liverpool, 1991), 13–50.
8 S. Lieu, *Select Letters of Libanius* (Liverpool, 2003).
9 A. F. Norman, *Libanius* vol. 1 (Loeb Classical Library) contains the speeches for Julian. Vols. 2 and 3 include a selection of his other important speeches.
10 Maud Gleason, "Festive satire: Julian's *Misopogon* and the new year at Antioch," *JRS* 76 (1986), 106–20.
11 Alan Cameron, *Claudian: Poetry and Propaganda at the Court of Honorius* (Oxford, 1970); M. Roberts, *The Jewelled Style. Poetry and Poetics in Late Antiquity* (Ithaca NY, 1989).

12 J. Harries, *Sidonius Apollinaris and the Fall of Rome* (Oxford, 1994); C. E. Stevens, *Sidonius Apollinaris and his Age* (Oxford, 1934).

13 Both are edited in one volume by Alain Chauvot, *Procope de Gaza, Priscien de Césarée. Panégyriques de l'empéreur Anastase 1ᵉ* (Bonn, 1986).

14 Alan Cameron, "The Roman friends of Ammianus," *JRS* 54 (1964), 15–28.

15 E. D. Hunt, "Christians and Christianity in Ammianus Marcellinus," *CQ* 35 (1985), 186–200; "Christianity in Ammianus Marcellinus revisited," *Studia Patristica* 24 (1993), 108–13; and especially, T. D. Barnes, *Ammianus Marcellinus* (Cornell, 1998), 79–94.

16 For the structure of the history, see Barnes, *Ammianus Marcellinus*, 20–31, who argues that what is preserved may in fact be the second half of a work in 36 books, which covered the period up to Constantine in brief, before launching into the expansive treatment of the surviving books.

17 He is thus both the subject and the inspiration for J. F. Matthews, *The Roman Empire of Ammianus Marcellinus* (London, 1989).

18 C. D. Gordon, *The Age of Attila. Fifth-Century Byzantium and the Barbarians* (Michigan, 1960), is an attempt to remedy the deficiency by producing a patch-work narrative based on translations of the surviving historical fragments.

19 R. P. C. Blockley, *East Roman Foreign Policy: Formation and Conduct from Diocletian to Anastasius* (Leeds, 1992); A. D. Lee, *Information and Frontiers: Roman Foreign Relations in Late Antiquity* (Cambridge, 1993).

20 The extent of Zosimus' dependence on earlier writers (Dexippus of Athens, Eunapius, and Olympiodorus) is controversial and the subject of much discussion. See especially F. Paschoud's commentary on Zosimus for analysis at all levels. W. Liebeschuetz, "Pagan historiography and the decline of the empire," in G. Marasco, *Greek and Roman Historiography in Late Antiquity* (Leiden, 2003), 187–218, argues that Zosimus contributed more than is generally supposed to his history.

21 R. P. C. Blockley, "The development of Greek historiography: Priscus, Malchus and Candidus," in G. Marasco, *Greek and Roman Historiography in Late Antiquity*, 289–315. At 312 he incomprehensibly criticizes Priscus for "vagueness, lack of interest in detail, over moralizing, poor strategic analysis, weak causation."

22 Evagrius 5.24 confirms that Zosimus' narrative ended in the reigns of Arcadius and Honorius.

23 For the issues see Wolfram Brandes, "Anastasios o dikoros, Endzeiterwartungen und Kaiserkritik in Byzanz um 500," *Byz. Zeitschr.* 90 (1997), 24–63; M. Meier, *Justinian. Herrschaft, Reich und Religion* (Munich, 2004), 25–8.

24 It has been conjectured that he had access to official war bulletins on the Roman side (Howard-Johnson) or reports on the campaigns that were made public by Anastasius at Edessa (Trombley). But Ps-Joshua makes no mention of these, and this would not explain the quality of information which he had from the Persian side.

25 A. Kaldellis, *Procopius of Caesarea. Tyranny, History, and Philosophy at the End of Antiquity* (Philadelphia, 2004).

26 B. Croke and J. Crow, "Procopius and Dara," *JRS* 63 (1983), 143–59. See the volume of *Antiquité Tardive* 8 (2000) devoted to a reappraisal of *Buildings*.

27 The historian may be identical with Bishop Jordanes of Croton, who accompanied Pope Liberius to Constantinople in 551 (one class of manuscripts of the *Getica* call the author *episcopus*). He would have been based near the monastery of Vivarium where Cassiodorus had retired and thus had access to Cassiodorus'

work at that time. A. Momigliano, "Cassiodorus and the Italian culture of his time" *PBA* 41 (1955), 207–45, accepts the identification, but this is contested by P. Heather, *Goths and Romans* (Oxford, 1991), 34–67.

28 P. Heather. "Cassiodorus and the rise of the Amals: Genealogy and the Goths under Hun domination," *JRS* 79 (1988), 103–28.

29 Michael Whitby, "Greek historical writing after Procopius: Variety and vitality," in Averil Cameron and Lawrence Conrad (eds.), *The Byzantine and Early Islamic Near East I. Problems in the Literary Source Material* (Princeton, 1992), 25–80.

30 A. Kaldellis, "The historical and religious views of Agathias: a reinterpretation," *Byzantion* 69 (1999), 206–52.

31 Averil Cameron, *Agathias* (Oxford, 1970); "Agathias on the early Merovingians," *Annali della scuola normale di Pisa* 37 (1968), 95–140; "Agathias on the Sassanians," *Dumbarton Oaks Papers* 23–4 (1969–70), 1–150.

32 M. Meier, *Das andere Zeitalter Justinians* (Göttingen, 2004), 235–45, 405–12.

33 Michael and Mary Whitby, *The History of Theophylact Simocatta* (Oxford, 1986).

34 A. H. M. Jones, "Notes on the genuineness of the Constantinian documents in Eusebius' Life of Constantine," *Journal of Ecclesiastical History* 5 (1954), 196–200 (reprinted in *The Roman Economy. Studies in Ancient Economic and Administrative History*, ed. P. A. Brunt, 1974, 257–62); S. Mitchell, "Maximinus and the Christians: a new inscription from Pisidia," *JRS* 78 (1988), 105–24.

35 T. D. Barnes, "The editions of Eusebius' *Ecclesiastical History*," GRBS 21 (1980), 191–201; cf. *Constantine and Eusebius*, 126–47. For later composition see R. Lane Fox, *Pagans and Christians* (London, 1985), 633–4, 774 n. 33; A. Louth, "The date of Eusebius' *Historia Ecclesiastica*," *JTS* 41 (1990), 111–23; D. S. Potter, *The Roman Empire at Bay* (London, 2004), 655 n. 59.

36 P. R. Amidon, *The Church History of Rufinus of Aquileia Books 10 and 11* (Oxford, 1997).

37 D. Rohrbacher, *The Historians of Late Antiquity* (London and New York, 2002), 135–49.

38 Michael and Mary Whitby, *Chronicon Paschale 284–628 AD. Translation with Notes and Introduction* (Liverpool, 1989), xvii.

39 C. Mango and R. Scott, Theophanes Confessor, *Chronicle of Byzantine and Near Eastern History AD 284–813* (Oxford, 1997).

40 Fergus Millar, *The Emperor in the Roman World* (London, 1977).

41 T. Honoré, "The making of the Theodosian Code," *Zeitschrift der Savigny-Stiftung, Römische Abteilung* 103 (1986), 133–222; J. Harries, "The Roman imperial quaestor from Constantine to Theodosius II," *JRS* 78 (1988), 148–72; J. Harries and I Wood (eds.), *The Theodosian Code* (London, 1993); J. F. Matthews, *Laying Down the Law. A Study of the Theodosian Code* (New Haven, 2000); T. D. Barnes, "The Theodosian Code," in G. W. Bowersock et al. (eds.), *Late Antiquity* (Cambridge Mass., 1999), 721–2; "Foregrounding the Theodosian Code," *JRA* 14 (2001), 671–85.

42 R. MacMullen, "Judicial savagery in the later Roman empire," *Chiron* 16 (1986), 43–62, reprinted in MacMullen, *Changes in the Roman Empire* (Princeton, 1990).

43 The English translation of S. P. Scott is available on-line at www.constitution.org/sps/sps.htm.

44 T. Honoré, *Tribonian* (London, 1978).

45 T. M. Charles-Edwards, "Laws in the western kingdoms between the fifth and the seventh centuries," *CAH* 14, 260–87.

46 R. H. Barrow, *Prefect and Emperor. The* Relationes *of Symmachus* AD *384* (Oxford, 1973).
47 A selection has been translated by S. J. B. Barnish, Cassiodorus: *Variae* (Liverpool, 1992).
48 T. D. Barnes, *The New Empire of Diocletian and Constantine* (Cambridge Mass., 1982).
49 O. Seeck, *Notitia Dignitatum* (Berlin, 1876) also includes texts of the two urban *notitiae* and the provincial gazetteers. R. Goodburn and P. Bartholomew (eds.), *Aspects of the Notitia Dignitatum* (Oxford, 1986). R. Grigg, "Inconsistency and lassitude: The shield emblems of the Notitia Dignitatum," *JRS* 73 (1983), 132–42, argues that the blazons are largely artistic inventions. For the date of the eastern section, see C. Zuckerman, *Antiquité Tardive* 6 (1998), 137–47.
50 See especially A. H. M. Jones, *The Later Roman Empire* II (Oxford, 1964), 1417–50.
51 R. MacMullen, *Corruption and the Decline of Rome* (Yale, 1988), 174.
52 Fergus Millar, *A Greek Roman Empire: Power, Belief and Reason under Theodosius II, 408–50* (Berkeley, 2006).
53 S. Lancel, *Actes de la Conférence de Carthage* (4 vols. Paris, Sources Chrétiennes 194 [1972], 195 [1972], 224 [1975] and 373 [1991]).
54 W. Mathisen, *People, Personal Expression, and Social Relations in Late Antiquity* (2 vols., Ann Arbor, 2003).
55 S. Mitchell, *Anatolia* II (Oxford, 1993), 73–84.
56 Y. Azéma, *Théodoret de Cyr. Correspondance* I (Paris, 1982), 44–56.
57 See N. McLynn, *Ambrose of Milan* (Berkeley, 1994), 308 for a specific example.
58 M. R. Salzman, *The Christianization of the Roman Aristocracy* (2003).
59 C. Lepelley, *Les cités de l'Afrique romaine au bas-empire* I. *La permanence d'une civilisation municipale* (Paris, 1979).
60 E. Sironen, *The Late Roman and Early Byzantine Inscriptions of Athens and Attica* (Helsinki, 1997); C. Roueché, *Aphrodisias in Late Antiquity* (*JRS* monograph, London, 1989).
61 L. Robert, *Epigrammes du bas-empire*, Hellenica IV (1948); C. Roueché, "Benefactors of the late Roman period," *Actes du Xe Congrès international d'épigraphie grecque et latine* (Nimes, 1992, publ. Paris 1997), 353–68.
62 Simon Corcoran, *The Empire of the Tetrarchs* (Oxford, 2000); Michael Crawford, "Discovery, autopsy and progress: Diocletian's jigsaw puzzles," in T. P. Wiseman (ed.), *Classics in Progress. Essays in Ancient Greece and Rome* (British Academy/Oxford, 2002), 145–63.
63 Fergus Millar, *The Roman Near East 31* BC–AD *337* (Harvard, 1993), 190–4.
64 D. Feissel, "Les inscriptions des premiers siècles byzantins (330–641)," in *Atti del XI congresso internazionale di epigrafia greca e latina* (Rome, 1997, publ. 1999), 577–89.
65 C. Roueché, "Acclamations in the later Roman empire: New evidence from Aphrodisias," *JRS* 74 (1984), 181–99. Other bibliography in Feissel's article (see previous note). For the phenomenon as a whole see now H.-U. Wiemer, "Akklamationen im spätrömischen Reich. Zur Typologie und Funktion eines Kommunikationsrituals," *Archiv für Kulturgeschichte* 86 (2004), 27–73.
66 D. Howlett, *Insular Inscriptions* (Dublin, 2004).
67 M. Handley, "Inscribing time and identity in the kingdom of Burgundy," in S. Mitchell and G. Greatrex, *Ethnicity and Culture in Late Antiquity* (Wales and London, 2000), 83–102.

68 S. Mitchell, *Anatolia* II (Oxford, 1993), 91–108; W. Tabbernee, *Montanist Inscriptions and Testimonia. Epigraphic Sources Illustrating the History of Montanism* (Macon, 1997); S. Mitchell, "An apostle to Ankara from the New Jerusalem. Montanists and Jews in late Roman Asia Minor," *Scripta Classical Israelica 24* (2005), 207–23. For Jews see the excellent regional collections for Egypt (W. Norbury and D. Noy), Western Europe including Rome (D. Noy), Asia Minor (W. Ameling), the Balkans and Syria.

69 F. R. Trombley, *Hellenic Religion and Christianization* II (Leiden, 1994), 247–373; "Christian demography in the *territorium* of Antioch (4th–5th c.): Observations on the epigraphy," in I. Sandwell and J. Huskinson (eds.), *Culture and Society in Later Roman Antioch* (Oxford, 2004), 59–85. New studies of this material are forthcoming from R. Haensch and M. Mango.

70 P.-L. Gatier, "Les inscriptions grecques d'époque islamique (VIIe VIIIe siècles) en Syrie du Sud," in P. Canivet and J.-P. Rey-Coquais (eds.), *La Syrie de Byzance à l'Islam* (Damascus, 1992), 145–57.

71 F. Kolb, *Herrscherideologie in der Spätantike* (Berlin, 2001); S. MacCormack, *Art and Ceremony in Late Antiquity* (1981).

72 R. R. R. Smith, "The public image of Licinius I: portrait sculpture and imperial ideology in the early fourth century," *JRS* 87 (1997), 170–202.

73 R. R. R. Smith, "Late antique portraits in a public context: honorific statuary at Aphrodisias in Caria," *JRS* 89 (1999), 155–89.

74 R. R. R. Smith, "Late Roman philosopher portraits from Aphrodisias," *JRS* 80 (1990), 127–55; Alan Cameron, *Porphyrius the Charioteer* (Oxford, 1971).

75 A. H. M. Jones, *The Later Roman Empire* (Oxford, 1964), 712–66.

76 W. Liebeschuetz, *The Decline and Fall of the Ancient City* (Oxford, 2001).

3

The Roman Empire from Diocletian to Alaric

| 250 | 300 | 350 | 400 | 450 | 500 | 550 | 600 | 650 |

Prelude

In the spring of 283 the Roman emperor Marcus Aurelius Carus died before the walls of the Persian city of Ctesiphon, struck by a bolt of lightening. His son, M. Aurelius Numerianus, who had accompanied him on campaign, was hailed to succeed his father by the army, but soon perished himself. The sources say that he was taken ill with an eye infection and confined to a litter, in which he was ambushed and killed by the praetorian prefect Aper. News of the assassination was kept from the troops, and the victim's body was hidden by Aper until the moment when he could seize power himself, but the crime was betrayed by the stench of the putrefying corpse. The story reached its dénouement on November 20, 284, at Nicomedia in Bithynia, when a council of army officers chose one of their number, Valerius Diocles (later Diocletianus), as the new Augustus. Diocletian addressed the troops for the first time at his inauguration, called upon the sun god to avenge the death of his predecessor, and struck a dagger into Aper, who was standing next to him. He swore an oath that he himself had played no part in the death of Numerian or willed his own accession to power. The coup was not yet complete, for Carus' elder son Carinus still retained control of the western part of the empire. Diocletian led his forces into Illyricum and confronted Carinus at the battle of Margus, near Viminacium, a short way east of modern Belgrade. Carinus succumbed, not apparently to Diocletian's forces but on account of the hatred he had incurred in his own ranks. We are told that he had denounced and condemned innocent men and seduced the wives of his officers. At the end he was slain by one of his tribunes, whose wife he had debauched.

This version of the accession of Diocletian derives from a group of fourth-century Latin accounts, which were largely drawing on a single source.[1] It depicts the key elements in imperial accessions during the third and fourth centuries: the selection of the candidate by an inner circle of military officers, the ruler's address to his troops, calling on the support of the gods for the new regime, and their acclamation of the candidate.[2] These and other procedures can be identified in many other imperial proclamations of the period. However, the accounts of Diocletian's accession raise problems that recur throughout the study of the later Roman Empire, which should be highlighted from the outset. Firstly, and transparently, the narrative is almost wholly apologetic for the new regime. It suggests that Diocletian was a reluctant nominee to imperial power and had no part in the death of his predecessors; on the contrary he had actually avenged Numerianus' presumed assassin, Aper. He might even have suffered defeat by Carinus' forces, had these not turned against their leader in justified outrage at his excesses. This was the authorized version of events, and it is full of implausibilities. How had the murder of Numerian passed unnoticed? Why had Aper failed to seize the initiative that he had created by his crime? Why in any case had he allowed Diocletian to be acclaimed Augustus, if this is what he had plotted for himself? If Diocletian was genuinely a reluctant ruler, not responsible for overthrowing his predecessors, why should he have led an army against Carinus in Illyricum, instead of offering loyal support to him? Why then admit almost to losing the decisive battle and attribute his opponent's fall to his own moral degeneracy? A precise answer to all these questions is beyond our reach. Imperial coups d'état were not the subject of investigative journalism at the time, and the intrigues and plots which brought down or created emperors spawned self-interested rumor and accusations, not dispassionate enquiries. However, a reasonable reading of the evidence would acquit Aper of conspiracy and suggest that he had been the senior military officer who remained loyal to house of Carus, but had been killed by the new man whose cause had been promoted by a rival group of army officers. The logic of usurpation then determined Diocletian's attack on Carinus, while the story that he had been killed by one of his own officers diverted attention from the crime of the usurper to those alleged against the incumbent emperor.[3]

Behind the false certainties offered by the official sources, there are important features of the narrative that no propagandistic distortion could obscure. Firstly, the drama of Diocletian's accession was acted out across the main axis of power that joined the northern and eastern frontiers of the Roman Empire (Map 3.1). The route that led Carus into battle against the Sassanian Empire and ended before the walls of Ctesiphon had been trodden before him by the emperors Trajan in 114, Lucius Verus in 165, and Septimus Severus in 198. It was to be followed again by Galerius in 298, and most famously by Julian in his ill-starred Persian campaign of 363. Nicomedia, at the hub of communication between the Balkans and Asia Minor, had grown steadily in importance since Trajan's day and was soon to become Diocletian's own imperial capital.[4] Finally the decisive encounter between the rival rulers occurred in the middle Danubian region, midway along the main military highway between the western and eastern provinces. This was the critical zone for imperial civil wars, in military terms a much more significant frontier than the outer boundaries of the empire. The conflict of Diocletian and Carus at Margus presaged the battles between Licinius and Constantine at Cibalae in 316, the army of Constantius and Magnentius at Mursa in 351, and Eugenius and the forces of Theodosius at the river Frigidus in 394.

Army commands and military power gave usurpers the capacity to seize political control of the Roman Empire. The emperors themselves were serving military officers, and they achieved their positions with the help of demonstrable support from the army; both from the officers who organized the dynamics of accession, and from the regular troops, whose raucous shouts and acclamations formally bestowed the title of Augustus on new rulers. Events between 283 and 285 were defined by the use of extreme political violence: covert and public assassinations; the manipulation of judicial processes, and civil war. In these struggles for power the winners took all, and losers were not permitted to survive to mount a future challenge.

The accession of Diocletian is often held to have ended the so-called period of military anarchy, which had lasted since the fall of the Severan dynasty in 235, and brought an era of stability to the Roman world. However, much remained unchanged by the new order. We need only to look ahead to the years 363–4, when the events of eighty years before were virtually replayed.[5] The emperor Julian led a large military expedition to Ctesiphon. After initial successes against Sassanian forces he too died on Persian soil, struck by an unknown hand during a skirmish as his troops withdrew northwards beyond the river Tigris. No Caesar was on hand to succeed him, and the officers of the imperial army, which combined forces from the western and eastern empire,

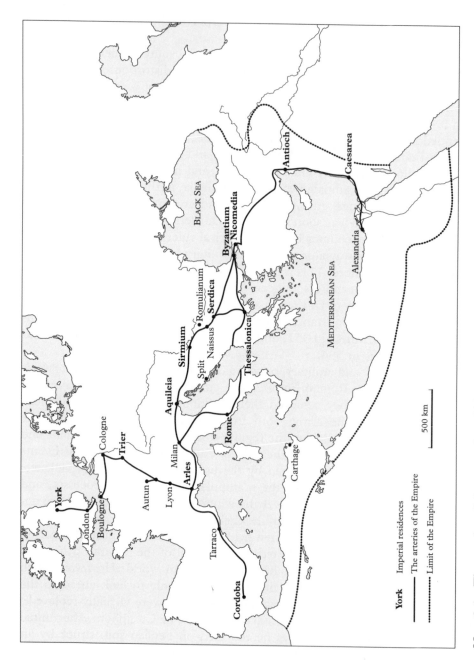

Map 3.1 The empire of the tetrarchs c.300

York Imperial residences
—— The arteries of the Empire
········ Limit of the Empire

500 km

wrangled over the succession. The first name to be proposed was a compromise figure, the aged praetorian prefect Salutius Secundus, but he disqualified himself (or perhaps was seen as unacceptable by the officer circle) on the grounds of his advanced years and lack of military qualifications.[6] A younger candidate then emerged, perhaps as the candidate of junior officers rather than the high command. Flavius Iovianus was a tribune of the *domestici*, the palace guard, who had escorted the body of Constantius from Tarsus to Constantinople in 361 and may well, therefore, have been related to the imperial family.[7]

Jovian's reign proved shorter even than that of Numerian. In the crowded days after Julian's death the Roman army withdrew from its exposed position beyond the Tigris. A route was chosen through desert country across Upper Mesopotamia to Nisibis, and the march brought the army to near starvation. The price of its rescue was a peace treaty which ceded much of Mesopotamia, including the city of Nisibis, to the Sassanians, and relinquished Rome's title to a group of small provinces beyond the Tigris, which had been acquired in 298. Jovian himself drew back to Antioch in Syria and then made a winter journey across Anatolia towards Constantinople. He ceremonially assumed the consulate on January 1, 364, at Ancyra, and among other legislative acts, rescinded Julian's famous law which forbade Christians to be professional teachers (*CTh.* 13.3.6). In February he continued his journey and reached the small town and staging post of Dadastana in eastern Bithynia on February 17. The following day he was found dead in his bed, allegedly suffocated by fumes from a brazier which had been placed in his newly-decorated bedroom.

Once again the main imperial highway (later to be known to Christians as the Pilgrims' Road to Jerusalem) witnessed a bizarre imperial death, which was followed, like that of Numerian eighty years earlier, by the choice of a new emperor (Ammianus 26.1–5). The entourage of officers again considered candidates, and opted for Valentinian, who had recently been appointed by Jovian to command a legion which was stationed in Ancyra. The new man was rushed to join the army at Nicaea, where he mounted the platform to be acclaimed Augustus by the troops. Within a month he co-opted his brother Valens to be his colleague, and in May both set out westwards for Naissus on the boundary of Thrace and Lower Moesia, where they parted ways. Valens returned to the East, while Valentinian made his way to the western provinces, where he spent the remaining eleven years of his reign securing the troubled frontier from Germanic attacks and incursions.

The events of 363–4 are recorded in detail by the greatest Latin historian of the fourth century, Ammianus Marcellinus, who had accompanied Julian's Persian expedition. In contrast to the situation that followed the fall of Numerian and Carinus, alternative versions of the deaths of Julian and Jovian circulated freely. Neither Jovian nor Valentinian had been directly implicated in his predecessor's death, and they had no need to produce a sanitized version of their succession to power. However, the main features of the events of 363/4 uncannily matched the precedent of 283/4. The theater of political activity extended across the same long and narrow stage, the military roads that extended from eastern Mesopotamia to the central Balkans. In each case an emperor died on an eastern campaign, their successors succumbed on the highway across northwest Asia Minor, and the emperors after them were elevated to power in the leading cities of Bithynia, Nicomedia, and Nicaea. Once again a cabal of officers moved to present their chosen candidate to be hailed by the campaigning army. Diocletian, Jovian, and Valentinian all came from similar backgrounds. They were middle-ranking military men, aged in their thirties or early forties, who had been born in the provinces of Illyricum: Diocletian from Salona in Dalmatia, Jovian from Singidunum in Moesia, and Valentinian from Cibalae in Pannonia. None of this may be regarded as coincidental. These narratives reflect both the realities of power and the political and military imperatives which shaped life at the highest levels of the Roman state of the later third and fourth centuries.

What are the lessons of this prelude? Reconstructing a historical narrative for the fourth century is a necessary task, but an almost impossible one. Apart from the twenty-five-year period covered by Ammianus Marcellinus, which included the reign of Jovian, the narrative sources are brief, and usually tendentious or confused. Gibbon made the point in his famous adieu to Ammianus when his own account reached the period after the battle of Adrianople in 378: "It is not without the most sincere regret that I must now take leave of an accurate and faithful guide, who has composed the history of his own times without indulging the prejudices and passions which usually affect the mind of a contemporary."[8]

Careful sifting of the evidence usually makes it possible to reconstruct events in chronological order, and to identify time, place, and actors in historical transactions. But questions of causation or motivation are always obscure, subjective, and distorted. The way that most of our sources presented great events in imperial history was usually determined by the victors, who created a narrative and expounded an interpretation that justified their own role in events. This is particularly true at moments of regime change. The higher the political stakes, the greater the likelihood of spin and distortion.

A Military Monarchy 284–395: Overview

From the accession of Diocletian to the death of Theodosius I (284–395), the Roman state was ruled by warrior emperors, who strenuously campaigned against internal rivals and defended its frontiers against external enemies. Then, for more than two centuries until the accession of Heraclius in 610, emperors and their courts became sedentary. Emperors were based at Constantinople in the East and Ravenna (or for short periods at Rome) in the West, and evolved a style of ruling that was radically different from what had gone before. Thus the basic framework of political and military activity in the earlier part of late antiquity up to 395 continued the pattern of the third century. In political terms the main features of the fourth-century empire resembled those of the principate that had been founded by Augustus. After 395 the eastern emperor and his court were permanently resident at Constantinople. As emperors ceased to take part in campaigns themselves and became palace-based, the empire's ability to defend the northern frontier and retain the western provinces was critically reduced.

The beginning of the Byzantine Empire is sometimes placed around 395. That label cannot of course apply to the western provinces. From the late fourth century the borders of the western empire became porous, and north European tribal groups, speaking early forms of the German language, infiltrated the regions adjacent to the former frontiers. Eventually, by the end of the fifth century, all the former western provinces of the empire had been transformed into kingdoms of a hybrid nature. They retained Roman legal systems and other institutions, but were ruled by tribal Germanic kings. Here, therefore, was a political transformation much more radical than anything experienced in the East. Out of these conditions emerged the earliest structures of medieval Europe.

The history of the Roman state in late antiquity was forged in an environment of warfare, battle, and military activity. It has been estimated that more than two-thirds of the annual state budget, the income derived from taxation, tribute, and the lease of imperial lands, was expended on soldiers' wages and benefits, on supplying and equipping the armies, and maintaining the military infrastructure.[9] This modern assessment is broadly confirmed by the remark of a sixth-century military manual that military wages took up most of annual imperial revenues.[10] The Roman army was overwhelmingly the most important component of the organized Roman state.

Throughout the fourth century the aims and motives of Roman wars were essentially threefold. Firstly, they were designed to maintain the integrity of the empire within established frontiers against barbarian enemies. Secondly, they were fought on Roman territory by rivals for power; bloody civil wars are a leitmotif of late Roman history. Thirdly, and no less importantly, warfare provided the armies, especially their elite squadrons, with their chief occupation, fighting, and were the source of the spoils and booty that motivated the soldiers. Each of these themes requires elaboration, and is illustrated from the detailed record of Ammianus. His extensive, colorful, and often gripping description of the events of 353–78 presents the many faces of Roman warfare. A recent study suggests that his narrative omitted no significant engagements from this period.[11] There were skirmishes and ambushes on either side of the northern river frontiers with Germanic barbarian groups. There was internecine warfare among these groups themselves (cf. *Pan. Lat.* XI [3], 16.1–2). Punitive Roman expeditions were sent beyond the Rhine and the Danube to assert Roman authority over their often elusive foes. There were pitched battles with the barbarians, successful against the Alemanni at Strasburg in 357, disastrous against the Goths at Adrianople in 378. Warfare in the east included large-scale sieges of the contested cities of Mesopotamia (Amida, Nisibis, Bezabde), as well as the cumbersome and draining logistic preparations for major invasions of Sassanian territory. No less important were the bloody campaigns fought on Roman soil, usually in the central Danubian region, between rival claimants to power.

Evaluation of the institutions of the Roman army and their economic implications belongs in a later chapter, but it is important to give military history pride of place during the first century of late imperial history, from the accession of Diocletian in 284 until that of Theodosius in 379. One of the critical, but little emphasized, aspects of this history is that throughout this period the rulers were expected to lead all major campaigns in person, and almost always did so. The youthful Constantine, serving as a cavalry officer, personally seized a Sarmatian warrior by his hair and threw him in triumph at the feet of his commander Galerius, and led his troops through the marshes against the enemy.[12] In 302 Constantius I had to be hauled up by a rope when the gates of the Gallic town of Langres were hurriedly shut to keep out an Alemannic raid, while the Caesar was outside. His army managed to rescue him five hours later and 60,000 Alemanni are said to have paid with their lives (Eutropius 9.23; Orosius 7.25). In 355 it was only after a long discussion that Constantius II relinquished personal command of a minor sortie against the Alemannic Lentienses along the south side of Lake Constance to his general, the *magister militum* Arbitio (Ammianus 15.4). Julian paid with his life when he recklessly plunged into a minor rearguard engagement without putting on his body armor (Ammianus 25.3). The next emperor to be lost in battle was Valens, who simply vanished in the pandemonium of the battle of Adrianople against the Goths in 378 (Ammianus 31.13). Adrianople was the first time that a Roman army suffered a major defeat at the hands of barbarians, and almost the last occasion, it seems, that any Roman emperor led an army into battle in person for more than two hundred years. The defeat changed the role and character of Rome's monarchy.

The burdens of warfare were without question the main reason why Diocletian created an imperial college to aid him in his ruler's task. Maximianus had been made Augustus in 286, and the second surviving panegyric of the period, delivered in 291, proclaimed the concord and unity which existed between the two emperors. They fulfilled the twin roles of Jupiter and Hercules in ruling a subdued and pacified world (*Pan. Lat.* XI [3]). In 293 two Caesars were added to the team, Constantius, who may have been Maximianus' praetorian prefect and was already marred to his daughter Theodora,[13] and Galerius, who married Diocletian's daughter Valeria (Lactantius, *DMP* 50. 2; Diagram 3.1).

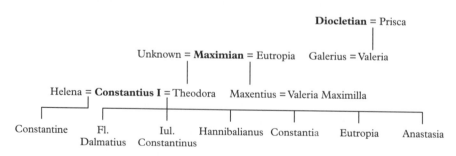

Diagram 3.1   The first tetrarchy

Much modern speculation has been expended on the political origins and the motivation behind this new coalition, the first tetrarchy. Its main objective was to achieve a manageable division of imperial powers, and it led to an unofficial territorial division of the empire:

> Since the burden of the wars, which we have already recorded, was pressing more fiercely, the empire was divided into four parts, and all the territory lying beyond the Gallic Alps was entrusted to Constantius, Africa and Italy was given to Herculius [Maximianus], the shores of Illyricum as far as the Pontic strait to Galerius, while Valerius [Diocletian] retained the remainder. (Aur. Victor, *Caes.* 39.30)

The Age of Diocletian and Constantine

The formation of the late Roman state extended over half a century, from Diocletian's seizure of power in 284 until the death of Constantine in 337. The entire period witnessed almost continuous warfare against internal and external enemies. There were struggles in the West against the Germanic tribes along the Rhine frontier and in Britain against the usurper Carausius. In the East there were revolts in Egypt and a major war with Persia, which culminated in a favorable peace treaty in 299. In the years that followed the victory against the Sassanians, Galerius also secured the Danube frontier.

As the threat of war emerged on all fronts, new imperial residences developed in the frontier regions of the empire. Maximianus was usually based at Milan or Aquileia in northern Italy, relinquishing his former headquarters at Trier to Constantius after 293. Diocletian and Galerius held court at Sirmium, Serdica, and Thessalonica in their European provinces, and at Nicomedia and Antioch in the East. These strategic and administrative centers contained palaces to accommodate the imperial court, garrison quarters for troops accompanying the emperors, and amphitheaters and circuses for shows and imperial ceremonials.[14] Formal public ceremonies were an important ingredient of imperial power. The Latin historians noted that Diocletian increased the distance between the emperor and his subjects by requiring them to prostrate themselves in his presence. Modern commentators have sometimes interpreted this as a move to Orientalize the monarchy.[15] This habit at the imperial court can be traced back to the Severan period, but it is evident that under the tetrarchs such practices evolved into a much stricter court ceremonial, which deliberately increased the literal and metaphorical distance between the rulers and their subjects.[16]

The imperial residences became showplaces for Roman power and the most important locations for representing imperial culture. Panegyric speeches, such as the ones for Maximianus, simultaneously expounded the emperors' virtues and achievements and proclaimed the loyalty and devotion of their subjects. The occasions chosen were the five- or ten-year anniversaries of the ruler's term of office, their birthdays, or the successful conclusions of campaigns. They lauded the generic imperial virtues of courage, strength, foresight, and mercy, and hailed specific achievements, notably successful campaigns. They offered speakers the opportunity to add personal thanks to the rulers for offices they had been given, or to ask for future favors, particularly for the cities of Gaul. The message of the speeches is interwoven with religious propaganda and ideology. This is strikingly evident in the second panegyric for Maximianus of 291, in which the speaker developed at length the equation of Diocletian with Jupiter and Maximianus with Hercules, which had led the emperors to adopt the names Iovius and Herculius respectively.[17] There is no doubt that the themes covered in the panegyrics were approved by the emperors themselves, at least in outline. Sometimes their wishes were explicit, as in the instance where Maximianus had charged the orator of 289 to pass quickly over his suppression of the Bagaudae. But in most cases the choice of topics will have been evident to all parties.

The ideas and style which suffused the panegyrics were also a dominant influence on other media of imperial self-presentation. Key political slogans and images became ubiquitous and were disseminated by coin types. Again the allusions might be generic, for instance to the VIRTUS and CONCORDIA AUGUSTORUM, or to the FELICITAS TEMPORUM, or they might refer to specific occasions and events. The coins also contain a full repertoire of imperial portrait types. Since Augustus, Roman rulers had used their own image to project the main moral and political characteristics of their reigns in a visual medium. The tetrarchs developed stern and vigilant portraits; square jawed, wide eyed, with the cropped hair and stubble beards of campaigning soldiers. In a ground-breaking study of the imperial portraiture of this period, R. R. R. Smith argues that these images embodied a radical new imperial idea and style. The visual record emphasized two features above all; the collegiality of the emperors, and their moral fundamentalism. Collegiality is expressed most famously in the multiple portraits of the four rulers, carved in porphyry which had been extracted from the imperial quarries in Egypt, clasping one another in an embrace of soldierly solidarity. Moral severity radiates from their harsh and unsmiling gaze (Plate 3.1).[18] Official propaganda represented the tetrarchy as a united team of two senior and two junior members. At the same time it was acknowledged that Diocletian was the dominant member of the group. The potential strains as well as the reality of the relationship were well caught by the later emperor Julian, in his satirical essay on the *Caesars*, as he describes the tetrarchs entering the banquet of the gods:

> Diocletian led the procession in his pomp, bringing with him the two Maximianuses and my grandfather Constantius. These held one another by the hands, and did not walk in line with him but they surrounded him like a sort of dancing troupe. They were like bodyguards, wanting to run out in front of him, but he kept preventing them, for he did not want to claim more than they in any way.[19]

Inscriptions focused the moral language of the panegyrics into lapidary formulae. Apart from dedications to the piety, courage, justice, and concord of

Plate 3.1 The four rulers of the first tetrarchy. This statue made from porphyry, the hard purple granite of the imperial quarries in Egypt, was probably originally erected at Nicomedia, Diocletian's capital. It was transported and displayed at Constantinople,where it was popularly known as the Philadelphion, "brotherly friendship" (see chapter 9, p. 314). After the sack of Constantinople by the crusaders in 1204 it was taken to Venice, where it now stands at the corner of St Mark's cathedral (DAI Rome)

the emperors, imperial edicts were enveloped in a wash of moralizing and propagandistic rhetoric. The obscure, but grandiloquent opening sentences of the famous price edict provide a good example:

> Public honour, Roman dignity and Roman majesty require that the good fortune of our state be administered in a trustworthy manner and properly adorned. Alongside the immortal gods it is right to congratulate the state by recalling the wars that we have successfully fought, at a moment when the world is in a tranquil condition, placed in the lap of deepest calm thanks to the benefits of peace, for which labour has been expended with copious sweat. Thus we, who by kind favour of the gods have repressed the seething plunder previously inflicted by barbarian nations by slaughtering those people themselves, have reinforced the calm which has been established for all time with the necessary defences of justice. (*ILS* 642)

The passage emphasizes the effort that had been required to achieve this state of blessed tranquility, and the god whose endeavors had inspired and stood behind the emperors was indisputably Hercules.

A variety of propagandistic media projected the ideology of the tetrarchic rulers, and justified the power of the reigning emperors within the Roman world. Their purpose was not missionary, to win over new supporters, but was to create a sense of moral and political purpose. They envisaged no opposition or alternative to the emperors' authority, but were addressed to the loyal mass of imperial subjects.

Relief sculpture on official buildings commemorated imperial victories. However, these were portrayed as a precursor of the peace and justice that the warrior emperors had secured for their people. The sculptured panels of the victory arch at Thessalonica, probably erected between 303 and 305, celebrated Galerius' triumph over the Persians. The centerpiece was a panel depicting the two Augusti enthroned above two symbolic figures that may represent heaven and earth. They are flanked by the standing figures of their two Caesars in the act of raising two female figures to their feet. These doubtless represent the subject regions of the empire. Behind and around this scene stand the gods, protecting and supporting the empire's rulers.[20]

The core political program of the tetrarchy was promoted in the ceremonies which Diocletian held in Rome in 303 to commemorate the ten-year anniversary of the creation of the tetrarchy. A relief on the arch of Constantine, completed in 315, depicts the later emperor delivering a speech from the rostra in the Roman forum, amidst a gathering of magistrates and military officers, in front of a five-columned monument. This had been erected for the celebrations of 303. Two of the five inscribed and sculpted bases of these columns bore inscriptions which hailed the successful outcome of ten years of rule by the Caesars, and twenty years of the Augusti, *Caesarum decennalia feliciter; vicennalia imperatorum*. The base for the Caesars, which is still extant, depicts battle trophies on either side of the inscription, and shows on its other three sides one of the Caesars completing a sacrifice, a procession of armed soldiers and civilians in togas, and the combined sacrifice of ox, sheep, and pig, which was offered to the war god Mars. The largest column bore a statue of Jupiter, the others carried images which depicted the geniuses of the two Augusti and the two Caesars. This presented the essence of tetrarchic rule, which had brought order and peace to the Roman world under the religious authority of the supreme god Jupiter.[21]

Such propaganda was not confined to the main imperial residences. The tetrarchs made enormous efforts to project the image of the revived Roman state throughout the provinces. Architectural monuments were a favored medium. In several cities of Syria and Egypt existing buildings were demolished and the central civic squares were surgically enlarged to accommodate a new building type, the *tetrakionia*, the "four columns." These comprised rectangular groups of four high podium bases, each in turn surmounted by four columns and baldachin roofs. These podia supported over-life-size statues of the tetrarchs, identified by dedicatory Latin inscriptions. These monuments served no practical function but literally thrust the presence of the ruling college into the urban communities of the eastern provinces.[22]

Another decisive innovation of the tetrarchic period was the use of Latin for all edicts published by the emperors, in the eastern as well as the western parts of the empire.[23] The famous edict which set maximum prices for goods and services, as a means of controlling military costs, is exclusively known from copies set up in the eastern provinces, but in every case the text was carved in Latin, a language that few of the local inhabitants would have been able to understand. Latin was the language used for the imperial edicts which authorized measures against the Christians. Eusebius, who preserves the text of several of these documents, points out in these cases that his own versions are translations of the originals.

Diocletian was not only concerned with the projection of monarchic power but with measures of real substance. The first systematic attempts to codify Roman law, in the form of the Gregorian and Hermogenian codes, date to the time of Diocletian. Although these are not explicitly known to be the result of an imperial initiative, they clearly foreshadow the great codification of Roman law in the fifth and sixth centuries under Theodosius II and Justinian. The Gregorian Code, published around 292, consisted of some sixteen books, which gathered imperial legal rulings issued since the mid-second century, arranged by topic. The Hermogenian Code, published in 295, seems to have been a supplement to this, compiled by Aurelius Hermogenianus, the author also of a six-book digest of Roman civil law, who later held the office of praetorian prefect. Both collections were evidently designed as guidance for governors and other imperial officials, and for the lawyers on their staffs.[24] But they also symbolized the intention of the tetrarchs to re-forge the empire into a secure and unified political structure, upheld by a framework of law and justice. Systematic publication of the rulings of the emperors, and hence of the laws of Rome, was one of the major institutional developments of the late empire.[25]

In 296 the tetrarchs reformed the procedures of the Roman census, replacing the irregular periodic census held in the provinces with regular five-year cycles. This was matched by a comparable attempt to set a uniform measure for the units of tax assessment, the *caput* and the *iugum*. The whole idea is set out in an edict by the prefect Aurelius Optatus, which introduced these measures to Egypt in 297:

> The levy on each *aroura* according to the classification of the land, and the levy on each head of the peasantry, and from which age to which, may be accurately known from the recently issued divine edict and attached schedule, copies of which I have prefaced for promulgation with this edict of mine. Accordingly, seeing that in this too they have received the greatest benefaction, the provincials should make it their business in conformity with the divinely issued regulations to pay their taxes with all speed and by no means wait for the compulsion of the collector, for it is proper to fulfill most zealously and scrupulously all the loyal obligation, and if anyone should be revealed to have done otherwise after such bounty, he will risk punishment. (*P. Cairo Isidore* 1, trans. Lewis and Reinhold, *Roman Civilization* 2, 419)

This highly unpopular attempt to introduce more stringent tax collection led to resistance, which is reflected in Lactantius' *On the Deaths of the Persecutors*. It was followed by other measures to regulate the monetary economy. A currency edict of September 301 re-tariffed the imperial coinage at twice its previous face value, an attempt doubtless to keep pace with inflation. Two months later the edict of maximum prices was intended to cap rising costs and prevent avaricious profiteering. The consumers that the emperors most wanted to protect were not the generality of their subjects, but soldiers. It appears, however, that prices were in fact pegged at a level below market rates and were therefore unsustainable. The experiment collapsed almost at once amid general rancor, reported by Lactantius: "there was much blood shed over small and cheap things, nothing went on sale and price increased all the worse, until the law was abandoned after many deaths" (*On the Deaths of the Persecutors* 7.6–7).

In May 305, in accordance with a long-planned intention, Diocletian dissolved the first tetrarchy. He and Maximianus retired from office, and their Caesars Galerius and Constantius were promoted to Augusti in their places. Two new Caesars were nominated to the vacancies, Galerius Valerius Maximinus, the son of Galerius' sister, and Fl. Valerius Severus, whose relationship to the other members of the ruling college is uncertain. The new arrangements did not cater for the ambitions of Constantine and Maxentius, the sons of Constantius and Maximianus respectively, and a civil war ensued. This was not resolved until Diocletian was called from retirement to convene a conference at Carnuntum in Pannonia, which created a new tetrarchy in November 308. Galerius, Maximinus, Constantine, and Licinius, who was a protégé of Galerius, became the new rulers, with Galerius and Licinius as the official Augusti, and Maximinus and Constantine as the Caesars. The latter pair demanded and were given the rank of Augusti soon afterwards. Diocletian and Maximianus were confirmed in retirement, and Maxentius was again sidelined.

Plate 3.2 The Imperial Bath House at Trier, the empire's northern capital in the fourth century, which was for long periods the residence of the emperors Constantius, Constantine, Constans, Valentinian, and Gratian (S. Mitchell)

The conference at Carnuntum also produced one of the latest documents which illustrates the religious and political ideals of the original tetrarchy, an inscription which commemorates the building of a Mithraeum by the rulers:

> The most religious Jovian and Herculian Emperors and Caesars restored the sanctuary for the unconquered sun god Mithras, the promoter of their empire. (*ILS* 659)

This text combined the Jupiter–Hercules theology, which Diocletian had developed to represent the politico-religious aspirations of the tetrarchy, with another central strand of late Roman imperial religion, the worship of the unconquered sun, Sol Invictus, who was fused, as often in this period, with Mithras, who was especially popular in military contexts.

Galerius and Maximinus now withdrew from the theater of civil war to the East, basing themselves at Thessalonica and Antioch respectively, while Licinius remained in Illyricum at Sirmium and Constantine in Gaul at Trier (Plate 3.2). However, the fundamental instability due to Maxentius' claims was still not removed. Maximianus retired to southern Gaul, while Maxentius himself, although not formally acknowledged by the tetrarchic college, established himself as Augustus in Italy, Rome and North Africa.

In 310 Constantine moved against Maximianus, who had once again claimed imperial power, and forced him to commit suicide near Massilia. Galerius died in May 311, leaving the empire ruled by a triumvirate of Augusti: Licinius, Constantine, and Maximinus. In 312 Licinius and Constantine converged on Maxentius. Constantine delivered the decisive blow. After crossing the Alps and fighting minor engagements at Turin and Verona (*Pan. Lat.* [IX], 5–13, 10.19–26), Constantine's army defeated Maxentius' forces at the battle of the Milvian bridge, on Rome's doorstep on October 28, 312. Maxentius himself perished in the waters of the Tiber. The Senate now recognized Constantine as the senior Augustus, and he made a pact with Licinius at Milan in February 313, which was concluded by the marriage of Constantine's sister, Constantia, to his fellow emperor. After the death of Galerius in May 311 Maximinus, still officially Augustus in the East, took control of Asia Minor and occupied the palace at Nicomedia. In 313 he launched an invasion of Licinius' territory, but was defeated in a battle at Adrianople, fled east across Anatolia, and committed suicide in Tarsus in the summer of that year (Lactantius, *On the Deaths of the Persecutors*, 45–49).

The Emergence of Constantine

Constantine was the senior figure in the new dyarchy. He was probably born around 273 at Naissus (Niš) in Lower Moesia, the eldest son of Constantius by Helena, reputedly a woman of humble origin. In later years Constantine was to found a city named after her at Drepanum near Nicomedia, and the mistaken belief became current that this had been her birthplace. More likely she had been born, like Constantius, in the Danubian province of Dacia Ripensis. Several sources indicate that before he rose to prominence in 305 Constantine had served as a military officer, a *tribunus*, in the service of Diocletian and Galerius. The anonymous Latin account of his career, written at the end of the fourth century, describes him as being held hostage, and this is not misleading, since he may clearly have had aspirations to succeed Constantius even before the dissolution of the first tetrarchy (*Origo Constantini imperatoris, Anon Val.* 2). The same source also declares that he was a courageous soldier, and this is not to be doubted.

The turbulent events of 305 to 312 proved the making of Constantine. Three traditional strands of Roman political life were interwoven in the struggles of these years: dynastic claims to power, the support of the armies, and the harnessing of religious propaganda. The artificial imposition of the tetrarchic system devised by Diocletian proved weaker than dynastic claims when power was transferred to a new ruler. Diocletian himself had implicitly recognized this fact when he used marriage connections to bind the Caesars, Constantius and Galerius, into the ruling coalition. The father–son combinations of Constantius and Constantine, and Maximianus and Maxentius were resilient and politically effective. Galerius compromised with Constantine, admitting him to the imperial college in 306. Maxentius proved his mettle by six effective years of defiance from his base at Rome. The panegyric of 310, delivered in praise of Constantine shortly after the downfall of Maximianus in 310, puts forward a manifesto for the primacy of familial claims to power:

> I will begin with your origin, because very many people up till now perhaps do not know it, but those who esteem you most do. The relationship of a grandson flows down to you from that divine Claudius, who first restored the lax and lost discipline of the Roman empire, and destroyed in land and sea battles huge bands of Goths who had poured forth from the gaping jaws on the Pontus and the mouths of the Danube. . . . The ancient prerogative of the imperial house advanced your own father, so that you should stand at the highest step, supreme over the fate of human affairs, the third emperor after two members of your family had been princes. Among all the sharers of your majesty, you have this status above all, Constantine, that you were born an emperor, and so great is the nobility of your origin, that the grant of empire added nothing to your honour.
> (*Pan. Lat.* VII [6], 2)

The flimsy claim that Constantine was in fact the grandson of the emperor Claudius Gothicus appears here for the first time.[26] It was designed to secure Constantine's position as the senior emperor against the aspirations of Galerius, Licinius, and Maximinus, who could boast no such lineages, and against Maxentius, who had only been preceded by his father as Augustus. By this time it must have been clear to all that the aim of the tetrarchy, to divorce imperial power from family succession, was dead. The rivals for power played the old game of dynastic politics for all it was worth.

The emperors also depended on the support of their troops. Backing from the praetorians, who had certainly been induced by the prospect of substantial donatives, impelled Maxentius' bid at Rome, and he also relied on the influence of his father Maximianus to win over troops from Severus, whose position was vulnerable to this dynastic challenge. Maxentius' own hold over the praetorians, however, proved sufficient to enable him to resist his father, when Maximianus attempted to supplant his son and resume power himself. Constantine meanwhile, having been acclaimed by his father's army in 305 and 306, had consolidated his popularity with them by throwing the defeated kings of the Alemanni and the Franks to the beasts in the arena.[27] Civil wars aroused hopes of rich pickings; the prizes at stake were not modest plunder from barbarian villages, but the substantial wealth and lands of Roman rivals. It is fair to guess that military loyalty to a commander was never stronger than in civil wars fought against their own kind. A telling document in this context is the bronze inscription found at Brigetio in Pannonia, containing a letter issued at Serdica in June 311 by Licinius. It offered the soldiers of the Balkan armies a huge reduction in their tax liabilities, by allowing them exemption for up to five *capita* (heads) in their households, when these were assessed for their normal obligations to the military *annona*, in place of the usual two. The purpose was to secure their loyalty in the forthcoming war with Maximinus, who was simultaneously attempting to seal the loyalty of his eastern subjects by targeting tax reductions on those who denounced the Christians.[28]

There is a striking parallel to this offer in a constitution of Constantine which probably dates to 320, the period of Constantine's own struggle with Licinius. The emperor entered the imperial army headquarters, amid the acclamations of his military prefects, tribunes, and other leading figures of the regime. He was confronted by veterans, due for discharge from service, who presented a demand: "Constantine Augustus, to what purpose have we been made veterans if we have no special grant of imperial privileges?" As the emperor made it clear that he was willing to hear their petition, a spokesman made the specific demand that veterans be exempted from providing compulsory public services. Constantine, in what was evidently a stage managed gesture, granted the request: "Be it known that it has now just been conceded to all veterans by my munificence that no one of them shall be compelled by law to perform a compulsory municipal service."[29]

The power struggles of the early fourth century were played out in a growing atmosphere of religious rivalry. Religious reform had been the bedrock of the new order imposed by Diocletian. World dominance was secured under the guidance of the two gods Jupiter and Hercules. This religious ideology was ubiquitous: The porticos of the theater of Pompeius at Rome were renamed the *porticus Iovia* and the *porticus Herculia* and dedicated respectively to the genii of Iovius Augustus (Diocletian) and Herculius Augustus (Maximianus); the gates of Grenoble were labeled *porta Iovia* and *porta Herculia*.[30] It is important to emphasize that although this new state religion gave prominence to traditional gods, it assumed a radically different form from earlier official cultic activity at Rome. There may even have been influence from Christian ideas, due to the similarity between Christian belief in God the Father and God the Son, and the roles assigned to Jupiter as *rector caeli*, and Hercules as *pacator terrarum*.[31]

The promotion of new Roman gods was accentuated by the demonizing of foreign enemies. The clearest example of this is the letter which was sent to a proconsul of Africa about how to deal with the sect of the Manichees, perhaps in 297. The introduction is highly illuminating for the religious temper of the tetrarchic period. "The language is filled with significant words to denote ancient Roman virtue and new Persian vice."[32] It argued that in times of peace the wicked tended to introduce ignorant and foolish doctrines, threatening the moral order. Established religion must not be criticized by a new one, and it was a most serious matter to tamper with what had been laid down since antiquity. The emperors had a responsibility to punish those who propagandized new sects.

The legislation of this period included laws against the Manichees (*Mosaicarum et Romanorum legum collection* XV.111; trans. in Stevenson, *New Eusebius*, 267 no. 236) and against eastern groups which allowed incestuous marriages (*CJust.* 5.5.2). These measures provide a ready context for understanding the most famous of Diocletian's religious actions, the decision taken in 303 to outlaw Christianity and to set in motion what has become known as the Great Persecution. This received so much attention from Christian writers, especially

Lactantius and Eusebius, that it is easy to set these events out of proportion. Lactantius, always given to highlight a colorful incident or anecdote, identi-fied the origin of the persecution at the occasion of a ritual, during which the *haruspices* (priestly diviners) were unable to detect the usual favorable signs in the entrails of sacrificial victims, and blame was cast on Christians who were present at the ceremony.[33] He claimed that Diocletian, under the strong influ-ence of Galerius, who had in turn been swayed by his rabidly pagan mother, consulted first his court and senior military officers, and then the oracle of Apollo at Didyma, before issuing an edict on February 23, 303, the Roman festival of Terminalia, from the imperial residence at Nicomedia. Although the wording of the edict is not preserved, its terms resembled the outlawing of the Manichees. Churches were to be destroyed, and copies of the scriptures sought out and burned. Christians were to be stripped of any rank or honor they held, and were legally downgraded, to be liable to torture. Since they would be required to swear a pagan oath, they were effectively denied the right to take any action in a Roman court. The main church in Nicomedia, which stood provocatively in full view of the palace, was razed to the ground by the praetorian guard, but the effects of this measure were initially relatively limited.

Thanks to the Christian writers we can follow the dissemination of the edict through the empire in a way that is impossible for other imperial legislation. Letters were sent to provincial authorities in 303 and 304 which urged them to play an active role in arresting and imprisoning clergy. Later sources, con-cerned with the origins of the Donatist controversy, provide a vivid account of the hunting down and handing over of scriptures to be burnt in the African city of Cirta.[34] In effect everything depended on the zeal and enthusiasm of the Roman authorities locally. This applied to the emperors themselves, as well as to provincial governors. The Christian tradition is unanimous that Constantius in Trier did little to trouble the Christians. Lactantius says he confined himself to destroying some churches, but even this was denied by Eusebius.[35] Outside Africa there is almost no trace of persecution in the western provinces. In any case the edict was reluctantly rescinded by Galerius on the eve of his death in May 311, apparently following similar actions taken by Constantine as early as 306, and by Maxentius perhaps in 308.[36]

In the East the most energetic anti-Christian action came from the new emperor Maximinus, whose actions must have been closely observed (although they may have been exaggerated) by Eusebius, who was living in Caesarea, the emperor's residence from 306 to 308. After the death of Galerius in 311, Maximinus contrived to persuade eastern communities to send him petitions demanding that persecution be carried on with full vigor, and in response to these propounded a doctrine of pagan belief, which reasserted the powers of the traditional gods and their influence on world affairs:

Who is so obtuse as not to see that the benevolent concern of the gods is responsible for the fertility of the earth, for keeping the peace, and defeating unrighteous enemies, for curbing storms at sea, tempests and earthquakes, which have only occurred when the Christians with their ignorant and futile beliefs, have come to afflict almost the whole world with their shameful practices.[37]

We must place the most dramatic and far-reaching religious event of the early fourth century, Constantine's conversion to Christianity, in this context. On the eve of the decisive battle with Maxentius Constantine was convinced that a solar apparition that he had experienced should be interpreted as a promise of victory from the God of the Christians. Armed with this new conviction, and placing, we are told, the sign of the cross on the shields of his soldiers, he led his outnumbered troops to a bloody but decisive victory at the Milvian bridge over the river Tiber. The nature of his vision and conversion are discussed below in chapter 8. It is generally acknowledged that there was a close affinity between the Christianity which Constantine endorsed in 312 and contemporary solar worship. The nature of his vision suggests that at the decisive moment of his imperial career, Constantine's belief in a supreme solar deity and belief in the Christian God were virtually convergent.

After the twin victories over Maxentius and Maximinus in 312 and 313, the relationship between the victors was uneasy and strained. The bond between the two Augusti was symbolically forged by the marriage of Constantine's sister Constantia to Licinius. Licinius was now Augustus in the East but also in effective control of the Danubian region.

Constantine's personal ambition far outweighed his collegial instincts, and were spurred when his second wife Fausta gave birth to a son, Constantinus, in spring 316. Between October 316 and January 317 he had defeated Licinius' forces first at Cibalae in Pannonia and then near Adrianople in Thrace. On March 1, 317, a new pact was made which confirmed Constantine and Licinius as Augusti, and appointed three Caesars: Constantine's sons Crispus (by his first marriage) and Constantinus, and Licinius' own infant son born to Constantia in 315, also called Licinius. The boundary between eastern and western rulers was set on the Thracian frontier. Constantine now controlled the entire empire as far as his own birthplace, Naissus. In the following years Fausta provided her husband with a quiverful of dynastic ammunition: Constantius, born in 317, a daughter Constantina, Constans born in 320 or 323, and another girl, Helena (Diagram 3.2). From 317 to 324 Constantine consolidated his power-base in Illyricum, and in 324 was ready for a final reckoning. Starting from Thessalonica, he defeated Licinius' troops at Adrianople in July and besieged Byzantium. His victory came at a land and sea battle at Chrysopolis on the Bosporus, followed soon after by Licinius' surrender at Nicomedia. Before the end of the year Constantine proclaimed the foundation of a new city at Byzantium, which was to bear his own name, Constantinople, and by spring 325 both Licinius and his son had been put to death in Thessalonica. The way was thus opened for the final phase of Constantine's reign.

From 324 until his death in 337 Constantine was sole Augustus. His second and third sons by Fausta, Constantius and Constans, were promoted to the rank of Caesar in 324 and 333. Meanwhile Crispus was executed in 326, accused of having an adulterous relationship with his stepmother Fausta, and Fausta

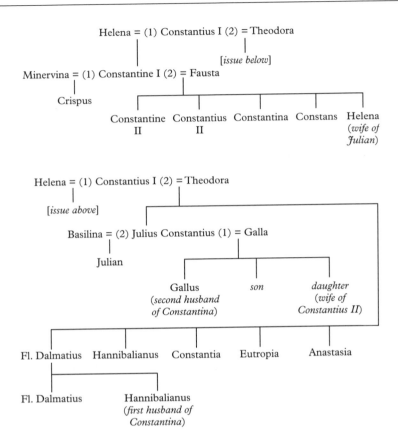

Diagram 3.2   The Constantinian dynasty (from G. W. Bowersock, *Julian the Apostate* [London, 1978], 35)

herself perished soon afterwards, apparently suffocated to death on the emperor's orders. The sources predictably provide divergent accounts of these sensational and sinister imperial secrets. The pagan historian Zosimus, who paints an unrelentingly hostile picture of Constantine, alleged that the emperor's conversion resulted from these events, as the Christians were the only sect that could offer him absolution for his crimes, through the rite of baptism, which in Constantine's case was deferred until his death bed.[38]

After the defeat of Licinius Constantine continued an aggressive frontier policy, designed to secure the Danube for Rome and to subordinate barbarians living north of the river. Stone bridges were built across the Rhine, at Cologne in 310 and across the Danube at Oescus in 328, protected in each case by forts on the north banks of the rivers. The purpose of the bridge at Cologne is illuminated by a contemporary panegyric:

Furthermore, by building the bridge at Agrippinensis you defy the remnants of the defeated tribe and compel them never to abandon their fears but to be in constant terror, and to keep outstretched their hands in submission. However, you are doing this more for the glory of your empire and to embellish the frontier, than to create an opportunity to cross into enemy territory whenever you wish. . . . (5) Certainly it brought you at its inception the submission of the enemy, who came in supplication for peace and brought well born hostages. So no one can doubt what they will do when the bridge is complete, if they are so servile when it is only just started. (*Pan. Lat.* [VI], 13.1–5, trans. Rodgers and Nixon)

These remarks make clear that the bridges were not designed to further extensive campaigns across the riverine boundaries of the empire. They made a conspicuous statement of Roman power, but also enabled traffic to pass across the frontier.

Christian sources show that Constantine was heavily engaged with the affairs of the church between 312 and the fall of Licinius. The compact at Milan in 313 proclaimed religious toleration for all, but particularly favored the Christians, since it brought a definitive end to the persecution. More than that, it provided both for the restoration of Christian property, and for those who had obtained possessions confiscated from Christians to be compensated at the state's expense.

Constantine was at once involved in the problem of the Donatists in Africa. The issue was quite simply to establish which was the official universal church in the province. A complicated feud had developed between a rigorist group, whose members reckoned that all who had compromised during the persecution were traitors to the church, and those who took a less severe line. The consecration of Caecilian as bishop of Carthage, probably in early 312, was challenged by the Donatist faction. Apart from the deeply held principle, there were material matters at issue, notably which party should benefit from privileges and imperial benefactions to the church (Eusebius, *HE* 10.5–7). In one of his letters Constantine denounced the Donatists as persons of unstable mind. But when they appealed, they received a remarkably even-handed reply from the emperor. A schism was to be avoided at all costs.

By engaging with the Donatist dispute Constantine began to formulate a new view of his own responsibilities for religious affairs, and this was the first step towards a new style of Christian imperial rule. He saw himself as responsible to God for the unity and harmony of the earthly kingdom which he ruled:

What greater obligation is imposed on me by my own intent and the bounty of my sovereign, than that, dispelling errors and cutting short all rashness, I should bring it about that everyone displays true piety, simple concord and the worship fitting for God Almighty. (Optatus, app. 7.34a, trans. Edwards)

Constantine now began, unsystematically, to accommodate the church and its personnel within the wider institutions of the empire. He exempted clerics from civic liturgies (*CTh.* 1.16.1–2) and from taxation (*CTh.* 16.2.10). To balance this generosity, he also excluded rich persons from holding clerical office (*CTh.* 16.2.6). He gave bishops rights of jurisdiction under Christian law between

Christian litigants (*CTh.* 1.27.1 [318] and *Constitutiones Sirmondianae* 1 [333]), and rescinded the penalties placed by Roman laws on celibacy or on childless couples, thus endorsing the Christian reverence for celibacy and virginity.[39] Virtually from the moment of his conversion he began to endow church construction to further the worship of the Christian God. The great basilica of John Lateran was constructed at Rome between 312 and 315 on the site of a cavalry barracks, which had housed the equestrian bodyguard of Constantine's rival Maxentius. Further major church building followed at Rome, culminating in the first Church of St Peter on the site of the Vatican, in the new city of Constantinople, at the holy sites of Palestine, and at a small number of pagan cult centers in the East.[40]

Other legislative measures were more ambiguous. In 321 a law was issued to the effect that Sunday should be a rest-day for those working in cities, although country dwellers were allowed to work their fields (*CJust.* 3.12.2). Slaves could be manumitted, but other legal business was forbidden. Eusebius interpreted this as the designation of Sunday as the "Lord's Day," a day of Christian prayer (*VC* 4.18.1), but in view of the blurred distinction, in Constantine's own perception, between sun worship and Christianity, the motivation behind this action was certainly not simply to promote Christian worship. Eusebius adds that Constantine instructed military units to address a prayer to the sun, to be acknowledged as the one god and bringer of victory to the emperor and his family (*VC* 4.20). This was similar to a prayer to the sun which Licinius had asked his own army to offer before their decisive battle with Maximinus in 313 (Lactantius, *On the Deaths of the Persecutors* 46). Constantine's measure would have been offensive to few, and made formal accommodation between pagan and Christian worship easier than it had been.

Religious antagonism was built into the final struggle with Licinius, but the doctrinal conflict between him and Constantine was clearly exaggerated in the context of the civil war between them (see below, chapter 7). In 325 Constantine adopted his most prominent role in ecclesiastical politics, when he arranged for the first ecumenical council to be convened at Nicaea. It was almost certainly at this gathering that he made his most famous statement relating to his own role as a religious, as well as a political, leader:

> Hence it was not without reason that once, on the occasion of his entertaining a company of bishops, he let fall the expression that he himself too was a bishop, addressing them in my hearing with the following words: "You are bishops (*episkopoi*) whose jurisdiction is within the Church: I also am a supervisor (*episkopos*), ordained by God to overlook affairs outside the Church." And truly his measures corresponded with his words; for he watched over all his subjects with an episcopal care, and exhorted them as far as he could to lead a godly life. (Eusebius, *VC* 4.24, trans. Stevenson [adapted])

The central point of this statement was that Constantine acknowledged his own responsibilities towards the non-Christian inhabitants of the Roman world.

Although he was a Christian by passionate personal conviction, and promoted the interests of the church by many of his actions and decisions, he was also committed to the well-being of the empire as a whole.

The Successors of Constantine

In the final years of his reign Constantine had widened the circle of the ruling dynasty. Two grandchildren of the collateral family line of Constantius and Theodora were promoted to high office in 335. Hannibalianus was made "king of kings and of the Pontic regions," while his younger brother Dalmatius was appointed Caesar and placed in charge of Thrace, Macedonia, and Achaea. The political context of these new arrangements is far from clear, but in any case they were soon overtaken by the dynastic crisis which occurred at the death of Constantine on May 22, 337. None of the Caesars had been raised to the status of Augustus, and an interregnum extended until September 9. During this period Constantine's army, which Zosimus says would tolerate no emperor apart from Constantine's sons, is said to have taken matters into its own hands and murdered rival claimants to power, including Dalmatius, Hannibalianus, and all the other male descendants of Constantius and Theodora apart from Gallus and Julian, aged twelve and six years old respectively. Most sources, beginning with Julian himself, suggest that Constantius was the instigator of the murders.

The next phase of imperial history is poorly documented, until the surviving narrative of Ammianus Marcellinus picks up the story in 354. However, the main theme is continuing rivalry for power between Constantine's successors and other usurpers, resulting in a series of dynastic murders and civil wars. Constans, the ruler of the western empire, displaced his elder brother Constantine II from Africa and Italy, but was overthrown himself by Magnentius, a senior military commander of barbarian origin (from a community of *laeti*, German settlers, in northern Gaul), who executed a successful coup d'état at Autun on January 18, 350. Constantius, who had been dealing with sustained Sassanian aggression along the eastern frontier during the 340s, brought his troops into Europe to deal with the usurpation. His first major action was to neutralize the impact of Vetranio, another commander who had been proclaimed emperor by his troops in Pannonia in March 350. He then moved against Magnentius. Constantius secured his dynastic position by arranging for his nephew Gallus to marry his sister and raising him to the rank of Caesar. The first battle of the civil war was fought at Mursa on September 28, 351 (Map 3.2). The defeated Magnentius escaped to Gaul, where he joined his brother Decentius, whom he had appointed as his own Caesar. Their resistance was undermined by attacks from across the Rhine by the Alemanni, which had been subsidized by Constantius. The end came at the battle of Mons Seleuci, near Gap in the French Alps. Defeat led the rebels to take their own lives in August 353 (Zosimus 2.53).

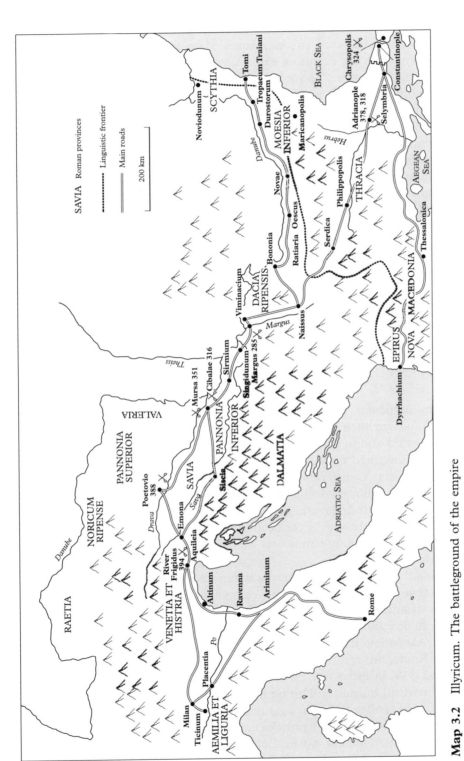

Map 3.2 Illyricum. The battleground of the empire

Constantius was thus now sole ruler of the empire. His personality and ruling style are vividly depicted by Ammianus Marcellinus, whose detailed history begins for us with the events of 354. Constantius is represented as being harsh and irritable in temper, and notably prone to baseless suspicion of would-be conspirators and rivals, a tendency which was exacerbated by the flattery of his courtiers. As the historian puts it, these encouraged the belief that the fate of the entire world hung on the slender thread of the emperor's own life. This sentiment correlated precisely with the tone of panegyric oratory in the fourth century, which relentlessly propounded the view that the empire's well being in every respect depended on the vigilance, providence, and courage of the emperors.

The drastic sequence of usurpation, civil war, and dynastic murder which characterized the empire during the 350s led to wider insecurity. Zosimus accurately summarizes the situation at the beginning of his third book:

> Everywhere (Constantius) saw the Roman empire being dismembered by barbarian incursions: the Franks, Alemanni and Saxons had already taken forty cities on the Rhine and left them in ruins by carrying off countless numbers of their inhabitants and untold spoils; the Quadi and Sarmatians had very boldly overrun Pannonia and Upper Moesia; and the Persians were continually harassing the East, whereas previously they had been inactive for fear of being attacked by Gallus Caesar. (Zosimus 3.1, trans. Ridley)

Gaul in particular had been devastated first by the war requisitions of Magnentius and then by the consequences of his defeat. The Alemanni were incited to raid and devastate the country, and the appointment of Silvanus to deal with them had ended in a self-inflicted catastrophe. It was against this background that Constantius appointed a new Caesar, Gallus' younger half-brother Julian, who was summoned from his studies at Athens to the court at Milan in 355 to undertake imperial responsibilities. Julian's cause was championed by Constantius' wife, the beautiful but childless Eusebia, and his position at the heart of the ruling family was strengthened by marriage to the emperor's sister Helena.

During the late 350s the empire was exposed to more external pressure than at any time since the 290s. Julian campaigned with unexpected energy and success against Frankish and Alemannic incursions in Gaul throughout this period. In 355 and 356 Constantius, based at Milan, also mounted expeditions against Alemannic tribes in the upper Rhine valley. In 357 he paid a famous visit to Rome, but returned to the Balkan frontier headquarters at Sirmium in 358 and 359, in order to deal with threats to the middle Danube area from the Sarmatian Limigantes. During the emperor's long absence in the West, the Sassanian king Sapor II increased pressure on the Mesopotamian front, capturing the city of Amida (Diyarbakır) in 359. Constantius returned to the East, spent the winter of 359–60 in Constantinople, and in the following spring marched as far as Cappadocia, before he heard news that his Caesar Julian had been proclaimed Augustus by his troops in Paris. Even so, the Sassanian threat was too serious to ignore (the frontier cities of Bezabde and Singara were taken in 360), and he continued to make a show of strength in Syria and across the Euphrates in Mesopotamia over two campaigning seasons, before finally turning back from Antioch to face the threat of civil war in autumn 361. A confrontation with Julian loomed, but Constantine died in Cilicia at the road station of Mopsucrene, in the foothills of the Taurus mountains, on November 3, aged forty-four.

Julian

Julian is by far the best documented emperor of the fourth century. This contrasts with the relative brevity of his reign (he was sole emperor for only twenty months), but is to be explained above all by his unorthodox religious position, namely his opposition to Christianity and his attempt to rekindle a coherent pagan theology at the heart of the Roman state. This, combined with the dramatic events of his reign and his evidently charismatic personality, attracted the admiration and attention of pagan intellectuals and writers. Thus Julian's near contemporary, Ammianus, who served under him both in Gaul and on the Persian campaign, devoted the bulk of his surviving work to Julian's role in public life. Books 15–21 cover the period from his accession as Caesar to the death of Constantius in 361, and books 22 to 25 his rule as sole emperor until his death in Persia in July 363. Ammianus openly acknowledged that his admiration for Julian lent his account many of the features of a panegyric:

> The great improvements which his valour and good luck enabled him to bring about in Gaul surpass many of the heroic actions of former times, and I shall therefore describe them one by one in due order. I intend to employ all the resources of my modest talent in the hope that they will prove adequate for the purpose. My narrative, which is not a tissue of clever falsehoods but an absolutely truthful account based on clear evidence, will not fall far short of a panegyric, because it seems that the life of this young man was guided by some principle which raised him above the ordinary and accompanied him from his illustrious cradle to his last breath. (Ammianus 16.1, trans. Hamilton)

Ammianus was not above criticizing Julian openly on several occasions, for instance for his excessive love of blood sacrifice, and for his unfair law banning Christian teachers, and at other times presents his actions in such a way as to imply criticism. In fact, as these examples show, his own conception of paganism differed from Julian's.[41] His portrait of his hero is based more on admiration for his achievements as a leader of men, than on sympathy for his religious position. Ammianus' portrait can be compared with that of Zosimus, who devotes book three of his history to Julian. Zosimus' main source, here as elsewhere in his fourth century narrative, was the largely lost work of another pagan writer, Eunapius. Zosimus, however, dwelt even less on the religious issues than

Ammianus, focusing almost exclusively on Julian's achievements as a military leader, in particular during the Persian campaign, which occupied the whole of the second half of the book.[42] In the same mode as the pagan historians are the avowedly panegyric speeches of Mamertinus, a Gallic supporter, delivered in praise of the new ruler when he received the consulship in January 362, and the oration which was delivered after Julian's death by the Anthiochian rhetor Libanius.[43] On the other side there is the hostile Christian tradition, notably the fourth oration of the Cappadocian Gregory of Nazianzus, who had been a fellow student with Julian in Athens in the mid-350s. The fullest narrative presentation of the Christian view of Julian is book three of the *Church History* of Socrates. In addition to this rich and diverse tradition we can hear the voice of Julian himself, preserved not merely in the letters and edicts which he issued as emperor, but more importantly in private speeches, letters, and treatises.

After the murder of his father and several close relatives in 337 Julian was transplanted from Constantinople to an imperial estate near Caesarea in Cappadocia, where he began his education. His mother tongue was Greek, not Latin, and during the 340s and early 350s he developed into a passionate and highly gifted intellectual, becoming absorbed in Christian and classical literature, and in Neoplatonic philosophy. After Cappadocia, his studies took him to Nicomedia, Pergamum, and Athens, where he encountered two of the outstanding Christian talents of his generation, the future bishops Basil of Caesarea and Gregory of Nazianzus. During this period he was also attracted to pagan religious rituals, and Eunapius, in his life of the sophist Maximus of Ephesus, gives an account of a theurgic ritual attended by Julian, which had the effect, as Julian later averred, of converting him to belief in the old gods. Julian later claimed that this conversion had taken place in 351, although he remained outwardly an observer of Christianity until the moment of his final break with Constantius in 361 (see further in chapter 8).

Thus, the Caesar who took over command in Gaul in 355 was radically different in character, background, and education from his imperial predecessors. The imperial example which he consciously followed was that set by the philosopher emperor Marcus Aurelius, who, like Julian, spent much of his reign conducting wars along Rome's frontiers. Julian's literary tastes and education gave him other models to emulate, most notably the tragic warrior hero of the Iliad, Achilles, and Alexander the Great. Another figure from the past whose shadow hung over him was that of a Roman general and man of letters, whose rise to power was also based on successes won against barbarian enemies in Gaul, Julius Caesar.

Julian's aspiration to match the feats of these mighty predecessors gives the lie to the idea that he was primarily a dilettante figure, reluctantly dragged into imperial power. He was popular with his troops but frequently at odds with his senior officers, who had been appointed by Constantius to provide a strategic lead in the West. Notably he came into conflict with Florentius, the praetorian prefect, over the administration and the tax regime of Gaul. Florentius was eager to press hard to extract tax revenues and military supplies.

Julian's concern was to restore well-being to the region, and perhaps thereby to ensure its support in a future civil war. Ammianus was as lavish in praise of Julian's fairness and generosity towards the provincials as he was of his military successes:

> Finally, to say nothing of the victorious battles in which he routed the barbarians, who often fell fighting to the last, the benefits which he conferred on impoverished Gaul when it was at the last gasp are most clearly illustrated by this fact: when he arrived, he found that twenty-five gold pieces per head were exacted by way of tribute; when he left, seven sufficed to meet all demands. This was like bright sunshine breaking through dark clouds, and was greeted everywhere with dances of joy. (Ammianus 16.5)

Julian achieved his single greatest military success in 357; the victory of his own 13,000 troops over an army of 60,000 Alemanni led by the overconfident king Chnodomar at the battle of Strasburg. Credit for the victory was variously assigned. Ammianus tells us that Constantius' courtiers denigrated Julian, calling him Victorinus as he so frequently reported victories over the Germans in his dispatches, and ascribed the successes to the emperor. In fact credit might properly be claimed first and foremost by Julian's troops, and the officer group under his praetorian prefect Florentius. Julian had marched his troops twenty-one miles across the Jura mountains to within view of the enemy and then proposed that they should rest for the night before engaging. The troops themselves and their officers had simply overruled this excess of caution and impelled him to join battle at once, before the Alemanni could slip away across the Rhine to safety. The result was one of Rome's most crushing victories against a barbarian enemy, which re-established their control over the Rhine frontier for fifty years (Ammianus 16.12).

The success of the war along the Rhine contrasted with the difficulties which Constantius faced, and he ordered detachments from some of Julian's best troops to be sent to the East. Julian raised no initial objection, except to point out that some recent German volunteers had been enlisted on condition that they should not serve beyond the Alps. However, the conflict of interest swiftly developed into a crisis. The senior military commanders in Julian's army were naturally inclined to obey Constantius' orders. The troops convened in Paris, where Julian entertained their officers to a banquet on the eve of their departure. At first light next morning soldiers surrounded Julian's quarters, hailing him as Augustus, and by the middle of the day, protesting, Julian had been lifted up on the shields of his Germanic soldiers, equipped with a makeshift diadem, and proclaimed Augustus. Arguments have raged ever since as to whether he had orchestrated the whole affair, or was simply swept along by the tide of events. Julian defended himself from charges of complicity in the *Letter to the Athenians* (281c–286d). Ammianus provides a dramatic account, which leaves the question of responsibility ambiguous (Ammianus 20.4). The pagan historian Eunapius, whose work was used by both Ammianus and Zosimus in constructing their versions, was clear that Julian orchestrated the usurpation. Modern commentators are disinclined to give Julian the benefit of the doubt. Constantius certainly would not have done so.[44]

The progress of the usurpation unfolded over the next twelve months, as information and correspondence passed from one end of the empire to the other. A careful diplomatic letter sent by Julian asked Constantius to approve his elevation, but was predictably rebuffed. Constantius' uncompromising reply was the moment of truth for Julian. Mindful of the fate of his half-brother Gallus, who had been summoned from the East and executed by the suspicious emperor in 354, Julian prepared for civil war.

In the autumn of 361 Julian began his move east, shipping troops down the Danube as well as overland towards Sirmium. A contingent was sent to besiege Aquileia, which had been seized by two legions loyal to Constantius, while he advanced to Naissus and the strategic Succi pass, which controlled the access to Constantinople. The long march to the East must have been crucially important for Julian, as it gave him the opportunity to cement the loyalty of his own officers and men. During the advance he used every means to rally support for his cause, soliciting support from provincial communities and signaling his impending arrival to the east Balkan provinces. The *Letter to the Athenians* was written at this time, explaining Julian's conduct in relation to Constantius both before and during his term in Gaul, and justifying his decision to accept the title of Augustus. In January 362 the new consul Claudius Mamertinus devoted much of his panegyric to the emperor to an account of this formative journey. Constantius rallied his own forces and prepared to bring them west for the battle, but died before the march was long under way. Julian entered Constantinople unopposed, as sole emperor, in December 361.

Julian was immediately responsible for many decisions relating to the administration of the empire. It is difficult to identify these as part of specific policies or guiding principles. However, Julian's approach to government seems to have been more deliberate than that of other emperors. This is clearest in the way he tackled religious issues and introduced many measures that were designed to curb Christian influence and advance pagan institutions, to be discussed in a later chapter (see below, chapter 8). However, we can see a deliberate plan behind several other measures, which cohere with what we might expect from a ruler with his distinctive combination of experience and intellectual background. Julian was a passionate student of Greek culture, imbued in the literature, philosophy, and religious ideas of Classical Greece. It is not surprising, therefore, that he was prepared to champion the old ideal of the classical *polis*, the autonomous city-state. He restored to cities the right to collect taxes and revenues from their own lands, and allowed them to enlarge their councils. Meanwhile he attempted to reduce the state's own tax demands, and in particular tried to alleviate the financial burdens on city councilors, the *curiales*. These may all be seen as attempts to shore up the system of city-state government, which had underpinned the political arrangements of the early Roman Empire, but had become seriously eroded by state intrusion, increasing tax demands, and the enlargement of the imperial administrative bureaucracy through the third and fourth centuries. Julian's desire to put the clock back was not restricted to his religious initiatives.

Julian developed and put into practice his ideas of government, statecraft, and religious ideology against the background of his main undertaking, an invasion of Persia, which would reverse the setbacks which Rome had suffered on the eastern frontier under Constantius. He surely hoped that success in this undertaking would demonstrate the efficacy of his religious reforms, in bringing the Roman world back to belief in the old divine order, after the misguided imperial mission begun by Constantine to supplant this with Christianity. Moreover, his aspirations were kindled by contemplation of his own military successes. For five years he had campaigned with conspicuous distinction in Gaul. In securing the Rhine frontier he had had to contend with not only the barbarian threat, but also with the conflicting strategies of Constantius' generals, and had emerged as their military superior. When it came to the ultimate test of Roman military command in the fourth century, victory in civil war, he had prevailed, albeit by default, over a rival whose prowess in these matters was legendary:

> Constantius, though he suffered grievous defeats in foreign wars, prided himself on his successes in civil conflicts, and bathed in the blood which poured in a fearful stream from the internal wounds of the state. (Ammianus 21.16)

Julian left Constantinople in May 362, and reached Antioch a month later. There followed a period of eight months, in which troops were assembled and preparations made for the Persian expedition. The period proved too long for the patience of the predominantly Christian people of Antioch, and the relationship between the emperor and the host city worsened rapidly as a grain shortage, exacerbated by the growing demands of the troops, drove up prices and led to insupportable profiteering by dealers. Julian found himself in conflict with Christians and pagans alike in religious matters. The relationship between city and emperor is memorably encapsulated in the self-mocking speech, the *Misopogon*, which Julian addressed to the Antiochenes at the festival of the New Year.[45]

The emperor left the city at the head of 65,000 troops on March 5, 363. The high point of the campaign was a hard-won victory over a large Sassanian force outside the walls of Ctesiphon, but the city itself appeared impregnable. Julian now led his troops northwards on the far side of the Tigris, aiming to join a large contingent of Roman forces which had been sent into Upper Mesopotamia under the command of Sebastianus and Julian's relative Procopius. On June 26 the emperor fell victim of a spear wound, and died in the evening, allegedly reliving the final hours of his philosophical hero Socrates and discoursing with his last words on the immortality of the soul (Plate 3.3).

As we have seen (above p. 51) it fell to his successor Jovian to extricate the Roman forces from their exposed situation, at the price of surrendering control

Plate 3.3 The Death of Julian. This Sassanian royal relief at Taq-e Bostan in northwest Iran depicts the gods Mithras to the left with a radiate crown, and Ahura-Mazda in the center, conferring the ring of royal power on the Sassanian king, Ardashir II. Under the king's feet lies the trampled body of his defeated enemy, who is recognizable from the thin features and goatee beard as the emperor Julian, who had been defeated by Ardashir's predecessor, Sapor II (S. Mitchell)

of the provinces beyond the Tigris which Galerius had claimed from Persia in the treaty of 299. More significant than this sacrifice was the handover to the Persians of Nisibis, a city which had three times endured sieges, and defied attempts at capture by Sapor II, in 338, 346, and 350.

Julian was the last emperor in direct line of descent from Constantine, and a new dynastic era began with the accession of Valentinian and Valens in 364. Looking back over the saga of civil wars and usurpations which overshadowed the Roman Empire in the fourth century, it is important to appreciate the role played by dynastic politics. When Constantius brushed aside the feeble challenge of Vetranio in 350 he needed to do little more than remind his troops of the generosity they had experienced from his father Constantine, and the oaths of loyalty they had sworn to the old emperor's children. The choice of the obscure Jovian to succeed Julian was probably connected to the fact that he was a relative of Constantius, not merely one of the emperor's pall-bearers. In the following generation Gratian, the son of Valentinian, was to strengthen his own position as Augustus by marrying Constantius' daughter. It is thus hardly a surprise that the beginning of the new regime of Valentinian and Valens was immediately called into question by a relative of Julian, Procopius, who mounted a serious challenge from his base in Constantinople, Constantine's own foundation, and in northwest Asia Minor. A detail noted by Ammianus confirms that Procopius was well aware of the need to play the dynastic card:

> Procopius hit upon a particularly effective way of winning their support by personally carrying about in his arms the small daughter of Constantius, whose memory they cherished, and stressing his relationship with that emperor and Julian. Another favourable circumstance was that Faustina, the child's mother, happened to be present when he received certain items of the imperial insignia. (Ammianus 26.7, trans. Hamilton)

The rebellion lasted more than a year until May 366 and demonstrated two things. Firstly, it attested to the continuing force of sentiment in favor of the Constantinian dynasty, which guaranteed support for Procopius even when his military position was desperate. Secondly, it showed the solidarity of the senior military hierarchy in support of the two Pannonian officers whom they had placed in power (see above, p. 51). They prevailed, but securing the Valentinian succession had been a close run thing.

Valentinian and Valens

After taking control of the western part of the empire in 365, Valentinian relied largely on diplomacy rather than outright warfare to maintain the frontier along the Rhine and the upper Danube, which had been established by Julian's campaigns. Ammianus noted that "even his harshest critic cannot find fault with his unfailing shrewdness in matters of state, especially if he bears in mind that it was a greater service to keep the barbarians in check by frontier barriers than to defeat them in battle" (Ammianus 29.4). In pursuit of this policy Roman forces were brought up to strength by energetic levies of barbarians and provincials in Gaul (Zosimus 4.12), and he constructed or refurbished the entire chain of forts and watch posts, and consolidated strategic bridgeheads along the river frontier.[46] The fruits of this policy are illustrated by the treaty which was agreed with the Alemannic king Macrianus in 374:

> A courteous invitation to come to the vicinity of Mainz was sent to the aforesaid king, who was himself clearly inclined to come to terms. . . . On the day appointed for the conference (Macrianus) stood majestically erect on the very bank of the Rhine, while his countrymen clashed their shields around him. From the other side the emperor, also attended by a host of officers of various ranks amid a display of gleaming standards, embarked in some river boats and came within a safe distance of the shore. . . . A pact of friendship was concluded with solemn oaths. The king who had been a source of such trouble withdrew mollified. From that time on he was to prove our ally. (Ammianus 30.3, trans. Hamilton)

Such ritualized diplomacy was typical of frontier relations with barbarian tribes at this date. Valens had dealt with the Gothic leaders on the Danube in an almost identical fashion in 369. For a moment it created the illusion that the wholly disproportionate relationship between the Roman Empire and minor Germanic tribal leaders was a transaction between equal sovereign partners. The principle was embedded in the Roman idea of a *foedus*, a treaty of alliance between nominally equal forces, in which the two parties swore to abstain from hostilities and to help one another against their enemies.

In the early 370s attention switched to the middle Danubian region and Valentinian's home province of Pannonia, where the defense of the frontier was in the hands of the *magister militum* Equitius, who had dowsed the last flickering embers of the revolt of Procopius, and had been responsible for building forts along the Danube, as part of the wider aim of securing the northern riverine frontier:[47]

> By the imperial order of our masters Valentinian, Valens and Gratian, greatest of emperors, and by the instruction of the illustrious man, commander of the cavalry and infantry, the count Equitius, Toscanus, the commander of *legio I Martiorum*, together with the soldiers entrusted to his command, constructed this fort, whose name is Commerce (for which purpose it had been built) from its foundations and brought it to its final completion in forty-eight days during the consulship of our master Gratian Augustus and the most distinguished man Probus. (*ILS* 775 [near Gran in Pannonia], dated to 371)

This inscription reveals the double nature of such positions. They were both military strongpoints and locations for commercial dealings with the barbarians. The economic advantages of being able to trade with neighboring provinces explains the readiness of tribes living near the frontier to prefer stable peace to resistance to Rome, and the Quadi and Marcomanni of modern Moravia and Slovakia had a long history as friendly barbarians.[48] We may compare the situation on the lower Danube frontier, where relations with Gothic tribes were on exactly the same footing. There is evidence for cross-border trade in the pattern of finds of Roman coins found in Gothic-held territory in the mid-fourth century.[49]

In 375 Valentinian spent three months at Carnuntum, and then led a punitive raid from Aquincum against barbarian villages across the river. After he returned to Brigetio representatives of the Quadi approached him seeking an amnesty and were admitted on the urging of Equitius. Their pleas involved shifting the blame for anti-Roman behavior onto foreign brigands who had infiltrated their territory near the river, but they included a reference to the affront which Roman fort-building across the Danube posed to them. This drove the irascible Valentinian into a fit of apoplectic anger, and he died of a seizure (Ammianus 30.6). Peace was made nevertheless, for the emperor's leading generals ordered that the bridge across the Danube, which had been built to enable an invasion of barbarian territory, was demolished (Ammianus 30.10).

A Changing World

The succession to Valentinian had fundamental political consequences for the nature of the Roman state. During a serious illness in 367 Valentinian had promoted Gratian, who had been born in 359, to the rank of Augustus. Gratian thus became the first of the so-called child emperors. He took up residence at Trier. Now the two leading generals of the western armies, Merobaudes and Equitius, summoned Valentinian's widow Justina, who had formerly been married to Magnentius, and her four-year-old son to Aquincum, where the latter was declared Augustus, Valentinian II. The object was to prevent the appearance of a conspicuous power-vacuum in the most important military area of the empire, at a time when the western emperor Gratian was still a mere sixteen-year-old boy. However, the manner of the promotion of a new child Augustus demonstrated with unambiguous clarity the power of the emperor's generalissimos, and their actions heralded an era when such men dominated the state in political as well as military matters.[50] Valentinian and Valens are presented as imposing imperial figures, prone to anger and to abrupt and decisive judgments. However, this blustering exterior conceals genuine weaknesses. The new emperors lacked the dynastic authority of Constantine and his successors, and owed their position to the officers who had organized the succession to Jovian in 364. Army commanders and the holders of the great offices of state not only had key roles throughout this period in forming and executing policy, but also for arranging the composition of the imperial house. During the 370s and 380s the destinies of Gratian, Valentinian II, and Theodosius I, as well as that of the usurper Magnus Maximus, were decided not by the senior emperors at the time, but by cliques of senior political and military figures. This was a new version of rule by an oligarchy, which had been Rome's fate for much of its history.[51]

In the eastern empire Valens was initially concerned with the frontier in Thrace. Three thousand Goths had come to Constantinople in 365 in support of Procopius, and despite their protests that they were merely honoring the treaty obligation owed to Constantine, Valens intended revenge.[52] Valens carried out invasions of Gothic territory from his base in Lower Moesia at Marcianopolis. In 367 a fort was built at Daphne, a pontoon bridge was flung across the Danube, and troops scoured the lowlands, while the Goths took refuge in the mountains of the Serri (Carpathians).[53] In 368 floods prevented invasion, but in 369 Valens crossed the river at Noviodunum, harried the tribe of the Greuthungi, and forced the Gothic leader Athanaric to flee for his life. The Goths sued for peace, "reduced to want by the interruption of their trade." Valens' commanders tested the barbarians' good intentions, and a treaty was struck between Athanaric and Valens, who met on boats in mid-Danube, secured by an exchange of hostages. Athanaric was probably the grandson of Ariaricus who had made the Gothic treaty with Constantine in 332.

Two speeches by Themistius present a view of official policy towards the Goths.[54] *Oration* 8, delivered on March 28, 368 in Marcianople, condemned earlier regimes for over-taxation and stressed the cost of foreign wars; *oration* 10, delivered in Constantinople in early 370, explained and justified the peace deal:

> And so the barbarian went away highly contented, in the grip of contrary emotions at once both confident and fearful, both contemptuous and wary of his subjects, cast down in spirit by those aspects of the treaty in which he had lost his case but exulting in those in which success had fallen to him. . . . Although the profit that comes from the give and take of business transactions was enjoyed by both races in common, Valens established only two of the cities which had been founded along the river as trading posts. . . . He built some completely new border forts and furnished others with what they required:– higher walls, water supply for forts, provision dumps, ports on the coastline, full complements of soldiers in the garrisons, armaments. (Themistius, *Or.* 10.135, trans. Moncur)

Valens had been unable to conquer the Goths; further campaigning was not cost-effective; and agreement broadly on Roman terms was the best solution. Goths were only allowed to do business at two crossing points on the river.

Hitherto tribute or subsidies had been paid to friendly Gothic chieftains, but this ceased with the new agreement, which echoed Valentinian's rebuttal of the Alemannic delegates to Milan in 365:[55]

> No one saw gold coin counted out for the barbarians, countless talents of silver, ships freighted with fabrics or any of the things we were in the habit of tolerating before, enjoying the fruits of peace and quiet that was more burdensome than the incursions, and paying yearly tribute, which we were not ashamed to do, although we refused to call it by that name. (Themistius, *Or.* 10.135, trans. Moncur)

It is clear from the comparison with Valentinian's actions on the upper Danube, that the emperors were conducting a policy that had been agreed for both halves of the empire.

Foreign policy can be observed in other frontier areas. During the early 370s there had been trouble in the African province of Mauretania, when Firmus, the son of the pro-Roman king Nubel, organized a revolt provoked by anger at abusive Roman rule, and was even declared emperor. Like many of the Germanic tribal leaders he had served in Rome's forces.[56] Between 368 and 371 there had been a growing dispute over control of Armenia, which almost escalated into a full-scale confrontation between Rome and Persia. However, Roman intervention was forestalled by the Gothic threat to Thrace which had emerged between 376 and 378, and the situation was defused by the death of the belligerent Sassanian king Sapor II in 379 (Ammianus 30.2).[57] During the 380s three Sassanian rulers followed one another in rapid succession and were as preoccupied with internal security as their Roman counterparts. An agreement was reached based on a division of Armenia, into a smaller western zone, under Roman protectorate, and the east (Persarmenia) which looked towards Persia. Sapor III appears during this period to have allowed freedom of worship to the Christians in his empire, and this will have reinforced the entente with Rome. Relations between the two great powers were thus placed on a friendly footing which was only rarely disturbed before the beginning of the sixth century.[58]

A major new factor came to a head in 376; the encroachment of the Huns onto the main territory occupied by the Goths in the great river valleys of the Don, Dnieper, and Dniester. According to a fragment of Eunapius "the Scythians had been defeated and destroyed by the Huns and were being utterly extirpated. Those who were captured were massacred with their wives and children. There was no limit to the savagery employed in the killings" (Eunapius fr. 42.1). Their threat is made clear in a famous excursus of Ammianus, although the portrayal of these nomadic horsemen of Mongolian origin owes much to classical stereotyping of barbarians, and in particular to Herodotus' famous account of the Scythians:

> They have squat bodies, strong limbs, and thick necks, and are so prodigiously ugly and bent that they might be two-legged animals, or the figures crudely carved from stumps which are seen on the parapets of bridges. . . . They are totally ignorant of the difference between right and wrong, their speech is shifty and obscure, and they are under no constraint from religion or superstition. . . . This wild race, moving without encumbrances and consumed by savage passion to pillage the property of others, advanced robbing and slaughtering over the lands of their neighbours till they reached the Alans. (Amianus 31.2, trans. Hamilton)

The Alans (earlier known as the Massagetae) were an Arian race from north of the Caucasus: "tall and handsome, with yellowish hair and frighteningly fierce eyes. They are active and nimble in the use of arms and in every way a match for the Huns, but less savage in their way of life" (Ammianus 31.2).

Ammianus' account of these movements of barbarian peoples beyond the Danube needs to be treated with caution. The Romans would have had access to little reliable information about the Huns and the Alans, and their main source would have been the Goths themselves, pleading to be allowed across the river into the empire. The Huns themselves had only a minor role to play in the events of the next twenty years, although it is significant that they were responsible for an invasion of Asia Minor in the mid-390s, exactly at the period when Ammianus was writing his history.[59] They only emerged as a sustained threat to Rome in the second quarter of the fifth century. By this period they had coalesced from nomadic groups of mounted raiders into a coherent political force, and their leaders occupied permanent settlements in the eastern part of modern Hungary.[60] During the 370s it is more likely that they presented a high nuisance value, rather than an existential threat to the settled peoples between the Don and the Danube. Accordingly in searching for the reasons that led first the Gothic Tervingi, and then the Greuthungi to cross the Danube en masse in 376, we should probably lay much more stress than contemporary accounts do on the attractions of life in the Roman provinces to the barbarians, especially as economic conditions north of the Danube had probably worsened since the new frontier agreement reached in 369.

Admitting the Gothic tribes, although a historical inevitability with countless precedents in Roman frontier policy,[61] proved catastrophic in the short term. The official agreement to allow the Tervingi into the empire was sullied by serious abuses on the Roman side which alienated the newcomers. Meanwhile the Tervingi, commanded by Fritigern, were joined by the Greuthungi, who had crossed the Danube against Roman wishes. Eunapius (fr. 42) suggests that 200,000 fugitives were introduced into Thrace in this way. They were reinforced by other groups of Goths who were already in service as part of the Roman army and were quartered at Adrianople in Thrace. Summary orders for transfer to Asia and mistreatment at the hands of the civilian magistrates at Adrianople drove these Gothic auxiliaries to rebel and join their fellow countrymen. There were skirmishes and a major encounter at the battle of *Ad Salices* (north of Marcianopolis) in 377. Valens himself came to Constantinople, and then advanced to Adrianople. Hindsight suggests that he should have waited for reinforcements from the western emperor Gratian, but he miscalculated Gothic strength and ventured battle on his own. He and perhaps 10,000 Roman troops lost their lives at Adrianople. According to Ammianus this was the biggest military setback for Roman troops since Cannae, and the emperor's body was never recovered. The Goths, although they failed to capture Adrianople and Constantinople, occupied Thrace and Illyricum blocking communications with the West (Zosimus 4.24.3). The death of Valens marked the end of an epoch. This was virtually the last occasion on which a Roman emperor led his troops into a major encounter until Heraclius' campaigns in the seventh century.

Theodosius I

The death of a ruler inevitably provoked an imperial crisis, and that of an emperor on the battlefield, from which his body was not recovered, an acute one. Theodosius was the son of one of the most prominent military figures under Valentinian, and his father's achievements were crowned by the campaign during which he suppressed the dangerous revolt of Firmus in Mauretania. His son obtained his first major military command in Illyricum in 373/4 and won victories over the Sarmatians, but both men fell drastically from favor in the maneuverings that made Valentinian II Augustus in 375. The father was executed, the son dismissed from service. The later view of Theodosius' accession was that he had been called by Gratian from his home in Spain to rescue Rome from a devastating defeat by barbarians. He did so with such speed and effect that Gratian appointed him as his colleague (Theodoret, *HE* 5.5–6). In fact the chronology between the death of Valens at Adrianople on August 9, 378, and Theodosius becoming emperor on January 19, 379, rules out this sequence of events. A strong argument has been made to support the view that he was called back out of retirement to resume a military position in the middle Danube region in 377, thus being the strongest candidate for imperial promotion in the crisis of the following year.[62]

The central issue for the empire was how to deal with the Goths. Although they had been unable to capture the cities, Zosimus says that they occupied the whole of Thrace, and the city dwellers and garrisons were unable to leave the fortifications that protected them (Zosimus 4.25.2).

After the ending of Ammianus' history in 378 the historical record of the remainder of the fourth century becomes extremely fractured and hard to reconstruct. On January 19, 379, Theodosius was made Augustus by Gratian, and given charge of Dacia and Macedonia in eastern Illyricum. By autumn 380 Theodosius had withdrawn to Constantinople, but reinforced the garrisons of cities in Macedonia, which had hitherto been forced to supply food to the Goths (Zosimus 4.31.5–32.3). On January 11, 381, the Gothic leader Athanaric was driven out by a domestic conspiracy and took refuge with the Romans in Constantinople, where he was buried splendidly at his death two weeks later.[63] This may have been connected with new thinking about how to deal with the Goths in Thrace, which placed more emphasis on accommodation, rather than outright military victory.[64] In 381 troops sent by Gratian from the West, led by the barbarian generals Bauto and Arbogast, drove the Goths out of Macedonia and Thessaly and back to Thrace. The pressure was maintained in 382, and the Goths seem to have been expelled from Illyricum by September 382. An agreement was concluded on October 3, 382. Rome claimed that the Goths surrendered: "We have seen their leaders and chieftains, not making token concessions of a tattered banner, but giving up their weapons and swords with which up to that day they had held sway, and clinging to the knees of the emperor." But the Goths were to be partners as well as subjects, "sharing their tables, military ventures and public duties." Moreover, peaceful cooperation between Romans and Goths was not yet a reality but remained a hope for the future: "at present their offences are still fresh, but in the not too distant future we shall have them sharing our religious ceremonies, joining our banquets, serving along with us in the army and paying taxes with us" (Themistius, *Or.* 16, 302; trans. Errington).

As a result of the treaty of 382 the Tervingi and parts of the Greuthungi were allowed to settle on the south bank of the Danube in the provinces of Thracia and Dacia Ripiensis, retaining their own social structure and military organization. According to the *Notitia Dignitatum* of 394 the Roman army of the West included Gothic units of Visi and Tervingi. The disappearance of earlier leaders such as Fritigern, Sathrax, and Alatheus may be part of the price the Goths had paid, but essentially this was what the Tervingi had asked for in 376. The agreement which they reached with Theodosius was analogous to that struck between Constantine and the Goths in 332, with the essential difference that now the Goths were settled *inside* the empire. Why had Theodosius and Gratian agreed to this? Firstly, they had suffered a major defeat at Adrianople. Secondly, they had been unable to regain the upper hand decisively between 379–381. Thirdly, the line of defense along the Danube against Huns (Zosimus 4.34.6), and Alans (Ammianus 31.11), on the lower stretches of the river, and against Sarmatians (Ammianus 31.4) and Lentienses (Ammianus 31.10) in the middle Danubian region, was stretched very thin. Fourthly, and probably critically, it was a growing problem to recruit sufficient Roman manpower. Every soldier recruited into a fighting unit was one less tax-payer to the state, and one less *colonus* available to till the land.[65] It was better to enlist the Goths to defend this frontier, than to have them as an enemy within.

There scarcely seems to be sufficient evidence to form a judgment about what legal status the Goths now held in the Roman Empire. On one view they should be regarded as *dediticii*, enemies who had surrendered and now operated under Roman patronage.[66] On a more traditional interpretation the deal of 382 was an epoch-making *foedus*, a full Roman treaty between notionally equal partners.[67] In practice the position of the Goths was profoundly ambiguous. They were both subjects of the emperor on imperial soil and loyal subjects of their own tribal rulers. Where did they stand between obedience to Rome and autonomy?

Theodosius and his successors in general were more concerned with internal developments than with frontier defense. Conflicts between Romans and Goths now took place for the most part within the empire. Civil war recurred in the western part of the empire through the 380s and 390s. Internal matters were also dominated by religious issues, or, more precisely, by the determination of the emperors and certain bishops to establish orthodoxy at all costs. This led to them showing much higher levels of intolerance towards pagans, Jews, or heretical Christian sects (see below, chapter 7). Imperial power, interpreted in the narrow sense as the personal authority of the emperor, diminished. The youthful Gratian, the child Valentinian II, and the pious Theodosius were not active military figures, such as Valentinian or even Valens had been. Theodosius inevitably established himself as the dominating figure of the age, but with the appointment of his sons Arcadius, aged six in 383, and Honorius, aged eight in 393, as Augusti, he perpetuated the political precedent set by the promotion of Valentinian II (Plate 3.4). By placing the dynasty's hopes for the future in children, Theodosius acknowledged that senior and experienced political and military men held the reins of power.

In 383 Magnus Maximus, a senior military figure of Spanish origin, who held a command in Britain, mounted a successful challenge to Gratian's rule in the western empire. As with the usurpation of Julian, the sources predictably hesitate between ascribing the initiative to him or to his soldiers.[68] Gratian at any rate had allegedly caused resentment by showing favoritism to barbarian soldiers, notably to a group of Alans, at the expense of his Roman troops. Whatever the immediate causes of Maximus' coup, the main issue was surely Gratian's youth and incapacity to provide military leadership in the style which Valentinian had established for the western provinces. Moreover Maximus, as a Spaniard, might have expected to become an acceptable partner to his compatriot,

Plate 3.4 The base which was set up by the emperor Theodosius I in the hippodrome at Constantinople in 389 to celebrate his victory over the usurper Magnus Maximus, and which supported an imperial trophy, an obelisk, brought from Egypt. The scene depicts the four key members of the imperial dynasty: Theodosius himself, Valentinian II to his left, and Theodosius' two sons, Arcadius and Honorius, who were to succeed him. Officials of the court, bearded in the fashion of the period, surround the imperial group. In the lower tier defeated barbarians offer tribute and supplicate the emperor's clemency (DAI Istanbul)

Theodosius. Gratian's soldiers, led by his general Merobaudes, defected, and the emperor was killed at Lyon on August 25, 383. Maximus retained control of the western provinces north of the Alps until 387. He took up residence in Trier, as Valentinian had done, and began negotiations with Valentinian II in Milan, and more importantly with Theodosius in Constantinople, with a view to legitimizing his position. The dealings in the West involved the powerful bishop of Milan, Ambrose, who acted on behalf of Valentinian. Valentinian II effectively rejected Maximus' terms, which would have established the latter as by far the senior partner, as in the relationship of a father to a son (Ambrose, *ep.* 24). By the end of 384 the battle lines were drawn along the Alpine border. Meanwhile Theodosius was content to recognize Maximus as co-Augustus.

Maximus launched a successful invasion of northern Italy in 387, which displaced Valentinian, and sent the young emperor, his mother Justina, and sister Galla hurrying east to Thessalonica, the easternmost imperial residence in Illyricum, and readily accessible from Constantinople. This was the moment of choice for Theodosius. There were strong arguments for continuing the compact with Maximus. Valentinian was not only militarily weaker than Maximus, but his own family favored Arian Christianity and was in visible conflict with the religious orthodoxy which Theodosius had energetically promoted since the Council of Constantinople in 381. Maximus in contrast was powerful, orthodox, and from the same background as Theodosius. The latter's decision to support Valentinian, taken in the later months of 387, was thus a surprise. Zosimus provides an explanation, which persuaded Gibbon and should also persuade us. Justina offered Theodosius the prospect of marriage to her beautiful daughter Galla, to take the place of his first wife, Aelia Flacilla. Her family meanwhile would revert to Christian orthodoxy.[69] Dynastic and religious solidarity could thus be achieved. The episode reveals the influence that women could exercise in the imperial court, a trend which was to become conspicuous and important through the first half of the fifth century.

Once the political and dynastic decision had been taken, Theodosius left his elder son Arcadius as Augustus in Constantinople, and marched swiftly west through Sirmium to Aquileia. Maximus was taken by surprise, seized, and executed. Theodosius continued to Milan, which remained his base until the middle of 391, when he returned to Constantinople. During these two years his clear priority was to restore order and stability to the western empire. The period is famous for his encounters with Ambrose in Milan, who attempted to assert moral and religious authority not only over the emperor but over imperial policy (see below, chapter 7), but Theodosius also reached an accommodation with the western senatorial aristocracy.[70] The emperor's visit to Rome in 389 was the occasion for the delivery of Pacatus' Latin panegyric, one of the key sources for his reign.

Valentinian II was dispatched after the death of his mother Justina in 388 to Trier. He was under the control of Arbogast, the Frankish *magister militum*, who had certainly been appointed by Theodosius, and the relationship is vividly portrayed in an episode which occurred at Vienne, related both by the church historian Philostorgius and by Zosimus, when Arbogast simply ignored an attempt by the emperor to dismiss him from office.[71]

Theodosius treated Valentinian much as Constantius had the young Julian, expecting him to play the role of imperial figurehead, but entrusting real power to generals appointed by himself. As during the 350s, the policy led to a usurpation, not this time on the part of Valentinian, but led by a cultivated nobleman Eugenius, who made common cause with Arbogast. Valentinian probably committed suicide at Vienne in May 392, and after a short delay Eugenius was pronounced Augustus.[72]

Eugenius made every attempt, as Maximus had done, to win recognition from Theodosius, seeking the help of Ambrose as an intermediary and minting coins in the name of Theodosius and Arcadius. He also wooed the support of the largely pagan aristocracy of Rome, a fact which was to enhance the pagan religious atmosphere which surrounded him in the coming conflict. A year later Theodosius definitively rejected Eugenius' overtures by raising his own younger son Honorius to the rank of Augustus, and set out for the West in 394, as he had done against Magnus Maximus. In September 394 his largely barbarian troops, including twenty thousand Goths, overcame Eugenius' men, who were also mostly of Frankish or Germanic origin, at the battle of the river Frigidus on the road between Aquileia and Emona. Eugenius' troops, it is said, entrusted their fortunes to the pagan gods Hercules and Jupiter, while Theodosius' barbarians were protected by the *labarum*, the Christian talisman. Ten thousand Goths fell during the battle, and resentment that their sacrifice had not been justly rewarded by Theodosius and his successor Honorius was one of the chief spurs to Alaric's insubordination over the next fifteen years. The treaty established in 382 between Goths and Romans, which had held firm up to this point, now began to splinter.[73] The victorious Theodosius made his way to Rome and returned to Milan, where he died on January 17, 395.

The reign of Theodosius saw the beginnings of a major shift in the role of the emperors themselves. After 380 it became increasingly unusual for emperors to reside in frontier areas. Theodosius stayed for most of his reign in Constantinople, leaving the city for prolonged periods only to suppress the usurpations of Maximus and Eugenius. Meanwhile his western counterparts also began to restrict their movements. Gratian's activities extended from Trier to northern Italy and to Viminacium on the Danube, corresponding to those of Valentinian I, but his assassination by the followers of Magnus Maximus at Lugdunum in August 383 forced a reappraisal of this pattern. The child emperor Valentinian II was confined to northern Italy, mostly to Milan or Aquileia, until he was driven to seek refuge at Thessalonica. He was reinstated to the Rhineland after the defeat of Maximus, but this was the last time a Roman emperor established a foothold so far north. After the death of Theodosius, Arcadius who had been Augustus since 383, lived continuously at Constantinople, interrupted only by short summer visits to Ancyra in Galatia, while Honorius, Augustus since 393, was resident in Italy, initially at Milan and after 402 for the most part at Ravenna. Ravenna and Constantinople were thus established as the twin centers of imperial power for the remainder of late antiquity.

Stilicho and Alaric

The death of Theodosius left his two sons, the eighteen-year-old Arcadius and the ten-year-old Honorius, as reigning Augusti in Constantinople and Milan respectively (Map 3.3). Thus the political stage was set for other big players to assume the roles which were beyond the capabilities of the youthful emperors. The most powerful figure in the western empire was the general Flavius Stilicho, who had been *magister peditum* (master of the infantry) at the western court since 391. He had already been marked out for prominence by his marriage in 384 to the emperor's niece Serena, and Ambrose's commemorative oration

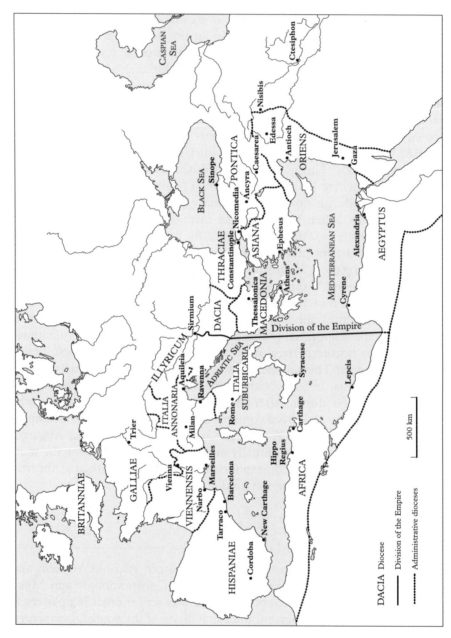

Map 3.3 The administrative dioceses of the empire in 395

DACIA Diocese
—— Division of the Empire
······· Administrative dioceses

for Theodosius, a work that had been commissioned by Stilicho, implies that he had been entrusted with the care both of the dying emperor's sons and with the empire itself.[74] The year 395 is sometimes seen as the moment when the eastern and western empires parted ways. However, this will not have been apparent to contemporaries, who were aware that this was a division of responsibilities precisely as favored by Valentinian and Valens in 364. In this case, however, the driving political force came not from the youthful rulers but from the men who dominated their courts and controlled their armies.

Stilicho's dominance is to be explained both by the youth of Honorius and by the fact that there was no secure ruling caste in the western part of the empire. In the East there had been more continuity. By 395 Arcadius was almost of an age to rule in his own right, and had grown up in the court that had served Theodosius. The dominant figure in 395 was the praetorian prefect Rufinus, but during the same year he was murdered in a political coup. Now the most influential figure in Arcadius' court was the eunuch Eutropius, who had arranged the emperor's marriage to Eudoxia, the daughter of the Frankish general Bauto, who may have been the father of the western warlord Arbogast.

Between East and West a new force had to be taken into the equation. The large band of Gothic warriors that had turned the battle of the Frigidus in favor of Theodosius had suffered enormous casualties, but failed to gain the material rewards that they demanded for their loyalty: gold, grain, and land for settlement. Alaric, now aged in his mid-twenties and married to a sister of the Gothic leader Athaulph, emerged as a major leader after the battle. He had already commanded a Gothic band that had tried to prevent Theodosius passing through Thrace on his return from the West to Constantinople in 391 (Zosimus 4.45, 48). Zosimus reports that he had expected to be rewarded with a command for himself as *magister militum* (Zosimus 5.5.4). After causing mayhem in Thrace and Macedonia, Alaric now took his Goths east to Constantinople and appears to have struck a deal with Rufinus. In 395–6 Alaric and his men invaded Greece. Athens was ransacked, although a pagan legend, told by Zosimus, implied that the Goths were deterred from attacking the city by visions on the city walls of the goddess Athena and Achilles (Zosimus 5.6.1). The invasion of Greece could be interpreted as a maneuver to forestall Stilicho's advance eastward, or even be a response to moves that Stilicho had already made.[75] Stilicho came to the aid of the Peloponnesians but allowed the Goths to cross over to Epirus, which they occupied.

The rise of Alaric and his followers between 395 and 410 led to the collapse of an important internal frontier, dividing the eastern from the western empire. The Goths were now able to move within the whole of Illyricum from Aquileia and the Julian Alps to Thrace, thus creating a third force in the struggle between East and West. The wider context and purpose of Alaric's activities from this time until the fall of Rome are hard to clarify, due to the inadequacies of Zosimus' narrative and the partisanship of the only contemporary source, Claudian. Apart from many uncertainties of detail, there is a major issue. Was Alaric the leader of a national movement, the rallying point for the Goths, who had originally settled in Lower Moesia after the battle of Adrianople, and were now in search of more land and better living conditions? Or was he the leader of a substantial group of *foederati*, fighting in Rome's service, but potentially biddable by the rival rulers of the eastern and western empire, and out for the best terms and conditions that he could obtain for his followers? There is a parallel to be drawn between Alaric's position, and that of the rival Gothic bands led by Theoderic the Amal and Theoderic Strabo in relation to the eastern empire in the 470s and 480s. At both periods, Gothic self-definition, as an independent *ethnos* or as Roman federate allies, was surely fluid, and must have depended both on the particular circumstances in which they found themselves and on the perspective of the observers of their position. Alaric's followers seem to have been unable to feed themselves from their own produce, and were always dependent on provisions supplied by the Roman authorities. This implies that they possessed no land and argues against the hypothesis that they should be identified with the Goths who had settled after Adrianople in eastern Moesia.[76]

From 397 to 405 the only narrative source, Zosimus, says nothing about Alaric. Claudian, the court poet and panegyricist, indicates that he was made general in command of cavalry and infantry (*magister utriusque militiae*) by the eastern administration in 399.[77] The significance of this position was that Alaric could now legitimately acquire the supplies needed to support his own men through the Roman provisioning system. When the eastern government stopped their supplies in 401 (Jordanes, *Get.* 146), Alaric and his men moved into northern Italy, where they were held at bay by Stilicho at the battles of Pollentia and Verona during the spring and summer of 402. Stilicho now changed his tactics and began to use the Goths as allies in his aim to secure Illyricum for the western empire. Alaric received the insignia of *magister utriusque militiae* for Illyricum not from Arcadius but from the western court. The Goths initially occupied territory on the boundary of Dalmatia and Pannonia, but moved back to their former possessions in Epirus, from which they threatened Thessalonica.[78]

Stilicho's plans to recover Illyricum with Alaric's help were interrupted in 405/6 by an invasion across the Rhine and the Danube of another Gothic chieftain Radagaisus, at the head of an army of Gauls and Germans, said to number 400,000 men. Stilicho, aided by Alans and Huns as well as thirty regiments of the Roman field army, forced Radagaisus to surrender near Ticinum in Liguria. Many of the barbarians were enslaved, depressing slave prices in Italy, while as many as twelve thousand warriors were enlisted in Roman forces.[79] The inhabitants of Italy and Rome in particular expressed their relief at being saved from this new barbarian invasion. A triumphal arch was dedicated by the Senate and people of Rome, and the *prafectus urbi*, Pisidius Romulus, erected statues to honor the emperors and Stilicho himself, by whose counsels and fortitude the city had been saved.[80] Stilicho returned in triumph to Ravenna where he received news from Honorius that the western provinces, including Britain, had rebelled under the leadership of a usurper, Constantine III (Zosimus 5.26–7).

The forces of the western empire, which had been unable to prevent the attack of Radagaisus, were also powerless to stop large numbers of barbarians, including Vandals, Suebi, and Pannonians, from crossing the Rhine in late 406 and early 407.[81] Insecurity inevitably led to usurpations. Three uprisings are attested between 406 and 408, headed respectively by Marcus, Gratianus, and finally Flavius Claudius Constantinus. The last of these managed to recover some control of the Rhine frontier and northern Gaul, where the cities of Mainz, Worms, Reims, and Trier had been overrun, and established his residence in Provence at Arles (Zosimus 6.5).

Meanwhile Alaric and his men gave up waiting in Epirus for Stilicho to support their efforts to take control of Illyricum. They returned westwards, attacking northeastern Italy and the province of Noricum, and threatened Stilicho with further incursions if he did not pay the money which had been promised to them during their stay in Epirus. Stilicho consulted the emperor Honorius and the Senate in Rome. The majority of senators voted to attack Alaric, but Stilicho cowed them into honoring their agreement with Gothic leader. His arguments, as reported by Olympiodorus, the source of Zosimus, revealed the role which Alaric had been set up to play:

> Alaric had stayed so long in Epirus by arrangement with Honorius, in order to make war on Arcadius and detach Illyricum from the East and add it to the West. This would already have been done if letters from the emperor Honorius had not arrived to prevent his march to the East, in expectation of which Alaric had spent so much time there. (Zosimus 5.29.7–8, trans. Ridley)

The sum required was enormous; 4,000 pounds of gold, to be raised from the wealth of the senatorial class at Rome. Quoting Cicero, Lampadius, one of the senators and perhaps identical with the *praefectus urbi* of 398, observed that such a gesture bought not peace but servitude.

In the spring of 408 news came of the death of the eastern emperor Arcadius. This provoked a dispute between Stilicho and Honorius, both of whom wanted to travel to Constantinople to take control of the succession. Stilicho prevailed, and arranged for Honorius to go west to Gaul to deal with Constantine III, while he and Alaric fulfilled their former ambitions in the East. However, opposition was led by a court official, Olympius, who alleged that Stilicho's real ambition was to set up his own son Eucherius to succeed Arcadius. A violent mutiny broke out at Ticinum among the troops assembled to begin the campaign against Constantine. In an atmosphere of tense uncertainty there was increasing polarization between Roman and barbarian troops. Stilicho decided to treat with Honorius at Ravenna, but was seized and killed by the emperor's guards (Zosimus 5.34). Soldiers loyal to Honorius thereupon perpetrated a massacre of thousands of barbarians who were quartered in Italy, including women and children. Up to thirty thousand of the survivors sought protection and redress by joining Alaric (Zosimus 5.35).

Alaric now had to deal directly with Honorius. He initially made modest financial demands and requested permission to move his army from Noricum into Pannonia, where they would presumably have settled. Honorius, advised by Olympius, his *magister officiorum*, refused cooperation, and Alaric resolved to march on Rome, bypassing Honorius who was holed up in Ravenna. Through the autumn of 408 Alaric besieged the city of Rome. Serena, Stilicho's widow, was put to death on suspicion that she was ready to betray the city to Alaric. Hunger gripped the inhabitants, and pagan priests even negotiated with Innocentius, bishop of the city, about reviving the old cults in the hope of securing divine protection. Negotiating under duress, the besieged agreed to pay a prodigious quantity of gold, silver, and other precious goods to the Goths to relieve the blockade, and an embassy was sent to Honorius to persuade him to make a peace with Alaric, who would henceforth fight in defense of the Roman Empire. Honorius was again dissuaded from making an agreement by Olympius, who was implacably hostile to any plan that seemed to revive Stilicho's policy of working with Alaric. Instead five legions were summoned from Dalmatia to protect Rome in future. Their commander, Valens, imprudently engaged Alaric in open warfare and lost his whole force.

During 409 abortive peace negotiations were carried out between Iovius, Honorius' praetorian prefect, and Alaric. The latter scaled down his demands to the point that he renounced his claims for an office for himself, and indicated that he would be satisfied with land in the two Norican provinces, which lay exposed to the Danubian frontier and paid little tax to the treasury. He would take any grain that could be made available to his hungry people and dropped his demands for gold. On these modest terms there could be friendship between his people and the Romans. Iovius rejected even these conditions on the grounds that all those who had taken office from Honorius since the fall of Stilicho had sworn an oath never to make peace with Alaric (Zosimus 5.48–51).

Alaric resumed the blockade of Rome, seized the harbor at Ostia, and cut off the food supply from Africa. The Senate at this point, as they had done in 408, yielded to his demands.[82] These included the appointment by Alaric of Priscus Attalus, Honorius' praetorian prefect, to be emperor at Rome. Attalus in turn gave Alaric the military command that he had asked for, the post of *magister utriusque militiae*. Alaric now besieged Honorius in Ravenna, while Attalus was expected to secure the province of Africa. When the new emperor failed to fulfill his half of the bargain, Alaric stripped him of his position in summer 410.[83] Negotiations were resumed with Honorius, but a renegade Gothic force, led by Sarus, attacked Alaric and led him to abandon his diplomacy and turn on Rome (Zosimus 6.13). The city was captured by assault on August 24, 410, and given over for three days for the Gothic forces to plunder.

Jerome wrote that his morale was broken and he could no longer dictate for weeping, now that the city of Rome, which once had conquered the entire world, was captured (Jerome, *ep.* 127, 12). Although the episode was to resonate in the contemporary imagination, it offered no solution to Alaric's predicament. After a mere three days, during which the population took refuge in the city's churches and were in large part spared by the Goths, who were themselves Christian, he marched his men south to Campania, but was prevented by a storm which wrecked his fleet from crossing to Sicily, where he hoped no doubt to obtain grain, other supplies, and perhaps land. Returning northwards through Italy he fell ill and died at Consentia in Bruttium in the early months of 411.

The Goths in Constantinople

Events in the East during this period followed a radically different course, but one which was also decisive for the evolution of the eastern empire. After the murder of Rufinus in 395 there was a brief power struggle. The generals of the eastern armies were outmaneuvered by the eunuch Eutropius, who was the leading official in the emperor's household, his *praepositus sacri cubiculi* (Zosimus 5.8–10). Eutropius was able to consolidate his own position and increase the stability of the eastern court to such effect over a four-year period that the threat from Stilicho was neutralized, and Alaric was effectively enlisted as an agent of the eastern government by being offered the position of *magister militum* for Illyricum. Eutropius took over the senior military command in the East in person, and was responsible for defeating the Huns, who had been raiding Asia Minor and threatening Syria during the period from 395–8 (Claudian, *In Eutrop.* I, 236ff.).[84] He was given the rank of *patricius* and made consul in 399.

The Goths, however, posed very serious problems for the eastern as well as the western empire, as become clear from a complicated political crisis that boiled over in Constantinople between 399 and 401. Part of the background to these events were the major policy issues raised by the incorporation of Goths in the empire, whether they were simply settled on provincial land as refugees from the pressures of other barbarian groups, or were accommodated as *foederati*, and thereby expected to supply substantial military support to the imperial armies when called upon. Clearly many Romans in positions of authority held the view that the Goths were always dangerous intruders, especially at times when the empire was in crisis or under threat, and that they should be dealt with by drastic measures. These issues were emphasized during the later 390s both by the activities of Alaric, and by the heavy dependence of the Roman armies on Gothic units both in the west and in the east. The dangers of this were highlighted in the speech *On Kingship* (*De Regno*) by Synesius of Cyrene, which purported to have been delivered in the presence of the emperor Arcadius himself, perhaps in the period 397–99.[85] It seems extremely unlikely that this was really the case, since the work contains blisteringly frank criticism of the emperor's conduct and policy.[86] There were two central points. Firstly, Arcadius should exchange his palace for the camps of his armies, and revert to the style of rulership of emperors before Theodosius, sharing the hardships of his soldiers, and campaigning in person to deter and defeat Rome's external enemies. Secondly, he should place no reliance on Scythian, that is Gothic, allies, but fight with Roman troops.[87]

In 399 a Gothic commander, Tribigild, led a rebellion of Gothic troops, who had been settled in central Asia Minor, against Eutropius. Another Gothic leader, Gainas, was sent to quell the uprising, but joined his compatriot and turned on Arcadius, demanding the dismissal and execution of Eutropius and other leading members of the regime. He achieved this aim, but, in obscure circumstances, the Gothic garrison in Constantinople itself was set upon by the local population, and seven thousand of them were massacred when they took refuge in a church designed for Arian worshippers. Fravitta, another Gothic leader appointed *magister militum* by Arcadius, compelled Gainas to flee over the Hellespont and into Thrace, and then to seek refuge beyond the Danube, outside the empire. Here he was confronted and killed by the first major Hunnic leader whose name is known to us, Uldin. The motivations and apparently numerous changes of allegiance of the protagonists in this bewildering civil war are portrayed from different perspectives by the various sources and remain today virtually impenetrable.[88] The outcome for the emperor was better than might have been predicted. Fravitta himself was done away with in 401, and the Gothic issue thereafter disappears from view. The Gothic groups and leaders in the East had not been able to sustain a coordinated challenge to Constantinople or establish themselves as a permanent presence in the East, as Alaric and his followers were able to do in the West. The eastern empire had survived the crisis more by skilful political action than by military means, and this was to be the watchword of imperial policy until the death of Arcadius in 408 and throughout the reign of his son Theodosius II. Western barbarian commanders and units were largely excluded from the military establishment and their place taken by Armenians, renegade Persians, Isaurians, and others. Even more important, warfare was seen as an instrument of last resort in foreign policy, and the security of the empire was maintained by diplomacy with Persian rulers, and by paying subsidies and thus securing the peace with major barbarian groups, above all the increasingly powerful Huns.

NOTES

1 Aur. Victor, *Caes.* 38.3; Eutropius 9.18–20; SHA [Carus] 8.2–9.3; Festus, *Brev.* 24; Hieron. *Chron.* 225. The source was the so-called *Kaisergeschichte*, written around 337 or perhaps later. See T. D. Barnes, *The Sources of the Historia Augusta* (Brussels, 1978), 66–8.
2 F. Kolb, *Herrscherideologie in der Spätantike* (Berlin, 2001), 25–7.
3 For modern discussion see H. W. Bird, "Diocletian and the deaths of Carus, Numerian and Carinus," *Latomus* 35 (1976), 127–32; F. Kolb, *Diocletian und die Erste Tetrarchie* (Berlin, 1987), 10–21.
4 B. M. Levick, "Pliny in Bithynia, and what happened afterwards," *Greece and Rome.*
5 The main narrative is Ammianus 25.5–10.
6 But Zosimus 3.36.1 has an alternative version, that Salutius was a candidate not at the death of Julian but of Jovian; T. D. Barnes, *Ammianus Marcellinus* (Cornell, 1998), 140 n. 48.

7   Ammianus 21.16.21; T. D. Barnes, *Ammianus Marcellinus*, 139.

8   E. Gibbon, *History of the Decline and Fall of the Roman Empire* (rev. edn. J. B. Bury London, 1929), 3, 128.

9   R. Macmullen, "The Roman emperor's army costs," *Latomus* 43 (1984), 571–80; H. Elton, *Warfare in Roman Europe AD 350–425* (Oxford, 1996), 118–27; B. D. Shaw, "War and violence," in G. W. Bowersock et al. (eds.), *Late Antiquity* (Cambridge Mass., 1999), 130–69 at 141.

10   Anonymous, *Peri Strategikes (On Generalship)*, 2. 18–21.

11   H. Elton, *Warfare in Roman Europe AD 350–425* (Oxford, 1996), 47–8.

12   *Anon. Val.* 2.3.

13   *Pan. Lat.* X (2), 11.4; with Barnes, *The New Empire of Diocletian and Constantine* (Cambridge Mass., 1982), 125–6.

14   W. E. Kleinbauer, "Palaces," in G. W. Bowersock et al. (eds.), *Late Antiquity*, 628–30.

15   Victor, *Caes.* 39.4; Eutropius, *Brev.* 9.26; Ammianus 15.5.18. H. Stern, "Remarks on the *adoratio* under Diocletian," *Journal of the Warburg and Courtauld Institutes* 17 (1954), 184–9.

16   F. Kolb, *Herrscherideologie in der Spätantike* (Berlin, 2001), 38–46.

17   *Pan. Lat.* XI (3), 2.3; VII (6), 8.2; IX (5), 8.1.

18   R. R. R. Smith, "The public image of Licinius I: Portrait sculpture and imperial ideology in the early fourth century," *JRS* 87 (1997), 170–202. See H. P. L'Orange, *Art Forms and Civic Life in the Later Roman Empire* (Princeton, 1965).

19   Julian, *Caes.* 315a–b; cf. F. Kolb, *Herrscherideologie in der Spätantike*, 32.

20   F. Kolb, *Herrscherideologie in der Spätantike*, 158–62; M. S. Pond Rothman, "The panel of the emperors enthroned on the arch of Galerius," *Byzantine Studies* 2 (1975), 19–40; "The thematic organization of the panel reliefs on the arch of Galerius," *AJA* 81 (1977), 427–54.

21   H. Brandt, *Geschichte der römischen Kaiserzeit von Diokletian bis zum Ende der konstantinischen Dynastie (284–363)* (Berlin, 1998), 64–8.

22   W. Thiel, "Tetrakionia. Überlegungen zu einem Denkmaltypus tetrachischer Zeit im Osten des römischen Reiches," *Ant. Tard.* 60 (2002), 299–326.

23   S. Corcoran, *The Empire of the Tetrarchs* (rev. edn. Oxford, 2000).

24   T. Honoré, *Emperors and Lawyers* (second edn. Oxford, 1994); S. Corcoran, "The publication of law in the era of the Tetrarchs – Diocletian, Galerius, Gregorius, Hermogenian," in A. Demandt et al. (eds.), *Diokletian und die Tetrarchie. Aspekte einer Zeitwende* (Berlin and New York, 2004), 58–72.

25   P. Garnsey and C. Humphress, *The Evolution of the Late Antique World* (Cambridge, 2001), 52–70.

26   R. Syme, "The ancestry of Constantine," *Bonner Historia Augusta Colloquium 1971* (1974), 237–53.

27   Eutropius, X.2.4–3.

28   *AÉ* 1937, 232; with T. D. Barnes, *The New Empire of Diocletian and Constantine* (Cambridge Mass., 1982), 232–3. For Maximinus, see S. Mitchell, "Maximinus and the Christians in AD 312: A new Latin inscription," *JRS* 78 (1988), 105–24.

29   *CTh.* 7.20.2. See J. F. Matthews, *Laying Down the Law* (New Haven, 2000), 37. There are difficulties in establishing both the date and the location of the event.

30   *ILS* 621, 622, 620.

31   W. Liebeschuetz, *Continuity and Change in Roman Religion* (Oxford, 1979).

32 S. Corcoran, *The Empire of the Tetrarchs* (Oxford, 2000), 136.

33 Lactantius, *DMP* 10.1–5; cf. Eusebius, *HE* 8.1.7.

34 *Gesta apud Zenophilum*, CSEL XXVI, 186–8 (Stevenson, *New Eusebius*, 273 no. 240).

35 Lactantius, *DMP* 15.7; Eusebius, *HE* 8.13.13; *VC* 1.13.2.

36 Galerius: Lactantius, *DMP* 33.11–35.1; Eusebius, *HE* 8.16.1, 17.1–11; Constantine: Lactantius, *DMP* 24.9; Maxentius: Eusebius, *HE* 8.14.1.

37 Eusebius, *HE* 9.7.8–9.

38 Zosimus 2.29; see F. Paschoud, "Zosime 2.29 et la conversion de Constantin," *Historia* 20 (1971), 334–53.

39 S. Corcoran, *The Empire of the Tetrarchs*, 320.

40 Eusebius, *VC* 4.

41 T. D. Barnes, *Ammianus Marcellinus* (Cornell, 1998), 166–86.

42 Zosimus 3.9.4 is the only overt mention of Julian's paganism, and is represented as part of his oppositional stance to Constantius.

43 Mamertinus, *Pan. Lat.* XI (3); excellent translation and commentary by S. Lieu, *The Emperor Julian. Panegyric and Polemic* (Liverpool, 1986); Libanius, *Or.* 18 (in A. F. Norman, Loeb *Libanius* vol. 1).

44 G. W. Bowersock, *Julian the Apostate* (London, 1978), 46–54. Others have argued that Julian's ambitions to elevate himself to Augustus were conceived well before 360.

45 M. Gleason, "Festive satire: Julian's *Misopogon* and the new year at Antioch," *JRS* 76 (1986), 106–19.

46 Ammianus 28.2, 30.7; Symmachus, *Rel.* 2. See H. von Petrikovitz, "Fortifications in the north-west Roman Empire from the third to the fifth centuries AD," *JRS* 61 (1971), 178–218 at 184ff. and 215ff.; J. F. Matthews, *Western Aristocracies and the Imperial Court AD 364–425* (rev. edn. Oxford, 1990), 32–3.

47 *ILS* 762 (before August 367), 774 (370), 775 (371).

48 L. F. Pitts, "Rome and the German 'kings' on the middle Danube in the first to fourth centuries AD," *JRS* 79 (1989), 45–58.

49 See P. Heather and J. Matthews, *The Goths in the Fourth Century* (Liverpool, 1991), 92, a chart showing coin finds from the time of Constantine and Constantius in the region (65% of bronze coin in hoards and 70% of single finds come from 320–60; the figures for silver coin are 70% and 55% respectively). This is clear evidence for the effect of the open frontier.

50 Zosimus 4.19; Ammianus 30.10; J. F. Matthews, *Western Aristocracies*, 64. For the political circumstances, whose consequences were felt until the accession of Theodosius in 379, see R. M. Errington, "The accession of Theodosius I," *Klio* 78 (1996), 438–53.

51 Detailed analysis by J. F. Matthews, *Western Aristocracies*, 32–100; D. Potter, *The Roman Empire at Bay* (London, 2004), 533–51.

52 Ammianus 26.10.3 (3,000 Goths), 27.4 and 5 (treaty); Zosimus 4.7.2 puts the figure at 10,000.

53 Ammianus 27.5; Zosimus 4.10–11.

54 Translation and commentary in P. Heather and J. F. Matthews, *The Goths in the Fourth Century* (Liverpool, 1991), 13–50.

55 See Julian, *Caesares* 329a and Themistius, *Or.* 10, 205, 13ff. (trans. in Heather and Matthews, *The Goths in the Fourth Century*).

56 Ammianus 29.5; J. F. Matthews, in Goodburn and Bartholomew, *Aspects of the Notitia Dignitatum* (1986).

57 See R. C. Blockley, "The division of Armenia between the Romans and the Persians at the end of the fourth century AD," *Historia* 36 (1987), 222–34; G. Greatrex, "The background and aftermath of the partition of Armenia in AD 387," *The Ancient History Bulletin* 14.1–2 (2000), 35–48. Ammianus' account is supplemented by the narrative of Faustus *FHG V 2, 201–310*; N. G. Garsoian, *The Epic Histories attributed to P'awstos Buzand* (Cambridge Mass., 1989); N. Baynes, *Byzantine Studies and Other Essays* (London, 1955), 186–208.

58 See note 79.

59 G. and M. Greatrex, "The Hunnic invasion of the East of 395 and the fortress of Ziatha," *Byzantion* 69 (1999), 65–75.

60 P. Heather, "The Huns and the end of the Roman Empire in the West," *English Historical Review* 110 (1995), 4–41.

61 G. E. M. de Ste Croix, *The Class Struggle in the Ancient Greek World* (London, 1983).

62 R. M. Errington, "The accession of Theodosius I," *Klio* 78 (1996), 438–53. See *Pan. Lat.* XII (2), 10.2–3 for the key point, that Theodosius was first summoned back to a military command, and subsequently called to be Augustus.

63 P. Heather, *Goths and Romans* (Oxford, 1991), 154.

64 R. M. Errington, "Theodosius and the Goths," *Chiron* 26 (1996), 1–27, esp. 8–15; P. Heather, *Goths and Romans*, 157–92.

65 These aspects were emphasized by the orators who justified imperial policy towards the Goths, Themistius, *Or.* 8, 10 and 16, 211a–b; Ammianus 31.4.8; Pacatus (*Pan. Lat.* [II], 32.3–4).

66 F. M. Ausbüttel, "Die Deditio der Westgoten von 382 und ihre historische Bedeutung," *Athenaeum* 66 (1988), 604ff.; followed by Errington, *Chiron* 26 (1996), 22.

67 A. Demandt, *Die Spätantike* (Berlin, 1989), 127.

68 Sulpicius Severus, *Martin* 20.3; *Dialogues* 2.6.2; and Orosius 7.34.9 suggest that the soldiers took the initiative; against, Zosimus 4.35.4.

69 See discussion by F. Paschoud, *Zosime II²* (Paris, 1971–89), 436–8.

70 J. F. Matthews, *Western Aristocracies and the Imperial Court AD 364–425* (rev. edn. Oxford, 1990), 223–52.

71 Philostorgius 11.1, 132, 5–13 (Bidez Winckelmann); Zosimus 4.53.

72 B. Croke, "Arbogast and the death of Valentinian II," *Historia* 25 (1976), 235–44; Paschoud, *Zosime II²* (Paris, 1971–89), 455–8.

73 A. Demandt, *Die Spätantike* (Berlin, 1989), 135–6. The sources for the battle are collected, translated and discussed by Paschoud, *Zosime II²* (Paris, 1971–89), 474–500.

74 Ambrose, *De obitu Theodosii (On the Death of Theodosius)*, 5; A. Cameron, "Theodosius the Great and the regency of Stilicho," *HSCP* 73 (1969), 247–80.

75 So T. S. Burns, *Barbarians within the Gates of Rome. A Study of Roman Military Policy and the Barbarians c. 375–425 AD* (Indiana, 1984), 148–82.

76 W. Liebeschuetz, *Barbarians and Bishops* (Oxford, 1990), 48–85 for detailed analysis.

77 Claudian, *In Eutrop.* II, 214–18; *de bello Gothico* 496–7, 535–9.

78 Sozomen 8.25.4 = 9.4.4. For Alaric in Epirus, acting on behalf of Stilicho, see Zosimus 5.29.1, 5, 7; 48.2. See Paschoud, *Zosime III¹* (Paris, 2003), 191–204, for critical analysis of Zosimus' very confused account, which up to 5.25 probably derived from Eunapius. 5.26.1 is Zosimus' own transition and 5.26.2ff. derived from Olympiodorus.

79 Orosius 7.37.16; Olympiodorus fr. 9.
80 *ILS* 798, 799, 1278 (Stilicho's name being erased from the last two).
81 Zosimus 6.3.1; Jerome, *ep.* 123, 15.
82 Zosimus 6.6.2–3; Sozomen 9.8.1.
83 Zosimus 6.7.5, 9.2–3, 12.2.
84 W. Liebeschuetz, *Barbarians and Bishops*, 96–100. The main source for Eutropius' activities during these years are the vigorous denunciations of Claudian, *In Eutropium* I and II. For the Huns in Asia Minor, see p. 198.
85 For the date see W. Liebeschuetz, *Barbarians and Bishops*, 106; Alan Cameron, J. Long, and L. Sherry, *Barbarians and Politics at the Court of Arcadius* (Berkeley, 1993), 107–9.
86 H. Brandt, in F. Chausson and É. Wolff (eds.), *Consuetudinis Amor. Fragments d'histoire romaine offerts à J.-P. Callu* (Rome 2003), 57–70, argues that the speech was delivered in Arcadius' presence, and is an exceptional example of *parrhesia*, the free-speaking of a ruler's philosophical advisor.
87 The detailed interpretation of the speech is fraught with difficulties. See T. D. Barnes, "Synesius in Constantinople," *Greek, Roman and Byzantine Studies* 27 (1986), 93–112; P. Heather, "The anti-Scythian tirade of Synesius' *de regno*," *Phoenix* 42 (1988), 152–72; W. Liebeschuetz, *Barbarians and Bishops*, 105–7; Alan Cameron et al., *Barbarians and Politics at the Court of Arcadius* (Berkeley, 1993), 103–42.
88 W. Liebeschuetz, *Barbarians and Bishops*, 111–25.

4

The Roman Empire of the Fifth and Sixth Centuries

Preface

The history of the Roman Empire in the fifth century cannot be reconstructed in the same way as in the fourth century. The reasons are partly due to the nature of the sources. No secular historical account survives in a complete form. There is not even a Zosimus, still less an Ammianus Marcellinus, to provide a narrative framework. Even for church affairs the ecclesiastical historians tend to offer a generic rather than an annalistic picture of events that occurred reign by reign.

However, the reasons for the changing historical picture also reflect the nature of events and the character of the empire, especially after the death of Arcadius in the East and the fall of Rome in the West. The roles played by the emperors changed radically. At least until the death of Theodosius the emperors in person had been the commanding political figures in the Roman state. They occupied strategically-placed imperial palaces and traveled ceaselessly with their troops and members of their courts to control the empire's trouble spots and its threatened frontiers. They accompanied their armies into battle in person. They visibly took personal responsibility for the state's diplomatic and military successes, and were called to account for its failures. Successes were measured in victory titles, while failures might take a form such as Theodosius' act of atonement in Milan for the massacre at Thessalonica. After the child emperor Theodosius II succeeded Arcadius in 408 there was a major transformation. The eastern emperor was confined almost exclusively to Constantinople, just as his western counterpart after 411 was based at Ravenna. Both imperial courts were physically secure behind a protective barrier on the land side, but provisioned from the sea. Emperors only left the protection of their capital cities for brief periods – Arcadius in the early fifth century made summer visits to Ankara on a regular basis; western rulers periodically visited Rome.

One obvious reason for the splintering of the imperial power base was the literal division between eastern and western empires. This was not the case *de iure*. The Roman Empire remained a legal and constitutional unity until the sixth century. Even after the line of western rulers ceased with Romulus Augustulus in 476, the emperors in Constantinople never abandoned their claim to rule the Latin West. Zeno in 489 dispatched the Goth Theoderic to reclaim control of Italy from the German king Odoacar. Justinian in the 530s launched the largest campaigns of his reign to bring Africa and Italy back into the empire after the lineage of Ostrogothic kings founded by Theoderic had come to an end. However, for practical purposes the shrinking Roman territories in the Latin West and those in the Greek-speaking East remained distinct political entities, and their fates were separate.

Thus, as the empire fragmented, it makes sense to look at its political history in segments. We need to look in turn at the eastern court in Constantinople, above all in the age of Theodosius II, who reigned until 450, and at his western counterparts, first Honorius up to 423 and then Valentinian III. The first half of the fifth century saw the rise of the most powerful of the non-Germanic groups, the Huns, culminating in what has been called the empire of the Huns, ruled by Attila. Meanwhile after the fall of Rome to Alaric in 410 we see the rapid emergence of Germanic barbarian groups in the West, who took control of most of the western provinces: Vandals in Spain and Africa; Visigoths in Spain and Aquitaine; Burgundians on the upper Rhine and southern Gaul; Franks on the lower Rhine and in northern and central Gaul. Illyricum, as ever, was contested territory. After the eclipse of Hunnic power in the 450s, the dominant groups were the large bands of Gothic warriors in Pannonia and Thrace, respectively controlled by Theoderic the Amal, the later king of Italy, and Theoderic Strabo. Their history in turn was entangled with that of a new dynasty at Constantinople, the Isaurian family and followers of Zeno. These Isaurians were virtually a tribal group from within the eastern empire, and although Zeno was recognized as the legitimate emperor in Constantinople, the story of his reign, from 474 to 491, resembled that of the Gothic chieftains as much as it did the regimes of his imperial predecessors. Only with the accession of Anastasius in 491, and the subsequent reigns of Justin and Justinian, lasting until 565, is it possible again to form an impression of a unified empire.

One consequence of the changing imperial role at the end of the fourth century was that much of the effective power passed into other hands. Powerful figures close to the emperors became increasingly significant players in the high politics of the fifth century, whether family members, as in the case of the influential women of the Theodosian family, dominant individuals at court, or generals in command of the field armies. However, it was not simply a matter of power being exercised by proxy, with emperors acting as mere figureheads for other members of their regimes. The relocation of the emperors to their capitals reduced their ability to intervene directly in local or regional matters. The impact of this development, however, differed between the eastern and western empire. In the eastern provinces, which were not disturbed by any serious military threats during the fifth century, the imperial system of administration and bureaucracy proved highly effective. There was no disintegration or loss of control. The civic base of the empire remained intact. State taxes were gathered. Provincial communities sent petitions to the emperors or his officials to complain of administrative injustice or other matters, and these were handled according to strict protocols by the offices of state in Constantinople. In the West, by contrast, Rome not only relinquished military control to the growing power of the barbarians, but also ceased to maintain its administrative structures and secure its tax base. Thus the Roman state began to break up, with divisions appearing between the landowning aristocrats of Gaul and those of Italy, even regardless of the overall loss of Roman control to the Germanic kingdoms.

The Reign of Theodosius II

The eastern court of Theodosius II in Constantinople has not impressed modern historians. Gibbon was responsible for drawing a picture of an indolent and

ineffective emperor, dominated by women and eunuchs.[1] A. H. M. Jones'
epigrammatic judgment of the era was that the successors of Theodosius I
reigned rather than ruled the empire.[2] Yet, judged by normal criteria, they did
so with outstanding success. The regime was stable. Reigns were long, and
rulers died, in most cases, in their beds. Paradoxically, the very fact that
emperors came to the throne in their childhood led to long and secure terms
of office. Theodosius II, the seven-year-old boy who succeeded his father
Arcadius in 408, was unchallenged emperor of the East until he died after a
riding accident in 450. In the West Arcadius' younger brother Honorius lived
until 423. His half-sister, Galla Placidia, daughter of Theodosius I by his first
marriage, married Flavius Constantius, whom Honorius named as co-Augustus
in 421. Constantius died within months of this elevation, but she lived on as
Augusta until 450. Their son Valentinian III, born in 419, was installed as
western emperor in 425, and ruled until 453. The imperial women more than
matched the longevity of their men folk. Pulcheria, Theodosius II's elder sister,
was named Augusta in 414, outlived her brother, and married and thereby
legitimized the position of his successor Marcian, before she died in 453. She
organized Theodosius' marriage in 421 to an Athenian noblewoman, Athenais,
who was renamed Aelia Eudocia, became Augusta in 423, and lived until 460.
Their daughter, Licinia Eudoxia, was betrothed as a child to Valentinian III,
and married him in 437. She too outlived her husband (Diagram 4.1).[3]

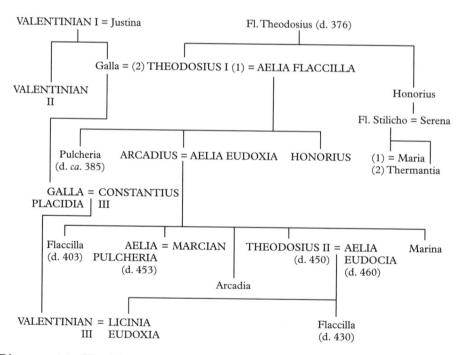

Diagram 4.1 The Theodosian dynasty (from K. W. Holum, *Theodosian Empresses*
[Berkeley 1982], 133)

The style of the fifth-century court in Constantinople was radically different from that of the pre-Theodosian age. As emperors were confined to the palace and the city, the intricacies of political life become an *arcanum imperii*. While this fact inevitably generated much speculation about tensions and power-struggles within the court, which are duly reflected in our sources,[4] there are few indications of how emperors actually operated at work, or of how policy was formed in the palace. We need, however, to be cautious in accepting everything that we are told. The picture of the Theodosian age, as re-interpreted in due course by Gibbon, Jones, and other modern writers, derives from fifth-century sources. Priscus of Panion said of Theodosius that he was "unwarlike, lived a cowardly life and obtained peace by money payments not by force of arms, while all his actions were under the influence of eunuchs" (Priscus fr. 3). The ninth-century chronicle of Theophanes judged him to be indecisive and swayed by every breath of wind (Theophanes, *Chron.* 5941, 101 de Boor). However, Priscus' judgment is evidently affected by the fact that he himself had taken part in an embassy to Attila the Hun on Theodosius' behalf. At that moment in the late 440s he had witnessed Hunnish power at its height and observed how Attila cynically and ruthlessly exploited his position to maximum Roman disadvantage. Moreover Priscus was actually writing when the policy of buying the barbarians off with subsidies, which were the hallmark of Theodosius' strategy, had been reversed by Marcian in the 450s, but at a period when Attila was no longer a threat. Moreover, the dominant political force of Theodosius' final years had been the eunuch Chrysaphius, and Priscus reflected the *post mortem* denigration that Chrysaphius suffered, as his religious policies were overturned.[5]

The record for Theodosius' foreign policy as a whole shows an effective grasp of strategic realities, and suggests caution but not inertia.[6] The greatest threat inevitably came from the barbarian groups in Illyricum and Thrace, in particular from the domination of Attila. A fragment from Priscus' history sets out Theodosian policy:

> The Romans complied with all Attila's instructions, and treated them as the command of their master. For not only were they taking precautions not to engage in a war against him, but they also were afraid that the Persians were preparing war, and that the Vandals were disturbing the peace at sea, and that the Isaurians were inclined to engage in brigandage, and the Saracens were mounting raids into their eastern empire, and that the tribes of Ethiopia were in rebellion. For this reason they swallowed their pride and obeyed Attila, but tried to prepare for military action against the other peoples, gathering their forces and appointing commanders. (Priscus fr. 10)

Peace was maintained on the eastern frontier with the Persians, apart from hostilities in 421–2 when Roman forces intervened to support a Christian group that was in conflict with Zoroastrian fire-worshippers (Theodoret 5.37 and 39; Socrates 7.8.18 and 20). The emperor, of course, did not take part in the campaign, but he is credited with supporting it to the fullest effect (Socrates

7.18.37). Forces were sent to the western empire on three occasions: in 424 to depose the usurper John, who threatened the succession of Valentinian III, and in 431 and 441, when fleets were sent, without success, to challenge the Vandal domination of Africa. There were no major offensives in the Balkans or Illyricum, and thus scope was left for the growth of Hunnic power, but archaeological evidence shows that Roman defenses were maintained along the lower Danube, which could be provisioned from the sea, and a military presence was maintained there (Priscus fr. 9.2). Above all, Theodosius' praetorian prefect Anthemius took the crucial decision to build the powerful outer ring of land walls around Constantinople, securing the city from barbarian threats (Socrates 7.1.2). Cyrus of Panopolis, the protégé of the empress Eudocia, who was the most powerful politician at Constantinople between 439 and 442, added the city's sea walls,[7] and further repairs were made to the land walls after an earthquake in 447 by the praetorian prefect Constantine, at the time of an urgent threat from the Huns.[8] There is a strong likelihood that the long walls built some 65 kilometers west of Constantinople, stretching across Thrace from the Black Sea to the Sea of Marmara, were also Theodosian in origin, for their existence is implied by the Ostrogothic campaigns of the 470s.[9] Victories were commemorated in inscriptions and monuments as they had been before. In the early 420s a new column was erected in the Hebdomon square, already adorned with similar monuments from the time of Theodosius I, with an inscription identifying the imperial statue:

> Our Lord Theodosius, pious and fortunate Augustus, Emperor and most mighty triumphant conqueror of barbarian races, eternal and universal victor, in accordance with the prayers of his sisters, rejoices on high.[10]

The reference in the inscription to the emperor's sisters is a remarkable acknowledgment of their importance to the regime, which the sources make no attempt to conceal. Arcadius' wife, Aelia Eudoxia, had borne her husband four daughters during the nine years of their marriage from 395 to 404. The eldest, Flaccilla, died in infancy, but the others, Pulcheria, Arcadia, and Marina, survived with their brother. Pulcheria, in particular, became a dominating figure. The importance of this formidable female presence in Constantinople need to be emphasized. As members of the imperial family, they were enormously wealthy and maintained huge households in the city. Between them the three surviving sisters owned five palaces, each with retinues of dependents. Quarters of the city were named after Marina and Pulcheria, and a branch of the imperial civil service was created for the latter after she established a separate household following Theodosius' marriage.[11] On this basis, as well as thanks to the strength of her personality, Pulcheria exercised enormous influence over the court.

The most detailed overall picture of this influence and of the character of the reign of Theodosius comes from the church historians Socrates, Sozomen, and Theodoret, who all wrote during the emperor's lifetime.[12] Their accounts of the period pay much attention to imperial piety. Socrates emphasized that the emperor's sheltered origins did not prevent him from developing good sense, resolution, and the ability to endure hardship, qualities which he had obtained from Christian self-discipline rather than from military training (Socrates 7.22.2):

> He made the palace into nothing so much as a monastery (*asketerion*). He and his sisters used to rise at dawn and sing antiphonal hymns to the divinity. He knew the holy books by heart and could carry on discussions of the sacred texts with the bishops he met like a long established priest. He collected the holy books and commentaries on them even more enthusiastically than Ptolemy Philadelphus [had collected books for the library at Alexandria]. (Socrates 7.22.4)

The ruler's devotional character was not merely a private matter. On one occasion he led the crowd in community hymn-singing in the hippodrome as a means of stopping a winter snowstorm. Socrates sums up the effect of such occasions in a comment which typifies his understanding of the Constantinople of Theodosius: the whole city became a church. It was characteristic of the age to project this fusion of imperial piety and public policy (Socrates 7.22.15–18).

Pulcheria, who had taken a vow of perpetual virginity which was not to be broken until she contracted a morganatic marriage with Marcian in 450, was evidently the main instigator of this religious development. Women in the political culture of the ancient world had usually achieved influence through their marriages or their children. Sozomen shrewdly observed that Pulcheria exercised her influence through her virginity. He explained that

> not yet fifteen years old, she adopted a most wise and divine resolution. From the first she dedicated her virginity to God and instructed her sisters to adopt the same way of life, so that they should not introduce another man into the palace and remove every basis for jealousy and plotting. (Sozomen 9.1.3)

Sozomen implies that she was mainly an influence on Theodosius while he was still too young to manage his own affairs (Sozomen 9.1.2), but this understates her role. In any case it is certainly misleading to suppose that he, as a minor, remained under her *tutela*, until he reached adulthood. There were only two years between them in age. Her authority was due to strength of character not to legal niceties, and events were to show that her influence endured and became stronger in his later years. The most hostile picture that survives of Pulcheria comes from the pen of the militant pagan Eunapius, who included a long digression on her baneful influence on public life, even though the scope of his own history did not extend chronologically beyond the fall of Rome. It was during Pulcheria's reign that provincial governorships and the higher posts of *vicarii* of the dioceses were openly put up for sale, and court judgments were settled in favor of the one who could pay most (Eunapius fr. 72.1). The force of the criticism is much diminished not only by Eunapius' rabidly anti-Christian prejudice, but also because the selling of offices was an intrinsic feature of the system of government.[13]

Pulcheria and her sisters inevitably became major players in the bitter religious controversies of the period and the ecclesiastical politics behind the great councils of Ephesus in 431 and 449, leading up to Chalcedon in 451. As well as working behind the scenes, Pulcheria took part in the official correspondence of the councils, thus adding further complexity to the lines that entangled the church and the state in these matters. Pulcheria was closely associated with the emergence of the doctrine of the two natures of Christ, opposed by Cyril of Alexandria, which emerged as the accepted theological position after the first Council of Ephesus in 431 and led to the deposition and exile of Nestorius, the bishop of Constantinople. In his *Address to the Pious Emperor Theodosius on the Correct Faith* of 431 Cyril described Pulcheria as "she who takes part in the care and administration of your empire." He deliberately contrasted her with Eudocia, in whom the hopes for the dynasty resided.[14] Specifically Pulcheria and her sisters promoted the cult of the Virgin Mary as the Mother of God (*Theotokos*) on a large scale, leading to the dedication of several Marian churches in Constantinople and the adoption of Marian theology as a central part of Christian belief. It is likely enough that enthusiasm for the cult of Mary had been widespread at an earlier period, especially among women, but the influence and patronage of the Theodosian empresses gave it a major new impetus and high public prominence. The spiritual and practical alliance between charismatic ecclesiastical leaders and wealthy and influential women was nothing new in the recent history of Christian society. St Jerome had attracted the total commitment of some of the wealthiest aristocratic women of Rome, taking several of them into exile with him to Bethlehem after 386. John Chrysostom, bishop of Constantinople, had forged an alliance with Olympias in opposition to Arcadius' wife the empress Eudoxia at the beginning of the fifth century. Similar alignments were maintained at an imperial level by Pulcheria during the 430s.

Pulcheria is credited with selecting her brother's bride, Athenais, the cultivated daughter of the sophist Leontius, who was a leading figure in the philosophical school in Athens. Athenais was baptized, renamed Eudocia and raised to the rank of Augusta in 423, two years after the marriage. She inevitably came into conflict with Pulcheria, and their rivalry infected the political atmosphere of the 420s and 430s. Her sophisticated cultural outlook and literary connections aggravated the rivalry and led in 437 to her being sent by Theodosius on pilgrimage to the Holy Land. This re-established her pious credentials, although her renewed influence when she returned to the court probably owed at least as much to the fact that her daughter, Licinia Eudoxia, had married the western emperor Valentinian III in 437. She had thus also accomplished her main dynastic role.

The imperial women did not achieve power on their own. Theodosius depended throughout his reign on powerful men: Anthemius who was praetorian prefect of the East from 405 until he was dismissed by Pulcheria in 414, Helion, master of offices from 414 to 427, Cyrus of Panopolis, who combined the post of praetorian prefect and prefect of the city from 439 to 442. At the beginning of the 440s, he was responsible for building Constantinople's sea walls to strengthen the land defenses built by Anthemius, and earned dangerous popularity with the people for introducing other facilities, including street lighting.[15] He was eclipsed by Chrysaphius, whose status as a eunuch and position within the court earned him greater revilement from subsequent historians. It is evident that the influence of these men lay in their individual qualities and their personal standing with the emperor, rather than in the different offices that they held. The record tends to paint these ministers as sinister and corrupting figures. The truth is that they were indispensable, as powerful advisors are to any regime. Military authority was monopolized by a series of generals of Alemannic–Gothic origin, Plintha, Ardaburius, and the latter's son Aspar, who was to play the role of kingmaker in the succession both of Marcian in 450 and Leo in 457.

For posterity the outstanding achievement of the Theodosian empire was the codification of the Roman law of the post-Constantinian period and its publication in the *Codex Theodosianus*. The result of this extraordinary enterprise was a handbook of Roman public law, designed for the practical guidance of magistrates and judges, which superseded the compilations of the tetrarchic period. The work was completed in 437, shortly after Theodosius' daughter married Valentinian III, and a year later an official copy was presented to the Roman Senate, where it was received, as it had been in Constantinople, by acclamation. As its contents, composed in the ornate and rhetorical Latin of legal judgments, were drawn from eastern and western provinces alike, the publication of the code is the clearest reminder that no one in high office thought of the Roman Empire as divided between East and West. Roman law was to remain the foundation and chief symbol of imperial unity throughout late antiquity.[16]

Socrates, in his unassuming, clear-thinking style, presented the age of Theodosius as eirenic and tolerant, reflecting the emperor's own character.[17] Church and state were in harmony; imperial success was grounded not in military might but in piety; conflict was resolved by discussion; violence was under control. The emperor achieved his successes "without warfare and struggle" (Socrates 7.22). Of course neither this nor Sozomen's very similar judgment was impartial; both offered a view of the reign that Theodosius wished to promote. But it is hard to avoid the conclusion that in the first half of the fifth century the Roman Empire, at least in the East, was more harmonious and at ease with itself than at any time since the second century AD.

The Western Empire and the Barbarians 411–455

The western provinces had been unprotected by Roman troops when a combined force of Vandals, Alans, and Suebi crossed the frozen Rhine in midwinter 406 (Zosimus 6.3.1; Jerome, *ep.* 125). This revelation of the vulnerability of the Gallic provinces led inevitably to usurpations. The most serious of these was that of Constantine III, who moved into Gaul from his British base and established himself at Arles. This led to a bewildering series of conflicts which did not begin to resolve until 414 when the beginnings of a new political order began to take shape. Symbolically a key moment was the marriage in Narbonne of Athaulph, Alaric's successor, to Galla Placidia, Theodosius I's daughter by his first marriage, and half-sister of Honorius. Orosius' history *Against the Pagans* (a work which had been commissioned by St Augustine to set the fall of Rome into the context of Roman history and demonstrate that it had not occurred due to the neglect and anger of the pagan gods) contains a famous account of this event:

> Athaulph was then the king in charge of the Gothic peoples. He had succeeded to the throne after the capture of the city of Rome and the death of Alaric, and had taken as his wife Placidia, the sister of the emperor. . . . I heard a person from Narbo, of high military rank under Theodosius, a man also of devout, prudent and serious character, relating in Bethlehem, a town of Palestine, to the priest Jerome, that he had been a close friend of Athaulph at Narbo and had often heard him say on oath, that he had first ardently desired to obliterate the Roman name and to render and name the entire territory of the Romans the empire of the Goths, so that, to speak vulgarly, what had been Romania should become Gothia, and that Athaulph should become what Caesar Augustus had once been. But when he had discovered from much experience that the Goths were totally incapable of obeying the rule of law because of their untempered barbarism, and that the laws of the state ought not be defied, since without them a state is no state, he had gradually chosen to seek glory for himself by restoring to its former state and enhancing the Roman reputation through the use of Gothic might, so that he might be considered by posterity as the author of the revival of Rome, after he could not be its transformer. (Orosius 7.43)

The marriage did not last and in the short-term the entente with Athaulph collapsed, but the Romans enlisted the Goths as allies against the Germanic tribes, which had taken control of much of Spain since 409; the Suevi and the Hasding Vandals in the northwest, the Alans in the center, and the Siling Vandals in the south of the Spanish peninsula.[18] In 418 Honorius' general Constantius escorted the Visigoths back across the Pyrenees to Aquitania, where they settled in the valley of the Garonne between Toulouse and Bordeaux and established a kingdom that lasted until 507. He also reorganized the provincial council of the so-called seven provinces of Aquitania, part of a wider attempt to bring order to the whole region. Constantius married Galla Placidia on January 1, 417 (Olympiodorus fr. 33). By 419 the union produced a daughter, Honoria, and a son, the future emperor Valentinian III, who was born in July 419. In that year Constantius was named consul for the third time, and in 421 he was raised to the rank of Augustus. He was to die suddenly later in the same year but the future of the western Roman dynasty was now mapped out. The outcome of the decade since the fall of Rome had been better than the Romans might have reasonably hoped for. Spain and northern Gaul had slipped from their control, and the defense of Britain had been abandoned (Zosimus 6.5.3, 10), but the regime of Honorius had consolidated its control of Italy, Africa, and southern Gaul. The Goths controlled Aquitania until their defeat by the Franks in 507.[19]

In the West, the large Germanic incursion that is dated to the last day of 406 may have been a decisive moment in the break-up and eventual collapse of the western empire. Peter Heather has analyzed the long-term consequences in a fine study. The gradual cession of territory to the invaders meant a loss of revenue and power. The local landowning elites of the western provinces began to make compacts with the newcomers or look to their own defense. This promoted the slow dissolution of the old empire over two or three generations.[20] The large number of barbarian groups began to put the western provinces under perceptible pressure from the beginning of this process. Goths, Suevians, Burgundians, Alans, and Vandals all claimed and were conceded land on which to settle, with the result that the empire relinquished a significant part of its revenue from taxable land. As it became clear that the empire was less able to protect them, local landowners now began to waver in their loyalty to Rome and their readiness to pay taxes. Tax revenues also fell, as areas, including Britain in 410, seceded and looked to their own defense. Moreover, remissions had to be given to war-torn areas, including Italy in 413 (*CTh.* 11.28.3, 12), and Sicily in 440, and this put an increasing burden on other regions. The issue became acute in 439, when the Vandals took Carthage and cut off the income that the western empire derived from Africa. This provoked an ineffective counter-offensive led by Aspar from Constantinople.

Honorius died childless in August 423, and, after an unsuccessful usurpation, was succeeded by Valentinian III. Like Theodosius in the East, Valentinian III depended on a highly effective military commander to give him political credibility in the western empire. Flavius Aetius, son of Gaudentius, a senior figure under Honorius, had quashed the usurper John, who had threatened the accession of Valentinian, with a large force of Huns, to whom he had been sent as a hostage during his youth.[21] This intervention brought its own problems, as Aetius' men clashed outside Ravenna with a force sent by Theodosius II, and blood was shed, before Galla Placidia produced money enough to buy off the Huns and send them back to the middle Danube regions (Philostorgius 12.14).

In 430 Aetius had to call on his Hunnish connections again to consolidate himself against a challenges from Bonifatius and Sebastianus, who held high commands in Africa and were rivals within the western military hierarchy. But from 433 he retained the position of *magister utriusque militiae* unchallenged until his death twenty-one years later. During this period he succeeded in maintaining the stability of Gaul and protecting the interests of its Roman landowners, despite the collapse of the old frontiers. Aetius made no attempt to prevent the growth of Hunnic power in the Danubian regions, and indeed depended on the support of the Huns to maintain his own position. This period saw Illyricum fall under the domination of Attila, whose threats to the empire were only checked by a continuous flow of tribute payments from Constantinople (see below, chapter 6). In 451 Attila, by choosing to lead an expedition against the West, relieved the pressure on the eastern empire. This enabled Marcian to reverse Theodosius II's policy and withhold tribute payments. Attila now pursued western ambitions, encouraged by Valentinian III's sister Honoria, who offered herself to him in marriage to avoid alternative arrangements made by the emperor. Attila took his forces into Gaul, to claim his share of the western empire, but was checked at the battle of the Catalaunian Plain, by a coalition of Aquitanian Visigoths under Theoderic and Roman troops under Aetius. The next year the Huns invaded Italy and plundered Aquileia, Milan, and Ticinum, but a famous parley between Attila and Pope Leo spared the city of Rome. A year later Attila was found dead, choked by a nosebleed after wedding-night excesses with a Gothic princess.[22] In 454 Valentinian III had Aetius executed, but was himself killed a year later by two of Aetius' followers.

In 411 the Germanic peoples who had crossed the Pyrenees had used lots to divide the Spanish peninsula.[23] The Suebi in the northwest corner of the peninsula were set upon by the Vandals, but saved by Roman forces. The Siling Vandals moved to the south. After capturing Hispalis and the port of Cartagena in Baetica in 428, they crossed the Strait of Gibraltar in the following year, with their eyes on richer pickings in Africa. The wealthy cities and fertile lands of Africa had been a target of barbarian ambitions previously, both for Alaric in 411, when he reached Sicily after the sack of Rome, and for the Visigoths under Athaulph in 414. Africa and its capital Carthage represented a larger prize than anywhere that had fallen to the barbarians except for Rome itself. The Vandal ruler Gaiseric organized his followers into eighty contingents each of a thousand persons (including non-combatants) for the sea passage. The figure suggests that the Vandals' fighting strength was around 20,000.[24] They had already operated over many years in Spain, and their ability to organize the sea passage for such a large group implies a growing level of social organization and collective discipline. This was certainly consolidated during their prolonged but systematic expansion westwards across the African provinces, which only achieved its final goal, the capture of Carthage, in 439. It was during this long march that the identity of the Vandal kingdom was forged.[25] The case of Hippo, St Augustine's bishopric, which withstood a Vandal siege for more than a year before it fell in July 431, shows the strength of local opposition. A first stage of the Vandal incursion continued until 435, when a treaty with the Romans ceded them Mauretania and western Numidia.[26] The offensive was resumed against the eastern provinces of Africa Proconsularis and Byzacena, which were covered with small cities.

Carthage, the capital and one of the great cities of the Mediterranean, fell in 439. The Vandals thus gained greater leverage over the western Roman Empire than any other barbarian group. They became an immediate threat to Rome and Italy, and may only have been deterred from invasion by the naval expedition of 441 which was dispatched to the western Mediterranean by Theodosius

II. In 442 the Vandal conquest of Africa was acknowledged in a new treaty agreed with the western emperor, which reversed the terms of 435. Wealthy Proconsularis and Byzacena were now Vandal territory, while Numidia and Mauretania reverted to Roman control. The agreement with Rome was placed on a firmer footing than before.

Marcian, Leo, and the End of the Western Empire

At the death of Theodosius in 450 no clear successor was in view, and Pulcheria was virtually sole empress for a month-long interregnum. She and the *magister militum* Aspar resolved the issue by choosing a Thracian military officer Marcian, who had served under Aspar and now married Pulcheria.[27] After the removal of Chrysaphius, Marcian called another ecumenical council, held at Chalcedon in 451, which reversed the decisions of Ephesus and asserted the new orthodox doctrine of the dual nature of Christ, that he was both fully human and fully divine in his two natures. The rugged church politics displayed at Chalcedon indicate some significant realignments in ecclesiastical authority. Leo the bishop of Rome, who passionately opposed any hint of Monophytism, engaged with the issues on the side of Constantinople as no western church leader had done before. The growing rivalry between Constantinople and Alexandria culminated in the decision that the patriarchate of Constantinople should rank second in the Christian world after Rome.[28] The enforcement of the decisions taken at Chalcedon was the result of a coalition between the secular state and the powerful bishops of Rome and Constantinople. This was the culmination of Theodosian policy in the first half of the fifth century.

Marcian enjoyed good fortune in his foreign policy. After the death of Attila, as his sons disputed with one another in feuds among the loose assemblage of tribes that he had controlled, the threat from the Huns gradually evaporated. Marcian discontinued the tribute payments which had drained Theodosius' Constantinople, and was able to reduce taxes to the approval of the Senate. By his death in 457 the treasury was reported to be in substantial surplus.[29]

Marcian was succeeded in February 457 by another senior military figure, Leo. According to the detailed account recorded by Constantine Porphyrogennitos in the tenth century, he was the first emperor to be raised aloft on the shields of his soldiers, in a gesture that recalled the practice of the Germanic troops that had proclaimed Julian Augustus in Paris in 360. He was then escorted to the church of the Holy Apostles, to be crowned by the bishop of Constantinople This was the first coronation at which the patriarch is recorded as playing this role, and this further confirmed growing authority of the Constantinopolitan Church (Constantine Porphyrogennitos, *De Caer.* 1.91). The most powerful military figure in Constantinople was the general Aspar, of Alan origin, whose influence can be traced back to the 420s.

Leo's reign in the East and the bewildering succession to Valentinian III, who had been murdered at Ravenna in 455, heralded an era of great uncertainty and confusion in the empire as a whole. The balance of power was evenly divided between the eastern and western Roman courts and the major barbarian groups, especially the Vandals in Africa and the Ostrogothic groups, which began to dominate Illyricum as Hunnic power declined. In the East there was a new element, the rise of Isaurian leaders and their followers from the Taurus Mountains in southern Asia Minor, who were effectively another barbarian state located within the frontiers of the eastern empire. The interplay of these competing ethnic groups was to last for more than a generation, until the establishment of a new order by the long reigns of Anastasius in the East between 491 and 518, and of the Ostrogothic king Theoderic, who ruled from Ravenna after the collapse of the western empire from 493–526.

Leo's reign lasted until 474. Our best source for the events of the 450s and 460s after the fall of Attila is the *Getica* of Jordanes, which incorporates reliable detail from otherwise lost sections of Priscus' history. His account of the battle of river Nedao, at which the Germanic tribal groups began to gain the upper hand over the Huns, describes the anarchic situation:

> There an encounter took place between the various nations Attila had held under his sway. Kingdoms with their peoples were divided, and out of one body were made many limbs not responding to a single impulse. Being deprived of their head, they madly strove against each other. They never found their equals ranged against them without harming each other by wounds mutually given. And so the bravest of nations tore themselves to pieces. (Jordanes, *Get.* L, 261, trans. Mierow = Priscus fr. 25)

This period saw the initial rise of the Ostrogoths, a tribal name first mentioned by Claudian in 392, when they were connected with the Greuthungi (Claudian, *In Eutrop.* 2, 158). The Ostrogothic tribes evolved as the dominant Germanic tribal peoples of the Balkans, clearly distinguished from their Visigothic cousins, who were settled in Aquitaine.

The Isaurians now also emerged to provide a counterweight to the Ostrogoths, particularly in the struggle for political control at Constantinople. Isauria, the mountainous area of southern Asia Minor between Iconium and Seleucia, had never been fully integrated into the structures and ideology of the Roman Empire. During the fourth and fifth centuries the region was in effect a large enclave of barbarian territory within the frontiers of the eastern empire, enclosed by a *limes Isauricus*.[30] Civic life was barely established in the mountainous interior of the country, and the future imperial family came a from a village called Rusumblada, which was only later to achieve the title of a city, Zenonopolis. The elder Zeno had helped to defend Constantinople from Attila in 447, and even at that date was seen as a contender for imperial power. The Isaurians, unlike the Goths and other Germanic barbarian groups, were nominally Catholic Christians, not Arians, and thus not debarred from imperial rank on sectarian grounds. Zeno's son, known by his native name Tarasikodissa, became a trusted intimate of the emperor Leo, and was promoted from being *comes domesticorum* to praetorian prefect of the East. He married Ariadne, the emperor's daughter, and replaced his Isaurian nomenclature with the Greek name of his father, Zeno. The Isaurian group was heavily involved when the "dynasty of Aspar and his sons" fell under suspicion of treachery in 471 and were murdered in the palace. Aspar's surviving supporters fled to Thrace to join the Ostrogoths under Theoderic Strabo.[31] There was resistance to Leo's attempt to designate Zeno emperor, but it was adroitly circumvented. When Leo died in 474, he was succeeded by Zeno and Ariadne's infant child, also called Leo, who reigned under his father's protection. The young Leo died a few months later leaving Zeno as sole emperor.

The Fall of the Western Empire

Throughout Leo's reign in Constantinople the drama of the western empire based at Ravenna began its last act. In 455 the murderers of Valentinian III put forward as his successor the senior Roman senator, Petronius Maximus, who married Valentinian's widow, Licinia Eudoxia, while her elder daughter Eudocia was offered to his own son Palladius. But Eudocia was already betrothed to Huneric, son of the Vandal king Gaiseric, and the Vandals intervened.[32] They plundered Rome for fourteen days, inflicting far greater losses than Alaric's Goths had in 410, thereby earning themselves the reputation which their tribal name preserves today (Procopius, *Bell. Vand.* 1.5). The emperor was killed and the Vandals took Eudoxia and her two daughters into captivity. In the following years, Gaiseric refused the requests of frequent embassies from Constantinople and from Ravenna that the imperial women be released, and continued to harass the Italian and Sicilian coastal cities (Priscus fr. 31).

Flavius Ricimer, grandson of Vallia, who had succeeded Athaulph as ruler of the Visigoths between 415 and 418, now made his first appearance, commanding Italy's defenses on behalf of the new Roman ruler, the Gallic senator Flavius Avitus, who was named emperor at Arles in July 455.[33] Avitus was soon replaced by Majorian (John of Antioch fr. 202). During his short reign Majorian undertook a campaign in Spain against the Visigoths, then launched an expedition from Spain against the Vandals, who had been preventing the corn ships reaching Rome. On returning to Italy in the summer of 461 he was executed by Ricimer.[34] After an interregnum Ricimer nominated another Italian senator, Libius Severus, to be Augustus, who survived until 465.

After Libius Severus' death in 465, Ricimer and the Senate at Rome asked Leo to supply a replacement from Constantinople. The choice fell on Anthemius, grandson of Theodosius II's powerful minister, and he reached Rome in April 467. Ricimer agreed to marry his daughter Alypia. The prospects of stability appeared to have improved now that the ruler was appointed with the eastern emperor's blessing, and he had formed an alliance through marriage with the kingmaker in the West.[35] However, the credibility of the regime was damaged by its military failures. Rome gave ground to the Franks, Burgundians, and

Visigoths in Gaul, and the combined naval expedition of the eastern and western empires against the Vandals in 468 ended in humiliating failure. Tensions developed after 470 between Anthemius, who was resident at Rome, and Ricimer in Milan, leading to civil war in 472. The combatants divided on ethnic lines, with the civilian population of Rome and the senators taking the side of Anthemius, while the barbarians resident in Italy supported Ricimer. They included the Scirian Odoacar, who was to become king of Italy after the final collapse of the western empire. Rome fell to Ricimer after a five-month siege in July 472. Anthemius was beheaded by Ricimer's nephew, the Burgundian prince Gundobad (John of Antioch fr. 209.1).

Ricimer now appointed the eastern senator Olybrius as Augustus,[36] but within weeks both general and emperor had died, each it seems of natural causes. Ricimer's place was assumed by Gundobad, who appointed Glycerius, *comes domesticorum*, to be emperor. Leo promptly sent his own man, Julius Nepos, a relative by marriage of Zeno's wife Verina, with a force to displace Glycerius. The latter, after a reign of eight months, gave up without a fight, was allowed to assume the post of bishop of Salona.[37]

The confusion and weakness of the western rulers had encouraged the ambitions of the barbarians settled in Gaul, the Visigoths under Euric, and the Burgundians under their leader Gundioc. The Burgundians established pacts both with the Gallo-Roman landowners and with the Visigoths to support Arvandus, the praetorian prefect of Gaul from 464 to 469. Arvandus formed a treasonable plot against Anthemius with the Visigothic king Euric.[38] The conspiracy was betrayed when leading members of the Gallic provincial council intercepted a letter from Arvandus to Euric:

> This seemed to be a document sent to the king of the Goths, urging him not to make peace with the Greek emperor, demonstrating that he ought to launch an attack on the Britanni north of the Loire, stating firmly that the Gallic provinces should be divided with the Burgundians according to the law of the nations, and very many other mad things in the same manner, such as might rouse an aggressive king to fury, a pacific one to shame. (Sidonius, *ep.* 1.7.5)

Arvandus was reprieved from a death sentence and sent into exile, but the alliance in Gaul disintegrated, with the Burgundians and the Roman population now making common cause against the Visigoths. A final attempt to assert control over Gaul from Italy was made by Nepos, who appointed the Pannonian officer Orestes to take command. In August 475, however, Orestes turned against his emperor. Nepos fled Rome to Dalmatia. Orestes named his own son Romulus to take his place, the last Roman emperor, who was known immediately after his fall in 476 as Augustulus.[39] Orestes, however, lost credibility among the barbarian troops on which he relied (Procopius, *Bell. Goth.* 1.5), and their leader Odoacar assumed control of the western empire.

Gaiseric, the Vandal king, had played a vital role in the unfolding demise of the western empire. He had, by some margin, the longest reign of any of the barbarian rulers, stretching from 428 until his death in 477. The conquest of Africa had forged his people into a formidable force, and they were a major naval as well as a land power. By the capture of Carthage the Vandals became the only barbarian group to exercise lasting control over a major Mediterranean city, and the importance of this was symbolized by the bronze coins struck for Gaiseric, depicting the king on the obverse, between the letters of the legend KARTHAGO.[40] The attack on Rome in 455 demonstrated *de facto* what was already clear, that Italy and the central Mediterranean islands were vulnerable to his naval power. Naval expeditions from Constantinople had twice failed to make an impression on the defenses of Africa, and in 468 a combination of low cunning, good luck, and the use of fire ships enabled him to destroy the largest fleet to appear in the Mediterranean during late antiquity, the 1,100 ships sent by Leo and Anthemius together in 468 (Procopius, *Bell. Vand.* 3.6.10–27). For both Roman courts this was not only a military but an economic catastrophe, as they had expended more than 64,000 pounds of gold and 700,000 of silver in financing the armada.[41]

The sea power of the Vandals in the central Mediterranean was the counterpart to the threat posed by the Hunnic forces in Illyricum during the 440s. Both Gaiseric and Attila in the early 450s were on the verge of making marriage alliances with the house of Valentinian III. Both barbarian groups proved capable of deploying their military supremacy to optimum political effect. They received formal embassies from eastern and eastern Roman emperors alike, and used the threat of their military supremacy to conduct diplomatic business which went far beyond their local or regional interests. The politics of the Roman world between 440 and 480 depended on an elaborate balance of power between the western court in Ravenna, the Huns in Illyricum, the eastern emperor at Constantinople, and the Vandals in Carthage.

Zeno and Odoacar

The events of Zeno's reign are obscure and complex. The only continuous narrative to have survived is by Evagrius, in book three of his *Ecclesiastical History*. Zeno's rule overlapped with the final collapse of the empire in the West, and the fates of the two halves of the Roman world were not independent of one another. Leading roles in both east and west were played by members of a single Germanic family; Armatus, who was a critical figure in the power struggles at Constantinople, and Odoacar, his brother, who ruled the rump of what had been the western empire, after the deposition of Romulus Augustulus.

Zeno's accession to the eastern throne in 474 provoked an immediate conspiracy involving Verina, the widow of the previous emperor Leo, her brother, the *patricius* Basiliscus, their nephew Armatus, *magister utriusque militiae* for Thrace, and Patricius, a former *magister officiorum*.[42] For a two-year period Zeno was driven from his capital by this rival group, who were aided by the Ostrogoths of Thrace under Theoderic Strabo. After 476 Zeno was reinstated, but failed to establish full control, having bargained away much of his power to his rivals. He called upon the Ostrogothic group led by Theoderic the Amal to do battle with the Thracian group under Theoderic Strabo. However, the Gothic leaders saw through this strategy of divide and rule. As Theoderic the Amal put the situation to his namesake,

> While remaining at peace the Romans expect the Goths to wear each other down. Whichever of us fails, they will be the winners with none of the effort, and whichever of us destroys the other side will benefit only from a Cadmeian victory and be left in diminished numbers to face Roman treachery. (Malchus fr. 18.2)

Theoderic Strabo now joined forces with the Amal. Their forces advanced towards Constantinople but were repulsed at the long walls across Thrace. Zeno made terms with Strabo and managed initially to outwit Theoderic the Amal. By the end of 479 Theoderic the Amal had established a base on the coast of Epirus, where Alaric had been based eighty years before, but was at war with Zeno and Theoderic Strabo.

Zeno's own position throughout his reign was weakened by rivalry with Illus, a fellow Isaurian, who had the support of many of the Isaurian troops in Constantinople, but the two united in successfully resisting a coup by Marcianus, grandson of the emperor of 450–7. Theoderic Strabo may have been party to the plot; at all events he was replaced as commander of the garrison army by Illus' brother Trocondes. Deprived of his livelihood and status, Theoderic Strabo attacked Greece, but died as a result of a riding accident on the road between Philippi and Maximinopolis (Evagrius, *HE* 3.25). Meanwhile Theoderic the Amal accepted new overtures from Zeno to support him against Illus, and was appointed *magister utriusque militiae praesentalis* and made consul for 484, the first time that a barbarian from outside the empire reached this rank.

After 484 most of the Thracian Goths joined Theoderic the Amal or enlisted in forces which were sent to fight in the East. The dispute between Zeno and Illus now became more acute and led to a civil war. Zeno defeated Illus at Antioch in September 484, and then besieged him at the Isaurian fortress of Papirion, where he managed to resist until 488. The involvement of the powerful Isaurian factions had embroiled Asia Minor, at the heart of the eastern empire, in open warfare for the first time since the episode of the Gothic leaders Tribigild and Gainas in 400.

During this war doubts were raised about the loyalty of Theoderic the Amal, and in 486 he again revolted against Zeno, advancing from Thrace to Constantinople and cutting off the city's water supply. Zeno paid off Theoderic after negotiations, and it was mutually decided that the Ostrogoths should go to Italy to recover the situation in the West, where no emperor had ruled since the fall of Romulus Augustulus, ten years earlier. There is a clear comparison to be made here between the roles played by Theoderic and by Alaric at the end of the 390s, when the latter was given effective command of Roman as well as his own forces in Illyricum, and, with or without direct instructions from the eastern empire, invaded Italy and attacked Stilicho in 402.[43]

Odoacar, Onoulph, and Armatus, the three children of the union of Ediko, Attila's trusted legate, and his Scirian wife, rose to powerful positions between the death of Attila in 453 and the battle of the river Bolia in 469, when the remnant portion of the declining Hunnic empire finally yielded to the emergent Ostrogoths. Both Armatus and Onoulph came to Constantinople, while Odoacar turned West. Odoacar was active in Noricum around 470,[44] and is attested as a bodyguard of Ricimer in Italy during his struggle with Anthemius (Procopius, *Bell. Goth.* 1.6). By 476 he was the leader of a mixed group of barbarians fighting in Italy, who declared him king on August 23, 476 (Jordanes, *Get.* 242, 291). Within a fortnight he had killed Orestes and banished the last emperor Romulus from the palace in Ravenna to an estate on the bay of Naples (*Anon. Val.* 8.37–8). This takeover coincided with the coup of Basiliscus against Zeno in Constantinople, in which Odoacar's brother Armatus was intimately involved, and the two episodes were surely connected. Zeno, now supported by Armatus, had regained power in the East, and Odoacar obliged Romulus Augustulus, as his last act, to send a senatorial embassy to Zeno, proposing that no second emperor was now required in the West but that Odoacar should be given the rank of *patricius* to wield authority on the Roman behalf. This coincided at Constantinople with an embassy from the almost forgotten figure of Julius Nepos, who had been appointed Augustus by Leo in 474. Zeno proposed that Nepos should be recognized as emperor, with Odoacar as his *patricius* (Malchus fr. 14).

Nepos was murdered in 480, but Odoacar brought a decade of relative stability to Italy, and to Dalmatia, which was now attached to it. Gaul was largely left to its own fate. Between the regions controlled by the Merovingian Franks, the Visigoths and the Burgundians there were two Roman enclaves, in mid-France around Soissons, and in Provence around Arles. From 457 to his death in 464 the effective leader of these regions was Aegidius, *magister militum per Gallias*, who with Merovingian help managed to reclaim Lyon from the Burgundians and defend Arles from the Visigoths. He was succeeded in 469 by his son Syagrius. Gregory of Tours indicates that both Aegidius and his son were treated as kings rather than as Roman officials by the Franks (Greg. Tur., *Hist.* II. 12, 27), and Syagrius was killed in 486 at the battle of Soissons by Merovingian forces under King Chlodwig.

In 488 Zeno reached his understanding with Theoderic the Amal, that the latter should take his Ostrogothic followers away from Thrace to overthrow Odoacar in Italy. Open warfare, with victories on either side extended from August 488 until Theoderic, supported by Visigothic forces sent from Toulouse by Alaric II, defeated Odoacar at the battle of Adda on August 11, 490, and besieged his rival in Ravenna (*Anon. Val.* 11.50–56). After a three-year siege an agreement was negotiated by the city's bishop, according to which the two leaders would rule Italy in concert. On March 5, 493, Theoderic entered the city; and on the Ides of March he murdered Odoacar with his own hands. He was to rule Italy from Ravenna until 526.

Anastasius

Zeno died in 491 and was succeeded by Anastasius, a sixty-year-old court official. According to Evagrius he was chosen by Ariadne, Zeno's widow, who married him, just as Pulcheria had married Theodosius II's successor Marcian in 450 (Evagrius, *HE* 3.29). The choice was not uncontroversial. Anastasius was considered to have unorthodox religious views, and his position was not confirmed before he had sworn an oath and made a written deposition that he would make no alterations to the creed or to arrangements within the church, in other words that he would respect Chalcedonian orthodoxy, which was upheld by the Constantinopolitan patriarchy (Evagrius, *HE* 3.32). The Isaurians, whose leaders were removed from power at the beginning of Anastasius' regime, attempted a rebellion and marched from their homelands in southern Asia Minor on Constantinople, but were defeated by Anastasius' forces at Cotiaeum in Phrygia in 492. This was the start of a seven-year guerilla campaign against the Isaurian heartlands. Their new leader, Longinus, was eventually captured, and the Isaurian strongholds in the mountains were razed. This extended campaign was vital for maintaining the security of the eastern empire, as the Isaurians had been able to threaten and interrupt the land routes between Constantinople and Antioch, which was the main base for warfare on the eastern frontier. The Isaurians had also posed an immediate threat to the rich olive-producing hill farms of Cilicia along the southeastern coast of Asia Minor, which sent much of their produce to supply the *annona* requirements of Constantinople. During this period Anastasius issued an edict which reduced the tolls paid by Cilician ship-owners passing through the Hellespont. This may have been a reward for their loyalty during the rebellion (*SEG* 1984, 1243).[45] The scale of the Isaurian threat is revealed by the fact that before their final defeat they received a subsidy of 5,000 pounds of gold annually from Constantinople, a sum substantially greater than that paid to any of the barbarian groups in the Balkans (Evagrius, *HE* 3.35).[46]

During the 490s the Bulgarians emerged as a new threat in Thrace and Illyricum. Anastasius' response was to reinforce the long wall which ran across Thrace some sixty kilometers west of Constantinople, creating a new military command to maintain its defense.[47]

One very memorable work was completed by the same emperor, the so-called long wall, which is well positioned in Thrace. This is about 280 *stades* distant from Constantinople, and links the two seas over a distance of 420 *stades* in the manner of a channel. It made the city almost an island instead of a peninsula, and for those who wish provides a very safe transit from the so-called Pontus to the Propontis and the Thracian sea, while checking the barbarians who rush forth from the so-called Euxine sea, and from the Colchians and the Maeotic lake, and from the regions beyond the Caucasus, and those who have poured forth over Europe. (Evagrius, *HE* 3.38)

Procopius, writing from his vantage point in Constantinople, stressed the wall's more obvious and immediate purpose, to protect the wealthy prize of Constantinople against barbarian attacks from Thrace.

The most detailed account of events under Anastasius is provided by the chronicle of John Malalas, book 16.[48] The emperor recognized Theoderic as monarch in Italy in 497,[49] and offered no interference as the Ostrogothic king began to extend his authority across Illyricum as far as Margus and Sirmium. Anastasius renounced Roman aspirations to wield direct military influence over the West, although he intensified diplomatic contacts not only with the Ostrogoths but also with the Franks and Burgundians. The focus of his policy was to maintain Roman authority in the East. This made excellent sense as the western kingdoms still acknowledged Constantinople's authority. The Burgundian king avowed that it was more important to him to be a subject of Anastasius than to be his own master (Avitus of Vienne, *ep.* 93; Danuta and Wood, pp. 148–50), and Gregory of Tours reported that the Frankish king Clovis was honored with the rank of consul (Greg. Tur., *Hist.* 2.38).

There was a significant religious shift during Anastasius' reign. Zeno had unsuccessfully attempted to unite the church behind the formula of the *Henotikon*, which attempted to reconcile Monophysites to Chalcedonians. Rather than leading to doctrinal unity, the permissive and tolerant intentions which lay behind the *Henotikon* encouraged the separate churches to pursue their own forms of worship (see below, chapter 8). The Monophysites were in the majority throughout Syria and Egypt, and their doctrines were favored by Anastasius, who thus increasingly came into conflict with the monks, clergy, and ordinary people of Constantinople. Religious tension at Constantinople reached a climax in 512, when the emperor was almost deposed during a major confrontation in the hippodrome (see below).

The confrontations of 512 provoked another challenge stemming from religious dissidence. This was mounted by Vitalianus, commander of the Gothic *foederati*. The imperial forces eventually prevailed thanks to the first recorded use of "Greek Fire," the combustible sulfur mixture which was targeted on the enemy ships as they attempted to cross the water. Malalas implausibly suggests that the proposal to use this new weapon had come from the Athenian philosopher Proclus (Malalas 16, 16; Evagrius, *HE* 3.43).

Anastasius' court was more favorable to cultural activity than any since the time of Theodosius II. Priscian, who wrote a Latin verse panegyric for the emperor, and John the Lydian, who began a successful legal career during his reign, both emphasized that the emperor appointed men of learning to official positions. Literature, especially poetry, enjoyed a renaissance after a fallow period which stretched back to the 440s.[50] This concern for culture was matched by building activity both in Constantinople and in the other major cities of the

East. Anastasius' own position was emphasized by having his statue erected on the column in the Forum Tauri, which had been built by Theodosius I. Reputedly he carried out building work in numerous provincial cities, "including walls and aqueducts; he dredged harbours, constructed public baths from their foundations and provided much else in every city" (Malalas 16, 13). These claims are clearly confirmed in the case of the newly founded frontier bulwark of Dara in Mesopotamia (see below).

This building activity was made possible by his decision to restrict Roman military ambitions. The state's income from taxation was well in excess of its spending needs. Procopius tells us that at Anastasius' death the treasury contained its highest ever surplus, 320,000 pounds of gold (*Secret History* 19.7). One of his most conspicuous acts, given pride of place in the surviving panegyrics of Priscian and Procopius of Gaza, was his decision to abolish the tax on urban services known as the *chrysargyron*, an act of imperial generosity which was publicized and celebrated by burning the tax records before the assembled people of Constantinople in the hippodrome. The Syriac *Chronicle* of Ps-Joshua the Stylite records that the news of the imperial decision reached Edessa in 497/8, immediately after the conclusion of the Isaurian war, and was greeted by a week-long festival (see below, chapter 5). The emperor could readily afford the gesture now that the annual tribute of 5,000 pounds in gold was no longer required to pay off the Isaurians. The *chrysargyron* was certainly worth substantially less than this to the treasury, and may in any case have been hard to collect, as well as unpopular. Evagrius records that Anastasius' generous and spectacular gesture was marked by the public burning of all documents connected to the previous collection of the tax. He thereby ostentatiously annulled all existing debts to the treasury.[51] Despite the grand gesture in revoking the *chrysargyron* Anastasius acquired a reputation for greed.[52]

The War with Persia

The only serious external wars under Anastasius were on the eastern front. Acute problems emerged with Persia for the first time since the 420s. Religious issues played only a marginal role in the conflict. There was a large Christian population in the Persian Empire, which had grown after the triumphs of the Monophysites at the councils of Ephesus in 431 and 449, when many Nestorians fled from the Roman Empire. In the course of the fifth and sixth centuries the Nestorians created numerous churches, the largest religious network in Persia outside the framework of the official Mazdaeic cults.[53] However, despite some signs of intolerance shown by the Persian priestly caste, outbreaks of persecution and martyrdom in Persia during this period were due to the conflicts of Nestorians with Monophysites, not of Christians with the Sassanid authorities.[54] In the later sixth century the treaty between Rome and Persia of 562 guaranteed tolerance to the Christians in Persia, including the right to build churches, conduct services, and sing hymns of praise to God.[55] This tolerance continued into the seventh century under Khusro II, and Nestorians took advantage of the political order provided by the Sassanian empire to proselytize in distant Asia, reaching China as early as 635.[56]

Peace between Rome and Persia was maintained though most of the fifth century on the basis of diplomatic understandings. Procopius records a story that the emperor Arcadius, on his deathbed in 408, had entrusted his infant son Theodosius II to the guardianship of the Sassanian king Yazdgird I (399–420), as a device to protect against usurpation.[57] Socrates noted that amicable relations between Roman and Persians were sustained by Yazdgird's tolerant, even sympathetic, attitude towards Christians, although this was undermined by the hostility of the *magi*, and attitudes hardened under Yazdgird's successor Bahram V Gur (420–39) (Socrates 7.8.1–20; Theodoret 5.39). A war broke out in 421 but ended a year later with a fifty- (or one hundred-)year truce in favor of the Romans.[58] These terms were renewed around 441 and an undertaking was added by both sides not to build additional fortifications close to the border that separated the Roman from the Sassanian Empire (Procopius, *Bell. Pers.* 1.2). In political terms the main factor in Roman–Persian relations was their common fear of the Huns. The Persians paid regular tribute to the Kidarite and Hepthalite Huns, who occupied a strong position at Gorgo (Gurgan), on the plains of Hyrcania east of the Caspian and adjacent to the Sassanian frontier. To the west of the Caspian Sea the Caucasus Mountains were a defensible barrier running to the Black Sea, important both to the Persians and the eastern Roman Empire. In the sixth century John Lydus explained how Jovian had reached an agreement with Sapor II, after the defeat of Julian, that both sides would contribute to the costs of securing the Caucasus, and that the Persians built and sent garrison troops to a fortress Biraparach, to prevent barbarian incursions (John Lydus, *de mag.* 3.52). In 467, in the reign of the Sassanian king Peroz (459–84), Rome abandoned an agreement to provide money subsidies to the Persians to maintain this garrison.[59] However, the main source of grievance was the status of the vital frontier city of Nisibis, where import and export dues were imposed on trade between the two empires:

> Jovian preferred peace above everything: and for the sake of this he allowed the Persians to take possession of Nisibis for one hundred and twenty years, after which they were to restore it to its former masters. These years came to an end in the time of the Greek emperor Zeno, but the Persians were unwilling to restore the city, and this thing stirred up strife. (Ps-Joshua, *Chron.* 7, trans. Wright)

During the 490s Anastasius argued that Nisibis should be restored to the Romans to provide revenue to support their wars in Ethiopia and against the barbarians in Europe.[60] Meanwhile the Sassanian king Kavad 1 (488–97/499–531), after overcoming serious internal rebellions early in his reign, renewed demands for the subsidies to be paid. When these were refused, war broke out.[61] The Persians took control of Armenia and northern Mesopotamia. Anastasius responded by sending large forces to Edessa, where the Goths and other *foederati* proved a particularly unwelcome burden to the local population (Ps-Joshua, *Chron.* 86, 93–96; see below, chapter 5).

In 504 the Romans recovered Amida, the main city of northern Mesopotamia, by a payment of 1,000 pounds in gold, and two years later a seven-year truce was agreed. Anastasius now began to fortify the village of Dara, a well watered position on a tributary of the river Chabur, as a counterweight to the frontier city of Nisibis.[62] The former village was equipped with baths, cisterns, churches, an administrative palace, and a column in honor of the emperor, as well as covered porticos and storehouses, and was renamed Anastasioupolis. Dara remained a standing provocation to the Sassanians, as it conspicuously breached the terms of the agreement of 441, but the seven-year truce stretched on beyond the death of Anastasius and into the reign of Justin.

Neither side was strong enough to defeat the other, or sufficiently well equipped and well organized to mount sustained campaigns in its rival's territory.[63] The centers of power on both sides lay far distant from their mutual frontier. Both empires were also seriously challenged by other powers: the Sassanians by the Hepthalite Huns, and in the later sixth century by the western Turkic tribes who were impinging on their eastern frontier; the Romans by continued threats and challenges from barbarians in Europe and from the Vandal settlement in Africa. Thus both had a vested interest in maintaining the peace, which had lasted through most of the fifth century. The hostilities under Anastasius interrupted this pattern only to a limited degree. Higher levels of belligerence later in the sixth century reflected the personalities of the respective rulers, Khusro I and Justinian.

Justin

Anastasius died in 518 at the age of ninety, to be succeeded by an emperor utterly different from him in character and background. Justin, the sixty-six-year-old commander of the palace guard, was born a peasant in a village near Skopje, Scupi, a city which was later to be re-founded and renamed Romulia Iustiniana. He was reputedly illiterate, Latin- rather than Greek-speaking, and, like most Latin Romans, was Chalcedonian rather than Monophysite in his religious sympathies. No event in late Roman history more vividly demonstrates that the highest offices of empire were accessible to individuals from the humblest backgrounds.[64] An official version of the circumstances under which he took power is preserved in a long description by Constantine Porphyrogennitos.[65] Potential opposition from the group close to Anastasius, and especially from those who opposed Justin's Chalcedonian leanings, was swiftly curbed by a series of political assassinations, and the transfer of power to the new regime was relatively smooth. The monks and the hierarchy of the Constantinopolitan Church were all in favor of a strong supporter of Chalcedon, and the people are reported to have been won over by cash distributions. Justin was careful to stress the legitimacy of the proceedings by writing an official letter to the Pope at Rome, in which he announced that "we have been elected to the empire by the favor of the indivisible Trinity, by the choice of the highest ministers of the sacred palace and of the senate, and finally by the election of the army" (*Collectio Avellana* 141). His own obscure family was now brought to the center of Roman politics, and the new regime favored individuals from Illyricum, and in particular Justin's own family members, as surely as that of Zeno had thrust Isaurians into the limelight.[66] Justin soon adopted his nephew, Flavius Petrus Sabbatius, now called Iustinianus, who was to succeed him in 527. Justinian was rapidly promoted to be *comes domesticorum*, commander of the praesental armies at Constantinople, *patricius*, and consul in 521. He was made co-Augustus a few months before his uncle's death (Malalas 17, 422, 18; *Chron. Pasch.* 527).

Justinian: The Years of Ambition

The reign of Justinian is much more exhaustively documented than those of his predecessors, thanks above all to the survival of the works of Procopius, the last great historian of antiquity. Like his predecessors, Ammianus Marcellinus and Priscus, Procopius was not merely a chronicler, but a participant in the events that he described. He had been appointed to the staff of the general Belisarius, when the latter was made *comes* of Mesopotamia in 526,[67] and this close relationship colors his narrative, both favorably and unfavorably at different stages of Belisarius' career. He was present for much of the fighting in the wars on the eastern frontier, against the Vandals in Africa, and against the Goths in Italy.[68] The campaigns in these three areas provide the dense and detailed material of the eight books of his *History of the Wars*. These narratives are more concerned with events and actions than with causes and motivation. Procopius, however, although he only rarely obtrudes his own voice to comment on events, used the structure and form of the historical narrative as a whole to provide a personal commentary and judgment on the behavior both of groups and of individuals. The juxtaposition of successful and unsuccessful episodes, the implicit contrast between speech and action, the clear connection between immoral, careless, or self-interested behavior and its consequences provide a moral framework through which the world of Justinian was presented to his readers. Procopius uses all the tools of classical historiography to provide as serious and comprehensive an account of Justinian's Roman Empire at war with its enemies as Thucydides had of the wars of Athens and Sparta in the fifth century BC. In an important recent study, Anthony Kaldellis argues that Procopius created a sophisticated intertextual dialogue between his work, and that of the great classical philosophers and historians as one means of conveying coded judgments on contemporary affairs.[69] In the unpublished *Secret History*, which was probably written around 550, at the same time as the *Wars*, Procopius produced an alternative view of the events described in the *History of the Wars*, which was concerned to get behind the facade of what had happened. This is

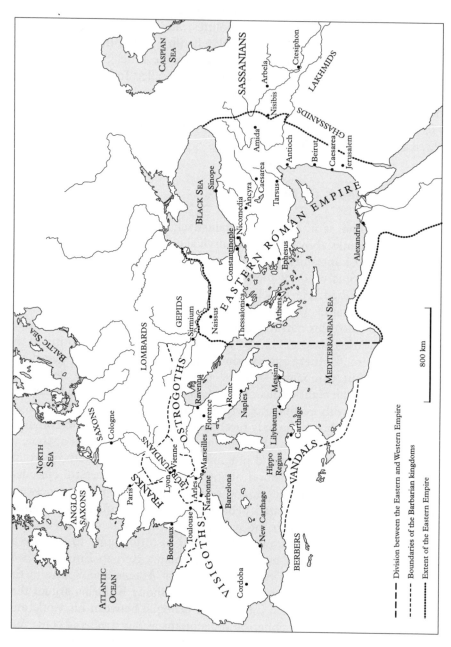

Map 4.1 The Roman Empire and the barbarian kingdoms around 525

ATLANTIC
OCEAN

BALTIC SEA

NORTH
SEA

ANGLO-
SAXONS

SAXONS

Cologne

Paris •

FRANKS

BURGUNDIANS

Lyon
Vienne

LOMBARDS

GEPIDS

Sirmium

Naissus

BLACK SEA

Sinope

CASPIAN
SEA

SASSANIANS

Arbela •

Ctesiphon •

LAKHMIDS

Bordeaux •

Toulouse

VISIGOTHS

Narbonne

Marseilles
Arles

Barcelona

New Carthage •

Cordoba •

OSTROGOTHS

Ravenna

Florence

Rome •

Naples •

Lilybaeum

Messina

Carthage •

Hippo
Regius •

VANDALS

BERBERS

MEDITERRANEAN SEA

Thessalonica

Athens •

EASTERN ROMAN EMPIRE

Constantinople

Nicomedia

Ancyra

Caesarea

Tarsus

Ephesus

Antioch •

Beirut

Caesarea

Jerusalem •

Amida •

Nisibis

GHASSANIDS

Alexandria •

800 km

- - - Division between the Eastern and Western Empire

- - - Boundaries of the Barbarian kingdoms

· · · · Extent of the Eastern Empire

a bitterly hostile analysis of the unscrupulous personal behavior of the crucial political figures: the emperor Justinian and his wife Theodora, the general Belisarius and his wife Antonina, the praetorian prefect John the Cappadocian, and the lawyer Tribonian. The *Secret History* looks into the black heart of a corrupt and evil imperial regime behind the closed gates of the palace. The *Wars* shows the impact of this sinister empire on the world that Justinian was bent on dominating. It is critical to remember that in the *Wars* the author was chronicling high affairs of state while the main protagonist, the emperor himself, was alive and active. This imposed obvious limits on what could be said. Most of Procopius' predecessors – Tacitus and Cassius Dio, Suetonius and Ammianus Marcellinus, to say nothing of Zosimus writing under Anastasius – had written about emperors who were dead. They had been able to integrate criticism, sometimes undisguised in its partisanship, in their narratives. Procopius did not have that option open to him. The *Secret History* was his solution.

Procopius' works are indispensable for any reconstruction of the historical events of the Justinianic period, but is obviously not without his limitations. The information he provides can be incomplete, misleading, or demonstrably inaccurate. His presentation was affected by *parti pris*. Thus the books of the *Persian Wars* are sometimes distorted by encomiastic misrepresentation of Procopius' commander-in-chief and patron, Belisarius. His *Buildings*, which was designedly written in praise of Justinian's achievements, enormously exaggerates and distorts the emperor's contribution, often attributing to Justinian what had in fact been accomplished by his predecessors, or dressing up insignificant repairs as major undertakings.[70] The view into the black box of the *arcana imperii*, which is provided by the *Secret History*, is also not untainted by Procopius' individual prejudices.[71]

Moreover, even on its own terms Procopius offers only a very partial picture of the empire in the mid-sixth century. His perspective is largely a Roman one, drawn from the viewpoint of a member of the Constantinopolitan elite. The subject matter, in the *Wars* at least, is deliberately restricted to campaigns and foreign policy, with only occasional excursuses on internal or domestic affairs that were more or less relevant to this narrative of warfare, battles, and diplomacy. He was nevertheless fully aware of the importance of the religious moralizing that was central to Justinian's self-representation, and the religious motivation that ran through imperial foreign policy.

Procopius affects not to have more than an outsider's pagan knowledge of Christian institutions: bishops are referred to as pagan priests (*hiereis*), churches as temples, monks are prefaced with an apologetic "so-called." He also writes virtually nothing about the religious issues that divided the Christian world, above all the doctrinal conflicts between the Chalcedonians and the Monophysites, which dominated church and civic affairs. This was one of the key topics on which he was fundamentally at variance with the emperor whose reign he chronicled. Whereas Justinian was driven to persecute heretics by religious zeal, "in order to gather all men into one belief as to Christ" (*Secret History* 13.7), Procopius shared the view that it was "a foolish thing to undergo any suffering in the name of a senseless dogma" (*Secret History* 11.25–26). Procopius turned a blind eye to the undercurrents of Christian feuding, and was alienated by the extremism that the emperor encouraged.

No emperor began his reign with more confidence and aplomb than Justinian. He had been well prepared by the role he had played in his uncle's reign, during which he eventually achieved the position of co-emperor, and when Justin died on August 1, 527, the succession was inevitable and unopposed. Justinian's early years in power were marked by extraordinary self belief. He was determined to consolidate the Roman Empire as a universal kingdom, ruled in justice before God. A first step was to codify and publish the entire corpus of Roman law on a definitive basis. This is the best guide to understanding how Justinian conceived his imperial mission. The *Codex Justinianus* was a revised compilation of the three existing late Roman law codes, which had been published under Diocletian and Theodosius II, and of the new legislation, *novellae*, produced by subsequent emperors. The work was completed in fourteen months. In January 530 Justinian asked his lawyers to undertake a much larger task, to produce an edited selection based on the existing collections of private legal rulings and discussions by earlier jurists. This came to be known as the *Digest* or Pandect of Civil Law, which was an epitome in fifty books, based on more than 1,500 classical legal texts, mostly dealing with private law. The man who was principally responsible for delivering this project was the quaestor to the palace, Tribonian, who, as well as being a lawyer of extraordinary energy, also possessed an immense private library, which must have served as the basis for the compilation. The *Digest* was ready by December 533. The commission also completed a third major undertaking, the *Institutes* of Justinian, a comprehensive handbook, designed for instructing jurists in Roman legal principles. Finally the legal team set to work on a revised second edition of the *Codex Justinianus*, which was completed in 534. In December 533 a law was passed which reorganized legal training. The law schools at Berytus and Alexandria were closed, leaving only those at Rome and Constantinople to provide a five-year syllabus. The aim was clearly to standardize legal education. After the completion of the *Digest* a law was passed which quite simply forbade the publication of new commentaries on existing laws. This was designed to draw a line under the whole undertaking. The enterprise was intended to be definitive. This enormous body of legal writing, mostly compiled in Latin, the emperor's own native tongue as well as the official language of imperial authority, was the most compelling articulation of the ideology and nature of the Christian Roman Empire ever to have been devised.

The great Justinianic codification of existing Roman law amounts to one of the largest bodies of Latin prose literature that survives from antiquity. It was for this reason above all that Roman law continued to be used as the foundation of organized western society until the early modern period. However, by the second quarter of the sixth century Latin, the language of law and administration, was being overhauled in Constantinople by the use of Greek, which was spoken by most of the eastern empire's inhabitants and was the language of culture and of the eastern church.[72] Justinian's own subsequent legislation, his *novellae*, were mostly issued in Greek. These appeared in rapid succession until the mid 540s, but only sparsely thereafter. The contrast between energy at the beginning of his period of rule and the inertia of his later years is characteristic of Justinian's reign as a whole.[73]

Although the regime was explicitly based on legislation that had been built up over centuries by his predecessors, Justinian's conception of the law differed from theirs. The prologue to the *Institutes* brackets military power with the force of law as the two main instruments by which the Roman Empire was mastered. However, human law was explicitly shaped by the guiding hand of God, and the *Institutes* begin with the invocation "in the name of our Lord Jesus Christ." The union of divine and secular authority is articulated even more clearly by the preface to one of Justinian's own early laws:

> The greatest gifts which God in his mercy has granted to mankind are priesthood and empire. The former serves God's requirements, the latter controls man's affairs and is concerned with them. These two authorities, originating from the same source, provide order to human life. (Justinian, *Nov.* 6, praef.)

Justinian approached the question of organizing religious doctrine with the same urgency that he brought to the codification of Roman law. He himself was a passionate proponent of Chalcedonian orthodoxy, and his beliefs were not merely those of casual convenience but based on personal conviction. In particular he adhered to the so-called theopaschite formula, that "the one who suffered in the flesh is God and one of the Trinity." This encompassed the Chalcedonian view of the two natures of Christ, that he was both wholly man and wholly God, and expressed the belief that Christ's suffering was completely compatible with his Godhead. Leading representatives of the Monophysites, the main opponents of this doctrine, were called to the capital in 528 to discuss and agree on the doctrine that Justinian expounded. He introduced a far more authoritative and high-handed approach to religious matters than any of his imperial forerunners. In 536 a council pronounced that "it was fitting that nothing be done in the holy Church contrary to the emperor's will and command." However, it is evident that even Justinian had to reckon with the fact that the Monophysites were too numerous and well organized simply to be extirpated or converted to the Chalcedonian view by the arbitrary redefinition of doctrinal terms. Remarkably the emperor's own wife, Theodora, had strong Monophysite sympathies, and entertained Monophysite bishops and other religious leaders in the palace. Procopius cynically suggested that the division between the two was contrived:

> For a long time, it is true, they were supposed by all to be diametrically opposed to each other at all times in both their opinions and their way of living, but later it was realised that this impression was purposely worked up by them in order that their subjects might not, by getting together in their views, rise in revolt

against them, but that the opinions of their subjects might be at variance regarding themselves. (*Secret History* 10, 13–14)

Dialogue and theological debate, in which the emperor himself was adept, remained the means by which the disputing wings of the Church would have to be united. Justinian was obliged to temper his beliefs to practical realities. When Ghassanid Arab leaders, who were Christian Monophysites, approached Theodora and asked for new clergy to be sent from Constantinople, she prevailed on her husband to send two bishops, Theodore and Jacob Bar' Addai, who in turn created an entire church hierarchy of thirty bishops and innumerable clergy across eastern Syria and Mesopotamia. The region thereby became a Monophysite stronghold.[74] Another important Monophysite figure was John, bishop of Ephesus, who was charged by Justinian in 542 to carry out extensive missionary work in Anatolia to convert the residual pagan populations of Phrygia and Lydia. His *Lives of the Eastern Saints* and his partially preserved *Church History*, which both survive in Syriac versions, presented an account of the eastern church that was sympathetic towards the Monophysites.[75] It appears that Justinian was prepared to bide his time, before attacking this central conflict of faith.

In practice, the empire was a maelstrom of diverse religious communities. The successive church councils had never managed to homogenize religious belief, or even religious practice. From the viewpoint of the imperial church some of these sects were irredeemably heretical, and these were swiftly and drastically outlawed. In the first half of 527, even before the death of Justin, Justinian passed laws against the Manichees and the Samaritans of Palestine (*CJust.* 1.5.12, 18–19). Repeated imperial legislation throughout the late empire had treated the "accursed Manichaeans" more repressively than any other religious group,[76] and the word Manichee itself had become a byword for extreme heresy, a term of abuse in religious polemic rather than a description of a particular form of belief. The Samaritans were an ethnic religious group, closely akin to the Jews, whose worship centered on sacrifice on Mount Gerizim in Palestine, north of Jerusalem. There had been violent conflicts between the Samaritans and local Christians in 484, during the reign of Zeno, and after a Samaritan attack on Christians during the Easter festival at Neapolis (Nablus), their mountain-top temple was replaced by a Christian church. Procopius in the *Buildings* alleged that Justinian converted them to a pious Christian way of life (Procopius, *Buildings* 5.7). In fact the legislation that forbade Samaritan religious activities amounted to the abolition of the Samaritan race. Large numbers of them are said to have sought sanctuary with the Persian king Kavad.[77] Those that remained mounted a major revolt in 529. Procopius, who himself came from Caesarea in Palestine, close to the Samaritan homeland, says that the sensible inhabitants of this region, with its mixed population and diverse religious traditions, made it their business to avoid religious confrontation. However, the Samaritans were goaded by the imperial decision:

The majority, feeling resentment that, not by their own free choice, but under the compulsion of the law, they had changed from the beliefs of their fathers, instantly inclined to the Manichaeans and to the polytheists, as they are called. And all of the farmers, having gathered in great numbers, decided to rise in arms against the emperor, putting forward as their own emperor a certain brigand, Julian by name, son of Savarus. (Procopius, *Secret History* 11.26–27)

The insurrection was crushed with massive military force. One hundred thousand rebels are said to have been put to death, and the Christian inhabitants of the region suffered in future from having to pay the huge annual land-tax. After achieving some respite around 550 the Samaritans revolted again in 556.

The Montanists of Asia Minor were another target of violent repression. This Judaizing sect had established a very strong hold across the interior of Asia Minor. Anti-Montanist moves were undertaken in 529, and in November 530 a law banished Montanist clergy from Constantinople (*CJust.* 1.5.18, 3, 5–7, 12; 1.5.20.3–7). These early actions were to culminate around 550 in a major pogrom, conducted by troops, against the spiritual center of the heresy, the Phrygian town of Pepuza, which Montanists regarded as the New Jerusalem. Montanism was a Judaizing form of Christianity, and for this reason the attack on Pepuza may well be compared with the attack on the Samaritans. The Montanists and other sects, which celebrated Easter at the time of the Jewish Passover, laid particular emphasis on the Christian teaching of St John's Gospel and the Book of Revelation.[78] It is no coincidence that in the 550s, as the onslaught on Pepuza took place, Justinian encouraged and supported the building of a great basilica church for St John at Ephesus, the supposed site of the evangelist's tomb, thus reclaiming the saint for the imperial form of orthodoxy. Pepuza is said to have been destroyed.[79]

Other heretical groups were treated severely, but less drastically. Early legislation was issued against the Nestorians and other groups that had been anathematized at Chalcedon. Justinian also mounted a final major onslaught on the institutions of paganism. The aim of his law of 529 was not simply to abolish pagan practice but to require pagan households to be baptized into Christianity (*CJust.* 1.11.10). Pagan teaching was a focus of attack, and the thrust of Justinian closed the philosophical school at Athens, which had become the most important center for non-Christian Neoplatonic teaching in the later empire. The staff of the academy fled to Persia.[80]

War on the Eastern Front

The first years of Justinian were marked by missionary fervor, to destroy all remnants of heresy or paganism, and to use every means available to create compliance with orthodoxy. Christianity was also to be spread beyond the boundaries of the empire. Religion was a motivating factor in several foreign policy initiatives of the late 520s, which began in 526, the last year of Justin's reign. There is little doubt that Justinian, who now shared power with his uncle, was responsible for this aggressive policy. The hostilities with the Sassanians in the Caucasus region in 526 were prompted by religious differences. There were three kingdoms aligned south of the Caucasus between the Black Sea and the Caspian; Lazica in the West, Iberia in the center, and Albania in the East. When Kavad, the Persian king, tried to impose fire worship on the Iberians, their Christian ruler Gougenes appealed to Justin to protect the region. Despite long-standing Persian influence among the Lazi, their ruler Ztathius, dressed in a mixed Roman-Persian garb, was converted to Christianity, baptized, and officially crowned by Justin.[81] The crucial details about Ztathius' conversion are omitted from Procopius' account, yet they are an indication of Roman motives.

The Romans also extended their grip in the Colchian region by subduing the highland people of Tzani, who "changed their way of life to a more civilized one, enlisted in Roman levies, and ever since have joined the Roman army against its enemies. They also changed their beliefs for a more pious way of life, all of them having become Christians" (Procopius, *Bell. Pers.* 1.15.25). In 527 Malalas tells us that Gord, the king of the Huns living near the Crimean Bosporus, also came to Justin in Constantinople and was baptized. Returning to his people he attempted to impose Christianity on them, meeting furious resistance from the Huns' pagan priests. Justin then followed up his initiative by sending a fleet manned by Gothic soldiers to impose peace on the Bosporan area (Malalas 18, 432–3). From the moment that hostilities with the Persians had been resumed in 526, it was Roman policy to turn the Black Sea into a Christian lake.

Religion and trade are the keys to understanding Roman intervention at the southern extremity of the eastern frontier, around the Arabian Sea. The Romans supported the Christian ruler of the Ethiopian Axumites in a successful war against their neighbors in the Yemen, the Himyarites (Homeritai). The latter, who followed a form of Judaism, had been interfering with Christian traders traveling through the Yemen from the East to do business with the Axumites. Their king Dimnos now sent an embassy to Alexandria, offering his subservience to the Roman Empire and asking that a bishop and clergy be sent them to baptize his people.[82] Procopius has a much fuller and more detailed account of these events, explaining the circumstances under which the Axumite Ethiopians imposed a new Christian ruler on the Himyarites. Justinian's role was to send an ambassador, Julianus, to require the two nations, on account of their both being Christian, to join together as allies against the Persians. Procopius indicates that one of the Romans' important objectives was to establish the Ethiopians as the key middle-men in the silk trade between India and Constantinople, thereby intercepting the profits which the Persians were making from this (Procopius, *Bell. Pers.* 1.20). The religious motives of the Romans

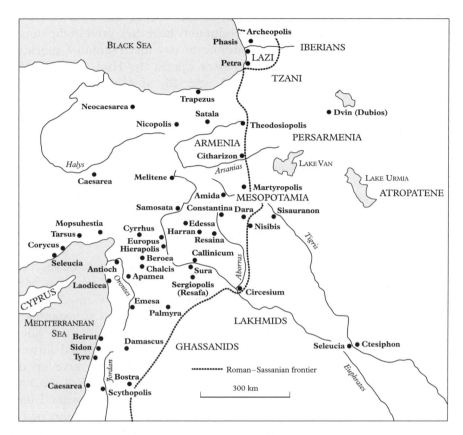

Map 4.2   The Roman–Sassanian frontier in the sixth century

appear from another detail. Justinian also ordered the demolition of the pagan sanctuaries at Philae in the upper Nile valley, which had been maintained up until Procopius' own times (Procopius, *Bell. Pers.* 1.19.36–7).

Justinian had adopted a more aggressive stance against Persia from the moment that he became sole ruler. His first order was given to Belisarius, the commander in Mesopotamia, to build a new frontier fortification at Mindouos, even closer to Nisibis than Dara was (Procopius, *Bell. Pers.* 1.13–14). The Sassanian attempt to prevent the fortification of Mindouos gave Justinian a *casus belli,* and he appointed Belisarius to full command of the troops of the diocese of Oriens, with instructions to make for Nisibis. The main front was in Mesopotamia, the traditional cockpit of warfare between the two empires (Map 4.2). Control of Nisibis since 363 gave the Persians an enormously important forward position, which reduced the strain of moving troops long distances through hostile territory before they could make significant incursions into Roman territory. Dara had been built as a bulwark against invasion along this route, and was the crucial position at the center of the Roman defense system. A large scale battle was fought outside the walls of Dara in 529. The Persians were defeated, but obdurately held their ground diplomatically, demanding that the Romans continue to pay the traditional subsidy to pay for the defense of the Caucasus passes against the Huns, and that they demolish their illegal forts at Dara and especially at Mindouos (Procopius, *Bell. Pers.* 1.16).

In 529 a Saracen raid, led by the Lakhmid leader Alamundaras (al-Mundhir), exposed Syria's weak defenses and almost reached the walls of Antioch in 529 (Malalas 18, 445). In 531 a combined force of Sassanians and Saracens, avoiding the heavily fortified and garrisoned cities of Mesopotamia, crossed the middle Euphrates near Callinicum, and headed again for Antioch. Roman troops forced them to retreat but suffered serious losses in a battle on the Euphrates, although the Persian force was unable to deliver a decisive blow.[83] Belisarius was recalled to Constantinople and the eastern command transferred to Mundus.

In September 531 the long-lived Sassanian king Kavad died, to be succeeded by Khusro (Chosroes) I. Khusro himself was faced by internal rebellion. Meanwhile, in January 532, Justinian's own attention was entirely focused on events at Constantinople, the catastrophic week-long Nika riot in Constantinople, which ended with 30,000 dead. These events helped to persuade both sides to agree to end a war that neither could win. The Romans returned fortresses which they had occupied in Persarmenia, while the Persians gave up their claims to control Lazica. The Iberians were allowed the choice of remaining in exile in Lazica under Roman rule, or returning to their homeland under Persian protectorate. The Romans abandoned Mindouos, but maintained the fortifications and their garrison at Dara. They also agreed to pay an indemnity of 11,000 pounds of gold as their contribution to the cost of the Caucasus garrison (Procopius, *Bell. Pers.* 1.22).

Such were the basic terms of the so-called Endless Peace. The outcome was highly satisfactory from the Roman point of view. All the major gains that had been made between 526 and 529, especially around the Black Sea, had been retained and consolidated. The Mesopotamian bulwark around Dara had held firm, and the cities of northern Mesopotamia and Syria had been spared serious damage. Moreover, the Persian threat was blunted by the Sassanian regime's internal fragility (Procopius, *Bell. Pers.* 1.23).

The Nika Riot

The Nika riot, a blood-bath that led to over 30,000 fatalities and the burning of many of the most prestigious buildings in Constantinople, was and remains the most discussed as well as the most mysterious event of Justinian's reign (Plate 4.1).[84] Procopius' summary account is prefaced by a description of the intense and violent rivalry of the circus factions, the Greens and the Blues, that afflicted the public life of the cities of the empire:

Plate 4.1 Porphyrius the charioteer. The victory monument for Porphyrius, the most successful charioteer and darling of the Constantinopolitan hippodrome in the early sixth century. He is being crowned by a female figure, who is identified by the inscription as the personified Fortune of the city of Nicomedia. This large monument was decorated with reliefs and inscriptions on all four sides, and originally stood on the central *spina* of the race track (Alan Cameron)

(The partisans) care neither for things divine nor human in comparison with conquering (one another) in these struggles; and it matters not whether a sacrilege is committed by anyone at all against God, or whether the laws and the constitution are violated by friend or by foe; even when they are perhaps ill supplied with the necessities of life, and when their fatherland is in the most pressing need and suffering, they pay no heed if only things are likely to go well with their faction (*meros*); for so they name the bands of partisans . . . I for my part am unable to call this anything but a disease of the soul. This, then, is pretty well how matters stand among the people of each and every city. (Procopius, *Bell. Pers.* 1.24.5–6)

Procopius presents a view of the Nika rioting from the perspective of the imperial authorities, and his account is full of details that could only have been available to a palace insider. This condemnation of the circus partisans, therefore, was certainly close to the emperor's own view of them. Justinian in fact had made a priority of curbing partisan violence from the early 520s, and had taken strong measures against the factions from the moment he became coemperor in April 527:

He established secure, orderly conditions in every city of the Roman state and dispatched sacred rescripts to every city so that rioters or murderers, no matter to what faction they belonged, were to be punished; thus in future no one dared to cause any kind of disorder, since Justinian had struck fear into all provinces. For a short period the factions at Antioch were on friendly terms. (Malalas 422, 14–22, trans. Jeffreys-Scott)

Riotous behavior, often orchestrated or exacerbated by the factions, which were capable of mobilizing large numbers of followers, was a central feature of life in the great cities of the later empire, especially Constantinople. The circus factions in Byzantine cities were the organized partisans of the chariot races and other forms of popular entertainment. However, although they had no consistent ideological or religious aims, the circus factions were the only means by which the mass of the people could be organized, and if necessary mobilized. There had been huge riots in Constantinople in 496, 501, and 507, involving bloodshed, the fall from power of leading politicians, and enormous destabilization. In 512 pro-Chalcedonian riots organized by the factions had led to the proclamation of a usurper, Areobindus, and almost toppled the emperor Anastasius.[85] At the beginning of the seventh century they were to be closely involved in the deposition of the emperor Maurice and the succession of Phocas.[86] The reasons for the phenomenon have been much discussed. The mass of the people in ancient cities (including many members of the wealthier classes as well as the urban poor) were an enormous potential force, which became aware of their power through the organization provided by the factions. The style of government of the late Roman Empire had removed the constitutional buffers between the emperor and his people. Political business was mostly carried out within the walls of the palace. The point at which the rest of the population could make its feelings known was precisely in the hippodrome, where the emperor and his leading officials appeared at the races before the people. It was inevitable that the circus should provide the focal point for political discontent. The social environment of great pre-modern cities was also of critical significance. Constantinople, like Rome, Alexandria, and Antioch, had an enormous population, and the eastern *metropoleis* had grown substantially in size during the mostly peaceful and prosperous years of the fifth and early sixth century. The majority of inhabitants were nevertheless poor and under-employed. Moreover, family ties and traditions, and links to a well defined social hierarchy were certainly weaker for many urban dwellers than they had been in the small cities and villages of the Mediterranean. In addition, the huge religious and political changes that the Roman Empire underwent through late antiquity, while they provided new structures of authority, also contributed to deracination and a loss of social equilibrium. The social mixture was explosive, and its ingredients were also well known to the ruling authorities. Justinian, like other emperors, was well aware of the problems posed by Constantinople's unruly inhabitants. Much more difficult was the question of how to control them. Troops were often called in to deal with rioting in Alexandria, Antioch, and above all Constantinople.

Events in early January 532 ran for a little more than a week. Partisans rioted after the races on Saturday January 10, and this led to the arrest of seven ringleaders by the city prefect Eustathius. Five were hanged to death, while two, one from each faction, literally escaped the gallows (execution on the *furca*), fled from the city, and found refuge in a monastery across the Bosporus in Chalcedon. At the next race meeting, on Tuesday, the crowd asked the emperor to pardon the escapees. There was no response until the twenty-second race of the day, when the partisans resorted to a united chant of the single word Nika, "victory," which has given the events their name. They rampaged to the headquarters of the city prefect, set free the prisoners they found there, and burnt it to the ground. The emperor, unmoved, ordered that the games continue on the following day, as programmed. The crowd now demanded that the city prefect be dismissed from office, in company with the praetorian prefect, John the Cappadocian, and Tribonian, the head of the legal commission. The last two men were the most prominent civilian figures of Justinian's radical government. Justinian, astonishingly, acceded to these demands, but as the riot did not abate, sent in his general Belisarius, whose troops killed many insurgents. The rioters set fire to public buildings, and the church of Haghia Sophia was destroyed. The next day the rioters made for the house of Probus, a grandson of Anastasius, whom they planned to put forward as a rival imperial candidate. Probus was not to be found, and his house too went up in flames. As the arson attacks intensified, Justinian called in fresh troops from Thrace. On Sunday morning he made a second appearance before the people in the hippodrome, clasping a copy of the gospels, with an offer of an amnesty for the rebel leaders. However, the response of the crowd was to put forward two other grandchildren of Anastasius, Hypatius and Pompeius, as imperial candidates. Their availability is extraordinary, since both had actually been sent home from the palace by the emperor the previous day. When a rumor spread that Justinian had fled, Hypatius accepted the imperial role offered to him, and was on the verge of leading an assault on the palace. At this critical juncture Justinian ordered a final intervention by three military commanders. Narses distracted and split the mob by cash distributions, while Belisarius and Mundus, both fresh from the eastern front, led their troops in an assault which slaughtered 30–35,000 people. The ringleaders were arrested, Hypatius and Pompeius executed, and numerous leading figures sent into exile.

One of the most significant aspects of the whole episode was the publicity which it received from the emperor himself.[87] Justinian made announcements of his own victory and claimed to have removed tyrants in every city (Malalas 476, 22–477, 1). This propaganda evidently made much of the fact that a would-be usurpation had been foiled. However, it is clear from the sequence of events that regime change had not been the immediate objective of the rioters, and the relatives of Anastasius, far from being major threats, were little more than straw men. Surviving members of Anastasius' family were subsequently rehabilitated. Rather, the real target of Justinian's actions were in fact his actual victims, the almost countless masses who paid with their lives. Procopius makes it clear that Justinian's guiding motive was to curb the unruly violence of the people, as organized by the circus factions. The troops who perpetrated the massacre of Sunday January 18, 532, were instruments of terror, designed to achieve this purpose. The question then arises whether the emperor's decisions and actions during the riots and burning of the city were purely responsive, or whether this was a situation that he had deliberately provoked, or one that he sought to exacerbate by his handling of the crisis, so as to justify the enormous level of violence with which it was repressed. In either case, the reports found in several of the sources, which suggest that the emperor vacillated during the crisis (Procopius tells the story that it was only a speech from his wife Theodora that prevented Justinian from taking flight from the city by sea, *Bell. Pers.* 1.24.32–37), are wholly incredible. No explanation of Justinian's handling of the Nika riot is likely to be correct that does not take account of the fact that Justinian during his early years was as decisive and self-confident a ruler as any that the empire had known in its history.

One of the effects of the Nika riot had been the devastation of a large area of the center of Constantinople. The *praetorium* of the city prefect had been burnt to the ground on the second day of the disturbances. There was much greater destruction as events approached their bloody climax, including the burning of the church of St Sophia and many buildings along the central avenue, the Mesê. By chance or by design the devastation presented the emperor with an opportunity to leave a permanent mark on the city. A great new square was laid out east of the imperial palace and south of the hippodrome. A new cistern of massive proportions was excavated beneath the courtyard alongside the imperial basilica, which housed the law library and

Plate 4.2 St Sophia. Justinian's great church, which was converted into a mosque when Constantinople fell to the forces of Mehmet the Conqueror in 1453. Here it is seen from the west, roughly along the line of the main street of Constantinople, the Mesê (S. Mitchell)

accommodated the courts of justice. Roman architecture, as ever, combined display with functionality.

Above all work began on the great domed church of St Sophia, which still stands in Istanbul today not only as the most spectacular church of late antiquity, but as an inspiration to the religious architecture of the Renaissance Christian and of the Ottoman Islamic tradition (Plate 4.2). The architects were Isidore

of Miletus and Anthemius of Tralles. Grand civic churches in the later fifth
and sixth centuries were no longer the echoing barn-like basilicas of the age
of Constantine. The most prestigious structures now tended to be cruciform,
with a domed roof above the central meeting point of the four arms of the
cross. The design of St Sophia shifted the emphasis away from the cross to the
dome itself, from Christ crucified to Christ resurrected. The 180 foot dome
of St Sophia, like that of its smaller predecessor at the Pantheon of Rome, was
a metaphor in stone for the vault of heaven. The materials for its construction,
above all the polychrome marble used for columns and the wall paneling, were
assembled from all parts of the eastern empire. The power of the building lay
in its monumentality and the unity of its design. The mosaics carried no figured
decoration but the sign of the Cross, repeated again and again. The message that
it conveyed was quite simply that imperial Christianity had triumphed.[88] The
building was completed in five years and dedicated in 537. The achievement
of Justinian and his architects is measured in Procopius' description of the
building's spiritual impact:

> Whenever anyone enters this church to pray, he understands at once that it is not
> by any human power or skill, but by the influence of God, that this work has
> been so finely turned. And so his mind is lifted up toward God and exalted,
> feeling that He cannot be far away, but must especially love to dwell in this place
> which He has chosen. (Procopius, *Buildings* I, 1.61)

The design stretched contemporary technology to the limit, and the arches
threatened to collapse under their own weight (Procopius, *Buildings* I, 67–78).
In 557 the dome collapsed, and was reconstructed only by a supreme effort
of Justinian's final years. The newly dedicated church received its second
encomium in a poem of Paul the Silentiary.

The Reconquest of the West: Africa

In 530 an upheaval occurred in the Vandal kingdom when Gelimer usurped
the authority of the elderly king Hilderic. The latter had established friendly
ties with Constantinople precisely as a precaution against this eventuality, and
after concluding his first truce with Khusro in spring 531, Justinian, despite
opposition from his advisors, his generals, and the soldiers themselves, who had
had no time to recover from the eastern campaigns, switched his attention to
Africa.[89] His decision to intervene, which was encouraged by rebellions against
the Vandals in Libya and Sardinia (Procopius, *Bell. Vand.* 3.10.21–34), demonstrated the aggressive self-confidence that was his hallmark.

The main expeditionary force to Africa, under the command of Belisarius,
consisted of 10,000 infantry and 5,000 horsemen, and included substantial
numbers of *foederati*. Barbarian allies comprised 400 Heruli and 600 mounted
Massagetic archers (Huns). The force embarked on a fleet of 500 transports

(capacity 3,000–50,000 *medimini*) manned by 30,000 Ionian, Egyptian, and Cilician sailors, as well as 92 warships, crewed by 2,000 oarsmen from Constantinople itself (Procopius, *Bell. Vand.* 3.11.1–16). The scale of the expedition was large, but the planners will have been mindful of the unsuccessful attempt on the Vandals in 468. Gelimer meanwhile, startlingly oblivious of the impending invasion, sent a force of 5,000 men and 120 ships under the command of his brother Tzazon to recover Sardinia (Procopius, *Bell. Vand.* 3.11.22–24).

The main force left the harbors of Byzantium in early spring 533, accompanied by Procopius himself. Crucial support in Sicily depended on an agreement that Justinian had made with the Ostrogothic queen Amalasuntha, Theoderic's widow (Procopius, *Bell. Vand.* 3.14.5–6). The anecdotal allusions of Procopius' account reveal the logistic and diplomatic preparations which supported this major imperial enterprise. Procopius describes how he himself, acting as an intelligence officer, had gathered information from a contact in Syracuse that Gelimer was still unaware of the impending attack (Procopius, *Bell. Vand.* 3.14.10–13).

It is likely that the original aim of the expedition had simply been to overthrow Gelimer and reinstate Hilderic. But the news that the Vandals were preoccupied by the revolts in Sardinia and Libya and wholly unprepared to resist, encouraged greater ambitions. At an early stage it became apparent that the reconquest of Africa was possible. The expedition established a bridgehead in Africa, won the support of the local population, and defeated a Vandal force in the field ten miles from Carthage. The city's fortifications were in disrepair, and the inhabitants in any case welcomed the Roman army. While the Vandals that remained sought sanctuary in the Arian churches of the city, Belisarius occupied the royal palace on the Byrsa, where he and his entourage dined, it is said, on the feast that had been prepared the previous day for Gelimer (Procopius, *Bell. Vand.* 3.21.17–25). Gelimer, who fled to take refuge in a mountain stronghold, was compelled by hunger to surrender after a three-month blockade in spring 534 (Procopius, *Bell. Vand.* 4.5–7).

In Constantinople accusations were made against Belisarius that he aimed to become king of Africa, but these dissolved in the euphoria of Justinian's triumph. The emperor took pains to ensure that credit for the recovery of Africa fell only to himself.[90] The spoils of war included even the treasures from the Jerusalem temple, which had been taken by Titus to Rome in 70 and by the Vandal Gaiseric to Carthage in 455. Both Belisarius and Gelimer did obeisance to Justinian and Theodora in the hippodrome. Procopius records that Gelimer was minded to quote the Book of Ecclesiastes from Hebrew scripture: "vanity of vanities, all is vanity." He was consigned to an estate in Galatia. The children of Hilderic, the last legitimate king, and the descendants of Valentinian II, whose daughter Eudocia had married Huneric, were also rewarded with pensions. On January 1, 535, Belisarius became consul and celebrated by disbursing huge cash handouts to the people of Constantinople derived from the Vandal spoils (Procopius, *Bell. Vand.* 4.9).

However, the triumphant conclusion to this first phase of the African war, was followed by complexity, confusion, and ambiguities. Belisarius was replaced by a new generalissimo, Solomon.[91] Lightning campaigns against the Vandals were replaced by prolonged warfare between the occupying force and the local Moorish (Berber) population. Taxation, which was imposed according to new and more stringent schedules by the conquerors, provoked predictable resistance from the inhabitants of the Roman cities (Procopius, *Bell. Vand.* 4.8.25). During the course of 535 Solomon defeated the Moors in two major battles in Byzacium, inflicting massive losses on the men and enslaving the women and children (Procopius, *Bell. Vand.* 4.11–13).

In the late summer of 535 Justinian also broadened the front of his attack on the Roman West. Belisarius was sent to Sicily, which was to be the springboard for the reconquest of Italy. Belisarius over wintered in Syracuse; Solomon in Carthage. It was at this time that disasters were portended by a remarkable occlusion of the sun, which lasted for more than a year (see below, chapter 10). Between 536 and 539 there was a series of major rebellions among the occupying forces in Africa, led by the dissident Roman commanders Totzas and Maximus. Many of the barbarian troops fighting on the Roman side sympathized with the Arian Christianity of the Vandals. Some of them married Vandal women and laid claim to their landholdings, rather than relinquish these to imperial ownership. The Moorish population was not slow to take advantage of Roman disunity. Order was with difficulty restored by sending a new commander from Constantinople, Justinian's nephew Germanus, and by the return of Solomon to the region in 539. Ominously Procopius remarks that under Solomon "Africa became a powerful source of revenue and in other respects prosperous." Taxes, this implies, were rigorously collected. Solomon's military objective was to subdue the Moors who controlled the highlands of Mount Aurasius (Procopius, *Bell. Vand.* 4.19–20.30). Further west Mauretania Caesarea remained in Moorish hands except for its capital Caesarea (Cherchel), which was only accessible to the Romans by sea (Procopius, *Bell. Vand.* 4.20.30–33).

The Invasion of Italy

The triumph of 534 encouraged much larger ambitions in Constantinople, to recover control of Italy from the Ostrogoths and to reconquer the heartlands of the western empire in Italy. While the driving impulse for this policy surely came from Justinian, Belisarius, and the militant inner circle of the regime, the situation among the Ostrogoths themselves presented the Romans with an opportunity and a pretext.

After the death of Theoderic in 526, there was a power struggle in his family over the succession, which involved Amalasuntha, Theoderic's daughter, her ten-year-old son Athalaric, and Theoderic's nephew, Theodahat. Procopius portrays a scene of cultural conflict within the Gothic elite, which was split between a Romanizing group, including most of Theoderic's family and associates, and others who held to more barbarous, Germanic, and warlike ways. Coin portraits and sculptures of Amalasuntha depict her in a fashion that resembled the style of the Roman court of Constantinople.[92] This split no doubt represented the genuine political option which the Ostrogoths faced in coming to an accommodation both with the western empire, which they had inherited, and with the eastern Romans, who had come to reclaim it.

Amalasuntha's supremacy was then challenged by Theodahat, who owned large possessions in Tuscany. Both parties approached Justinian for support, although neither can have conceived that it was in the emperor's mind to reestablish direct Roman rule over Italy. Justinian's motives for intervening were religious as well as political. Although the Arian Ostrogoths had not interfered with the Catholic Church hierarchy in Italy, the presence of a heretical regime would have been an affront to Justinian's militant orthodoxy. He sent two bishops to Italy to confer with the bishop of Rome, and a senatorial legate, with an official letter to Amalasuntha. This complained about Gothic conduct in the recent wars, and especially objected to their request for the return of Lilybaeum in Sicily:

> Do not act in this way, emperor, but remember how when you were mounting your expeditions against the Vandals, not only did we not obstruct you, but with great enthusiasm provided a passage against the enemy and a market for the purchase of all the most essential supplies, and especially the great quantity of horses, which provided you with the most important means of overwhelming the enemy. (Procopius, *Bell. Goth.* 5.3.23)

The conflict between Amalasuntha and Theodahat sharpened after the death of the youthful Athalaric. Theodahat had the queen murdered by three leading Goths whom she had antagonized during the succession struggle after Theoderic's death. His actions provided Justinian with further cause for extending his military intervention in the West (Procopius, *Bell. Goth.* 5.4).

The undertaking to reclaim Roman control of Italy had enormous ramifications among the barbarian kingdoms of the West. In particular, the Franks used the conflict as an opportunity to extend their influence into northern Italy. The Roman military strategy was two-pronged. Mundus, the Gepid *magister militum* in Illyricum, was to invade Dalmatia, targeting the port of Salona, while Belisarius was to take a larger force, made up of 4,000 regular troops, 3,000 Isaurians, and *foederati*, first to Sicily and then into Italy. Belisarius' forces crossed the straits of Messina and, heartened by high-level Gothic defections, laid siege to Naples, which fell after a twenty day siege. The resistance of its inhabitants, headed by the Jews who were rightly alarmed at the prospect of being ruled by the fanatical Christian Justinian rather than the tolerant Ostrogothic regime, was notable but unavailing (Procopius, *Bell. Goth.* 5.8–10). Theodahat had done nothing to organize help for them and was rightly suspected by his own people of selling out to the Romans. A force of Gothic cavalry assembled in early December south of Rome, and replaced him with

Vitigis, a commander who had won his laurels in the battle for Sirmium. In a letter to his people crafted for him by Cassiodorus, the new king marked the change of style and intention betokened by his accession:

> You must know that I was not chosen in the privy chambers but in the wide open fields; I was not sought among the subtle debates of sycophants, but as the trumpets blared, so that the Gothic race of Mars, roused by such a din and longing for their native courage, might find themselves a martial king. (Cassiodorus, *Var.* 10.31)

Vitigis left behind a garrison of 4,000 men in Rome in support of bishop Silvestris and the Roman Senate, before he moved north to Ravenna. Here he married a reluctant Matasuntha, the daughter of Amalasuntha, and secured his dynastic position by marital rape. Gothic soldiers were summoned from throughout Italy and provided with arms and mounts. This move mobilized all his troops except those who were needed to protect Ostrogothic territory in Gaul from the Franks (Procopius, *Bell. Goth.* 5.11.10–29).

After the capture of Naples southern and central Italy fell into Belisarius' grasp. Silvestris, the bishop of Rome, invited the invading Romans to occupy the city after negotiations which allowed the Gothic garrison of 4,000 to withdraw to Ravenna (Procopius, *Bell. Goth.* 5.14–15). Belisarius organized his garrison of 5,000 men into a tenacious defense of the huge circuit walls, fourteen miles long, which were now partly enclosed from the north and east by seven Gothic camps. Procopius provides an extended and dramatic account of the siege of Rome, which began with a major three-week assault in late February and early March of 537. The climax of the siege were two major Roman counteroffences at the Vivarium, the enclosure used for stabling wild animals destined for the Roman arena, and at the Porta Salaria, in which 30,000 Goths are said to have died. Belisarius celebrated the victory, or the reprieve, but promptly evacuated the women and children from the city and sent urgently to Justinian for reinforcements (Procopius, *Bell. Goth.* 5.17–25).

The rigors of defending Rome, under siege through 537 into 538, were relieved by sallies and skirmishes outside the walls, which are recalled with much anecdotal detail in the vivid reportage of Procopius, who himself was present as a senior member of Belisarius' staff.[93] Prolonged resistance had been possible because the Goths were never able to seal off the city, despite having gained control of the harbor at Portus. Nevertheless famine and disease became acute in the early months of 538. Belisarius countered the growing demoralization by announcing that a fleet from Constantinople had arrived in Campania, and sent Procopius himself to round up whatever troops he could find in the Naples region and bring them to Rome in the guise of a relieving force (Procopius, *Bell. Goth.* 6.3–4.5). He was aided by Belisarius' wife Antonina (Procopius, *Bell. Goth.* 6.4.6–20).

In March 538 the promised relieving force finally docked at Naples. The arrival of these reinforcements brought despair to the Goths, who were already suffering themselves from severe food shortages and pestilence. An armistice was declared and a deputation consisting of one Roman and two Goths parleyed with Belisarius.

The arguments which were deployed laid out the political positions of the two sides with perfect clarity. The Goths argued that they had legitimate authority to control Italy. The emperor Zeno had charged Theoderic, whom he had already appointed to be a Roman consul and a *patricius*, to oust the usurper Odoacar and to take legitimate control of his Italian kingdom. This Theoderic had done. His regime had preserved the laws and administrative forms of the Roman government, and been scrupulously tolerant of Catholic religious practice. Romans indeed had held all the high state offices in the Gothic kingdom, and consuls were appointed not by him but by the eastern emperor. Belisarius, accordingly, had no business to threaten this legitimate sovereignty. The case was a powerful one. Indeed in 509 Anastasius had explicitly legitimized Theoderic's position. However, it was crudely swept aside by Justinianic realpolitik. Belisarius riposted that Theoderic's mission to depose Odoacar had been undertaken on behalf of the emperor with the view of freeing Italy from its tyrant and reclaiming it for the empire. Theoderic had failed to give to the emperor the land that was his. The barbarians, making no headway with the central case, offered to yield up Sicily, an essential requirement if the eastern empire was to keep a grip on Africa, but received the sarcastic answer that they could have the island of Britain, far larger than Sicily, in return. The implication was that the Goths had no more right to give the Romans Sicily than the Romans had to give them Britain. The Gothic embassy moved to its bottom line, offering to negotiate the sovereignty of Naples and Campania, and indicating a readiness to pay annual tribute to Constantinople. The rebuff was that Belisarius had no powers to negotiate about territory which was owned by someone else, the emperor. The only agreement reached was to send embassies to put the matter before Justinian in person (Procopius, *Bell. Goth.* 6.6).

The endgame now began. As the Goths made final attempts to infiltrate Rome through the aqueducts, a ploy that had worked successfully for Belisarius at Naples (Procopius, *Bell. Goth.* 6.9). Roman cavalry advanced into Picenum, and marched into Ariminum (modern Rimini), at the invitation of its Roman inhabitants. Rimini lies a day's march from Ravenna. Vitigis promptly ordered his forces to abandon the siege of Rome and to make all speed to protect the Gothic capital. Thus on March 30, 538, one year and nine days since the city had been invested, the Goths burnt their camps and began to withdraw. For most of their forces this meant crossing the Tiber at the Milvian bridge. Belisarius rushed his troops back to the scene, to inflict maximum damage on the confused mass of Gothic troops who were struggling to escape across the river (Procopius, *Bell. Goth.* 6.10).

The Gothic position in central Italy was critically undermined by the arrival of fresh forces from Constantinople, 5,000 troops led by the eunuch Narses, and 2,000 Germanic Heruls, under their own commanders (Procopius, *Bell.*

Goth. 6.13.15–18). Narses met Belisarius at Firmum, and persuaded him of the urgency of relieving John, the Roman Commander at Ariminum. A soldier from the besieged force arrived with a message that John's men could only hold out for another week. Forces, coordinated with considerable military skill, converged from the sea and by two overland routes to put the Goths to flight. The famished commander emerged with his exhausted troops (Procopius, *Bell. Goth.* 6.17–18.2). The Goths escaped to Ravenna.

The invading force now clearly had the momentum of victory with them, but discord among the Roman generals led to catastrophe in Liguria. Bickering between the commanders prevented the Romans from coming to the relief of Milan. The starving inhabitants and tiny garrison were forced into negotiations. The soldiers were surrendered into captivity, but in late March 539 Milan was razed to the ground, its male population was massacred, and the women handed over to the Burgundians as slaves (Procopius, *Bell. Goth.* 6.21). The remainder of the Ligurian cities surrendered. As news of the disaster came in and was reported by Belisarius to Justinian, the lesson was drawn. Narses was recalled and Belisarius confirmed as commander with full powers (Procopius, *Bell. Goth.* 6.22.1–4).

Much of 539 was taken up in a war of attrition in which the Romans held the upper hand. The Goths, defending the strongholds of Auximum and Urbinum, were at the mercy of famine, and indeed the country dwellers, who had been prevented by the warring parties from planting crops the previous year, were reduced to extreme distress and starvation, described with chilling realism by Procopius. With staring eyes, jaundiced, their skin desiccated and furrowed by emaciation, 50,000 were estimated to have perished from hunger (Procopius, *Bell. Goth.* 6.20.23–33). The Roman troops were provisioned by supplies brought into Ancona (Procopius, *Bell. Goth.* 6.24.14). After a six-month siege Auximum and Faesulae capitulated and their garrisons defected to Belisarius, pledging loyalty to the emperor (Procopius, *Bell. Goth.* 6.27.25–34).

Belisarius now closed in on Ravenna, where Vitigis' position continued to deteriorate. It was agreed that a Gothic deputation should seek surrender terms from the emperor. This secured a better offer than they might have hoped, and better than Belisarius was prepared for his part to concede, namely that Italy south of the Po should revert to the empire, that the Ostrogoths should retain the Transpadana, and that the royal treasures in Ravenna be divided between the two sides. Then, in a surprising turn, a group of Gothic nobles suggested to Belisarius that they would surrender to him if he were to accept the title of emperor of the West. Belisarius gave every appearance of compliance, telling his own men that he now had plans to secure full control of Theoderic's kingdom, and his opponents that he was ready to accept the proposal. He thus marched in and occupied Ravenna in May 540. Royal property was seized, but the other inhabitants were allowed to retain their private wealth. Belisarius announced that he himself would be returning to

Byzantium, summoned by Justinian to take command again on the eastern front (Procopius, *Bell. Goth.* 6.28–30).

Procopius' account of these events, written largely from the perspective of Belisarius, makes too little of the fact that the general's behavior led directly to one of the gravest political misjudgments of Justinian's reign. The Gothic embassy to Justinian arrived in Constantinople at exactly the moment that the empire faced renewed invasion from the Persians. The emperor and his advisors were well aware that they lacked the resources to continue large-scale warfare on two fronts (to say nothing of the situation in Africa), and accordingly offered a highly rational deal. By reclaiming Italy as far as the Po, including the western capital of Ravenna, the campaign of reconquest could be considered a resounding success. The Goths could now continue the role to which they had long been accustomed, providing military protection to the empire, along its northern frontier, securing the Alpine passes especially against the growing threat of the Franks. Rome and Italy could then enjoy a period of peace and recovery, as well as serving as a major source of tax revenue for the state. Belisarius' mutinous and arbitrary behavior, motivated by his vain belief that the agreement "would prevent him from winning the decisive victory of the whole war, when it was possible to do so with no trouble, and leading Vitigis a captive to Byzantium" (Procopius, *Bell. Goth.* 6.29.4), undermined the successes that his campaign had achieved, and led directly to a further generation of misery for Italy and to a weakening of imperial power.

For Procopius the return of Belisarius in 540 marked a turning point in the attempt to reconquer the western empire.

> But the other leaders, who were inclined to be on a level with one another and had their minds fixed on nothing except private gain, had already begun to despoil the Romans and to put the subject population at the mercy of their soldiers. They themselves no longer heeded what had to be done and were unable to command their troops' obedience. And so they committed many errors and all the affairs of the Romans were ruined in a short time. (Procopius, *Bell. Goth.* 7.1.23–24)

With this unmistakable echo of Thucydides, Procopius invited his readers to judge Justinian's Italian expedition as his classical predecessor had viewed Athens' grandiose attempt to conquer Sicily and the West nearly a thousand years before. The vision of reconquest carried with it the seeds of its own collapse. But Procopius' analysis is faulty and the blame is better laid at the door of Belisarius himself.

The fifteen years of Justinian's reign which stretched from his accession in 527 to the outbreak of the plague in 542 were a time of extraordinary achievement and ambition. He had taken over at a propitious moment. Justin had inherited an enormous amount of surplus revenue from Anastasius in 519, and this had hardly been touched. The new emperor, driven by a personal religious mission and a sense of his own destiny, launched an imperial program un-matched since the age of Augustus. The political will of the new regime is surely symbolized by the decision to collect, edit, and publish the entire corpus of Roman law, and then establish it as the unchanging template of order and authority within the Christian empire. The limits of this empire were expanded and redefined. From the Crimean Bosporus to Ethiopia, peoples and king-doms along the eastern border were secured for Christianity. After the initial, almost fortuitous success in Africa, a plan formed to reclaim the western Mediterranean for Roman orthodoxy from the Arian barbarian kingdoms. The mob in Constantinople, senatorial rivals, doubters, and critics had been intimid-ated into silence by the carnage that followed the Nika riots.

Much of this was due to Justinian's own demonic energy, the relentless drive of a man who boasted that he never slept. The atmosphere of his early years is captured in the memoirs of the bureaucrat John Lydus:

> When the state was being tossed from side to side by waves and storms of this sort, fate proffered a counterweight which served to combat the apathy of the old days, by placing Justinian, the most sleepless of all emperors, in charge of the common good, a man who thought that it was a punishable offence in his own life, unless everyone under his direction remained perpetually vigilant and did battle to their utmost for the state, so that they should take control not only of the possessions which once belonged to the Romans, when these had simply been lost thanks to the indolence of his predecessors, but also even of those of their enemies in addition to these. (John Lydus, *de mag.* 3.55)

Justinian himself, of course, claimed the impulse that he channeled into empire was divine inspiration:

> Hope in God is our sole recourse for the existence of the monarchy. It is that which assures the safety of our rule and empire. It is necessary that all our legislation flows from this principle, which is for it the beginning, the middle and the end. (Justinian, *Nov.* 109, preface)

Around himself he assembled one of the most astonishing groups of ministers known from any period of Rome's history. Belisarius, who was only the most distinguished of several highly effective and charismatic military leaders; John the Cappadocian, praetorian prefect, responsible for the empire's finances, bitterly hated by many of his contemporaries but supremely effective; Tribonian, who put previous lawyers in his shadow; Anthemius and Isidore, the architects of St Sophia; and Procopius himself, the historian of the age. This constellation of talents was driven by the same purpose and ambition that motivated the emperor. It was surely their collective aim, above all by the instrument of reconquering the lands that had slipped away from Roman control, to establish an empire of enduring power and restore the dominion of Augustus and Constantine. By the year 540 this was an aim that must have seemed within their grasp (Map 4.3).

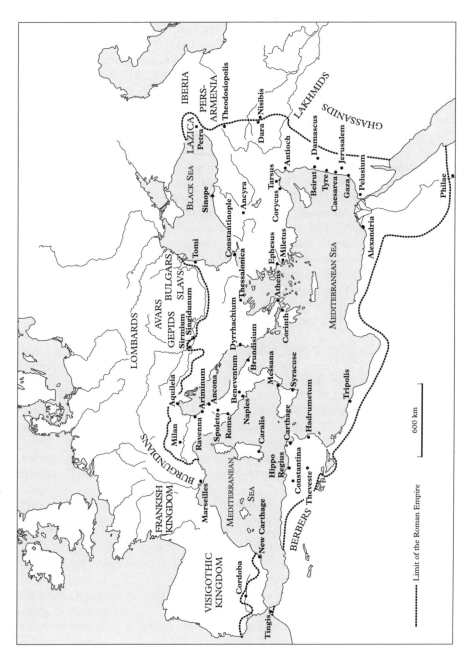

Map 4.3 The new Mediterranean empire of Justinian

LOMBARDS

AVARS

GEPIDS

BULGARS

SLAVS

IBERIA

LAZICA

PERS-ARMENIA

LAKHMIDS

GHASSANIDS

BLACK SEA

Theodosiopolis

Nisibis

Dara

Petra

Sinope

Constantinople

Ancyra

Tomi

Singidunum

Sirmium

Thessalonica

Ephesus

Miletus

Athens

Corinth

Tarsus

Corycus

Antioch

Damascus

Jerusalem

Beirut

Tyre

Caesarea

Gaza

Pelusium

Alexandria

Philae

MEDITERRANEAN SEA

LOMBARDS

Dyrrhachium

Brundisium

Messana

Syracuse

Tripolis

Aquileia

Ariminum

Ancona

Benaventum

Rome

Naples

Caralis

Hadrumetum

Carthage

Milan

Ravenna

Spoleto

BURGUNDIANS

FRANKISH KINGDOM

Marseilles

MEDITERRANEAN SEA

New Carthage

Hippo Regius

Constantina

Theveste

BERBERS

VISIGOTHIC KINGDOM

Cordoba

Tingis

············· Limit of the Roman Empire

600 km

NOTES

1 E. Gibbon, *Decline and Fall of the Roman Empire* (London, 1929).
2 A. H. M. Jones, *The Later Roman Empire* I (Oxford, 1964), 173.
3 See K. Holum, *Theodosian Empresses* (Berkeley, 1982).
4 See Alan Cameron, "The empress and the poet: Paganism and politics at the court of Theodosius II," *Yale Classical Studies* 27 (1982), 217–89.
5 E. A. Thompson, *The Huns* (rev. edn. Oxford, 1996), 203–24.
6 A positive judgment in Evagrius 1.19.
7 Alan Cameron, "The empress and the poet: Paganism and politics at the court of Theodosius II," *Yale Classical Studies* 27 (1982), 240–2.
8 *CIL* III 734 = ILS 823; Marcellinus *comes* 447.
9 M. Whitby, "The long walls of Constantinople," *Byzantion* 55 (1985), 560–83; J. Crow, "The long walls of Thrace," in C. Mango and G. Dagron (eds.), *Constantinople and its Hinterland* (Aldershot, 1995), 109–24; J. Crow and A. Ricci, "Investigating the hinterland of Constantinople. An interim report on the Anastasian long wall," *JRA* 10 (1997), 232–62.
10 K. Holum, *Theodosian Empresses* (Berkeley, 1982), 110; B. Croke, "Evidence for the Hun invasion of Thrace in AD 422," *GRBS* 18 (1977), 347–67.
11 K. Holum, *Theodosian Empresses* (Berkeley, 1982), 130–46.
12 G. Zecchini, "Teodosio II nella storiografia ecclesiastica," *Mediterraneo Antico* 5 (2002), 529–46; J. Harries, "Pius Princeps: Theodosius II and fifth-century Constantinople," in P. Magdalino (ed.), *New Constantines* (Belfast, 1994), 35–44.
13 C. Kelly, *CAH* 13, xxx; "Empire building," in G. W. Bowersock et al. (eds.), *Late Antiquity* (Cambridge Mass., 1999), 170–95, esp.178ff. Kelly offers a more positive appraisal of corruption than R. MacMullen, *Corruption and the Decline of Rome* (New Haven, 1989), 122–70.
14 E. Schwartz, *Acta Conciliorum Oecumenicorum* I.1.1.44.
15 Malalas 361, 14–362.18. *Chron. Pasch.* 450 has a detailed but wrongly placed account of Cyrus.
16 J. F. Matthews, *Laying Down the Law* (New Haven, 2000); T. D. Barnes, "Theodosian Code," in G. W. Bowersock et al. (eds.), *Late Antiquity* (Cambridge Mass., 1999), 721–2.
17 See T. Urbaincsyk, *Socrates of Constantinople. Historian of Church and State* (Ann Arbor, 1997), a clear and perceptive study.
18 Orosius 7.40.10; *Chron. Min.* II.18.
19 P. Heather, *Goths and Romans* (Oxford, 1991), 221–5; P. Heather, "The emergence of the Visigothic kingdom," in H. Elton and J. Drinkwater, *Fifth-Century Gaul. A Crisis of Identity?* (Cambridge, 1992).
20 P. Heather, "The Huns and the end of the Roman Empire in the West," *EHR* (1995), 4–41, a sophisticated and detailed analysis, which attempts a global explanation of the collapse of the western empire, spanning a century of events from 376 to 476.
21 Greg. Tur. 2.8, quoting the history of Renatus Frigeridus.
22 Jordanes, *Get.* XLIX, 254–8 on the death and funeral of Attila.
23 Hydatius, *Chronicle* 49. For the earlier history of the Vandals, see H. Wolfram, *The Roman Empire and its Germanic Peoples* (California, 1997), 169–61.

24   Victor of Vita 1.1. W. Goffart, *Romans and Barbarians ad 418–584. Techniques of Accommodation* (1980), 231–5, argues that the figure is historically baseless.

25   H. Wolfram, *The Roman Empire and its Germanic Peoples*, 166.

26   *Chron. Min.* 1, 474; Isidore, *Historia Vandalorum* 74.

27   Evagrius 2.1 with Whitby's note; K. Holum, *Theodosian Empresses* (Berkeley, 1982), 208–9; R. W. Burgess, "The accession of Marcian," *Byz. Zeitschr.* 86/7 (1993/4), 47–68 emphasizes the role of Aspar.

28   Council of Chalcedon canon 28; trans in J. Stevenson, *Creeds, Councils and Controversies* (London, 1989), 361–2 no. 248.

29   John Lydus *de mag.* 3.43. R. L. Hohlfelder. "Marcian's gamble: A reassessment of eastern imperial policy towards Attila," *American Journal of Ancient History* 9, 1 (1984), 54–69.

30   J. Rougé, "Les Isauriens au IVe siècle," *REA*; J. F. Matthews, *The Roman World of Ammianus Marcellinus* (London, 1989); B. D. Shaw, *Journal of the Economic and Social History of the Orient* 33 (1990), 199–233, 237–70; H. Elton "The Isaurians in the sixth century" in S. Mitchell and G. Greatrex, *Ethnicity and Culture in Late Antiquity* (Wales and London, 2000), 293–307.

31   John Malalas 371, 9–372, 2; *Chron. Pasch.* 467; Candidus fr. 1.

32   John of Antioch fr. 201, 6 (*FHG* IV, 615); Marcellinus *comes* I, 304.

33   Sidonius Apollinaris, *carm* 7, 297, 316. This is from Sidonius' panegyric of Avitus.

34   Majorian's martial virtues are highlighted in Sidonius' panegyric, *carm.* 5. For another side of his character, see Sidonius' long account of attending an imperial banquet with Majorian and his court in 461, *ep.* 111.

35   Sidonius delivered a panegyric for Anthemius, *carm.* 2, when he took the consulship in January 468, and was in Rome for the wedding of Ricimer and the emperor's daughter Alypia, *ep.* 1.5 and 1.9.

36   F. M. Clover, "The family and early career of Anicus Olybrius," *Historia* 27 (1978), 169–96 = *The Late Roman West and the Vandals* (Variorum, 1993) III.

37   Priscus fr. 65; John of Antioch fr. 209.2; cf. the epitome of Malchus by Photius, Blockley, Malchus *testimonia* 1.

38   Jordanes, *Get.* 237f.; Sidonius *ep.* 3.9; 3.17.3.

39   *Anon. Val.* 37; *Chron. Min.* 1. 308.

40   F. M. Clover, "Carthage and the Vandals," in *The Later Roman West and the Vandals* (Aldershot, 1993), VI, 13.

41   Candidus fr. 2; Procopius, *Bell. Vand.* 3.6.2 gives an even higher figure.

42   These events have been treated in detail by P. Heather, *Goths and Romans* (Oxford, 1991), 272–308. See also W. Liebeschuetz, *Barbarians and Bishops* (Oxford, 1990), 80–3, for a comparison between these events and the role played by Alaric.

43   W. Liebeschuetz, *Barbarians and Bishops*, 58–64.

44   Eugippius, *Life of Severinus*; *Anon. Val.* 10.45–47.

45   See S. Mitchell, "Olive production in Roman Asia Minor," in S. Mitchell and C. Katsari (eds.), *Patterns in the Economy of Roman Asia Minor* (Wales and London, 2005).

46   For events in Isauria, see F. Hild and H. Hellenkemper, *Tabula Imperii Byzantini: Kilikien und Isaurien*, vol. 1 (1990), 40–2.

47   Evagrius, *HE* 3.38; Justinian, *Nov.* 26 pr (535).

48   Much of the information in Malalas is also duplicated in *Chron. Pasch.* For a modern account see C. Capizzi, *L'imperatore Anastasio I (491–518). Studio sulla sua vita, la sua opera e la sua personalità* (1969).

49 *Collectio Avellana* (this is a collection of imperial and papal letters covering the period 367–553) 113.4; *Anon. Val.* 64.

50 Fiona Nicks, "Literary culture in the reign of Anastasius I," in S. Mitchell and G. Greatrex, *Ethnicity and Culture in Late Antiquity* (Wales and London, 2000), 183–203, a good survey of the cultural climate, including the use of Greek and Latin.

51 Evagrius, *HE* 3.39 is the fullest account (see Whitby's commentary). For Edessa see the Ps-Joshua, *Chron.* 31. For the abolition of the *chrysargyron* as a high point of the panegyrics of Priscian and Procopius of Gaza, see Alain Chauvot, *Procope de Gaza, Priscien de Césarée. Panégyriques de l'empéreur Anastase 1ᵉ* (1986).

52 Whitby, note on Evagrius, *HE* 3.42, collects the references.

53 E. Winter and B. Dignas, *Rom und das Perserreich* (Berlin, 2002), 55–6.

54 G. J. Reinink, "Babai the Great's *Life of George* and the propagation of doctrine in the late Sassanian empire," in J. W. Drijvers and J. W. Watt, *Portraits of Spiritual Authority in Late Antiquity* (Leiden, 1999), 171–93.

55 Menander prot. fr. 11.

56 G. Fowden, *From Empire to Commonwealth* (Princeton, 1993), 121–4.

57 Procopius, *Bell. Pers.* 1.1–10. An agreement in the reverse direction was declined, on advice by Justin I in 518, when Cabades proposed that he should adopt his third son Chosrhoes. The suggestion was quashed by the objections of the quaestor Proclus, who gave extremely cautious lawyer's advice: such a move would effectively make Chosrhoes heir to the Roman Empire itself. The plan was dropped; Procopius, *Bell. Pers.* 1 11.1–25.

58 Malalas 14, 23 (p. 364); cf. Sozomen 9.4.1; Eudoxia wrote a poem to celebrate the Roman triumph, Socrates 7.21.8.

59 Priscus fr. 47 (*FHG* IV, 107–8). R. C. Blockley. "Subsidies and diplomacy: Rome and Persia in late antiquity," *Phoenix* 39 (1985), 62–74; Z. Rubin, "Diplomacy and war in the relations between Byzantium and the Sassanids in the fifth century AD," in P. Freeman and D. Kennedy (eds.), *The Defence of the Roman and Byzantine East* (Oxford, 1986), 677–95. In the sixth century, in 562, another resolution was found: the Sassanids were to be responsible for opposing Huns, Alans, and other barbarians in the Caucasus, while the Romans were to send no more troops to the region and to give up their influence there, Menander prot. fr. 11 (*FHG* IV, 206–17). For an analysis of developments in this region during the fifth and sixth centuries see D. Braund, *Georgia in Antiquity* (Oxford, 1994), 268–314.

60 Ps-Joshua, *Chron.* 18; 20. Cf. E. Winter and B. Dignas, *Rom und das Perserreich, Zwei Weltmächte zwischen Konfrontation und Koexistenz* (Berlin, 2002), 158–9.

61 Procopius, *Bell Pers.* 1.7.1–4; Ps-Joshua, *Chron.* 20, 24; G. Greatrex, *Rome and Persia at War 502–32* (Liverpool, 1998), 73ff.

62 Evagrius 3.37; Zacharias of Mytilene, *HE* 7.6.; Malalas 16, 10 (p. 399); B. Croke and J Crow, "Procopius and Dara," *JRS* 73 (1983), 143–69 argue that Procopius is highly misleading, attributing to Justinian construction for which Anastasius seems to have been responsible; L. M. Whitby, "Procopius' description of Dara (Buildings II. 1–3)," in P. Freeman and D. Kennedy, *The Defence of the Roman and Byzantine East* (Oxford, 1986), 737–83.

63 L. M. Whitby, "The Persian king at war," in E. Dabrowa, *The Roman and Byzantine Army in the East* (Krakow, 1994), 227–63.

64 On Justin I see Klaus Rosen, "Justin I," *Reallexicon für Antike und Christentum* 19 (1999), 763–78.

65 *De caer.* 1.3; see discussion by J. B. Bury, *Later Roman Empire* II (London, 1923), 15–19.

66 J. B. Bury, *The Later Roman Empire* II, 19.

67 Procopius, *Bell. Pers.* 1.1.3; 1.12.24.

68 Averil Cameron, *Procopius in the Sixty Century* (London, 1985), 13–15.

69 A. Kaldellis, *Procopius of Caesarea. Tyranny, History, and Philosophy at the End of Antiquity* (Philadelphia, 2004).

70 See B. Croke and J. Crow, "Procopius and Dara," *JRS* 73 (1983), 143–59.

71 Averil Cameron, *Procopius and the Sixth Century* (London, 1985), 49–66, especially 63–5.

72 G. Dagron, "Aux origines de la civilisation byzantine: langue de culture et langue d'état," *Revue historique* 241 (1969), 23–56.

73 G. Downey, *Constantinople in the Age of Justinian* (Oklahoma, 1960), 68–79; D. Liebs, *CAH* 14, 238–59.

74 W. Frend, *The Rise of the Monophysite Movement* (Cambridge, 1972), 284ff.

75 Michael Whitby, "John of Ephesus," in G. W. Bowersock et al. (eds.), *Late Antiquity* (Cambridge Mass., 1999), 526–7. For his mission to convert the pagans in Asia Minor, see Michael Whitby, "John of Ephesus and the pagans: Pagan survivals in the sixth century," in M. Salamon (ed.), *Paganism in the Later Roman Empire and in Byzantium* (Krakow, 1991), 111–32.

76 W. Liebeschuetz, *Barbarians and Bishops* (Oxford, 1990), 147.

77 *CAH* 14, 478, 598.

78 S. Mitchell, "An apostle to Ankara from the new Jerusalem. Jews and Montanists in late Roman Asia Minor," *Scripta Classica Israelica* 24 (2005), 207–23.

79 For a comprehensive study of the documentary evidence for Montanism in Asia Minor, see W. Tabbernnee, *Montanist Inscriptions and Testimonia. Epigraphic Sources Illustrating the History of Montanism* (Washington, 1997).

80 Alan Cameron, "The last days of the Academy at Athens," *Proceedings of the Cambridge Philological Society* 195 (1969), 7–29; Edward Watts, "Justinian, Malalas, and the end of Athenian philosophical teaching," *JRS* 94 (2004), 168–82; R. Lane Fox, "Movers and shakers," in A. Smith (ed.), *The Philosopher and Society in Late Antiquity* (Swansea, 2005), 19–50 at 32–41. R. Lane Fox, "Harran. The Sabians, and late-Platonist 'movers'," in A. Smith (ed.), *The Philosopher and Society in Late Antiquity* (Swansea, 2005), 231–44, refutes the supposition that the philosophers returned to the empire in 532 and settled at the pagan stronghold of Carrhae in Mesopotamia.

81 Malalas 17, 413–14; D. Braund, *Georgia in Antiquity* (Oxford, 1994), 271–87.

82 Malalas 18, 433–4; see J. B. Bury, *Later Roman Empire* II (London, 1923), 322–7.

83 Malalas 18, 461–5; Procopius, *Bell. Pers.* 1.17–18; see Averil Cameron, *Procopius and the Sixth Century* (London, 1985), 146–7; 157–8.

84 J. B. Bury, "The Nika riot," *JHS* 17 (1897), 92–119, is a famous and fundamental treatment, matched a century later by G. Greatrex, "The Nika riot: A reappraisal," *JHS* 117 (1997), 60–86. All the standard works on the later empire and on Justinian contain substantial discussions. The most radical modern analysis is by M. Meier, "Die Inszenierung einer Katastrophe: Justinian und der Nika-Aufstand," *ZPE* 142 (2003), 273–300.

85 G. Greatrex, *JHS* 117 (1997), 63–7.

86 Alan Cameron, *Circus Factions* (Oxford, 1976); Michael Whitby, "The violence of the circus factions," in K. Hopwood (ed.), *Organised Crime in Antiquity* (Wales, 1998), 229–53; W. Liebeschuetz, "The circus factions," *Convegno per Santo*

   Mazzarino, Roma 9–11 Maggio 1991 (Saggi di storia antica 13, 2002), 163–85; W. Liebeschuetz, *The Decline and Fall of the Roman City* (Oxford, 2001), index s.v. factions.

87 M. Meier, *ZPE* 142 (2003), 275–6.

88 R. Cormack, *CAH* 14, 902–5.

89 J. B. Bury, *Later Roman Empire* II (London, 1923), 124–50.

90 M. McCormick, *Eternal Victory. Triumphal Rulership in Late Antiquity, Byzantium and the Early Medieval West* (Cambridge, 1986), 65, 125; M. Meier, *ZPE* 138 (2002), 287.

91 Procopius, *Bell. Vand.* 4.19.3–4 summarizes his virtues, but needs to be read with a critical eye, as Procopius was a close associate and admirer of Solomon.

92 See the sculpted head reproduced by R. Browning, *Justinian and Theodora* (1971), fig. 6.

93 Procopius, *Bell. Goth.* 6.1–2. He claims to have catalogued 67 Gothic–Roman engagements up to December 536, the end of the second year of the war, which were to be followed by two final ones before the siege was lifted (*Bell. Goth.* 6.2.37–8).

5

The Roman State

The Anatomy of the Empire

In the time of Constantine the late Roman Empire was the most highly developed imperial system of the ancient world. The capacity of the emperors and their administrations to command the obedience of their subjects depended on complex and interlocking systems of governance. The most important of these was the creation of a symbolic system of authority, which presented imperial power as an inevitable part of world order. This was embodied in an ideology of rulership (*Herrschaftsideologie*). The idea of empire, based on the specific virtues and capacities which rulers possessed, was presented to the people in ritualistic and symbolic forms of action, through ceremonies, and through artistic media such as architecture and sculpture. Imperial victory was a key feature of this ruling ideology, as was the notion that emperors ruled as regents of God under divine protection. Emperors presented themselves as guarantors of the cosmic order and custodians of every aspect of their subjects' well-being.

Armies and military force preserved this order, and provided the means by which rulers could protect the interests of the empire and its inhabitants. Security, however, necessarily came at a price. Soldiers' pay and the state's other military needs required systems of taxation. Taxation, the bureaucratic equivalent of old-fashioned tribute, was one of the features that distinguished the Roman Empire from the barbarian kingdoms of the West. Empires claimed and asserted the right to levy revenue from their subjects, and the tentacles of the Roman tax system stretched across all communities.

The empire also provided a source of authority capable of resolving conflicts without resorting to violence and warfare. Emperors and their representatives acted as judges, and this entailed the existence of a system of justice, enabling subjects to bring complaints and disputes to the imperial authorities, who would be responsible for legal decisions. Such decisions might be made simply on the basis of perceived fairness, but written laws were a means by which mere transient authority was made permanent. The empire was held together by Roman law and the administration of justice.

Empires depended not only on the organizational capacity of the rulers to deploy military power, to raise taxes, and to resolve disputes in accordance with the law, but also on the willing consensus of the majority of their subjects. The people of the empire recognized its authority. Rulers and ruled had a common conception of the political system as a whole, and a shared view of what the Roman Empire stood for. This entailed the subjects' acceptance of the emperors' right to rule, which had been established over generations of historical experience. Empires fostered a collective consciousness and memory about the past.[1]

All aspects of imperial rule presupposed complex and effective systems of communication. At one level means of communication were designed for moving persons and products throughout the empire, between the peripheries and the centers, between producers and consumers, from peaceful areas to trouble spots. The state placed a high priority on building and maintaining roads, and organizing an overland transport system. Harbors, shipping, and sea transport were also essential to the empire's existence, especially to the eastern empire based on Constantinople (see below, chapter 9). However, the communication of information was even more important than the movement of men and materials. The coherence of the empire depended entirely on the reciprocal capacity of rulers and subjects to convey information and decisions to one another, both in spoken, but above all in written, form. For the empire to be governable verbal communication had to be systematically organized into recognized official channels, by which the demands and wishes of the subjects were transmitted to the authorities in provincial or imperial centers, and responses, again conforming to standard protocols, sent back and otherwise disseminated among the empire's communities.

Propaganda and Ideology

How did the Roman state meet these necessary conditions for maintaining the empire from Constantine to Justinian? The later Roman Empire relied on an elaborate ideology of rulership, which was projected in the grand style by official works of art and literature, and also at a routine level by many aspects of political communication.

A notable example drawn from political life in late antiquity, which was designed precisely to emphasize both the hierarchy of power and the ideological unity of the Roman Empire, was the use of acclamations on public occasions. These repeated, rhythmical chants were a ubiquitous phenomenon in public life. Our sources preserve detailed records of several such occasions. One was the forty-three acclamations which hailed the publication of the Theodosian Code in the Senate at Rome on December 25, 438.[2] Seventy-five acclamations greeted the appearance of a new provincial governor in Osrhoene, delivered on behalf of the city of Edessa in April 449.[3] Twenty acclamations, perhaps of the early sixth century, which were subsequently inscribed on columns at Aphrodisias in Caria, were delivered in honor of a prominent local citizen and benefactor, Albinus.[4] A remarkable acclamatory dialogue was staged in the hippodrome of Constantinople during the events of the Nika riot between members of the Green and Blue factions and a speaker for the emperor Justinian.[5] Acclamations took a distinctive ritualized form, although their wording was naturally appropriate for the particular occasion that they celebrated. They began with an invocation to God, and followed this immediately with good wishes for the emperor's health and long life, for his continued rule and for his victories. These then normally led to acclamations on behalf of the Senate, of the great state officeholders, and of imperial officials. A law of 380 explicitly indicated that a group of senior civilian officials, namely the *quaestores sacri palatii*, the *magistri officiorum*, and the *comites utriusque aerarii*, were entitled to be hailed by acclamations, as were the praetorian prefects (*CTh.* 6.9.2). Acclamations on major state occasions might be delivered either in the presence of the emperor, or, much more frequently, in his absence. They were delivered by groups gathered for such occasions, and thus symbolically expressed the wishes of the whole people. These rituals, repeated across the empire on countless occasions, echoed not only the ideology but the power structure of the Roman Empire, and were designed to validate the role of the emperors at the summit of the imperial hierarchy of authority.[6]

The standardized formulae of acclamations had their written counterparts in all official documentation of the state's activities. The imperial titles at the beginning of public inscriptions and other documents embodied the message that the powers of the emperor were eternal and unchallengeable. At the same time they differentiated between individual rulers. The images and wording used on imperial coinage were conceived in the same way. They identified the particular ruler responsible for issuing the coinage by using a coded pattern of symbols that linked him to his predecessors. A coin could thus be identified in the first instance as an imperial issue, and then as that of a particular emperor. The charisma of the divinely appointed rulers was thus routinized, but their authority was not diminished. Panegyric oratory promoted the idea of imperial rulership in a more sophisticated way, but conformed to similar principles. While individual speeches were tailored to the achievements and policies of particular rulers, they drew on a repertoire of themes that characterized the role of all just and righteous rulers. One of the most significant developments of this imperial ideology was the gradual integration of Christian ideas within a tradition that had its origins in classical ideas about kingship. However, apart from the late works of Eusebius, his *Tricennial Oration* and the *Life of Constantine*, which develop an original and new ideology of Christian rulership,[7] it is striking that overt Christian symbolism is remarkably absent both from the panegyrics written for fourth-century rulers, and from the monuments set up for them.

Christian symbolism also played only a limited role in the public art of the fourth century. This point is demonstrated by two of the most elaborate imperial monuments of the period; the arch of Constantine in Rome, and the sculpted reliefs on the base of the obelisk set up by Theodosius I in the hippodrome at Constantinople.

Constantine's arch, set up next to the Colosseum by the Roman Senate and people, honored the emperor at his *decennalia* in 315, on the occasion of the tenth anniversary of his becoming Augustus (Plate 5.1). It is instructive to distinguish the general from the specific message conveyed by its famous decorative reliefs. Recent research has shown that the arch was not originally designed for Constantine. Foundations appear to have been laid in the early empire for a structure that was never built. The realization of the plan was taken in hand by Maxentius, during the five-year period from 307–12, when he claimed the title of Augustus and was effective ruler of Italy and Africa. Two-thirds of the building, as far as the lofty *attica*, wholly constructed from spolia, and including the famous series of re-used imperial relief tondos and panels, had been completed before Maxentius' death in 312. The Constantinian portion consists of the attic story, which was made from brick and merely faced with marble cladding. This includes the prominent dedicatory inscription, and the statues of barbarians, placed at the top of the pilasters of the façade. In addition, a one-meter-high frieze was slung like a girdle round the piers of the arch, and depicted the victories of Constantine in the campaign against Maxentius, his *adventus* into the city of Rome, and his address and liberalities to the people (Plate 5.2). Above the frieze at the west and east ends, two tondos were added by the Constantinian sculptors, one showing the Sun god, the other the Moon goddess. The design of the frieze was essentially conventional. It combined the themes of the emperor's triumph over a usurper, his civility towards Rome's

Plate 5.1 The Arch of Constantine at Rome (DAI Rome)

dignitaries, and his generosity towards the Roman *plebs*, and portrayed them in
the visual equivalent of a panegyric speech. The Constantinian carving is often
crude and schematic, but this is in part due to the fact that the sculptors had
to work on scaffolding *in situ*, rather than prepare their work in a workshop
beforehand. The aesthetic and visual impact of the Constantinian frieze is overshadowed by the program designed for Maxentius. This involved the selection
and re-use of eight great circular tondos from a monument built for Hadrian,
all showing the emperor in scenes of hunting or sacrifice, another set of Antonine
friezes, perhaps for Marcus Aurelius, displaying the emperor engaged in a further
sequence of great public occasions, which were placed in the *attica*, and two
enormous frieze blocks, placed on either side of the central passageway, from
a monument for Trajan, with scenes of a battle and of the victorious emperor.
The redeployment of these earlier sculptures, which must already have been
familiar to Roman viewers, deliberately evoked the new emperor's place in the
succession of great rulers of the past, but it is of course important to realize
that the new emperor for whom they were originally designed was Maxentius.
Constantine saw fit to inherit all the essentials of his predecessor's design,
before he (or his advisors) devised the new frieze which commemorated the

Plate 5.2 The Arch of Constantine. Constantine (the head is missing), seated, surrounded by members of his court, distributes largesse to members of the Roman aristocracy, who are depicted wearing the heavy togas of Roman citizens (DAI Rome)

overthrow of the usurper. The only modification to the early imperial sculptures was to re-fashion the imperial heads into the likenesses of Constantine and his father Constantius. We see precisely the same affirmation of the legitimacy of imperial rulership in the comparisons that writers of the fourth century made between the emperors of their day and their illustrious predecessors. The arch and its sculptural program signified the embodiment of Roman power in the person of the emperor and the ritual authority of the principate itself. The achievements of Constantine were subsumed in this larger picture.[8]

The Theodosian base in Constantinople presents another strategy. The twenty-meter-high obelisk was erected on the central *spina* of the hippodrome to commemorate the victory of Theodosius I over another usurper, the *tyrannus* Magnus Maximus (Plate 5.3). One set of reliefs, on the lower part of the socle, showed scenes of chariot racing, pantomimes, and dancers, as well as a vivid representation of the laborious transport and setting-up of the obelisk itself. The main pictorial program was displayed on the upper part of the base. The four sides of the monument displayed the emperor in a series of key symbolic relationships. On two of them he appears seated in the loggia which overlooked the arena, accompanied by the other family members with whom he shared power; Valentinian II, and his designated successors Arcadius and Honorius.

Plate 5.3 The obelisk of Theodosius I, erected on its decorated base in the hippodrome at Constantinople. The later church of St Sophia is in the background (DAI Istanbul)

Plate 5.4 The Theodosian Base in the Hippodrome, front side, depicting musicians and dancers below the imperial loggia (DAI Istanbul)

In both these scenes the emperors were variously accompanied by high civilian and military dignitaries and by members of the armed imperial bodyguards. They thus represent the ruling heart of the empire. However, it is equally important that the reliefs also depict packed rows of spectators, the common people of the city, who in this context represented the mass of the emperor's subjects. In reality, after the fourth century, contact between the emperor and the common people was largely restricted to ritualized moments such as this one. The base of the Theodosian obelisk is the first monument to depict the crucial encounter of the east Roman ruler with his people in the hippodrome (Plate 5.4).[9] The stone monument thus mirrored in idealized form the actual encounters between the ruler and his subjects which took place in the same location. By including the most important members of the imperial family and leading figures of the state, the monument asserts the legitimacy and authority of the whole dynasty.

These two monuments carry only the barest hints of Christianity. The inscription on the Arch of Constantine contains the famously ambiguous phrase *instinctu divinitatis*, "by the impulsion of a divinity," to allude to the divine help which Constantine acknowledged had been behind his victory over Maxentius.

The Theodosian base depicts a solitary military standard, decorated with the Christian *labarum* (the *chi-rho* sign) beside the imperial box on the northeast side. In this respect there is a marked contrast with an equally famous monument from the early part of Justinian's reign, the surviving panel of the carved diptych, now in the Louvre, known as the Barberini ivory (Plate 5.5). This was

Plate 5.5   The Barberini ivory (Louvre, Paris)

not a great public monument, but an infinitely precious miniature, akin in style to the exquisite ivory diptychs which were commissioned to commemorate the holders of the consulship in late antiquity.[10] The central panel shows the imperious figure of the emperor, on his rearing horse, ramming his lance into the ground, in a gesture of triumphant conquest. He is attended by figures representing a barbarian, Victory, and Mother Earth. The panel to the left of this (and doubtless also its lost counterpart on the right) showed a bare-headed official presenting him with a statue of victory. The narrow frieze along the base shows further barbarian subjects bringing offerings of a basket of grain, a wreath, and an ivory tusk, as well as a lion and a panther. The whole composition is best interpreted as a symbolic representation of the reconquest of Africa. The iconography of these panels developed classical themes of triumphal rulership, but the upper frieze emphatically manifested the religious ideology, which Justinian himself had introduced into all representations of imperial power. In front of a tondo held up by two angels it depicts the bust of Christ, holding his right hand in a gesture of blessing over the emperor.[11] This explicit acknowledgment of God's might and guiding authority is characteristic of almost all forms of official communication under Justinian, but it is important to recognize that this is also an innovation of this period.

There is a further instructive contrast to be made between this image of the emperor, triumphant in battle, and the dedication mosaic of the Church of S. Vitale in Ravenna, dating to 548. This shows the emperor carrying a basket of offerings. To his left is bishop Maximinus, founder of the church, and three bare-headed clergy, to his right are two civilian courtiers and four armed soldiers of the bodyguard, standing behind an oval shield, decorated with the *labarum* (Plate 5.6). The overall impression is now devotional, not triumphant, and was determined not only by the ecclesiastical context of the mosaic, but also by the change in the political atmosphere during the later part of Justinian's reign.

The symbolic system and visual language of power, which is to be found in all late Roman imperial iconography, was also adopted and manipulated with an equal sureness of touch by the rival empire of the Sassanians. A magnificent series of rock monuments from the central areas of the Persian Empire in the third century depicts the rulers in attitudes of triumph over foreign enemies, piety towards their supreme god Ahura-Mazda, and authority over the courtiers and officials that surrounded them. The finest and best-known of these reliefs date to the third century and depict Sapor I, victor over three Roman emperors, and the mightiest ruler of the third century AD, commanding the twin worlds of Persia and Rome, "king of the Arians and the Non-Arians" as his inscriptions describe him. However, it is also instructive to compare another set of reliefs from Taq-e Bostan in northwest Persia, which probably dates to the reign of Khusro II, the rival of Heraclius in the early seventh century. The main panel depicts the king, clad in heavy armor, astride his warhorse (Plate 5.7). Above this he is shown again, being crowned by the divinity, the great god Ahura-Mazda, on whose protection the state depended, and accompanied by a female figure, presumably his royal consort, who is shown holding the severed

Plate 5.6 Church of S. Vitale, Ravenna. The mosaic depicts the emperor Justinian, surrounded by clergy, including the bishop of Ravenna, Maximinus, who is identified by the inscription, with three soldiers of the palace guard, their shields displaying the *labarum* (DAI Rome)

head of one of his enemies. The whole composition, a wall of sculpture five meters high, is recessed in an arched vault. At the front the tondos of the arch carry winged victory figures that mirror the pose of the angels on the Barberini ivory.[12] The overall composition of this great rock monument of late Sassanian Iran is strikingly similar to the Justinianic ivory miniature.

Military Security

The emperors had absolute power and authority, and ruled by means of an elaborate bureaucratic system. This need not be described or analyzed in detail, a task that has been done with unmatchable authority by A. H. M. Jones in *The Later Roman Empire*. One important feature of the system was the functional division between civilian administration and military command. The main army commands were now given to the "masters of soldiers" (*magistri militum*), and to other senior commanders including "counts" (*comes*) and "dukes" (*duces*), who were subordinate to them. These headed the complex and fluid structure of the late Roman armies.

Plate 5.7 Taq-e Bostan. The Sassanian king, Khusro II, clad in heavy armor, mounted on his war horse. Khusro II was Rome's nemesis during the first twenty years of the seventh century, bent on a policy of destroying the Roman Empire (S. Mitchell)

The pattern of Roman military organization was considerably complicated by the regional division of the empire. When the empire was divided between two or more emperors, each was at the head of his own military hierarchy, and this multiplied the number of offices. Lactantius made the famous charge that by creating the tetrarchy Diocletian quadrupled the size of the Roman army, thereby creating an intolerable tax burden on the civilian population (*On the Deaths of the Persecutors* 7.2). This cannot be literally true. There is a tendency both in the ancient sources and in modern scholarship to exaggerate the size of the Roman armies in late antiquity. The sixth-century bureaucrat John Lydus claimed that Diocletian's army numbered 435,266 soldiers and sailors (John Lydus, *de mens.* 1.27), and Zosimus reckoned that in 312 the combined forces of the western empire alone numbered 286,000 (Zosimus 2.15). The *Notitia Dignitatum*, which reflects the putative conditions around 400 in the East and the 425 in the West, has been interpreted to suggest troop numbers as high as 600,000.[13] However, these high figures contrast with the actual numbers given for troops engaged in major campaigns, especially after the end of the fourth century, when overall Roman military capacity became appreciably weaker than it had been. Procopius, for instance, says that the largest army ever to fight the Persians was assembled by Anastasius in 502 (Procopius, *Bell. Pers.* 1.8.4). The well informed *Chronicle* of Ps-Joshua the Stylite puts the figure for this force at 52,000 (Ps-Joshua, *Chron.* 54). Agathias

Military Commanders				
Magister Militum (*Oriens*) Usually based at Antioch	*Magister Militum praesentalis equitum* (cavalry, Constantinople)	*Magister Militum praesentalis peditum* (infantry, Constantinople)	*Magister Militum* (*Thrace*) Usually based at Marcianopolis?	*Magister Militum* (*Illyricum*) Usually based at Thessalonica
Bucellarii (mounted guards of the commander, about 15,000 troops in total)				
Comitatenses (mobile field armies, about 150,000 troops in total)				
Limitanei (frontier garrisons, up to 400,000 troops in total)				

Diagram 5.1   The Roman high command and the military structure

observed that in its weakened state at the end of Justinian's reign the army numbered only 150,000 and was no longer equal to the task of defending the empire (Agathias 5.13). This figure seems broadly credible for the mobile field armies, although it does not account for the sedentary frontier garrisons.[14] At all events it is important to draw a distinction between overall military numbers, which included the regional garrisons of *limitanei*, and the much smaller figures which represent the manpower available for active campaigning (Diagram 5.1).

The units of the late Roman army fell into three main categories.[15] The *limitanei* were garrison troops, who resided in the frontier areas of the provinces. They contrasted with the *comitatenses*, the mobile field armies, which accompanied the emperors on campaign during the fourth century and were available for expeditionary deployment later, and the *palatini*, units which were attached to the forces that were based in the imperial capitals themselves, especially at Constantinople. In the fifth and sixth centuries their counterparts in the field armies were elite bodies of troops with personal connections to the commanders, who were informally known as *bucellarii*, after the baked biscuit which was the staple military ration. However, it is unlikely that the distinction between these categories was completely clear cut, and the field units certainly made up numbers from the frontier garrison units when need arose. The field armies also drew their recruits to an increasing degree from barbarians, who thus became integrated into Roman forces.

Rome made military use of barbarians in numerous ways.[16] Barbarians who were taken captive as a result of Roman campaigning during the fourth century were often resettled in small groups in frontier areas. They were known as *Laeti* and were liable to be enlisted or press-ganged into army service.[17] In 382 the Goths in Thrace were offered the status of allies, *foederati*, by treaty with the Romans, which enabled them to retain their own social structures and tribal leadership. It was even more significant that the most important military leaders in the western empire in the fifth century had large personal followings of barbarian soldiers. These included Stilicho, who commanded 35,000 federate followers at his death in 408 (Zosimus 5.35.6). According to Olympiodorus,

Constantius, the western general who became Augustus in 421, had a large retinue of barbarian soldiers, which he bequeathed to Placidia, Honorius' sister (Olympiodorus fr. 38). Other major military figures of the first half of the fourth century were Bonifatius, who attempted to mount a usurpation from Africa supported by Gothic federates (Possidius, *Life of Augustine*, 18), and above all Aetius, whose political predominance in the West between the 430s and the 450s was due to the large following of Hunnic mercenaries that he could command.[18] They were followed in the next generation by Marcellinus, whose power base was in Dalmatia, and above all by Ricimer, the kingmaker of the western empire in the third quarter of the fifth century.[19] It is important to note that these warlords were only influential in the western part of the empire. Their actions contributed as much as anything to the collapse of Roman authority in the West. In the East, even during the grievous instability of the Isaurian dynasty of Leo and Zeno, generals with private armies never took control of the civil hierarchy. Under Justinian Belisarius is reported to have been accompanied by a retinue of 7,000 barbarian horseman (Procopius, *Bell. Goth.* 7.1.19–20). Procopius, however, only drew attention to this huge retinue in the context of Justinian's decision, which was unchallenged, to deny his general the opportunity to parade in a second triumph.

The exact terms under which barbarians were recruited were evidently fluid and flexible, and Procopius indicates that by the sixth century federate troops included many soldiers who might previously have been classified as Romans.[20]

> Now at an earlier time only barbarians who were enlisted among the *foederati*, those, namely, who had come into the Roman political system not in the condition of slaves, since they had not been conquered by the Romans, but on the basis of complete equality. For the Romans call treaties with their enemies *foedera*. But at the present time there is nothing to prevent anyone from assuming this name. (Procopius, *Bell. Vand.* 3.11.3–4, trans. Dewing)

Some groups of barbarians operated within Roman army structures; others, especially those with strong and effective leaders of their own, have the appearance of free agents. The latter could be a serious threat to the internal security of the state, if their leaders chose to defy the orders of their political masters, as was clear in the cases of Alaric and Gainas at the beginning of the fifth century, and of Theoderic the Amal and Theoderic Strabo in the time of Zeno; but in general these barbarian troops were effective, well trained for war, and probably posed no greater problems of discipline than Roman troops. The *Chronicle* of Ps-Joshua the Stylite provides graphic detail of the abusive behavior of Gothic troops quartered in Edessa during Anastasius' Persian campaign, but their behavior was not significantly worse than that of Roman troops billeted on civilian populations at other times and places (Ps-Joshua, *Chron.* 93–95).

These diverse categories of the Roman army were all supported by the state systems of military pay, provisioning, and transport. The armies were able to provide security across the huge area of the empire thanks to their mobility and the logistic infrastructure that supported them. Rome's military capacity was

built on an extraordinary communication system, which was capable of conveying information, manpower, arms, and provisions between its regions. On
land there was an engineering miracle, the road system, and its administrative
counterpart, the organization of state transport liturgies, which were provided
by local communities. Although inscribed milestones become rare after the fourth
century, the literary evidence, notably of Procopius in *Buildings*, indicates that
at least the major roads were maintained until the mid-sixth century, and the
Justinianic law code indicates that the system for requisitioning official transport continued to function at this period (*CJust.* 12.11.1–23). The supposed
collapse of this system, and the replacement of wheeled transport by camels,
has been suggested as a major reason for the Islamic conquest of much of the
eastern empire in the seventh century, but this remains contentious.[21]

The passage of rulers, officials, and soldiers along the roads of the empire had
a huge impact on provincial life in the later empire. Fourth-century emperors
were constantly on the move between the empire's trouble spots. It has been
estimated that Diocletian throughout his years as emperor must have moved
an average ten miles every day, a statistic that makes the praise of his tireless
care of the empire a fully comprehensible feature of the panegyrics of the age.
Emperors were accompanied by a large entourage of advisors and officials, and
of course by military units, amounting to several hundreds of people, and the
demands made by these traveling administrations were immense. The complex
preparations and demands that were necessary on such occasions are vividly
illustrated by a dossier of correspondence from Panopolis in the Thebaid
(Upper Egypt), involving the procurator of the lower Thebaid *nome* (the senior
Roman regional official), who was issuing requisitioning orders in advance
of the imperial visit, the *strategos* in charge of the district of Panopolis, and
the president of the local council. The local population had to be organized to
provide food equipment, transport, and billeting. Perhaps the most extraordinary aspect of the whole business is the intensity of written communication that
it generated. This included not merely the surviving correspondence between
the principal players, but the plethora of requisitioning orders, accounts,
receipts, and other paperwork that the correspondence implies.[22] One consequence of the growing emphasis on the official use of the road system was
that the communication network itself, rather than the cities that it connected,
became a main focus for imperial attention.[23] Road stations (*mansiones*) were a
prominent feature of the imperial landscape, and could become the focal point
of substantial settlements. The finest archaeological example of this phenomenon in the eastern Roman Empire is the *mansio* at the foot of the pass that
carries the main road from Pamphylia in southern Asia Minor into the interior
at the Döşeme Boğazı (Plate 5.8).[24] The structure, measuring about twenty
by thirty meters and secured from the exterior by lockable doors, had a suite of
substantial rooms adjoining a courtyard, where pack animals could be unloaded
and stabled. It stood immediately beside the main highway, but was not
isolated. Around it was a cluster of stone houses, cemeteries, and at least two
churches. This is the archaeological counterpart of a road station that is well

Plate 5.8   The *Mansio* beside the Roman road that ran through the Döseme Boğazı in southern Turkey from the Pamphylian plain to the interior of Asia Minor (S. Mitchell)

documented in the literary record, the birthplace and home of the Galatian saint Theodore, which lay at Sykeon, on the border between Bithynia and Galatia on the main road that led across Asia Minor from Constantinople to Syria.[25] As land communications between the eastern and western parts of the empire became less secure in the fifth century, maritime communication was a factor of increasing significance. Constantinople depended on the sea, and by the sixth century maritime transport both of goods and troops had become more important than land communications. Shipbuilding and the maintenance of secure harbors were both essential to the success of the late Roman state (see below, chapter 10).

All forms of state activity, but above all army costs, were supported directly or indirectly by Roman taxation. Most Roman taxation was related to land and landownership. Agriculture was the largest economic activity in the empire, and land was the most important reservoir of invested wealth. By contrast city-dwellers paid much less tax, often none at all. There were vigorous protests in the time of the tetrarchy, when Diocletian and his colleagues conducted new censuses and attempted to levy an urban poll tax throughout the empire in order to meet the budgetary requirements of the state, which had been rigorously calculated.[26] Later levies on the income of urban craftsmen were similarly unpopular.

There is general agreement that one of the achievements of Diocletian was to reform the entire Roman taxation system and place it on a more unified basis. Theoretically, at least, universal censuses were conducted at fifteen-year intervals. These counted and registered individuals for the poll tax, and assessed their property, in terms of quantity and quality, for the land tax. The outcome in the early fourth century was a general system of assessment known as *iugatio-capitatio*. The empire's subjects were liable to provide levies in kind, known as *indictiones*, and compulsory labor for state projects (*operae*), as well as money contributions. Both types of contribution could be commuted into cash. The fifteen-year census period was known as the indiction cycle. One indication of the universal impact of Roman authority in the late empire is the very common use of indiction years as a way of dating documents, including funerary inscriptions, throughout the eastern empire in the fifth and sixth centuries. The tax system was put into practice by a very large number of minor and middle-ranking officials in the capitals and throughout the provinces, under the overall supervision of the praetorian prefects. No ancient source survives to explain the principles or general procedures of Roman taxation, and our understanding of the details of the system is based on often uncertain inferences from individual tax documents, or from passing references in the historical sources. This creates an impression of great complexity, but in general the tax system of the later Roman Empire appears to have been simpler and more rational than it had been in the Augustan period. This is partly due to the systematic organization which Diocletian and his successors brought to the problem, and partly to the fact that tax collection was now almost exclusively handled by imperial officials, rather than being a task delegated to city administrations, as it had been during the early empire.

Tax was always felt as an imposition by those who paid it. The inhabitants of the empire frequently sought tax remission at an individual or a community level, and this was one of the commonest forms of benefaction that emperors could confer on their subjects. The impact of taxation at a local level, and the ways in which burdens were alleviated by an imperial benefaction are well illustrated by the *Chronicle* of Ps-Joshua the Stylite, concerning the city and territory of Edessa in Osrhoene around 500. The *Chronicle*'s entry for the year 497/8 is dominated by the report that the emperor Anastasius had issued an edict which remitted the tax paid by artisans and manufacturers, the *chrysargyron*.[27] The decision was proclaimed in all the cities of the empire. The Edessenes had hitherto paid 140 pounds of gold every four years.

> The whole city rejoiced, and they all put on white garments, both small and great, and carried lighted tapers and censers full of burning incense, and went forth with psalms and hymns, praising the emperor, to the martyr church of St Sergius and St Simeon, where they celebrated the eucharist. They then re-entered the city and kept a glad and merry festival during the whole week, and enacted that they should celebrate this festival every year. All the artisans were reclining and enjoying themselves, bathing and feasting in the court of the church and in all the porticoes of the city. (Ps-Joshua, *Chron.* 31, trans. Wright)

In 499/500 the territory of Edessa was devastated by locust infestations. Peter, the metropolitan bishop, undertook an embassy to the emperor at Constantinople to ask for remission of the land and poll tax, the *synteleia*, but this did not prevent the provincial governor from using violence against the local landowners to extract the contribution that was due and sending it to Anastasius. The emperor kept the tax, but agreed to a remission of two *folles* per head by the villagers, while city dwellers were freed from the obligation to draw water for the Greek garrison (Ps-Joshua, *Chron.* 39). In 500/1 the food shortage continued. Villagers were reduced to eating bitter vetch or withered grapes in the countryside, or crowded in to beg in the city, gleaning scraps of vegetables from the filthy streets. The governor, Demosthenes, reported the famine conditions in person to the emperor, and brought back with him a considerable sum which was used to obtain bread for the city's relief. But disaster could not be avoided and deaths from famine and disease through the winter from November to March ran at 100–130 per day. The harvest gathered in June and July 501 brought some respite (40–44).

During this period edicts also reached Edessa from Anastasius concerning entertainments. The first, in August 499, addressed to all the Greek cities of the empire, abolished wild beast shows (*kynegia*) in the amphitheater (34). The second, which arrived in May 502, made dancers (*orchestai*) illegal (46). In October 502 the Persian king Kavad launched an offensive against the Roman Empire and laid siege to Amida, while his Arab ally Na'mân attacked the region of Carrhae (Harran) and Edessa. Anastasius refused to meet the Persian demands for money and sent Greek forces to the cities of the region. The people of Edessa were ordered to bake 630,000 *modii* of bread for the troops at their own cost, although it seems that the flour was mostly brought in by the army from Egypt. In December 503 an edict came from Anastasius to remit the land and poll tax, the *synteleia* (66). In May 504 more wheat was brought to Edessa to be made into bread for the soldiers by the local people (850,000 *modii*). The conditions of war caused extreme famine, which led even to cannibalism in Amida, which had been occupied by the Persians, but the Roman troops in Mesopotamia received their supplies.

> To the Greek troops, however, nought was lacking, but everything was supplied to them in its season, and came down with great care by order of the emperor. Indeed the things that were sold in the camps were more abundant than in the cities, whether meat or drink or shoes or clothing. All the cities were baking soldiers' bread (*boukellaton*) by their bakers, and sending it to them, especially the Edessenes; for the citizens baked in their own houses this year too, by order of Calliopius the hyparch, 630,000 *modii*, besides what the villagers baked throughout the whole district, and the bakers, both the strangers and natives. (Ps-Joshua, *Chron.* 77)

During this year (504/5) Mar Peter, the bishop, again went to the emperor to ask him to remit the tax (*synteleia*). The emperor rebuked him for having neglected the charge of the poor in bringing the petition, saying that God himself would have put it into his heart, if it had been right, without anyone persuading him, to do a favor to the blessed city. However, while the bishop was still in Constantinople, he authorized the remission of taxes for all Mesopotamia. He also remitted one-third of the taxes of the district of Mabbôg-Hierapolis (78). His conduct is consistent with an edict issued in 496 that all tax reductions were to be authorized by Anastasius in person (*CJust.* 10.16.13).

These extracts, written by a well-informed author about events which he had witnessed himself, serve to illustrate how the empire was governed in practice. Major initiatives can be traced back to the emperor himself. The decision to abolish the *chrysargyron*, a tax on urban manufacture, was greeted at Edessa, as elsewhere, with unfeigned enthusiasm. His successor Justin commended Anastasius for his skill at working to a tight budget (*CJust.* 2.7.25 pr.), and the contemporary panegyrics of Priscian and Procopius of Gaza are full of praise for his fiscal and financial competence. On the other hand the orders to abolish wild-beast shows and pantomime performances are evidence of his puritanical religious predilections. The role of the provincial governor revealed here was to ensure that taxes were collected in full, even to the extent of using violence to extract them. No doubt he would have been held accountable for any shortfall. The emperor might choose to be generous, but this was not a liberty permitted to his servants.

Remissions were obtained by petitioning the emperor. The narrative indicates that there were two spokesmen of sufficient status to achieve the desired results. One was the provincial governor himself, Demosthenes, who successfully obtained a grant-in-aid from the emperor for the city during the second year of an acute famine, which caused very high mortality. The other was the city's bishop, who undertook two embassies in five years to Constantinople, on each occasion to ask for remission of the city's *synteleia*, that is the composite land and poll tax of its inhabitants.

The passage also provides dramatic evidence of the impact of war. The Sassanian king declared war on the empire as a result of Anastasius' decision to discontinue the subsidy which the Romans paid to the Persians to maintain the Caucasus garrison against the Huns. Such decisions were the outcome of international politics at the highest level. The consequences, however, were felt locally, in the Mesopotamian frontier area, which not only suffered from the enemy invasion (Amida was occupied after a Persian siege), but also from the consequences of Roman mobilization. Edessa provided provisions and billets for the mainly Gothic troops of the field army that had been sent to the front. Baking bread for the army became a task for every household as well as for the professional bakers. As we have seen their efforts were poorly repaid by the indiscipline and abuses of the soldiers (see above). It required another Episcopal petition, employing tact rather than indignation, to gain tax relief in compensation for this.

Ruling the Empire

The structure of the central administration essentially comprised a supreme authority, the emperor, and his chief ministers, who operated within strict

Praetorian Prefect of Illyricum (Thessalonica)			Praetorian Prefect of the East (Constantinople)		
Office of the Dioeceses (*Scrinia Dioecesum*)					
Illyricum	Thracica	Asiana	Pontica	Oriens	Aegyptiaca
Provinces					
Macedonia I	Europa	Asia	Bithynia	Cilicia I	Aegyptus
Macedonia II	Rhodopa	Hellespontus	Honorias	Cilicia II	Augustamnica I
Thessalia	Thracia	Phrygia Pacatiana	Paphlagonia	Cyprus	Augustamnica II
Hellas	Haemimontus	Lydia	Galatia I	Isauria	Arcadia (Heptanomia)
Creta	Mysia II	Pisidia	Galatia Salutaris	Syria I	Thebais Inferior
Palaea Epirus	Scythia	Lycaonia	Cappadocia I	Syria II	Thebais Superior
Nea Epirus		Phrygia Salutaris	Cappadocia II	Euphratensis	Libya Superior
Dacia Mediterranea		Lycia	Helenopontus	Osrhoene	Libya Inferior
Dacia Ripensis		Insulae Cycladum	Pontus Polemoniacus	Mesopotamia	
Dardania		Caria	Armenia I	Phoenicia	
Mysia I			Armenia II	Phoenicia Libanensis	
Pannonia				Palaestina I	
				Palaestina II	
				Palaestina III	
				Arabia	

Diagram 5.2 Praetorian prefectures, dioceses, and provinces under Justinian (after R. Talbert [ed.], *The Barrington Atlas of the Greek and Roman World* [Princeton, 2000], 102, and A. H. M. Jones, *The Later Roman Empire* II, 1456–61)

procedures and protocols. This pattern was replicated locally by the governors of provinces, and the vicars in charge of the dioceses of the empire (Diagram 5.2). The former were for the most part simply designated by the term iudex, judge, which indicated the most important aspect of their duties. Both at the capital and in the provincial centers magistrates were supported by a substantial staff of lawyers and other advisors. To a very large degree political decisions were

Emperor			
[Senators]	[Prefect of the city (Constantinople)]	Cabinet (*consistorium*)	
Master of Offices (*magister officiorum*)	Chief legal officer and imperial spokesman (*quaestor sacri palatii*)	Minister for imperial expenditure (*comes largitionum sacrarum*)	Imperial chamberlain (*praepositus sacro cubiculo*)
Palace guard (*scholae Palatinae et excubitorum*)		Minister for imperial property (*comes rei privatae*)	
Imperial agents and couriers (*schola agentum in rebus*)		Minister for imperial revenues (*comes patrimonii*)	
Legal officers and administrators (*schola notariorum*)			
Archives (*scrinia memoriae*)			
Correspondence (*scrinia epistularum*)			
Petitions (*scrinia libellorum*)			
Logistics (*scrinia dispositionum*)			
Weapons and armouries (*fabricae*)			
State transport (*cursus publicus*)			

Diagram 5.3   The organization of civilian government at Constantinople (after D. Feissel, in C. Morrisson [ed.], *Le monde byzantin* I [2004], 79–110)

made in passive mode, as responses to petitions and letters which were addressed by individuals or communities, sometimes via provincial governors or other officials, to the central authorities. At the highest level the power of decision resided with the emperor in person, who was supported by the ever expanding entourage of the imperial court, a centralized and largely civilian administration, which during the fourth century accompanied the rulers on their travels or was based in the regional capitals of the empire. In the East, during the fifth and sixth centuries, these officials were concentrated in the imperial city of Constantinople, which was home to a very large population of highly educated civil servants, responsible for articulating the emperor's decisions (Diagram 5.3).

A remarkable, newly published inscription from the site of Didyma, renamed Justinianopolis, in western Asia Minor illustrates the mechanics of the imperial bureaucracy, and the elaborate procedural dance that was played out by subjects and officials (Plate 5.9). The matter in question concerned the community's

Plate 5.9 Didyma. Inscribed rescript of Justinian of 533 (DAI Berlin)

land tax. In 533 the people of Didyma, which had recently been promoted to civic status and received the name Justinianopolis, requested that their annual land tax of sixty-one gold pieces should be made the responsibility of their large neighbor Miletus, and levied out of the income produced by land that had been newly reclaimed from the sea, as a result of the progressive silting in the lower Maeander valley. Six main steps can be identified in securing this imperial favor, four of which were directly recorded on the inscription. The people of Justinianopolis submitted a petition to the main financial official of the eastern empire, the praefectus praetorio Orientis, who at this time was Justinian's famous minister, John the Cappadocian. The prefect, who evidently approved the request, then presented the petition in the form of a report to the emperor. Justinian responded on April 1, 533, by granting the favor with a legal enactment called a "divine pragmatic sanction." On the following day (extraordinary testimony to the vigilant efficiency of Justinian's government in his early years), the imperial decision was officially adopted at a formal meeting of the office of the prefect, and endorsed not only by the prefect of the East but also by his fellow prefects, who were responsible for Illyricum and for Italy (which was still, at this date under Ostrogothic rule), and by an Augustalis, another official responsible for financial administration in Asia. The ruling was then sent to the governor of the province of Caria, to which Justinianopolis belonged, who added his own instructions for the enforcement of the imperial decision. The inscribed dossier, which was erected by the beneficiaries themselves, combines Greek and Latin language and script in a way that is typical of late Roman bureaucracy. Even more striking to the reader than the complex interplay of official languages is the use of a particular form of Latin lettering for the heading of the record of the formal meeting in the prefect's office. This is visible in the middle of the photograph. This style of script can be identified as the so-called "heavenly letters" (*litterae caelestes*), used on papyrus documents for the headings of similar official documents which have been recovered both from fifth-century Egypt and from late sixth-century Ravenna.

The Didyma inscription presents the maturation and distillation of Roman government in action, more than half a millennium after the basic practices of imperial rule had been forged in the early principate.[28] It is extremely significant that by the time of Justinian the center of power had been fixed in one location, Constantinople, for nearly 150 years, a period which had seen the growth of a highly unified and centralized style of government, explicitly based on universal law, which responded, in theory at least, to the needs and demands of the subjects.[29] The central archives of the empire were now literally housed in the vault beneath the seats of the hippodrome, adjacent to the imperial palace, an enormous repository of bureaucratic power.[30] The term "Byzantine" in the popular imagination has come to mean a tortuous, abstruse, and devious style of government. The facts of the matter were quite the reverse. Roman government in the sixth century AD was more rationally organized than it had ever been. The imperial decisions themselves formed part of a growing corpus of Roman law. The lawyers and rulers of the later empire were increasingly aware of the need to codify these decisions, which in turn served to guide the judgments of their successors. Roman civil law was first systematically organized under the tetrarchy, but these codes were eclipsed by the *Codex Theodosianus*, completed for Theodosius II in 437/8, and the code of Justinian, published in a revised edition in 533. This body of written laws became increasingly important as the explicit basis of judicial decisions (see above, chapter 4).[31]

High standards were expected of public officials, and many chapters of the *Codex Justinianus* set out regulations and an overall code of conduct. In 479 the emperor Zeno addressed a law to the praetorian prefect of the East, which required that all officials with judicial powers, that is the top ranks of the administration, should remain accessible in the place where they had exercised their office for a minimum of fifty days, "so that every one may have ample opportunity to file complaints against them, for theft or for other crimes; and that everyone may be defended from injury by his successor." Under these circumstances civil litigation concerning officials had to be concluded within the fifty days, but officials facing criminal charges had to remain in their province indefinitely, until the case was concluded (*CJust.* 1.39.1, 3). It is particularly striking that legislation of this type was being introduced during one of the most lawless and anarchic periods of the eastern empire, as Zeno strove to retain his authority in the face of rival claimants to power. It is easy to be skeptical about the claims to probity which are embodied in the evidence of the laws, but the ideology of good governance and justice was internalized by the officials themselves. This is clearly demonstrated by the language of inscriptions and the iconography of the statues which were set up in their honor, but also at their expense, in provincial cities.[32]

The growing importance of Roman law as a central institution of the empire was related directly to the spread and growth of Roman citizenship. Citizenship had been the most important institution of the early Roman Empire for creating a sense of communal identity and ideological unity among its inhabitants.[33] Rome from an early date had offered citizenship to deserving wealthy individuals, or even to whole communities which had given outstanding service. This created a restricted category of provincial subjects who had access to the protection of Roman law, as well as other social advantages. As the number of Roman citizens grew during the first century AD, holding Roman citizenship ceased to be such a clear mark of privilege, and a new distinction was introduced in the early second century between more and less wealthy citizens, defined as "more honorable" and "more humble," *honestiores* and *humiliores*, who were liable to differential penalties in the penal code.[34]

In 212 the emperor Caracalla (M. Aurelius Antoninus) issued a decree which gave Roman citizenship to virtually all the free inhabitants of the empire. This had various consequences. Some observers saw it as a cynical measure to increase state revenues, since certain taxes, including the inheritance tax, were only levied from Roman citizens. However, it would be mistaken to interpret the measure only in a restricted or negative way. Inscriptions and papyri show that over the next two generations the majority of the inhabitants of the empire advertised their new citizen status by taking the imperial first name Aurelius. The measure certainly helped to create a broad ideological unity for the empire during the third century, when it was faced with severe external pressures and internal political disorders. Diocletian and his colleagues in the tetrarchy, who themselves came from inconspicuous provincial backgrounds, could never have refashioned the public face of the Roman state, based on an ideal of *Romanitas*, if the way had not been prepared by other social developments during the third century.

The use of the new citizen name "Aurelius" ceased to be widespread after 260, and was rare after the end of the third century. Most Romans in late antiquity were known simply by a single given name, which contained no clues to whether they were Roman citizens or not. There are some exceptions to this pattern. Flavius, the family name of the Constantinian dynasty, was given to ever larger numbers of prominent persons between the fourth and sixth centuries. In almost every case, however, they appear to be in one sense or another imperial officials in the service of the state, and "Flavius" functioned as a title of office rather than a personal name.[35] The numbers of Flavii rose inexorably between the fourth and sixth centuries, corresponding to the increasing number of state officials during this period. A small group of very prominent Romans continued the early imperial practice of using several names (most typically the *tria nomina* combination of *praenomen*, family name, and *cognomen*), but accentuated this by the practice of polyonymy, that is accumulating a long sequence of Roman names that mirrored the widespread connections of their family. However, this was an affectation of a small part of the ruling senatorial aristocracy, both at Rome and Constantinople, which self-consciously advertised its continuity with the elite of the early empire, and used multiple names as a way of showing off their illustrious pedigrees. It is clear that citizenship in itself was no longer a mark of distinction; multiple names were now used only as a marker of high status.[36]

It is hard to know the means by which the inhabitants of the empire were formally identified as citizens after this ceased to be made clear from their nomenclature, but this should not obscure the most significant consequence of Caracalla's citizenship measure. This was that the majority of the empire's inhabitants now considered themselves to be Romans, subject to Roman civil and criminal law, and the representatives of the state regarded them in this light also. This assumption underlies Augustine's discussion throughout his *City of God*, which contrasts virtual universal citizenship in the secular Roman Empire with membership of the heavenly kingdom of God.[37] The Christian faith, or more precisely orthodox Catholic belief, which was adopted as the state religion, naturally emerged as another unifying factor alongside Roman citizenship during the fourth century. The famous and programmatic edict of Theodosius I, which began his reign in 380, was an order that all his subjects, *cunctos populos*, should be followers of the universal religion, Catholic Christianity, and this form of ideological and religious unity remained the goal of all the emperors who succeeded him (see below, chapter 8). The culmination of this process was achieved under Justinian. As Geoffrey Greatrex has argued in an important paper, it was the normal practice of contingents in Roman armies of the sixth century to advertise their separate ethnic origins, for instance as Heruls, Moors, Huns, Armenians, or Isaurians. Many of them also continued to use personal names of ethnic origin. This did not prevent them also from being Romans, a label that was used very flexibly. The critical quality shared by all the warriors in the armies of Justinian was that they were Chalcedonian Christians.[38]

Social and Cultural Transformations

Cities were essential to the ordered world of the Roman Empire at all periods. They focused the political and other organized activities of the empire's subjects. Although the biggest cities with very large populations often generated high levels of urban violence, cities in general were rarely centers of resistance or opposition. Civic life, however, changed substantially between 300 and 600. Even at the beginning of the period cities had ceased to be independent, self-governing communities, whose magistrates maintained local order and security, and administered civic finances with little or no interference from the imperial administration. The days had also mostly passed when members of the local landowning elites maintained city institutions and financed public buildings and services by their private generosity. By the early fourth century the cream of the provincial aristocracy were making their careers in state service.[39] Rather than seeking local magistracies and high-priesthoods, they became members of the growing band of provincial and imperial administrators. Many palace officials were also lawyers, and legal training, based on command of Latin as well as Greek, became the most important component of higher education in late antiquity, overshadowing the traditional forms of *paideia*, Greek education, which derived from an advanced mastery of Greek grammar, rhetoric, and culture in the wider sense.[40] The conflict between the two forms of education was already apparent in the third century to an educated Greek of eastern Asia Minor, the future bishop Gregory of Neocaesarea (known in Christian hagiography as Gregory the Wonder-worker), who summed up the challenge of mastering Roman law in a famous passage:

> A quite different form of study takes a terrible grip on my mind and binds my mouth and my tongue, if ever I wish to say the least thing in the Greek language – our admirable laws, by which the affairs of all those that live under the rule of the Romans are regulated, which neither can be composed nor studied thoroughly without great labour, being as they are wise and accurate and varied and admirable, and in a word most Hellenic, but expressed and transmitted in the language of the Romans, which is impressive and pretentious and wholly suited to the imperial power – but none the less burdensome for me. (Gregory Thaumaturgus, Address to Origen 1, 6–7, trans. Fergus Millar)

Through the fourth century the council (*ordo*) of the *curiales* remained the defining institution of the cities. The councilors were generally the heads of the better-off families, and they took collective responsibility for city finances. In practice this often amounted to little more than fulfilling compulsory obligations for their communities (civic liturgies), ensuring that a city met its tax obligations to the empire, and organizing supplies and transport for Roman troops. Meanwhile most of the serious decisions regarding public buildings and services, as well as the running of local courts of justice, were carried out by provincial governors, aided by the members of their staff. Power thereby became more centralized. The picture of civic life in the fourth century is accordingly a bleak one, at least as seen through the eyes of the *curiales*. The reasons for this development were religious and cultural, and not merely the result of bureaucratic developments. City life in the early Roman Empire had been sustained by strong and diverse local religious traditions. Much of community life, financed by the generous public spending of city notables, was connected to civic religion and the holding of festivals, which emphasized the diversity and variety of Greek pagan culture. However, by the beginning of the fourth century this pagan community culture, based in the cities, had virtually expired. Christianity, although it took many different forms, was explicitly a universal religion, and it contributed strongly to a centralized uniform culture, as it was adopted and supported by the state.

This had inevitable consequences for city institutions. The members of the local *ordo* recede from view. Mentions of city councils and councilors in inscriptions and literary sources become sparse after 450, although the law codes indicate that the emperors were anxious for them to survive as effective bodies. However, the decline of city councils is not evidence for a social revolution. Provincial society continued to be dominated by the wealthier individuals, and these are identified by the later sources as *ktetores* or *possessores*, terms which emphasize their status as landowners. Meanwhile the term *oiketor*, householder, comes to replace the earlier Greek term *politês* or the Latin *civis*. The emphasis is switched from the community to the individuals, but the latter, simply by virtue of their social status and economic position continued to exercise various forms of civic leadership. The gradual demise of earlier city institutions did not spell the end of the cities themselves.[41] From the mid-fifth century eastern cities frequently seem to have relied on men with the title "father of the city" (*patêr tês poleôs*), who were generally wealthy local men but appointed by the central authorities.[42] Bishops also played an increasingly important part in secular administration, often acting as spokesmen in petitions to the imperial authorities or as recipients of imperial letters. The general evolution of the cities, therefore, turned away from formal constitutional structures, based on elected officials and councilors, to control by prominent and powerful individuals, who were not directly answerable to their communities, and to religious leaders.[43]

Traditional Roman society was strongly hierarchical, and social standing was determined by a combination of wealth, office, lineage, service to the state, and political or military success. In the later empire, merit was increasingly favored over inherited privilege; service and effectiveness were generally regarded as more important than lineage.[44] This is exemplified most dramatically by the

Constitutio Antoniniana (212)	CTh 7.18.1 (365)	Ammianus 14.7.1; CTh 10.12.2; 13.3.5	Notitia Dignitatum	CTh 16.5.52 (412)	CTh 16.5.52	
Citizenship	Social division	Social ranking	Social titles	Social hierarchy	Graded penalties	Social status
cives Romani	honestiores	honorati (possessores, nobiles)	illustres	illustres	50 pounds gold	Imperial aristocracy
			spectabiles	spectabiles	40 pounds gold	
				senatores	30 pounds gold	
			clarissimi	clarissimi	20 pounds gold	
			perfectissimi (equestrians)			
		Curiales (decuriones)		sacerdotales	30 pounds gold	Civic aristocracy
				principales	20 pounds gold	
				decuriones	5 pounds gold	
	humiliores	Plebei (negotiatores, provinciales)		negotiatores	5 pounds gold	Urban commoners
				plebei	5 pounds gold	
dediticii (laeti)		coloni	coloni liberi adscripticii	circumcelliones	10 pounds silver	Rural commoners
				coloni	Physical beating	
servi				servi		

Diagram 5.4 The social hierarchy of the Roman Empire in the third and fourth centuries (from A. Demandt, *Die Spätantike* [Berlin, 1989], 505)

backgrounds of the emperors. The most extreme example is the emperor Justin, who had risen from being an illiterate peasant, through long years of service in the palace guard, to be hailed as successor to the aristocratic Anastasius in 519. Christianity probably encouraged this development. The moral authority of the clergy rested not on wealth, social status, and education, but on the demonstration of Christian virtues and holiness.

Although Roman society offered major opportunities for social and professional advancement, particularly through state or military service, it was certainly not democratic or egalitarian. The universal category of Roman citizens was marked by increasing social differentiation. The legal sources, supported by documentary sources such as inscriptions and papyri, enable us to reconstruct the theoretical social league table of the empire which had evolved by the beginning of the fifth century. This is shown in a very elegant schematic representation of the ranks of late Roman society, devised by Alexander Demandt for his splendid handbook on late antiquity (Diagram 5.4).

There was a steady inflation in honors and titles, which was driven by the opportunities within the system for upward social mobility. Members of the town councils, the *decuriones* or *curiales*, aimed at achieving equestrian rank in order to evade their local civic duties, while officials serving on a provincial governor's staff and certain military officers were also rapidly promoted to equestrian status. The result was a devaluation of equestrian rank. Members of the equestrian order who actually held public office, for instance as provincial governors, began to acquire the titles of lower-ranking senators (*clarissimi*).

The most prominent senatorial offices were the city prefectures at Rome and Constantinople; and the provincial governorships of Asia and Africa. Although the number of genuinely influential senatorial offices was relatively small, senatorial prestige remained high, and was further increased when Constantius II founded a second body in Constantinople, which was referred to a "senate of second rank" (*Anon. Val.* 30). While the Senate at Rome was drawn from "the better part of the human race" (Symmachus, *ep.* I. 52), that is the richest landowning families of the western empire, its counterpart in Constantinople was initially assembled from leading families in eastern cities or from able and ambitious lawyers and rhetoricians. Rome's senators had little regular contact with the emperors, but those in Constantinople, especially after 395, formed a social class that overlapped heavily with members of the resident imperial court.[45]

The creation of this new senatorial aristocracy provided Constantinople with an elite class around the emperor, which supplied the state with officials and senior military officers. The pool from which they were drawn ranged widely. The military men were often career soldiers, including many of barbarian origin. However, civilian officials either belonged to existing senatorial families, or came from the curial class of the cities of the provinces. The draining of talent away from the cities was a source of tension for two reasons. There was a clear danger that those left behind would simply be less well qualified to govern their cities effectively. More obviously, those who entered imperial service were exempted from fulfilling local liturgies and thus deprived the cities of an important financial resource. A good deal of legislation during the fourth and fifth centuries shows the emperors trying to limit these exemptions to the uppermost tier in the Senate, the *illustres*, but once a senator had obtained this immunity his family members retained it in perpetuity. In return, as senators attached to Constantinople, they acquired new obligations, to provide symbolic gifts of gold at the emperors' accession and on his quinquennial anniversaries, and in particular to sponsor games in connection with their otherwise largely honorific urban magistracies (quaestorship, praetorship, consulship).

The *senatorii* or *synkletikoi* were particularly prominent in the eastern provinces of the empire. They in their turn produced a more prestigious sub-group of *consulares* or *hypatikoi*, meaning those who had held the consulship or held senior governorships. These adjectives applied not only to officeholders but to members of their families. These terms were less about holding a particular office than about belonging to a social group. The senatorial class itself evolved into the three ranks of *illustres*, *spectabiles*, and *clarissimi*, and by 530 in the reign of Justinian only the *illustres*, made up from consuls, patricians, and an inner circle of senior magistrates and officers, formed the Senate itself. While sons inherited the lowest senatorial rank, the clarissimate, from their fathers, higher rank and office had to be earned by their own efforts.

The most vivid and tangible evidence for the prominence and high social status of the leading senators derives from the cities of the eastern empire, Asia Minor in particular, which erected statues and honorific inscriptions, usually in verse, to commemorate provincial governors or men of local origin who had made distinguished careers for themselves in imperial service.[46] The milieu where this phenomenon has been most intensively studied is the city of Aphrodisias, the metropolis of the province of Caria. The relevant inscriptions have been presented in exemplary fashion by Charlotte Roueché. These brief verse texts, written in elevated and often obscure language, advertise generic virtues rather than specific accomplishments. Governors in particular might be praised for their knowledge of the law and their devotion to justice.[47] The statuary that accompanied these inscriptions has been subjected to highly revealing analysis by Bert Smith.[48] The individuals who were honored in the late fourth and fifth centuries at Aphrodisias were provincial governors, whose statues were erected in three of the most important public spaces of the city: in front of porticos outside the theater, in the street beside the council house, and close to the main bath building. The statues, placed on high composite bases made from reused materials, depicted the men they honored in the full formality of ceremonial garb. Senators were entitled to wear a new style of Roman toga, which perhaps deliberately distinguished them from other citizens, who had been entitled, since Caracalla's edict, to wear the older-fashioned garment.[49] Other leading figures were clad in a long heavy cloak, the *chlamys*, which first appears in the military entourage of the Theodosian court at Constantinople, although it was not restricted to military officers. Leading men of local origin tended to be dressed in the less formal *himation*, characteristic of the Greek civic aristocracy. There was considerable variety in beard and hair fashions, but the styles adopted clearly mirrored those found on monuments of Constantinople, to be seen, for instance, on the reliefs of the great base of Theodosius I in the hippodrome. The statues and their bases also carried symbols linked with their office, the baton of a consul, bundles of scrolls typical of provincial officials, alluding to the mass of petitions and other paperwork that their duties involved, or, more rarely, an ink-well (Plate 5.10). This repertoire of accessories precisely corresponded to those depicted on the miniature ivory diptychs, which were produced at Constantinople to commemorate individual consulships in the fourth and fifth centuries. Diptychs and statues together illuminate the grandeur of state office.

A comparable system of social ranking grew up within the organization of the church. There was considerable overlap between this and the secular state hierarchy, with the result that many influential individuals in society at large also acquired prominence in the church. This particularly applies to bishops.

Plate 5.10 Aphrodisias. Statue of Oecumenius, a senator and provincial governor, erected at Aphrodisias, capital of the province of Caria, in the late fourth century (Aphrodisias excavation, from *JRS* 92 [2002], pl. XXII)

However, the church respected values which were of little account in secular society: poverty, renunciation, ascetic self-discipline, and holiness in general, and thus created an honorable role for humble church servants, local priests, hermits, and monks. As the institutions and ideology of Christianity increasingly permeated the upper reaches of the state and were explicitly recognized in law giving, so humble persons began to acquire influence through their religious credentials.

Late Roman attitudes to status were certainly influenced by Christian ideas, including the view that all men were equal before god. Being human was a great leveler. There was no room in this ideology for the elaborately-graded social hierarchy of traditional Roman thought. This approach finds expression in late Roman epitaphs, which ceased to distinguish individuals by rank or title or even patronymic, but simply call them by a single (Christian) name and refer to them as slaves of god.

The explicit and implicit contradictions between traditional Roman and Christian social ideas complicate the picture of late Roman society. However, in broad terms traditional Roman ideas gave way to Christian conceptions. This is a result both of a readiness to recognize individual merit, which made promotion to high rank possible for people from humble backgrounds, and of the gradual fusion of state and church institutions, as the institutions of the Roman Empire became more explicitly Christian. The distance between the classical model of the second century and the Christian one of the sixth century is exemplified by the fact that the key men in Justinian's regime could come from a great variety of educational, cultural, and ethnic backgrounds: Justinian and Belisarius, Latin speakers, were from Thracian soldier families; Tribonian from Pamphylia in southern Asia Minor, Procopius of Caesarea, and John from the Lydian city of Philadelphia came from old Greek civic backgrounds, although all three had followed a legal training in Constantinople; John the Cappadocian was from eastern Anatolia where the civic tradition had been much weaker. The generals Solomon and the eunuch Narses came from Mesopotamia and Armenia respectively, frontier areas with complicated and mixed cultural traditions. The common factor that held the ruling elite together was loyalty to the Roman state, based on their shared Christian beliefs.

As the structures of Roman society evolved between the third and sixth centuries, so social attitudes changed. The tone was set by the large numbers of officials and military personnel from the upper ranks, who formed the governing class of the empire. In cultural terms this extended elite, who may have numbered as many as 30,000 in the empire as a whole, drew on four main traditions.

Hellenic *paideia*, which derived from rigorous education based on classical models, had been the ideal of the Greek cities which had flourished in the early Roman Empire. The foundations of this in Greek civic life and classical religious and philosophical traditions were systematically undermined by religious and social developments of the later empire. Classical culture, which continued to shape the mentality of the educated class of the cities of the Greek

East in the fourth and early fifth centuries, still found outstanding exponents in the sixth century, and the *litterati* made a great show of their knowledge of classical mythology,[50] but it was the preserve of a small minority of the population. Greek *paideia* by now had little relevance to the empire's administrative needs, and contributed little to social advancement.[51]

Expertise in Roman law, on the contrary, was increasingly prized. Lawyers possessed a sophisticated practical skill which led directly to careers in the imperial administration. It was thus by far the most favored form of higher education for talented young men looking for careers, or with ambitions to influence society around them. The rhetoric of Roman law combined high-flown grandiloquence with cumbersome bureaucratic jargon. In its way it was as abstruse and hard to master as the elevated style of Greek pagan intellectuals, and the subject was thus reserved for those with the talent and training to master its intricacies.

The church provided a separate cultural tradition. The Bible, a comprehensive body of sacred literature in written form, was the basis for the education of a substantial literate minority, especially in the eastern part of the empire, who became deacons, priests, or bishops, and also comprised many who entered monasteries or nunneries, or lived ascetic lives as hermits. Christianity provided a different form of intellectual framework from secular forms of learning. At the highest level it was heavily influenced by Greek philosophy, which gave theologians the tools to debate the questions about the relationship of the Father to the Son, and about the divine nature of Christ, which dominated the agenda of church councils through the entire period. More broadly the Bible itself supplied churchmen, especially bishops, with an inexhaustible quarry of moral examples which were applied in their sermons or in the judgments of church courts. This formed the basis for a Christian code of conduct which shaped the lives of many of their congregations. It is clear that a majority of the clergy could read and write. One of the humbler ranks in the church hierarchy was precisely that of a reader (*anagnostes*). This skill may have been as important as their pious credentials in advancing them as spokesmen and leaders for their communities.

Finally, we have to reckon with the growing influence of popular culture, and the uneducated beliefs of largely illiterate people. As more people in positions of authority were drawn from a wider pool of the population, they introduced much less sophisticated ideas to the class of decision makers. Ramsay MacMullen has argued that the pervasive presence of popular superstitious beliefs had a large impact even among educated representatives of late Roman society. However, the nature of the source material from the late Roman period may be largely responsible for this impression. A much larger proportion of popular literature, ranging from saints' lives to local chronicles, survives from late antiquity than it does from the early empire, and provides insights into the outlook of the lower classes. Members of the elite continued to work at a high level of rational sophistication.[52]

NOTES

1 Clifford Ando, *Imperial Ideology and Provincial Loyalty in the Roman Empire* (Berkeley, 2000).

2 John Matthews, *Laying Down the Law* (New Haven, 2000), 31–54.

3 Alan Cameron, *Circus Factions* (Oxford, 1976), 237–44; H.-U. Wiemer, *Archiv für Kulturgeschichte* 86 (2004), 35–44, 66–73 (German translation of the Syriac original).

4 C. Roueché, "Acclamations in the later Roman empire: New evidence from Aphrodisias," *JRS* 74 (1984), 181–99.

5 Alan Cameron, *Circus Factions*, 318–33.

6 H.-U. Wiemer, "Akklamationen im spätrömischen Reich. Zur Typologie und Funktion eines Kommunikationsrituals," *Archiv für Kulturgeschichte* 86 (2004), 27–73, is the best modern discussion.

7 See Averil Cameron and Stuart Hall, *Eusebius, Life of Constantine* (Oxford, 1999), 27–39.

8 J. Curran, *Pagan City and Christian Capital. Rome in the Fourth Century* (Oxford, 2000), 86–90; J. Elsner, "From the culture of spolia to the cult of relics: The arch of Constantine and the genius of late antique Rome," *PBSR* 68 (2000), 149–84; R. R. Holloway, *Constantine and Rome* (New Haven, 2004).

9 F. Kolb, *Herrscherideologie in der Spätantike* (Berlin, 2001), 225–42.

10 Alan Cameron, "Consular diptychs in their social context," *JRA* 11 (1998), 385–403.

11 E. Kitzinger, *Byzantine Art in the Making. Main Lines of Stylistic Development in Mediterranean Art 3rd–7th Century* (Cambridge Mass., 1977), 96, 176.

12 For the Sassanian reliefs, see G. Herrmann, *The Iranian Revival* (Oxford, 1977).

13 A. H. M. Jones, *Later Roman Empire* I (Oxford, 1964), 683–4.

14 A. H. M. Jones, *Later Roman Empire* I, 679–89; discussion by D. Potter, *The Roman Empire at Bay* (London, 2004), 455–9, for the fourth century.

15 The best recent survey of the late Roman army is by Michael Whitby, "Recruitment in Roman armies from Justinian to Heraclius (ca 565–615)," in Averil Cameron (ed.), *The Byzantine and Early Islamic Near East III* (Princeton, 1995), 61–124, which is more wide-ranging in chronology and subject matter than its title suggests. Hugh Elton, *Warfare in Roman Europe AD 350–425* (Oxford, 1996), is an excellent study of the evidence from the early part of late antiquity, and debunks many commonly held views.

16 For the fourth century see R. MacMullen, *Corruption and the Decline of Rome* (New Haven, 1988), 199–204.

17 H. Elton, *Warfare in Roman Europe AD 350–425*, 129–34.

18 E. A. Thompson, *The Huns* (Oxford, 1996), index s.v. Aetius; T. Stickler, *Aetius. Gestaltungsspielräume eines Heermeisters im ausgehenden weströmischen Reich* (2002).

19 P. MacGeorge, *Late Roman Warlords* (Munich, 2002).

20 The complexity of these categories emerges from H. Elton, *Warfare in Roman Europe AD 350–425*, 91–4.

21 R. W. Bulliet, *The Camel and the Wheel* (Cambridge Mass., 1975); D. F. Graf, "Camels, roads and wheels in late antiquity," in E. Dabrowa (ed.), *Donum Amicitiae. Studies in Ancient History* (Electrum 1, Krakow, 1997), 43–9.

22 T. C. Skeat, *Two Papyri from Panopolis in the Chester Beatty Library* (Dublin, 1964); C. Adams, "Transition and change in Diocletian's Egypt: Province and

empire in the late third century," in S. Swain and M. Edwards (eds.), *Approaching Late Antiquity* (Oxford, 2004), 82–108.

23 S. Mitchell, "The cities of Asia Minor in the age of Constantine," in S. N. C. Lieu and D. Montserrat (eds.), *Constantine. History, Historiography and Legend* (London, 1998), 52–6.

24 For recent survey reports see S. Mitchell, in *JHS Archaeological Reports* 45 (1998/9), 173.

25 S. Mitchell, *Anatolia* II (Oxford, 1993), 122–4.

26 T. D. Barnes, *The New Empire of Diocletian and Constantine* (Cambridge Mass., 1982), 227–32.

27 See Evagrius 3.39. The law itself is cited at *CJust.* 11.1.1–2.

28 D. Feissel, "Un rescrit de Justinien découvert à Didymes," *Chiron* 34 (2004), 285–365.

29 See Jill Harries, *Law and Empire in Late Antiquity* (Cambridge, 1999); Jill Harries and Ian Wood (eds.), *The Theodosian Code: Studies in the Imperial Law of Late Antiquity* (London, 1993); Simon Corcoran, *The Empire of the Tetrarchs, Imperial Pronouncements and Government AD 284–324* (Oxford, 2000); J. F. Matthews, *Laying Down the Law* (New Haven, 2000).

30 John Lydus, *de mag.* 3.19–20; see C. M. Kelly, "Later Roman bureaucracy: Going through the files," in A. Bowman and G. Woolf (eds.), *Literacy and Power in the Ancient World* (Cambridge, 1994), 161–76.

31 For the administrative and political workings of the empire see now the detailed studies of Fergus Millar, F. Millar, *A Greek Roman Empire. Power and Belief under Theodosius II, 408–50* (Berkeley, 2006), and D. Feissel in C. Morrisson (ed.), *Le Monde Byzantin* I (Paris, 2004), 79–110.

32 R. R. R. Smith, "Late antique portraits in a public context: Honorific statuary at Aphrodisias in Caria," *JRS* 89 (1999), 185–8.

33 A. N. Sherwin-White, *The Roman Citizenship* (2nd edn. Oxford, 1974).

34 P. Garnsey, *Social Status and Legal Privilege in the Roman Empire* (Oxford, 1970).

35 S. Mitchell, "Ethnicity, acculturation and empire in Roman and late Roman Asia Minor," in S. Mitchell and G. Greatrex (eds.), *Ethnicity and Culture in Late Antiquity* (Wales and London, 2000), 117–50 at 137–8.

36 Alan Cameron, "Polyonymy in the late Roman aristocracy: The case of Petronius Probus," *JRS* 75 (1985), 164–82; Benet Salway, "What's in a Roman name? A survey of Roman onomastic practice from c.700 BC to AD 700," *JRS* 84 (1994), 124–45.

37 P. Garnsey and C. Humfress, *The Evolution of the Late Antique World* (Cambridge, 2001), chapter 4; T. Honoré, "Roman law AD 200–400: From cosmopolis to Rechtstaat," and P. Garnsey, "Roman citizenship and Roman law in the late empire," in S. Swain and M. Edwards (eds.), *Approaching Late Antiquity* (Oxford, 2004), 109–32, 133–55.

38 G. Greatrex, "Roman identity in the sixth century," in S. Mitchell and G. Greatrex (eds.), *Ethnicity and Culture in Late Antiquity* (Wales and London, 2000), 267–92.

39 Fergus Millar, "Empire and city, Augustus to Julian: Obligations, excuses and status," *JRS* 73 (1983), 76–96; reprinted in *Rome, the Greek World and the East*, Volume 2 (Chapel Hill, 2004), 336–71.

40 Fergus Millar, "The Greek East and Roman law; The dossier of M. Cn. Licinius Rufinus," *JRS* 89 (1999), 90–108; reprinted in *Rome, the Greek World and the East*, Volume 2, 435–64.

41   A. Laniado, *Recherches sur les notables municipaux dans l'empire protobyzantine* (Paris, 2002); usefully reviewed by F. Haarer, *JRA* 17 (2004), 735–40.

42   C. Rouaché, *GRBS* 20 (1979), 173–85; C. Rouaché, *Aphrodisias in Late Antiquity* (1989), 77–8; D. Feissel, *Inscriptions de Cilicie* (Paris, 1987), 215–20.

43   See especially W. Liebeschuetz, *The Decline and Fall of the Roman City* (Oxford, 2001), 104–36. For the *curiales* see A. Laniado, *Recherches sur les notables municipaux dans l'empire protobyzantine* (Paris, 2002).

44   On the formal organization of late Roman society, see above all A. H. M. Jones, *The Later Roman Empire* I (Oxford, 1964), 523–62, and A. Demandt, *Die Spätantike* (Berlin, 1989), 276–96. My discussion is heavily dependent on these.

45   J. F. Matthews, *Western Aristocracies and the Imperial Court* (2nd edn. Oxford, 1990), 1–31; A. H. M. Jones, *The Later Roman Empire* I (Oxford, 1964), 523–62; A. Demandt, *Die Spätantike* (Berlin, 1989), 276–88.

46   M. Horster, "Ehrungen spätantiker Statthalter," *Ant. Tard.* 6 (1998), 37–59.

47   The fundamental discussion of these epigrams in L. Robert, *Epigrammes du Bas-Empire*, Hellenica IV (1948).

48   C. Rouaché, *Aphrodisias in Late Antiquity* (1989), nos. 36–52, 62–5; R. R. R. Smith, "Late antique portraits in a public context: Honorific statuary at Aphrodisias in Caria," *JRS* 89 (1999), 155–89; R. R. R. Smith, "The statue monument of Oecumenius: A new portrait of a late antique governor from Aphrodisias," *JRS* 92 (2002), 134–56.

49   For the phenomenon at Ephesus, see C. Foss, "Stephanus, proconsul of Asia, and related statues," *Okeanos. Essays for I. Sevčenko* (Harvard Ukrainian Studies 7 1983), 196–217, reprinted in *History and Archaeology of Byzantine Asia Minor* (Aldershot, 1990), ch. 3.

50   Alan Cameron, "Poetry and literary culture in late antiquity," in S. Swain and M. Edwards, *Approaching Late Antiquity* (Oxford, 2004), 327–54.

51   P. Brown, *Power and Persuasion in Late Antiquity* (Wisconsin, 1992).

52   R. MacMullen, "Cultural changes and political changes in the 4th and 5th centuries AD," *Historia* 52 (2003), 465–95; see also P. Heather, "Literacy and power in the migration period," in A. Bowman and G. Woolf (eds.), *Literacy and Power in the Ancient World* (Cambridge, 1994), 177–97.

6

The Barbarian Kingdoms

250	300	350	400	450	500	550	600	650

The Origins of the Germanic Kingdoms of the West

Rome had grown accustomed to, and had made use of, German barbarians since the beginning of the empire. The image of a bearded northerner cowering before an armed legionary had become a visual cliché for celebrating Roman victories. Classical civilization, based on the civic life of the Mediterranean, defined itself by the contrast with unkempt, skin-clad barbarians from the north. But German soldiers were good warriors, and had been recruited into the Roman armies since the time of Julius Caesar and Augustus. In the third and early fourth centuries the proportion of barbarians serving in the armies increased drastically, and the number of officers of Frankish, Alemannic, or Vandal origin is astounding.[1] Barbarian commanders in the West such as Bauto, *magister militum* from 380 to 385, Arbogast, *magister militum* from 388 to 394, and Stilicho, his successor, were influential at the highest level. Sulpicius Severus observed that in 394 Frankish mercenaries controlled military affairs, Arbogast's accomplices took over the civil administration of the western empire, and Valentinian II, confined to the palace at Vienne, was virtually reduced to the status of a private citizen (Sulpicius Severus, cited in Greg. Tur., *Hist.* II, 9). Bauto's daughter Eudoxia married the emperor Arcadius; Stilicho married Serena, the niece of Theodosius I. Members of the imperial family continued to intermarry with leading barbarian families throughout late antiquity.[2] Such alliances were based on a recognition of mutual benefits, not on shared culture. These barbarians, however, had been enlisted into the Roman Empire on Roman terms. They acquired Roman titles and offices, and clearly used Latin as their main language. There is little evidence that any of them was tempted to operate as a fifth column for their tribe or people of origin.

To most barbarians conditions of life appeared much better in the Roman Empire than outside it. Large-scale immigration across the Rhine and Danube had occurred since the first century AD.[3] Some of the newcomers were refugees from political or demographic pressures, others were economic migrants attracted by the lure of gain in the Roman market economy. Immigrants tended to be broken into small groups and dispersed, and ceased to exist as ethnic or tribal groups.

Both Roman sources and archaeological evidence present a generally homogeneous picture of barbarian society beyond the Rhine and the Danube up to the fourth century.[4] The various tribes lived in small sedentary agricultural villages, which formed into cantons that were controlled by local leaders. The barbarian communities living closest to Roman territory tended to be richer. They had better opportunities for trade with the provinces, and their leaders also often received Roman subsidies, usually paid in silver denarii. Much of this surplus wealth was recycled into the purchase of Roman luxuries, including wine and material goods. These exchanges helped to create a stable environment beyond the frontier, and the barbarians living in these regions not only had close commercial relations with the Roman provinces, but also adopted Roman building styles.[5]

The equilibrium of the northern frontier zone was destabilized not so much by tension between Romans and barbarians as by internal conflicts on either side. During the third and fourth centuries larger barbarian confederations, notably of Alemanni, Franks, and Goths, were able to take advantage of weakness along the Roman *limes*, leading to extensive raiding and to some, usually temporary, infiltration and settlement in the Roman provinces. Fourth-century emperors regularly campaigned against such groups both inside and beyond the imperial boundary to restore the traditional lines of defense along the Rhine and Danube, and they also broadly attempted to maintain the policy which had been successful in the early empire. After his successful campaigns against the Goths, Constantine restored the practice of paying subsidies to Gothic leaders, and maintaining an open frontier for lively commercial exchanges. Valens in 369, after reinforcing the garrisons along the lower Danube, made a short-lived attempt to restrict access to two crossing points.[6]

The consequences of the Roman civil wars of the mid-fourth century are apparent in Ammianus' account of Gaul under Julian. The Alemanni took advantage of the war between Constantius and Magnentius, and overran large parts of eastern Gaul before they were decisively defeated at the battle of Strasburg in 357. In 358 Julian campaigned against the Salian Franks and the Chamavi, who had occupied territory around Tongres in Belgica. The Franks approached him, promising to keep the peace if they were allowed to remain on the land they had settled and which they regarded as their own. Julian appeared to concede the request and offered them gifts, but then terrorized them with an unexpected military attack. Then, "using his victory as a favourable opportunity to show mercy, he accepted their surrender with their goods and families." Nevertheless both the Franks and the neighboring Chamavi were allowed to remain in their settlements (Ammianus 17.8).

Terror played a large part in Roman frontier policy. Roman brutality is most blatantly on show in Constantius' campaign of 358 against the Sarmatians and the Limigantes. First the Sarmatians and the Quadi, who had often been useful allies of the Romans in the past but had recently been engaged in sporadic raiding in Pannonia and Moesia, were cowed by a brutally rapid attack. Those who could not flee, rooted to the spot by fear, were butchered. Those who escaped watched their country being put to the sword. It fell to an earlier favorite of the Romans, Zizais, to plead for mercy:

At the sight of the emperor he threw away his weapons, flung himself prostrate to the ground, and lay apparently lifeless. He aroused greater pity because, at the moment when he should have spoken, fear choked his utterance; after several attempts, interrupted by sobs, he was hardly able to set forth his request. At last he recovered himself and was told to rise. Kneeling, and with his voice once more under control, he begged forgiveness and pardon for his past offences. The multitude of his followers who were admitted to join in his petition remained dumb with fear as long as the fate of their superior hung in the balance, but, when he was told to stand up and gave them the long-awaited signal to add their entreaties to his, they all threw down their spears and shields and stretched out their arms in supplication, striving to outdo even their prince in the humility of their appeal. (Ammianus 17.12, trans. Hamilton)

Butchery and humiliation, which sufficed for the Sarmatians and Quadi, escalated to genocide against several cantons of the Limigantes. These initially defied a Roman order to leave their lands, but they begged for their lives when threatened with massive force and promised to pay an annual tribute, to provide a levy of able-bodied men for the army, and a supply of slaves. Two groups, the Amicenses and the Picenses, were ordered to cross the Danube and approach the imperial camp. The area was staked out, with troops in ambush on either sides. The emperor "warned them in mild terms not to behave with violence." As the barbarians threw down their shields, the praetorian cohorts formed a battle wedge, known in soldiers' jargon as the boar's head, and in half an hour had massacred them to the last man. Worse was to follow:

> No sooner had the hostile tribes been overthrown than the families of the slain were dragged forth in droves from their humble huts, without distinction of age or sex, to exchange the proud independence of their former life for the degraded status of slaves. A brief space of time sufficed to reveal piles of corpses and throngs of prisoners. So, excited by the heat of battle and the prospect of loot, our men betook themselves to the destruction of those who had fled from the fight or were lying concealed in their huts. Thirsting for barbarian blood they tore down the frail thatch and slaughtered those within; even a house built of the strongest timbers could not preserve its inmates from death. At last, when everything was on fire and there was nowhere left to hide, the survivors, finding every avenue of escape cut off, either refused to yield and perished in the flames, or else came out and escaped one form of torment only to fall at the hands of their enemies. Some . . . entrusted themselves to the depths of the river nearby. . . . Some of these died by drowning, others were pierced by missiles and perished; so much blood was spilt that the whole stream foamed with it. Thus with the help of two elements the rage and courage of the victors destroyed the Sarmatians. (Ammianus 17.13, trans. Hamilton)

No passage in Ammianus' history better illustrates the savage brutality of a military emperor of the fourth century. Constantius was a devout and observant Christian,[7] ascetic in his personal conduct, and scrupulous and incorruptible in the conduct of state duties. However, when it came to the exercise of imperial power, he was utterly ruthless. He had been hardened by civil war. Ammianus remarked that he "prided himself on his success in civil conflicts, and bathed in the blood which poured in a fearful stream from the internal wounds of the state" (Ammianus 21.16, trans. Hamilton). Barbarian enemies of Rome fared worse even than the usurpers who challenged him.

There was an enormous transformation between the world of the Germanic barbarians depicted in the pages of Ammianus, and that of the kingdoms that supplanted the western provinces in the fifth century. The process of change may be traced back on the Roman side to Valens' decision in 376 to admit the Gothic tribe of the Tervingi into Thrace, and the six years of turmoil in the eastern Balkans which saw the Roman defeat at Adrianople and Valens' death in 378, and was concluded by Theodosius I's treaty with the Goths of 382. The new policy of according the Goths the status of independent allies within the empire was highly controversial, but forced by Rome's financial constraints and manpower shortages. It was argued that the Gothic treaty was a means of acquiring more soldiers without levying more taxes. Objections to using German barbarian troops prevailed in the East, especially after the suppression of the revolt of Gainas in 400, but the Goths were now a permanent fixture in the central regions of the empire.

This set the stage for the emergence of a new breed of barbarian leader, the warrior chieftains who emerged to command Germanic contingents, which either fought for Roman masters or rampaged in pursuit of their own goals across the western empire. Alaric is the prime example. Initially the strength of the Goths in the empire was limited, but as a result of the internal conflict between East and West in 390s Alaric emerged as a formidable force. His military ability and battle successes established his prestige and status. Fighting on behalf of Stilicho entitled him to provisions, pay, and logistic support from the Romans, which enabled him to build his followers into a coherent band of professional soldiers. After the fall of Stilicho, Alaric also attracted barbarian federates and escaped slaves to his core group of Visigothic followers, reaching a total of 40,000 men (Zosimus 5.35 and 42). All of these were dependent on him for the necessities of life: provisions for them to function as a campaigning group; monetary rewards; arms, weapons, and mounts; and ultimately land for themselves and their families to settle. The organization of Alaric's followers into an effective fighting force during the long years of campaigning helped to create a new type of community and forge a Visigothic nation.

Similar experiences can be identified behind the emergence of other major barbarian groups in the fifth century. The Vandals, who crossed into the empire in 406, spent the next generation carving out temporary homes for themselves in Spain, fighting against Romans, Suevians, and Goths. They were joined by a group of Alans (*Chron. Min.* II. 19), and the later official title of the barbarian rulers of Africa was *rex Vandalorum et Alanorum* (Victor of Vita 2.9, 3.3). A total of 80,000 barbarians is reported to have crossed into Africa in 429, including old men, children, free persons, and slaves. This count was made to estimate the number of ships needed to ferry the people across to Africa, in eighty groups, each of a thousand persons, and so the women were also presumably included in this figure.[8] Their unity, as one of the most effective and coherent barbarian groups of the fifth century was evidently forged in the long years of campaigning and migration. A similar experience led to the formation of the Ostrogothic kingdom under Theoderic the Amal. In all these cases strong leaders were able to bequeath effective tribal groups to their successors, and thus led to the creation of lasting dynasties.

One of the most disputed matters concerning these barbarian groups is the question of whether land was specifically assigned to them by Roman authorities, and how this was achieved. In the eastern Balkans and Thrace, where the first Gothic immigrants were settled in the 370s and 380s, there seems to have been little at stake. The newcomers are described in a remarkable passage of the sixth-century Gothic historian Jordanes:

Now there were other Goths as well, who are called the lesser Goths, a very large people, whose priest and primate Ulfila is said also to have taught them how to write. Today these Goths live in Moesia and inhabit the region of Nicopolis towards the foot of Mount Haemus: a people large in numbers but impoverished and unwarlike, with no resources except for herds of various sorts of animal, pasture and the forest for wood. They have little fertile land for growing wheat or other varieties of cereal. As for vines some of them are even unaware that they exist in other places, and buy their wine from the neighbouring regions. Most of them live on milk. (Jordanes, *Get.* 267)

There were few cities in the region, and no well established landowning class to contest possession of the land with the newcomers. Almost all of the existing settlers would either have been impoverished peasants, ex-soldiers, and their dependants, who were sociologically and even ethnically hardly distinct from the newcomers. At this level barbarians were absorbed without causing long-term disturbances. Jordanes' description draws attention to the important influence of Ulfila, one of the most important church leaders of the fourth century, who was not only responsible for creating the first Gothic Christian community but also for determining that Arianism, at least until the 380s, was the dominant form of Christianity in the churches of the region as a whole.[9]

In the West matters were more complicated and contentious. The classic theory is that land allotments were modeled on Roman laws concerning *hospitalitas*, the billeting of soldiers in civilian settlements. A law of 398 issued by Arcadius and Honorius laid down that one-third of the space in a house was to be made available to soldiers and those on state business when required (*CTh.* 7.8.5). This is turn has been linked to a law issued by the Burgundian king Gundobad in the early sixth century. This refers to a former state of affairs in which Burgundians had obtained one-third of the bondsmen and two-thirds of certain lands where they had settled, in accordance with the regulations covering *hospitalitas*, but that in cases where these Burgundians had subsequently received benefactions of land or retainers from the king himself, they should return both the land and its tied laborers to their original owners (*Lex Burgundionum* 54). These and other passages have been interpreted in a different sense by Walter Goffart, to refer not to the barbarians obtaining title to the land itself, but being able to claim one-third of the tax revenues that they generated for the state.[10] The theory may indeed explain some of the relevant evidence, especially as there are indications that the Roman tax budget was sometimes conceived as being made up of one-third portions, which were then assigned for specific areas of expenditure, such as military pay or payment to barbarian *foederati*. However, a number of passages from sixth-century writers indisputably refer to actual land divisions, and suggest that the traditional interpretation should in general still be preferred. A passage from a letter written by Cassiodorus on behalf of Theoderic, addressed to the Roman Senate in the last years of the fifth century, praised the praetorian prefect Liberius Venantius for managing to increase state revenues by efficiency savings rather than by raising taxes. It continues with a complicated allusion to land division between Goths and Romans: "It is my delight to mention how, in the assignment of one-third shares (*tertiae*), he unites both the estates and the hearts of Goths and Romans. . . . Behold, a new and wholly admirable achievement: division of the soil joined its masters in good will" (Cassiodorus, *ep.* 2.16.5–6). Another, earlier letter of Theoderic written by Cassiodorus to a pair of his officials, one Gothic, the other Roman, also alludes to authorized land division, and the state of the law regarding claims against illegal usurpation of land:

> If, after the date when, by God's favour, I crossed the river Isonzo, and the realm of Italy first received me, a barbarian occupier has seized the estate of a Roman, without a warrant taken from any assigning officer, he is to restore the property before that time, since the thirty-year limitation is clearly an objection, I decree that the plaintiff's claim is to fail. For I want only those matters brought to judgement which I condemn as acts of seizure made in my reign, since there is no room left for idle accusations when the obscurity of many years has passed. (Cassiodorus, *ep.* 1.18.2–3, trans. Barnish)

Procopius also indicates that the Goths in Italy partitioned the lands which Odoacar had previously given to his followers (Procopius, *Bell. Goth.* 5.1.28). The evidence of Cassiodorus in particular seems incompatible with the idea that measures assigning land to barbarians should usually be interpreted as references not to the land itself but to the tax income that it produced.[11]

In general, however, it appears that the arrival of barbarian groups and their demands for land were less disruptive than one might have expected. Certainly there is no evidence for tensions such as are generated by the existential struggle in the modern world between Israelis and Palestinians over a territory to which both lay claim. Various explanations may be offered for this. The numbers of the migrating barbarian groups were never overwhelming, in proportion to the settled peasantries of the western provinces. Some groups, like the minor Goths described by Jordanes, occupied marginal areas that were thinly populated in any case. Even Alaric was prepared at one stage to exchange land in Noricum for a more distant and exposed territory during his negotiations with Honorius (Zosimus 5.36). In such frontier areas the ethnic and cultural differences between Germanic barbarians and the lower strata of provincial society were not large. Above all, the newcomers, ready and able to fight, were a welcome source of military strength both to the state and to the Roman landowners in the West, who had proved incapable of defending the western provinces either against internal or external enemies. Although they regarded Germanic barbarians with aristocratic distaste, the senatorial elite of southern Gaul, whose attitudes are reflected in the writings and career of Sidonius Apollinaris, were always ready to come to agreements with Visigoths and Burgundians if it could secure their own and their communities' interests.

The Huns

Ammianus devoted the most famous of all his ethnographic excursuses to an account of the Huns and the Alans, who were supposed to have been responsible for driving the Gothic tribes settled between the rivers Dnieper and Dniester south to the river Danube. The Huns, he reported, lived east of the Sea of Azov near the frozen ocean, and were abnormally savage. Their faces were deeply scarred by gashes that were cut in their children's cheeks, but hairless, like those of eunuchs. "They have squat bodies, strong limbs, and thick necks, and are so prodigiously ugly and bent that they might be two-legged animals, or the figures crudely carved from stumps which are seen on the parapets of bridges" (Ammianus 31.2, trans. Hamilton). They virtually lived on horse-back, roaming over mountains and forests, indifferent to hardship, and never settled to cultivate the land. They were formidable mounted archers, a fact confirmed by a fragment of Olympiodorus (fr. 19) who noted that their leaders (*reges*, "kings") were notable for their skill with the bow. This famous descrip-tion should not be interpreted too literally. Ammianus presented the Huns ac-cording to a familiar ethnographic schema, which contrasted savage, untamed nomadic peoples, who knew no laws, with their settled and civilized counter-parts. He also drew on Herodotus' famous account of the Scythians, which had provided all subsequent classical writers with a model depiction of the horse-riding warriors of the steppes. However, it is at least clear that they were racially distinct from the Germanic peoples, and Ammianus emphasized their alien appearance by comparing them immediately with the tall, fair-headed Alans, with their fierce direct gazes, who joined the Huns in their early raids. Claudian and Jerome, Sidonius and Jordanes all mention the terror and repulsion caused by their physical appearance.[12]

Ammianus may also be misleading when he implies that the Gothic tribes were forced to cross the Danube into the empire by the Huns irresistible onslaught. The Tervingi waited at the river for several weeks before word came from Valens that they were to be admitted into the empire in 376 (Ammianus 31.3–4). In reality the situation was very confused. Some Goths still remained in settlements north of the Danube (Ammianus 31.4.13; Zosimus 4.35.1, 37–9). There is also evidence that groups of Huns had themselves crossed the frontier of the empire, and were recruited into Roman forces by Theodosius I and Valentinian II during the 380s.[13] Since, according to Ammianus, the Huns had no king or overall leader but operated in bands "under the improvised command of their chief men," it would be a mistake to see them as a coherent threat at this period. The first major Hunnish raid on the Roman Empire descended not on the Balkan region but was directed through the Caucasus against Asia Minor in 395, extending south as far as Syria. Tribigild, who was in command of Gothic troops stationed near Nacolea in Phrygia, recorded a notable success against a Hunnic group in 398. It may be that Ammianus, writing in 390s and impressed by these events, exaggerated the influence that the Huns had exercised on Gothic movements in 376.

The first Hunnic leader named by contemporary sources was Uldin, who was responsible for capturing and beheading the Goth Gainas when he fled from the emperor across the Danube after his failed coup in 400. The Roman government of Arcadius rewarded him with the offer of a treaty, and six years later he reappears on the Roman side at the head of a force of Huns that defeated the Germanic barbarians who had invaded Italy under Radagaisus in 405/6 (Orosius 7.37.8; Zosimus 5.26.3–5). It may in fact be the case that increasingly numerous and effective groups of Huns had been responsible in the first instance for driving Radagaisus and his numerous tribal followers out of their homes. The events of 405 were followed on December 31, 406, by another huge multi-ethnic incursion across the upper Rhine, consisting of Vandals, Alans, and Suevi. About the same time it appears that the Burgundians moved from settlements in the area between the upper Rhine and the Danube to new homes west of the Rhine. The numbers crossing into the empire at this date were very large, with figures for armed men numbered in the tens of thousands; and overall numbers in the hundreds of thousands. Hunnic pressure may be the reason for this mass migration, which resembled that of the Tervingi and Greuthungi across the lower Danube in 376. Mounted bands of marauders would have readily terrorized settled Germanic villages in search of plunder and land to support their way of life.[14] However, we should not discount the possibility that the multi-ethnic forces introduced at the beginning of 407 had in fact been brought into Gaul by Honorius and his advisors, faced as they were by the prospect of a civil war with Constantine III. By 408 Uldin had taken his followers to Castra Martia in Dacia Ripensis, and boasted that nothing was beyond the Huns to achieve "He pointed to the sun and declared that it would be easy for him, if he so desired, to subjugate every region of the earth that is enlightened by that luminary" (Sozomen 9.5.2–3).

Almost all that we can say about the realities of Hunnic society at this period is based on analogies with better documented nomadic groups of the Asiatic steppe. E. A. Thompson suggests that small groups of families, living in tents and moving between grazing grounds, formed camps of about fifty to sixty people, and these in turn might fuse into clans several hundred strong. Groups of clans in turn operated in concert to form tribes, with a population of some thousands. The sources include the names of several Hunnic tribes, such as the Akatziri, who occupied territory east of the Black Sea in the mid-fifth century,[15] and the 7,000 Kutrigurs, who menaced Constantinople in 559 (Agathias 5.22). It is implausible that the threat of the Huns to the settled peoples of eastern Europe was posed by teeming hordes of mounted warriors, since pastoral economies were incapable of supporting such concentrations of population. However, rapidity of movement and the terror that the Huns inspired by their behavior and appearance will have been powerful reasons why enemies overestimated their numbers. For the most part Hunnic forces attested on specific occasions numbered between 200 and 1,200. Larger forces could only be maintained with the support of the Roman commissariat (Zosimus 5.50.1).[16]

The eastern response to the Huns, and to other threats from the Balkans, was to build the new walls of Constantinople in 413 and to strengthen the Danube fleet in 412 (CTh. 7.17.1, cf. 7.16.2). Up to this point relations between the Huns and the Roman Empire had been good, thanks to the close links established by the western generalissimo, Aetius, who had spent time among them as a hostage. The western chronicles indicate that Aetius had been able to use Hunnic forces to control other barbarian groups, including the Visigoths in 425, 430, and 436, the Franks who gave trouble in 428 and 432, and also the Bagaudae of western Gaul and the Burgundians in 436–7. However, in 440 the Huns, now under the joint leadership of Attila and his brother Bleda, who were doubtless inspired by the Vandal success, refused to cooperate with Rome and launched a major invasion across the Danube. This setback was aggravated by growing Vandal pressure in Africa. In 442 Aetius had to cede the wealthy provinces of Proconsularis and Byzacena to the Vandals, receiving in exchange the poorer regions of Numidia. The overall loss of tax revenue led to the introduction of a 4 percent sales tax and the cutting of tax exemptions.

These extreme pressures on the empire ushered in a twelve-year period, during which the Huns were able, without inflicting an outright military defeat, to impose their will on both the eastern and the western empire. The historian Priscus, who himself took part in a critical embassy to Attila in 449, is an extraordinarily valuable source of information about this period of Hunnic domination.[17] His fragments, above all the account of the embassy of 449, are the cornerstone of our understanding of Hunnic affairs and Roman foreign policy in the mid-fifth century.

In 435 the Hunnic king Rua was succeeded by the brothers Attila and Bleda. At the fort of Constantia on the north bank of the Danube opposite Margus they negotiated a treaty which determined Hunnic relations with the eastern empire for the next twelve years. Romans were to receive no more fugitives from the Huns and surrender those they had. The ransom price for Roman prisoners was raised from one to eight gold *solidi* per head; the Romans were not to support barbarian tribes which fought the Huns. Markets were to be set up where Huns and Romans could do business. The Romans were to pay an annual sum of 700 gold pounds (up from 350) to keep the peace. Two refugees from a ruling Hunnic family who had fled to the Romans were returned to Attila and Bleda, and executed on territory controlled by the Huns within view of the Thracian fortress of Carsium (Priscus fr. 2). Terror was an essential ingredient of Hunnic diplomacy, and fear of the Huns is cited as the major reason why the Romans agreed to much harsher terms when the peace was updated in 447. After defeating a Roman army in the Thracian Chersonesus, Attila had launched a major attack on Constantinople, and the city was preserved only after its inhabitants made a supreme effort to repair the walls of Theodosius, which had been thrown down by an earthquake. The new agreement stipulated the payment to the Huns of 6,000 gold pounds owing in back tribute, future annual payments of 2,100 pounds, and a ransom price of 12 pounds per Roman prisoner. Priscus dwells at length on the privations which Attila's new demands inflicted on the inhabitants of Constantinople (Priscus fr. 9.3).

In 449 the eunuch Chrysaphius, then at the height of his powers in Theodosius' court, hatched a plot to persuade one of Attila's closest associates, Edeko, who had come on an embassy to Constantinople, to assassinate his master. Priscus himself was a member of the reciprocal embassy to Attila, and thus narrates not only the encounter of the Roman group with the Huns but also the unfolding drama of the assassination plot, which was betrayed to Attila at a very early moment by Edeko (Priscus fr. 11–14).

Attila's Huns were completely transformed from the nomads of Ammianus' description. Attila himself dominated all around him with the terror and cunning of a tyrant. He was supported by a close entourage consisting of clan leaders and members of his own family, including many sons. The overriding characteristics of Attila's regime were intimidation, greed, and the remorseless exercise of power. The economic basis of his authority came from two sources. From 435 to 450 the Huns milked the eastern Roman Empire for everything they could extract: booty from the looted cities of the Danube region, escalating tribute requirements from the state treasury in Constantinople, ever larger ransom demands for captive prisoners, and the expectation of lavish gifts for every representative who undertook embassies to meet the Romans. The other basis of the Hunnic economy was trade. Frontier trading posts are one of the keys to understanding the interface between Romans and barbarians along the length of its northern frontier. Sources identify these fairs at Margus, Viminacium, Naissus in the Balkans, and at Cherson in the Crimea. For their part the Huns, or their subjects, could deliver horses, skins, furs, and slaves. What they sought, above all, were the luxuries of the Roman Empire: jewelry, costly textiles, spices, costly foods, wine. Attila's village encampment, at an unlocated site in the Hungarian plain west of the Carpathian Mountains, could even boast a bathhouse, built from stone that had been laboriously carted from the Roman province of Pannonia. It had been built by a prisoner of war captured during the Hunnic seizure of Sirmium in 441. Trade was not only essential for the growth of Hunnic power but also helps to explain the readiness of the east Romans to opt for a policy of appeasement, by paying tribute, rather than attempting a military confrontation. The wealth acquired by Attila's people had to be spent. Large sums will have been used in buying the allegiance of a kaleidoscopic medley of Germanic peoples and other barbarians extending west almost to the Rhine and east to the fringes of the Caucasus. But much of the cash would have found its way back into the empire, used as payment at the frontier fairs for the luxuries and comforts that the empire had to offer. Two episodes from the diplomatic exchanges between the Huns and the court at Constantinople underline the crucial importance of trade to the barbarians, and the fact that the border that divided their territory from the Romans was not primarily intended as a military frontier but as a crucial location of trade and exchange. In 449, when Edeko came to Constantinople after Attila's destructive incursions of the previous years, he asserted the Huns' claim to a broad strip of land south of the Danube, extending from Pannonia to Thrace, which the Huns had conquered.

Furthermore, he said that the market in Illyria was not on the bank of the Danube, as it had been before, but at Naissus, which he had laid waste and established as the border point between the Scythian and the Roman territory, it being five days' journey from the Danube for an unladen man. (Priscus fr. 11.1, trans. Blockley)

Some years after the fall of Attila, in the reign of Leo, the former's sons came to the emperor with the request that "a peace treaty should be made and that in the old manner they should meet with the Romans at the Danube, establish a market and exchange whatever they received" (Priscus fr. 46, trans. Blockley). They were sent away empty-handed by the emperor, who ruled that since they had done much damage to Roman territory, they should not have access to Roman trade.

Priscus provides many insights into the mixture of cultures and languages which were to be heard around Attila's encampment: Gothic, Latin, the Hun's own language (of which only a single word seems to be recorded), and even Greek. At the heart of his narrative Priscus reported his encounter with a native of Greece, who had become a businessman at Viminacium, doubtless profiting from the cross-border trade, until he became the prisoner and slave of Attila's close associate Onegesius. He had won his freedom by the courage he had displayed in a war against the Akatziri, but opted to stay in his new home. Priscus reports (or rather invents) the discussion they shared about the virtues of life on either side of the Roman frontier, a topic that is better interpreted as a rhetorical commonplace than as a faithful report of their exchange of views.[18] The Greek emigrant to the Huns argued that he lived a life of comfort and leisure. Above all he had no taxes to pay, and he was spared the inequalities of Roman law, and the attentions of corrupt judges and their assessors. It is striking that a similar point is made by the Christian historian, Orosius, when he alluded to Romans who chose to live among the barbarians, poor but free, rather than among the Romans burdened by oppressive taxes (Orosius 7.41.7). Priscus' response is a rather frigid presentation of an ideal Roman *Rechtsstaat*. The arguments he presents have an academic feel to them – the shadow of Plato hangs over this ideal republic – but their emphasis precisely on the rule of law is significant. Amid the cultural and ethnic confusion of the eastern as well as the western empire in the mid-fifth century, nothing defined *Romanitas* more surely than its written laws.

The Germanic Kingdoms of Western Europe in the Fifth Century

The most important historical development of the fifth century in the West was the emergence of the Germanic kingdoms, which engulfed the former western provinces of the empire: The main groups were the Visigoths in southwest Gaul and Spain, the Burgundians in the upper Rhone valley, the Merovingian Franks of northern and central Gaul, and the eastern Goths, based in Pannonia through the third quarter of the century, who were to take control of Italy under Theoderic. In addition, the ethnic and political landscape included

Suebians in northwest Spain; Saxons, who were active in the English Channel and on the European Atlantic seaboard; Thuringians and Scirians east of the Rhine and in the upper Danube basin; as well as robust relics of Roman provincial society in Gaul, such as the group that formed around Aegidius and Syagrius in the Soissons district; the old landed aristocracy of Provence, who produced a Roman emperor in the person of Avitus; and the shadowy Bagaudae, attested in the western areas of Brittany and in northern Spain, who may have been peasant insurgents, or the armed followers of regional landowners.

The major groupings, by organizing armed forces under recognized leaders, were able to assert their status as independent kingdoms, based on permanent occupation of territory within the former Roman dioceses of Gaul and Spain. The legitimacy of each kingdom depended not only on its innate political and military authority, but also on its relationship to the Roman emperors, from whom all claimed recognition. Institutionally, the fifth century kingdoms combined Germanic tribal practices with those of Roman provincial society. The most important of these was the retention, usually in modified form, of Roman legal practices, which were embodied in new written law codes. For the most part German kings ruled their subjects with Roman methods and tools. The populations of these kingdoms were mixed. The majority were evidently the indigenous Roman provincial inhabitants, of all classes and stations from the simplest peasants to the great landowners, who perforce recognized in the Germanic tribal kings a new set of authorities to replace their former Roman governors. The tribal rulers required land for themselves and their followers. The nature of this land settlement, as discussed above, is both obscure and controversial, although it is fundamental to our understanding of how these kingdoms functioned in economic and social terms.

This revolutionary change to the political environment of the western provinces destabilized existing power structures. The urban centers, which had been the main focal points of Roman authority, declined, particularly in northern and central Gaul, and yielded ground to power based in rural landholdings. The tendency to retain wealth in the countryside rather than concentrate it in urban centers had always been an important aspect of Gallic society. Meanwhile, civic leadership at a local level was increasingly a matter for the church and its bishops. These played a leading role in championing their communities, intervening to protect local people from the newcomers, and mediating between the Roman and German peoples. Religion, however, remained a major means of differentiation between the Romans and most of the Germanic groups. The Christian Roman population of the western provinces had been almost universally Catholic and Trinitarian since the pioneering years of the mid-fourth century. The Germanic tribal peoples were mostly Arian. Religious polarization, while rarely a source of overt friction (as it was in Vandal Africa), remained nevertheless a crucial strategy which helped to perpetuate the distinction between the old and new populations. Religious allegiance also helped to define the stance of specific Germanic groups to the Roman Empire. Thus when the Frankish king Clovis adopted Christianity towards the end of the fifth century he was baptized a Catholic by bishop Remigius of Reims. This aligned him as a potential ally of the eastern Roman emperors and marked his opposition to the Arian Visigoths. In like manner the majority of the Burgundians declared themselves to be Catholic as part of their strategy to align themselves as far as possible with Roman interests during their power struggles with their neighbors.

The Visigoths

In 416 the Visigothic king Vallia sent Galla Placidia, the widow of his predecessor Athaulph, back to her brother the emperor Honorius. In return in 418 the Romans concluded a treaty with him, which handed over to the Goths the province of Aquitania Secunda, the valley of the Garonne. Vallia was succeeded in 418 by Theoderic I, who expanded Gothic control west towards Provence and the Rhone valley.[19]

Aetius, supreme commander in the western empire, relying largely on Hunnish forces, was successful during the later 430s in containing Theoderic's ambitions and protecting the administrative centers of Arles and Narbonne, but Rome suffered two serious setbacks which restricted its ability to impose its authority in Gaul. One was the fall of Carthage to the Vandals in 439, which led both the eastern and western emperors to look to the defenses of Rome, Italy, and Constantinople against the real threat of Vandal sea-power. The Romans now had to come to terms with the economic stranglehold over the empire, which was implicit in Vandal control of African grain exports and tax revenues. The other was the growing power of Attila's Huns, who withdrew cooperation from Rome, and for a decade virtually held Ravenna and Constantinople to ransom by a combination of threats of war and demands for tribute.[20] As Valentinian put it in a letter to Theoderic I, "the Huns do not overthrow nations by means of war, where there is an equal chance, but assail them by treachery, which is a greater cause for anxiety" (Jordanes, *Get.* XXXVI, 188, trans. Mierow). The Roman population of southern Gaul had to look to its own defense.

In 451 the Huns switched the focus of their attention from Constantinople to the West, and invaded Gaul with a force that also included the Amal-led branch of the Ostrogoths, under Valamir, Thiudomer, and Vidimer, and the Gepids under Ardaric (Jordanes, *Get.* XXXVIII, 199). A group of Alans resident at Orleans and led by Sangiban promised to hand the city to Attila. Metz, the largest city of northern Gaul, was stormed and burned on May 7, leaving only the Oratory of St Stephen unscathed (Greg. Tur., *Hist.* 2.6). The Huns had reached Orleans before they were confronted with a determined coalition led by Aetius. His allies included all the Germanic groups in Gaul: Saxons, Burgundians, Franks, as well as Armoricans from Brittany, Riparians from the Rhineland settlements, and Olibriones, former Roman soldiers (Jordanes, *Get.* XXXVI, 191). Attila withdrew as far as the Champagne country. A territorial skirmish between Franks and Alans preceded the main battle, which claimed enormous casualties, including the Visigothic king Theoderic himself. The Huns were driven to take refuge in their wagon laager, but confusion and division prevented their enemies from securing an outright victory. Aetius persuaded Theoderic's son Thorismund not to avenge his father's death in the aftermath of the battle, advising him to return to Toulouse and secure his kingdom before his position was usurped by his brothers, who had not joined him on the campaign. Aetius' alleged motive was to prevent the Goths from destroying the Huns completely and then challenging Roman power. He was also mindful that his own power rested largely on the Hunnish forces that he had been able to command throughout his career.[21]

Aetius' advice to the Visigoths was prophetic. Thorismund was murdered in 453 and succeeded by his younger brother Theoderic II, who began to show the ambition that Aetius had feared. In 455, as the western empire had been shaken by the Vandal capture of Rome, the Visigoths promoted the Gallic aristocrat Avitus, an erstwhile tutor of Theoderic II, who had been praetorian prefect of Gaul in 439 and had helped persuade the Visigoths to resist Attila in 451, to succeed the short-lived Petronius Maximus as emperor.[22] The Visigoths then took his authority to attack the Suevi in Spain. In 456 Theoderic defeated his brother-in-law, the Suevic king Rechiar, at the battle of the river Orbigo, and his followers took control of southeastern Spain. The Visigothic position in Spain was strengthened after the fall of Majorian, and extended to include Narbonne in 461, but they were confined on their northern border by the independent Roman kingdom of Aegidius (Greg. Tur., *Hist.* 2.9, 11, 12).

The effectiveness of the Visigoths as rulers depended on their ability to work with the great estate-owning families of Gaul and Spain. The Goths provided military security and stability, while the old provincial aristocracy maintained civil law, the institutions of the Catholic Church, and normal economic structures. Warfare fought against their neighbors on all fronts, including Saxons, Bagaudae, Burgundians, and the kingdom of Aegidius, provided the Goths with booty, while the land of Provence and Aquitaine continued to yield a level of prosperity which was reflected in the survival of important cities through the region: Bordeaux, Toulouse, St Bertrand de Comminges, Carcassonne, Narbonne, Marseilles, and Arles. The correspondence of Sidonius shows that between the 450s and the 480s the landowners of Aquitaine, Provence, and the Auvergne continued to maintain an impressively high standard of living in their rural estates.

Sidonius Apollinaris, who married the daughter of the emperor Avitus, and was to become bishop of Clermont-Ferrand in the Auvergne in 469, is the prime witness to the society and culture of southern Gaul. His poetry includes panegyrics for leading figures of the period, while his letters reflect the artificially civilized manners of the landed gentry, based on farming and hunting, western classical culture, and Christian piety. They offer a sanitized view of the often tense relations between Goths and Romans.[23] He is responsible for the fullest pen portrait of any Germanic ruler of the fifth century in a letter

addressed to Avitus' son Agricola. The transparent intention is to idealize the
king. "The rule of God and nature's order have adorned his personality with
gifts of consummate felicity, and his character is such that not even jealousy
can deny it the praise which is its due" (Sidonius, *ep.* 1.2.1, trans. Anderson).
After an admiring page on the king's personal appearance and his careful
grooming, Sidonius explained the course of a royal day: pre-dawn religious
devotions with his Arian clergy (a matter, according to this Catholic observer,
of form rather than conviction), a morning spent in administrative cares,
inspecting the treasury and the stables.[24] A short siesta is followed by games
of backgammon, which provided opportunities for defeated rivals to ask for
difficult favors, followed by a further round of petitions. Dinner may be accompanied by the music of stringed instruments (the Goths favored a sort of three-
stringed guitar),[25] or the diversion of a court jester. Armed nobles stand
alongside the king, skin-clad Gothic retainers mutter among themselves behind the throne-room awnings, and marshals organize access. This remained
a Germanic, not a Mediterranean court, and the palace was protected by
sentries and night guards watching the treasury. Leisure and pleasure came
from hunting, archery, and fine dining with weighty conversation. "You may
see there the elegance of the Greeks, the generosity of the Gauls, the swiftness
of Italy, public pomp, private attentiveness and kingly discipline."[26] Sidonius
does his best to assimilate what he had seen of the Gothic court with his own
compatriots' ideals of aristocratic country life. The king's counselors appear
elsewhere in Sidonius' pages, "old in years but green in wisdom," assembled
at dawn in their greasy linen shirts, short animal skin coats, and high boots of
horse-hide, laced up below the knee (Sidonius, *Carm.* 7, 452–7).

Theoderic was murdered by his younger brother Euric in 465. Euric's reign
until 484 spanned the fall of the last Roman emperor in the West, and his robust
external policies surely sprang from the realization that western emperors had
had their day. As Jordanes put it,

> Now Euric, king of the Visigoths, perceived the frequent change of Roman em-
> perors and strove to hold Gaul by his own right. (Jordanes, *Get.* XLV, 237)

During the early 470s he defeated a force of Brittones and sought to control
the Auvergne. The region resorted in the main to self help. Sidonius appealed to
Avitus, a relative of the emperor, to protect Clermont-Ferrand by interceding
with the Visigoths:

> The Goths time and again despise and reject their own territory of Septimania,
> so that they may control and occupy this little corner even though they have
> devastated it. But it is right for you, standing between them and the Roman
> state, under God's command to devise a more peaceful way, because, although
> they have broken through the restraints of the old boundaries and with all their
> courage or rather all their might are extending the boundaries of their violent
> occupation as far as the Rhone and the Loire, your authoritative voice by the

dignity of its pronouncements will cause both sides to moderate their actions, so that our people will learn what it should deny them when it is asked, and our enemies will cease to demand what they are refused. (Sidonius, *ep.* 3.1.4–5)

Arles and Marseilles were captured in 476. Euric's ambitions gave a harder edge to Gothic policy vis-à-vis the Romans in Gaul. The religious conflict with Roman Christianity and the Catholic clergy intensified,[27] and Sidonius himself was imprisoned in Toulouse in 475–6. This consolidation in Gaul was followed by Visigothic campaigns in Spain, including the annexation of Tarraconensis.

It is a clear reflection of the fallen empire that Euric was the first Visigothic ruler to give his name to a law code, the *Codex Euricianus*. Now the Goths "first acquired the institutes of law in writing; previously they were held only by custom and tradition."[28] Germanic kings, not Roman emperors, had become the sovereign authority even in the field of written law.[29] Euric's code was drafted in Latin and closely modeled on Roman precedent and principle, as was to be expected, but it was concerned with local issues, in particular property and land disputes. Practical application and enforcement depended on local arbitrators, who were chosen with the agreement of the disputing parties. The law itself covered the needs of Goths and Romans alike, and was evidently devised by Roman experts under Gothic supervision. One of these was probably Leo, a close advisor of Euric, who had once invited Sidonius to take up historical writing.[30] Leo's role emerges in outline in a remarkable letter from Sidonius, sent to accompany the dispatch of a Latin translation of Philostratus' *Life of Apollonius*, which Leo had requested from him:

> Put aside for a little while those acclaimed speeches which you compose as the royal mouthpiece, by which the famous king himself at one moment strikes fear into the hearts of races across the sea, at another, as a victor from on high, schemes a treaty for barbarians trembling by the river Vachalis, and at another, as he constrains the people throughout the boundaries of the extended portion of his kingdom by force of arms, so he constrains armed force by laws. (Sidonius, *ep.* 8.3.3)

Leo, we may assume, played the role of a Themistius or a Cassiodorus for his royal employer. Euric's court was increasingly bi-cultural, as it was certainly bilingual. The king had attempted unsuccessfully to attract the services of Sidonius as a regular panegyricist;[31] his wife Ragnahild, however, was gratified with six flattering elegiac couplets, which were minutely inscribed on a silver drinking cup (Sidonius, *ep.* 4.8.4–5). Latin gained ground in court circles, and was inevitably the language of law, although German remained the language of power and political exchange. The Visigothic kings would hardly have used Latin to communicate with the other Germanic kingdoms, but even in dealing with an embassy from the western court, Euric used an interpreter.[32] Euric's rising cultural aspirations corresponded to his growing political influence. In a poem which was clearly written to gratify the king, Sidonius presented Euric's court as the destination of diplomatic embassies from the length and breadth of the ancient world: Saxons and Huns, Burgundians and Ostrogoths. Even the Persian king himself was prepared to offer payment – tribute – if Euric refused to send troops to help the eastern emperor.[33]

Euric died in 484 and was succeeded by his son Alaric II, who ruled until 507 and further strengthened the Visigothic position in Gaul. Whereas Euric had steered his people through the transition from dependent to independent Germanic kingdom, Alaric was fully on terms with the demise of Roman political authority in the West. Perhaps for that reason he seems to have been more comfortable with appropriating Roman legal institutions. The law code which was issued in his own name, the *Breviarium* of Alaric published in 506, was in essence a digest of Roman laws and opinions, derived from the classical jurists, which had been compiled by a *consilium* or committee of Roman legal experts (*prudentes*), in consultation with priests and provincial notables, all under the supervision of one of the king's Gothic retainers, the *comes* Goiaricus.[34] This, as John Matthews argues, was a body of law designed not with the purpose of distinguishing between Goths and Romans, but of bringing them together under a common authority. Its Roman nature and origins are dramatically illustrated by the inclusion of Valentinian I's interpretation of a law contained in the Theodosian Code, that no Roman, male or female, should marry a barbarian wife of any race, subject to a capital penalty.[35] In parallel to the integration of the two races under a single system of law and government, Alaric also sought to reconcile the majority Catholic population of his kingdom with the Arianism of the Gothic ruling class at a council concluded at Agde in September 506.[36]

Alaric established a crucial marriage alliance with the Ostrogoths by marrying Theodegotha, the daughter of Theoderic the Amal, probably soon after the latter replaced Odoacar as king in Italy in 493. Visigothic power in Gaul lasted until 507, when Alaric was defeated and killed at the battle of Vouillé (or Voulon), south of Poitiers, by the Franks.[37]

The Burgundians

The greatest saga of the post-Roman age, the *Niebelungenlied*, the basis for Wagner's Ring operas, has its historical roots in one of the smaller Germanic kingdoms of fifth-century Gaul, that of the Burgundians.[38] In 413 the short-lived Roman usurper Iovinus awarded to his Burgundian ally Gundahar (Gunther) a kingdom west of the Rhine around Worms. The kingdom was virtually destroyed by Aetius commanding an army of Hunnish mercenaries in 435,[39] but in 443 Aetius resettled Burgundians around and south of lake Geneva.[40] These *foederati*, ruled by the brothers Gundioc and Chilperic, served the Roman Empire in the west against Attila. In 456, after the fall of the Gallic emperor Avitus, they extended their influence as far south as Lyon. They lost ground to the martial emperor Majorian (Maiorianus) and the Roman magnate Aegidius, who claimed Lyon in 458, but after the fall of Majorian in 461 the Burgundians recovered their southern possessions and extended them to the valley of the Drôme. This was with the approval and connivance of Ricimer, who had married Gundioc's sister, and appointed Gundioc to the Roman rank of *magister militum*. When the emperor Zeno sent an easterner, Anthemius, to replace Libius Severus as emperor, the praetorian prefect of Gaul, Arvandus, claiming to represent the interests of the Gallic aristocracy, proposed that his prefecture be divided between the Visigoths and the Burgundians. Gundioc's younger son Gundobad was also made *magister militum* by Ricimer, and led the campaign against Anthemius, strangling him with his own hands in Rome in 472. After the death of Gundioc in the early 470s, Chilperic adopted a pro-Roman stance against the Visigoths, who were attempting to seize the Rhone valley, and challenged their authority over the Auvergne. The Burgundians also took on the Alemanni in the region of the Jura and the Vosges. The relationship between their rulers and the western court, which was fostered during the hegemony of Ricimer, consolidated Burgundian status as Rome's most favored federate allies and the ties were strengthened by a new treaty between Chilperic and Rome in 474.[41]

Sidonius, in humorous hendecasyllables which parody Catullus (his addressee was called Catullinus), had categorized his "seven-foot Burgundian patrons" as archetypical Germans:

> Why, even if I had the skill, do you order me to compose a poem for Dione, lover of Fescennine verse, when I am situated among bands of hairy folk, having to put up with German conversation, and to praise with a wry face the songs sung by gluttonous Burgundians, who have greased their hair with rancid butter. (Sidonius, *Carm.* 12, 1–6)

But this little satire belied the strong Burgundian inclination to adopt a Roman cultural identity. Until the fall of the western empire, it seems clear that the Burgundians still identified themselves as Roman *foederati*.[42] Under Valentinian I, around 369, the Burgundians claimed kinship with the Romans (Ammianus 28.5.11–13). This affinity was demonstrated by their religious politics. Many Burgundians were Catholics, not Arians.[43] Clotild, daughter of Chilperic, the Burgundian wife of the Frankish king Clovis, is credited by Gregory of Tours with pushing him towards Catholicism (Greg. Tur., *Hist.* 2.28–31). According to Gregory, Chilperic's brothers, Gundobad and Godigisel, were both Arians, along with their followers. Chilperic fought a civil war with Godigisel, who was based in Vienne and supported by Clovis, and Gundobad, who controlled Avignon. Gundobad eventually prevailed, but was persuaded to adopt the Catholic faith by Vienne's influential bishop Avitus (Greg. Tur., *Hist.* 2.34). Acting on Gundobad's behalf in 499, Avitus had been able to obtain recognition from the Pope that the bishop of Vienne among the Burgundians, not the bishop of Arles among the Visigoths, should be the chief metropolitan of all Gaul.

A remarkable feature of Burgundian *Romanitas* was the tradition they established of using the Roman system of consular dating for inscriptions and legal documents. The practice is particularly conspicuous in the epigraphic record for the century between 480 and 580, but continued until the mid-seventh century. It thus outlasted the practice of dating by consuls in Italy itself, and continued long after the demise of the independent kingdom of Burgundy in 534. The practice marked the region and the Burgundians apart from their neighbors, and shows clearly that ethnic identity could be asserted not only by stressing indigenous traditions, real or fictive, but also by the ostentatious adoption of an external cultural marker.[44] It is notable that almost all the acts of Gallic church councils in the first half of the sixth century use this consular dating system as a badge of their Roman affiliations.

Gundobad's son, Sigismund, who married Theoderic the Amal's daughter Ostrogotho sometime before 497, and succeeded his father in 516, also became a Catholic.[45] Avitus was one of his close advisors, and it was Avitus, writing on Sigismund's behalf, who averred to Anastasius, the emperor in Constantinople, that "my people is yours," and that the Burgundians would serve Rome rather than fight for their own independent interests (Avitus, *ep.* 93, trans. Shantzer and Wood p. 144). Sigismund was duly rewarded from Constantinople with the rank of a *patricius*. Social and political reasons were surely responsible for the changing religious allegiance of the Burgundians. The shift from Arianism to Catholicism indicated that they were aligning themselves with the provincial population of the Rhone valley and the Auvergne, who were led by influential families of the former Roman aristocracy, and organized by their powerful and effective Roman bishops. They thus turned their backs on the Visigoths, whose influence in southern France in any case ended with the defeat of Alaric by Clovis in 507.

Like the Visigoths, the Burgundians enjoyed the cooperation of Romano-Gallic landowners and aristocrats, who provided them with a professional cadre of diplomats, administrators, and legal experts. The most striking of these was Syagrius, great-grandson of a Roman consul and a man of high literary culture, to whom Sidonius wrote a teasing letter about his mastery of the German language in which he was able to correct the Burgundians themselves:

> It is incredible to relate how amazed I am that you have grasped a knowledge of the German language with such facility. . . . The bowed elders of the Germans are amazed as you translate their letters, and have taken you on as a judge and arbitrator in their business with one another. (Sidonius, *ep.* 5.5.1 and 3)

Sidonius, who comically pretended to fear that Syagrius might forget his Latin culture, called him a Solon among the Burgundians, who discussed their laws. Syagrius may have had a hand in creating the Burgundian law code. The Burgundian law codes that have survived were created somewhat later than those of the Visigoths. A *lex Gundobada* of around 500 was followed in 519 by the *lex Romana Burgundionum*, which was concerned with the legal distinctions between Burgundians and Romans under the conditions created by the arrival of Germanic newcomers into the former Roman provinces, and the *Lex Constitutionum*, modeled in form on the Theodosian Code, which was drawn up under Sigismund.[46] Gregory of Tours observed that Gundobad instituted milder laws among his people, to stop them treating the Romans unjustly (Greg. Tur., *Hist.* 2.33).

The Franks

The Franks first appeared among Rome's enemies in northern Gaul in the later 250s. In 286 the new emperor Maximianus made a treaty with the Frankish king Gennobaudes,[47] as a consequence of which many Franks entered Roman service. It was alleged at the time of the supposed revolt of the Frankish officer Silvanus in 355 that "a large number at that time had influence in the palace" (Ammianus 15.5.5, cf. 11). Such men became Christians. Silvanus was murdered as he sought sanctuary in a chapel in Cologne (Ammianus 15.5.26). Frankish *foederati* probably made up the largest non-Roman contingents of the fourth-century army in the Roman West.[48] Meanwhile independent Franks were an established force in northeast Gaul by 350. Some of these figures preserved their status both within the Roman and the Frankish hierarchy, notably the warrior Mallobaudes, who had a military career which spanned more than twenty-five years from Constantius to Gratian, when he is described simultaneously as count of the household troops and king of the Franks, *comes domesticorum et rex Francorum.*[49] The Franks Bauto and Arbogast, who dominated the youthful Valentinian II, played an increasingly prominent role in the western empire towards the end of the fourth century.

After the middle of the fifth century, the king of the Salian Franks, Childeric, became a major power in northern Gaul.[50] He supported Aegidius in his battle against the Visigoths in 463, and helped another Roman *comes*, Paulus, to defeat the Scirian Odoacar and an army of Saxons at Angers in 469. He was succeeded around 481 by his son Clovis. Clovis extended Frankish power by defeating Syagrius, son of Aegidius, in the neighborhood of Soissons, in the 480s, and the Alemanni and Riparian Franks along the Rhine in he following decade. The decisive moment in his career was the battle of Vouillé/Voulon near Poitiers of 507, in which he defeated the Visigoth Alaric II. Had it not been for the intervention of Theoderic the Amal with Ostrogothic forces in 508, he would have been able to extend his kingdom to the Mediterranean.

The ethnography of northern Gaul in the early fifth century was a complicated matter, as Procopius recognized. In an interesting passage, he drew a clear distinction between the free Germans (his designation for the Franks), the native people called the Arborychi, which is probably a mistake for the Armorici who lived in Brittany and northwest Gaul, and the Roman military settlers in the frontier areas, who should surely be identified as Germanic, that is Frankish *foederati*:

> But as time went on, the Visigoths forced their way into the Roman Empire and seized all Spain and the portion of Gaul lying beyond the Rhone river and made

them subject and tributary to themselves. By that time it so happened that the Arborychi had become soldiers of the Romans. And the Germans, wishing to make this people subject to themselves, since their territory adjoined their own and they had changed the government under which they lived from of old, began to plunder their land and, being eager to make war, marched against them with their whole people. But the Arborychi proved their valour and loyalty to the Romans and showed themselves brave men in this war, and since the Germans were not able to overcome them by force, they wished to win them over and make their two peoples kin by intermarriage. This suggestion the Arborychi received not at all unwillingly; for both, as it happened, were Christians. And in this way they were united into one people and came to have great power.

Now other Roman soldiers also had been stationed at the frontiers of Gaul to guard it. And these soldiers, having no means of returning to Rome, and being unwilling to yield to their enemy who were Arians, gave themselves together with their standards and the land, which they for long had guarded for the Romans, to the Arborychi and the Germans. And they handed down to their descendants all the customs of their fathers which were thus preserved, and this people has held them in sufficient reverence to guard them up to my time. For even at the present day they are clearly recognised as belonging to the legions to which they were assigned when they served in ancient times, and they always carry their own standards when they enter battle, and always follow the customs of their fathers. And they preserve the dress of the Romans in every particular even as regards their shows. (Procopius, *Bell. Goth.* 5.12.12–19, trans. Dewing)

Gregory of Tours implies that the Franks under Childeric had mainly been pagans. "They fashioned idols for themselves out of birds and beasts: these they worshipped in place of God and to these they made their sacrifices" (Greg. Tur., *Hist.* 2.10, trans. Thorpe). Excavations at the location of Childeric's tomb, which was discovered in the seventeenth century, produced evidence for horse sacrifices, but this may not be sufficient to prove that Childeric himself was a pagan. The royal burial may have been accompanied by traditional pagan practices.[51] Clovis at first worshipped idols made of stone, metal or wood, not gods (Greg. Tur., *Hist.* 2.29). Gregory of Tours says that he adopted Catholic Christianity after his marriage to the Burgundian princess, Clotild, and as a consequence of a victory over the Alemanni around 496, which could be attributed to God's support.[52] However, conversion did not come out of a blue sky, and the date is also in dispute. Clovis' and Childeric's earlier paganism had certainly been rooted in native traditions of leadership. They invented a lineage for their dynasty which went back two generations to a bull-like creature, which had mated in the sea with the wife of a Frankish noble, Clodio. She have birth to Merovech, the eponymous founder of the Merovingian dynasty and supposed father of Childeric (Greg. Tur., *Hist.* 2.9). Such a lineage was better suited to tribal Germans than to successor kingdoms of the Roman Empire. On the other hand, the Franks who had reached high rank under the emperors had all been Christian, and Christianity had also made headway among the people as a whole, as Procopius indicates. At the end of the narrative of Clovis' baptism by Remigius, bishop of Reims, Gregory reveals that the king's sister Lanthechild was converted at the same time from her former Arian ways. Clovis' approach to Christianity was certainly a more gradual process than Gregory of Tours suggests. The main significance of Clovis' shift to Catholicism was political and signaled his ambition to take on the mantle of Roman power. Avitus, bishop of Vienne, underlined Frankish aspirations to become a major ruler in the post-Roman world in a letter to the king: "Your faith is our victory . . . Greece no longer has only a single catholic ruler" (Avitus, *ep.* 49). The king of the Franks, this implied, could now assume the rule of a western emperor. Gregory of Tours described Clovis emerging from the pool of baptism "like a new Constantine" (Greg. Tur., *Hist.* 2.31). By adopting Catholicism, Clovis not only appealed to the non-Arian Roman inhabitants of the Visigothic kingdom, but also attracted support from Constantinople. The eastern emperors had been aware of the growing power of the Franks since the mid-fifth century. Childeric's tomb contained a large hoard of gold *solidi* minted for eastern emperors, and Leo had summoned a Frank, Titus, to Constantinople, where he had fallen under the spell of the Stylite saint Daniel (*Life of Daniel* 60–3). The eastern emperor, Anastasius, awarded Clovis a consulship in 508, and Clovis himself took on the trappings of a victorious emperor:[53]

Letters reached Clovis from the emperor Anastasius to confer the consulate on him. In St Martin's church he stood clad in a purple tunic and the military mantle, and he crowned himself with a diadem. He then rode out on his horse, showered gold and silver coins among the people present all the way from the doorway of St Martin's church to Tours cathedral. From that day on he was called consul or Augustus. (Greg. Tur., *Hist.* 2.38, trans. Thorpe)

Clovis died in 511, and chose to be buried, like Constantine and in striking contrast to his father Chilperic, in another Church of the Holy Apostles, at Paris.[54]

Clovis was survived by four male children. It now became the custom for the Frankish kingdom to be divided between the previous ruler's surviving sons. The three sons of Clotild, his second wife, were involved in disputes with each other over the Burgundian kingdom, which they occupied in 524. Their power was overshadowed by Clovis' eldest son, Theoderic I, and his son Theodebert I, who succeeded him in 533. They controlled the west bank of the Rhine from the North Sea to the Alps, and Theodebert took full advantage of the situation in 536 when Justinian's Roman forces undertook the reconquest of Italy. The Franks offered their support both to the Romans and to the Ostrogoths, acquired control of Provence from the latter, who were too hard pressed to defend it themselves, and then marched into northern Italy in 539. They sacked Milan and took control of much of Liguria. Procopius offers the partisan eastern view that Theodebert and his 100,000 barbarous followers had not yet abandoned paganism and conducted human sacrifice among their captives.[55]

They began to sacrifice the women and children of the Goths whom they had found at hand and to throw their bodies into the river as the first fruits of war.

For these barbarians, though they had become Christians, preserve the greater part of their ancient religion; for they still make human sacrifices and other sacrifices of an unholy nature, and it is in connection with these that they make their prophecies. (Procopius, *Bell. Goth.* 6.25.1–18, trans. Dewing)

Theodebert was succeeded by Theodebald, who had to cede control of northern Italy to the Romans in 548, and who died in 555. This left the way open for the two surviving children of Clotild, Childebert I and Clothar I, to assert their claims, and after the former died in 558, Clothar I became king of all the Frankish peoples until his death in 561. His four sons, Charibert I, Sigebert I, Chilperic I, and Guntram, divided the kingdom as the sons of Clovis had done before, now basing it on four royal residences at Paris, Reims, Soissons, and Orleans.[56] However, there was no corresponding territorial division of Gaul, and each leader had supporters in all areas. The nature of the Frankish kingship was not territorial. Their title to rule was based on their lineage, and the personal following that each could command both among their own people and among the post-Roman landowners. Rulers displayed their power through royal progresses through their realms.

> In the patchwork political fabric of Merovingian Gaul, whose single name conceals a complex web of towns and local elites, the consensus between sixth-century ruler and ruled was constantly exemplified by the *adventus* ceremony. The quintessentially Merovingian institution of the "royal circuit" or *circuitus regis* of a wandering monarchy became so essential a trait of rulership that a seventh-century Frank assumed its roots reached into the Roman past.[57]

The situation was inherently unstable. Charibert I died in 567 and this led to a civil war between Sigebert and Childeric, who both claimed the area of Tours and Poitiers. Guntram, in dispute with Sigebert, joined Chilperic, but he made his peace with Sigebert after Chilperic was defeated near Reims in 575. Chilperic's wife Fredegund hired assassins to murder Sigebert, whose kingdom now passed to his son Childebert II, while he was still a minor. Chilperic died in 584 also leaving a young son, Clothar I, to follow him. In 592 Childebert II inherited the possessions of Guntram, who had no male children, and thus emerged as the strongest of the group, but when he died aged 25 in 596, his kingdom was again divided between his two sons Theodebert II and Theoderic II.[58]

The historical and social fabric of sixth-century Gaul is presented in extraordinary detail by the works of Gregory of Tours, who was born in 538 into one of the major Gallo-Roman families, became bishop of Tours, like many other members of his family, in 573, and died c.594. His *Book of Histories* (most often translated as *History of the Franks*), began with a summary of biblical history and covered events of the fourth and fifth century on the basis of narrative sources available to Gregory, some of which are now lost. For the generation of Clovis' children he will have drawn on oral tradition, and the narrative becomes more detailed. The later books deal with events that happened during his own adult lifetime, and are recorded in a dense chronicle of Herodotean richness. It is evident that Gregory compiled his history as events occurred, continually updating the record until 591. He seems to have used the same process of incremental composition in other surviving works, most notably the lives of martyrs and saints, and the miracles they performed.[59] The huge body of Gregory's writings reflects the outlook of the Christian aristocracy of Gaul a century after Sidonius. The world had changed radically. The balance between Christian and classical allusion had shifted completely in favor of the former. The style and language of Gregory are simple and direct, contrasting with Sidonius' ornate and self-conscious sophistication. The historical world of the Roman Empire, which was still the main cultural frame of reference in fifth-century Gaul, was now no more than a background to a world in which the outlines of medieval Europe are already clear.[60]

Ostrogothic Italy

Theoderic the Amal had gained the position of a Roman insider during the 480s in Constantinople. Zeno had made him a "son in arms," appointed him *magister utriusque militiae praesentalis* and *patricius* in 476. His status was reaffirmed in 484 when he was awarded a consulship. Moreover, from this period he and members of his family were given the titular Roman family name Flavius, which had been employed as a sign of rank since the Constantinian period.[61] When he left the East to recover Italy from Odoacar, he did so in the name of Zeno:

> Zeno . . . made Theoderic a patrician and a consul and gave him a great sum of money, and sent him to Italy. Theoderic stipulated with him that if Odoacar should be vanquished, in return for his own labours he would only rule provisionally (*praeregnare*) in his place, until Zeno should come himself. So, when Theoderic the patrician came from the city of Novae (in Moesia) with his Gothic people, he had been sent by the emperor Zeno from the eastern parts of the empire with the purpose of defending Italy for himself. (*Anon. Val.* part 2, 11, 49)

This was confirmed by Anastasius in 497 in response to an embassy which Theoderic dispatched to Constantinople. Anastasius sent the deputation back to Ravenna with the so-called *ornamenta palatii*, which had been returned to him by Odoacar.[62] Although Theoderic is said to have dressed in a purple robe,[63] these *ornamenta* were a sign of regal, not imperial, rank. His garb depicted a king in the classical style, in contrast to the skin-clad Visigoths, Euric and Alaric. Theoderic conducted himself as an emperor might have been expected to have done. He undertook a major state visit to Rome to celebrate thirty years of rule and this was described at length in his anonymous biography. The visit was accompanied by grain distributions to the poor, and the reconstruction of the palatium and the city walls (see below, chapter 9).

A speech to the people of Rome was duly inscribed, *more Romano,* on a bronze tablet (*Anon. Val.* part 2, 12, 65–70). The date was 500, and he reckoned his rule to have begun not from the defeat of Odoacar, but from the moment in 470 when he had taken over leadership of the Amal Goths. Although Theoderic's conduct was demonstrably imperial in manner, he avoided making claims to be emperor. This protocol is respected in the chancery style of Cassiodorus, whose collection of letters, the *Variae,* preserves a representative sample of official correspondence from Theoderic's court.[64] Latin inscriptions from Italy also generally respected this custom, referring to Theoderic as *rex,* sometimes with the added words *dominus noster,* which had long been customary for emperors. Only one text makes the larger claim that he was an Augustus. This was carved on two bases near Terracina, to celebrate the reclamation of the Appian way from encroachment by the Pomptine marshes, which had flooded agricultural land and threatened communications along the main route from Rome to Naples.

> Our lord the glorious and famous king Theoderic, victorious and triumphant, the perpetual Augustus, born for the good of the commonwealth, guardian of liberty and propagator of the Roman name, tamer of the nations, has restored the route and places of the via Appia at Decem Novium (the nineteenth milestone), that is from Tripontium to Terracina, to the public use and safety of travellers, by wonderful good fortune and the favour of God. Under all previous princes, they had been flooded through the marshes converging from either side. Caecina Mavortius Basilius Decius, right honourable and illustrious, former Urban Prefect, former Praetorian Prefect, former ordinary Consul and Patrician, from the glorious house of the Decii, toiled industriously on the task imposed, and served with good fortune the most clement prince. To perpetuate the glory of such a lord, he led the waters into the sea through many new channels, and restored the ground to its all too ancient dryness, unknown to our ancestors. (*ILS* 827, trans. Barnish)[65]

The language of this inscription is so traditional, embodying phrases that had been used of emperors since the time of Augustus, and the role of Theoderic so closely resembled that of imperial benefactors who had backed the Senate in their care for Italy, that we should surely regard the reference to Theoderic as Augustus as an exaggerated aberration, rather than a designation of his formal status.

At a later date Procopius summed up Constantinople's view of Theoderic:

> He himself secured the supremacy over both Goths and Italians. And though he did not claim the right to assume either the garb or the name of emperor of the Romans, but was called *rex* to the end of his life, for thus the barbarians are accustomed to call their leaders, still, in governing his own subjects, he invested himself with all the qualities that appropriately belong to one who is by birth an emperor. For he was exceedingly careful to observe justice, he preserved the laws on a sound basis, he protected the land, and kept it safe from the barbarians dwelling round about, and he attained the highest possible degree of wisdom and manliness. And although in name Theoderic was a usurper (*tyrannos*), yet in fact

he was as truly an emperor as any who have distinguished themselves in this office from the beginning; and love for him among both Goths and Italians grew to be great, and that too contrary to the ordinary habits of men. (Procopius, *Bell. Goth.* 5.1.25–29, trans. Dewing)

Theoderic's claims to be a just ruler, in the manner of Trajan, are projected most clearly in Cassiodorus' correspondence, whose twelve books may well have been published in direct emulation of an earlier imperial advisor, the younger Pliny. Cassiodorus was a member of one of the wealthiest senatorial families of Italy, with properties in Bruttium, whose members had served the emperors over at least three generations (Cassiodorus, *Var.* 1.3 and 4). In the role of *quaestor*, that is chief legal officer and spokesman for the regime,[66] he wrote official letters, edicts, and other documents for Theoderic and his successors, Athalaric, his daughter Amalasuntha, Theodahat, and Vitigis, and also issued documents in his own right as Praetorian Prefect of Italy. The format of letters dealing with administrative matters regularly began with a paragraph of generalities, laying down the principles on which the regime operated. This was followed by details on the matter in hand, sometimes accompanied by observations or even lengthy digressions of a philosophical nature. Thus the corpus as a whole supplies three different perspectives on the conduct of Ostrogothic rule. Firstly, it laid down principles of justice and standards of public behavior. These were not innovative, but were careful restatements of the traditional virtues of the just ruler, conducted within an overtly Christian moral framework. Secondly, it provided specific information about political and legal issues that had to be resolved by a court decision. Thirdly, it gave a flattering view of the high cultural level of the Gothic court.

It is revealing that neither Theoderic nor his successors issued a code of laws in their own name, as the other Germanic kingdoms did in the fifth and sixth centuries.[67] They worked entirely within the Roman framework of government, using Roman officials, mostly senior members of the Senate, and operating with Roman law. Theoderic stated in a letter to his armor-bearer:

We are pleased to live according to Roman law, which we desire to avenge by our force of arms. What benefit would we gain from having removed barbarian disorder if we could not live under the rule of law. (Cassiodorus, *Var.* 3.43)

All this was consonant with the conception of the Ostrogothic kingdom as a part of the Roman Empire, subservient in theory and diplomatic protocol to the eastern empire. This was the role that Theoderic had fulfilled all his life as a Gothic leader, and his conception of his own position did not change with his transfer from a base in eastern Illyricum to Italy. He achieved the vision which had been contemplated by Athaulph at his marriage to Galla Placidia in 415, of a Roman Empire reliant on and protected by Gothic strength. "The glory of the Goths is to be guardians of civilisation" (Cassiodorus, *Var.* 9.14).

Theoderic did not lose sight of his Gothic heritage. Jordanes' *Getica*, written in Constantinople in 551 contains a lengthy preamble covering the early history of the Gothic people, identified with the ancient Getae, and the genealogy over seventeen generations of the Amal family. Jordanes tells us that he based his work on Cassiodorus' Gothic history. The nature and extent of this debt are a matter for discussion,[68] but a letter of Athalaric to the Senate of Rome, written on September 1, 533, demonstrates that Cassiodorus was the key literary figure in promoting the history of the Amal lineage. His purpose was not to provide accurate information about the past but to confer a glorious antiquity on the house of the Amals.[69] We may compare the similar aspirations of the Isaurians, when they came to prominence in the 460s, to identify an antique and noble heritage for their people. The historian Candidus contended that the name and the race of the Isaurians were derived from the biblical Esau.[70] It is also valuable to compare Theoderic with Clovis, his near contemporary. Clovis also claimed a mythical descent, but could trace this back for only two generations to his grandfather. Theoderic's own legitimate ancestry also goes back no further than to his grandfather, Valamir.

Theoderic also remained a Germanic leader of his Gothic followers.[71] He had, of course, been a warrior throughout his early adult life. In a panegyric Ennodius, bishop of Milan, reminded his listeners that this was a king who led his forces into battle, and defeated his enemies by main might. Fighting the Gepids in 488 Theoderic led by example:

> Whoever seeks a path through the enemy's ranks follow me; whoever seeks an example for battle look at me and no one else. Bravery does not ask about numbers; few must take the burdens of war upon themselves, many enjoy the fruits. The Gothic army will be judged by what I do, and the tribe will triumph in my deeds.

Before the battle of Verona with Odoacar in 489 he is said to have taken leave of his mother as a classical Spartan might have done:

> Mother, known to all peoples through your son's honour, you know that you have given birth to a man. Today is the day when the battlefield will prove the manhood of your son. With arms I must show that the fame of my ancestors does not come to an end with me. Without reason would we invoke the deeds of our ancestors if we had none of our own to show. (Ennodius, *Panegyricus* 19ff., 32)

This was probably the last occasion, at the age of thirty-eight, that he fought in person. After he became sole ruler of Italy, Ostrogothic campaigns were led by other generals.

Theoderic had brought a large group of around 100,000 Goths into Italy, including 20–25,000 fighting men. Their settlements, according to the written sources and the archaeology, were to be found in the Po valley and guarding the main Alpine passes, along the Adriatic coast with concentrations around Ravenna and in Picenum, in southern Italy around Naples, in Sicily and across the Adriatic in Dalmatia.[72] Other Germanic groups were attracted to join his kingdom, including the Rugi, but according to Procopius these refused to intermarry with the Ostrogoths, preserving their discrete bloodlines and ethnic identity (Procopius, *Bell. Goth.* 7.21–23). This carries the obvious implication that they lived in separate settlements. The cultured voice of Cassiodorus insinuates that the rule of law in Theoderic's Italy had brought back years of stability under a powerful empire, but beneath the rhetoric and in the parts not reached by the smooth governance of senatorial officials, there is also a view of Gothic settlements, led by local strong men, such as Quidila at Nursia (Cassiodorus, *Var.* 8.26), and a network of Gothic as well as Roman counts of the cities, charged with defense and the administration of justice.[73] These men held their positions with Theoderic's approval, but they owed their positions to their own personal qualities and the authority they enjoyed at a local level. They appear from the pages of Procopius' narrative of the wars in Italy as responsible for local resistance to the Roman forces: Pitzas in Samnium (Procopius, *Bell. Goth.* 5.15.1–2); Hildebad at Venice (*Bell. Goth.* 6.29.41, 7.1.25–27); Sisigis on the western boundary of the Cottian Alps (*Bell. Goth.* 6.28.28–35). Thus individual Gothic leaders outside the king's circle commanded local garrisons during the wars, and arbitrated between Goths and Italians in peacetime.[74] The true nature of the Ostrogothic kingdom is surely demonstrated by the events that followed Theoderic's death (Plate 6.1). There was no stability to the succession. During peace time Amal rule continued under Amalasuntha's invalid and irresponsible son, Athalaric, and Theoderic's unwarlike but vindictive nephew, Theodahat. But when the Roman army advanced up the Italian peninsula in 536, Theodahat was displaced to make way for a warrior unconnected to the Amal family, Vitigis, who in turn was supplanted by Totila after the fall of Ravenna to Belisarius. The claims that prevailed as the kingdom changed hands were not dynastic but those of military prowess and authority among the Goths at large.

Cassiodorus draws a picture of Theoderic as a ruler thoroughly assimilated to the prevailing Roman ethos, but also offers insights into the relationships which held the Gothic tribal people together. Some leading Romans learned the German language, as Syagrius had done in Burgundy. Cyprian, who was Theoderic's *comes sacrarum largitionum*, was trained in three languages, Latin, Greek, and German, and his children also learned language and weapon skills from the Goths (Cassiodorus, *Var.* 5.40.5, 8.21.6ff.). A greater number of Goths certainly mastered Latin, and although the newcomers were generally easily distinguished from the Roman inhabitants of Italy, in many contexts they must have lived alongside one another, adopted language and customs, and begun to intermarry.[75]

Theoderic pursued dynastic politics with the neighboring kingdoms of the West. He himself married Audofleda, sister of the Frankish king Clovis. His daughters Theodogotha and Ostrogotho married respectively Alaric II, king of the Visigoths, and Sigismund, king of the Burgundians, while his niece Amalaberga was given to Herminafrid, king of the Thuringians. The marriage policy was matched by diplomatic initiatives. Cassiodorus drafted impeccable missives to advertise his friendly intentions. The senator Boethius, in a fascinating

Plate 6.1　Mausoleum of Theoderic at Ravenna (DAI Rome)

letter, was asked to design and build a water-clock, to be presented to the Burgundian ruler Gundobad (Cassiodorus, *Var.* 1.45 and 46). The versatile Boethius was then asked to find a skilled musician, a cithara player, who could be sent to the court of Clovis. Theoderic accompanied this with a plea for the life of the king of the Alemanni, lately defeated by Clovis, who was seeking Theoderic's protection (Cassiodorus, *Var.* 2.40 and 41). These initiatives date to 506, the year before the decisive triumph of the Franks over the Visigoths. As the storm clouds gathered in Gaul, Theoderic attempted to keep the contestants apart by a vain flurry of diplomatic correspondence, addressed to Alaric, to Clovis, to Gundobad, and to the lesser kings of the Heruls and the Warni. Neither the letters nor the diplomacy of the Ostrogothic envoys who carried them availed.[76]

NOTES

1   R. MacMullen, *Corruption and the Decline of Rome* (New Haven, 1989), 199–201.
2   A. Demandt, *Die Spätantike. Römische Geschichte von Diocletian bis Justinian 284–565 n. Chr.* (Berlin, 1989), 504 table g.
3   G. E. M. de Ste Croix, *The Class Struggle in the Ancient Greek World from the Archaic Age to the Arab conquests* (London, 1983).
4   H. Elton, *Warfare in Roman Europe AD 350–425* (Oxford, 1996), 15–44, deconstructs and demythologizes barbarian society.
5   L. F. Pitts, "Relations between Rome and the German 'kings' on the middle Danube in the first to fourth centuries AD," *JRS* 79 (1989), 45–58.
6   P. Heather and J. F. Matthews, *The Goths in the Fourth Century* (Liverpool, 1991), 17–26.
7   N. McLynn, "The transformation of imperial church-going in the fourth century," in S. Swain and M. Edwards (eds.), *Approaching Late Antiquity* (Oxford, 2004), 235–70 esp. 242–50.
8   H. Wolfram, *The Roman Empire and its Germanic Peoples* (California, 1997), 163. The figure is questioned by W. Goffart.
9   Philostorgius 2.5; P. Heather and J. F. Matthews, *The Goths in the Fourth Century* (Liverpool, 1991), 133–53.
10 W. Goffart, *Barbarians and Romans AD 418–584. The Techniques of Accommodation* (Princeton, 1989).
11 S. J. B. Barnish, "Taxation, land and barbarian settlement in the western empire," *PBSR* 54 (1986), 170–95; W. Liebeschuetz, "Cities, taxes and the accommodation of the barbarians: The theories of Durliat and Goffart," in W. Pohl (ed.), *Kingdoms of the Empire: The Integration of Barbarians in Late Antiquity* (Leiden, 1997), 135–51.
12 E. A. Thompson, *The Huns* (Oxford, 1999), 56–7.
13 E. A. Thompson, *The Huns*, 36.
14 Compare the contemporary situation in Darfur, southern Sudan, where the village populations have been driven from their homes over the Sudanese border into refugee camps by the mounted Janjaweed militia.

15 E. A. Thompson, *The Huns*, 105.

16 E. A. Thompson, *The Huns*, 46–68.

17 C. Zuckerman, "L'Empire d'Orient et les Huns; notes sur Priscus," *Travaux et Mémoires* 12 (1994), 159–82.

18 Compare the speech on the topic "A man recalling the Scythians to their nomadic existence, since they are falling ill through living in cities," which was improvised by the Cilician sophist Alexander in the second century, Philostratus, *Lives of the Sophists* 572; a similar point in Salvian, *On the Governance of God* 5.4ff.

19 H. Wolfram, *History of the Goths* (California, 1988), 172–246; H. Wolfram, *The Roman Empire and its Germanic Peoples* (California, 1997), 145–58; E. A. Thompson, *Romans and Barbarians* (Madison, 1982); P. Heather, "The emergence of the Visigothic kingdom," in J. Drinkwater and H. Elton (eds.), *Fifth-Century Gaul: A Crisis of Identity* (Cambridge, 1992), 84–92.

20 P. Heather, in *CAH* 14, 8–12.

21 Jordanes, *Get.* XLI, 216; Greg. Tur., *Hist.* 2.7. Gregory of Tours attributes the success of the coalition mainly to the prayers of the bishop of Orleans. Jordanes' analysis may be retrospective and designed to flatter Gothic self-esteem.

22 See Sidonius Apollinaris, *Carm.* 7 (Panegyric of Avitus), 295–356, 431–602.

23 C. E. Stevens, *Sidonius Apollinaris and his Age* (Oxford, 1933); J. Harries, *Sidonius Apollinaris and the Fall of Rome AD 407–85* (Oxford, 1994). W. B. Anderson, *Sidonius. Poems and Letters* (Loeb Classical Library, 2 vols., Cambridge Mass., 1936 and 1965) has a valuable introduction and useful notes.

24 Theoderic's predecessor Athaulph had been assassinated while inspecting the royal stables.

25 Sidonius, *ep.* 5.5.3; cf. Cassiodorus, *Var.* 2.41.4 (Theoderic the Amal sends a cithara player to the Frankish king).

26 Sidonius, *ep.* 1.2.6.

27 Sidonius, *ep.* 7.6.4–10 on the retreat of the Catholic Church in the face of Euric's aggressive stance.

28 Isidore of Seville, *Historia Gothorum* 35 (MGH, *Chron. Min.* II, 281).

29 See J. Harries, "Legal culture and identity in fifth-century Gaul," in S. Mitchell and G. Greatex (eds.), *Ethnicity and Culture in Late Antiquity* (Wales and London, 2000), 45–57 at 55.

30 Sidonius, *ep.* 4.22. Surely this would have been a history to exalt the status and lineage of the Goths, like the work which Cassiodorus later wrote for Theoderic's Ostrogoths. Sidonius turned down the invitation.

31 Sidonius, *ep.* 8.9.6, declining to add to the short commissioned poem in praise of Euric which this letter also contains.

32 Ennodius, *Life of Epiphanius*, 89f., p. 95.

33 Sidonius, *ep.* 8.9.5; a fifty-nine line hendecasyllable poem.

34 H. Wolfram, *History of the Goths* (California, 1988), 195–7. See the excellent essay of P. Heather, "Literacy and power in the migration period," in A. Bowman and G. Woolf (eds.), *Literacy and Power in the Ancient World* (Cambridge, 1994), 177–97.

35 *CTh.* 3.14.1 with J. F. Matthews, "Roman law and barbarian identity in the late Roman West," in S. Mitchell and G. Greatrex, *Ethnicity and Culture in Late Antiquity* (Wales and London, 2000), 31–44 at 36.

36 H. Wolfram, *History of the Goths* (California, 1988), 200–2.

37 H. Wolfram, *History of the Goths*, 190–3.

38 P. Amory, "Names, ethnic identity and community in fifth and sixth century
    Burgundy," *Viator* 25 (1994), 1–30; I. Wood, "Ethnicity and the ethnogenesis of
    the Burgundians," in H. Wolfram and W. Pohl, *Typen der Ethnogenese unter
    besonderer Berücksichtigung der Bayern* (Vienna, 1990), 53–69; H. Wolfram, *The
    Roman Empire and its Germanic Peoples* (California, 1997), 248–59.

39 Socrates 7.30; *Chron. Gall.* a 435, 600.

40 *Chron. Gall.* a 443, 600.

41 H. Wolfram, *The Roman Empire and its Germanic Peoples*, 253.

42 D. Boysson, "Romano-Burgundian society in the age of Gundobad," *Nottingham
    Medieval Studies* 32 (1988), 91–118.

43 Note *Inscriptiones Latinae Christianae Veteres* I no. 44, the grave of a *protector
    domesticus* (a Roman military title), who was son of a man of the royal family of
    the Burgundians, buried in a Catholic cemetery at Cologne.

44 Mark Handley, "Inscribing time and identity in the kingdom of Burgundy," in
    S. Mitchell and G. Greatrex, *Ethnicity and Culture in Late Antiquity* (Wales and
    London, 2000), 83–102.

45 For the religious situation among the Burgundians see Avitus, *ep.* 8, 23, 29, 31,
    discussed by D. Shanzer and I. Wood, *Avitus of Vienne: Letters and Selected Prose*
    (Liverpool, 2002), 221–32.

46 T. M. Charles-Edwards, *CAH* 14, 284–7. See P. Amory, "The meaning and
    purpose of ethnic terminology in Burgundian laws," *Early Medieval Europe* 2
    (1993), 1–28.

47 H. Wolfram, *The Roman Empire and its German Peoples* (California, 1997), 48–9.

48 T. Anderson Jr., "Roman military colonies in Gaul, Salian ethnogenesis and the
    forgotten meaning of *Pactus Legis Salicae* 59.5," *Early Medieval Europe* 4 (1995),
    129–44.

49 Ammianus 30.3 and 31.10. H. Wolfram, *The Roman Empire and its German
    Peoples*, 66.

50 E. James, *The Franks* (Oxford, 1988); I. Wood, *The Merovingian Kingdoms 450–
    751* (London, 1994); John Moorhead, *The Roman Empire Divided 400–700*
    (London, 2001), 66–94.

51 John Moorhead, *The Roman Empire Divided* (London, 2001), 73–5. Compare I.
    Wood, *CAH* 14, 423, for the retention of pre-Christian beliefs about the dead,
    even by Catholic bishops.

52 The conversion of Clovis has been a major discussion point, of obvious interest to
    the history of modern Christian France as well as in its Frankish context. Recently
    M. Spencer, "Dating the baptism of Clovis," *Early Medieval Europe* 3 (1994), 97–
    116, argues for Gregory's dating in 496. Danuta Shanzer, "Dating the baptism of
    Clovis," *Early Medieval Europe* 7 (1998), 29–57, argues on the contemporary
    evidence of Avitus, *ep.* 46, for conversion to Catholicism in 508, not from paganism
    but from a form of Arianism.

53 M. McCormick, *Eternal Victory. Triumphal Rulership in Late Antiquity, Byzantium,
    and the Early Medieval West* (Cambridge, 1986), 335–42.

54 Greg. Tur., *Hist.* 2.38. I. Wood, "Gregory of Tours and Clovis," *Revue Belge de
    Philologie* 63 (1985), 249–72; "Clovis," in G. W. Bowersock et al. (eds.), *Late
    Antiquity* (Cambridge Mass., 1999), 382–3.

55 For another view of the Franks, from Constantinople, see the works of Agathias,
    analyzed by Averil Cameron, "Agathias on the early Merovingians," *Annali della
    scuola normale superiore di Pisa* 37 (1968), 95–140.

56   Greg. Tur., *Hist.* 4.22.

57   M. McCormick, *Eternal Victory*, 332.

58   See R. Collins, *CAH* 14, 116–21.

59   See P. Brown, *The Cult of the Saints. Its Rise and Function in Latin Christianity* (Chicago, 1981); R. van Dam, *Saints and their Miracles in Late Antique Gaul* (Princeton, 1993).

60   English translation of Gregory of Tours, *History of the Franks*, by Lewis Thorpe, with introduction (Harmondsworth, 1974).

61   H. Wolfram, *The Roman Empire and its Germanic Peoples* (California, 1997), 199–203; for Flavii see G. Keenan, *ZPE* 11 (1973), 33–63; 13 (1974), 283–304; 53 (1983), 245–50.

62   *Collectio Avellana* (CSEL 35), 113, 4; *Anon. Val.* part 2, 12, 64.

63   Cassiodorus, *Var.* 1.2.

64   See S. Barnish, *Cassiodorus, Variae* (trans. Liverpool, 1992), xii n. 7. See G. Vidén, *The Roman Chancery Tradition. Studies in the Language of the Codex Theodosianus and Cassiodorus' Variae* (Gothenburg, 1984).

65   The context is clarified by a letter of Theoderic to one of his *apparitores*, and to the Roman Senate of 507, Cassiodorus, *Var.* 2.21 and 32.

66   See J. Harries, "The Roman imperial quaestor from Constantine to Theodosius II," *JRS* 78 (1988), 148–72.

67   P. Heather, "The historical culture of Ostrogothic Italy," *Atti del XIII congresso internazionale di studi sull'Alto Medioevo* (Spoleto, 1993), 317–53.

68   A. Momigliano, "Cassiodorus and the Italian culture of his time," *PBA* 41 (1955), 207–45; S. J. Barnish, "The genesis and compilation of Cassiodorus' Gothic history," *Latomus* 43 (1984), 336–61; P. Heather, *Goths and Romans* (Oxford, 1991), 34–67.

69   P. Heather, "Cassiodorus and the rise of the Amals: Genealogy and the Goths under Hun domination," *JRS* 79 (1989), 103–28. See further Heather, "The historical culture of Ostrogothic Italy," *Atti del XIII congresso internazionale di studi sull'Alto Medioevo* (Spoleto, 1993), 317–53.

70   Photius, *Bibl. cod.* 79 (Blockley, Candidus fr. 1).

71   P. Heather, "Theoderic king of the Goths," *Early Medieval Europe* 4 (1995), 145–73.

72   See P. Heather, "Theoderic king of the Goths," 156, fig. 2, based on V. Bierbrauer, *Die Ostgotischen Grab- und Schatzfunde in Italien* (Spoleto, 1975).

73   See for example Cassiodorus, *Var.* 1.18, 2.20, 3.13, 7.3, 8.28 (from Barnish's selected translations).

74   For all this see P. Heather, "Theoderic king of the Goths," *Early Medieval Europe* 4 (1995), 145–73.

75   P. Amory, *People and Identity in Ostrogothic Italy 489–554* (Cambridge, 1997) argues that criteria for ethnic identity were elusive and flexible, and that the distinctions between Goths and Romans, presented in Cassiodorus' *Variae*, are too clear-cut. But the differences between Goths and Romans are maintained in Procopius, and are also broadly established in the archaeology.

76   Cassiodorus, *Var.* 3.1, 2, 3, 4.

7

From Pagan to Christian

The later Roman Empire underwent an unprecedented level of religious change. At the center of this transformation was the conversion of pagans to Christians in the fourth century, when it seems likely that more than half the inhabitants of the Roman world converted to Christianity. The eradication of paganism was by any standards rapid, but it was not instantaneous. Many people, at all levels of society, stuck to their old beliefs and practices, and significant pagan groups were to be found in the fifth and even the sixth centuries. The impact of this religious revolution is evident in almost every aspect of the history of late antiquity. It remains, however, a challenging task to explain how and why this process occurred, and to evaluate its significance. These simple questions in turn raise a series of complicated historical problems. Neither pagans nor Christians formed homogeneous groups. Conversion itself can be seen both as an individual and as a collective phenomenon, sometimes adopted voluntarily, at others as a result of force and coercion. If we use the metaphor of a journey to describe the progress from one side to the other, it is clear there were many different starting points and destinations, that some pagans had much further to travel to become Christians than others, and that not all the traffic was in one direction. Certain features of pagan polytheism were more easily discarded than others, and many communities that called themselves Christian undoubtedly retained and perpetuated pre-Christian traditions.

There is also a larger consideration. How large a place did religion occupy in public and private life? Was conversion to Christianity of overwhelming importance in determining how individuals or communities related to one another? Did religious preferences largely determine people's social and political behavior, or was there plenty of secular space within which people could fraternize, intermarry, and conduct business regardless of each others' beliefs?

This chapter begins with a general account of the religious scene in the Roman Empire in the third century AD, drawing attention to the main aspects of pagan polytheism before the conversion of Constantine. It then considers the importance of state policies towards traditional paganism and Christianity during the main period of transition in the third and fourth centuries. Chapter 8 is concerned with conversion, and examines the importance of religion in shaping communal identities in the later empire.

There are serious difficulties in assessing the balance between paganism and Christianity in late antiquity, particularly during the fourth century. Most of the mainstream written sources available to us are Christian, and they belittle or suppress the evidence for paganism.[1] Pagan rituals were often represented as the activities of a deluded minority. Christian writing at the beginning of our period had been predominantly apologetic, offering a defense and justification for the faith in the face of criminalization by the Roman state and the critique of Greek intellectuals. After the conversion of Constantine the tone and format of this literature changed to become assertively triumphalist. Christian authors had no interest in providing a realistic view of the strength of paganism, whether numerically or in other ways. Meanwhile secular authors of the fourth century, who were by no means all pagans, preferred to mention Christianity as little as possible. The brief historical epitomes, which document the period of the tetrarchs and Constantine, scarcely mention religious issues at all. Even Ammianus Marcellinus, who was fully aware of the nature and significance of Christianity, and may have been a Christian himself for some of his life, pushes all aspects of Christianity to the margins of his narrative, usually excluding it altogether from view.[2]

Other sources are also difficult to evaluate. Inscriptions, especially religious dedications, are the richest single source of information about pagan cults in the Roman Empire. They occur in great numbers during the second and third centuries, but become rare in the fourth.[3] However, this is at least as much to do with a change in epigraphic habits of commemoration as it is with the abandonment of paganism. An exception must be made for the city of Rome, where the epigraphic habit remained strong and pagan cults are well attested, at least in the senatorial class until around 400. Archaeology may offer a more dispassionate and objective record, but the archaeology of cult is a problematic area. It is very rare to find archaeological evidence for the construction or even for the major rebuilding of pagan temples after the mid-third century. On the other hand material evidence for monumental church building is also sparse before the mid- or later fourth century in any part of the empire. Thus the most dynamic period of religious change from 250–350 has left little mark in monumental archaeology.[4]

Later paganism was also camouflaged and obscured by the distortions of its opponents. After the religious re-orientation of the Roman state, which was achieved by Constantine and his successors, all pronouncements or actions by emperors and their officials were also either explicitly or implicitly Christian. This characteristic became more pronounced as affairs of state and church became inextricably bound to one another. This creates an illusion that non-Christian religions had disappeared or had been marginalized. But much religious activity, like many other aspects of life in the late Roman world, was beyond the reach of the state.

In any case, many aspects of society and culture in late antiquity were thoroughly imbued with pagan traditions. At the highest political level emperors developed a style of rulership which increasingly distanced them from the populations that they ruled. The huge gap between rulers of large territories and their subjects in the ancient world was one that was invariably bridged by cult.[5] In the later Roman Empire, ritualized behavior which emphasized the emperors' power and authority became an even more prominent part of political life.[6] Inevitably, therefore, many aspects of ruler worship survived in the late empire. Of course, both in literature and in representational art formulae were found to distinguish between the nature of divinity, in a Christian sense, and the charismatic power of the emperors. Both Constantine and Justinian were the agents of God's will, not divine beings themselves, but this did not prevent Eusebius from portraying Constantine as virtually a second Christ (Eusebius, *VC* 4.71), or Procopius from envisaging Justinian as a supernatural daemonic force (Procopius, *Secret History* 12). Priscus, in his famous account of the embassy to the Huns in 449, records how the separate groups of Romans and Huns that were encamped together on the road from Constantinople to Serdica became embroiled in a violent argument about the qualities of their respective rulers, Theodosius II and Attila. To the Roman party the question was incomprehensible, for how was it possible to make a comparison between a mere man and the emperor, a god (Priscus fr. 11.2)? The contradiction, at least to a modern student of the period, between Christian belief and the notion of ancient rulers as divinities appears most starkly in Procopius' *Secret History*. Procopius bitterly attacked Justinian and Theodora for requiring even members of the Senate to perform an extreme and humiliating form of *proskynesis*, corresponding to the conduct of slaves before their masters. The ideology of this despotism, which reflected similar practices in the contemporary Sassanian court, was that all mankind should abase themselves before the omnipotent and virtually divine authority of the emperor (Procopius, *Secret History* 30, 21–30).[7]

Pagan traditions also remained ineradicably embedded in the high culture of late antiquity. This was partly due to the enduring appeal to educated people of classical literature. But it was also the result of an educational system which was based on the study of grammar and rhetoric. The language of public life in the eastern part of the empire was a sophisticated and artificially elaborated form of literary Greek, which had been mastered by those who were the products of this system.[8] However, it was only possible to master language at this level through the study of literature, and that unavoidably meant a familiarity with pagan mythology, philosophy, and rhetoric.[9] The wealthy elite of the cities of the eastern Roman Empire, and also, to a lesser extent, their counterparts in the Latin-speaking West, were reared on classical learning and the pagan religious ideas that were embedded in it. Famously Julian the Apostate attempted to ban Christians from teaching this traditional syllabus. A Christian teacher was by definition guilty of gross hypocrisy if he rejected the moral substance of the works he was expounding.

> I think it absurd that men who expound the works of these writers should dishonour the gods whom they used to honour. Yet, though I think this is absurd, I do not say that they ought to change their opinions and then instruct the young. But I give them the choice; either not to teach what they do not think admirable, or, if they wish to teach, let them persuade their pupils that neither Homer nor Hesiod nor any of these writers who they espoused and have declared to be guilty of impiety, folly and error in regard to the gods, is such as they declare. (Julian, *ep.* 42, 423a–b, trans. Stevenson)

Julian's legislation was short-lived, and was rejected by Christians as well as by pagans. Specific literary genres, notably epic poetry and panegyric oratory, retained the hallmarks of paganism throughout late antiquity. The longest Greek epic that survives is the *Dionysiaca* of Nonnus, written in Egypt around the middle of the fifth century by a poet who was also responsible for rendering St John's Gospel into hexameter verse.[10] The fusion of Christian piety with the high culture of the pagan tradition is particularly evident in literary circles around the court of Theodosius II at Constantinople (see above, chapter 4). It was left to Justinian to follow through the logic of Julian's law in legislation that forbade all pagan teaching (*CJust.* I.5.18, I.11.10).

Of course the illiterate inhabitants of the ancient world, the great majority, had at best only indirect access to this sophisticated literature. During the fourth and fifth centuries there was a shift away from the traditional learning and elaborate rationality of what we call the classical world to much less sophisticated ideas. However, much of the writing of the fourth and fifth centuries, notably saints' lives, letter collections, and accounts of miracles, reveals popular super-stitions and beliefs that are absent from more sophisticated genres of literature. After 300, as power in the empire began to slip from the civic elites and was transferred to the many thousands of state bureaucrats, and as the size of the clergy was vastly enlarged, so many more people in positions of authority were drawn from a wider pool of the population. These brought a less educated approach to decision making. The ideas and educational values of the elite were diluted by the popular beliefs of the masses.[11]

Pagan traditions were also tenaciously preserved among the lower classes. Most of the evidence relating to popular festivals in the ancient world comes from late antiquity. The religious changes of the period could not obliterate pagan practices and cultural attitudes which were engrained in society itself.[12] There is abundant evidence from late antiquity that non-Christian festivals and rituals continued to be celebrated throughout the empire.[13] Most notable were traditional calendrical celebrations, associated with particular times or seasons of the year, but not strongly attached to specific pagan gods. These included the Brumalia and Saturnalia, staged in November and December respectively, festivities associated with the winter solstice and the spring equinox, and above all the celebration of New Year's Day, the Kalends, which was frequently deplored by Christian preachers, but left in place by imperial legislation (*CTh.* 16.10.3 [341]; 8 [382], 17 [399], 12.1.145 [399]).[14] A notable event which was widespread in the Near East was the popular festival of the Maiuma, which involved night-time spectacles of pantomime, parties, and, according to the unreliable hostile testimony of the preacher John Chrysostom, naked female bathing.[15] The event spread throughout the empire, to fifth-century Aphrodisias in Caria, to sixth-century Constantinople, and to the port of Ostia in the West.[16] Christian leaders objected resolutely, but largely in vain, to these events.

Religious Pluralism in Late Antiquity

Paganism in the third-century Roman Empire took many different forms. In the forefront were the mainstream public cults of the Graeco-Roman cities. Throughout the empire the inhabitants of the provinces, especially those living in cities, identified their local gods with members of the Graeco-(Roman) pantheon. Although in many cases the indigenous origins of these cults remain identifiable, the practice of giving the gods familiar Greek names gave a unified appearance to public religion.

This unity was reinforced by the broadly similar institutions and patterns of religious practice.[17] Cult activity was most conspicuous at major temples in towns and cities, and was often associated with large public festivals. Animal sacrifice was the most important form of ritual observance, but the festivals included ceremonial processions, public feasts, and especially games, competitions, and other spectacles. Many festivals from the first to the third centuries were associated with emperor worship, which enhanced rather than competed with traditional cult in provincial cities. Gladiatorial contests were a form of spectacle closely linked to the imperial cult. All this activity was expensive to mount and was only made possible by the disposable surplus wealth to be found in prosperous cities. Temple building and public festivals were either financed by the cities themselves or by donations from members of the local aristocracy. Sometimes individual families also paid the expenses of the priesthoods. This was in essence a city-based religious system. Cults and ritual activity was integrated into the institutions of the *polis* and funded to a considerable degree by the euergetism of private benefactors.

Social and economic changes during the third century had a big impact on the pattern of religious behavior. The most important of these was the decline of the city-states as viable and independent economic units with the freedom to dispose of their own surplus wealth. Aristocratic generosity, which had sustained the boom in public civic paganism since the later Hellenistic period, and which had reached a climax in the cities of the second and early third centuries AD, occurred while the empire was mostly at peace. New temples, lavish festivals, musical and athletic games were also a particular feature of the empire's peaceful provinces. The overall tax burden of the empire was generally affordable, and the most urbanized areas of the empire were not exposed to intense requisitioning or direct demands by Roman armies. These conditions changed during the third century, especially after the end of the Severan period, when increased taxation and militarization affected the ability and the willingness of Rome's richer subjects to pay for buildings and local festivals. Local elites no longer voluntarily spent their surplus wealth to enhance the public facilities of the cities. It is significant that in the fourth and fifth centuries public civic building was rarely initiated by members of the local elite but by provincial governors or other Roman officials.[18] When the empire's fortunes revived at the end of the third century thanks to the energetic measures of the tetrarchs, the initiative came not from provincial cities but from the central authorities.[19] Meanwhile *polis*-based religion declined along with other institutions of the city-states.

This did not bring civic paganism to an immediate end. Although smaller cities succumbed to the pressures, large centers, and especially the capital cities of the new provinces, provide evidence for continued urban vitality. The municipalities of Roman North Africa remained viable until the end of the fourth century, and their leading families continued to finance local civic cults until the time of Augustine.[20] But the overall impact of social and economic changes was to shift attention away from showy public festivals, which were supported by and served the interests of the urban elites, to popular and less formal aspects of paganism. Augustine, who had spent his student years in the aggressively secular environment of Carthage, encountered enthusiastic pagan festivities of this sort during his years as bishop of Hippo. In 409 he deplored blatant pagan impieties in the town of Calama:

> At the June 1st festival, the impious ceremony of the pagans was celebrated without hindrance from anyone, with such impudent audacity as was not ventured in Julian's day: an aggressive crowd of dancers in the precinct passed directly in front of the church doors. And when the clergy attempted to prevent such an outrageous thing, the church was stoned. (Augustine, *ep.* 91.8)

But he was fighting not only against pagan traditions but the government line. Ten years earlier Honorius had issued a law to the proconsul of Africa which expressly permitted these activities:

> When by our salutary law we forbade the practice of sacrilegious rites, we were not giving our authority for the abolition of the festivals which bring the citizens together for their communal pleasure. In consequence we decree that, according to the ancient customs, these forms of entertainment should be available to the people, although without any sacrifice or illegal superstition. (*CTh.* 16.10.7 = *CJust.* 1.11.4)[21]

Blood sacrifice, the defining activity at the heart of pagan ritual, was banned, with gradually increasing effect, throughout the Christian empire,[22] but animals were still slaughtered at feasts, which retained most of the elements of pagan festivities. Libanius at Antioch in the late 380s explained how the practice continued and might avoid Christian sanction:

> But for a banquet, a dinner, a feast and the bullocks were slaughtered elsewhere (not in temple grounds): no altar received the blood offering, no single part of the victim was burned, no offering of meal began the ceremony nor did libations follow it. If the people assemble in some beauty spot, slaughter a calf or a sheep or both, and boil or roast it, and then lie down on the ground and eat it, I do not see that they have broken the laws. . . . Even if they were in the habit of drinking together amid the scent of every kind of incense, they broke no law, nor yet if in their toasts they sang hymns and invoked the gods. (Libanius, *Or.* 30.17ff.)

In modern Islam animal sacrifice has no place within the religious ritual, but the blood sacrifice of a victim at the end of the fasting month of Ramadan is a universal feature of Moslem societies.

It is, however, open to question whether these non-Christian rituals were fully pagan, or whether they had been tacitly accepted as part of popular everyday culture, whose religious overtones could be ignored. Of course they were deplored by bishops and other Christian authorities, but so too were other diversions such as circus spectacles and wild beast hunts in the amphitheater, which were as popular with Christian as with pagan spectators. Christians perpetuated many forms of popular pagan activity by disregarding their religious associations and re-branding them as secular or even as Christian events. We may compare the persistence of May Day and other festivals in Christian Europe, or the secular festival of Nourouz (New Year's Day) in contemporary Iran, which attracts criticism from zealots, but the latter is universally celebrated by the people and tolerated even by a strongly religious regime. One of the literary works of the fourth century which points towards a desacralization of popular festivities was the almanac of Dionysius Philocalus, produced in Rome in 354, which assembled lists of emperors and consuls, city prefects and bishops of Rome, as well as publishing the ecclesiastical calendar of the Roman Church juxtaposed with that of the non-Christian holidays of the civic year.[23]

It is much harder to classify the private religious beliefs and practices which played a large part in people's lives across the empire. Magical practices were ubiquitous, and belief in their effectiveness was widespread. People called on supernatural powers to achieve their personal goals in love, life, and business, or to thwart their rivals. Practitioners of magic, amateur or professional, drew on an eclectic medley of religious traditions. So magic texts refer to Greek, Near Eastern, Jewish, and Christian divine powers and demonic forces. People hedged their bets by calling on gods of all sorts to help them. However, it would be mistaken to see all this as merely random activity. Magic comprised a complex cultural system with its own recognized patterns and rules for curses and binding spells, spirit consultations and exorcisms.[24] Belief in magic cut across other divisions, being common to pagans, Jews, and Christians, and was prevalent among all social classes. In the later empire accusations of sorcery were common in tense and competitive political environments, among the upper classes of the major cities, and around the fringes of the imperial court.[25] Laws against magic and consulting astrologers were usually more concerned with the politically subversive implications of these activities than with the rituals themselves.[26] Legislation about magic, however, implicitly concedes that there was an enormous body of "superstitious" activity which could not be suppressed. The social significance of magic may be compared with that of exorcism in this period. One third of Rome's clerical establishment in AD 251 consisted of exorcists; and exorcism, which had its origins in Palestinian Jewish practice, is portrayed as an essential remedy against demonic possession by Christian sources from the Gospels themselves, through the main Christian apologetic writers of the second and third centuries, to countless lives of saints between the fourth and sixth centuries.[27] It spread beyond Judaeo-Christian circles and became part of a shared culture of magical activity.[28]

While magical practices assumed the existence of an almost unlimited number of daemonic forces, which might be marshaled to support or oppose human endeavors, it is also clear that monotheistic religious ideas were widespread. The notion that the universe was dominated by a single supreme god can be traced back to archaic Greek thought. The idea became a mainstream one in Greek philosophy and can be traced in the Platonic, Aristotelian, and Stoic traditions.[29] The growing numbers of Jews and Christians, at all levels of the population, helped to spread monotheistic ideas even among those who did not fully subscribe to them. Paradoxically, it was not difficult to reconcile pagan monotheism with the pattern of polytheistic worship in Greek cities. Educated and also less sophisticated members of the population could see the logic of the argument that there should be one supreme god, to whom other divinities were subordinated. During the third century AD the oracle at Claros in Asia Minor propounded the view that there was a single god in heaven, known from many inscriptions as Theos Hypsistos ("Highest God"), to whom other divine beings, including the Olympian divinities were subordinate. Another oracle put out by Zeus Philios at Antioch in 311 offered a theology in which Zeus was the supreme deity, whose protective authority covered all the local civic gods and goddesses.[30] In competition with the growing influence of Christianity, various forms of pagan monotheism emerged after the mid-second century and into late antiquity. Particularly important were the beliefs propagated by the so-called Chaldean oracles, a religious movement based in the Syrian city of Apamea.[31]

The most distinctive characteristic of Christianity was not that it was a monotheistic religion, which was by no means out of place in the spectrum of religious activity in the later Roman Empire, but that it was based on formal commitment to beliefs about Jesus' divinity. Christians believed that they would be redeemed through Christ's self-sacrifice, and consequently achieve eternal life.[32] Their sacred books, especially the Gospels, the Acts of the Apostles, and Paul's letters, taught them that God had sent his son in human form to redeem mankind; that he had suffered for men, died on the cross and risen again; and that through his sacrifice his followers would find redemption from their own sins and eternal life in the kingdom of heaven. Christians through their faith would thus find salvation in the world to come. Those who denied Him forfeited their own redemption. Christians were distinguished not only from pagan polytheists, but also from other monotheists, including the Jews, whose religion was based not on the belief in redemption but on adherence to righteousness and God's law. Faith in Christ the redeeming god, which was at the core of Christian self-definition, was extraordinary by pagan and Jewish standards. It could be tested very simply. Do you believe that Jesus is the son of God, came to earth to redeem us, and rose from the dead? Those who subscribed to these claims considered themselves, and were considered by others, to be Christians. Those who called themselves Christians could be assumed to hold these beliefs.

Christian faith was represented by powerful symbols. Most important of these were the Easter festival and the sign of the cross, which simultaneously represented Christ's death and the locus of his resurrection, and thus became central expression of Christian belief in redemption. In the search for Christian unity during the later Roman Empire it became essential to define the precise nature of Christ. The fundamental tenets of the faith had to be sharpened and presented in a form that was universally recognized and acceptable. The innumerable versions of the creed which were put forward and debated during the fourth and early fifth centuries were intended to supply this essential requirement. Between the ecumenical councils of Nicaea in 325 and Constantinople in 381 the relationship of Christ to God was the central theological and political issue for all believers. In the fifth century the debate shifted to the related issue of the nature of Christ himself, whether he had the dual nature of God and Man, or whether these two aspects were fused into a single divine nature. The first of these two positions was finally upheld by the Council of Chalcedon in 451, which thereby defined Christian orthodoxy for the remainder of antiquity in the East. However, this was only achieved at the expense of creating an unhealable split between orthodox Chalcedonians and other Christians, mainly in Syria, Egypt, and the eastern frontier areas of the empire, who upheld the Monophysite position of believing in the one nature of Christ (see below, chapter 8).

Christian Diversity

By the beginning of the fifth century the religious landscape of the Roman Empire had changed irrevocably. Christian writing from the mainstream tradition of patristic literature is responsible for the impression that religious belief, with certain exceptions, had been homogenized into a universal pattern of Christian orthodoxy. In practice this profoundly misrepresents the real situation. There were major divisions even within the mainstream Christian tradition, represented by the schismatic groups within the church itself; Donatists in Africa, Melitians in Egypt, and by Arians at odds with the followers of the Nicene Creed across most of the East for much of the fourth century, and by Monophysites irreconcilable with Chalcedonians in the later fifth and sixth centuries (see chapter 8). These were huge fault lines, which emperors and the ecclesiastical politicians of late antiquity strove to bridge with the theological formulas devised at the ecumenical councils of Nicaea in 325, Constantinople in 381, Ephesus in 431 and 449, Chalcedon in 451, and Constantinople again in 553.

However, there were also innumerable smaller groups, heretics in the eyes of the state and the mainstream church. Epiphanius, the late fourth-century bishop of Salamis in Cyprus, gathered information from throughout the East as he compiled the case studies that went into his *Panarion*, a handbook of remedies that were to be used against eighty heresies that he had identified and described.[33] The work is a compendium of often outlandish beliefs and practices, and of the arguments and practices that were to be deployed against them. Heresies thrived in rural regional strongholds. In the 370s Basil, one of Epiphanius' correspondents, wrote a lengthy canonical letter from Caesarea in Cappadocia to his fellow bishop, Amphilochius of Iconium, and provided detailed instructions for dealing with the ascetic heretical groups of Apotactites, Saccophori, Encratites, and Cathari, who flourished in the territory of Iconium and its neighboring cities (Basil, *ep.* 188.1, 199.47). These groups are all well attested by inscriptions and it is evident that Nicene orthodoxy was a minority creed in the fourth and fifth centuries in this region, as in most of the rest of

central Anatolia.[34] Heretical groups were also numerous in northern Syria, especially among the Syriac-speaking communities of monks and hermits in the
country regions. These presented a particular challenge to Theodoret, bishop
of Cyrrhus, who wrote a lengthy treatise designed to combat heretical ideas,
which concluded with an exposition of true belief.[35] Augustine's *On Heresies* is
the main work in this tradition written in the western part of the empire. The
fight against heresy was also an imperial priority. In age-old fashion Roman
religious unity was seen as a way of guaranteeing political and military success.
Nestorius, bishop of Constantinople, told Theodosius II, "give me the earth
undefiled by heretics, and in return I will give you heaven. Help me to destroy the
heretics and in turn I will help you to destroy the Persians" (Socrates 7.29.5).
The reality was different. The military commands under Theodosius were
controlled by Arian barbarians, and even sometimes by pagan generals and
political leaders. Nestorius was driven into exile by his theological enemies
within three years of assuming office.

To judge from the frequency with which they are mentioned in Roman
legislation, the religious groups which were regarded as posing the greatest challenge to the supremacy of the orthodox church were the Jews, the Manichees,
and the Montanists. Each represented different strands in the religious traditions
of the eastern Roman Empire, with complex histories and separate origins.
Jewish communities were to be found throughout the Roman Empire. Christian
and state attitudes towards the Jews were highly ambivalent. Ambrose displayed
intransigent anti-Jewish convictions in an ugly form in his letter to the emperor
Theodosius concerning the destruction of the synagogue at Callinicum in 388.[36]
Such views helped to inflame the violent hostility that was shown towards Jews
in the major imperial cities, above all at Alexandria in 414–15, where a notorious
pogrom was organized by the bishop Theophilus. On the other side there is
important evidence for close contact, mutual sympathy, and interest between
Christian and Jewish communities. As during the early empire, large numbers
of non-Jewish sympathizers throughout the cities of the Diaspora were attracted
to synagogues and participated in Sabbath worship. The two best-documented
examples in the late empire of this phenomenon are to be found in Asia Minor.
At Sardis a wing of the gymnasium building was converted during the fourth
century into a synagogue.[37] The location of this conspicuous building itself
demonstrates that Jewish worship was completely integrated into the city's community life. However, it is particularly telling that many of the features of the
synagogue, including the fine mosaics and marble wall-cladding were paid for
not by Jews but by non-Jewish sympathizers, the god-fearers (*theosebeis*). It is
impossible for us to tell now whether these sympathizers had made their way
towards Judaism from paganism, or whether they had in fact been Christians.[38]
A similar picture can be seen at Aphrodisias, which has produced the most
important epigraphic evidence relating to Judaism in late antiquity. A tall marble
slab carries two lengthy texts. The first, probably dating to the fourth century,
seems to be the dedication of a building to commemorate the dead and ease
the grief of the community, set up by a funeral association called the *dekania*

of the lovers of wisdom and praise-singers. Its members included thirteen Jews, three Jewish converts (*proselytai*), and two god-fearers. The second, which is probably later in date, simply has the names, patronymics, and profession designations of members of the community, nearly half of whom were not Jews but god-fearers. Again there is no way of telling whether these had come to the synagogue from pagan backgrounds or from the church.[39]

This epigraphic evidence indicates that Jewish communities thrived in late antiquity and attracted non-Jewish sympathizers to the synagogues. This was precisely the situation at Syrian Antioch. The Jews of Antioch had lived peacefully with their pagan and Christian fellow-citizens since the early imperial period, and may have amounted to 15 percent of the local population. They were to be found both in the city and in the countryside, and were well integrated in the wider community. Highly educated Jews were on good terms with their pagan counterparts. In the late fourth century the Jewish patriarch, the leader of the entire Palestinian Jewish community, corresponded with Libanius, and his son nearly became one of the sophist's pupils (Libanius, *ep.* 1098). In 386–7 the preacher John Chrysostom delivered a series of sermons, which virulently attacked the common practice of Antiochene Christians of attending worship at the synagogue.[40] This was during a period of notable religious intolerance in Syria, when Cynegius Maternus, the zealous praetorian prefect of Theodosius I, was giving Christian monks their head in attacking pagan shrines, and it also coincided closely enough with the Christian attack on the synagogue at Callinicum, on the province's eastern frontier. John Chrysostom's incitements to religious hatred would have met no official opposition from the Roman authorities. However, in Antioch itself, it is evident that in general Christians and Jews lived in harmony, to the extent of taking part in one another's religious festivals.[41]

There is also plentiful evidence for close cooperation and even shared worship among the Jews and the non-orthodox Christians of Asia Minor. The two largest Christian sects of rural Anatolia were the Montanists, a millenarian movement, whose spiritual center was the obscure Phrygian town of Pepuza,[42] and the Novatians, who had numerous followers both in the large cities of Asia Minor and in the rural hinterland. Between the 360s and the 380s the Novatians split into two groups over the question of the date of Easter. The city communities followed orthodox practice, as laid down at the Council of Nicaea. However, Novatians in the country areas obdurately maintained the practice of celebrating Easter according to the lunar calendar on 14 Nisan, with the result that they were called *quartodecumani* (*tessareskaidekatitai*). Sozomen and Socrates, the church historians of the mid-fifth century, both have lengthy discussions of the debates concerning the date of Easter and refer to these practices. Socrates, who may well have been a Novatian himself, from the Constantinople community, indicates explicitly that, as a result of a decision taken at a synod in Phrygia, the rural Novatians not only celebrated Easter on the same date as the Passover, but actually attended the Jewish Passover festival (Socrates, *HE* 4.28.17), precisely the behavior of god fearers who frequented Jewish synagogues. This point is emphasized in the reference to this synod in Theophanes' *Chronographia* (Theophanes, *Chron.* 5867).[43] A remarkable set of documents attached to the acts of the Council of Ephesus of 431 shows the Monophysite representatives at the council receiving reports from their emissaries who had been sent to the region of Lydian Philadelphia, where they received depositions of orthodox faith from individuals who had formerly been *tessareskaidekatitai*.[44] It was also the practice of the Montanist communities to celebrate Easter on 14 Nisan, and an inscription from Ankara shows that the organization of the Montanist Church there was very closely modeled on that of Jewish diaspora communities.[45] Relations between Jews and Christians were close and complex. They are also systematically misrepresented by orthodox Christian sources.[46] The rhetoric of the Christian emperors, to be found in their laws about the Jews, often creates the impression of extreme intolerance and hostility, but closer attention to the detail shows that they preserved many of the Jews' privileges, including particularly their freedom to worship.[47] Persecution was sporadic and a product of local conditions, not of systematic policy.

The Montanists were one of the main heresies attacked by Epiphanius in the *Panarion*. He distinguished several different branches of the Montanist Church, calling them variously Pepuzianoi, Montanists, named after their founder, or Priscillianoi, after Priscilla, one of their first prohetesses. Epiphanios identified one group as Quintillians, the followers of another prophetess, Quintilla. She, it was said, had experienced an extraordinary vision of Christ, dazzlingly dressed in a woman's clothes, who imbued her with wisdom, declared that Pepuza was a holy place, and foretold that Jerusalem would descend there from heaven (Epiphanios, *Pan.* 48.14.1–3, 49.1.2–3). Such sensational and titillating stories were a standard way of belittling the beliefs of heretics. In fact, the Montanists offered a genuine challenge to the authority of the orthodox church. They were inspired by the books of the New Testament that had the closest affinity to Judaism, the Gospel of John, and the millenarian prophecies of the book of Revelation. They challenged orthodoxy in particular by their faith in the New Prophecy, that God's will continued to be revealed to them after the apostolic age by their own prophets. It was for this, not for their interpretation of doctrine, that they were repeatedly outlawed by Roman legislation. In the *Secret History* Procopius records that, when threatened with military force to convert to orthodox Christianity, the Montanists committed mass suicide by burning themselves to death in their churches at Pepuza (*Secret History* 11.23).[48]

The Manichees also faced furious intolerance that originated in the legislation of Diocletian and his colleagues. Although Mani, the founder of the sect, was of Mesopotamian origin, the fact that beliefs of the Manichees incorporated Mazdaan ("Zoroastrian") dualism caused them to be equated with Rome's eastern rival, the Persian Sassanian empire.[49] Ironically, Manichaeism was persecuted by the Persians as well as by the Romans. The religion was a sophisticated and original mixture of Persian, Christian, Jewish, and other beliefs. It had an internal hierarchy of priests, "the elect," who were bound to a life of chastity, and a wider circle of devotees known as hearers. Mani himself was the self-proclaimed prophet of Jesus' revelation. He spread his teachings by missionary work that went far beyond the boundaries of the Roman and Sassanian empires as far as China, and he ensured that his message would last by producing a large body of scripture, which became the focus of his followers' beliefs.[50] The most famous Manichee convert, the young Augustine, was attracted not only by the exclusivity and dualistic theology of Manichaeism, which seemed to offer a solution to the world's moral problems, but also by their resplendent holy books (Augustine, *Confessions* 5.7.12).

The Manichees were a renewed target of Roman legislation from the time of Theodosius I, and always seem to have been a secretive sect, meeting in "nefarious retreats and wicked recesses." Certainly there are no epigraphic or archaeological remains of Manichaeism, as there are of Montanism and of Judaism. However, collections of their scriptures found their way into libraries, and some of the main evidence for their beliefs and activities comes from finds of Coptic manuscripts, including those in the gnostic library of Nag-Hammadi in Egypt. Edicts outlawing Manichaeism were issued under most emperors until the time of Justinian. In 383 they were banned from inheriting property (*CTh.* 16.7.3, May 383, Constantinople) and from assembling for worship (*CTh.* 16.5.11, May 383, issued in Padua). It was precisely in this year that Augustine, now at Rome, admitted that he was losing his enthusiasm for their beliefs (*Confessions* 5.10.18–19). Under Zeno, and under Justin and Justinian between 520 and 527, acknowledged Manichees were exposed to exile or the death penalty (*CJust.* 1.5.11–12).[51] By the later fifth century the name Manichee seems to have become an all-purpose term of abuse for an extreme heretic. Even the emperor Anastasius was labeled a Manichaean for his Monophysite tendencies.

We may conclude that despite the best efforts of church leaders, the eastern Roman Empire remained a variegated patchwork of diverse religious beliefs and practices. Although legislation against Jews, pagans, and heretics appears throughout the period, and appears to reflect a high level of religious intolerance, emperors and administrators were conscious of the need to hold a balance between rival religious communities. Until the time of Justinian tolerance of diversity was much more normal than outright religious warfare.

Christianity and the State: Outlawry and Tolerance

During the third and fourth centuries the emperors faced difficult choices in their religious policies. The mainstream Christian tradition made much of persecution and martyrdom, presenting it as a virtual rite of passage through which the church had to pass before emerging in triumphant domination. This perspective is highly misleading. The episodes of persecution by the state were relatively short. Both Christians and pagans were powerful groups and the rulers of the empire during the main period of religious change could not lightly afford to alienate either side.

Christianity was one of a very small number of religious sects that had been outlawed by the Roman Empire. Christians were an object of casual persecution in Rome as early as the 40s and had been scapegoated for the crime of incendiarism after the great fire of AD 65. Reporting on those events, Tacitus says that the Christians were adherents of a pernicious superstition and were condemned on account of the detestation of the human race. It is unclear whether they are to be understood as the objects or the agents of this hatred, but the episode, as represented by Roman writers, cast the tiny Christian community in fundamental opposition to the values of the Roman state (Tacitus, *Annals* 15.44). Some fifty years later the younger Pliny, who conducted trials of persons charged with being Christians in the northern Anatolian province of Pontus, makes clear that their crime was precisely that of being Christian. Their religion was illegal in itself. He introduced a simple test at these hearings to establish their guilt or innocence. If they were prepared to invoke the gods and make a reverential offering with wine and incense to a bust of the emperor and statues of the gods, and abjured Christ, they would be acquitted (Pliny, *ep.* 10, 96–97). Other evidence shows that this should not be understood as a loyalty oath to the emperor and the imperial cult, but as a practical means of establishing that they were no longer Christians.[52]

At the same time both Pliny and the emperor Trajan recognized that Christian behavior was not inherently threatening. Although Christianity was a capital crime, punishable by death, its followers were rarely actively persecuted. The majority of cases which resulted in the execution of Christians before the middle of the third century involved more or less fanatical extremists, in particular followers of the Phrygian Montanist sect, who deliberately challenged the authorities and thus courted their own martyrdom.[53] Christians themselves were at odds over the desirability of such extreme and provocative behavior. From early days the movement was divided between a moderate majority, who led unobtrusive and inoffensive lives, and those who defied not only the state but all normal conventions by their behavior. The writer Lucian ironically portrayed Christians in the 170s as poor wretches who had convinced themselves that they would live for ever, and so despised death. They did not value worldly goods and shared their property in common, following a naive and literal interpretation of Christ's teaching that all men were brothers. Their gullibility made them easier dupes for Lucian's own butt, the trickster Peregrinus (Lucian, *Peregrinus* 11–16).

Christian numbers before 200 were very small, probably to be counted in tens not hundreds, except in the huge metropolitan cities of Alexandria, Antioch, Carthage, and Rome itself.[54] These communities grew significantly in the first half of the third century, a point that was noticed by Origen, the greatest of the early theologians (*De principiis* 4.1.1–2), and we in fact possess reliable figures for the size of the clerical establishment at Rome in 251; 155 persons, who ranged in rank from church doorkeepers to the bishop, and 1,500 widows who were supported by the church's charity (Eusebius, *HE* 6.43).

In 249 the emperor Trajan Decius issued an edict which required that all the empire's inhabitants sacrifice to the gods. Decius' officials employed the census rolls, the administrative mechanism which made possible systematic tax collection, to enforce individual compliance with the order. This was a significant new development. Generally in Graeco-Roman paganism regulations concerning sacrifices offered on behalf of the emperors, or for any other reason, were communal events, not matters for individual responsibility. Decius' measure, in contrast, required everyone, or at least all householders, to stand up and be counted. Moreover, it was a significant step towards exercising centralized control, directed by the emperor himself, over pagan religious practice. It is inconceivable that the edict was universally effective, but it was certainly enforced in parts of Egypt, where numerous certificates of sacrifice written on papyri (*libelli*) have been found. Its effects are also apparent at Smyrna in the province of Asia, where the proconsul of the year 250, who is independently known to have been an enthusiastic pagan, tried and condemned to death a number of non-compliant Christians, including the priest Pionius.[55] It is debated whether the measure was originally intended to target Christians as such, or was a general measure designed to coordinate religious observance at a time of difficulty for the empire, but its undoubted effect was to place the Christian communities under severe pressure. The bishops of Rome and Alexandria were executed, and Cyprian, the bishop of Carthage, whose letters are a vital source for the effects of the edict in North Africa, fled to the countryside.[56]

The edict brought into the open the opposition between Christianity and the state's interests that had usually remained latent. Persecution was renewed in 257 by the emperor Valerian, and this led to the arrest and trial of Cyprian himself. Christian sources preserved a supposed record of two hearings in which the bishop was tried by successive proconsuls of Africa, Aspasius Paternus in 257 and Galerius Maximus in 258, the first of which led to his exile, the second to his execution. The wording of the exchanges between the governors and the bishop is significant:

> *Paternus*: The most sacred emperors Valerian and Gallienus have honoured me with letters, wherein they enjoin that all those who do not observe the religion of Rome, shall make profession of their return to Roman rites; I have accordingly made enquiry as to how you call yourself; what answer do you make to me?
>
> *Cyprian*: I am a Christian, and a bishop; I know no other gods beside the one and true God, who made heaven and earth, the sea and all things therein; this God we Christians serve, to him we pray day and night, for ourselves, for all mankind, for the health of the emperors themselves. (*Acta proconsularia*, CSEL III.3, 110; trans. Stevenson)

This appears to be the first time that the phrase "Roman religion," *Romana religio*, appears in a contemporary source. It reflects the ideas that lay behind Decius' initiative, to articulate a concept of a unified pagan state religion, which, intentionally or not, became a direct counterpart to Christianity.

The anti-Christian climate of the 250s eased after the death of Valerian in Persian captivity in 260, and the consensual model of mutual tolerance between the state and Christians was resumed. This was a period of considerable religious innovation in the Roman world. Aurelian, who made strenuous efforts to restore unity and order to an empire that was under threat of fragmentation, promoted worship of the sun god, Sol Invictus, to a dominant place in the state cults and presented himself as a god, working for mankind's interests as Sol's earthly partner. The period also witnessed a growing emphasis on monotheistic beliefs, at the level of popular cult, among intellectuals and in the ruling elite. Christians began to be found in the upper levels of society, a fact which had important implications for the nature of Christianity itself, as Origen had already acknowledged in the 230s:

> I admit that at the present time perhaps, when on account of the multitude of people coming to the faith, even rich men and persons in positions of honour, and ladies of refinement and high birth favourably regard adherents of the faith, one might venture to say that some become leaders of Christian teaching for the sake of a little prestige. (Origen, *Contra Celsum* 3.9, trans. Chadwick)

By 300 Christians were to be found in the Roman Senate, in the imperial entourage, and in the Roman army.[57] They had thus become part of the state's most important institutions. Christian leaders became increasingly confident of their role in society. In 270 a group of church leaders from Asia Minor and Syria had appealed to the emperor Aurelian to intervene in their internal dispute with Paul of Samosata, the bishop of Antioch, and the emperor had ruled in their favor and for the deposition of Paul. This was a clear precursor to the involvement of fourth-century emperors in major church affairs.[58] T. D. Barnes has argued forcefully that Christians formed "the dynamic element in Roman society and that by 300 no emperor could rule securely without the acquiescence of his Christian subjects."[59]

The renewed period of persecution under the tetrarchy came as a serious shock. Diocletian's restoration of the Roman state was based on a systematic re-invention of Roman religion. This did not resemble Aurelian's sun cult, which was not difficult to reconcile with Christianity, but involved the re-affirmation of central features of traditional paganism. Diocletian promoted the worship of Jupiter as the supreme divine being, adopted Hercules as a major emblem of imperial ideology, and refocused attention on the main figures of the Olympian pantheon. The emperors were explicitly associated with Jupiter and Hercules, and were themselves viewed as gods with Olympian attributes and qualities.[60] As had happened under Trajan Decius, when the emperors launched a new religious initiative which was specifically designed to reinforce the integrity of the Roman Empire, this threw a spotlight on un-Roman activities (see chapter 3). The decision in February 303 to renew persecution of the Christians was taken in the same spirit. The persecution between 303 and 312 recreated the hostile climate of the 250s. As then, anti-Christian measures were targeted on individuals, as is shown by the universal proclamation of 304/5, which ordered that all members of civic communities should sacrifice and make offerings to the pagan gods (Eusebius, *Martyrs of Palestine* III.1).[61]

The tide of the conflict between the Roman state and the church was of course reversed by the conversion of Constantine to Christianity and the measures which were introduced immediately after 312. From 313 until 324 Constantine ruled the empire jointly with Licinius. After the defeat of Maximinus Daia in summer 313, the latter controlled the eastern provinces, where the majority of Christians lived. Although Constantine was now an avowed Christian, Licinius' religious allegiance is less clear. According to Lactantius, Licinius approved the wording of a monotheistic prayer to be used by his soldiers before the decisive battle with Maximinus' troops. This invoked the supreme and holy god and was certainly acceptable to Christians, but should probably be understood as a deliberate formula of generalized monotheism (Lactantius, *On the Deaths of the Persecutors* 46). When the two rulers met in Milan in February 313 they agreed the text of an edict on religious toleration which was promulgated in both halves of the empire. While this entailed full restoration of privileges and property to Christians who had suffered under the persecutions, and promised state funds to compensate pagans who had unwittingly acquired confiscated property from Christians, the main point was to establish freedom of worship throughout the empire, a policy on which both emperors were ready to agree (Lactantius, *On the Deaths of the Persecutors* 48; Eusebius, *HE* 10.5.2–14). An inscription from a military camp in Lower Moesia indicates that the soldiers of the garrison were required to make an annual dedication of an image of the sun god, with incense, candles, and libations, at the express order of Licinius and his son (*ILS* 8940). This probably dates to the period when Licinius was at open war with Constantine, but the latter is unlikely to have been acutely uncomfortable with the religious implications of this action. Constantine's own Christian views were themselves much influenced by solar monotheism, all the more so as the decisive event in his own conversion had been the Christian interpretation of a spectacular solar halo.[62]

As relations between Constantine and Licinius deteriorated, and civil war broke out between them, it was virtually inevitable that the difference in their religious positions was emphasized. Constantine fought under the banner of the God who had given him victory over Maxentius, while Licinius became increasingly mistrustful of Christians in his part of the empire. In the *Life of Constantine* Eusebius tells us that Licinius restricted Christian rights of assembly, prevented bishops from holding synods, and curbed the tax privileges which Constantine had offered to the clergy.[63] In the final version of the *Ecclesiastical History* he alleged that Licinius revived the systematic persecution of Christians (*HE* 10.8.10–18). However, these actions probably amounted to no more than measures taken against subjects who were under reasonable suspicion of taking sides with Constantine, and fiscal rigor was a general feature of Licinius' administration. There is no evidence for the extreme religious polarization that had occurred during the great persecution.

Constantine's victory at the battle of Chrysopolis on the Bosporus in 324, followed a few month's later by the death of Licinius in custody, was celebrated as a further victory for the Christian cause, and the years 324–5 witnessed a series of triumphalist gestures. Constantine himself expounded his own views on God's providence and his own place in history in the Oration to the Saints, delivered to an assembly of bishops, perhaps at Nicomedia, on Good Friday 325.[64] His chief Christian adviser, Ossius, bishop of Cordoba, had made strenuous efforts to resolve the doctrinal split among the eastern Christians between the followers of the priest Arius and the bishop of Alexandria, and the largest ever gathering of church leaders came together at Nicaea in June 325 to agree a program of ecclesiastical unity and an organizational framework for the church. During the same period a decision was taken to create the new imperial city of Constantinople at the site of Constantine's latest victory.

Also in 324 the emperor wrote a series of letters to his subjects relating to Christianity, which are reproduced in Eusebius' *Life*. A long letter to the inhabitants of the eastern provinces celebrated the outcome of the war and the end of the persecutions as a vindication of God's judgment and as a reward for those who had retained faith in Him. The letter reiterated at length the numerous provisions and measures of restitution to restore Christians to the status, positions, and wealth they had possessed before the civil wars (Eusebius, *VC* 2.24–42). A second letter encouraged bishops to see to the reconstruction of damaged or abandoned churches, and promised them state aid (*VC* 2.46.1–3). A third, addressed to all his eastern subjects, commemorated the triumph of the Christian cause, but concluded with a significant and emphatic plea for religious tolerance:

> For the general good of the world and of all mankind, I desire that your people be at peace and stay free from strife. Let those in error, as well as the believers, gladly receive the benefit of peace and quiet. For the sweetness of fellowship will be effective for correcting them and bringing them to the right way. . . . Persons of good sense ought to be convinced that those alone will live a holy and pure life, whom you call to rely on your holy laws. Those who hold back, let them keep, if they wish, their sanctuaries of falsehood. (*VC* 2.56.1–2, trans. Hall and Cameron)

It is important to distinguish the rhetoric from the substance of these imperial pronouncements. Constantine was a passionate convert to Christianity, and often used violent language to describe those with whose views he disagreed, including schismatic and heretical Christian groups as well as pagans.[65] In Christian company he reveled in his religious convictions, flattered bishops by paying attention to their interests and wishes, and sought in return their approval, which was willingly and enthusiastically provided. His biographer and panegyricist Eusebius articulated the view of Constantine as a Christian man of destiny. He was buried in the church of the Holy Apostles, which he had built in Constantinople, in a sarcophagus surrounded by twelve cenotaphs designated for Christ's apostles. The symbolism placed him almost on a level of equality with Christ himself.

However, Constantine was also a secular political leader, who had survived a murderous series of civil wars. For his own regime to succeed he had to defuse the confrontational religious politics of the tetrarchic era. He must also have been aware that, however rapidly the Christian population was growing, Christians were still far outnumbered in the empire by pagans. The letter to the provincials of 324 is the prime document which attests to the politics of religious reconciliation. His famous remark made to a company of bishops, that he himself was perhaps also a bishop, appointed by God to watch over those outside the church, shows his awareness of his wider responsibilities. The remark was very likely intended as a riposte to those who were looking for a more aggressive imperial stance in regard to paganism (*VC* 4.24; see above, chapter 3).

Constantine, like all emperors, was concerned about the subversive threat of magic and divination. He also demonstrated a missionary vigor in closing certain pagan sanctuaries that appeared immoral or were in other ways particularly offensive to Christians. Thus a ban on sacred prostitution led to the closure of temples at Aphaca, and at Heliopolis in Phoenicia the temple of the popular healing god Asclepius at Aegae in Cilicia was pulled down, and offensive pagan altars and statues removed from the holy site of the Oak-Tree of Mamre near Hebron, where God had appeared to Abraham (Eusebius, *VC* 3.51–8). However, it is far from clear in these cases that the words were matched by actions, and pagan cult activity continued long afterwards at the major temple sites.

One measure – the complete ban on sacrifice – has been interpreted in a much more confrontational sense, as a body blow aimed at pagan cult. Eusebius mentions a law "restricting the pollutions of idolatry . . . so that no one should presume to set up cult objects, or practice divination or other occult arts, or even to sacrifice at all" (*VC* 2.45, trans. Hall and Cameron). Another law of 341, ascribed to Constantius but more probably issued by his brother Constans, also refers back to a measure of Constantine which forbade sacrifice (*CTh.* 16.10.2). The significance of this legislation has been much disputed. The ban on sacrifice has been taken by Barnes and others as a key to understanding Constantine's religious intentions, evidence of a deliberate policy to cut the heart out of the old paganism. This seems to place too much weight on a flimsy foundation. If Constantine did propose such a sweeping measure, it was rapidly rescinded to make way for the conciliatory approach found in the letter to the eastern provincials in 324:

> My own desire is for the common good of the world and the advantages of all mankind, that your [that is, God's] people should enjoy a life of peace and undisturbed concord. Let those, therefore, who still delight in error, be made welcome in the same degree of peace and tranquillity which they have who believe. For it may be that this restoration of equal privileges to all will prevail to lead them into the straight path. Let no one molest one another, but let every

one do as his soul desires. Only let men of sound judgement be assured of this, that those only can live a life of holiness and purity, whom thou call to rely on your holy laws. With regard to those who will hold themselves aloof from us, let them have, if they please, their temples of falsehood; we have the glorious edifice of your truth. (Eusebius, *VC* 2.56)

This breathes the same spirit of reconciliation as the Edict of Milan of 313, while at the same time proclaiming and advocating the superiority of the Christian faith. If there was a ban, it seems to have applied only to sacrifice in contexts associated with magical practices and divination, as Eusebius virtually implies and is in fact explicitly attested in a law of Constantine of 321 (*CTh.* 9.16.1–4).[66]

Most of the surviving sources for the period of nearly forty years that separated the defeat of Licinius in 324 from the accession of Julian to sole power in December 361 were written from a Christian perspective and dealt with church affairs, with which the emperors were closely involved. Christians were seriously divided among themselves during this period (see below, chapter 8) and their bishops expended little time and energy in attacking the pagans, now that their own faith was securely anchored as the state's religion. Legislation continued to be passed that favored the church, but few active measures were undertaken to repress paganism. It appears that Constantine and his sons had no major interest in sharpening the division between pagans and Christians. The emperors retained the title of *pontifex maximus*, implying that they took responsibility for pagan cults, and they continued to use this authority in a traditional way. Constantine himself wrote a letter in 326/7 to the people of Hispellum in Tuscany, granting them permission to erect a temple of the imperial cult, a *templum Flaviae gentis*, in honor of his own dynasty, provided that the sanctuary was not "defiled by the deceits of any contagious superstition," a reference to traditional blood sacrifice (*ILS* 705).

Constantius II's position is less well attested than that of Constantine. His personal commitment to Christianity was at least as great as that of his father, and he became closely involved in ecclesiastical politics. Part of a law of Constantius stated that "it is our pleasure that the temples shall be immediately closed in all places and in all cities, and access to them forbidden, so as to deny to all abandoned men the opportunity to commit sin" (*CTh.* 10.16.4). Sources also list a number of temples, in addition to these closed under Constantine, which were re-commissioned by Julian and are therefore likely to have been subject to restrictions under Constantius.[67] In 357, during his visit to Rome, Constantius II saw that the pagan priestly colleges were brought up to strength, while at the same time he removed the pagan altar of Victory from the Senate House (Symmachus, *Rel.* 3.7).

Julian brought a halt to legislation in favor of the Christians, and withdrew the privileges they had received from his predecessors. Christian clergy were no longer exempt from taxation, lost their right to receive free grain distributions, and were required to fulfill financial duties to their cities as *curiales*. Bishops no longer enjoyed the power to act as judges. Julian made no attempt to instigate active persecution, but sought to undermine the church in other ways (Theodoret, *HE* 1.11). Christians who had been exiled as a result of internal church disputes were recalled with the purpose, Ammianus claimed, of rekindling this disabling strife (Ammianus 22.11). Julian's own religious views, as attested by his writings, were complex. They reveal a man prepared to push his convictions to the limit and force the issue with Christian opponents. The famous edict which declared that Christians were morally unfit to serve as teachers of grammar, philosophy, or rhetoric was the act of an emperor intent on placing Christians beyond the pale of acceptability.[68] Augustine later saw this as a clear act of religious intolerance (*City of God* 18.52). It is not surprising that inscriptions set up in Julian's honor should have revived the charged vocabulary of the 250s, and hailed him as *restitutor libertatis et Romanae religionis*, "restorer of liberty and the Roman religion" (*ILS* 752). For an eighteen-month period the politics of religious confrontation were revived.

Julian's reign was too brief to have had long-lasting effects on religious practice in the empire, but it is striking that his successors avoided adopting an extreme religious position, and did not copy the intolerant stance that he had taken up. Jovian in fact took advantage of Julian's drastic initiative in stripping clergy of their tax privileges, and only restored them to a third of the level at which they had been set by Constantine and Constantius, a level which was maintained until the mid-fifth century (Theodoret, *HE* 1.11.3, 4.4.6). However, he ostentatiously advertised a policy of religious toleration. This is apparent from the speech addressed to him in Ankara on January 1, 364, by the political philosopher Themistius. Themistius himself was not a Christian, but a pagan with philosophical religious views. Ironically, he was not held in favor by Julian, who preferred other intellectual advisors, but acted as spokesmen for all the Christian emperors of the period who were based in the East: Constantius, Jovian, Valens, and Theodosius I.[69] The speech implies that Jovian allowed all his subjects to take part in rituals according to their individual inclinations. Themistius argued that it was appropriate to encourage healthy competition between people of different religious persuasions, to avoid falling into indolence and lethargy. Religious activity was compared to a race in which all the competitors strove to reach the same goal, even if they did not all travel by the same route. The metaphor as well as the argument strikingly anticipates that of Symmachus in his famous *relatio* to Valentinian II, pleading for the restoration of the pagan altar of victory at Rome. In an even more remarkable passage, the speech portrays god the creator delighting in the diversity of his worshippers, Syrians, Greeks, and Egyptians, each organizing their affairs in their own way. In this tripartite division the Syrians are evidently to be understood as the Christians (Themistius, *Or.* 567b–70c). Jovian is credited with making religious laws relating to pagan cult that may be compared to Constantine's, "opening the temples, but closing the haunts of imposture, allowing lawful sacrifices but giving no license to those who practice the magic arts."[70]

Jovian's policies were continued in the East by Valens and in the West by his elder brother Valentinian. A law of 371 implies that they had passed measures of religious toleration at a previous date (*CTh.* 9.16.9). Themistius' speeches should be interpreted as articulating the views of the emperors he served,[71] and oration 6 (delivered exactly a year later than the speech for Jovian) puts a different emphasis on religious plurality, perhaps in deference to Valens' own more pronounced Christian standpoint. It emphasizes that humanity was united in spiritual kinship and shared moral goals. Men competed in virtue, but also shared feelings of shame when they behaved wickedly. They occupied the earth as property held in common and came to one another's aid when help was needed. All recognized and depended on a supreme divinity as their father, even if they perceived him in different ways (*Or.* 6.77a–c). This speech presents a deliberately vague form of political monotheism to justify Themistius' advocacy of a continued policy of mutual tolerance between pagans and Christians. The whole approach was succinctly summarized by Ammianus in his obituary notice for the emperor Valentinian:

> His reign was distinguished for religious tolerance. He took a neutral position between opposing faiths, and never troubled anyone by ordering him to adopt this or that mode of worship. He made no attempt to fasten his own beliefs on the necks of his subjects, but left the various cults undisturbed as he found them. (Ammianus 30.9, trans. Hamilton)

Valentinian died of a stroke in 375, and was succeeded by the juvenile Gratian. After the death of Valens in 378, Theodosius, already a key military figure in the army of Illyricum, was acclaimed emperor in January 379. On November 24, 380, he entered Constantinople, having brought some calm and stability to the eastern Balkans. The relationship between the state and the church was about to undergo rapid change. Both Valens and Valentinian had kept their distance from ecclesiastical controversy; but their successors Gratian and Theodosius embraced it. Both were strong adherents of Nicene Christianity, the prevalent orthodoxy of the western empire. Theodosius' personal piety had been forged during his Spanish upbringing, while Gratian was under the strong influence of the most formidable churchman of the last quarter of the fourth century, Ambrose of Milan, who presented the youthful ruler with a two-volume treatise *On the Faith* (*De Fide*) in 379.[72] Immediately after Adrianople Gratian had issued an edict of religious tolerance for all but the Manichees and two extreme Arianizing sects. However, a law of August 379 prescribed the Catholic faith for all (*CTh.* 16.5.5). In February 380 Theodosius matched this with the most famous religious edict pronounced by any Roman emperor of late antiquity, known from the first words of the Latin text as *Cunctos Populos*:

> We desire that all the peoples who are ruled by the guidance of our clemency should be versed in that religion which it is evident that the divine apostle Peter handed down to the Romans, and which the pope Damasus and Peter, bishop of Alexandria, a man of apostolic sanctity, adhere to. . . . We command that those persons who follow this rule shall have the name of catholic Christians. The rest,

however, whom we judge to be demented and insane, shall sustain the infamy of heretical dogmas, their meeting places shall not receive the name of churches, and they shall be smitten first by divine vengeance and secondly by the retribution of our own initiative, which we shall assume in accordance with divine judgement. (*CTh.* 16.1.2)

Unlike Constantine, who had been baptized only on his death bed, Theodosius had been anointed into the church in Thessalonica in 380 when faced with a life-threatening illness, and ruled accordingly as a full initiate of the Christian community. The command that his subjects should follow the tenets of Catholic orthodoxy, laid down by the Council of Nicaea, was intended above all to impose a united Christian doctrine. Theodosius' intentions were confirmed two days after his arrival in Constantinople on November 24, 380, when he dismissed its Arian bishop and replaced him with the orthodox Gregory of Nazianzus (Socrates, *HE* 5.8.11; Sozomen 7.5.1). Further laws outlawing heresy followed before one hundred and fifty eastern bishops assembled for the second ecumenical Council of Constantinople, held in May 381, and which approved an updated version of the Nicene Creed.[73]

The storm did not break at once over the pagan cults. In 382 Theodosius allowed a pagan temple to be re-opened at Edessa, provided that no sacrifices were carried out there (*CTh.* 16.10.8), and a verse inscription carved on an imperial equestrian statue at Constantinople called Theodosius "a second Helios," harking back to the deliberately ambiguous religious language of the early Constantinian period (*Anth. Pal.* 16.65). However, in the same year in the West, Gratian refused to accept the robe of the *pontifex maximus* when it was presented to him by members of the Roman Senate,[74] and took three measures that decisively undermined traditional paganism in Rome. He stopped imperial subsidies for the city's main cults, he abolished the salaries of the Vestal Virgins, and he once again ordered the removal of the altar of Victory from the Senate House.

Gratian was killed in the war with the usurper Magnus Maximus in 383, and was succeeded in the West by the very young Valentinian II. This offered the opportunity for the famous appeal that the altar be restored, sent to Valentinian by the pagan prefect of the city, Symmachus, who spoke for the still influential group of pagan senators at Rome (Symmachus, *Rel.* 3). These prominent men, the main guardians of late paganism, had revived and maintained the traditional cults through the middle and into the later years of the fourth century.[75] Their request and the core of the argument was put in memorable words:

We ask, then, for peace for the gods of the homeland, for the divine heroes. It is equitable that whatever all worship be considered one. We gaze upon the same stars, the sky is common to us all, the same world envelops us. What difference does it make by what judgment a person searches out the truth? So great a mystery cannot be arrived at by one path. (Symmachus, *Rel.* 3, 10, trans. Boniface Ramsay)

The emperor was brow-beaten into rejecting their petition by the arguments of Ambrose which were set out in two long letters, the first delivered even before the formal presentation of Symmachus' petition, the second celebrating the *fait accompli* of its rejection (Ambrose, *ep.* 72 [17] and 73 [18]). The Christian poet Prudentius related the whole episode in hexameter verse a few years later.

In the eastern provinces anti-pagan measures are particularly associated with the praetorian prefect of the East of 384–8, Maternus Cynegius, a Spanish associate of the emperor. Enlisting the aid of grim and fanatical monks, and urged on by his zealous wife, Cynegius supervised the destruction of temples at Edessa in Osrhoene, at Apamea in Syria, and in Egypt. At Antioch the pagan orator Libanius, who was clearly aware that Maternus was acting without explicit imperial authority, protested to Theodosius in his speech in defense of the temples, which vainly reminded the emperor of the tolerance of his predecessors (*Or.* 30.4).

The praetorian prefect and his followers may have exceeded their instructions from the emperor, but there was no respite for pagans from this destructive zeal after Maternus' death in 388. In the course of his campaign against Magnus Maximus, Theodosius himself came to Milan in 389/90. Theodosius and his court had been used to dominating ecclesiastical affairs in Constantinople and this generated an atmosphere of tension between the emperor and the strong-willed bishop in Milan (Sozomen 7.12). Ambrose now insisted that the emperor in church should not take his place among the clergy, but in a position subordinate to the priesthood at the front of the congregation (Sozomen 7.27.8–9). In a first trial of wills, Ambrose put pressure on the emperor not to punish an eastern military leader for the wanton destruction of the Jewish synagogue at Callinicum in Syria and pay for its repair, and urged him not to rein in the monks who had destroyed a heretical Christian conventicle (Ambrose, *ep.* 74; this is an edited version of *ep. extra collectionem* 1a [40], 6–8).[76] Then, in one of the most dramatic confrontations of church and state power in late antiquity, he forced the emperor to do thirty days penance. In 390 there had been a riot in Thessalonica during a festival when the local military commander Botheric, probably the *magister militum* for Illyricum, had arrested a favorite charioteer. The rioters killed Botheric himself and in retaliation Theodosius ordered punitive (but probably selective) reprisals against the population (Sozomen, *HE* 7.25; Rufinus, *HE* 12.18; Theodoret, *HE* 5.18). The punishment, carried out by the soldiers who had served Botheric, escalated out of hand and led to the massacre of 7,000 innocent – and Catholic orthodox – citizens of Thessalonica as reprisal for the murder of an Arian Germanic general. Ambrose, who was involved with a synod of Gallic bishops at the time when Theodosius and his court were taking the punitive decision, wrote a private letter to Theodosius to tell him that he would not be present to participate in the *adventus* ceremony when Theodosius came to Milan after the massacre. He also suggested a resolution to the issue: he would administer the sacrament, if Theodosius did public penance. This appears to have been Ambrose's diplomatic solution to a highly charged political crisis. Theodosius agreed to comply, securing his own reputation for piety, as he deflected the odium which his orders had aroused.[77]

The campaign against the pagans reached a climax soon afterwards. In early 391 Theodosius reiterated in emphatic form earlier rulings designed to outlaw sacrifice and to restrict activities in pagan sanctuaries:

> Let no one defile himself by conducting sacrifices; let no one slaughter an innocent victim; let no one enter a pagan sanctuary, spend time in a temple or gaze in reverence on statues that have been shaped by mortal hands. (*CTh.* 16.10.10)

The order was directed at senior state officials, for the most part provincial governors in the Italian provinces, who exploited the advantage of their position to enter temples and conduct formal pagan rites.[78] Four months later a law in similar terms was sent to the *comes* of Egypt and the military commander there (*CTh.* 16.10.11). As had happened in Syria during the 380s, local action went much further than the emperor's intentions. In the summer of 391, amid riotous opposition from the pagan population of Alexandria led by the philosopher Olympius, Theophilus, the bishop of Alexandria, called on imperial troops to destroy the Serapeum, the largest pagan sanctuary in the Roman Empire. A church in honor of the emperor Arcadius was built on the site (see below, chapter 9).

Theodosius' drive to suppress paganism turned to outright war in 394, during the conflict with Eugenius. In the final stages of the uprising the usurper, supported by the *magister militum* Arbogast, his pagan Frankish sponsor, sought help from the remaining pagan senators at Rome, promised to restore their religious privileges, and brought back the sacred statue of Victory into the Senate House. This was sufficient for Theodosius to present the war against him as one of pagans against Christians. In the accounts of the deciding battle at the river Frigidus, it was alleged that Eugenius' camp stood under the protection of Hercules and Jupiter (Augustine, *City of God* 5.26). The tide of battle turned in the second day, when a fierce wind from the East set in behind Theodosius' troops and enabled them to inflict a defeat on the enemy after their own serious losses of the previous day. The reversal of fortune was hailed as a decisive victory of the Christian God over His pagan enemies.[79]

The issue whether to outlaw or tolerate pagan practices became less urgent in the fifth century. The measures taken to repress sacrifice and to destroy major pagan cult centers under Theodosius I certainly coincided with the growth in Christian numbers among the population at large, so that they were certainly in a majority in the empire at large. This is demonstrated by the accelerating pace of church building in the late fourth and early fifth centuries. Major temples in many eastern cities began to be converted into churches during the first half of the fifth century, a phenomenon that is only sporadically attested at an earlier date.[80] Under Theodosius II laws continued to be passed which banned pagans from imperial service and from acting as judges (*CTh.* 16.10.21 [415], 16.10.23 [423]). Some of the legislation of this period simply repeated

earlier imperial pronouncements against pagans, while simultaneously acknowledging that they had been ineffective. Both Marcian in 451 and Leo in 472
repeated earlier laws that banned sacrifice, and Leo in 468 made it illegal
for pagans to become lawyers (*CJust.* 1.11.7–8, 1.4.5). Nevertheless Theodosius
II, in keeping with the consistently eirenic approach which characterized the
whole period of his reign, avoided confrontational legislation and instructed
his praetorian prefect Asclepiodotus to ensure that Christians did not attempt
violence against Jews or pagans who were not involved in disorderly or other
illegal conduct (*CTh.* 16.10.24).[81] Emperors and their advisors were much
more consumed by the internal divisions of the church.[82]

The issue of paganism only re-emerged significantly at the beginning of
Justinian's reign. His stance is drastically revealed by the preface to the publication of the law code:

> All people who are ruled by the administration of our clemency shall practice
> that religion which the divine Peter the Apostle transmitted to the Romans. We
> command that those who follow this law shall embrace the name of Catholic
> Christians. (*CJust.* 1.1.1)

The first book of the Justinianic Code was concerned with religious legislation,
leaving no doubt that the emperor's legislative priorities were significantly
different from those of his predecessors. Active measures were taken to eradic-
ate pagans for the first time in nearly 150 years. Justinian was responsible,
perhaps in 531, for a law that aimed at comprehensive repression of pagans
and of Manichees. Pagans were defined as those who had not received or agreed
to undergo baptism. Those who refused were banned from practicing as teachers or being employed by the state. Their children were to be forcibly educated
in Christian doctrine. Those who defied the law would be punished by exile
and confiscation of their property (*CJust.* 1.11.10).[83] Outright Christian intolerance of other forms of religious practice and belief was a new hallmark of the
Justinianic regime.

NOTES

1 R. MacMullen, *Christianity and Paganism in the Fourth to Eighth Centuries* (New
   Haven, 1997), 3–5.
2 T. D. Barnes, *Ammianus Marcellinus* (Cornell, 1998), 79–94.
3 J. Geffcken, *The Last Days of Graeco-Roman Paganism* (English trans. S.
   MacCormack, Amsterdam, London, New York, 1978).
4 E. Sauer, *The Archaeology of Religious Hatred in the Roman and Early Medieval
   World* (Stroud, 2003).
5 Simon Price, *Rituals and Power. The Roman Imperial Cult in Asia Minor* (Cambridge,
   1985), 1–22, 234–48; K. Hopkins, *Conquerors and Slaves. Sociological Studies in
   Roman History* (Cambridge, 1978), 197–242.

6   F. Kolb, *Herrscherideologie in der Spätantike* (Berlin, 2001).

7   A. Kaldellis, *Procopius of Caesarea* (Philadelphia, 2004), 128–42.

8   R. Kaster, *Guardians of Language. The Grammarian and Society in Late Antiquity* (Berkeley, 1988).

9   Alan Cameron, "Poetry and literary culture in late antiquity," in S. Swain and M. Edwards (eds.), *Approaching Late Antiquity* (Oxford, 2004), 327–54.

10   W. Liebeschuetz, "The use of pagan mythology in the Christian empire, with particular reference to the *Dionysiaca* of Nonnus," in P. Allen and E. Jeffreys (eds.), *The Sixth Century. End or Beginning?* (Brisbane, 1996), 75–91.

11   R. MacMullen "Cultural changes and political changes in the 4th and 5th centuries," *Historia* 52 (2003), 465–95.

12   For pagan survivals in popular culture, see above all R. MacMullen, *Christianity and Paganism in the Fourth to Eighth Centuries* (New Haven, 1997).

13   G. W. Bowersock, *Hellenism in Late Antiquity* (Ann Arbor, 1990).

14   M. Meslin, *La fête des kalendes de janvier dans l'empire romain* (Brussels, 1970).

15   C. Roueché, *Performers and Partisans at Aphrodisias in the Roman and Late Roman Periods* (London, 1993), 188–9, citing John Chrysostom, *Homilia in Matthaeum* 7.6.

16   C. Roueché, *Aphrodisias in Late Antiquity* (London, 1989), 71–3.

17   R. MacMullen, *Paganism in the Roman Empire* (New Haven, 1981); R. Lane Fox, *Pagans and Christians* (London, 1985).

18   A. H. M. Jones, *LRE* I, 732–63; W. Liebeschuetz, *The Decline and Fall of the Roman City* (Oxford, 2001), 169–202 on civic finances. See also S. Mitchell, "The Cities of Asia Minor in the age of Constantine," in S. Lieu and D. Montserrat, *Constantine. History, Historiography and Legend* (London, 1998), 52–74. The picture was not completely clear-cut. Some evidence can be found in the later fourth century for civic euergetism in the larger cities, notably Antioch.

19   P. Brown, *The Rise of Western Christendom* (2nd edn. Oxford, 2003), 56.

20   C. Lepelley, *Les cités de l'Afrique romaine au bas-empire* I. *La permanence d'une civilisation municipale* (Paris, 1979), 359–69.

21   See C. Lepelley, *Les cités de l'Afrique romaine* I (Paris, 1979), 371–85.

22   F. W. Trombley, *Hellenic Religion and Christianization c. 370–529* (Leiden, 1993), 1–97.

23   H. Chadwick, *The Early Church* (London, 1967), 154; M. R. Salzman, *On Roman Time. The Codex-Calendar of 354 and the Rhythms of Urban Life in Late Antiquity* (Berkeley, 1990).

24   C. A. Faraone and D. Obbink (eds.), *Magika Hiera. Ancient Greek Magic and Religion* (Oxford, 1990); B. Ankarloo and S. Clark (eds.) *Witchcraft and Magic in Europe. Ancient Greece and Rome* (London and Pennsylvania, 1999), especially the surveys of Richard Gordon and Valerie Flint; D. Ogden, *Magic, Witchcraft and Ghosts in the Greek and Roman Worlds. A Sourcebook* (Oxford, 2002).

25   P. Brown, "Sorcery, demons and the rise of Christianity: From late antiquity into the middle ages," in *Religion and Society in the Age of Saint Augustine* (London, 1972), 119–46.

26   A. A. Barb, "The survival of magic arts," in A. Momigliano (ed.), *The Conflict between Paganism and Christianity in the Fourth Century* (Oxford, 1963), 100–25.

27   R. MacMullen, *Christianizing the Roman Empire AD 100–400* (New Haven, 1984), 27–8.

28   D. Ogden, *Magic, Witchcraft and Ghosts in the Greek and Roman Worlds. A Sourcebook* (Oxford, 2002), 166–71.

29   M. Frede, "Monotheism and pagan philosophy in later antiquity," in P. Athanassiadi and M. Frede (eds.), *Pagan Monotheism in Late Antiquity* (Oxford, 1999), 41–67.

30   S. Mitchell, "The cult of Theos Hypsistos," in P. Athanassiadi and M. Frede (eds.), *Pagan Monotheism in Late Antiquity* (Oxford, 1999), 81–148. The literature on pagan monotheism is expanding rapidly.

31   P. Athanassiadi, "Apamea and the Chaldaean oracles: A holy city and a holy book," in A. Smith, *The Philosopher and Society in Late Antiquity* (Swansea, 2005), 117–43.

32   Stressed by K. Hopkins, "Christian number and its implications," *Journal of Early Christian Studies* 6 (1998), 185–226, at 220.

33   Epiphanius, *Panarion*, translated by P. Amidon.

34   S. Mitchell, *Anatolia* II (Oxford, 1993), 96–108.

35   T. Urbaincsyk, "The devil spoke Syriac to me," in S. Mitchell and G. Greatrex, *Ethnicity and Culture in Late Antiquity* (Wales and London, 2000), 253–65; T. Urbainczyk, *Theodoret of Cyrrhus: The Bishop and the Holy Man* (Michigan, 2002).

36   Ambrose, *ep.* 74; an edited version of the letter which also survives as *ep. Extra coll.* 1. See N. McLynn, *Ambrose of Milan*, 298–309.

37   Jodi Magness, *American Journal of Archaeology* 109 (2005), 443 argues that the conversion of the structure for use as a synagogue did not occur until the sixth century.

38   For a full review of the Sardis evidence see W. Ameling, *Inscriptiones Judaicae Orientis* II. *Kleinasien* (Tübingen, 2004), 209–97. The inscriptions are published by J. H. Kroll, *Harvard Theological Review* 94 (2001), 15ff.

39   W. Ameling, *Inscriptiones Judaicae Orientis* II. *Kleinasien* (Tübingen, 2004), 71–112 no. 14 (Aphrodisias); A. Chaniotis, "The Jews of Aphrodisias: New evidence and old problems," *Studia Classica Israelica* 21 (2002), 209.

40   R. L. Wilken, *John Chrysostom and the Jews. Rhetoric and Reality in the Late Fourth Century* (Berkeley, 1983).

41   J. Hahn, *Gewalt und Religiöser Konflikt* (Berlin, 2004), 139–45.

42   W. Tabbernee, "Portals of the Montanist New Jerusalem: The discovery of Pepuza and Tymion," *Journal of Early Christian Studies* 11.1 (2003), 87–93.

43   S. Mitchell, *Anatolia* II, 98–9.

44   Fergus Millar, "Repentant heretics in fifth-century Lydia: Identity and literacy," *Scripta Classica Israelica* 23 (2004), 111–30.

45   S. Mitchell, "An apostle to Ankara from the New Jeruslaem," *Scripta Classica Israelica* 2005, in press.

46   Fergus Millar, "The Jews of the Graeco-Roman diaspora between paganism and Christianity AD 312–438," in J. Lieu, J. North, and T. Rajak (eds.), *The Jews among Pagans and Christians in the Roman Empire* (London, 1992), 97–123.

47   Fergus Millar, "Christian emperors, Christian church and the Jews of the Diaspora in the Greek East, CE 379–450," *Journal of Jewish Studies* 55 (2004), 1–24.

48   W. Tabbernee, *Montanist Inscriptions and Testimonia. Epigraphic Sources Illustrating the History of Montanism* (Macon, 1997), 17–47, 471–6.

49   Translated in Gardner and Lien, *Manichaean Texts from the Roman Empire* 116–18. Diocletian's legislation is contained in a letter sent to the governor of Egypt.

50   D. Potter, *The Roman Empire at Bay* (London, 2004), 302–14.

51   I. Gardner and S. N. C. Lieu, *Manichaean Texts from the Roman Empire* (Cambridge, 2004), 145–50.

52 Fergus Millar, "The imperial cult and the persecutions," in W. den Boer (ed.), *Le culte des souverains dans l'empire romain* (Fondation Hardt Entretiens 19, Geneva, 1973), 145–65 (repr. in *Rome, the Greek World and the East, Volume 2. Government, Society, and Culture in the Roman Empire* [Chapel Hill, 2004], 298–312).

53 A. R. Birley, "Die freiwilligen Märtyrer. Zum Problem der Selbst-Auslieferer," in R. von Haehling (ed.), *Rom und das himmlische Jerusalem. Die frühen Christen zwischen Anpassung und Ablehnung* (Darmstadt, 2000), 97–123.

54 R. Stark, *The Sociology of Early Christianity* (Princeton, 1997), K. Hopkins, *Journal of Early Christianity* 6 (1998), 185–226.

55 R. Lane Fox, *Pagans and Christians* (London, 1985), 460–8; L. Robert (ed. G. W. Bowersock and C. P. Jones), *Le martyre de Pionios, prêtre de Smyrne* (Washington, 1994).

56 J. B. Rives, "The decree of Decius and the religion of the empire," *JRS 89* (1999), 135–54.

57 D. Potter, *The Roman Empire at Bay* (London, 2004), 314, and discussion at n. 51; W. Eck, "Das Eindringen des Christentums in den Senatorenstand bis zu Konstantin dem Grosse," *Chiron* 1 (1971), 381–406; T. D. Barnes, "Statistics and the conversion of the Roman aristocracy," *JRS* 85 (1995), 134–48.

58 Eusebius, *HE* 7.30, 19–21; F. Millar, *The Emperor in the Roman World* (Cornell, 1977).

59 T. D. Barnes, "Christians and Pagans under Constantius," in *L'Église et l'Empire au IVe Siècle* (1989), 301–38 at 308.

60 W. Liebeschuetz, *Continuity and Change in Roman Religion* (Oxford, 1972).

61 For details of the persecutions, see S. Mitchell, "Maximinus and the Christians: A new Latin inscription from Pisidia," *JRS* 78 (1988), 105–24.

62 P. Weiss, "The vision of Constantine," *Journal of Roman Archaeology* 16 (2003), 237–59. See below pp. 257–60.

63 See Eusebius, *VC* 1. 51–3; but Licinius' speech in *VC* 2.5 is surely an invention.

64 The date and location of the Oration to the Saints have been much discussed. I have followed the conclusion of T. D. Barnes, "Constantine's speech to the assembly of the saints: Place and date of delivery," *JTS* 52 (2001), 26–36. See also R. Lane Fox, *Pagans and Christians* (London, 1985), arguing for Antioch in the same year.

65 For example, Optatus, *Tract*, app. 5 has Constantine saying of the Donatists that "It is as clear as day that their madness is of such a kind that we find them abhorrent even to the heavenly dispensation: so great a madness persists in them when, with incredible arrogance, they persuade themselves of things that it is not right to say or hear, repudiating the equitable judgement that had been given by the will of heaven." Compare Eusebius, *VC* 2.66 (Constantine's letter to Arius and Alexander).

66 S. Bradbury, "Constantine and the problem of anti-pagan legislation in the fourth century," *Classical Philology* 89 (1994), 120–39.

67 Discussion in P. Heather and D. Moncur, *Politics, Philosophy, and Empire in the Fourth Century. Select Orations of Themistius* (Liverpool, 2001), 48–57.

68 G. W. Bowersock, *Julian the Apostate* (London, 1978), 78–93 for a sharp characterization of Julian's hard-line views.

69 J. Vanderspoel, *Themistius and the Imperial Court. Oratory, Civic Duty, and Paideia from Constatius to Theodosius* (Michigan, 1995); R. M. Errington, "Themistius and his emperors," *Chiron* 30 (2000), 861–904.

70 Themistius, *Or.* 567b–70c. See the translation and commentary of P. Heather and D. Moncur, *Themistius, Select Orations. Politics, Philosophy, and Empire in the Fourth Century* (Liverpool, 2001), 137–96.

71 See P. Heather and D. Moncur, *Themistius, Select Orations*, 1–42, esp. 29–38.

72 N. Mclynn, *Ambrose of Milan* (Berkeley, 1994), 79–157 for lengthy discussion.

73 For Theodosian religious legislation, see J. H. W. G. Liebeschuetz, *Barbarians and Bishops* (Oxford, 1990), 146–53.

74 Zosimus 4.36.5; Alan Cameron, "Gratian's repudiation of the pontifical robe," *JRS* 58 (1968), 96–102.

75 See P. Brown, "Aspects of the Christianization of the Roman aristocracy," *JRS* 51 (1961), 1–11 (reprinted in his *Religion and Society in the Age of Saint Augustine* [London, 1972], 161–82); M. R. Salzmann, *The Making of a Christian Aristocracy. Social and Religious Change in the Western Roman Empire* (Harvard, 2002).

76 N. McLynn, *Ambrose of Milan*, 298–315, for a revisionist interpretation.

77 F. Kolb, "'Der Bussakt von Mailand.' Zum Verhältnis von Staat und Kirche in der Spätantike," in H. Boockmann et al., *Geschichte und Gegenwart: Festschrift für K. D. Erdmann* (Neumünster, 1980), 41–74; G. W. Bowersock, "From emperor to bishop: The self-conscious transformation of political power in the 4th century AD," *Classical Philology* 81 (1986), 299; P. Brown, *Power and Persuasion in Late Antiquity* (1992), 109–13; N. McLynn, *Ambrose of Milan*, 315–30.

78 N. McLynn, *Ambrose of Milan*, 331–2 for discussion. The measure would surely have been construed as hostile to the interests of pagan members of the Roman senatorial class.

79 F. Paschoud, *Zosime* II.2, 474–500 for the sources and discussion.

80 G. Fowden, "Bishops and temples in the eastern empire," *Journal of Theological Studies* 29 (1978), 53–78; J. Vaes, "Christliche Wiederverwendung antiker Bauten. Ein Forschungsbericht," *Ancient Society* 15–17 (1984–6), 305–443; S. Mitchell, *Anatolia* II (Oxford, 1993), 67.

81 P. Garnsey and C. Humphress, *The Evolution of the Late Antique World* (Cambridge, 2001), 132–69, esp. 152.

82 For the patchy evidence for pagan survivals see the excellent surveys of Michael Whitby, "John of Ephesus and the pagans: pagan survivals in the sixth century," in M. Salamon, *Paganism in the Later Roman Empire and Byzantium* (Krakow, 1991), 111–31, and K. Harl, "Sacrifice and pagan belief in fifth- and sixth-century Byzantium," *Past and Present* 128 (1990), 7–27.

83 Recent discussion by E. Watts, "Justinian, Malalas and the end of Athenian philosophical teaching," *JRS* 94 (2004), 168–82, at 177–82.

8

Conversion to Christianity and the Politics of Religious Identity

250	300	350	400	450	500	550	600	650

Three Conversions and their Consequences

Christians in the fourth century and throughout late antiquity were confident of their ability to absorb pagan traditions, and triumphantly aware that the tide of religious change was flooding in their direction. The period as a whole may be seen through Christian sources as a vast collective narrative of conversion, comprising innumerable episodes which fitted into this large picture. Two accounts loom large in the historiography, from each end of the fourth century; the conversion of the emperor Constantine, and the conversion of St Augustine. These have done more than anything else to shape perceptions of the phenomenon. They are counterbalanced by an equally famous conversion in the other direction, that of the emperor Julian.

Constantine

Constantine's conversion, which was a decisive turning point in Roman history, has been a subject of endless fascination. Both Eusebius in the *Life of Constantine*, which was completed shortly after the emperor's death, and Lactantius in *On the Deaths of the Persecutors*, gave accounts of a dramatic dream or vision which supposedly determined Constantine's religious allegiance to Christianity. Lactantius, writing around 314, reports the experience that came to the emperor on the eve of the decisive battle with Maxentius at the Milvian bridge two years earlier:

> The anniversary of Maxentius' accession, 27 October, was near and his first five years were drawing to a close. Constantine was directed in a dream to mark the heavenly sign of God on the shields of his soldiers and thus to join battle. He did as he was ordered and with the cross-shaped letter X, with its top bent over, he marked Christ on the shields. (*On the Deaths of the Persecutors* 44.3–6)

Eusebius has a much more elaborate version. The context is the moment at which Constantine sought divine help some time before the decisive battle. The emperor reflected that those who had placed their trust in many gods had failed to dislodge the tyrant Maxentius, and accordingly looked for support for his father's talisman, "the God who transcends the universe, the saviour and guardian of his empire."[1] This, then, is a classic narrative of transition from polytheism to monotheistic Christianity, which continues:

> This God he began to invoke in prayer, beseeching and imploring him to show who he was, and to stretch out his right hand to assist him in his plans. As he made these prayers and earnest supplications there appeared to the emperor a most remarkable divine sign. If someone else had reported it, it would perhaps not be easy to accept; but since the victorious emperor himself told the story to the present writer a long while after, when I was privileged with his acquaintance

and company, and confirmed it with oaths, who would hesitate to believe the account, especially when the time which followed provided evidence for the truth of what he said. About the time of the midday sun, when the day was just turning, he said he saw with his own eyes, up in the sky and resting over the sun, a cross-shaped trophy formed from light, and a text attached to it which said, "by this conquer." Amazement at the spectacle seized both him and the whole company of soldiers which was then accompanying him on a campaign he was conducting somewhere, and witnessed a miracle.

He was, he said, wondering to himself what the manifestation might mean; then, while he meditated, and thought long and hard, night overtook him. Thereupon, as he slept, the Christ of God appeared to him with the sign which had appeared in the sky, and urged him to make a copy of the sign which had appeared in the sky, and to use this as a protection against the attacks of the enemy. (Eusebius, *VC* I.28, trans. Cameron and Hall)

It has been questioned whether the very different versions of Lactantius and Eusebius can refer to the same event, but it seems best to combine them. Lactantius, although writing soon after the episode, had no access to the emperor's personal and detailed account. He accordingly offered a simple version of the dream before the battle which led Constantine to place a Christian symbol on his soldiers' shields. Eusebius also has the dream, which revealed God's will to the emperor, but before that a circumstantial account of what appears to be a miraculous event. The details were provided by the emperor in person, speaking under oath. It is evident that this cannot have been a private interview with Eusebius, who in any case was not an intimate associate of Constantine, but must have been relayed to a Christian audience in some formal setting.[2]

Scholars have naturally exercised themselves over the question of what, if anything, Constantine actually saw and interpreted as a heavenly vision. Eusebius implies that it occurred an unspecified time before the battle. In a highly convincing study Peter Weiss argues that an earlier account of the same vision can be found in the panegyric addressed by an anonymous Gallic orator to Constantine in 310, shortly after the death of Maximianus, and that this vision can be identified as a spectacular solar phenomenon.[3] The passage in question runs:

You learned that all the storms had abated, and all the tranquillity which you had left behind had returned. Fortune herself had so ordained matters that the successful outcome of your actions admonished you to make an offering of what you had vowed to the immortal gods at the very place where you had turned off the road to the most beautiful temple in the whole world, or rather to the very presence of the god, as you had seen him. For, Constantine, you saw, I believe, your Apollo in the company of Victory offering you laurel crowns, each of which bears the prophecy of thirty years rule. (*Pan. Lat.* VII [6] 12)

Weiss interprets the descriptions of Eusebius and of the panegyricist of 310 as corresponding to the appearance of a double solar halo, an optical effect caused by the refracted light from slanting sun hitting ice crystals in the upper atmosphere and producing a semicircular halo with intense crosses of light directly above and on either side of the sun. The appearance of such haloes, *coronae* in Latin, was readily interpreted as a victory signal, and this was the conventional meaning which the orator of 310 attached to the vision. From a pagan perspective, the divinity responsible was of course Apollo, the sun god himself, and the vision occurred close to the important sanctuary of Apollo Grannus, which lay on the main route across Gaul leading north to the imperial residence at Trier. The psychological effect of such a dramatic experience is not to be doubted. The nineteenth-century Alpinist, Sir Edward Whymper saw a comparably awe-inspiring halo with three crosses in the sky as he made his way down from the first successful ascent of the Matterhorn in 1865. Whymper recalled that "the ghostly apparitions of light hung motionless; it was a strange and awesome sight, unique to me, and indescribably imposing at such a moment."

The experience lived with Constantine and two years later its meaning was reinterpreted during the build-up to the battle with Maxentius. The three (or rather six) crosses of light were now understood in the Christian sense, and the victory which they heralded, in the form of the corona itself, was a sign from the Christian God, not Apollo. Eusebius takes evident relish in describing the role of the emperor's Christian advisors, among them certainly Ossius of Cordoba, who expounded their view that the crosses in the sky were a manifestation of Christ and a symbol of his triumph over death.[4] In the telling or retelling of this indelible scene, Eusebius translated the symbolic victory sign into the verbal message, "by this conquer."[5]

It is right to hail the vision as a decisive moment in late Roman history. Neither solar haloes nor critical battles were unparalleled events, but the coincidence of the two, and above all the religious and psychological response that they triggered in Constantine transformed a remarkable event into an epochal one. The vision itself was not the sole cause of Constantine's conversion. For the orator of 310 it was a manifestation of the sun god's power, and we may assume that this interpretation was perfectly acceptable to Constantine at the time. However, we cannot say that it was the vision which caused Constantine's conversion in 312, since by then the emperor, and his Christian advisors, were already looking for the Christian meaning that was confirmed to him by his dream. The most important difference was contextual. Whereas in 310 the vision had seemed only casually appropriate to Constantine's good fortune, coming after Maximianus' death and the evaporation of the minor threat of an Alemannic raiding party, in 312 it was treated as talismanic, a cosmic sign sent by God as an omen for the decisive engagement with Maxentius. Crucially the battle was won, and Constantine's belief in the talisman was confirmed. The close affinity between Christianity, which Constantine experienced and endorsed in 312, and sun worship is readily apparent from the reconstruction of his vision. The nature of the event will have reinforced his conviction that belief in a supreme solar deity and belief in God were virtually convergent. The imagery favored by the emperor after 312 reflects this. The great symbol of the conversion, the *labarum*, the new standard painted on the shields of the emperor's soldiers and then recreated in gold and jewelry, took its name not from Christian vocabulary but from the Celtic word used to denote the solar apparition.

> It was constructed to the following design. A tall pole plated with gold had a traverse bar forming the shape of a cross. Up at the extreme top a wreath woven of precious stones and gold had been fastened. On it two letters, intimating by its first characters the name "Christ," formed the monogram of the Saviour's title, *rho* being intersected in the middle by *chi*. These letters the emperor also used to wear upon his helmet in later times. (Eusebius, *VC* I.31.1, trans. Cameron and Hall)

The design deliberately fused the solar image of a six-pointed star with the almost identical *Chi-Rho* form of a christogram. The sun was the manifestation of Christ's power. As early as 315 the *Chi-Rho* symbol adorned Constantine's helmet as displayed on the silver medallion of Ticinum. His portraits, as Eusebius commented, show him with his gaze tilted up to the sky (Eusebius, *VC* 4.15). A new law was passed in 321 establishing the *dies solis* as the day of rest (*CTh.* 11.8.1).[6]

Constantine himself displayed his new religious convictions in different ways for different audiences, and met with a varied response. The panegyric address delivered in Constantine's presence in 313 referred to an unspecified divine will, *mens divina*, as the source of the emperor's victory:

> What god was it, what so present majesty, that exhorted you – when almost all your staff officers and generals were merely silently muttering but openly fearful – so that you, contrary to human advice, contrary to warnings of the haruspices, you yourself, on your own initiative, felt that the moment had come to liberate the city? For a certainty you share something with the divine mind, Constantine, something secret: that mind delegates care for us to lesser gods and deigns to reveal itself to you alone. (*Pan. Lat.* IX [12] 2.4f.)

In 315 the dedication by the Roman people and Senate of the Arch of Constantine also avoided an open allusion to Christ, preferring the neutral formula *instinctu divinitatis*:

> To the Emperor Caesar Flavius Constantinus Maximus Pius Felix Augustus, the Roman Senate and People dedicated this arch, decorated with his victories, because, by the prompting of Divinity (*instinctu Divinitatis*) by the greatness of his mind, he with his arm, at one moment by a just victory avenged the State both on the tyrant and on all his party. To the liberator of the city. To the establisher of peace. (*CIL* VI 1139, AD 315)[7]

However, in a letter addressed to the bishops of Africa, written in this period, Constantine provided a more personal and pointed view of his own conversion, and the consequences which it had for his own role:

The eternal and religious incomprehensible piety of our God by no means permits the state of man to stray too long in darkness, nor does it allow the hostile wills of certain men to be so strong that it does not grant an opportunity of conversion to the rule of righteousness by opening anew with its most glorious lights a path to salvation. I know this from many examples; I extrapolate the same conclusion from my own case. For there were in me at first things which seemed alien to righteousness, and I did not think that a power on high saw any of the things which I carried out inside the secret places of my heart. What fortune ought these things to have earned me? Surely one overflowing with every evil. But almighty God, sitting in the watch-tower of heaven, bestowed on me what I did not deserve: assuredly, what he has granted to me his servant by his heavenly benevolence cannot at present be described or enumerated. (Optatus, app. 5, letter of Constantine to the bishops in 314)

As far as we can judge, Constantine's own journey to Christianity had not been a long one. It seems clear that his father was an adherent of solar monotheism, a cult that was not only acceptable to many intellectuals but was also rooted in popular patterns of belief both in the western and eastern provinces, even though it was not a component of the civic paganism. Constantine from 312 was a Christian in the full sense of the word, believing that the supreme saving divinity should be identified with Christ. But he also accepted that the Christian God could be presented, without theological baggage, simply as the highest god, *summus deus*, a conception which was acceptable to a broad swathe of his subjects, especially in the eastern provinces.[8] Another significant figure from the early fourth century who made a step similar to Constantine's was the father of the Cappadocian bishop Gregory of Nazianzus. He had been a worshipper of the highest god, *theos hypsistos*. A party of bishops traveling to the Council of Nicaea in 325 is said to have converted him to Christianity.[9]

Much was changed by Constantine's conversion, above all Christianity itself. A cult that had been illegal became more favored than any other, and by 325 had evolved into the religion of the Roman state. Christian clergy were rewarded with privileges, and their leaders, the bishops, already highly effective community leaders who had brought their followers through a challenging and dangerous decade of persecution, were now entrusted with legal powers. More importantly they had the ear of the emperor himself. Pagan cults were restricted and undermined, without for the most part being suppressed. The emperor's own actions prompted a great flood of conversions. Eusebius, in his capacity of bishop, received a letter from Constantine requesting fifty ornamental leather-bound copies of the scriptures, which were to be prepared in the *scriptoria* of his city Caesarea and sent for the use of the swelling congregations of Constantinople (Eusebius, *VC* 4.36). By drawing attention to the size and zeal of their Christian populations, cities in the East successfully claimed privileges and benefits from the emperor.[10]

These events also transformed Christian society. Before 300 Christians had always been in a minority. They had emphasized their distinctiveness by strict adherence to the values that defined them. However, this stance inevitably raised questions about how Christians should behave in the secular world, and such issues preoccupied local church leaders at a series of church councils of the early fourth century, held at Arles in Gaul in 314, at Elvira in Spain soon afterwards, at Ankara in Galatia between 313 and 316, and at Neocaesarea in Pontus before 319. One issue was whether Christians should hold public office. In southern Spain the canons of the Council of Elvira ordained that any Christians who served as municipal priests and conducted sacrifices, having been baptized into the church should be excluded from communion, more especially if they had been involved in sponsoring gladiatorial shows or forms of lewd public entertainment (Elvira can. 2, 3). Ideally, at least, Christians should have as little to do with the secular world as possible. Clergy were not allowed to engage in trade or sell their wares outside the province in person, although they were not prevented from using agents on their behalf (Elvira can. 18). Usury was anathematized (Elvira can. 19). Strict morality and social discipline was imposed. Women who left their husbands without cause should never be received into communion, and baptized women could not remarry even after leaving an adulterous baptized husband (Elvira can. 8, 9). Bishops, priests, and deacons who had sexual relations with their wives were to be removed from the clergy (Elvira can. 33). The councils of Arles and Ancyra in 314 also tend to be very stringent on Christian discipline.[11]

Such ideals were impracticable. As Christian communities emerged from repression it became obvious that there was a large gulf between the conduct laid down by canon law and that of the mass of new recruits whose lives belonged firmly in the unredeemed secular world. As Henry Chadwick memorably put it in a discussion of the dilemma facing the church after the earlier persecution of Trajan Decius, the rapid growth in Christian numbers "highlighted the conflict between the primitive conception of the Church as a society of saints, and the now growing view . . . that it was a school for sinners."[12]

Christians very rapidly came to prominence as officeholders. There is a considerable debate about the proportions of pagans and Christians among high-ranking Christian officials in the fourth century, and the rate at which Roman senators converted from paganism. T. D. Barnes in a series of studies has challenged the majority view that Christians only came to outnumber pagans at these levels of the Roman hierarchy in the 370s or 380s, claiming that Constantine and Constantius both favored Christians to the extent that in both their reigns more than half the holders of senior government posts (*praefecti praetorio*, the *praefecti urbis* of Rome and Constantinople, the proconsuls of Africa and Asia, the counts of Oriens, and the *magistri militum*) were Christians.[13] Whatever view is taken of this discussion, it is clear that some of these offices were held by Christians from the moment of Constantine's conversion, and that such men from the first will have taken a very secular view of their Christian obligations. More importantly, as Christians and pagans had to work together in such contexts, there must have been a consensus between them, that their religious affiliations did not materially affect either their ability to hold office or to cooperate with one another.

The same must have been true of army service. It could be said that the army was made Christian by painting the sign of Christ on his soldiers' shields. Simply by fighting on behalf of Christian emperors, Roman soldiers adopted and advanced the Christian version of Roman ruling ideology, and armies became deeply permeated by Christianity during the fourth century. Plainly, merely belonging to a military unit of a Christian state in itself will have had little impact on the personal religious convictions of soldiers, who maintained many features of pagan traditionalism and were also well known for promoting and spreading eastern cults such as Mithraism and the worship of Jupiter Dolichenus in the western frontier provinces.[14] We should conclude that in state service, and probably in large parts of society at large, religious affiliation was a neutral factor, which did not impinge on or inhibit the way in which ordinary people led their lives.

The necessary compromises made by lay men and women encouraged the growth of more radical forms of Christian conduct. The rite of baptism was the crucial symbol which set apart the compromised Christians of everyday society from an elect brother- and sisterhood which aspired to the ideals of the ancient church. Constantine, as we have seen, underwent the ritual on his deathbed, precluding the possibility that he might sin before he was resurrected into another life (Eusebius, *VC* 4.61–62).

Julian

The story of Julian demonstrates a very different individual response to the complex religious environment of the fourth century. The issue of where paganism stood in relation to Christianity was put to the test after the death of Constantius in November 361, when Julian emerged by default as sole ruler of the empire. Immediately he declared his pagan convictions and initiated policies which were designed to reverse the measures taken in favor of Christians by his predecessors, and to restore the prestige and authority of the traditional religion:

> (He) directed in plain and unvarnished terms that the temples should be opened, sacrifices brought to their altars, and the worship of the old gods restored. To make this ordinance more effective he summoned to the palace the Christian bishops who were far from being of one mind, together with their flocks, who were no less divided by schism, and warned them in polite terms to lay aside their differences and allow every man to practise his belief boldly without hindrance. His motive in insisting on this was that he knew that toleration would intensify their divisions and henceforth he would no longer have to fear unanimous public opinion. Experience had taught him that no wild beasts are such dangerous enemies to man as Christians are to one another. (Ammianus 22.5, trans. Hamilton)

The roots of Julian's attachment to paganism can clearly be traced to his upbringing. He was born in the new imperial city of Constantinople in 332, the son of Constantine's half-brother Julius Constantius. When the emperor died in 337 the army, with the connivance of Constantius II who was the only one of the emperor's sons present in the city, massacred the collateral male descendants of Constantius I to guarantee the transfer of power to his sons. The only survivors of this blood-letting were Julian and his elder half-brother Gallus. The five-year-old Julian was removed, perhaps for safety's sake, to a country house near Nicomedia (Julian, *ep.* 4, Bidez-Cumont), the home of his mother Basilina's family, where his education was directed by the powerful bishop Eusebius. In 361, the year that he openly declared his bid for power, he recalled the details of the traumatic murders in his *Letter to the Athenians* (Julian 270c–d). At Nicomedia he was under the tutelage of a Christian eunuch Mardonius, who introduced him to classical Greek literature (Julian, *Misopogon* 352a–54a), and in 341 he was sent as a virtual exile with Gallus to an imperial villa in the interior of Asia Minor at Macellum, near Caesarea. Julian studied Greek literature intensively under the direction of another priest, George, before returning to Constantinople in 348. When George was later transferred to become bishop of Alexandria and was murdered by a riotous mob, Julian, who had just become sole emperor, confessed to coveting his library.[15] While his half-brother now became attached to the court, Julian pursued his education under the rhetoricians Nicocles and Hecebolius. He soon came in contact with the sophist Libanius, the leading practitioner of Greek rhetorical education of the period, and despite a temporary ban from attending Libanius' lectures, became his tutee.

In 351 he encountered the group of philosophers around Aedesius of Pergamum, who himself had studied with one of the great figures of Neoplatonism, Iamblichus of Chalcis. Julian was captivated by the circle of talented and charismatic speculative intellectuals who had studied with Aedesius: Eusebius from Myndus in Caria, Chrysanthius of Sardis, Priscus from Thesprotis in northwest Greece, and Maximus of Ephesus. The tendency in late Platonic speculation had been to emphasize the mystical at the expense of logic and reason. In the *Lives of the Sophists* Eunapius provides a lengthy account of Julian's encounter with the Neoplatonists. Eusebius was an advocate of rational argument, but Maximus practiced theurgy, claiming the ability to manipulate the gods and thus help mortals to achieve union with the divine world.[16] Although Eusebius understandably condemned such activities as the impostures of witchcraft and magic, Julian was captivated by the account he gave of a séance in which Maximus, by chanting hymns and burning incense, had caused a statue of Hecate to break into a smile, and the torches in the goddess's hands to burst into flame. The young man made his way directly to Ephesus, where Maximus was in residence, and became his devoted pupil (Eunapius, *Sophists*, 474–5). Julian himself, in his letter to the Cynic Heraclius, which defended his own preference for Platonic philosophy, identified this as the moment of his conversion from Christianity to paganism (Julian, *Or.* 7), and this was repeated by Libanius in his speech addressed to the emperor at Antioch on January 1, 363 (Libanius, *Or.* 12.34).

Julian's pagan beliefs defy summary. They were rooted in his devotion to Greek literary culture and Greek philosophy, which provided him with a moral and a cultural framework. He was a believer in divination, not least when reading signs that were relevant to his own future, he was impressed by theurgic magic and convinced of the importance of the key ritual of animal sacrifice. He developed his own speculative syncretistic idea of solar monotheism in his hymn to the sun, in which it appears that the god Helios may have been equated with Mithras. In this, as in other matters, his developed views were personal to himself, not matters of common belief even among pagan intellectuals. Moreover, he conducted his own life and his pagan devotions in a spirit of ascetic piety which was clearly based on Christian models. His paganism was thus a particular thing. Julian's religious convictions made him a very isolated figure, even among the religious intelligentsia of his own generation.[17]

On the other hand much of his public religious policy as emperor, both in deeds and words, presents a mirror-image of fourth-century Christianity. He was aware that his attempt to usurp power potentially faced formidable Christian opposition. Since the beginning of the fourth century Christianity had prevailed over pagan polytheism in Constantine's two civil wars against Maxentius and Licinius, and the most recent usurpation of Magnentius against Constantius had pitched Christian against Christian. Flying under a pagan banner would have been catastrophic, as he recognized from the outset.

> To frustrate any opposition and win universal goodwill he pretended to adhere to the Christian religion, from which he had secretly apostasized. A few only were in his confidence, and knew that his heart was set on divination and augury and all the other practices followed by the worshippers of the old gods. (Ammianus 21.2, trans. Hamilton)

Accordingly he ostentatiously attended a Christian service at the festival of Epiphany, January 6, 361, before declaring his hand against Constantius. As soon as the news of Constantius' death reached him, encamped at Naissus, the birthplace of Constantine, he advertised his paganism in dramatic fashion:[18]

> We worshipped the gods openly, and most of the army which accompanied me reveres them. We sacrificed oxen in public. We offered many hecatombs to the gods as expressions of thanks. The gods bid me to purify everything insofar as possible, and I obey them with enthusiasm. They say that they will give rewards for our labour, if we do not grow slack. (Julian, *ep.* 26, trans. Bowersock)

In his personal conduct, as Ammianus puts it, "Julian was so spectacularly and incorruptibly chaste that after the loss of his wife he never tasted the pleasures of sex" (Ammianus 25.4.1, trans. Hamilton). The view of pagan religion which he transmitted to his subjects by letters and edicts was built upon an elaboate moral basis which mirrored in detail that of the Christians. He matched Christian injunctions to charity, which were based on biblical texts, with his own arguments based on passages of Homer. To counter Christian mockery of the worship of idols, he set out elaborate and explicit arguments for revering and worshipping the gods' images, although he acknowledged that the gods themselves were not corporeal beings.[19] Unusually in the polemic between pagans and Christians in late antiquity he was prepared to name his enemies, albeit pejoratively, as "Galilaeans," who were pitched against the ranks of pagan "Hellenes."

In the letter which he wrote in the summer of 362 to Theodorus, high priest of the province of Asia, he sets out a bleak diagnosis of the condition to which pagan belief – Hellenism – had been reduced, and proposed remedies for it. In Asia Minor Julian had followed a precedent set by the tetrarch Maximinus during the time of the persecutions, when he had appointed provincial high priests responsible for maintaining the old cults in the provinces and supervising the rest of the priesthood.[20] On the other hand, he equally deliberately rejected the tetrarchic precedent of using persecution as a weapon against his enemies, since martyrdom had strengthened not weakened Christian resolve. There were three thrusts to his argument in the letter. Public rituals, especially sacrifice, should be revived and punctiliously observed; priests were to set examples of restraint and sobriety, avoiding the temptations of the theater and chariot-racing, excessive drinking and disreputable trades. They were to check on the conduct of other priests and members of their families, especially to prevent them backsliding into Christian observance; and they should engage in philanthropy to aid the poor (ep. 89).[21]

Julian reckoned that three specific features were at the heart of Christian success: their acts of charitable generosity, their care for the dead, and their virtuous conduct. All three were rooted in conditions of life in the Roman world, and were of particular importance among the poor. Agricultural and urban communities in antiquity were exposed to the risk of destitution and famine, brought on by failure of the harvest, the depredations of warfare, the greed of landowners, or the excessive demands of a predatory state. Without insurance or any state-sponsored forms of poor relief, the only recourse of communities was to self-help if this was forthcoming, it came in almost all cases from friends and neighbors in the villages and small towns of the empire, but many would have been unprovided for. Christianity appealed directly and unambiguously to the poor, both in ideology and in practice. The network of churches was capable of transforming God's providence into a tangible system of support for Christians. It is evident that many communities impressively lived out the injunctions of the Gospels to "love thy neighbor."

Death, like famine, was also an inescapable reality which pressed hard on every family. Life expectancy was low by modern standards; there were no forms of effective contraception; and infant mortality rates were horrendous, even among the aristocracy. Coping with premature death was thus an experience that every individual and every family faced, usually repeatedly. Christian faith could not ward off death, but it could and did dramatically transform it to a moment of hope and expectation, of resurrection to a new life. Places of burial became a particular focus for Christian gatherings. The persecuting emperors of the third and early fourth century were aware of this when they forbade Christians to assemble in their graveyards (Eusebius, *HE* 7.11.10–11). Aemilianus, deputy of the prefect of Egypt, summoned Dionysius, bishop of Alexandria, before him in 258 and banished him to Libya:

> I see at once that you are ungrateful and pay no attention to the clemency of our emperors. So you shall not remain in this city but be sent to the regions of Libya at a place called Cephro. . . . And neither you nor any of the others will be allowed to hold assemblies or to enter the cemeteries, as they are called. (Eusebius, *HE* 7.11.10)

The Christians, as this passage shows, had coined a new word, *koemeteria*, "dormitories," to signify their new understanding of death. Christians, their faith confirmed by baptism, slept, awaiting the resurrection to eternal life. Fifty years later during the great persecution of the tetrarchs, these cemeteries were places where Christians regularly assembled, and they were again singled out by the persecuting authorities. One of the unplanned consequences of persecution was to increase their symbolic significance. The cults which grew up around the early Christian martyrs were for the most part located in the cemeteries where the victims of the persecutions had been buried.

Finally, Christians of Julian's day impressed others by their dignified conduct. This may have been particularly conspicuous in contrast to the demeanor of their pagan priestly counterparts, which Julian admonishes in the same letter to Theodorus. Countless inscriptions from Roman provincial cities show that pagan priests in the second century AD had generally been wealthy and pious members of the municipal gentry, who were treated with honor and respect in their communities. However, by the fourth century they were few in number and their status in most provincial cities was sharply reduced.[22] It is hard not to be reminded of the story ruefully told by Julian himself in his satirical broadsheet *Misopogon*, addressed to the people of Antioch. He had ventured to the sanctuary of Apollo at Daphne near the city to celebrate the annual summer festival. The well-off citizens of Antioch boycotted the event, and instead of the expected feasting and sacrifice, he was met by a single priest who had brought a modest victim from his own house – a goose (Julian, *Misopogon*, 34–35).

It is not only with the hindsight of history that we may judge Julian to have been fighting a losing battle. We have the impression of an eccentric, highly intelligent and tirelessly active emperor cajoling and haranguing friends and small groups of convinced supporters to try to put together an imperial policy which simply enjoyed little popular support. Even Ammianus, a pagan sympathizer, declared that he was "superstitious rather than a genuine observer of religious rites," and regarded his anti-Christian campaign to have been ill-judged.[23] He overtly criticized his most publicized measure, the edict which forbade Christians to take up positions as rhetors and teachers in the cities of the empire.

Augustine

The conversion of Augustine, even more famous than that of Constantine, belongs in an entirely different context. Augustine was born at Thagaste, a small town in Numidia, in 354. Almost everything that we know about his life comes from his own writings, above all from the autobiographical *Confessions*, which he completed in 397, shortly after he had become bishop of Hippo Regius, a bustling harbor town seventy kilometers from his birthplace. The climactic moment of his narrative is the famous episode in a garden in Milan, when the thirty-two-year-old Augustine, already confronting a crisis in his personal and professional life, chose to renounce secular ambition and a marriage that had been planned for him (*Conf.* 6.13.23), in favor of baptism, sexual renunciation, and a life in the church, serving God.

This was not a conversion in the style of Constantine. Augustine traces his own journey in terms of his intellectual and psychological development. This had begun with a schoolboy passion for literature, especially Vergil, a training in rhetoric, nine years devoted to Manichaeism as a "hearer" (*Conf.* 5.6.10), a growing interest in philosophy, especially Neoplatonism, and, in the final months before the conversion, a reflective engagement with Christianity, which had been stimulated by the inspiring sermons of Ambrose who was then presiding over the church at the heart of the western empire in Milan (*Conf.* 5.13.23). Augustine's own career path was a glittering success story, all the more compelling for the fact that Augustine's account of it allows his readers to see the price that he paid for his achievements. Put in modern terms, he had won prizes for public speaking at school (*Conf.* 1.17.27), but his father Patricius, a townsman of slender means (*tenuis municeps*), could barely afford to send him to further education at Madauros, and Augustine had had to intermit a year for lack of funds (*Conf.* 2.3.6). He was probably only able to continue at the important center of Carthage (*Conf.* 3.1.1) thanks to the subvention of a wealthy neighbor Romanianus. He studied for four years in the African capital. Within eighteen months his father had died, and he himself began to cohabit with a woman, with whom he was to live for fifteen years, and who soon bore him a son (*Conf.* 4.2.2). His intellectual training was as an orator, but his quest for spiritual enlightenment led him to Manichaeism. On graduation in 375 he returned to Thagaste to teach for a year (*Conf.* 4.1.1, 2.2), before being offered the chance to teach rhetoric in Carthage itself. He remained there for eight years, finding the students as unruly and provoking as when he had been one of them. So when the opportunity to go to a higher post, greater financial rewards, and a better class of student presented itself at Rome, he seized the chance with the help of contacts, engineered by friends who had preceded him, and the support of his hometown patron, Romanianus (*Conf.* 6.8.13). In doing so he risked, as he was all too conscious, a perilous breach with the greatest influence on his life so far, that of his devout and determined mother Monica

(*Conf.* 5.8.15, 6.1.1). A year in Rome proved a trial and a disappointment. Augustine suffered from poor health, there was intense competition for students, and his private pupils did not pay their fees (*Conf.* 5.12.22). Luckily he had not lost his oratorical gifts, and when Manichee friends drew his attention to a competition, organized by the city prefect Symmachus, to find an official rhetorician for the imperial city at Milan, Augustine delivered a suitably accomplished piece on a prescribed theme and was selected for the post (*Conf.* 5.13.23). Thus, at just over thirty years of age, he had arrived on the threshold of a major career in imperial service.

Augustine's *Confessions* are a priceless record of a young man's qualities and ambition, and a tribute to the extraordinarily fluid social structures of the later Roman Empire. With solid family backing and a willingness to exploit contacts, a young man of exceptional ability had brought himself to the notice of the richest senator of the western empire, and the emperor himself. But such a dizzy ascent exacted its toll. A professional rhetor was a political servant of the regime and candor was not at a premium:

> How unhappy I was, and how conscious you made me of my misery, on that day when I was preparing to deliver a panegyric on the emperor! In the course of it I would tell numerous lies and for my mendacity would win the good opinion of people who knew it to be untrue. (*Conf.* 6.6.9, trans. Chadwick)

The moral conflict was sharpened for Augustine by the fact that he and a group of friends around him were immersed in Platonic philosophy, which inspired its followers to truth and honesty.[24] Augustine made the final step in the company of a group of friends who had made the same journey as he had – serious young men, who were all conscious of the need to make a choice between family life and secular achievements, and ascetic Christian devotion. Augustine withdrew to an estate outside the city, resigned his teaching responsibilities after due notice (*Conf.* 9.2.2, 5.13), and in the company of his mother and of another catechumen, Alypius, prepared himself with devotional reading to be baptized by his bishop, Ambrose.

Augustine's conversion was that of one of the rising stars of the western Roman Empire. It was not a move from paganism to Christianity. Both his parents were Christians. If Patricius was more noted for the breach than for observance of the faith, he was nevertheless a catechumen being prepared for the baptism which he received on his death bed (*Conf.* 2.3.7, 9.9.22). Monica, known to us from Augustine's painfully intimate diary of their relationship and the lengthy portrait of her in *Confessions* book 9, is for us one of the most extraordinary Christian figures of the fourth century.[25] Mother and son are depicted as presenting two complementary faces of Christian devotion; she, barely literate, he at the intellectual cutting edge of late Roman society. Their faith is fused in an extraordinary shared vision of divine bliss, which they achieved during the last days of her life at Ostia. Augustine describes the vision as a revelation achieved by dialogue and introspection:

Our minds were lifted up by an ardent affection towards eternal being itself. Step by step we climbed beyond all corporeal objects and the heaven itself, where, sun, moon, and stars shed light on the earth. We ascended even further by internal reflection and dialogue and wonder at your works, and we entered into our own minds. We moved up beyond them so as to attain to the region of inexhaustible abundance where you feed Israel eternally with truth for food. There life is the wisdom by which all creatures come into being, both things which were and which will be. (*Conf.* 9.10.24, trans. Chadwick)

The concept of this ascent to transcendence was clearly Neoplatonic. In his life of Plotinus, the greatest of the Neoplatonic philosophers, his pupil Porphyry wrote,

And it is said that he was tireless, guarding the purity of his soul and always hurrying on to the divine, which he loved with the whole of his soul; also that he made every effort to be released, "to escape from beneath the bitter wave" of the present "blood-gorged life." Thus it was that the god who has neither shape nor form, and is set above intellect and all that is intelligible, appeared to this daemonic man as time after time he drove himself on towards the first and transcendental god with his own reflections and according to the ways set forth by Plato in the *Symposium*. I, Porphyry, testify that I once drew close to this god and was united with him, being in my sixty-eighth year. To Plotinus, at any rate, the "goal ever near" was shown, for his end and goal was to be united with and close to the god above all. This goal he achieved four times, while I was with him, not virtually but in unspeakable actuality. (Porphyry, *Life of Plotinus* 23, trans. Edwards)

Augustine during his early life had taken the opportunity to probe into the range of religious and cultural choice that the western empire had to offer: the flamboyant virtuoso culture of Latin rhetoric; the recondite (and usually illegal) faith of the Manichean elect; and the highly speculative world of learning offered by Neoplatonism, which had first become accessible to Latin speakers through the translations of Marius Victorinus, made a generation earlier (*Conf.* 8.2.3). Members of his circle took astrology sufficiently seriously for Augustine to be tempted to dabble himself (*Conf.* 7.6.8–10). Both the home environment in which he grew up and the social circles of his early adult years offered him and his contemporaries a wide range of religious choice.[26] Within Christianity itself there was room both for devout and casual believers.

The *Confessions* are not simply a narrative of one man's conversion. The books present us with a spectrum of believers and unbelievers, and of social contexts which range from the secular hedonism of Carthage to reclusive meditation at Cassiciacum. Augustine's own story is interwoven with that of his younger *alter ego*, Alypius, another man of Thagaste, who had come to Rome to study law. There he obtained a minor treasury post, became addicted to gladiatorial games and the circus at Rome, and attached himself to Augustine, sharing his interest in the Manichees and attending his classes in rhetoric. He accompanied Augustine to Milan to take up a legal position, but also opted out of secular life to be baptized at the same time as Augustine. Both returned to Africa to become bishops. A third member of this tight group of friends, Nebridius, was baptized soon afterwards, returned to Africa, and persuaded his entire family to follow his example (*Conf.* 9.3.6).

An inspiration from the previous generation was the pagan Platonist, Marius Victorinus, lionized in cultural circles and tutor to the sons of senators in Rome. As a Platonist, Victorinus had publicly defended the pagan cults, which were both prominent and highly controversial in the 350s, but, first privately, and then publicly in church, he pronounced the Creed. In 362 he made a point of resigning his post as a philosopher when Julian's edict banned Christian teachers (*Conf.* 8.2.3–5.10). Augustine heard the story of Victorinus from the old priest Simplicianus, who had baptized Ambrose himself in 374. It was a narrative artfully told to coax intellectuals who were impressed by sophisticated Neoplatonism into accepting the apparent commonplaces of Christianity.

Another African Christian, Ponticianus, who was attached to the court, introduced Augustine and Alypius to the world of Christian asceticism and the monastic movement. This had been inspired by the life of the Egyptian hermit, Antony, which circulated in the West in two recent Latin translations. There were monasteries outside Milan too, set up by the encouragement of the bishop Ambrose, and Ponticianus told the story of two imperial agents at Trier, another imperial center, who had read the book and promptly decided to adopt the ascetic life themselves, persuading their fiancées to do the same (*Conf.* 8.6.14–15). Ponticianus himself had taken a moderate approach, keeping his secular post, while opting for baptism and a life of chastity.

Augustine's conversion was from a non-committal lukewarm Christianity to a passionate and life-consuming conviction, and to asceticism, and it took place among a group of upwardly mobile friends who were already making their mark in court circles. It should not by any means be taken as representative of the period in general. A large proportion of the inhabitants of Italy and the Latin-speaking western provinces was still pagan at this date. Augustine's own letters, written when he was bishop of Hippo, cannot disguise the number of non-Christians in proconsular Africa and Numidia.[27] The same was true in much of Gaul and northern Italy.[28] The public life of the municipalities of the Roman West throughout the lifetime of Augustine was resolutely secular.[29]

Politics and Christianity

The alliance of church and state pervaded the history of the later empire. After Constantine the hierarchical organization of the church was calqued on the Roman provincial system. Each city had its own bishop, whose diocese included all the villages and smaller settlements of the city's territory. He was responsible for the appointment of village priests. In parts of central Asia Minor there were also country bishops, *chorepiscopi*, who were responsible for large areas of landed estates where there were no cities. At the head of the church in each province was the metropolitan bishop. According to the rulings of the Council of Antioch in 341 he was responsible for convening twice-yearly meetings of the bishops subordinate to him to regulate church affairs. Bishops possessed substantial authority. They were, by definition, senior churchmen, who had held lower positions in the ecclesiastical hierarchy before obtaining office. At least in theory they were chosen by a procedure which took account of the views both of the common people and of senior clergy. A candidate would be acclaimed by his congregation and the appointment confirmed by his fellow bishops, usually at one of the regular provincial councils. It is important to draw a distinction between the nature of support available to a bishop and that enjoyed by laymen. In addition to relying on the usual network of connections, derived from aristocratic intermarriage, shared culture, and ties of mutual obligation, the bonds of favors owed and repaid,[30] bishops enjoyed strong local support from the common people. The church acted as an effective patron, especially to the poor, and bishops were able to call on huge crowds of supporters in times of need. The massed congregation, besieged in the main basilica of Milan, enabled Ambrose to prevail over the forces of Valentinian II and his mother Justina in 386.[31] The workers in the armaments factory and the women in the weaving mills of Caesarea in Cappadocia supported Basil in his struggle with Valens and Modestus, the praetorian prefect.[32] The close-knit fabric of personal power, which had been inherited and developed over centuries, was beginning to give ground to a rawer and cruder form of politics. The church now commanded growing resources; bishops had loyal support thanks to the protection that they could offer to their people.[33]

The power of individual bishops closely correlated to the cities where they officiated. Traditionally, the most important figure in the church was the bishop of Rome, the See of St Peter. Throughout late antiquity the authority of the bishop of Rome as the leading western ecclesiastical leader was scarcely challenged. The only period at which he was put in the shade was during the quarter century between 374 and 397 when Ambrose became bishop of Milan. Ambrose was a devout orthodox Christian, but his appointment was a political one and he had been transferred from a secular career, as provincial governor of Aemilia and Liguria, to succeed the Arian bishop of Milan, Auxentius. Milan during this period became the main western imperial residence, and Ambrose's tenure coincided with a period when the western empire was ruled by the very young Gratian and the child Valentinian II. This gave him unprecedented political leverage, which he exploited to the full. In the mid-380s he successfully intervened to neutralize the Arian influence of Valentinian's mother Justina, and was also closely involved in the negotiations between the court and the usurper Magnus Maximus. The position he had built up enabled him to impose his will even on Theodosius over two critical decisions, the affair of Callinicum and the massacre of 7,000 civilians at Thessalonica. Ambrose, however, was a quite exceptional figure who exploited unusual circumstances, and his career should not be seen as creating a precedent for other bishops.

Carthage, the other leading western bishopric, presented a different case. Christianity had laid down deeper roots in Africa than anywhere else in the western empire. Many of the country towns of Africa Proconsularis, Numidia, and Byzacena had acquired their own bishops during the third century. The African church evolved its own distinctive traditions, including the particular respect that was paid to age and length of tenure. Carthage was the key diocese. However, in the wider Mediterranean context Africa always punched beneath its weight, and the bishop of Carthage never wielded the influence of his counterparts at Rome, Constantinople, Antioch, or Alexandria. The reason was that Christian allegiance in Africa was split down the middle between the strictly African church of the Donatists, representing local traditions, and the Catholic Church, who were aligned with the interests of the Roman state (see below, p. 279). In 429 Africa was invaded by the Arian Vandals, who took Carthage itself in 439. This nullified the influence of the Catholic Church, whose members suffered serious persecution especially under the Vandal king Huneric from 477 to 484.[34] Until and beyond the Justinianic reconquest of Africa the region played no further significant part in wider church affairs.

In the East the two main bishoprics at the time of the Council of Nicaea in 325 were Antioch and Alexandria. The canons of Nicaea recognized the special authority which the bishop of Alexandria exercised over the other bishops of Egypt, Libya, and the Pentapolis (Nicaea can. 6). This authority was amply demonstrated through the long, but interrupted, career of Athanasius, who championed Nicene orthodoxy over fifty years against the diverse challenges of the Arians and in defiance of the emperor Constantius. The bishop of Antioch had influence throughout the whole administrative diocese of Oriens, which included most of the Levant and eastern Asia Minor. Antioch was chosen for a succession of major regional councils, in 325, 341, and 379, which prepared the ground for the major ecumenical councils of 325 and 381. Nicomedia was briefly prominent as an important see from the time of the great persecution until the death of Constantine, largely because the city was an imperial residence for much of this period, but its position was rapidly overtaken by the new foundation, Constantinople. When Theodosius I convened the worldwide Council of Constantinople in 381 the question of the powers of the great bishoprics was a central part of the agenda. The council resolved that the metropolitans should not be permitted to exert influence beyond their traditional boundaries:

The bishop of Alexandria must have the administration of the affairs of Egypt only, and the bishops of Oriens must administer Oriens only, the privileges which were assigned to the Church at Antioch by the canons of Nicaea being preserved; and the bishops of the Asian diocese must administer the affairs of the Asian diocese only; and those of the Pontic diocese of the Pontic diocese only; and those of Thrace the affairs of Thrace only. Moreover bishops may not without being invited go beyond the bounds of their diocese for the purpose of ordaining or any other ecclesiastical function. (Council of Constantinople, can. 2, trans. Stevenson)

However, the most provocative ruling concerned the new eastern capital: "the bishop of Constantinople shall have primacy of honor after the bishop of Rome, because Constantinople is the new Rome" (Council of Constantinople, can. 3). This resolution was a major affront to Alexandria, and sowed the seeds of contention that were to last through the fifth and sixth centuries. The doctrinal split between the Chalcedonians and the Monophysites after 450 found its political expression in the rivalry between the Monophysite bishops of Alexandria and their Chalcedonian counterparts at Constantinople.

The rivalry between Constantinople and Alexandria was overshadowed by an even more significant division. The supremacy of Rome was acknowledged in the East until the mid-fifth century, and the orthodox theological views of the bishop of Rome Leo, formulated in the *Tome* of Leo, helped to shape the doctrine of the two natures of Christ which was adopted at Chalcedon in 451. However, a major division began to appear as a consequence of canon 28 of the Council of Chalcedon, which placed Constantinople, not unreasonably, on a par with Rome, on the grounds that both were imperial cities. The bishops of Rome became more conscious of their political influence in the second half of the fifth century as the power of the western empire collapsed. They also took serious issue both with the emperor Zeno and with Bishop Acacius of Constantinople, when the former issued the letter known as the *Henotikon* which aimed to heal the split between the Chalcedonians and the Monophysites in the East. The Roman Church was opposed to any rapprochement with Alexandria, and excommunicated Acacius in July 484, producing what is known to history as the Acacian schism. This was exacerbated through the reign of Anastasius by the emperor's Monophysite views. In correspondence with the emperor, Gelasius, the bishop of Rome, articulated his objections to the *Henotikon*, that it was an attempt by the emperor, a secular authority, to lay down the law in a religious matter, over which he had no jurisdiction:

> There are in fact two powers, emperor, by which the world is governed by a sovereign ruler; the consecrated authority of the bishops and royal power. Of these the responsibility of the bishops is more weighty, since even the rulers of men will have to give account at the judgement seat of God. (Leo, Letter 104 to Anastasius)

The rift was not healed until Justin replaced Anastasius in 519. However, the distinction between secular and sacred responsibilities, to which the pope appealed, was effectively annulled by the principle that guided Justinian, that the emperor should wield power in all matters as God's agent.

It is evident from countless sources that individual bishops, especially those in charge of major sees, often became prominent political figures.[35] Certain clear distinctions need to be made between the political roles played by bishops in the later empire. It is obvious that almost all bishops became involved in the politics of the church itself. They attended provincial, regional, or ecumenical councils, which dealt with matters of doctrine and ecclesiastical discipline.

Throughout the great doctrinal controversies of late antiquity, between the Arians and champions of Nicene orthodoxy in the fourth century, and among Nestorians, Monophysites, and Chalcedonians in the fifth and sixth centuries, bishops became embroiled in political struggles in which no holds were barred. Church councils witnessed scenes of political chicanery and often of outright violence, while the imperial authorities intervened in the great ecumenical councils to impose decisions that were seen to be in the state's interest.

How far did bishops became seriously involved in secular matters? As long as civic government was still handled by municipal magistrates, and the councilors of cities retained a significant measure of local authority, it was unusual for bishops to intervene in civic administration. In the Latin-speaking provinces of Africa Proconsularis, Byzacena, and Numidia, secular and ecclesiastical administration remained distinct from one another until the first quarter of the fifth century. It is particularly striking that, although there are almost no traces of surviving pagan cults detectable in public building projects or in fourth-century civic inscriptions, these were not replaced by references to Christianity. The office of *flamen*, the priesthood of the municipal imperial cult, continued to be filled, but it was an office now devoid of religious content. Fourth-century municipal government in Africa was deliberately and self-consciously secular.

However, wherever municipal government was weak there was an opportunity for religious leaders, in particular for bishops, to take a leading role in local politics. The bishop of Alexandria, a city which had never been allowed to develop autonomous civic government, had always wielded immense power locally. This was demonstrated most vividly in the climax of the campaign against the pagans under Theodosius I, the destruction probably in 391 of the Serapeum in Alexandria. The bishop Theophilus called on violent Christian supporters to fight pitched battles with the pagans defending the sanctuary. Twenty-five years later Theophilus' nephew Cyril took these violent tactics to new levels in confrontations with the Jewish community in Alexandria (414), and with a residue of pagan intellectuals led by the philosopher Hypatia (415), who was torn limb from limb by the bishop's supporters. The hard core of these were his *parabalani*, supposedly teams of paramedics, who were organized into a virtual regiment of vigilantes. These prevailed in riots and stand-offs with Roman troops, and were hardly curbed by imperial legislation in 416 and 418.[36] In 431 Cyril took a posse of *parabalani* to intimidate other bishops at the Council of Ephesus, who helped him to impose his will in the deposition of Nestorius, bishop of Constantinople.

In Cappadocia in the later fourth century, where civic traditions were also very weak, church leaders assumed an active role in secular politics. This is demonstrated by the career of Basil, bishop of Caesarea from 370 to 378. He was prominent in sending petitions to provincial and imperial authorities, pleading for tax exemptions and other favors for members of his community. As the most important bishop of the whole area between Antioch and Constantinople, he was also the main mouthpiece of local objections to the decision of the emperor Valens to divide western Cappadocia into two provinces.[37]

Basil's influence in Cappadocia was not only due to his position in the church, but also to the fact that he was from one of the wealthiest landed families of eastern Asia Minor, and had profited from an education which made him one of the intellectual elite of the empire. In this he may be compared with Synesius, a wealthy, well-connected, and highly educated landowner from Cyrenaica, who had been one of the leading men of the province and had undertaken important embassies to Constantinople, before he was made bishop of Ptolemais two years before he died in 413. The most serious issues faced by the people of Cyrenaica in this period were concerned with their security from the incursions of native tribesmen, and as bishop in 412 Synesius organized the pickets that defended his city.[38]

In Illyricum bishops were exposed on the front line. At a moment of high tension in the 440s, when violence erupted between the Huns and the Romans at the emporium of Margus, the city's bishop was accused of having looted treasure from Hunnic royal tombs. The Huns, as well as their central demand for the restitution of fugitives (see above, p. 200), demanded the return of the treasure and launched a campaign in support of their claims which led to the fall of Viminacium. To avoid further losses, Roman opinion now swung towards handing over the bishop of Margus directly to the Huns. The bishop anticipated the decision, crossed over to the enemy, and secured safe conduct for himself at the price of guiding a large Hunnic force back to take over his city, which was duly despoiled.[39] Fortunately most bishops played a more edifying part. In the 470s Sidonius Apollinaris, having previously been the most prominent figure in the educated aristocracy of southern Gaul, had an even more active role to play, attempting, eventually to no avail, to secure his city, Clermont-Ferrand, against the Visigoths.[40] In the fourth and fifth centuries bishops in the areas exposed to barbarian raids and incursions were regularly called upon to use the wealth of the church to pay ransom demands to secure the release of prisoners.[41] Theodoret, bishop of Cyrrhus in Syria in the 430s and 440s, a period when the province was generally secure and at peace, actively championed his community by sending petitions to the authorities in Constantinople, pleading for tax remissions and other favors.[42] A century later it was the bishops of the cities of Syria who were mainly responsible for local leadership when the Persian forces invaded the province. They organized local military resistance, undertook embassies to the enemy, or collected money to buy immunity from attack and plundering. Inscriptions from Mesopotamia and Syria show that they were also responsible for building city fortifications.[43]

Religious Identities

The church had never been a homogeneous body before Constantine. The numerous separate Christian communities, each led by a bishop, had developed their own traditions and patterns of worship.[44] Although the intellectual climate of Christianity was changed by the enormous and challenging output of Origen in the early third century, for most Christians there was little systematic theology beyond the simple affirmations of their belief in Christ's resurrection and of man's prospective redemption.

Matters changed after Constantine became sole emperor in 324. It became the object of imperial policy to create a single unified church, and to ensure that the largest possible number of the empire's inhabitants belonged to this church. The reasons for this were both practical and ideological. In practical terms, members of the church, especially clergy, immediately began to receive favors and privileges from the emperor, and bishops even began to exercise judicial authority on the state's behalf. It was essential to know who were entitled to these rights, and choices had to be made between Christian groups which competed for the emperor's recognition. Ideological unity was even more important. The Roman Empire was an autocratic monarchy (although in practice supreme power was sometimes shared between two or more emperors), and it was explicitly recognized that the political system should be supported by an equally monolithic religious framework. Constantine himself made this clear when he became involved in the controversy about the theological ideas of the Alexandrian priest Arius, which were to divide eastern bishops for much of the fourth century:

> On the subject of divine Providence therefore let there be one faith among you, one understanding, one agreement about the Supreme; the precise details about these minimal disputes among yourselves, even if you cannot bring yourselves to a single point of view, ought to remain in the mind, guarded in the hidden recesses of thought. (Eusebius, *VC* 2.71.7, trans. Cameron and Hall)

Christians themselves also began to form into larger ideological groups than before. The initial impetus for this came in their responses to the persecutions. There were different views as to how resistance or compliance with the authorities' demands should subsequently be handled. In the wake of the Decian persecution, the Roman priest Novatus (or Novatianus) had become leader of an immensely influential schismatic community whose leaders argued that only God could forgive the sin of apostasy, thus denying that the churches' own bishops or other leaders could provide absolution. The circumstances which led to this split existed only in the aftermath of persecution, yet the ideas which underpinned the Novatian schism remained vigorous and alive in Constantinople and Asia Minor into the fifth century AD. The events of 303–13 revived the issue that had brought Novatianism into being, and the Novatian Church gathered strength in Constantinople and in the interior of Asia Minor, where it had many supporters up to the middle of the fifth century.[45] There is a famous anecdote from the Council of Nicaea, recalling an interview between Constantine and the Novatian bishop Acesius. The bishop explained his church's unbending view that only God could forgive the sins of those who had compromised their religion; thus Novatians could not join the Catholic Church, although there were no doctrinal differences between them. The bemused emperor replied that Acesius should take his ladder and climb up into heaven.[46] The Novatians managed to avoid violent open conflict with the mainstream Catholic Church for most of its existence, but this may be due to the fact that much of our evidence for it comes from the church historian Socrates, who may even have been a Novatian himself, and who produced a highly eirenic view of ecclesiastical history in support of his overall argument that under Theodosius II church and state flourished in harmony under the guidance of their pious emperor.[47] Even so, Constantius II, urged on by Arian bishops, had occasion to send four regiments of soldiers against the Novatians of rural Paphlagonia. According to a peasant from the region who claimed to recall these events, they were slaughtered by the local inhabitants wielding scythes and axes (Socrates, *HE* 2.38; Sozomen 4.21).

Another separate movement formed in the communities of the Egyptian Delta around bishop Melitius. He and his followers had refused to acknowledge the authority of Peter, bishop of Alexandria, because he had failed to keep open places of Christian worship during the persecutions, surrendered scriptures, and adopted a lenient line with compromised clergy after he returned to Alexandria (Sozomen 1.24; Athanasius, *Apology against the Arians* 71). A church council held at Ancyra under the rule of Licinius before 319 had dealt with similar issues in Asia Minor, and proposed a series of compromises, which allowed persons who had sacrificed to be re-admitted to communion, and even appointed to the priesthood, provided it was clear that they had acted under duress.[48] In Egypt the Melitians had simply formed their own rival church, in defiance of the authority of the bishop of Alexandria. At the Council of Nicaea a settlement was reached in the same spirit of reconciliation that had been extended to the Novatians: Alexandria would recognize Melitian clergy provided that the clergy acknowledged the authority of Alexandria. Melitius submitted for approval a register of twenty-nine bishops, seven priests and deacons in Alexandria, and a rural priest. Coexistence, however, was not tolerable to the next bishop of Alexandria, the formidable Athanasius, who had no intention of sharing power with any schismatic group in his region, especially as the Council of Nicaea had recognized Alexandrian control over all the bishoprics of Libya, Egypt, and the Pentapolis (Nicaea, can. 6). He went into battle against them in word and deed:

> The Melitians, on whatever grounds (for it is not necessary to mention the reason) were received. Five months, however, had not passed when, the blessed Alexander having died, the Melitians, who ought to have remained quiet, and to have been grateful that they were received on any terms, like dogs unable to forget their vomit, began to trouble the churches. (Athanasius, *Apology against the Arians* 59, trans. Stevenson)

The bishop, supported by extremist ascetics, conducted a campaign of violent intimidation against the Melitians, a tactic which anticipated the goings-on in Syria in the 380s orchestrated by Maternus Cynegius (see above). The Melitians responded with an elaborate menu of charges against Athanasius.[49] They alleged that he had ordered the smashing of the Eucharistic chalice of Ischyras, a

Melitian priest, that he had perpetrated further acts of violence against Ischyras and others, and that he was responsible for the murder of a respected confessor, Arsenius, whose severed arm was then used for magical purposes. The murder charge was dropped after Arsenius was discovered by Athanasius' men alive and well, but the broader charges of violence are indirectly confirmed by a papyrus letter, which records that some of Athanasius' men, assisted by a group of off-duty Roman soldiers, had kidnapped or beaten up various Melitian followers, and that Athanasius himself had confined leading members of the Melitian clergy respectively to the meat market, the camp prison, and the main military prison of Alexandria.[50] Athanasius was summoned to account for himself at a council held in Tyre in 335, which, after sending a far from impartial commission of enquiry to Egypt to establish the facts of the case, deposed him.[51] Athanasius escaped in a dinghy from Tyre and took ship to Constantinople, where he accosted a dumbstruck emperor, who was riding outside the city.[52] Constantine heard his case with sympathy, and sent a summons to the bishops at Tyre to reconvene at Constantinople. At that moment five leading opponents of Athanasius, led by Eusebius of Nicomedia, appeared after a headlong overland journey and played their trump card: they alleged that Athanasius had conspired to prevent the sailing of the freighters which brought the corn supply from Alexandria to Constantinople. Constantine, without formally deposing him, promptly banished Athanasius to Trier, at the opposite end of the empire.[53]

The most important separatist movement to be born out of the persecutions were the Donatists in North Africa. Serious divisions existed between Numidian Christians and the church in Carthage before Diocletian's edict of persecution, but the so-called Donatist movement took definitive shape in the prison at Carthage in 304, where Christians who had been arrested, condemned the behavior of those who had handed over scriptures to the authorities, the *traditores*.[54] They were above all incensed at the behavior of the bishop of Carthage, Mensurius, who not only condemned the confessors and would-be martyrs, but sent his deacon Caecilian to prevent family members and supporters from visiting the prisoners and bringing them food. Caecilian, who had already quarreled bitterly with Lucilla, a leading figure in Numidia, for her practice of ostentatiously kissing a supposed martyr's bone before taking communion, had used extreme violence in carrying out his instructions.[55] In 311, with the support of seventy Numidian bishops, this group objected to the appointment of Caecilian as bishop of Carthage, on the grounds that he had been ordained by a *traditor*, Felix of Aptunga, and appointed their own man, Majorinus, in his place. The dispute was referred by the proconsul of Africa to Constantine, who had ordered that benefits be given to the church in Africa. Constantine in turn referred the dispute to be decided by councils of bishops, the first chaired by Miltiades in Rome in 313, then, at the Donatists' request, by a conclave at Arles in Gaul in the following year. This set an important precedent for later procedures whereby emperors empowered church councils to resolve issues of ecclesiastical or theological significance, but it was a logical move for Constantine at a time when regional councils of bishops were dealing with issues raised by the end of the persecutions throughout the empire.

The rulings of these councils, supported by the emperor and eventually backed up by force, found for Caecilian and against the rigorists. Majorian had been succeeded by the Numidian bishop of Casae Nigrae, Donatus, who was to lead them until 355. Its opponents gave the name "Donatist" to the movement, but the Donatists naturally regarded themselves as representatives of the legitimate Catholic Church. They proved to be stronger and more effectively organized than their opponents. Constantine, motivated by his search for ideological unity especially during the conflict with Licinius, abandoned attempts at outright repression in 321. A decade later, he avoided a confrontation when the Donatists commandeered the main basilica at Constantina, by providing the Catholics with funds to build their own (Optatus, *On the Schism of the Donatists*, app. 10, trans. Stephenson, *A New Eusebius*, 312 no. 271).[56]

The African churches made up by far the strongest and most numerous Christian communities in the western Roman Empire before Constantine. They had produced leading Christian figures including Tertullian and Cyprian; Carthage was one of the largest Christian cities; and there was a dense network of small communities, led by bishops, across the hinterland of Africa Proconsularis and Numidia. The Donatists, whose strength was in the small towns and cities of Numidia, could claim to be the authentic representatives of African Christianity, and it is appropriate to re-label them, with Brent Shaw, as African Christians. In 336 they were strong enough to convene a regional council of 270 bishops, effectively one for every city of North Africa. It is doubtful whether their opponents, whose position rested on the official support they received from the state, could match this. The Donatist position was strengthened immeasurably by Julian's edict, which re-instated exiled clergy, and they surely were the driving force in the region for the rest of the fourth century. When Augustine was appointed bishop of Hippo in 395, the greatest challenge he faced was from this regional African religious movement. There were temperamental and religious differences between the two sides. The African Christians, deriving strength from the mythology of persecution and martyrdom, identified themselves as defenders of the church's integrity against compromise. The Catholics meanwhile had evolved a cosmopolitan tradition of inclusiveness.[57] The Roman state was irrevocably committed to the Catholic side. Donatists had been implicated and repressed during the regional rebellions in Mauretania led by Firmus in the 370s,[58] and in 397 by his brother Gildo.[59]

The conflict between the imperial and the regional church came to a head in 411. In October 410 Honorius wrote to his tribune and *notarius* Marcellinus with a curt order:

> Greeting! We abolish the new superstition and we command that the regulations in regard to Catholic law shall be preserved unimpaired and inviolate. (*CTh.* 16.11.3)

A council was summoned at Carthage in 411, and met in the largest building of the city, the baths of Gargilius.[60] Both sides turned out in full strength, 286 Catholic bishops against 285 put out by their African opponents. A roll was taken and the rival bishops identified themselves and their rivals, and were called to account one by one to match their signatures. Both sides provided teams of shorthand writers and secretaries, who checked the record word for word, and took down the proceedings, which lasted three days. They have survived virtually entire, the fullest documentation of any meeting that has come down from antiquity.[61] The two sides glared at each other across the aisle. The Donatists refused to sit, literally standing their ground, while their spokesman Petillianus truculently affirmed their real identity when their opponents declared them to be Donatists:

> We are simply bishops of the truth of Christ, our Lord – so we call ourselves and so it is usually noted in the public records. As for Donatus of holy memory, a man of a martyr's glory, although he is our predecessor and an embellishment of the Church of this city, we only accord him the sort of honour and status he deserves. (*Gesta Coll. Carth.* 2.10)

In the confrontation both sides strained to display their strength. Of the Catholics, Augustine reported that

> So many bishops were gathered from all of Africa and entered Carthage with great pomp and ceremony in a magnificent parade, that they turned the eyes and attention of the city's inhabitants upon themselves. (Augustine, *Ad Donatistas post Collationem* 25, 43)

The Donatists too had marched solemnly into the baths so as to impress their supporters with their numbers and their moral superiority (*Gest Coll. Carth.* 1.14.7–11, 29.2–4). Similar ostentatious tactics were employed by rival Arians and orthodox Christians in Constantinople at this period (Socrates, *HE* 6.8).

The council concluded as the emperor had intended, by refuting the claims of the Donatists on the central legal point. It relied on the simple fact that Constantine's rulings had found for Caecilian and his followers almost a century before. All the supplementary argument presented by Petillianus and his fellows was regarded as special pleading.

The Donatist struggle had begun with obscure quarrels among African communities which had escalated under the pressure of the persecutions. The supporters of the African church derived their moral strength from stories of martyrdom and their opponents' betrayals, and a rallying point in their indignation at the ordination of Caecilian. This was the kernel around which they had created their regional identity. They drew their strength from local roots, not from empire-wide diplomacy and alliances, and played little part in the doctrinal controversies of the fourth century. The rival group, against which they matched themselves, was a mirror organization, the Catholic Church, created and supported by the state. Although Donatist clergy were implicated in regional uprisings and some may have directly supported them, this was not a political movement directed against the empire, but an attempt to assert their role as the rightful church. After 411 the movement gradually faded from view. It is not plausible that this is due to the repressive measures taken against them after the Council of Carthage. State power had failed before, and had little impact beyond the major cities where troops and violence could be used. Nor did the moral force of the Donatist message dissipate. More convincing is Brent Shaw's subtler explanation, that Donatism, or African Christianity, ceased to be identified as such later in the fifth century because its counterpart, state-sponsored Catholicism, was also forced into retreat and marginalized by the Vandal invasion of the 430s. As the Germanic invaders imposed their own Arian orthodoxy, the Roman Empire lost its authority over the church in Africa and Catholics were persecuted. No doubt many of those who suffered for their doctrinal views at the hands of the Vandals were in fact former Donatists, but there were now no authorities to give them this label. In Arian eyes African Christians and their rivals were all simply the Catholics that they claimed to be.

Christianity played a major role in the formation of community identities in the empire at large, not merely at a regional level. In the midst of the Donatist dispute Constantine was drawn into an abstract doctrinal argument about the nature of Christ and his relationship to God the Father, which affected the entire Christian community in the eastern empire and spread thereafter to the West. The Arian question took its name from the Libyan priest Arius, whose arguments that Christ was subordinate to God provided the starting point of the controversy.[62] However, the label is also a misleading one. Arius certainly drew attention to a central matter of doctrine in the years leading up to the Council of Nicaea in 325, but the issues were not new in themselves and continued to be debated with increasing intensity across the eastern Christian world. The term "Arianism" and the label "Arian" were in any case mostly used in a pejorative sense by opposing churchmen, above all by Athanasius, who denounced their rivals as heretics. The argument was concerned with the central core of Christian belief, the nature of God, and the way in which his divinity was embodied in Christ.[63]

Arius' own views have to be reconstructed from three surviving letters quoted by hostile sources, and by verses from a poem called the *Thalia* (*The Banquet*), composed in the meter of the popular songs of sailors, mill workers, and muleteers, which were written after he was expelled from Alexandria by his bishop (Philostorgius, *HE* 2.2). According to one of his letters, quoted by the mid-fifth-century historian Theodoret, he taught

> that the son is not unbegotten, nor in any way part of the unbegotten; nor from any lower essence; but that by (the Father's) will and counsel he has subsisted before time, and before ages as fully God, only-begotten and unchangeable. And that, before he was begotten, or created, or defined, or established, he was not. For he was not unbegotten. We are persecuted because we say "the Son has a

beginning, but God is without beginning." We are also persecuted for this reason, that we say that he is from nothing. And we say this because he is neither part of God, nor of any lower essence. (Theodoret, *HE* 1.5.1–4; trans. adapted from Stevenson, *New Eusebius*, 324–5 no. 283)

Arius argued for the primacy, and therefore the superiority, of the Father to the Son. The Son was a "creature," created or made, the product of the will of the creator, not part of the substance of God. As the Son in human form possessed free will he was capable of virtue or vice. Socrates summarized Arius' position succinctly in his *Church History*: "If the Father begat the Son, he that was begotten has a beginning of existence. From this it is clear that there was (a state) when the Son was not. It therefore necessarily follows that He had his essence from the non-existent" (Socrates I.5; trans. Stevenson, *New Eusebius* no. 280).

Arius' opponents, led initially by Alexander, bishop of Alexandria, argued for the identity of Father, Son, and Holy Spirit, "One in Three," and that the Son was consubstantial and co-eternal with the Father, that the Son was the Lord's true Word and Wisdom, not one of his works and creatures. Alexander summoned a synod of bishops to establish which view was correct, and this concluded by banishing Arius from Alexandria and excommunicating his followers.[64] This had the effect of spreading rather than restricting the controversy. Arius was a senior and respected theologian. His subordinationist view of Christ's divinity had a highly respectable pedigree, traceable to the greatest Christian thinker of the third century, Origen, and also appealed on grounds of plain common sense. It is no surprise that he won important support from many eastern bishops, most notably from Eusebius, who was promoted from being bishop of Berytus to bishop of Nicomedia, and Eusebius of Caesarea, the writer of the *Ecclesiastical History*.

The split in the eastern church became apparent after 319, and conflicted with Constantine's drive to achieve church unity. The emperor wrote a lengthy letter admonishing both Arius and Alexander. He dispatched Ossius to reconcile them in Alexandria in 324 but failed to achieve a resolution (Eusebius, *VC* 2.63–72). Ossius (often reproduced in Greek sources as Hosius) then presided over a council in Antioch in April 325, and drafted a résumé of the outcome which is preserved in a Syriac version. The introductory paragraphs of this letter indicate that the issue was extremely serious in theological terms.

> Since the holding of a synod of bishops had been hindered in these parts, our first care was to investigate a topic that is most important of all and surpasses all others – in fact it comprises the whole mystery of the faith that is in us – I mean what concerns the Saviour of us all, the Son of the Living God. (Opitz, *Urkunde* 18, 36–41; trans. Stevenson, *New Eusebius*, 334–5 no. 288)

Antioch was a prelude to the great Council of Nicaea, held three months later in the presence of Constantine himself, and attended by nearly 300 bishops from the eastern and Danubian provinces, as well as by two deputies of the bishop of Rome. Constantine, who had specifically refused to travel to the East from Nicomedia as long as the controversy raged, had probably hoped that the doctrinal issues could have been cleared up at Antioch, in order that the gathering at Nicaea might concentrate on matters which more closely matched his own priorities: church unity, agreement on the date of Easter, and the hierarchy of authority within the church. As it was, the theological issue took precedence, and the issue had to be settled. Famously the bishops agreed a wording for the creed which placed Arius' views beyond the pale: Christ was begotten from the substance of the Father, not created from that which was not. Hosius and his associates insisted on the insertion of the key word *homoousios*, "consubstantial," which Arius and his followers had always repudiated, as for them it implied that God's essential nature was in some way divisible and diminished. The pressure for unity and the presence of the emperor achieved their purpose, and all but two Libyan bishops, who were exiled, signed up to the creed. A letter written by Eusebius of Caesarea to his church shows how he, like other sympathizers with Arius, reconciled themselves to the wording by the different senses they applied to its key terms.[65]

Despite Constantine's best efforts the decisions at Nicaea failed to resolve the dogmatic issues about the nature of Christian belief. During the final phase of Constantine's reign we enter an almost impenetrable thicket of ecclesiastical controversy, which was to extend up to the reign of Theodosius, when the issues were resolved, again by imperial *fiat*, at the Council of Constantinople in 381. The supporters of Arius remained numerous and influential, and their views were well rooted in a strong intellectual tradition. As early as September 325 Eusebius of Nicomedia and his associate Theognis of Nicaea had slipped into apostasy and were exiled by the emperor. However, within two years they were re-instated and Arius prepared a personal credal statement which persuaded Constantine that he too could be brought back into the fold.[66]

Let us summarize the main features of this formative period in the evolution of a universal church. The argument about doctrine which flared up between an Alexandrian priest and his bishop provided the setting for the first attempt by the church as a whole to define its core beliefs. The debate led churchmen to expound a range of views about the relationship of the Son to the Father. At one extreme was the Sabellianism of Paul of Samosata or Marcellus of Ancyra, which denied the Son any significant independence from the Father. This exaggerated monotheism could also be seen as a form of Christianity strongly influenced by Jewish theology. At the opposite end of the scale were the views of the Anomoeans, who argued that the Son was dissimilar to the Father and therefore did not share in his divinity. The doctrinal issue which occupied the Council of Nicaea, that is the choice between the theology of Arius and the creed that was imposed by Hosius and Constantine, in fact fell between these two extreme positions. Arius asserted that the Son was begotten to the Father, and thus subordinate to Him, the product of an act of creation where previously there had been nothing. The Nicenes, in contrast, asserted that he was of the same substance as the Father and had existed with him for all eternity.

After the death of Constantine, the party led by Eusebius of Nicomedia, which had taken its cue from Arius' ideas, and which was supported by Constantius in the East, united around the formula that the Son was "like in substance," *homoiousios*, to the Father, a position which was sufficiently close to the Nicene *homoousios*, for Hilary of Poitiers, a western bishop who was exiled to Asia Minor in 358, to argue at length that there was no important difference between these positions.[67]

It is unnecessary in this context to trace the dispute about the "Christian doctrine of God" in detail through the convolutions of fourth-century church politics. However, the imperial quest for church unity led inevitably to the consequence that much of the controversy was driven not by theology but by politics. Constantine, as far as we can judge from the admiring portrait of Eusebius in his panegyrical life, was genuinely prepared to let his bishops formulate their own views and reach their own decisions. Much confusion resulted during the 330s.

The dominating personality among the churchmen was the bishop of Alexandria, Athanasius, whose vigorous Nicene views and uncompromising tactics provoked extreme reactions both from his supporters and his opponents.[68] After he was banished to the West following the Council of Tyre in 335 much of the argument between the eastern and western church simply concerned whether or not he should be restored to the See of Alexandria. In 339 Athanasius took refuge in Rome, and the conflict within the church assumed a new dimension as the western bishops became embroiled for the first time on a large scale. Under the leadership of Julius, bishop of Rome, they espoused the cause both of Athanasius and of Marcellus, the former bishop of Ancyra, who had been one of the most unbending champions of Nicaea and had been exiled by a council at Antioch in 340 on a charge of Sabellianism, the heretical view that the Son was not only in substance indistinguishable from the Father but subsumed within him. They had the support of the emperor Constans, who had ousted his elder brother Constantine II in 340. The eastern bishops were broadly championed by Constantius, now resident for long periods at Antioch as he campaigned against the Persians on the eastern frontier. In the hope of avoiding a schism the two emperors summoned the bishops of East and West to a council at Serdica, modern Sofia. However, the two sides never met under one roof. The westerners refused to accede to the easterners' demand that they exclude Athanasius and his associates from the council, and their opponents withdrew to Philippopolis (Plovdiv), where they held their own conclave. The two groups formulated contrasting Nicene and Arianizing creeds and anathematized one another. The conflict was more about the eastern refusal to take back Athanasius and the western championing of Marcellus of Ancyra than the technicalities of dogma. As if to emphasize this, the western bishops, under the veteran chairmanship of Hosius of Cordoba, produced a series of canons which curbed the powers of individual bishops, in particular by restricting their movements and influence outside their own dioceses, but also asserted the authority of the bishop of Rome, the apostolic See of St Peter, over the rest of the church. This included the assertion that he had the power to reinstate clergy who had been deposed by a provincial council.[69] The eastern church rejected this out of hand. The emperors Constantius and Constans supported the causes of their respective bishops, and according to later church historians practically committed themselves to a civil war over the issue of restoring Athanasius in 345.[70] The bishops of Rome, following the lead of Julius at the Council of Serdica, who tried to claim the role of supreme arbiter in the church's affairs, became much more aware of their own importance.

Constantius intervened more actively in religious affairs than his father had done. As he relentlessly pursued the aim of achieving a unified church during the 350s, one of his victims was the aged Ossius of Cordoba, who wrote a vain letter of protest to the emperor in 356:

> Cease, then, these proceedings, I ask you, and remember that you are a mortal man. Be afraid of the day of judgement, and keep yourself pure against that day. Do not intrude into ecclesiastical matters, and do not give commands to us concerning them; but learn them from us. God has put into your hands the kingdom; to us he has entrusted the affairs of the Church; and, as he who should steal the empire from you would resist the ordinance of God, so fear on your part lest, by taking upon yourself the government of the Church, you become guilty of a great offence. It is written, *Render unto Caesar the things that are Caesar's, and unto God the things that are God's.* Neither, therefore, is it permitted us to exercise an earthly rule, nor have you, Sir, any authority to burn incense. (Athanasius, *History of the Arians*, 44; trans. Stevenson, *Creeds, Councils and Controversies*, 35–37 no. 24)

Ossius was neither the first nor the last bishop to make this complaint, more or less in the same words. When he emerged in the 350s as sole Augustus, Constantius was as eager as Constantine had been to create a single united church in the whole empire, and during the 350s he personally attended a sequence of councils, which aimed to win over the western church to the homoean views held by most of the eastern bishops. He finally succeeded in this aim through the twin councils of Ariminum and Seleuceia, held in 359 (which were the equivalent of an ecumenical council, but staged in separate western and eastern sessions), whose decisions were consolidated at the first Council of Constantinople in 360. Jerome was later to comment about the outcome of these gatherings, "that the whole world groaned to find itself Arian," but in fact the compromise formula was not far from the Nicene one.

The drive towards religious unity which was the central feature of the religious policies of Constantine and his sons was interrupted for twenty years by the attempted pagan restoration of Julian and then by the permissive tolerance of Valentinian and Valens. Valens has the reputation of being an Arian emperor, like Constantius before him, but this is an exaggerated view, supported by little more than the fact that most of the eastern bishops around him tended to hold homoean views, and he made no moves against the more extreme anomoeans or dissimilarian theologians, who argued that God's majesty was diminished by any admission that the Son derived any of his character and substance from the Father.[71]

The change of emphasis which followed the accession of Theodosius I was very marked. The new emperor came from a western Spanish background, and he and his associates were noted both for their piety and for their staunch adherence to Nicene views, which were universally adopted by the Latin churches.[72] Whereas the western Christians, dominated by the already powerful figure of Ambrose at Milan, were united and recognized the authority of Damasus, the bishop of Rome, the simmering ecclesiastical controversy in the East is graphically illustrated by the state of the great bishoprics around 380. There were two contenders for the See of Antioch, Paulinus, whose views were dangerously Sabellian, and the aging Meletius. A third claimant, the Arian Euzoius, had only disappeared from the scene a few years before. At Constantinople the Arian Demophilus had resigned, anticipating imminent dismissal by Theodosius, and been replaced by the orthodox Cappadocian theologian Gregory of Nazianzus. However, Meletius died in 381, during the early stages of the ecumenical council which Theodosius had summoned to Constantinople in 381, and Gregory resigned amid a storm of controversy, when he proposed that Paulinus be re-instated to succeed him.

In this atmosphere it is no surprise that Theodosius should have taken a more brusque line with the disputing factions than his imperial predecessors. Theodosius' pronouncement of the *cunctos populos* edict soon after his accession left the bishops with no illusions that they were under instructions to re-affirm the Nicene Creed as a universal article of faith. The ground had been prepared in the East by the Cappadocian fathers, especially Basil of Caesarea, whose writings on the Trinity explained the doctrine of a single divine essence (*ousia*) which was represented in three substances (*hypostaseis*), one in three and three in one. The object of the Council was not in this case to formulate a creed, as at Nicaea, but to impose it. This is evident from the beginning of the letter which the council addressed to Theodosius on concluding its business:

> Having then assembled at Constantinople according to the letter of your Piety, we in the first place renewed our mutual regard for each other, and then pronounced some short definitions, ratifying the faith of the Nicene fathers, and anathematizing the heresies which have sprung up contrary to it. In addition to this we have established certain canons for the right ordering of the Churches, all of which we have subjoined to this our letter. We pray therefore your Clemency, that the decree may be confirmed by the letter of your Piety, that as you have honoured the Church by the letters calling us together, so also you may ratify the conclusion of what has been decreed. (trans. Stevenson, *Creeds, Councils and Controversies*, 115–16 no. 91)

The dominant rival theological views which had made headway over the previous forty years were duly named and condemned as heretical. The hierarchical organization of the church and the new status of Constantinople was given special emphasis (see p. 274 above). Moreover the new bishop of Constantinople was effectively a political appointment, Nectarius, a palace official, who was rushed through all the stages of the priesthood (as Ambrose had been in

Milan seven years earlier) to take charge of the second place in the hierarchy of Christendom.

The Council of Constantinople thus set the seal on the imperial search for a single Christian identity. The settlement was imposed, not agreed by consensus, and was not immune to controversy, which was to re-ignite during the fifth century. However, the Nicene Creed, as expanded at Constantinople, remained the touchstone of Roman Christianity at the Council of Chalcedon in 451 and in the sixth century under Justinian.

There was another dynamic behind the drive to establish Nicene Catholicism as the religion of the Roman state. Nicene orthodoxy was distinguished from the Arian faith of the barbarians. In 376 the Gothic tribe of the Tervingi had negotiated an agreement with Valens to be allowed to cross the Danube and settle in the administrative diocese of Thrace. Christianity had first been introduced to the Goths by Ulfila, who had taken part in an embassy to Constantinople either in 336 or in 341 and had been consecrated as bishop *in partibus* by Eusebius of Nicomedia (Philostorgius, *HE* 2.5).[73] The Christian Goths were driven out by their pagan compatriots in the late 340s, and settled at Nicopolis in Lower Moesia, where Ulfila became an influential church leader. It was doubtless here that he devised a new alphabet and transformed Gothic from an oral into a written language, into which the Bible could be translated (Philostorgius, *HE* 2.5). In 376 he is said to have acted as a spokesman for the Goths in the negotiations that led to the Tervingi being allowed to cross the Danube at the time of the Hunnic incursions. An added motive for Ulfila's intervention would have been recent persecution of Christians among the Goths themselves.[74] The Tervingi were obliged to declare themselves to be Christian before they entered the empire. Christian priests on the Gothic side later acted as go-betweens between the Goths before the battle of Adrianople and the Romans (Ammianus 31.12, p. 433; 31.15, p. 440).[75] The church historians Socrates and Theodoret indicate that it was at this moment, under the influence of Eudoxius, the Arian bishop of Constantinople, that the Goths firmly took on Arian theological doctrines, concordant with those of the emperor Valens (Theodoret, *HE* 4.37, Socrates 4.33.5; cf. Sozomen 6.37.7), but Sozomen indicates that Ulfila, whose spiritual mentor was the Arianizing bishop Eusebius of Nicomedia, already espoused a primitivist, gospel-based form of Christianity and was hostile to the non-biblical Nicene formula of the *homoousion* (Sozomen 6.37.8–11).

Theodosius was fully cognizant of the religious difference between the Goths and the Romans as he campaigned in Illyricum in the aftermath of the debacle at Adrianople. The canons of the Council of Constantinople made a deliberate exception for the Goths to follow a creed which conformed with their simple adherence to a pre-Nicene apostolic church:

> The Churches of God which are among the barbarians must be administered according to the usage of the Fathers which has prevailed. (Stevenson, *Creeds, Councils and Controversies*, 116 no. 91, can. 2)

This must also have been acknowledged in the *foedus* of 382, which was to remain the basis of the compact between Goths and Romans within the imperial boundaries. Both sides may have been conscious of, but did not emphasize, the fact that the Goths henceforth adhered to the Arian belief of the emperor Valens, whom they had defeated in 378, while Theodosius and his Roman subjects were now neo-Nicene Catholics.

After 381 Arian beliefs ceased to play a significant role in the internal Christological controversies of the Roman Church, but they remained of fundamental importance for distinguishing the federal Germanic peoples.[76] Gothic Christianity was not made welcome in the cities of the empire. Ambrose of Milan drew on all his political resources to resist attempts by Justina, Valens' widow and mother of Valentinian II, to take over one of Milan's churches to hold an Arian Easter liturgy in 385 and 386. It is evident that Gothic troops were among those pressing for a church to be made available to them.[77] In Constantinople around 400 John Chrysostom banned Goths from conducting an Arian liturgy within the city, and their church was located outside the walls. A city church was designated for them where the Catholic mass was offered by Gothic-speaking clergy, and he himself preached there with the aid of an interpreter (Theodoret, *HE* 5.30). Socrates has a vivid description of the Arian and orthodox communities competing with one another in their processions through the city (Socrates 6.8).

Arianism among the Germanic kingdoms was deliberately maintained to mark the distinction between Romans and barbarians in the western empire through the fifth century, long after the Arian controversy had ceased to be an issue in internal church politics. Orthodoxy was thus not merely equated with being Christian, but with being Roman. Conversely, the barbarians were fully aware of the importance of their Arian identity in constructing their own ethnic cohesion. The Vandals strongly emphasized their Arianism, and used it not only as an active form of nation building, but accentuated their credentials by persecuting the Catholic provincial population in Africa. Another test case is provided by the Burgundians, whose leaders deliberately identified themselves more closely with the Romans than other barbarian groups in Gaul. Many of them turned to Catholicism (see above p. 209).

Roman writers have deliberately little to say about the nature of Christianity in the barbarian kingdoms. Sidonius Apollinaris described the daily routine of the Visigothic king Theoderic as a matter of routine rather than conviction (*ep.* 1.2.4). Catholic Romans were anxious to belittle this barbarian Arian form of Christianity. The monuments tell a different story. Theoderic, the Ostrogothic king, erected buildings in Ravenna, above all the great basilica of S. Apollonare Nuovo, that are as evocative of his Arian piety as the later Church of S. Vitale attests the Catholicism of the age of Justinian.

The struggle to achieve a single form of Roman–Christian identity continued to be the hallmark of imperial religious policy through the fifth and sixth centuries. Under the pious rulership of Theodosius II the impetus came not from the emperor himself, who was anxious to promote an ideology of reconciliation between rival doctrines and interpretations of scripture, but from the theological arguments advanced by highly polemical bishops. Nestorius, who became bishop of Constantinople in 428, advanced the view that there were two natures, both man and God, in Christ. This was a development of the theories of Theodore of Mopsuhestia. Both were representatives of the Antiochene school which was strongly opposed by the Alexandrian tradition of the one nature of Christ, that stemmed from Athanasius, but was now powerfully advocated by Cyril, who had been bishop of Alexandria since 415. Confined to Antioch, these views were an irritant to Alexandria, but from the mouth of the bishop of Constantinople, who now outranked him, they were an outright provocation. Moreover, Nestorius, at least in the eyes of his enemies, was a naïve and unsophisticated preacher, described as illiterate and ignorant by the church historian Socrates (7.32.10).

Much of the argument about the nature of Christ was abstruse, but it stirred passions when Nestorius drew the conclusion that the Virgin Mary could not be called "Theotokos," mother of God, but at best "Christotokos," mother of Christ, for she had only given birth to Jesus in his human incarnation, not to Jesus the divine word of God. This was the crucial point from which Cyril chose to attack Nestorius' position. Cyril then began to construct a theological alliance in which the crucial figures were the bishop of Rome, Celestinus, and the bishop of Jerusalem, Juvenal. Further arguments were developed to demonstrate that Cyril's view of the unified nature of Christ corresponded with the doctrine of Nicaea, which had been confirmed as the lynch-pin of orthodoxy at the Council of Constantinople in 381. The arguments were put to the test at another ecumenical council, which met in Ephesus in 431. Cyril left little to chance. A flotilla of ships from Alexandria carried not only the bishops of Egypt and Libya with their attendant clergy, but six hundred of the paramilitary *parabalani*, who were the bishop's enforcers in Alexandria. Cyril is reported to have bribed members of the imperial court in Constantinople to the tune of 2,500 pounds of gold. Nestorius' supporters were outnumbered and divided. Many of the bishops of Asia Minor, on whose territory the council was held, threw their weight behind Cyril. John, the bishop of Antioch, was delayed in his overland journey across Anatolia, and arrived only after the council had condemned Nestorius as a new Judas and stripped him of clerical rank. Cyril triumphantly wrote that the Nicene Creed was re-affirmed, that out of two natures a union was made in Christ, and that the Virgin Mary was confirmed as Mother of God (Cyril, *ep.* 39, 105c–106c, trans. in Stevenson, *Creeds, Councils and Controversies*, 313–17 no. 226).[78] The Nestorians were hounded from power and from the empire. Many communities fled to Persia and took refuge within the more tolerant religious environment of the Sassanid Empire (see above, p. 122).

The debate was far from over, and fueled two further ecumenical councils in the middle of the fifth century which polarized the views of the established church around the question of the nature of Christ and involved state intervention at the highest level. Cyril died in 444 and was succeeded at Alexandria by Dioscorus. Meanwhile the Antiochene theologians returned to their arguments about the two natures of Christ, led by Theodoret of Cyrrhus. Councils were called in rapid succession to address the issue of Christ's nature, at Ephesus in 449 and at Chalcedon in 451. This theological crisis claimed major victims including Dioscurus, the bishop of Alexandria, who pushed Cyril's views with an unscrupulousness that outmatched his predecessor, and Flavian, bishop of Constantinople, who was deposed by the Monophysite monks at the Robber Council of Ephesus. The bishop of Rome, Leo, played a decisive part by submitting the view of the western churches in the *Tome of Leo*. This contained a ponderous assertion that the distinctive character of each nature and substance remained unimpaired, but came together in the one person of Christ. As mediator between man and God, Christ was capable of death in one nature but not in the other. Thus in the whole and perfect nature of true manhood, one God is born (trans. in Stevenson, *Creeds, Councils and Controversies*, 336–44 no. 241, 3). The bishops who assembled at Chalcedon in 451, under extreme imperial pressure, agreed to a formula along similar lines:

> We all with one voice confess Lord Jesus Christ to be one and the same Son, the same perfect in Godhead, the same perfect in Manhood, truly God and truly man, the same consisting of a reasonable soul and a body, of one substance with the Father as touching the Godhead, the same of one substance with us as touching the Manhood, like us in all things apart from sin. (Stevenson, *Creeds, Councils and Controversies*, 350–54 no. 246, 4)

Chalcedon redefined orthodoxy in terms that were intended to bring a halt to the disputes of the Alexandrians and the Antiochenes. The emperor Marcian issued the optimistic and self-deluding edict that

> Controversy about the orthodox religious law (*lex*) of the Christians has been put away; remedies at length have been found for culpable error, and diversity of opinion among the peoples has issued in common consent and concord. From the different provinces the most religious bishops have come to Chalcedon in accordance with our commands, and have taught by clear definition what ought to be observed in the matter of religion. Therefore let profane wrangling cease. (trans. in Stevenson, *Creeds, Councils and Controversies*, 364–5 no. 250)

The official doctrine of the Roman Church was thus that Christ possessed two natures in one person. The theologians and common people of Alexandria were appalled. As they saw it, the facile and internally contradictory doctrine of Leo and of the Council of Chalcedon hardly differed from the heretical views of Nestorius himself. Nestorius, from exile in the Great Oasis, made the point in his *Book of Heracleides* (Stevenson, *Creeds, Councils and Controversies*, 349 no. 245). Doctrinal unity was achieved by imperial decree, but resulted in the permanent alienation of the Monophysite movement in the eastern empire.

The Council of Chalcedon created a gulf that was never bridged between the predominantly Monophysite regions of Syria and Egypt, and the orthodoxy which had been imposed from Constantinople and which was favored above all by the Christian West. The opponents of Chalcedon achieved a significant success in the early 470s during the interregnum of the usurper Basiliscus. Timothy, the bishop of Alexandria, supported by Peter the Fuller, bishop of Antioch, had persuaded Basiliscus to issue an encyclical letter. In terms of doctrine this insisted on adherence to the Nicene Creed of 325, and to the revised formulae that had been agreed at the Council of Constantinople in 381, and also accepted the conclusions reached at the two councils of Ephesus in 431 and 449. However, the encyclical anathematized the tome of Leo and the decisions of the Council of Chalcedon (Evagrius, *HE* 3.4). The central issue raised by this decision was more a matter of ecclesiastical politics than of doctrine. The Council of Chalcedon had underlined the leading position in the eastern church of the patriarchal bishop of Constantinople. Acacius, the patriarch of Constantinople, organized a vigorous lobby, supported by the monks of the capital, to have the encyclical reversed, and Basiliscus duly recanted. The revised statement deliberately avoided making any pronouncements about doctrine, but restored the authority of Constantinople

> For, on this account, we also enjoin that whatever has occurred during our reign, whether as encyclicals, or in other forms, or indeed anything else whatsoever concerned with faith and ecclesiastical organization, be null and void, while we anathematize Nestorius and Eutyches, and every other heresy, and all who hold the same opinions; and that there will be no synod or other investigation concerning this subject, but these matters will be unbroken and unshaken; and that the provinces, whose ordination the see of this imperial and glorious city controlled, should be returned to the most devout and most holy patriarch and archbishop, Acacius. (Evagrius, *HE* 3.7, trans. Whitby)

In 482 Acacius, the patriarch of Constantinople, prepared a new statement of belief designed to reconcile the two sides, which was labeled the *Henotikon*, the affirmation of Union. His main concern was to reconcile the imperial church and the views of Constantinople with the Monophysite theology propounded at Alexandria. The formula was an old-fashioned statement of Trinitarian belief, but avoided any direct assertion about the one or two natures of Christ: "For the Trinity has remained a Trinity even after one of the Trinity, God the Word, was made flesh" (Evagrius, *HE* 3.14). The *Henotikon* approved the anathemas of Cyril of Alexandria, but condemned heresies of all sorts, whether promulgated at Chalcedon or anywhere else. This document won the support of the bishops of Alexandria and Antioch, without persuading more extreme Monophysites.[79]

More seriously, the fact that Acacius had unambiguously entered into communion with the Monophysites provoked the wrath of Rome. In 484 the bishop of Rome excommunicated Acacius, initiating a split between the western church and Constantinople which was to last until the accession of Justin I in 519. In effect, instead of creating unity, the tolerant policy which lay behind the *Henotikon* led the separate churches to pursue their own forms of worship. Evagrius emphasizes the resulting confusion:

There were very many divisions both in the East and in the western regions and in Libya since the eastern bishops were not on terms with those in the West or in Libya, nor in turn were the latter with those in the Eat. The situation became even more absurd. For the prelates in the East were not even in communion with one another. (Evagrius, *HE* 3.30, trans. Whitby)

The obduracy of the East is fully explicable within the broader political context. The western empire had collapsed as a political entity a few years earlier, and however imposing the pope's ecclesiastical authority, it was more important for the East to strive for internal coherence and unity. This was especially urgent as the eastern provinces had now become war zones for the first time during the fifth century. The emergence of the Isaurians had caused widespread violence and civil war in the center and south of Asia Minor, there was serious tension with Sassanid Persia after the mid-480s, and hostilities on the eastern front were to break out in the middle years of the emperor Anastasius.

Anastasius' own beliefs showed strong Monophysite tendencies and appealed to the majority of the population of Syria and Egypt, but provoked opposition in the capital. Religious tension at Constantinople reached a climax in 512 when the emperor approved the addition of the words "who was crucified for us," to the Chalcedonian formula of the *trishagion*, "Holy God, Holy Mighty, Holy Immortal, have mercy on us!"[80] The Chalcedonians, fully in control of the church at Constantinople, interpreted this as implying that God himself was crucified, which was not a belief that could be reconciled with their two natures' theology. Opposition led by the monks of the city caused riotous demonstrations; much of the center of the city was burnt; a Syrian monk, who was held responsible for introducing the Monophysite formula to the *trishagion*, was beheaded, and his head paraded on a pole. A move was even made to promote Areobindus, a grandson of Aspar who was married to a descendant of Theodosius II, to replace the emperor. In this crisis Anastasius confronted the crowd in the Hippodrome and demonstratively laid aside his diadem. This was one of the great stage-managed political moments of the later empire. His address challenged them to face reality – the empire could not be ruled by the mob but only by a single ruler. The mob was manipulated into compliance. The emperor, now aged eighty-three, certainly did not rely exclusively on his own rhetoric and arguments. The rebellion was extinguished by arrests and executions (Malalas 16.19, 406.22–408.11).

The division between East and West, the Acacian schism, was brought to an end in 518 by the death of Anastasius. Anastasius' successor Justin, was a Chalcedonian, and immediately after his accession a delegation from Hormisdas, the bishop of Rome, formally put an end to the breach between the western church and Constantinople. Imperial religious policy was now actively controlled by Justin's nephew, the future emperor Justinian, and the new policies of the regime led to many Monophysite bishops in Syria, notably Severus the bishop of Antioch, being removed from their sees.

Justinian's personal influence now became the dominating factor in ecclesiastical politics. To a greater degree than any of his predecessors, he envisaged his own role as emperor in religious terms. Imperial policies were explicitly presented as an expression of God's will. "We continuously commit ourselves to all plans and actions in the name of Jesus Christ" (*CJust.* 1.27.2 preface). Moreover, the theological nature of Christian doctrine was a matter of passionate personal concern to him, especially in the later part of his reign. Procopius condemned him for spending long hours debating theological issues in the palace with clerics, to the detriment of his secular responsibilities (Procopius, *Bell. Goth.* 7.32.39). More than any other emperor, he spared nothing and no one in the quest for religious unity:

> For in his eagerness to gather all men into one belief as to Christ, he kept destroying the rest of mankind in senseless fashion, and that too while acting with a pretence of piety. For it did not seem to him murder if the victims chanced not to be of his own creed. (Procopius, *Secret History* 13.7, trans. Dewing)

At the heart of Justinian's own Christianity was his commitment to the so-called theopaschite formula, that one member of the Trinity had truly suffered on the cross. In essence this was closely associated with the Monophysite supplement to the *trishagion*, which had stirred up Chalcedonian opposition to Anastasius, and it was initially rejected by the bishop of Rome and the western church. However, negotiations during the 530s, which culminated at a council held in Constantinople in 536, produced a paradoxical resolution. Rome acknowledged the formula as an acceptable extension of Chalcedonian dogma, provided that Rome's own status as the supreme Church of Christendom was recognized by the great bishoprics of the East. Indeed the enhanced significance of the city of Rome at the head of the church was a major incentive for Justinian to undertake his war against the Gothic kingdom in Italy, thereby bringing secular as well as religious unity to the universal church. This created the appearance of the Roman Christian world united in its adherence to the orthodox doctrine of Chalcedon. The political context of these developments is important. Imperial politics after 532, when a peace treaty with Persia had been signed, were focused on the West, and the search for religious unity was an urgent concern for Constantinople and Rome. Alexandria was another matter. The emperor was obliged to depose its Monophysite bishop Theodosius in 538, and replace him with Chalcedonian candidates, who were supported by military force. The people of Egypt were mostly unmoved from their Monophysite convictions and continued to regard Theodosius as the true patriarch of Alexandria until his death in 566.

However, there was doctrinal confusion in Justinian's religious politics, including the potentially fatal flaw that the new Chalcedonianism in fact contained crucial ingredients of Monophysitism. It is symptomatic of the ambiguity that the emperor's own wife Theodora was well known for her Monophysite sympathies, and had several occasions to support and encourage Monophysite churchmen. It is also revealing that Justinian himself brought a completely different approach to religious politics than that of earlier emperors. Whereas his predecessors rarely played an active role in theological debate, but mustered state authority, and on occasion brute force, to enforce the decisions of church councils, Justinian preferred to engage in debate himself and enforce compliance through persuasion and argument.

In 553 Justinian convened a fifth ecumenical council to try and win over the dissident Monophysite East. The council agreed to retain the main dogma of Chalcedon, but condemned three crucial dogmatic works that expounded two-nature theology, written more than a century earlier by Theodoret of Cyrrhus, Ibas of Edessa and Theodore of Mopsuhestia. The attempted compromise was no more successful than the *Henotikon* had been. In the later stages of his reign Justinian was prepared to use force where persuasion failed. Vigilius, the bishop of Rome, had been literally kidnapped and brought to Constantinople, but refused to participate in the discussions. The remnants of the Roman Church in Italy effectively refused to acknowledge the council's authority. Meanwhile the Monophysites of Syria regarded the outcome as a half-way measure, which had failed to remove the objectionable features of Chalcedonian theology. Their conclusion was surreptitiously to declare their independence of Constantinople. Jacob Baradaeus (Bar-Addai), the bishop of Edessa from 542 to 578, identifying himself with the monks, hermits, and holy men of Syria and Mesopotamia, began the task of ordaining an entire alternative clergy to create the Jacobite Church of Syria. The result was a region split very much as fourth-century Africa had been by the Donatist controversy, between Monophysites, who were largely based in the country, drawing their strength from local holy men and the Syriac-speaking population, and Chalcedonian clergy, who had been appointed in the cities with the blessing of Constantinople.[81]

The aim of successive emperors since Constantine had been to achieve a unified Christendom within the Roman Empire. More than any other ruler Justinian attempted to make real what was proclaimed in his propaganda, that to be truly Roman was to be a Chalcedonian Christian.[82]

The failure of this imperial mission was sealed by the Monophysite schism in the eastern frontier provinces of Syria and Mesopotamia, which had forged a new religious identity of their own.[83] It is not a coincidence that this should have coincided with the failure of the empire itself to provide protection for these provinces against the invasions of Khusro I. The religious authority of Constantinople over the Near East stretched no further than the now waning might of its armies.

NOTES

1   Various sources suggest that Constantius was strongly inclined to monotheism, and perhaps was even sympathetic to Christianity. This could be true, but all the evidence dates after Constantine's conversion and may be part of a manufactured tradition. His father may at least be considered a Christian sympathizer. He had been conspicuously lenient when the persecution edict was issued. When in 313

the dissident Donatist church leaders in North Africa asked Constantine for an adjudication in their dispute with the bishop of Carthage Caecilian, they referred back to this episode: "O Constantine, most excellent emperor, since you come of just stock, and your father (unlike other emperors) did not persecute the Christians, and Gaul was immune from this crime, we beseech you that your piety may command that we be granted judges from Gaul" (Optatus, *On the Donatist Schism* 1.22).

2   T. D. Barnes, *Constantine and Eusebius* (Harvard, 1981), 266.

3   P. Weiss, "The vision of Constantine," *JRA* 16 (2003), 237–59. Sound historical theories have to be rigorous and productive. Weiss's interpretation convinces not simply because it addresses the numerous individual cruxes of the complex tradition, but also because it throws so much light on Constantine's religious outlook and policies later in his reign.

4   For the eschatological significance of the vision, see O. Nicholson, "Constantine's vision of the Cross," *Vigiliae Christianae* 53 (2000), 309–23.

5   Weiss's very full and detailed theory has been accepted by some, ignored by many, and sporadically contested, e.g. by O. Nicholson, "Constantine's vision of the Cross," *Vigiliae Christianae* 53 (2000), 311 n. 9; D. Potter, *The Roman Empire at Bay* (London, 2004), 354–9, 666 n. 103, 667 n. 119, but without substantive argument.

6   P. Weiss, *JRA* 16 (2003), 254–5.

7   There is a reference to a very similar inscription in Eusebius, *Life of Constantine* I, 40, where the key expression has been changed to "A sign of salvation" referring to the cross; see Hall and Cameron's commentary.

8   T. D. Barnes, "Monotheists all," *Phoenix* (2002), 142–62. See also E. D. Digeser, *The Making of a Christian Empire. Lactantius and Rome* (Cornell, 2000), 6–7, on the widespread acceptance among educated people of a supreme god, albeit they denied the divinity of Jesus. See also E. D. Digeser, "Lactantius, Porphyry and the debate over religious toleration," *JRS* 88 (1998), 129–46.

9   S. Mitchell, "The cult of Theos Hypsistos," in P. Athanassiadi and M. Frede (eds.), *Pagan Monotheism in Late Antiquity* (Oxford, 1999), 81–148, at 94–5.

10 Eusebius *VC* 4.37–9 for Constantia (formerly Maiuma) and Constantina near Gaza in Palestine. *MAMA* 7, 305 for Orcistus in Phrygia.

11 R. Lane Fox, *Pagans and Christians* (London, 1985), 664–7. For a selection of canons from these councils in translation, see J. Stevenson, *A New Eusebius* (London, 1987), 290–6, 313–14. The date of the Council of Elvira is disputed, but fell between 300 and 320. T. D. Barnes, *Constantine and Eusebius* (Harvard, 1981), 54, dates Elvira before 303; R. Lane Fox, *Pagans and Christians*, 664–5, after 312.

12 H. Chadwick, *The Early Church* (London, 1967), 119. R. A. Markus, *The End of Ancient Christianity* (Cambridge, 1990) is the fundamental modern study.

13 T. D. Barnes, "Statistics and the conversion of the Roman aristocracy," *JRS* 85 (1995), 35–47, contesting the conclusions of R. von Haehling, *Die Religionszugehörigkeit der höhen Amsträger des römischen Reiches seit Constantins I. Alleinherrschaft bis zum Ende der Theodosianischen Dynastie* (Bonn, 1978); R. MacMullen, *Christianity and Paganism in the Fourth to Eighth Centuries* (New Haven, 1997), 22, 58, 174 n. 70. See also D. M. Novak, "Constantine and the senate: An early phase in the Christianization of the Roman aristocracy," *Ancient Society* 10 (1979), 271–310; M. R. Salzmann, "How the West was won: The Christianization of the Roman aristocracy in the years after Constantine," in C. Deroux (ed.), *Studies in Latin Literature and Roman History* 6 (Brussels, 1992), 451–79; M. R. Salzmann, *The*

Making of a Christian Aristocracy. Social and Religious Change in the Western Roman Empire (Cambridge Mass., 2002).

14 Roger Tomlin, "Christianity and the late Roman army," in S. Lieu and D. Montserrat, *Constantine. History, Historiography and Legend* (London, 1998), 21–51; R. Haensch, "Le christianisation de l'armée romaine," in *L'Armée romaine de Dioclétien à Valentinien I* (Paris, 2004), 525–31. Army: A. Harnack, *Militia Christi. The Christian Religion and the Military in the First Three Centuries* (trans. Gracie, Philadelphia, 1981); J. Helgeland, "Christians and the Roman army from Marcus Aurelius to Constantine," *Aufstieg und Niedergang der römischen Welt* II.23.1, 723–834. An important inscription for a Christian soldier who left the army as a result of the persecution of Diocletian was published with full commentary by T. Drew-Bear, "Les voyages d'Aurelius Gaius, soldat de Dioclétien," in *La Géographie administrative et politique d'Alexandre à Mahomet. Actes du colloque de Strasbourg Juin 1979* (1981), 93–141.

15 Julian *ep.* 60 and 107 (Bidez); Ammianus 22.11.

16 E. R. Dodds, *The Greeks and the Irrational* (Berkeley, 1951), 283–311; Sarah Iles Johnson, "Theurgy," in G. W. Bowersock et al. (eds.), *Late Antiquity* (Cambridge Mass., 1999), 725–6.

17 R. E. Smith, *Julian's Gods: Religion and Philosophy in the Thought of Julian the Apostate* (London, 1995); P. Athanassiadi, *Julian. An Intellectual Biography* (London, 1992; first published as *Julian and Hellenism* [London, 1981]), P. Athanassiadi-Fowden, "A contribution to Mithraic theology: The emperor Julian's hymn to king Helios," *JTS* 28 (1977), 360–71.

18 G. W. Bowersock, *Julian the Apostate* (London, 1978), 61.

19 *Ep.* 89b (Bidez-Cumont), probably to the high priest Theodorus.

20 O. Nicholson, "The 'Pagan Churches' of Maximin Daia and Julian the Apostate," *Journal of Ecclesiastical History* 45 (1994) 1–10.

21 I accept the arguments of P. van Nuffelen, *Vigiliae Christianae* 55 (2001), 131–50 that the corresponding letter of Julian to Arsacius, high priest of Galatia, is not authentic but a composition probably dating to the 440s. According to this Julian announced that he would set up *xenodocheia*, charitable guest houses, in all the cities where strangers, pagans and non-pagans alike, would have their needs attended to. Grain and wine from the imperial *annona* were to be distributed from these establishments, one-fifth to the poor attendants of the pagan priesthood, the remainder to needy strangers. In this way pagans would be able to match the provisions that both Jews and Christians made for their own communities. However, as van Nuffelen points out, our actual evidence for Christian *xenodocheia* only begins with Basil's foundation at Caesarea in the 370s.

22 J. Geffcken, *The Last Days of Greco-Roman Paganism* (trans. S. MacCormack, Oxford, 1978).

23 T. D. Barnes, *Ammianus* (Cornell, 1998), 155–62.

24 See R. Lane Fox, "Movers and shakers," in A. Smith, *The Philosopher and Society in Late Antiquity* (Swansea, 2005), 19–50 at 25–31.

25 E. A. Clark, "Rewriting early Christian history: Augustine's representation of Monica," in J. Drijvers and J. Watt (eds.), *Portraits of Spiritual Authority in Late Antiquity* (Leiden, 1999), 3–23.

26 W. Frend, "The family of Augustine: A microcosm of religious change in North Africa," in Frend, *Archaeology and History in the Study of Early Christianity* (London, 1988), ch. VIII.

27   C. Lepelley, *Les cités de l'Afrique romaine au bas-empire* I (Paris, 1979) and 2 (Paris, 1981); "Les limites de la christianisation de l'État romain sous Constantin et ses successeurs" in *Christianisme et pouvoirs politiques* (1973), 25–41; "L'aristocratie lettrée paienne. Une menace aux yeux d'Augustin," in *Aspectes de l'Afrique romaine. Les cités, la vie rurale, le christianisme* (Bari, 2001), 397–413; D. Riggs, "Paganism between the cities and countryside of late Roman Africa," in T. S. Burns and J. W. Eadie, *Urban Centres and Rural Contexts in Late Antiquity* (Michigan, 2001), 285–300.

28   R. Lizzi, "Ambrose's contemporaries and the Christianization of northern Italy," *JRS* 80 (1990), 156–77.

29   S. Lepelley, *Les cités de l'Afrique romaine* I (Paris, 1979), 371–408.

30   R. MacMullen, *Corruption and the Decline of Rome* (Yale, 1988), 58–121.

31   N. McLynn, *Ambrose of Milan* (Berkeley, 1994), 170–208.

32   Mitchell, *Anatolia* II (Oxford, 1993), 79–80. N. McLynn, "Imperial churchgoing," in S. Swain and M. Edwards (eds.), *Approaching Late Antiquity* (Oxford, 2004), 235–70 discusses both episodes.

33   P. Brown, *Power and Persuasion in Late Antiquity* (Wisconsin, 1992), 71–158.

34   The persecution is recorded, and probably exaggerated, by Victor of Vita, *History of the Persecution of the Province of Africa in the Time of Gaiseric and Huneric, Kings of the Vandals*, English trans. by J. Moorhead (Liverpool, 1992).

35   T. D. Barnes, *Athanasius and Constantius* (Harvard, 1993), 176–8; H. Chadwick, *The Role of the Christian Bishop in Ancient Society* (Berkeley, 1980), 1–14; G. W. Bowersock, "From emperor to bishop: The self-conscious transformation of political power in the fourth century AD." *Classical Philology* 81 (1986), 298–307.

36   J. Hahn, *Gewalt und Religiöser Konflikt. Studien zu den Auseinandersetzungen zwischen Christen, Heiden und Juden im Osten des Römischen Reiches* (Berlin, 2004), 78–120.

37   S. Mitchell, *Anatolia* II, 73–84.

38   W. Liebeschuetz, *Barbarians and Bishops* (Oxford, 1990), 228–35.

39   Priscus fr. 6.1; E. A. Thompson, *The Huns* (Oxford, 1996), 87–8.

40   J. Harries, *Sidonius Apollinaris and his Age* (Oxford, 1994).

41   W. Klingshirn, "Charity and power: Caesarius of Arles and the ransoming of prisoners in sub-Roman Gaul," *JRS* 75 (1985), 183–203. The practice was especially prevalent in the areas terrorized by the Huns in the mid-fifth century, and also along the eastern frontier.

42   Y. Azèma, *Theodoret de Cyr. Correspondance* I (Paris, 1982), 46–56. Note especially Theodoret, *ep.* 79–81.

43   W. Liebeschuetz, *The Decline and Fall of the Roman City* (Oxford, 2001), 148–55.

44   R. Lim, "Christian triumph and controversy," in G. W. Bowersock et al. (eds.), *Late Antiquity* (Cambridge Mass., 1999), 196–217 at 200–1.

45   S. Mitchell, *Anatolia* II, 96–100.

46   S. Mitchell, *Anatolia* II, 96 n. 372. The Council of Nicaea canon 8 recognized Novatian ordained clergy, but deemed them subordinate to those of the Catholics.

47   T. Urbaincsyk, *Socrates of Constantinople. Historian of Church and State* (Michigan, 1997).

48   J. Stevenson, *A New Eusebius* (London, 1987), 313 no. 272 for translations of the key canons; S. Parvis, "The canons of Ancyra and Caesarea (314): Lebon's thesis revisited," *JTS* 52 (2000), 625–36; D. Potter, *The Roman Empire at Bay* (London, 2004), 412.

49   T. D. Barnes, *Athanasius and Constantius* (Cambridge Mass., 1993), 19–32.

50 H. I. Bell, *Jews and Christians in Egypt* (London, 1924), 53ff.
51 Sozomen, *HE* 2.25.3–8; J. Stevenson, *A New Eusebius* (London, 1987), 362 no. 302.
52 J. Stevenson, *A New Eusebius* (London, 1987), 363 no. 303, letter of Constantine cited by Athanasius, *Apology against the Arians* 36; Socrates, *HE* 1.34; Sozomen, *HE*, 2.28.
53 Socrates, *HE* 1.35.1–4. For background see M. J. Hollerich, "The Alexandrian bishops and the grain trade: Ecclesiastical commerce in late Roman Egypt," *Journal of the Economic and Social History of the Orient* 25 (1982), 187–207.
54 W. H. C. Frend, *The Donatist Church: A Movement of Protest in Roman North Africa* (3rd edn. Oxford, 1985), "Donatists," in G. W. Bowersock et al. (eds.), *Late Antiquity* (Cambridge Mass., 1999), 417–19. M. Edwards, *Optatus: Against the Donatists* (Liverpool, 1997).
55 See the Acts of the Abitinian Martyrs, 20, 881–917, 21, 957–60, in J.-L. Maier, *Le dossier de donatisme* I (Berlin, 1987), 86–9 (trans. D. Potter, *Roman Empire at Bay* [London, 2004], 404–5).
56 See the letters to the bishops and laity of Africa, in Optatus, *On the Schism of the Donatists*, app. 10 and 11; trans. J. Stevenson, *A New Eusebius* (London, 1987), 311–12 no. 270–1.
57 P. Brown, *Augustine of Hippo* (London, 2000), 212–25.
58 A. Demandt, "Die Feldzüge des älteren Theodosios," *Hermes* 100 (1972), 81–113; J. J. Matthews, "Mauretania in Ammianus and the Notitia," in R. Goodburn and P. Bartholomew (eds.), *Aspects of the Notitia Dignitatum* (Oxford, 1976), 157–86.
59 Claudian, *De bello Gildonico*; A. Demandt, *Die Spätantike* (Berlin, 1989), 141–2.
60 I follow the brilliant reconstruction of B. D. Shaw, "African Christianity: Disputes, definitions, Donatists," in *Rulers, Nomads and Christians in Roman North Africa*, ch. XI. See also P. Brown, *Augustine of Hippo* (London, 2000), 330–9.
61 S. Lancel, *Actes de la Conférence de Carthage en 411, tome 1–111* (Sources chrétiennes 1972–5), and *Gesta Collationis Carthagiensis anno 411* (Corpus Christianorum ser. Lat. 149A, 1974).
62 R. Williams, *Arius. Heresy and Tradition* (London, 1987); further bibliography in T. D. Barnes, *Athanasius and Constantius* (Cambridge Mass., 1993), 244–5 n. 50.
63 R. P. C. Hanson, *The Search for the Christian Doctrine of God. The Arian Controversy 318–381 AD* (Edinburgh, 1988) is the fullest recent treatment.
64 Sozomen, 1.5.1–6, trans. J. Stevenson *A New Eusebius* (London, 1987), no. 281; Opitz *Urkunden* 1.2 (Athanasius).
65 Letter of Eusebius, Socrates, *HE* 1.8, trans. J. Stevenson, *A New Eusebius* (London, 1987), 344–7 no. 291.
66 Socrates, 1.26.2ff., trans. J. Stevenson, *A New Eusebius* (London, 1987), 353–4 no. 295.
67 *Apologetica Responsa, Patrologia Latina* 10, 478–546.
68 T. D. Barnes, *Athanasius and Constantius. Theology and Politics in the Constantinian Empire* (Harvard, 1993); more briefly in "The career of Athanasius," *Studia Patristica* 21 (1989), 390–405; W. H. C. Frend, "Athanasius as an Egyptian Christian leader in the fourth century," in *Religion Popular and Unpopular in the Early Christian Centuries* (London, 1976), XVI.
69 Canons of Serdica 3 c; 3 b 6, trans. J. Stevenson, *Creeds, Councils and Controversies. Documents Illustrating the History of the Church AD 337–461* (London, 1989), 14–18 no. 9.

70 Socrates, *HE* 2.22.5 (reduced to the apparatus criticus in the *Griechische Christliche Schriftsteller* edition of Hansen on the grounds that it was a forgery. Even so it certainly stood in Socrates' text. The letter was cited by other fifth-century church historians, see Barnes, *Athanasius*, 89.)

71 For skepticism about Valens' Arianism, see R. M. Errington, "Christian accounts of the religious legislation of Theodosius I," *Klio* 79 (1997), 398–43; in general N. Lenski, *Failure of Empire: Valens and the Roman State in the Fourth Century AD* (Berkeley, 2002).

72 J. F. Matthews, *Western Aristocracies and the Imperial Court AD 364–425* (2nd edn. Oxford, 1990), 107–45.

73 T. D. Barnes, "The consecration of Ulfila," *JTS* 41 (1990), 541–5, argues for 336; P. Heather and J. F. Matthews, *The Goths in the Fourth Century* (Liverpool, 1991), 142–3, prefer 341. See Auxentius of Durostorum, *Letter on the Life and Beliefs of Ulfila (Corpus Christianorum Ecclesiae latinae* 87) (1982), 101–10.

74 This is the historical context of the martyrdom of St Sabas, describing Gothic persecution of their Christian fellows; translation in P. Heather and Matthews, *The Goths in the Fourth Century* (Liverpool, 1991), 111–17; cf. Basil, *ep.* 155, 164, and 165, which imply that details of the martyrdom were in circulation by 372.

75 P. Heather, "The Crossing of the Danube and the Gothic Conversion," *GRBS* 27 (1986), 289–318.

76 E. A. Thompson, "Christianity and the northern barbarians," in A. Momigliano (ed.), *The Conflict between Paganism and Christianity in the Fourth Century* (Oxford, 1963), 63ff.

77 Ambrose, *ep.* 75–7, and *Sermo contra Auxentium*. See N. McLynn, *Ambrose of Milan* (Berkeley, 1994), 158–219; A Lenox-Cunyngham, "The topography of the basilica conflict of AD 385/6," *Historia* 31 (1982), 353–63.

78 W. H. C. Frend, *The Rise of Christianity* (London, 1984), 752–62.

79 The controversy that ensued is described by Evagrius, *HE* 3.15–23.

80 Evagrius, *HE* 3.44; Malalas 16.19.

81 P. R. L. Brown, *The Rise of Western Christendom* (2nd edn. Oxford, 2002), 180–9.

82 G. Greatrex, "Roman identity in the sixth century," in S. Mitchell and G. Greatrex, *Ethnicity and Culture in Late Antiquity* (Wales and London, 2000), 267–92.

83 Garth Fowden, *Empire to Commonwealth* (Princeton, 1993), 100–37.

9

The Political Economy of the Later Roman Empire

Roman culture spread across the empire between the time of Augustus and the tetrarchy. The most striking aspect was an extraordinary level of uniformity which was stamped across the diverse regions from the Euphrates to the Atlantic seaboard. Almost all of the region was now urbanized. Cities and towns were found throughout Asia Minor, the Near East and the Mediterranean basin, across northwest Europe to the Rhine and into Britain, through the Balkans up to and beyond the Danube, and as far south as the desert and mountain fringes of Africa. By modern standards these cities were usually small, only rarely with more than 10,000 inhabitants, but as centers of economic exchange and local administration they were the key to the empire's organizational structure. They also provided places of entertainment and display. Display was particularly important in the political culture of the empire. Local landowners and other members of the wealthy classes showed themselves off and lived their public lives in these urban settings. They were also the focal points where imperial power was demonstrated to the empire's subjects. This resulted in one of the distinctive aspects of the Roman Empire, the culture of local aristocrats, whose wealth and authority was paraded in public buildings, often paid for out of their own funds, in statues for them and members of their families, and in grandiloquent inscriptions which praised their achievements. The emperors' might was also symbolically encapsulated in temples, sanctuaries, and other monuments to the imperial cult, also associated with inscriptions, which were set up in great numbers to commemorate particular events and achievements. The need to display resources and power through intelligible visible symbols was perhaps the most important reason for the development of the epigraphic habit, the culture of inscriptions that is such a telling feature of Roman civilization.

The smaller cities of the Roman Empire could never have existed in isolation. On the one hand, they were symbiotically inseparable from the rural territories which supported them, and where most of the population of the empire lived. Both the normal Latin word, *civitas*, and its Greek equivalent, *polis*, denote not the city in the narrow sense of an urban settlement, but the fusion of town and territory, its inhabitants and institutional structures. They represent an idea or a concept, not simply a place of habitation. On the other hand, cities were interdependent with one another. This was not merely a matter of crude economics, in that they often relied on other places for sustenance and survival, but rather that they thrived as part of a system. Being a city was a mark of status, and status is a worthless commodity without the opportunity for comparison. A city in isolation would lose most of its raison d'être.

The security of the empire was guaranteed by military power. During the late empire military pressures from external enemies and from civil war increased seriously. As a result military aspects of the empire became more apparent. The distinction between peaceful provinces and narrow, militarized, frontier zones, which had been the ideal of the so-called golden age of the second century, now gave way in the third century to a picture in which the difference between militarized and civilian zones, between soldier and civilian, and indeed between war and peace was blurred.

There were however limits to Roman military presence. Soldiers and the infrastructure necessary to support them could only be deployed on the basis of transport and communication systems. Effective imperial power was strictly determined by the network of road and sea communications which the Roman state had created and maintained. Paved roads linked the various regions around the Mediterranean with one another and criss-crossed provinces in networks that became denser and more pervasive as the empire evolved. Roads made it possible to move troops, officials, and administrators over long distances as swiftly as the conditions of a pre-mechanized age allowed. In this way rapid military deployment, the most important instrument of conquest in the hands of great generals such as Alexander, Pompey, or Julius Caesar, could be transformed into a routine of empire. This was never more evident than in the third and fourth centuries, a great age of road building,[1] when troops and generals were ceaselessly shuttled to confront trouble between the eastern and northern frontiers, or when rivals for power mobilized and marched their armies across the length of the empire to achieve their purposes.

Roads, however, were exploited to serve the empire in other ways. Provincial networks underpinned and sustained the urban settlement pattern. They ensured that towns were not isolated from one another and thus the city-based culture thrived. They also provided access to isolated rural areas and they were the conduits along which rural products could be moved into towns, or collected as a form of taxation and used to support armies. All major Roman roads were furnished with a regular system of way stations (*mansiones*, *mutationes*), where official road users could stay, where mounts could be changed, and wagons maintained. Supplying means of transport for official use was one of the most important services which the Roman state expected of its subjects. Cities were required to provide pack and draft animals, wagons, and other support for military and official traffic passing through their territory. This operated on a relay system, which was one of the keys to imperial power. Travelers with authorizing documents (which were known in the late empire as *evectiones*), and (it must be said) a good many others without authorization, were able to requisition local mounts and draught animals until they reached the boundaries of city territories. At this point the burden and responsibility passed to the next city. In a literal sense, the horse power supplied by the cities ensured that the roads of the empire could be used to their full potential.

The Roman Empire saw a prodigious increase in inter-regional mobility. This is confirmed by plentiful evidence from archaeology, epigraphy, and written sources for natives of one region moving to distant parts of the empire. This movement of peoples also contributed to a homogenization of imperial culture. However, the overland transport of products, especially bulky goods, was much more problematic. Local traffic, from farms and villages to the nearby town or market center will certainly have been intense, but the costs of land transport were high, and in practical terms simply unfeasible. It has been well put that a yoke of horses or oxen pulling a wagon loaded with grain would be likely to have eaten the load (or its equivalent) before they had traveled a hundred miles. Accordingly, overland inter-regional trade by private merchants was largely confined to non-bulky, high-value commodities. The Roman state was able to solve this problem through its power to requisition transport from local communities and create the relay system. This was beyond the capacity of even the wealthiest private producers and merchants.

Transport by sea was as important as land communication, and the Roman Empire witnessed an extraordinary explosion of mercantile activity in the Mediterranean. Seafaring was a dangerous activity, especially during the winter, and this confined the Mediterranean sailing season to the months between March and October. But the advantages of sea transport were overwhelming. Bulky goods could be moved over long distances in cargo vessels at costs that were a fraction of the real price of land transport; the wind may have been dangerous, but it did not have the appetite of draught animals. Marine traffic shaped the appearance of the Roman world. Coastal cities, with good harbors, were not dependent on a small hinterland for their food supply, but could import goods, at least potentially, from the entire Mediterranean and Black Sea region. In consequence settlements on the coast could grow to be much larger than those of the interior. The most populous cities of the Mediterranean world in antiquity – Rome, Constantinople, Carthage, Alexandria, Antioch, and Ephesus – were all directly on the coast or could be reached by a short riverine connection from their harbors. The Roman state organized sea transport as it had overland traffic, not by creating relays but by deals and contracts with large naval contractors. Above all, the enormous population of Rome itself had to be supplied with imported food; the harvests of the Nile Valley, brought by transport ships from Alexandria, and of the grain fields of North Africa, imported from Carthage. Oil came from Libya, Tunisia, and Southern Spain. The mercantile infrastructure needed to feed Rome had a tremendous impact on the coastal regions of western Italy. Ostia, the harbor town at the mouth of the Tiber, was developed into the Rotterdam of the ancient world, with huge harbor works built by the early emperors, especially Trajan. A major secondary unloading point for the transports from Alexandria and the eastern Mediterranean was Puteoli in the Bay of Naples, now linked by a canal and coasting network to Rome. Docks, harbors, granaries, and storage facilities were built at intermediate points along the long-distance sea routes. In the late empire, the sea routes to Rome were eclipsed by comparable networks for the supply of Constantinople, which was also sustained by foodstuffs brought by the imperial *annona* system, responsible for supplying a significant part of its population with grain, wine, oil, and other products.

Private merchants at sea did not face the practical constraints which restricted overland trade, and there was an enormous growth in traffic. The melancholy reflection of this is the high proportion of Roman wrecks that have been found in the Mediterranean compared to those of earlier or later periods. These, however, are a crucial boon to the study of the Roman trading economy. Each preserved and excavated wreck is effectively a time capsule, preserving an atomized fragment of the Roman economic system at the moment when disaster struck. Most merchant ships carried amphoras, closely packed below the decks, containing grain, olive oil, wine, fish sauce, and other staple commodities. The study of amphoras, taken together with the wrecks where many of them have been discovered, is the lynch-pin of archaeological investigation of the Roman economy. It is also important to recognize the importance of inland water transport, both along large navigable rivers (most notably on the great rivers of Gaul and on the Po in northern Italy) and along canal systems which began to be built in all parts of the empire from Britain to Egypt and Asia Minor.

The creation of the road system and the intensification of maritime trade also reflected technological advances in the building of ships, harbors, lifting devices, and warehouses, and in the design and mass production of carts and wagons. The most critical development of the Roman Empire was the harnessing of water power to generate the energy needed for grain mills and in the mining industry. The scale and impact of technological advances in classical antiquity have been consistently underemphasized until recently in modern scholarship. The reason for this is that the most familiar literary sources, on which scholarly work has been mainly based, were produced by members of the educated elite of the classical world, who rarely took any notice of the march of technology, a subject that fell beneath the level of their gaze. On the other hand a considerable body of technical literature survives from antiquity, and this is now supplemented by an abundance of archaeological evidence for technological developments. The sophisticated harnessing of water power underpinned large scale mining and ore-processing enterprises (especially in Spain in the first and second centuries) and quasi-industrial processes such as the cutting of marble blocks and large timbers with mechanical saws, as well as grain milling.[2] Mining for precious metals remained an important preoccupation of the late Roman economy, although it is evident that the disruption caused by the barbarian invasions and occupation of the Spanish provinces brought an end to large-scale mining, and probably contributed very substantially to the impoverishment of the western empire.[3] In the eastern empire, by contrast, there was a growing awareness in the upper levels of society of the importance of practical technologies and their value both in economic and military contexts. This is illustrated strikingly by the sustained interest shown by Procopius in feats of engineering, mechanical ingenuity, and technological innovation, which has even led a scholar to suggest, implausibly, that his educational background and training might have been that of an engineer not a lawyer.[4]

The Roman Empire was also united by a uniform monetary system. With only marginal exceptions all the precious metal coinage which circulated in the Roman Empire was produced under Roman supervision to a Roman standard. In the early empire the silver denarius was the principle denomination. Roman silver coin was minted at regional centers across the empire, from Lyon in Gaul to Alexandria in Egypt, and probably mostly entered into circulation in the form of soldiers' pay. Gold was minted much more sparsely, mostly for special occasions. A significant proportion of Roman gold coin was distributed in the form of gifts or subsidies to barbarian kings and chieftains outside the empire, and was used as a diplomatic tool in maintaining the security of the frontiers. Bronze coin in the western part of the empire was also an imperial monopoly after the first century AD, but the Greek cities of the East continued to enjoy the privilege of issuing their own bronze coinage for local needs, and local bronze coin was interchangeable with centrally minted Roman silver at fixed rates. The common coinage and monetary system made a major contribution to cultural uniformity, and this was reinforced by the use of coin legends. Almost every coin, of whatever denomination, carried the portrait, name, and titles of a living member of the imperial family, usually the emperor himself, on one side, and an emblem, again identified by a written legend, chosen to project a significant feature of imperial ideology on the other. As a monetary system Roman imperial coinage was more extensive geographically, and lasted for a longer period, than any other in world history.

The existence of a single, empire-wide monetary system does not necessarily imply that the empire as a whole acted as a single economic unit. Between northwest Europe and the Middle East there is some evidence, although it is difficult to measure and evaluate, of distinct economic zones, which prospered or faltered according to local conditions. The Roman Empire was large and complex, and there were certainly major regional variations. However, a significant measure of economic unity was certainly created by universal mechanisms such as tax, interregional trade, and the production and consumption of goods, which the state required to provision its armies and the populations of its capital cities.

All the features of the Roman Empire which have been discussed so far are more or less identifiable on the basis of visible – indeed sometimes very conspicuous – material evidence. Other defining institutions and characteristics have to be inferred less directly. Rural settlements were much less conspicuous than the cities. To an extent the pattern of villages and other types of rural community represents the continuation of regional, vernacular traditions in areas that came under Roman control. These often preserved native traditions and styles of building, although they were open to Roman architectural influence and betray the impact of empire in other ways. Roman rule brought significant changes to the patterns of land ownership, including the growth of rural estates, and new types of land exploitation. These had a lasting impact on provincial society. The stable conditions of the empire encouraged the consolidation of landownership and a trend towards the emergence of large or middle-sized estates. This reinforced the authority of the rich in the provinces and enabled them to pass their wealth and resources, in the form of land, to their heirs. The agrarian landholdings of elite and middle-ranking families throughout the Roman provinces underpinned the flourishing life of the cities. They also helped to create a stable conservative and conformist mentality in the provincial aristocracies. The emperors themselves acquired a great deal of property, confiscated from their enemies or inherited from their would-be friends, especially in the wealthiest regions of the empire such as Spain, Italy, Africa, Asia Minor, and Egypt. Imperial estates, which were generally divided up and leased out to long-term tenants, played a large part in the supply system of the armies and the imperial capital cities. Wealthy landowners, and above all the emperors, supervised their estates through agents, who were often freed ex-slaves or members of freedmen families.

Taxation was another universal feature of the Roman Empire whose effects are almost invisible. The main exception to this generalization is in Egypt, where innumerable papyri have been recovered which document the bureaucratic workings of imperial administration, including tax collection, precisely at the point where it affected the lives of individuals. However, because our main evidence for how taxation worked comes at this hum-drum level, it is difficult to reconstruct the big picture of taxation policy. In broad terms three types of taxes may be identified. Taxes were levied on individuals and the land they owned, and the levies made on heads (*capita*) and on acreage (*iugera*) were consolidated and rationalized into a single system at the beginning of the late Roman period under Diocletian, the system of *iugatio-capitatio*. The rates of the poll and land tax were fixed, not progressive, so they weighed more heavily on the poor than the rich. Taxes were also placed on the movement of goods, both at the frontiers of the empire and on provincial boundaries (*portoria*). Thus the growing trade and exchange of the Roman Empire yielded a significant cut for the state. Finally taxes were levied on transactions with monetary value: on inheritances, on the freeing of slaves, and on the sales of particular types of goods. Rates of payment varied to a small degree from one part of the empire to another, reflecting local traditions, but the essential precondition for Roman taxes as a whole was the existence of universal bureaucratic systems for assessing and collecting them. It was a major achievement of the Roman Empire, and one of defining characteristics that distinguished it from the barbarian kingdoms in the West, that it translated the practices of previous conquerors, who demanded tribute by right of conquest from their subjects, into permanent, institutionalized tax levies, which did more than anything to define the relationships of subjects to the political system which ruled and protected them.

The preceding pages have been designed to sketch in the broadest terms the social and economic conditions in the provinces under the Roman Empire. The emphasis has deliberately been placed on universal features which helped to create economic and cultural unity and can accordingly be identified as crucial defining elements of empire. It is now necessary to survey the cities and provinces of the empire on a regional basis. One purpose is to provide some idea of what the later Roman Empire looked like in material terms. Another is to identify variations within the overall pattern. The survey begins with the largest cities, whose evolution and history was directly determined by the political economy of the later empire. In the last generation most innovative work on the Roman Empire has tended to look away from the capitals to the provinces, and interpret the workings of the empire by starting at the peripheries. However, the old and new imperial capitals were by far the largest social units in the empire and in economic and social terms imposed patterns in the movement of goods which can be studied throughout and beyond the Mediterranean world.

Rome

Rome, by virtue of its name and historical traditions, was the center of the Roman world. By the time of Diocletian, Rome had long since ceased to be the main focal point of political and military power in the empire, but the Senate, "the better part of the human race" (Symmachus, *Rel.* VI.1), numbering some 600 members, including the richest landowning families of the western empire, retained high prestige. The senators' public role was largely ceremonial. The old republican offices of quaestor, praetor, and suffect consul were now taken by wealthy men in the early stages of a public career, and were marked not by administrative or judicial duties but by the obligation to pay for shows and spectacles to entertain the Roman people and impress one another with their wealth and style. The practice of the late fourth and early fifth centuries is described by Olympiodorus:

> Many of the Roman households received an income of 4000 pounds of gold per year from their properties, not including grain, wine and other produce which, if sold, would have amounted to one-third of the income in gold. The income of the households at Rome of the second class was 1000 or 1500 pounds of gold. When Probus, the son of Olybrius, celebrated his praetorship during the reign of the usurper John [423–5], he spent 1200 pounds of gold. Before the capture of Rome, Symmachus the orator, a senator of middling wealth, spent 2000 pounds when his son Symmachus celebrated his praetorship. Maximus, one of the wealthy men, spent 4000 pounds on his son's praetorship. The praetors celebrated their festivals for seven days. (Olympiodorus fr. 41.2, trans. Blockley)

Many members of the Senate were prodigiously wealthy, deriving their riches from land holdings in Italy and the other western provinces. They built huge villas in and around the city. Olympiodorus wrote that the great houses of Rome in his day were as large as good-sized cities, each containing its own race course, fora, temples, fountains, and various bath houses (Olympiodorus fr. 41.1). A century later Theoderic commended the wealthy Symmachus for the magnificence and good taste of his suburban villa, which "created public works of a sort in your own private dwelling," and on the strength of this commissioned him to supervise repair work on Pompey's theater (Cassiodorus, *Var.* 4.51). Both passages imply the growing tendency in late antiquity for the wealthy to spend lavishly on their private properties.

Diocletian was aware of the continuing importance of the Senate, and rebuilt the Curia, its meeting place. The building still stands in the Roman forum in the form that it then took. However, the tetrarchs spent little time in the city except in November 303, when Diocletian, prematurely, arrived to celebrate the twentieth anniversary of his accession to power. It is revealing that he left the city in haste, before the year was out, unable, according to Lactantius, to tolerate the free spirit of the Roman people (Lactantius, *On the Deaths of the Persecutors* 17.1–2). Similar antagonism is implicit in Ammianus' account of Constantius' visit in 357 (Ammianus 16.10). The great cities of the empire were the only places where emperors encountered a great mass of their ordinary subjects, and these meetings were fraught with tension and significance. The tenor of an imperial reign could be defined in such moments, and the despotic Diocletian chose to avoid a confrontation with a free-speaking *plebs*. Lactantius, however, does not mention another initiative of Diocletian in Rome which was equally representative of an emperor's relations with the people. In 305, the year of their abdication, the tetrarchs completed the *Thermae Diocletianae*, a monstrous bathing complex, with almost double the capacity of the Baths of Caracalla, capable of holding 3,000 bathers at a time, dedicating the building "to their own Roman people" (*ILS* 646).

Diocletian himself constructed another major monument in the Forum to celebrate his *vicennalia*, an ensemble of five columns erected next to the temple of Concord. Four of these supported statues of the tetrarchs, and were grouped behind a central column with a statue of Jupiter. This presented the religious ideas of the tetrarchy at the center of the empire. At the same time Diocletian also organized the celebration of the secular games, an event of major religious significance previously staged by the Severans in 204.

Ammianus called Rome the temple of the whole world (17.4), and implied that the Capitol remained the greatest pagan sanctuary of the empire (26.16.12), while Ausonius hailed it as the house of the gods (Ausonius XI.1). It was the symbolic center of the struggle between paganism and Christianity in the fourth century.[5] Senators, like the rest of the population, were divided in their religious allegiances, but leading senators can be identified as the main champions of paganism up till the last years of the fourth century.

Between 300 and 450 only one would-be emperor resided in Rome, Maxentius, son of Maximianus, who claimed the title of Augustus between 306 and his defeat by Constantine in 312. He restored Hadrian's temple of Venus and Roma, which had been destroyed by fire, and built the huge brick basilica, which stands at the east end of the forum and must have been designed as the setting for his public appearances as judge and ruler. The basilica was later dedicated by the Senate to Constantine, and the famous colossal head of Constantine, the best known of his portraits, was found there, implying that the building continued to serve a similar function after Maxentius' death (Aur. Victor, *Caes.* 40.26). As imperial visits to Rome became less frequent, the building may have been taken over as a ceremonial meeting hall and courtroom by the city prefect.[6] The best comparison for this building is the equally grandiose basilica, perfectly intact today, which was constructed by Constantine at the northern Gallic capital of Trier.

Constantine's most famous construction in Rome was the famous arch (see above, chapter 5). More significant in the long term were his church foundations. Work began on St John Lateran in the weeks following the victory of the Milvian bridge in autumn 312. The basilica was built on the demolished foundations of the barracks that had been occupied by Maxentius' cavalry bodyguard. Constantine's mother Helena is associated with another major basilica, the church now called S. Croce in Gerusalemme, which was attached to a palace where she now resided. Above all, Constantine ordered the building of a great church dedicated to St Peter, on the Vatican hill. The apostle's tomb had been identified and venerated in the catacombs at this site, but construction was no simple matter. It was necessary to build massive substructures, effectively reversing the direction of the hill slope, to achieve the correct orientation for the church. The emperor mastered and reconfigured the terrain to leave a permanent mark on the city's topography. The Church of the Lateran appears to have been the seat of the bishop of Rome, but it was the tomb and basilica of St Peter, combined with its location in the greatest city of the Mediterranean, that conveyed special authority on the leaders of the Roman Church. The bishop of Rome had no lasting rivals in the western empire, and was recognized as the senior patriarch by the Council of Constantinople in 381. After the fall of the last western emperor in 476 the Pope also became effectively the senior secular authority in the western Roman Empire.

None of Constantine's imperial successors matched these efforts. Constantius II paid a famous visit in 357, which has been immortalized in some of the best known paragraphs of Ammianus' history, written in Rome in the 390s.

> When he came to the Forum of Trajan, a creation which in my view has no like under the cope of heaven and which even the gods themselves must agree to admire, Constantius stood transfixed with astonishment, surveying the gigantic fabric around him; its grandeur defies description and can never again be approached by mortal men. So he abandoned all hope of attempting anything like it, and declared that he would and could imitate simply Trajan's horse, which stands in the middle of the court with the emperor on its back. Prince Hormisdas . . . remarked with oriental subtlety: "First, majesty, you must have a similar stable built, if you can. The horse you propose to fashion should have as much space to range in as this one which we can see." (Ammianus 16.10, trans. Hamilton)

In the event Constantius marked his visit by bringing to Rome an obelisk, which had been intended for the city by his father Constantine. This was one of several that the city acquired during late antiquity (Ammianus 17.4; *ILS* 736).[7]

The city, and especially the forum, continued to be a focus for the public commemoration of emperors and senators. Senatorial wealth was used to fund public entertainments in the Circus Maximus and the Colosseum, which was restored by Theodosius I. However, secular public building on a grand scale virtually ceased after the fourth century. The material damage inflicted by Alaric's Goths in 410 was repaired, but the psychological blow had a lasting effect. We should not, however, underestimate the amount of building that must have continued in the fifth-century city. The *Notitia Urbis* catalogues the buildings of the city, including 462 living quarters, 46,602 apartment buildings, 254 bakeries, 19 aqueducts, 11 major *thermae*, and 856 small bath houses. The effort required to service Rome's enormous population still dwarfed that of any other city of the empire. Looking back in the 530s, Cassiodorus reflected precisely on these conditions, which had changed by his own day:

> It is evident how great was the population of the city of Rome, seeing that it was fed with supplies furnished even by far off regions, and that this imported abundance was reserved for it, while the surrounding provinces sufficed to feed only the resident strangers. For how could a people that ruled the world be small in

number? For the great extent of the walls bears witness to the throngs of citizens, as do the swollen capacity of the places of entertainment, the wonderful size of the baths, and that great number of water mills which was clearly provided especially for the food supply. (Cassiodorus, *Var.* 11.39, trans. Barnish)

The pattern of public construction changed drastically in the fifth and sixth centuries. Virtually all new buildings were now churches, oratories, and, especially in the sixth century, monastic foundations. Fourth-century Rome contained relatively few Christian foundations. Apart from the great Constantinian basilicas and the huge extra-mural church of Saint Paul on the road to Ostia, the churches were inconspicuous and made no attempt to rival pagan religious architecture. The pattern then changed. Only two major basilicas, including the present church of S. Maria Maggiore, were built in the fifth, and only one, the Church of the Holy Apostles, in the mid-sixth century, probably dedicated by Justinian's general Narses after the final defeat of the Ostrogoths in the 550s. On the other hand, parish churches during this period spread to all parts of the city and were clearly marked by external porticos and courtyards. They thus acquired the characteristic appearance of public buildings, but their distribution through the wards of the city represents a change in their social function. They served Rome's neighborhoods, as the magnetic power of the civic center began to fade.

Rome suffered another critical blow when it was attacked and plundered by the Vandals under Huneric in 455. The city enjoyed a revival in political terms during the third quarter of the fifth century, as it became the focus of Ricimer's attempts to restore a stable western empire, and it benefited notably from the stability created by the Ostrogoth Theoderic's long reign from 483 to 526. Famously he visited the city in person in 500 in a manner appropriate to an emperor:

In celebration of his *tricennalia* he entered the palace in a triumphal procession among the people, staging circus games for the Romans. He made an annual grant to the Roman people and the poor of 120,000 *modii* of grain, and gave orders that each year two hundred pounds of gold should be taken from the wine tax and spent on restoring the palace or reconstructing the city walls. (*Anon. Val.* 2, 67)

The situation faced by Theoderic also illustrates the transformation that had overtaken the city. Much of the interior of the city was no longer inhabited, as Rome's population began to decrease. A conservative estimate puts the number of inhabitants in the fourth century at over 500,000. By the mid-sixth century the figure was not more than a tenth of this. Procopius indicates that the inhabitants and defenders were unable to man the nineteen-kilometer wall circuit during the long sieges of Rome in 537–8 and 546. Warfare and above all the plague must have hit the city hard in the 530s and 540s, but the root of Rome's decline lay in the collapse of its food supply, the life support system on which it had depended for over five hundred years. The city had always been supplied by a diversity of sources in Italy and overseas. Some of this was distributed without charge to free urban householders, but most was put on the market for sale at controlled prices. As in all ancient cities there was immense distress if the grain supply was interrupted, and shortages were greeted by violent rioting. The main staple, grain, was imported from Egypt, Africa, and Sicily. After the foundation of Constantinople Egyptian grain was diverted to the eastern capital, leaving Rome dependent on western sources. A critical moment came in 439 when the Vandals seized Carthage, the point of export for most of the African grain, and used their sea power to menace shipping out of Sicily. The vital change was not a direct embargo on shipping out of Carthage. There is no evidence that the Vandals, who set up a highly effective state in their new African environment, wished to curtail normal economic activity, but they were able to use their control of Carthage and their maritime strength as powerful bargaining weapons in dealing with the western empire. Moreover they cut off the African tax revenues, in kind as well as cash, to Rome. The loss of the African *annona*, combined with growing insecurity in the Mediterranean, will have driven up prices as it reduced Rome's supply. The situation was naturally compounded with the final fall of the western empire in 476. The ability of the city of Rome to feed its enormous population in earlier centuries had depended directly on its role as an imperial city which could impose tax demands on its subjects. Now it had to pay for what it consumed. The population accordingly shrunk to a level much closer to that of other larger cities of the later empire.

Constantinople

Constantinople possessed the most extraordinary natural advantages of any city in the ancient world. It was founded on a peninsula at the entrance to the Bosporus, which linked the Sea of Marmara with the Black Sea, and was protected on two sides by water and on the third by a narrow isthmus, which could easily be fortified. The sheltered inlet of the Golden Horn was a huge, and defensible, natural harbor. This was the point where all the land routes from Europe and Asia converged, uniting the eastern and western parts of the empire.

The strategic importance of the site was revealed by the events of the civil war between Constantine and Licinius, when the latter's fleet was defeated at the battle of Chrysopolis (Scutari). The victor chose to re-found the previously modest Roman city of Byzantium. Building began at the end of 324 and the foundation dedication was celebrated in the emperor's presence on May 11, 330. It is not clear what role Constantine intended for his new city. Having now achieved his aspiration to be sole ruler of the empire he could hardly envisage replacing Rome as its capital, and he had made a point of returning there to celebrate his own *vicennalia* in 326. Constantinople, rather, was modeled on the other imperial cities that had emerged during the tetrarchic period, comparable to but outshining Trier, Antioch, and nearby Nicomedia.[8]

Constantine left intact the old acropolis of Byzantium, containing the main pagan temples, which only lost their sacral character in the time of Theodosius I. The imperial palace, where the ruler would conduct business in seclusion, and the hippodrome, where his people could gather for racing and other spectacles, and to acclaim the emperor on his public appearances, also both lay within the earlier city limits. The imperial household moved into its new quarters and the future emperor Julian was born in the palace two years after Constantinople had been founded. The imperial residence probably originally took a form similar to Diocletian's palace at Split, or the imperial complex built by Galerius at Gamzigrad, Felix Romuliana, in modern Bulgaria (see below, chapter 10), but the building was enlarged by his successors until it extended south to the sea walls facing the Propontis. The hippodrome, with seating for 80,000 spectators, was an enlargement of a pre-existing stadium. The loggia for the imperial family and high officials was directly accessible from the palace and looked across the race track to the seating occupied by the circus partisans.[9] Adjoining the hippodrome on the north were two public buildings also incorporated from the former Roman city, the Baths of Zeuxippos, and a square with colonnades on four sides leading to a meeting hall for the city's Senate (later to be known as the Augustaeum).

Constantine now extended the city westwards. The *Mesê*, a broad colonnaded street, ran up the middle of the peninsula. Along this was placed the omphalos, an oval piazza, and at its center a porphyry column which carried a statue of the emperor, rendered in the guise of Apollo wearing a radiate crown. It is important to recognize that Constantine did not overwhelm his city with ecclesiastical foundations. The church historians say that he built a church for St Eirene (Socrates, *HE* 1.16), an extra-mural basilica for the local martyr St Mocius (Sozomen 8.17.5), and a church for St Acacius (Socrates, *HE* 6.23). The first church of St Sophia was completed by Constantius II. Eusebius naturally asserted that he created a city that was purged of pagan idol worship (*VC* 3.47), but Zosimus emphasized that he preserved a temple of the Dioscuri by the hippodrome and created sanctuaries for Rhea and for the Tyche of the Romans (Zosimus 2.30–31). Much the most important of Constantine's religious foundations was the shrine of the Holy Apostles (located on the site of the Ottoman Fatih mosque), which was designed and built towards the end of his life as his mausoleum. Here he was entombed at the center of a circular or cruciform building, elaborately decorated with golden ceiling coffers, in the midst of twelve cenotaphs, which symbolized the tombs of the apostles themselves (Eusebius, *VC* 4.58–60).

Constantine constructed new fortifications enclosing the peninsula about three kilometers west of the old walls of Byzantium and enlarged the area for building by extending the land mass into the sea both on the side of the Golden Horn and on the Sea of Marmara. A street grid was established to accommodate new settlers, and senators who had supported the emperor began to construct their own houses. Main streets ran north to docks on the Golden Horn and south to the Propontic shore. Two large harbors were built here, the first by Julian, the second by Theodosius. The *Mesê* continued to another intersection marked by a monument popularly known as the Philadelphion, a statue group which was supposed to depict the sons of Constantine embracing one another. The statue in question appears to be none other than the famous porphyry group depicting the four tetrarchs, probably originally from Nicomedia, which was taken to Venice by the crusaders after the sack of Constantinople in 1204 (Plate 3.1).[10] The public places of the city were adorned with statues and other monuments collected from cities in the eastern empire.

This was the template for the development of the New Rome. Provisions were made immediately to supply the city with tax grain from Egypt. According to the *Notitia* of about 425, the city had four large warehouses for storing provisions close to the Prosphorion harbor at Sirkeci on the Golden Horn, and two others close to the harbors on the Propontic side (*Notitia Urbis Constantinopolitanae*; Zosimus 3.11). In all the sources attest as many as twenty-one public granaries in the city. It has been estimated that four kilometers of quayside would have been needed to provide docking for the grain ships during the sailing season.

Securing the city's water supply was a major issue. Themistius, in a panegyric for Valens written in 376, evokes the image of a city dying of thirst before the emperor constructed an aqueduct over 1,000 stades (over 180 kilometers) in length, bringing the water to the city from the nymphs of Thrace (*Or.* 13, 167d). This enormous project multiplied by a factor of ten the amount of water available from springs close to the city. The water was stored in huge rectangular cisterns built on the hills, from which it could be distributed as required to the rest of the city. Large new cisterns were built in 421, in 459, during the reign of Anastasius, under Justinian in the 530s, and under Phocas in 609, attesting the increase in the city's population and the growth of its needs. Smaller underground cisterns were built for private houses.[11] The famous arches attributed to Valens, which are a conspicuous feature of Istanbul today, may however be part of the earlier Hadrianic system built for Byzantium. Constantius had begun to construct imperial baths, the *Thermae Constantianae*, in 345, but these were not finished until 427, and evidently lacked a water supply at least until Valens' day.

The public areas of the city were greatly expanded in the late fourth and early fifth centuries. Theodosius began work in 393 on a new civic center, the Forum Tauri, at Beyazit, where he erected a column which was a faithful copy of the Roman column of Trajan, Theodosius's great Spanish predecessor. A mounted statue of Theodosius set up in the same square deliberately evoked comparison with the bronze equestrian figure of Trajan at Rome. Theodosius thus realized in Constantinople the ambition that Constantius had conceived in 357 on his visit to Rome. In contrast to Rome, marble was readily available at Constantinople, brought from the quarries of Proconnesus in the Propontis, where architectural elements (column shafts, capitals, and gable pieces in particular) were prefabricated before being shipped to the building sites of the

Plate 9.1 The Golden Gate at Constantinople, constructed as a triumphal arch for Theodosius I, c. 390, and later incorporated into the fortifications of Theodosius II (S. Mitchell)

capital. The most imposing pieces to be identified are gigantic column drums intended for the Forum Tauri.[12]

The most representative monument of Theodosian Constantinople was the obelisk and its sculpted and inscribed base, probably set up in 391/2, which still stands in the spina of the hippodrome. The inscriptions displayed Greek and Latin verses which celebrated both the achievement of raising the obelisk to its new position (the task had been supervised by the prefect of the city Proclus) and Theodosius' defeat of the usurper Magnus Maximus (*ILS* 821). The reliefs are a visual realization of the power structure of the late Roman state and are a key to understanding the political relationship between the emperor and his subjects (Plate 9.1; see above, chapter 5).

The most important development of the early fifth century was the completion of new fortifications in 413, the walls built by Theodosius II's praetorian prefect Anthemius and rebuilt after an earthquake in 447.[13] Attackers were confronted by a twenty-meter wide moat, an outer wall five meters high, reinforced with circular and square towers, and behind them the main rampart, twelve meters high, also reinforced by massive towers (Plate 9.2). The towers served as barracks for the standing army in the city (*CTh.* 7.8.13). Constantius had started to build the sea walls, but these were reinforced and completed in the 440s, to meet the naval threat of the Vandals.

Plate 9.2   The Theodosian Walls of Constantinople (DAI Istanbul)

The fortifications of Constantinople were not breached until its fall to the crusaders in 1204.[14] The Theodosian walls increased the fortified area of the city by about 40 percent. It appears that this area was not largely devoted to new housing, but contained large villas, monasteries, churches, and several large cisterns. The wall of Constantine remained intact, dividing the city into an urban and a suburban region, both secured from attack. Further important protection was provided by the fifty-kilometer long ditch and land wall which was built across the Thracian peninsula from the south coast east of Selymbria (Silvri) to the Black Sea, and reinforced by a series of small garrison forts (see above, chapter 4).

As at Rome, the sharp growth in the number of churches in the city occurred not in the fourth but in the fifth and sixth centuries. During the ostentatiously pious regime of Theodosius II and Pulcheria, the *Notitia Urbis* lists fourteen churches, including the two earliest that survive today, the Church of the Theotokos at Chalkoprateia, the copper market west of St Sophia, built by Pulcheria, and the Church of St John Studios, near the new Theodosian walls. The biggest increase occurred in the time of Justinian. Procopius' *Buildings* describes thirty-four new foundations by the emperor himself, a list headed by the great surviving structures of St Eirene and St Sophia. The rapid expansion of church building is not only to be explained by the liturgical needs of the growing population, but by the ambitions of wealthy families, including the emperor's, to display their power by ostentatious ecclesiastical foundations.

The clearest example of this rivalry is provided by the Church of St Polyeuctus, built between the second and third hills of the city by Anicia Juliana, the matriarch of one of the wealthiest senatorial clans of Constantinople. The dimensions and design of her church deliberately matched the Old Testament blueprint for the Temple of Solomon at Jerusalem and the surviving dedicatory poem for the building asserted her claim to be matched as a builder with the emperors Constantine and Theodosius (*Anth. Pal.* 1.10).[15] Justinian rose precisely to this challenge in building his own greatest church, St Sophia, above the ruins that had been burnt to the ground in the Nika riot of 532. St Sophia, completed between 532 and 537, was the greatest building of the Justinianic period, the realization in stone and mortar of the emperor's personal sense of religious destiny. The achievement of Justinian and his architects is measured in Procopius' description of the building's spiritual impact:

> Whenever anyone enters this church to pray, he understands at once that it is not by any human power or skill, but by the influence of God, that this work has been so finely turned. And so his mind is lifted up toward God and exalted, feeling that He cannot be far away, but must especially love to dwell in this place which He has chosen. (Procopius, *Buildings* I, 1.61)

The initial design for the huge dome was too precarious, and the structure collapsed in an earthquake of 557 (Agathias V, 3–9), but the will to complete the project remained indomitable, even after the death of its two architects, Anthemius of Tralles and Isidore of Miletus. Reconstruction was completed in 562. Two contemporary accounts of the building survive, a lengthy description in Procopius' buildings (Procopius, *Buildings* I, 67–78), and a poem by Paul Silentiarius, written after the re-dedication of the great church in 562.[16]

Constantinople, like Rome, had an impact on the empire that extended far beyond its walls. It acted as a powerful magnet to settlers. Rich senators accompanied Constantine at the foundation, and there was continuous immigration by members of the ruling class, notably the Spanish clique that arrived in the wake of Theodosius I.[17] The poor inhabitants came in vast numbers for different reasons, attracted by the prospects of employment and a guaranteed food supply. Constantine made initial provision for the state *annona* to feed 80,000 inhabitants with grain brought from Alexandria. By the time of Justinian, the number of recipients may have reached 600,000.[18] As at Rome, the ultimate responsibility for distributing provisions lay with the city prefect. Although the practice had its origins in the distribution of free grain to citizens at Rome in the late republic, the creation of universal Roman citizenship had transformed the legal basis for the organization, and the state *annona* of the late empire was transformed into a service designed to support the proletariat of large cities. *Annona* systems existed not only at Rome and Constantinople, but also at Alexandria, Antioch, and even in the provincial Egyptian town of Oxyrhynchus.[19] The tentacles of the supply chain to Constantinople stretched into the Black Sea, to Egypt, the main source of grain, and to southern Asia Minor, which was one of the chief sources of olive oil. Procopius (*Buildings* 5.1.7–16) tells us that the island of Tenedos, at the entrance to the Dardanelles, became a major entrepôt, where large ships discharged their cargoes into smaller ones which could make their way more easily through the straits and into the Sea of Marmara. The time saved enabled them to make two or even three trips from Alexandria in a single season. The demands of the capital had a transforming effect on the economic structures of the regions that supplied the *annona*. Production concentrated in the hands of large-scale, well-organized producers. The primary trade in foodstuffs generated essential secondary industries, in particular the production of amphoras and shipbuilding. Merchant shipping was one of the major industries of the east Mediterranean. The continuing prosperity of Egypt in late antiquity and the growth of large estates there were due to the fact that the harvests of the Nile Valley found a permanent market outlet in Constantinople.

Alexandria

After Rome and Constantinople it is logical to look at Alexandria, Antioch, and Carthage. These were the next largest cities in the Mediterranean basin in antiquity. It is notoriously difficult to work out population figures for ancient cities, and there are wide margins for error. A cautious discussion suggests that Alexandria may have had a population between 200,000 and 400,000, and Antioch between 150,000 and 300,000.[20] In terms of size, Carthage was probably closer to Antioch than to Alexandria. It is no coincidence that Alexandria and Carthage were the ports through which grain was channeled to the two capitals. This guaranteed employment for countless shippers, dealers, porters, transport managers, ship-owners, bureaucrats, and businessmen. Both cities therefore were huge trading and service centers. Further, the fact that grain, in bulk, passed through these cities every year, meant that neither was likely to suffer acute shortages, and they could support urban populations that were much larger even than other port cities. Ammianus provides an example in the case of the governor of Africa in 370, Hymetius, who, at a time of famine, sold grain to the people of Carthage from the supplies due to be sent to Rome (Ammianus 28.1).

Our knowledge of late Roman Alexandria is extraordinarily uneven. Although we are well informed about ecclesiastical politics by the rich patristic sources and about administrative practices by the papyri, almost nothing remains at Alexandria of the city's early churches; and no papyrus documents and very few public inscriptions have been recovered from Alexandria itself.[21] Before the seventh century, the city was never in a war zone, subjected to a major siege, or at the center of military activity. It therefore appears only intermittently in the secular historians. Much of Alexandria's social and economic history has disappeared into a black hole.

The site at the western edge of the Nile Delta was chosen because its two harbors, protected by the offshore island of Pharos, made it the natural point of exchange between the Nile Valley, the most fertile and productive agricultural region of the Graeco-Roman world, and the Mediterranean waterway. A major canal linked Alexandria and its harbor with the western branch of the Nile, and it was cut off from the desert to the south by the shallow waters of Lake Mareotis. The city's hippodrome, half a kilometer long, which adjoined the great temple of Sarapis, was enclosed by the bend of the Nile canal.

The city was about five kilometers in length from east to west and up to two kilometers wide, surrounded by a fifteen-kilometer defensive wall.[22] Excavations along the main east–west street have identified one of the central *insulae* of the city plan. Large houses of the first and second century AD were extensively damaged in the third, abandoned in the early fourth, and replaced by public buildings in the mid-fourth century. These included a small theater, two suites of auditoria which have been identified as lecture rooms, and a public bath house. These structures, which were maintained until the seventh century, must have been the setting for some of the cultural and educational activity for which Alexandria was famous.[23] Throughout antiquity Alexandria's schools and the famous library, whose site has never been identified, were a magnet to trainee philosophers, public speakers, theologians, and doctors. It was a cultural powerhouse both in the pagan and the Christian tradition.

Alexandria was the residence of the prefect of Egypt until the office was replaced under Theodosius I by the *Praefectus Augustalis*. As far as we know the only emperor of late antiquity to visit the city was Diocletian himself, who campaigned in Egypt to reassert Roman control in Upper Egypt and Ethiopia and to suppress the internal rebellion of Domitius Domitianus.[24] In comparison to what is known from the other great population centers of the ancient world, this amounted to a power vacuum. Urban unrest, rioting, and major disturbances, which had to be suppressed by military intervention from the Roman garrisons of Lower Egypt, were a recurring feature of Alexandrian history. Church leaders were able to mobilize social networks in support of theological or other causes, and there were major religious confrontations in the fourth and fifth centuries.

The huge sanctuary of the Graeco-Egyptian god Sarapis, built by the Ptolemies and enlarged by the Romans in the Severan period, occupied one of the low hills on which the city was built, at the southwest corner, along the line of a road which led northwards to the so-called heptastadion, the kilometer-long causeway that divided the western from the eastern harbor. A statue of Diocletian was erected on a single tall column in the sanctuary area and marked it out as a focal point of Roman power. "Its splendour," said Ammianus, "is such that mere words can only do it an injustice, but its great halls of columns and its wealth of life-like statues and other works of art make it, next to the Capitol, which is the symbol of the eternity of immemorial Rome, the most magnificent building in the whole world" (Ammianus 22.16, trans. Hamilton).[25]

The destruction of the Sarapeum is one of the iconic moments in the Christian narrative of the overthrow of ancient paganism. In 391 the bishop of Alexandria, Theophilus, successfully petitioned Theodosius for permission to transform a temple of Dionysus into a church. A Christian mob broke into the holy of holies and mocked the phalluses and other pagan symbols they found there. The pagans reacted violently by killing some Christians and taking others who had been wounded into the great walled enclosure of the Serapeum. A siege followed. The Christians outside received support from the *Dux Aegypti* in command of Roman troops, and from the prefect Euagrius; the besieged pagans were spurred on by a philosopher Olympius, who told his followers that the destruction of pagan images did not impair the power of the ancient gods, which resided in heaven. Reports of Christian casualties were brought to the emperor Theodosius, who declared them to be martyrs, and the opening words of his edict, which denounced the pagans as guilty, were hailed with acclamation by the Christian mob, which proceeded to fall on the guards at the gate and stormed the sanctuary.[26] The destruction of the Serapeum, which represented a climax to the religious intolerance of the last years of Theodosius I, forced many pagan intellectuals to flee Alexandria.

The violent scenes were echoed a generation later, instigated by Theophilus' successor in the See of Alexandria, his nephew Cyril. He mobilized his followers first in 414 against the Jews, and then against pagan intellectuals in the city. The Jews had provoked hostility by attending theater performances on the Sabbath. They were goaded into violence by a rabble-rousing supporter of Cyril, who was arrested by the Roman prefect Orestes. In the course of events the Jews supposedly plotted to burn down a church, and Cyril used the opportunity to attack and brow-beat Orestes, and to organize Christian attacks on Jewish synagogues. Many Jews were killed (Socrates, *HE* 7.14–15). It emerges that they were in part at least the unwitting victims of a power struggle between Cyril and Orestes. In the following year a group of 500 monks waylaid the prefect in his carriage and stoned him. Other Alexandrians came to the Roman's rescue and arrested one of the perpetrators, who was tortured to death during his interrogation. The next year Christian violence claimed its most famous victim, the philosopher Hypatia, daughter of the Platonist Theon, who had left Alexandria when the Serapeum was destroyed. Hypatia had become a confidante of Orestes, who accordingly himself was accused of being a pagan. A Christian gang, led by a church reader called Peter, dragged Hypatia from her carriage to the city's main church, which had been constructed on the site of the former imperial temple, and murdered her in a hail of broken roof tiles. Her body was dismembered and incinerated. The church historian Socrates protested at these outrages, but Cyril escaped largely uncensored.[27]

The historical accounts of these episodes in Alexandria leave open many questions about their causes, but they provide a clear sense of their social context and illustrate the brutalization of local politics.[28] The bishops of the city could call on ill-educated supporters from the proletariat, who did not hesitate to employ extreme violence in a fanatical cause. It is revealing that the city councilors of Alexandria, an educated minority, petitioned the emperor in 416 in protest against the violence of the gangs of the bishop's supporters, the *parabalani.* Theodosius II responded only as far as ordering that their numbers should be limited in future to five or six hundred persons.[29]

Carthage

The picture of late Roman Carthage is also unbalanced by the preponderance of Christian source material. This includes the dossier of information relating to the conflict between African Christianity and imperial Catholicism, culminating in the verbatim records of the Council of Carthage in AD 411 (see above, chapter 8), and the *Confessions* of Augustine, the most prolific and important figure in the development of the western church. However, the city of Carthage itself, which lies under the sprawling suburbs of the modern city of Tunis, has remained largely unknown, at least until recent excavations carried out by international teams under the patronage of UNESCO.

Carthage possessed the largest sheltered harbor on the North African coast and occupied a crucial position in the layout of the western Mediterranean. The coastline westwards towards the Atlantic is a barricade of cliffs and mountains, exposed to northerly winds. Procopius observed that there were no harbors at all here (*Bell. Vand.* 3.15). Carthage itself, however, not only provided an anchorage, but was at the southern end of the shortest traverse to Europe, opposite Sicily, which was closer to Carthage than to Rome.[30] The city was linked by land routes to the hinterland of Numidia, one of which led up the valley of the Bagradas river. It drew most of its wealth in the form of agricultural produce, particularly grain and olives from the plains and hill slopes of Africa Proconsularis and Byzacena. The region was a network of small and medium-sized cities, interspersed with large rural estates, that had developed a civic culture which flourished into the fifth century. Like Alexandria, Carthage and its hinterland enjoyed a remarkable level of security from external threats. Few of the cities of Numidia and Africa Proconsularis possessed walls in the third and fourth centuries, and Carthage's own defenses were only built in 425, ironically just fourteen years before the city fell to the Vandals.[31]

The city was dominated by an acropolis, the Byrsa, and had a grid of planned streets, elaborate urban villas with mosaics, and the full repertoire of buildings for public entertainment – hippodrome, amphitheater, theaters and odeia, basilica churches, and bath houses, including the enormous *Thermae* of Antoninus.[32] Life in late-fourth-century Carthage is known to us, primarily and unforgettably, through the distorting lens of Augustine's *Confessions*. The *Confessions* focus on two aspects: the rowdy and bohemian lives of students, and the compulsive excitements of the public entertainment on offer in the arenas and the theaters, where the lewdness and the bloodletting posed moral challenges which were a source of obsession and repulsion to Augustine and his friends. The young man's confessions do not present a wider picture of the social and economic life of the city that might have emerged from Augustine's writings had he ever become its bishop.

Carthage fell to the Vandals in 439, and their kings occupied the former proconsular seat of government on the Byrsa. Genseric took control of the best land in Africa Proconsularis, Carthage's hinterland, and distributed it by lot to his warriors, who were to form a new hereditary landowning class.[33] The chief victims were the Catholic Church, which suffered confiscation and organized persecution at the hands of the Arian Vandals, and Carthage's senators, including members of the local city council and Roman senators with African properties. Some of these fled to Syria, others to Italy.[34] Those who remained are described as being enslaved to the barbarians. The Vandal presence, which was almost exclusively confined to the province of Proconsularis, is confirmed by the distribution of inscriptions and archaeological finds.[35] After the reconquest of Africa in 533, Justinian undertook measures to restore territory respectively to private landowners, to the state, and to the church. Procopius praises him for rebuilding the Theodosian defenses of Carthage and refurbishing the harbor front with new stoas and a public bath named the Theodoriane, after his wife. He built a monastery inside the sea wall, and churches of the Theotokos and of the local St Prima. Archaeological work in the city has located four substantial churches built at this period, confirming that the reconstruction of Carthage after the Vandals was mainly through religious foundations. It appears that the church buildings were maintained through the seventh century but like the rest of the city fell into decline, and the occupied area had shrunk significantly before it fell to the Arabs in 698.[36]

Antioch

The local history of Syrian Antioch in late antiquity is better documented than that of any other city in the ancient world apart from the two capitals. As it was the main headquarters and springboard for campaigns against the Sassanians, it became a military center and served as a long-term residence for campaigning emperors, such as Constantius and Julian. It features prominently in secular histories, especially Ammianus, and in much of the literature associated with Julian. It is the only provincial city of the eastern empire from which a local chronicle, the work of John Malalas, has survived, and it is the focus of the ecclesiastical history of Evagrius, which is concerned with secular as well as church affairs, especially in the fifth and early sixth centuries. Added to this is the rich texture of local information for the later fourth century to be found in the speeches and letters of the pagan Libanius, and in the writings of his near contemporary, the Christian priest John Chrysostom, and for the fifth century in the letters and other writings of Theodoret of Cyrrhus. It is hardly surprising that the quantity of modern work on Antioch is far greater than that on the other major centers of late antiquity.

Antioch extended along the east bank of the river Orontes at the foot of Mount Silpius. City walls, originally built by its Hellenistic founder Seleucus I, ran along the river frontage and then eastward up the mountain slope. They were repeatedly restored and rebuilt in late antiquity, notably under Theodosius I and Justinian. The city itself had a central colonnaded street, two miles long, famous for public street lighting. There is abundant evidence from all periods of major public building. A large octagonal church was under construction at the end of Constantine's life and was dedicated at the Council of Antioch in 341.

Antioch was not as large a city as Alexandria. After the fourth century, it ceased to serve as an imperial residence and declined in importance. It was not itself a sea port, but imports and exports were transported by a canal system that was designed to make the last section of the river Orontes navigable down to the port of Seleucia Pieria.[37] Both Diocletian and Constantius are known to have restored the harbor facilities, as it was critical for their major Persian campaigns, and it certainly was a conduit for military supplies up to the ill-fated expedition of Julian in 363.[38] There was an outer and an inner harbor, the latter secured by a chain. A fifth-century inscription contains a tariff of inspection-fees on imports via the port, which were payable to the *curiosi*, the imperial agents responsible for the state transport *annona* and requisitions systems. These were set at a lower level for short-haul trade from Phoenicia, Cyprus, and Cilicia than from Palestine and Egypt. *Annona* contributions certainly reached Antioch by sea. The emperors Anastasius and Justinian set up inscriptions at Antioch which published the levels of these fees as a measure to prevent extortion by officials (Malalas 470–1).[39]

We have good information about the city's food supply in the late fourth century. The best documented shortage occurred in 362–3, as the emperor Julian prepared to invade Persia. The build-up of troops and the presence of the huge imperial entourage aggravated the situation, and the emperor attempted to relieve the crisis by making available grain from imperial estates to the civic markets, but much of this was bought up by profiteers. Julian himself was blamed and hunger added a menacing edge to the tense relations between the emperor and the city population before he left on campaign.[40] It may have been in consequence that the emperor Valens, who spent much of the 370s in residence at Antioch, instituted an imperial corn distribution system for the city, and this continued in existence until the time of Justinian.[41] The periodic famines and grain supply crises, which are a leitmotif of Antioch's history in the late empire, suggest that local requirements could not be matched by maritime imports, and when the city was threatened by and fell to Persian attacks in 529 and 540, the imperial reaction in Constantinople was sluggish and half-hearted. The security of Antioch was not vital to the capital's own survival.

The transfer of at least some of the responsibility for the city's food supply to imperial officials is symptomatic of a major political change which is better documented at Antioch than anywhere else in the empire; the gradual decline in the economic independence and authority of the members of the city council, the local land-owning class, who here, as in almost every other city of the eastern Roman Empire, had hitherto been the mainstay of social order. The letters and speeches of Libanius imply that the number of active councilors had fallen sharply by the late fourth century. Their place was taken increasingly by a smaller number of imperial officials, often themselves local men who had made good. Salaried imperial officials and soldiers took over many of the political and economic functions of local landowners in a process which can also be observed in late Roman Egypt.[42] Thus during the late fourth and fifth centuries a middle tier of local government was squeezed out of existence. This widened the gap between the newly enriched landowners, who derived their income from state service, and the urban poor and the peasant population.

One consequence of this was the growing importance of patronage wielded by individuals who had access to the governor. In his speech *Against Mixidemus* Libanius illustrates how the target of his criticism had replaced a group of *officiales* as the patron of a group of villages, from whom he exacted produce and services, in return for the protection he offered. As country people became indebted to him, he was able to buy property, gradually building up large estates (Libanius, *Or.* 52). In his speech *On Patronage* Libanius depicts how villagers, by making payments of produce or gold, obtained the patronage of the commanding officers of the garrisons stationed among them, and then exploited this military protection to attack and plunder neighboring villages. They also relied on military protection when they refused to pay contributions to the tax levies which were being conducted by local councilors. It is clear that the web of patronage was not limited to locally-stationed soldiers, but stretched back to senior military officers, who prevented the senior provincial authorities from intervening on behalf of the councilors (Libanius, *Or.* 47).[43]

There were many consequences of this shift in the balance of local power. The constitutional basis of civic government was rapidly undermined. City councils began to be replaced by coteries of powerful notables who operated primarily in their own private interests, not in those of the city. Already by 370 the emperors had created a new office of *defensor civitatis*, defender of the city, ostensibly to prevent corrupt practice in the courts at the expense of the rural poor (*CTh.* 1.29.5). Small-scale landholding began to be replaced by large estates, and the new landowners were often powerful enough to be a law unto themselves, in a position to negotiate with or even defy the demands of the imperial government. Violence and dispossession in the countryside will have led many peasants to move to the city, and the population of Antioch certainly expanded in the fifth century, when its walls were extended to cover a larger area (Evagrius I.20). Meanwhile its richer citizens became wealthier than before. This is illustrated by the luxurious villas, decorated with some of the finest figurative mosaics of the late Roman period, which were excavated by the Princeton expedition to Antioch in the 1930s.[44] In material terms the city reached an apogee in the fifth century.

Despite the evidence for corruption and low-level rural violence, which is presented in Libanius' account of patronage, and the city's reputation for unruly popular behavior, which is conveyed by the accounts of Julian's stay in the city in 362–3, urban disturbances seem to have occurred rarely.[45] There was a reasonable level of religious harmony. Pagans and Christians appear generally to have avoided conflict, at least until the notorious campaign of

Maternus Cynegius, Theodosius' praetorian prefect of the East, who directed a vigorous campaign to close down and restrict the activities of the pagan temples in the 380s (see above, chapter 3). Relations between Christians and Jews were too harmonious for the comfort of John Chrysostom, who resorted to a major series of sermons designed to dissuade Christians from attending Jewish places of worship.[46] The episode that broke the calm in a serious way was the Riot of the Statues in 387. It is probably not a coincidence that this came at the end of the period when religious tension had been raised by the campaign of Cynegius Maternus. An imperial edict was read out to the city council announcing a steep rise in taxation. As the councilors mounted a petition to the governor of Syria to protest, and tried to enlist the help of Flavianus, the city bishop, rumors of what was happening reached the people, and a mob, led by a claque leader of one of the theater factions, stormed the palace of the provincial governor, and then vented its anger on the imperial images, first destroying wooden panels which carried Theodosius' portrait, and then overthrowing the bronze statues of the emperor, his wife Eudoxia, and son Arcadius in the forum. They attempted to burn down the house of a councilor who had spoken in favor of the tax rise, but were prevented by the appearance of mounted archers and a body of troops under the *Comes Orientis*, who arrested the ring leaders. While these were swiftly tried and punished, the city awaited its own punishment with growing anxiety that there would be wholesale retribution. The emperor dealt with the mutiny in two stages. His initial reaction was to strip Antioch of many privileges, including its title to be metropolis of the province, to cut off the *annona*, and to shut down the hippodrome, theaters, and bath houses. A commission of enquiry then sat to establish who was to blame, and ordered the imprisonment of several councilors. Our sources portray these events from two viewpoints, the pagan represented by Libanius, and the Christian by John Chrysostom. Theodosius chose to pay heed to Christian pleas for clemency. It was the embassy to Constantinople headed by the bishop that secured freedom for the prisoners and the restoration of the city's privileges. John Chrysostom was able to hail the news that the city would be spared further punishment in time for the Easter festival. The dénouement of these events implied a shift in the balance of local power, from the secular council to the Christian authorities.[47]

The sparse trickle of information for the fifth century includes Evagrius' detailed account of an earthquake which particularly affected the palace quarter of Antioch, the so-called New City (Evagrius 2.12). Recovery, with assistance from the emperor Leo, was evidently rapid, but Antioch was much more seriously affected in 525, firstly by a fire which destroyed the cathedral of St Stephen, and then by the largest earthquake in the city's history since 115, which allegedly claimed 250,000 lives including that of the bishop Euphrasios. A further shock in November 528 killed an additional 5,000 people. Imperial help was promised, but priorities in Syria switched from peace to war as the Persians renewed hostilities. The so-called eternal peace of 532 promised more than it delivered, and war broke out again in 539. In the following year the Persians descended on Antioch and took the city despite vigorous local resistance, which was led by the circus factions. Khusro I, the Persian king, reputedly took away 30,000 Antiochenes to found and populate a new city in Persia (Procopius, *Bell. Pers.* 2.14.6). Syria had effectively been left to its own devices by the emperor, since imperial forces were tied down in the increasingly bitter struggle to regain control of Italy. Procopius credits Justinian with an ambitious restoration program after the Persians had withdrawn, but his description implies that parts of the city had to be given up and the fortifications contracted. Streets and public buildings were rebuilt and a new church dedicated to the Theotokos (Procopius, *Buildings* 2.10.2–25).[48] Two years after it fell to the Persians the city was exposed to a more devastating menace; the plague. The earthquakes of the 520s had already dealt heavy blows to the growth in Antioch's population and general prosperity; warfare and repeated recurrence of the plague made the decline irreversible.

NOTES

1   See D. H. French, "The Roman road-system of Asia Minor," *Aufstieg und Niedergang der römischen Welt* II.7.2 (1981), 698–729, especially diagram 7 showing huge peaks for milestones set up under Septimius Severus, the tetrarchs and Constantine.

2   A. Wilson, "Machines, power and the ancient economy," *JRS* 92 (2002), 1–32.

3   J. Edmundson, "Mining in the later Roman Empire: Continuity or disruption?" *JRS* 79 (1989), 84–102.

4   J. Howard-Johnston, "The education and expertise of Procopius," *Ant. Tard.* 8 (2000), 19–30.

5   G. Fowden, *Empire to Commonwealth. Consequences of Monotheism in Late Antiquity* (Princeton, 1993), 45–50.

6   H. Brandt, *Geschichte der römischen Kaiserzeit von Diokletian bis zum Ende der konstantinischen Dynastie* (Berlin, 1998) 69–72.

7   See G. Fowden, "Nicagoras of Athens and the Lateran obelisk," *JHS* 107 (1987), 51–7.

8   Discussion by J. Vanderspoel, *Themistius and the Imperial Court. Oratory, Civic Duty and Paideia from Constantius to Theodosius* (Michigan, 1995), 51–61.

9   M. Whitby, "The violence of the circus factions," in K. Hopwood (ed.), *Organized Crime in Antiquity* (Wales, 1999), 229–53.

10 D. Feissel, "Le philadelphion de Constantinople. Inscription et écrits patriographiques," *Comptes-rendus de l'Académie des inscription et belles lettres* (2003), 495–521.

11 C. Mango, "The Water Supply of Constantinople," in C. Mango and G. Dagron (eds.), *Constantinople and its Hinterland* (Aldershot, 1995), 9–18. The aqueduct system has been investigated by J. Crow and A. Ricci, "Investigating the hinterland of Constantinople. Interim report on the Anastasian long wall," *JRA* 10 (1997), 253–62.

12   N. Asgari, "Proconnesian production of architectural elements in late antiquity,"
     in C. Mango and G. Dagron (eds.), *Constantinople and its Hinterland* (Aldershot,
     1995), 263–88.
13   W. Lebek, *Epigraphica Anatolica* 25 (1995), 107–53.
14   C. Foss and D. Winfield, *Byzantine Fortifications* (Pretoria, 1986); W. Karnapp
     and A. M. Schneider, *Die Stadtmauer von Konstantinopel*; A. M. Schneider, "The
     city walls of Constantinople" *Antiquity* 11 (1937), 461ff.
15   M. Harrison, *A Temple for Byzantium* (London, 1989) is an account of the excava-
     tion of this building and its interpretation.
16   Procopius, *Buildings* 1.1.20–78. Paul Silentarius, *Ekphrasis*. See Mary Whitby,
     "The occasion of Paul the silentiary's Ekphrasis of St. Sophia," *Classical Quarterly*
     35 (1985), 215–28.
17   J. F. Matthews, *Western Aristocracies and the Imperial Court* (Oxford, 1990), 101–21.
18   Socrates, *HE* 2.13; A. H. M. Jones, *Later Roman Empire* I (Oxford, 1964), 698.
19   J.-M. Carrié, "Les distributions alimentaires dans les cités de l'empoire romain
     tardif," *Mélanges de l'école française de Rome – antiqutité* 87 (1985), 995–1101;
     J. Rea, *The Oxyrhynchus Papyri* 40 (1979).
20   W. Liebeschuetz, *Antioch* (Oxford, 1972), 92–100.
21   C. Haas, *Alexandria in Late Antiquity: Topography and Social Conflict* (Baltimore,
     1997). R. Bagnall, *Egypt in Late Antiquity* (Princeton, 1993), based on rigor-
     ous analysis of documentary sources, deliberately excludes Alexandria from
     consideration.
22   An illustrated account in R. Bagnall and D. Rathbone (eds.), *Egypt from Alexander
     to the Copts. An Archaeological and Historical Guide* (London, 2004), 51–86.
23   J. Mackenzie, "Glimpsing Alexandria from archaeological evidence," *JRA* 16 (2003),
     35–63.
24   T. D. Barnes, *Constantine and Eusebius* (Harvard, 1981), 17–20.
25   J. McKenzie, S. Gibson, and A. T. Reyes, "Reconstructing the Serapeum in
     Alexandria from the archaeological evidence," *JRS* 94 (2004), 73–121; G. Fowden,
     Empire to Commonwealth (Princeton, 1993), 44–5.
26   Sozomen, *HE* 7.15; cf. Socrates, *HE* 5.16–17; Theodoret, *HE* 5.22; Rufinus,
     HE 11.22–27.
27   See K. Holum, *Theodosian Empresses* (Berkeley, 1982), 98–100.
28   For discussion see R. Alston, *The City in Roman and Byzantine Egypt* (London,
     2002), 285–92.
29   *CTh.* 16.2.42, 43.
30   W. Frend, *The Donatist Church* (Oxford, 1952), 25–31.
31   C. Lepelley, "The survival and fall of the classical city in late Roman Africa," in
     Aspectes de l'Afrique romaine. Les cités, la vie rurale, et le christianisme (Bari, 2001),
     85–104.
32   *Princeton Encyclopedia of Classical Sites* (Princeton, 1976), 201–2.
33   Victor of Vita I, 12–14; Procopius, *Bell. Vand. 3.5.11–17.*
34   Theodoret, *ep.* 2, 29, 33, 34; *Life of Fulgentius of Ruspa* (ed. G. Lapeyre 1929), 1.
35   Y. Modéran, "L'etablissement territorial des Vandales en Afrique," *Ant. Tard.* 10
     (2002), 87–122.
36   W. Frend, *The Archaeology of Early Christianity. A History* (London, 1996, repr.
     1997), 316–17; W. Liebeschuetz, *The Decline and Fall of the Roman City* (Oxford,
     2001), 101, 377.

37 D. van Berchem, "Le port de Séleucie de Piérie et l'infrastructure navale des guerres parthiques," *Bonner Jahrbücher* 135 (1985), 47–87.

38 W. Liebeschuetz, *Antioch*, 75–6.

39 *SEG* 35 (1985) 1523; G. Dagron, "Un tarif des sportules à payer aux *curiosi* du port de Séleucie de Pisidie," *Travaux et Mémoires* 9 (1985), 435–55; P. Petit, *Libanius et la vie municipale à Antioche au IVe siècle après J.-C.* (Paris, 1955), 305–22; G. Downey, "The economic crisis at Antioch under Julian the apostate," *Studies in Honour of A. C. Johnson* (Princeton, 1951), 312–21.

40 Julian, *Misopogon* 369–70; W. Liebeschuetz, *Antioch*, 127–8.

41 Justinian, *Nov.* VII.8 with W. Liebeschuetz, *Antioch*, 129.

42 W. Liebeschuetz, *Antioch*, 167–92.

43 W. Liebeschuetz, *Antioch*, 192–208.

44 D. Levi, *Antioch Mosaic Pavements* (Princeton, 1947).

45 J. Hahn, *Gewalt und Religiöser Konflikt* (Berlin, 2004), 122.

46 R. L. Wilken, *John Chrysostom and the Jews: Rhetoric and Reality in the Late Fourth Century* (Berkeley, 1983).

47 R. Browning. "The riot of AD 387 in Antioch: The role of the theatrical claques in the later empire," *JRS* 42 (1952), 13–20; P. Brown, *Power and Persuasion in Late Antiquity* (Wisconsin, 1992), 105–8; H. Leppin, "Pagan and Christian interpretations of riot," in H. Brandt (ed.), *Gedeutete Realität. Krisen, Wirklichkeiten, Interpretationen 3–6 Jht. n. Chr.* (Historia Einzelschr. 134, Stuttgart, 1999), 103–23.

48 Michael Whitby, "Procopius and Antioch," in D. French and C. S. Lightfoot (eds.), *The Eastern Frontier of the Roman Empire* (2 vols., Oxford, 1989), 537–53.

10

Society and Economy in the Mediterranean and the Near East

250   300   350   400   450   500   550   600   650

There was a profound divergence between the economic and social history of the eastern and western parts of the empire. The fundamental reason for this can be expressed in a single word – security. Until the middle of the sixth century most of the Roman East was free from war and invasion. During long periods of peacetime, urban culture thrived, the population rose both in the cities and in the countryside, and the economy benefited from long-term stability. The disastrous effects of war were only felt in the Thracian hinterland of Constantinople, and in North Syria and Mesopotamia, where the empire was exposed to Sassanian attacks in the sixth century. By contrast, the western provinces were exposed to continuous threats from Germanic barbarian groups and later from the Huns. Former provinces were successively relinquished to the invaders. This led not only to the collapse of the western empire in a political sense, but to a transformation of its economic and social structures. As the infrastructure created by Roman administration and taxation was removed, cities shrank in size and lost their significance, and populations were dispersed into villages with narrow economic horizons. Only the institutions of the church were resilient and adaptable enough to carry forward the legacy of the empire into the Middle Ages.

The Eastern Empire

The Near East

In the late empire the Roman diocese of Oriens, the modern Near East, comprised fourteen Roman provinces. The zone as a whole was the western half of the famous "fertile crescent," and in social and economic terms it was one of the most vibrant and flourishing areas of the Roman Empire. Its relative importance naturally increased after the empire was divided and the center of economic gravity shifted from the western to the eastern Mediterranean.

In the south the settled provinces of the Near East abutted the edge of the south Syrian and Arabian deserts. Between the permanent settlements and the true desert there is a broad zone of steppe, where the rainfall is too low to allow agriculture without the use of irrigation, but where livestock can be raised. This region was mainly exploited by small mobile populations of nomadic or semi-nomadic tribes, and settled agriculture was not possible outside the oases. Rome attempted to control this marginal region by coming to agreements and treaties with the tribal peoples, and sometimes maintained a small military presence at key locations. During the late fifth and sixth centuries their main allies were the Ghassanid Arabs, under the leadership of the Roman client Aretas (al-Harith b. Jabala).[1]

The most distinctive development in the Near East between the third and sixth centuries was the spread of settlements to parts of the region which had hardly been exploited previously. Marginal areas were now brought under cultivation and the population grew. The limestone massif of north central

Syria has been intensively studied. This hilly country, divided between the city territories of Antioch, Apamea, and their smaller, eastern neighbors, Chalcis, Beroea, and Cyrrhus, attracted enough rainfall to support mixed agriculture and was particularly well suited to olive cultivation. Between 700 and 800 village settlements have been archaeologically identified, with stone houses, churches, monasteries, and a small quota of public buildings. The smallest villages were occupied by only a few dozen inhabitants, but the larger ones often had several churches, and some even had public bath houses. They were occupied by well-off peasant families who drew a livelihood from a mixed agricultural economy, and especially from olive cultivation. The main market for surplus olive oil seems to have been the urban markets of northern Syria. Antioch and Apamea probably consumed most of the crop. It was no doubt the abundant supply of cheap olive oil which made it possible for Antioch to install public street lighting, so bright that "it made night as clear as day" (Ammianus 14.1.9). There is no evidence for crop specialization or monoculture, and the technology of oil production does not show the standardization found in the great oil producing regions of Tripolitania and Tunisia, but suggests simply a multiplication of individual production units.

No other part of the Roman Empire provides a better archaeological perspective on the spread of Christianity to a rural area. By the middle of the fourth century single-nave churches appear in the smaller settlements, while three-aisled basilicas on a simple pattern can be found in the larger villages.[2] Construction accelerated through the fifth and early sixth centuries with higher technical standards and more elaborate ornamentation.

The chronological pattern of finds suggests an initial spread of settlements through the second and first half of the third centuries, followed by a pause, and then rapid and continuous development from c.330 to 550. The steepest growth in the number and density of the settlements seems to occur during the peaceful fifth century between 410 and 480, with the graph leveling off thereafter. Calculations of the ratio between the number of rooms in the villages and the size of village territories suggest that Jebel A'la and Jebel Barisha between Antioch and Chalcis may have had populations of between 50 and 100 persons per square kilometer in the fifth and sixth centuries, reaching a total population of around 300,000 persons, a density higher than most of the rural areas of contemporary western Europe or western Turkey, and in any case presenting an extraordinary contrast with today's conditions, when these hills are almost deserted.

By the mid-sixth century the archaeological evidence suggests that the size and wealth of the villages had reached a plateau, and remained at the same level into the seventh century. The plague in 542, by reducing the level of population in the short term, may even have contributed to the viability of the communities, by reducing the demands on their agricultural resources. The discovery of a treasure of fifty-six silver pieces from the Church of St Sergius at the village of Kaper Koraon, all datable to the century from 540–640, with some of the best pieces clearly later than 577, indicates that some villages still possessed surplus wealth.[3] The suggestion that life continued broadly as before into the seventh century is partly confirmed by the excavation of the village site at Déhès, which shows that the village continued to flourish, although new building was rare after 550.[4]

The economic resilience of late sixth century Syria is also clear in the region further east, in the steppic territory east of Chalcis, and north of Jebel Balas. There had been few settlers here before late antiquity, but underground canals (*qanats*) were constructed to tap the water courses of Jebel Balat, and made irrigation possible. Two striking settlements emerged in the mid- or later sixth century, at Androna, where the structures include a barracks building dated to 558, and at Qasr Ibn Wardan, a complex which combines a church, rooms and stabling for soldiers, and a palatial residence dated to 564. The design and construction technique of the church show a clear awareness of developments at Constantinople. This could be the residence of a Ghassanid tribal chieftain who had responsibilities for the defense of this frontier zone, and was also a focus for cult among the recently Christianized population.[5]

As population levels increased in the limestone massif east of Antioch, it is certain that something similar occurred in the fertile and more accessible areas close to the city. A combination of satellite imagery and field survey in the Amuq plain north of Antioch has identified evidence for intense exploitation of these lowlands, as well as for irrigation channels and canals by which goods could be transported to the Orontes and into the city.[6] The finds substantially confirm the enthusiastic encomium of Antioch's territory to be found in Libanius' speech *In Praise of Antioch* (*Or.* 11).

The settlement evidence for the region of the Hauran, the basaltic region around Jebel Druze between Damascus and Bostra in southern Syria, has a broadly similar profile to that of the north Syrian limestone country. Villages, with associated field systems and traces of hydraulic engineering to collect and conserve rainfall, spread across the region from the first century, especially in the late third and fourth and in the sixth and early seventh centuries. There is evidence in the early imperial period that there were extensive imperial propert-ies in the region, and the estate centers were designated *metrokomiai*.

While Syria as a whole shows no evidence for economic decline before the end of the sixth century, there is a significant exception in the larger cities of northern Syria, above all Antioch and Apamea. Excavations at Apamea, a huge city "where all the nobility of Syria" had lived in the fifth century,[7] suggest that the formerly thriving city went into recession in the late sixth century. In 573 a Sassanian army led by Khusro II's general Adarmahan,

> captured Apamea . . . which of old was prosperous and populous but which had been largely ruined by time. After taking the city on certain conditions, since they had been unable to resist as the wall was lying on the ground through age, he burnt it completely and pillaged everything contrary to the agreements; he departed and went away, after enslaving the city and the adjacent districts. (Evagrius, *HE* 5.10, trans. Whitby)

Procopius clearly shows that the north Syrian cities were seriously damaged by the Sassanian invasions in the sixth century (see above, chapter 4 and below, chapter 11). Archaeology appears to confirm that they never fully recovered from this.

The cities of southern Syria, which were not the target of Sassanian attacks, were thriving centers until the middle of the sixth century. Inscriptions suggest that Justinian undertook to build the walls, an aqueduct, and a church at Bostra, but none of the is work is dated later than 540 (*Inscriptions grecques et latines de la Syrie* XIII.1, 540, 541). Damascus and Hama were both major urban centers through the sixth century. The cities of the Decapolis to the south probably reached their highest population levels in the first half of the sixth century. A recent survey shows that in all cases the pattern of urban living was not seriously disturbed either by the conflict between Rome and Persia at the beginning of the seventh century or by the Arab conquest and the coming of Islam. In this period the population of Beth Shean (Scythopolis) has been estimated at between 30,000 and 40,000 inhabitants, a level that could only be supported by a very complex and active economic infrastructure. The classical urban character of the city did not begin to change substantially until the late seventh and first half of the eighth centuries, a process which was finally sealed by a major earthquake in 749 (Plate 10.1).[8] Christian communities continued to build new churches into the seventh century. Dated mosaic

Plate 10.1   Scythopolis in Palestine. The end of the ancient city was caused by the earthquake of 749 (S. Mitchell)

inscriptions testify to new church construction at Gerasa in 559, 565, 570, and 611, and there is a final building inscription from 629. However, archaeological evidence suggests that some parts of the site were abandoned in the sixth century, and the rash of seven new churches built in the sixth or early seventh century may be more a testament to local piety, or even to anxiety in the face of threatening times, than to prosperity.[9] A small early mosque has been identified at Gerasa and a large one at Amman (Philadelphia), but in general the impact of the Islamic conquests on the physical structures of the cities was slight.[10]

A series of small market towns, including Elusa, Nessana, and Mampsis, all equipped with substantial churches and fortifications, developed in the northern fringe of the Negev region, previously a marginal region. Irrigation systems enabled the semi-desert environment to be cultivated, producing cereals, fruit crops, and vines. Nessana is remarkable for a find of papyrus documents, written in Greek and Arabic, which date to the seventh century, immediately following the Islamic conquest of Palestine. These include marriage documents, land titles, contracts of sale and other merchant records, evidence for the handling of church property, as well as documents relating to the poll tax and military requisitioning.[11] An archaeological counterpart to the papyrus finds from Nessana is the nearby site of Shivta, perhaps to be identified as the ancient village of Soubaita, where the state of preservation of the ancient buildings is remarkable even for this region. They date from the fourth to the eighth centuries, and the effect of the Arab conquest is marked not by destruction but by the building of a small mosque beside the southernmost of the site's three large churches in the eighth or ninth centuries. Two large pools next to this church and its central placement suggest that this was the focal point of the community. The settlement was a dense honeycomb of houses clustered in irregularly shaped but roughly even sized blocks, which were separated by streets three or four meters wide. Livestock pens encircle the village. About 2,000 inhabitants are estimated to have lived in the settlement, where 170 houses have been identified, mostly substantial stone structures with about seven rooms grouped round a central courtyard. The houses were mostly evenly sized between 250 and 550 square meters, implying a generally homogeneous population whose livelihood depended on livestock, cereal agriculture, vine and olive cultivation.[12] There had been no perceptible decline in the quality of life in the region through late antiquity up to and beyond the Arab conquest.

These small towns and large villages lay on the overland route, popularly known as the "spice road" and followed by Roman roads which are still well preserved today, that linked Petra and the Gulf of Aqaba with the Mediterranean port of Gaza. Gaza was one of the most thriving commercial and cultural communities of the Levant.[13] There is no reason to doubt that the prosperity of the communities in the northern Negev was dependent on their ability to sell surplus produce in this major trading port. To judge from finds of amphoras, wine exported from Gaza was a major commodity in eastern and even some western Mediterranean markets in the fifth and sixth centuries.[14]

In general the communities of southern Syria appear to maintain their levels of prosperity through to the Arab conquest and the first century of Islam.

Asia Minor

Asia Minor, divided between the dioceses of Asiana in the west, Pontica in the center and northeast, and Oriens in the southeast, was part of the secure heartland of the eastern Roman Empire. By the early imperial period, the old provinces of Asia, Bithynia, and Lycia were among the most urbanized and economically successful parts of the Roman world. Like Africa, most of the region remained unaffected by war. Social and economic conditions had favored the emergence of stable provincial elites, families which owned much of the land and expended their wealth in a sophisticated and ostentatious urban culture. Even modest cities contained an impressive range of public buildings. Athletic and cultural festivals were a particularly notable feature of life in the third-century cities.[15]

During late antiquity city culture can be studied more closely in Asia Minor than in any other part of the Roman Empire, thanks to an abundance of inscriptions and the archaeological remains of buildings. Several trends can be identified in late antiquity which point to the differences between the great flowering of cities in the second and third centuries and under the Christian empire that followed. The profile of public building was naturally affected by religious change. No new temples or sanctuaries were founded after the end of the third century and major centers of pagan worship fell into disrepair. In functional terms they were replaced by churches (and to a lesser extent by synagogues for the numerous Jewish communities), but the transition was a gradual one. The earliest church that is epigraphically attested in Asia Minor was built by a survivor of the Diocletianic persecution, the Novatian bishop and a member of a prominent local family, M. Iulius Eugenius of Laodicea Catacecaumene, in a part of central Anatolia which became largely Christian at an early date:

> Having held the office of bishop with much honour for twenty-five full years, and built up from its foundations the entire church and all the adornment around it – that is the colonnades, and the quadrangles with colonnades, and the paintings and the decorated screens and the water supply and the gateway with marble decoration – and having in a word constructed everything, and renouncing the life of men, I made for myself a tomb building and a sarcophagus on which I arranged for all these things to be inscribed. (*MAMA* I, no. 171)

This is a remarkable text. Apart from providing one of the most valuable documents of the persecution, it is a rare example of a text that shows a church leader taking credit for building a church in the manner of old-style city benefactors. Subsequent church building inscriptions, which are preserved in large numbers from Asia Minor and Syria, suggest that the costs of construction were usually the result of a collective effort by clergy and laymen.

Bishops frequently took the initiative for these buildings but did not present themselves as seigneurial benefactors to their communities. Eugenius of Laodicea, however, lived in the age of Constantine and still retained much of the outlook that had sustained civic life in the early empire. He was as ready as the emperor was to claim personal political credit for his actions, although these were now directed towards the institutions of the church. A more explicit Christian ideology, based on personal humility and acts of charitable giving, did not become well rooted until later in the fourth century.[16]

It was not until the last decade of the fourth century that existing buildings in the city centers began to be taken over and converted into churches. The evidence seems to be concentrated in two periods in particular, at the end of the reign of Theodosius I in the early 390s, when imperial legislation against pagans and heretics was particularly strident, and in the last decade of the reign of Theodosius II, reflecting the heightened religiosity of the court and the strong influence of the emperor's sister Pulcheria.[17] At Ephesus the major cathedral church of St Mary and the large baptistery next to it were built at the end of the fourth century, adapting the foundations of a large market basilica which had fallen into disrepair.[18] At Sagalassus, the metropolis of Pisidia, two large civic temples were literally turned inside out in the 440s to become the city's largest churches. The walls of the cella were re-erected along the line of the external colonnades, and the columns were placed inside the enclosed structure to divide the naves and support the roof. Additional building material was brought in from other Roman buildings, including the imperial temple of Antoninus Pius, and these spolia were systematically re-used for the new constructions.[19] A similar large-scale conversion occurred at Aphrodisias, also probably in the 440s, when the columns along the short east and west sides of the temple of Aphrodite were relocated to extend the long colonnades.[20] It is important to emphasize that such reconstructions represented major, well organized civic undertakings, and should not be seen as the random pillaging of available building stone.[21]

The rising force in late Roman society were those who made careers in the imperial government service. Such men avoided local liturgies and tax demands, and provided access to cash salaries and other opportunities for enrichment. It is overwhelmingly men in this category who became civic benefactors. The cities of Asia Minor and Greece in the fourth and fifth centuries produced numerous verse inscriptions composed in honor of imperial officials, usually provincial governors, who organized and funded public building or provided other forms of benefit for the cities where they served.[22] One consequence of this trend was that urban prosperity and visible evidence for organized public life in the later empire was increasingly focused in the more important centers, provincial capitals such as Ephesus, Sardis, Ancyra, Aphrodisias, and Side.

In addition to church building there was much other new construction of a secular nature. Most cities had put up fortifications either in response to the Gothic and Sassanian threats of the mid-third or during the fourth century. There is also ample evidence for new aqueducts, bath houses, and public fountains. Roman bathing culture flourished throughout the period, although it had distanced itself from previous associations with the pagan Greek culture of the gymnasium. Theaters and stadia were now used for a new types of entertainment. Horse racing and pantomimes remained major attractions not only in the great cities such as Constantinople and Antioch, but also in provincial capitals such as Aphrodisias in Caria.[23] It was rarely necessary to erect buildings *a novo*, but existing structures were renovated, adapted, and enlarged. The theater at Pisidian Antioch, for instance, was more than doubled in size at the beginning of the fourth century when the city became metropolis of the new province of Pisidia, and an arch, dedicated to the imperial college of 311, was built at the entrance to a tunnel which took one of the city's main streets underneath the wing of the enlarged auditorium.[24] Smaller structures such as *odeia* were also maintained. Many aspects of public cultural activity were transformed in the fourth and fifth centuries, mainly due to the religious change from paganism to Christian monotheism, but communal life continued, and urban populations had to be entertained as well as fed.

The major regional economic shift to be seen in late antiquity is towards the coastal regions of south Asia Minor. Large new urban settlements of stone-built houses and substantial churches were created along the southern Lycian shoreline from Finike to Kaş, notably on the island of Kekova and at the harbor towns of Tristomon (Üçağız) and Andriake. Access to these settlements was largely from the sea and they owed much of their prosperity to their position on the shipping routes from Alexandria, Syria, and Cyprus to the Aegean and Constantinople.[25] A remarkable example of the impact of the empire on a specialized local economy has been observed at the Lycian coastal settlement of Aperlae. This small city's livelihood depended on harvesting the mollusks which produced the royal purple dye, an imperial monopoly and status symbol. The shellfish were bred in off-shore fish tanks, and the processed dye-stuffs were then transported by a short paved road to an anchorage about a mile away. Beside this road stood the only milestone of Diocletianic date to have been recorded in the whole of Lycia, further testimony that imperial attention was focussed on this small place.[26]

The growth of coastal settlements also stimulated economic activity in the interior. The sixth-century *Life* of St Nicholas of Sion, who lived in the time of Justinian, provides a detailed picture which illustrates the interdependence of coastal and upland Lycia.[27] The villages, which were administratively dependent on the coastal cities, supplied them with products of the mountain country, including timber, cheese, and honey, as well as providing upland pasture and relief from the summer heat.

The most dramatic evidence for economic development in the late Roman period comes from the hilly limestone area of Rugged Cilicia, north and east of Seleuceia on the Calycadnus. By far the most important settlement here in late antiquity was the harbor city of Corycus. In the first three centuries Corycus remained only of local importance, but from the fourth to the sixth century the settlement boomed. It contained numerous large stone houses, churches, and bath houses, all enclosed within substantial fortifications. The cemeteries around the site have produced nearly 600 funerary inscriptions, carved on sarcophagi, which identify not only the persons who were buried there but their professions (*MAMA* III 200–788). There is an extraordinary diversity of urban trades, which indicate that Corycus was no ordinary harbor town but a major commercial entrepôt.[28] The texts mention substantial numbers of olive and wine merchants, ship owners, shipbuilders, sail-makers, and potters. They were often organized into guilds. This new city did not appear in a vacuum. There is a dense concentration of late Roman building along the coastline from Seleuceia eastwards, including Corycus' immediate neighbor Elaiussa-Sebaste, which it now overshadowed. The pattern of stone-built settlements, many with large churches and private houses containing fine mosaics, extends into the hinterland.[29] The economic key to the area's rapid development in late antiquity was trade, and the products which were exported were timber, wine, and above all olive-oil. Olive presses are to be found throughout the hinterland of Rugged Cilicia, as they were in the Syrian limestone massif. The Cilician production centers, however, had the advantage of being near to the sea, and thus the olive oil could be transported to the eastern empire's largest market, Constantinople, where it formed part of the *annona* ration for the population. A late-fifth-century inscription found at Abydus in the Dardanelles names the Cilicians as one of the major categories of ship owners who were involved in transporting the *annona* to Constantinople (see above, chapter 4).[30]

The eastern frontier zones

The nature, location, and economic impact of the Roman eastern frontier changed during the later empire. At the beginning of our period, Diocletian and the tetrarchs created an elaborate defensive system in the Near East which was typical of the early empire. Garrisons were stationed in Mesopotamia at Singara and Nisibis, on the middle Euphrates at Sura and at Circesium, along a frontier road, known as the *Strata Diocletiana*, which ran southwest from Sura to Damascus,[31] and from the city of Bostra through the oasis of Azraq to Dumatha in the Wadi Sirhan. The forts and milestones of the frontier were marked by grandiose Latin inscriptions dedicated by soldiers and army officers to Diocletian and his colleagues.[32]

Writing in the 520s, Malalas attributed to Diocletian the essential elements of the organization of Roman defense in Syria that was familiar in his own day:

> Diocletian also built fortresses on the *limes* from Egypt to the Persian borders, and stationed *limitanei* and *duces* for each province, to be stationed further back from the fortresses with a large force to ensure their security. (Malalas 308, trans. Jeffreys and Scott)

Soon after this date Procopius records warfare between the two Saracen confederations of the Ghassanids and the Lakhmids over an area called *Strata*, which was surely the former frontier road built by Diocletian (Procopius, *Bell.*

Pers. 2). Nevertheless, the organization of the defense of the region changed significantly between the end of the third and the sixth century. Responsibility was shared between a settled militia of *limitanei* and friendly tribes acting as Roman clients. By the end of the fourth century archaeology suggests that the forts along the steppic frontier southwest of the Euphrates were hardly manned by regular troops, although some reinforcement occurred during the early sixth century as open warfare was resumed against the Sassanian Empire.

The failure of Julian's Persian campaign in 363 was a serious blow to Rome, above all due to the loss of Nisibis, which had repeatedly resisted Persian sieges under Constantius and was described by Ammianus as the stoutest stronghold of the East (Ammianus 25.8.14). However, the treaty introduced a long period of peace, which was crucially important for the stability and prosperity of the Roman Near East in the fifth century. In the sixth century the status quo was disturbed by growing Persian aggression. Thanks to their advance bases at Singara and Nisibis, the Sassanians were a genuine military threat to Roman Syria. The cities of Mesopotamia and Osrhoene were attacked and besieged between 502 and 505, and again between 529 and 531. Syria itself was invaded and suffered seriously in 540 (see above, chapter 4). The Roman response was to create or reinforce the garrison towns along the potential invasion routes, at Amida (modern Diyarbakir), Circesium, Callinicum, Constantia, Rhesaina, and above all at Dara.[33] In each case a previously insignificant settlement was provided with permanent cavalry garrisons and imposing fortifications, usually high walls with closely spaced round towers. These outposts soon attracted much larger civilian populations than before, and generally received the status of cities. Sixth-century sources, principally inscriptions, indicate that out of sixteen sets of fortifications constructed in Syria at this period all but three were the work of the cities themselves, rather than the central Roman authorities. The defense of the empire had been sub-contracted to the local communities.[34]

There were also major developments in eastern Asia Minor. The Romans converted this open border into a fortified frontier, by creating a chain of walled strongholds along a line that ran almost exactly due north from Circesium on the Euphrates to the southeast corner of the Black Sea. It is difficult to date these changes precisely. Procopius ascribed to Justinian a great deal of work that had been undertaken by his predecessors. Much activity along the eastern frontier was certainly begun by Anastasius and carried on by Justin during the first quarter of the sixth century. The spur to this was the Persian invasion of 502 and the open hostilities in the East which lasted until 507. These were followed by an uneasy truce, but no real peace, so that modern historians have viewed the whole period from 502–32, when "eternal peace" was established between the combatants, as a single war.[35] There are good grounds for believing that much of the militarization of the zone was achieved during the strained intermission of hostilities between 507 and 529.[36] At the north end of the frontier was the fortress of Petra in Lazica, south of the river Phasis, which was re-founded by Justinian under the name Petra Pia Justiniana (Justinian, *Nov.* 28 [535]; Procopius, *Bell. Pers.* 2.15.10). It not only became the focus of warfare between the Romans and Persians during their struggle to control Lazica in 551, but was also the main harbor at the east end of the Euxine in the mid-sixth century.[37] Revealingly the remains of the site are dominated by a very large church, material evidence of the muscular and aggressive Christianity which was the hallmark of the empire of Justinian.

The main northern stronghold of western Armenia was Theodosiopolis (modern Erzurum), originally a hilltop fortress built by Theodosius II, but expanded by Anastasius into a city with a lengthy circuit wall.[38] This, like the construction of Dara (see below) was a response to the invasion of Kavad in 502, when the place had fallen to the Persians without resistance. Justinian is said to have built churches and monasteries (Procopius, *Buildings* 3.4.12–14), strengthened the fortifications, and made the city the headquarters of his general of the two Armenias (Procopius, *Buildings* 3.5.1–12). The fortresses of Pheison and Citharizon respectively guarded the routes between Persian Armenia and the districts of Sophanene and Arzanene (Procopius, *Buildings* 3.3.1–8). Citharizon, in a strategic position southeast of modern Bingöl, was the more important site and the headquarters of one of the two Roman field commanders in the region.[39]

Substantially more can be reconstructed from the history of Martyropolis–Maifaraqqin (modern Silvan). The city occupied a liminal position between the Roman Empire and the Persians, and controlled the southern access to the Bitlis pass, the only practicable route from Mesopotamia into highland Armenia around Lake Van.[40] The activities of Marutha, bishop of Martyropolis between 380 and 408, illustrate the cultural and religious interchange which became possible in the atmosphere of détente between Rome and Persia in the early fifth century.[41] When Martyropolis surrendered without resistance to the Persian invasion led by Kavad in 502, its citizens were able to preserve themselves from reprisals or deportation by returning to the king a gold chalice which had been presented to Marutha by Kavad's grandfather, Yazdgird I, and presenting him with two years' worth of taxation. Anastasius is said to have acquiesced when the Roman satrap of Sophanene, Theodorus, based at Martyropolis, was issued with his tokens of office by the Persians, since he thought that the city was indefensible. Justinian took a more robust approach and rebuilt the city walls (Procopius, *Buildings* 3.2.2–14).

Dara is the best studied of the eastern frontier positions (Plate 10.2). Anastasius took the decision to convert this frontier village, a day's journey northwest of Nisibis, into a fortified city in 505 and it took his name, Anastasiupolis (see above, chapter 4). The sources for the construction include a near contemporary reference in the Syriac *Chronicle* of Ps-Joshua, whose account is an invaluable reflection of the contemporary situation. Moreover, it shows that the fortification of Dara occurred in the context of other defensive building work along the Euphrates, largely organized and funded by local civic leaders:

> The emperor gave orders that a wall should be built for the village of Dara, which is situated on the frontier. They selected workmen from Syria, and they

Plate 10.2   The Fortifications of Dara in Mesopotamia (DAI Istanbul)

went thither and were building it; and the Persians were sallying forth from
Nisibis and forcing them to stop. (91) The excellent Sergius, bishop of Bîrtâ-
Kastra, which is situated beside us on the river Euphrates, began likewise to
build a wall at his town; and the emperor gave him no small sum of money
for his expenses. The Magister also gave orders that a wall should be built at
Europus, which is situated to the west of the river in the prefecture of Mabbug;
and the people of the place worked at it as best they could. (Ps-Joshua, *Chron.* 90,
trans. Wright)

Procopius' lengthy account of Dara, which he knew from his service under
Belisarius, exaggerates Justinian's contribution at the expense of Anastasius'.[42]

This sixth-century frontier from Mesopotamia to the Black Sea differed
radically from the early imperial *limes* along the upper Euphrates. The new
strongholds of the late empire were strategically sited castles, designed to
secure major routes (including access to the Black Sea) and to provide centers
from which the region could be controlled. They could only be bypassed at the
enemy's peril, for they cut off an attacker's lines of reinforcement, supply,
and retreat. The warfare of the period between Romans and Persians did not
involve pitched battles in the open plains, but assaults, sieges, and subversion
aimed at securing these positions.

At a local level the late Roman frontier was porous and economic life in the
frontier regions was typified by exchange and commerce, which often conflicted

with imperial attempts to control cross-border traffic. This is well described by Procopius for the people of Chorzanene in the highlands of northeast Anatolia, south of Erzerum:

> So the inhabitants of this region, whether subjects of the Romans or the Persians, have no fear of each other, nor do they give one another any occasion to apprehend and attack, but they even intermarry and hold a common market for their produce and together share the labours of farming. And if the commanders on either side ever make an expedition against the others, when they are ordered to do so by their rulers, they always find their neighbours unprotected. Their very populous towns are close to each other, yet from ancient times no stronghold existed on either side. (Procopius, *Buildings* 3.3.10–12, trans. Dewing)

This description shows local conditions in a zone where the imperial boundary cut through the region on an arbitrary basis, dividing peoples who had innumerable social, economic, and religious ties among themselves. In spite of this, the Romans and the Sassanians made a series of agreements that trade between the two empires should be restricted to a small number of trading posts. In 408/9 a regulation was introduced, that all cross-border trade was to be restricted to the three cities of Nisibis in Mesopotamia, Artaxata in Armenia, and Callinicum on the Euphrates (*CJust.* 4.63.4; the regulation was confirmed in 422, *CJust.* 4.63.6). These constraints on free trade remained in force through the fifth and sixth centuries, since the fully preserved treaty of 562 between Khusro I and Justinian states simply that Roman and Persian merchants of any sort should conduct their business in accordance with the old regulations at the established customs stations (Menander Protector fr. 6; see below, chapter 11). Procopius indicates that in the mid-sixth century the northern emporium for this long distance trade between the Roman Empire and the Far East was no longer Artaxata, but the nearby bishopric of Dubios (Dwin), eight days journey east of Theodosiopolis:

> In that region there are plains suitable for riding, and many very populous villages are situated in close proximity to one another, and numerous merchants conduct their business in them. For from India and the neighbouring regions of Iberia and some of those under the Roman sway they bring in merchandise and carry on their dealings with each other there. (Procopius, *Bell. Pers.* 2.25.2–3)

Tolls of 25 percent were imposed on imports to the Roman Empire from the East. It is clear that the merchandise involved in these transactions were not everyday goods but the luxuries of the East – precious metals, gems, spices, and silk. It had never been an economic proposition to transport low-value goods across the vast overland distances of these Asian routes. Conversely neither Rome nor Persia had the ability to prevent localized exchange in everyday goods across the imperial boundary. There is thus no contradiction between a state policy of restricted trade and free commerce throughout the border region.

Roman interest in access to eastern luxuries is most dramatically illustrated by the history of the silk trade. Silk was produced in a region called Serinda, to be identified with southern China, and traded both overland and by sea, through numerous intermediaries, to the West. All routes passed through the Sassanian Empire and were accordingly liable to heavy levies which were charged before they reached the Roman West. Justinian's interest in southern Arabia in 529 was aimed at restricting the Sassanian stranglehold on this trade (see above, chapter 4). Eventually the secret of silk production was cracked. In 551 missionary monks, returning from India, are said to have discovered and explained to Justinian how silk was produced, and were sent back to collect silk worms so that they could be bred in Constantinople, thus avoiding the need to obtain silk, at huge price, which had passed through the hands of the Sassanians (Procopius, *Bell.* 8.17.1–8).

Egypt

Egypt is often treated as a special case in regional or provincial studies of the Roman Empire. This is due to the nature of the documentation. Study of the society and economy of Egypt is mostly based on the documentary papyri, which present a huge scholarly challenge. These documents are almost always fragmentary, and require a very high level of technical analysis before they can be placed in a wider context that transforms them from being anecdotal fragments into pieces within an intelligible structure of administrative communication. Arguments that Egypt was unique, a world of its own, "serve in many cases mainly as an apology for scholarly unwillingness to come to terms with the quantity and difficulty of the papyrological evidence."[43] The converse of this argument is extremely important. Egypt is the one part of the Roman world where we can compare two categories of evidence for Roman rule in action: the information about legislation and administrative procedures in the law codes, and their actual application as revealed by the papyri. Where the two types of evidence point in the same direction there is a double historical gain. Firstly, we may have some confidence that they indicate how procedures actually worked. Secondly, we may reasonably suppose that the indications of the papyrological documentation should be broadly applicable to the rest of the east Roman world.[44] Egypt ought to provide important keys to wider questions, especially concerning the role of the state and the impact of tax demands on the development of provincial society and the regional economy.

However, it is also essential to recognize the limitations of the documentary data. The several Egyptian provinces, numbering from two to four according to changing Roman administrative arrangements, had been divided since pre-Ptolemaic times into districts called nomes, and almost all the papyri have been recovered from the administrative centers of the nomes, which acquired the title of *metropoleis* by the late Roman period.[45] The largest groups of documentary papyri come from the nome capitals of Oxyrhynchus, Arsinoe, Hermopolis, and Antinoopolis, all in the Heptanomia south of the Delta and north of the Thebaid, from Panopolis in the Thebaid, and from the villages of Theadelphia and Karanis, which were dependent on Arsinoe. They contain evidence for the organization of the census, tax collection, and the workings of the legal system at a middle range in the power spectrum. Out of picture at the top end is the center of Roman authority in Egypt, Alexandria. At the other extreme there is little to be heard from inhabitants of most village communities, especially those who did not speak or write in Greek, but used the vernacular language of everyday life, Coptic.

The history of Egypt in the early Roman Empire differed in one important respect from the normal pattern of the eastern provinces. Cities, defined as self-governing municipal units on the Greek model of the *polis*, were not created in most of Egypt before the beginning of the third century, when Septimius Severus permitted the nome capitals to appoint city councils for the first time. The purpose of this was doubtless in part to make the landowning classes responsible for the organization and payment of taxes to the Roman authorities, but the Severan reform also created a relatively cohesive urban elite, with common interests, which played a key role in Egyptian society for the following two centuries.[46] Councilors were generally rural landowners, whose powerbase now visibly shifted from their country estates to the urban centers. Towns thus began to acquire political dominance over the countryside.[47] A parallel development, tending in the same direction, was the decline of village-based pagan shrines, which preserved Egyptian religious traditions. By the fourth century there was a vacuum of culture and local leadership at village level, which seems rapidly to have been filled by the institutions of the church and Christianity. These conditions favored the Christianization of much of the Egyptian countryside even before the conversion of Constantine.[48] The towns meanwhile became centers of economic power and home to a Hellenized elite, which became the driving force of late Roman society.[49] The archaeological evidence for the urban settlements of late antiquity is now being taken seriously alongside the discussion of the papyri.[50] One of the consequences of the development of the nome *metropoleis* was that the overall culture of the inhabitants of the Nile Valley became closely assimilated to that of the east Roman world for the first time. Wine and olive production superseded the earlier reliance on the local staples of beer and beans as Egypt became part of Mediterranean society. Another product of this civic development was the extraordinary late flowering of Greek literature in Egypt, particularly at the city of Panopolis, the home of the poet Nonnus, in the fifth century.[51]

From the middle of the fourth century another crucial shift began to take place. The monetary economy of the Roman Empire rested on a gold standard, the introduction of the gold solidus by Constantine. This gold coinage was now used for the assessment and payment of taxes, for the remuneration of the growing numbers of imperial civil servants, soldiers, and other employees, and also for an increasing proportion of commercial transactions in the empire.[52] The classes of the imperial population who had readiest access to the currency were those paid in state gold, and they rapidly emerge as the nouveaux riches of late antiquity, using their wealth to acquire land, thus building up large estate holdings at the expense of earlier proprietors. The outcome of this process is best documented in fifth- and sixth-century Egypt, whose economy was increasingly dominated by large estate holders, who also held prominent positions in imperial service. The most famous example of this process is represented by the family of the Apions, which flourished from the late fifth to the seventh century and is attested as owning extensive property in at least three separate nomes. Flavius Apion, the first recorded member of the dynasty, was in charge of the commissariat which supplied Anastasius' forces at Edessa for the war in Mesopotamia in 504, and became praetorian prefect of the East under Justin in 518. His son Strategius was *praefectus Augustalis*, the highest imperial official in Egypt, in 523 and, like his father, reached the patriciate in Constantinople. His son, Flavius Apion II, was *dux* (military commander) of the Thebaid around the middle years of the sixth century and continued to hold high government positions in the area until his death in the late 570s. The last papyrus which explicitly refers to the family property dates to 625, during the period of Sassanian rule in Egypt. The size of the family holdings may be judged from the fact that it was responsible for two-fifths of the taxable revenue of Oxyrhynchus in the sixth century.[53]

The Western Empire

Africa

For the first century and a half of late antiquity Africa was protected by its geographical situation from many of the pressures that weighed on the rest of the empire.[54] The population was a mixture of indigenous peoples, collectively called Berbers (or simply *barbaroi*, barbarians) and long established immigrants, the majority from Italy, but also others from elsewhere in the Mediterranean.[55] Since the first century BC the region had enjoyed an enviable stability. The wealth of Africa derived in the first place from agricultural production. The large hinterland of Carthage in Africa Proconsularis and Byzacena was mainly taken up with cereal agriculture. In the early empire two-thirds of the annual harvest is said to have been exported to Rome. In the late second and third centuries oil production became a major feature of the interior of Numidia and Byzacena, and especially of the Tripolitanian hinterland. The territories of Lepcis Magna, Oea, and Sabratha were largely given over to producing oil, mainly for the Roman market. The pattern continued into the fourth century. Around 350 the anonymous author of the *Expositio totius mundi et rerum* remarked that Africa was wealthy in all things, including grain, fruit, trees, slaves, and textiles, but "it virtually exceeds all others in the use of the olive."

Collection of the *annona* was a priority in the later empire and recent study of the milestones of Africa Proconsularis, one of the main grain producing areas, indicates on-going repairs and the provision of road stations and collecting points to maximize efficiency in the collection of grain and other produce.[56] Like all tax collection in the late empire these methods were open to abuse and inevitably led to complaints. Aurelius Victor, in the *De Caesaribus* which he wrote around 360, noted: "the collectors were evil, open to bribery, cunning, roughnecks, grasping and almost naturally adapted to committing and concealing fraud." He should have known what he was talking about, as he describes his own father as being a poor African farmer (Aur. Victor, *Caes.* 33). The law codes also contain plenty of evidence for exploitation of this sort, but oppressive tax collection was an unavoidable feature of Roman rule at all periods, and we can no more take this as a reliable index of maladministration than the contrary description of Victor, bishop of Vita, who prefaced his account of the miseries brought by the Vandal invaders with the simple, and equally contestable assertion that the barbarians were unleashed on "a province that was peaceful and quiet and presenting a picture of a whole world in bloom" (Victor of Vita 1.1.3).

Settlement in the African provinces was based on a combination of small towns, *municipia*, and estates, which were made up from Berber villages. The towns were the focus for the public activities of provincial landowners, many ultimately of immigrant origin, and these preserved their civic institutions until the early fifth century. Local magistracies were a focus for aristocratic ambitions, and not only the secular but also the non-Christian religious institutions of small town life flourished later in North Africa than anywhere else in the empire. The epigraphic and archaeological evidence from the municipalities and colonies of Africa in the late fourth century evoke an age of independent, self-sufficient cities, whose magistracies and priesthoods continued to be filled by members of the local landowning families. Inscriptions imply that these men still spent much surplus income for the benefit of their home towns on buildings, games, and public festivals.[57] This picture need not correspond wholly to reality, and there is evidence from the law codes, as there is from elsewhere in the empire, that local councilors and others were increasingly reluctant to carry the burdens and expenses of office. However, it is beyond doubt that the African gentry were still anxious to keep up appearances.

Changes occurred in the fifth and sixth centuries, which have been summarized by Mattingly and Hitchner, in their invaluable recent survey of archaeological work on Roman Africa. Many fora ceased to function or played a reduced role in urban life. Some of their functions were replaced by buildings attached to churches, which often occupied part of the earlier fora. Temples in particular, and some bath buildings, fell into ruin; large peristyle houses were broken up into smaller units; shop fronts, workshops, and booths appeared along the street frontages. However, it is evident that these changes implied not so much an overall downturn in economic conditions as a change in social priorities.[58]

Under the settled conditions of the empire the native populations had a large stake in sustained peace and order. Many, in accordance with the early imperial laws, the *lex Manciana* and the *lex Hadriana*, became tenants on huge estates owned by the landed aristocracy, with rights of usufruct and inheritance, but paying a third of their produce as rent. The terms of these leases, which were attractive to long-term tenants, were still in force at the end of the fifth century.[59] As in Syria, the country villages of the Numidian uplands multiplied and became more densely populated between the second and sixth centuries. Productivity presumably rose as the population increased and Africa established itself as the economic powerhouse of the late Roman western Mediterranean. The diagnostic feature of this success was the penetration achieved by African ceramic production in western markets. The most widely distributed fine pottery ever produced in the ancient world was African red-slip. From the late first century until the end of antiquity, African red-slip table wares were found throughout the empire from Scotland to Ethiopia, and came close to mono-polizing the market in the wealthier parts of the western Mediterranean, in Italy, Gaul, and Spain. This was matched by the equally spectacular success of African oil exports. The production of the first amphoras designed specifically for the oil trade, the so-called "piccolo Africano" and "grande Africano," which appear in the last second and early third centuries, corresponds to the huge development and growth of Tunisian and Tripolitanian olive production. Combined with the enormous export trade in grain to Rome, these oil and ceramic industries made Africa the equivalent of a modern economic super-power. The favorable terms of the leases regulated by the *lex Manciana* and the *lex Hadriana* encouraged tenants to produce on a commercial basis for the market. Africa had good products to sell: fine table wares which wiped the floor with locally produced competitors, and abundant olive oil for the grow-ing needs of urban markets. An equally crucial factor was that roads, harbors, transport ships, and the human organization needed to operate large-scale exports had been developed to deliver grain and oil to Rome. Fine pottery and many other African products were sent to overseas markets on the back of the *annona* system. A third point not to be underestimated in the African economic success story was that the region was almost completely shielded from the burdens of warfare.[60]

The invasion of the Vandals had a major impact on political and religious conditions in Africa, but seems not to have inflicted heavy damage on the regional economy. The newcomers were now the main political authority, with the ability to impose their will by the threat of military force. The royal palace was sited on the Byrsa, the acropolis of Carthage, and Vandal confidence in their regional supremacy seems to be reflected in the fact that Carthage's city walls, which had been built under Theodosius I, were allowed to fall into disrepair in the mid-fifth century. Vandal warrior families predictably claimed some of the best land in Africa for themselves. There are remarkably few archaeological traces of their presence, but the handful of inscribed epitaphs for Vandals and the precise locations indicated by literary sources can almost all be plotted within the boundaries of Africa Proconsularis, forming Carthage's enlarged hinterland.[61] According to Procopius, Gaiseric took property from many African landowners and distributed it to his own people. These estates were still called *kleroi Bandilon* in Procopius' time. The Vandals effectively stepped into the shoes of the Roman authorities that had ruled Africa previously, and took over the existing administrative regime, including the tax system.

Archaeological evidence suggests that the export of goods and produce from Africa was not seriously impaired by the Vandal conquest, but very little Roman bronze coinage seems to have circulated in Vandal Africa, and the Vandals produced their own issues or re-circulated earlier types. The overall economic effects of the Vandal kingdom both within and outside Africa have yet to be fully assessed. There is some indication that goods that had previously been exported to Rome and Italy were now redirected westwards towards Visigothic Spain and southern Gaul. Rome was now presumably obliged to purchase grain that had previously been sent from Africa in the form of tax, and may have turned increasingly to Sicily as an alternative source of supply.

During the fifth and sixth centuries the Moors (Mauri), based in the Aures mountains, emerged as a prominent factor in ethnic and political conflicts. After the reconquest of Africa by Justinian, successive governors encountered much more significant resistance from Moors under tribal leaders, some of whom had served in the Roman army. The Roman reconquest of Africa seems to have damaged the local economy, above all due to the imposition of high levels of taxation (see below p. 381). Justinian's forces and successive east Roman commanders assumed not so much the role of liberators as of occupiers. There were aspirations to revive city life. Procopius has an eloquent passage extolling the rebuilding of the previously insignificant and waterless town of Caputvada, where Belisarus' forces had first set foot on African soil:

> Justinian . . . conceived the desire to transform this place forthwith into a city which should be made strong by a wall and distinguished by other constructions as worthy to be counted a prosperous and impressive city; and the purpose of the emperor has been realised. For the wall and the city has been brought to completion, and the condition of the territory is being suddenly changed. The country-dwellers have thrown aside the plough and lead the existence of a community, no longer going the round of country tasks but living a city life. They pass their days in the market place and hold assemblies to deliberate on questions which concern them; and they traffic with one another, and conduct all the other affairs which pertain to the dignity of a city. (Procopius, *Buildings* 6.6.13–16, adapted from trans. of Dewing)

However, little other evidence supports this optimistic picture of civic renewal outside Carthage, where a broader-based program of urban restoration seems to have been attempted. Fortifications were erected at many of the major cities, including Lepcis Magna, Sabratha, Theveste, and Sitifis, but the new defended circuits were much smaller than those of their fourth-century precursors, and sometimes cut directly across the central areas of the cities.[62] The aim of most of Justinian's building program was to maintain military control of the African provinces (Procopius, *Buildings* 6.5–7). In striking contrast with sixth-century Syria, where almost all city fortification was undertaken at local initiative, most of the building inscriptions relating to fortifications in Byzantine Africa indicate that they were constructed by the occupying force, including twenty-four erected by the praetorian prefect Solomon on behalf of Justinian.[63] The perceived insecurity of the country is in marked contrast to the Vandal period, when the fortifications of Hadrumetum had been deliberately removed (Procopius, *Buildings* 6.6.1). Indeed Procopius' account of the later years of the Byzantine reconquest of Africa, after the initial defeat of the Vandals, does little to hide the high level of conflict and disruption.[64]

The final eclipse of Romanized civic life in Africa came swiftly. Carthage was abandoned after the Arab conquest and replaced in 670 by the new foundation of Qayrawan. The Berber tribes, which had grown in strength during the period of east Roman rule, at first resisted but later offered support to the Arabs and provided much of the manpower that extended the Muslim conquests to the Atlantic and Spain.[65] Christianity was eclipsed, and despite the extraordinary manifestation of small-town culture and civic organization that had prevailed in African history between the second and fifth centuries, post-Roman Africa appears to owe less to its classical antecedents than any other part of the ancient world where city life had flourished.

Gaul

The Gallic provinces were at the heart of the western Roman Empire in late antiquity. The transformation of their political and social structures during the fifth century helps to define our understanding of the collapse of the empire itself. These changes were extremely complex. They involved the abandonment of the frontier defenses of the empire; the encroachment and emergence of new ethnic groups, speaking different languages; wholesale economic restructuring; and major religious realignments.

The third century had already presented an alarming preview of future events when the Rhine frontier had been exposed to major invasions by Germanic groups, which had been able to range and plunder extensively in northern Gaul. Their impact is dramatically illustrated by the discovery at the Rhine crossing of Rheinzabern of three boatloads of loot, which had been plundered from the villas of northeastern Gaul by a raiding party. The hoard contains numerous virtual replica sets of the tools and household equipment of these farms. The region of the Marne and the Somme in northern France was covered with small villas, evenly distributed across the countryside.[66] The armies of Germania Inferior and Germania Superior were heavily dependent on produce from the northern regions of Gaul, and the pattern of well equipped, evenly resourced rural estate centers implies that the organization of rural production to supply the garrisons was systematically standardized.[67] The settled but undefended population of this region was acutely vulnerable when the frontier defenses collapsed. The raiders went for these exposed rural targets. "They avoid the actual towns as if they were tombs surrounded by nets," wrote Ammianus of the Alemanni in the 350s (Ammianus 16.2).

Roman authority in Gaul was reasserted by the tetrarchs and Constantine. Their overriding aim was to re-establish the old frontier along the Rhine and across southern Germany to the upper Danube. As always Roman military power was made effective by a combination of good communications and effective garrisoned strong points. The frontier roads, ensuring communications between Neumagen, Trier, and Cologne and along the Rhine itself were repaired and garrisoned, and the critical route from Cologne through Tongres and Beauvais to Boulogne, the Channel port, was protected by fortlets. The north–south highway through France from Trier to Lugdunum and then south to Arles and Marseilles in Provence was another key to political control. This was also the route by which supplies moved, by road and river, from the Mediterranean to the northern frontier zone.

Up to the reign of Valentinian I, the emperors invested heavily in maintaining the status quo. Diocletian extended the legionary fort at Kaiseraugst perhaps to accommodate troops from *legio I Martia*. Constantine rebuilt the bridgehead fort at Cologne-Deutz (*ILS* 8937).[68] Julian's campaigns in northern Gaul, and those of Constantius' generals around the Alpine fringes, were aimed at securing the frontier from Alemannic incursions. This policy continued under Valentinian, who, like Julian, sometimes placed forts beyond the river. Within the *limes* it seems to have been policy to establish a zone 20–40 kilometers broad, where roads were protected by regularly-spaced forts and watch towers. Inscriptions attest numerous *burgi* along the upper reaches of the Rhine (*ILS* 8949, 371). Large numbers of similar fortifications were also built further east in the great Danube bend between Brigetio and Aquincum (*ILS* 762, 774–5).[69] During the fourth century fortified silos were built at larger farms near the Rhine.

The Gallic provinces also provided important tax revenues. This emerges clearly in the continuous arguments between Julian and the officials appointed by Constantius to operate in the province. Ammianus points out that oppressive taxation, in areas that already suffered both from the continuous presence of Roman troops and from constant barbarian threats, severely debilitated the provinces close to the northern frontiers.

> (Julian) knew that the irremediable damage inflicted by settlements or, to give them a truer name, unsettlements of this kind had often brought provinces to utter poverty; the very thing, as will be shown later, completely ruined Illyricum. (Ammianus 17.3, trans. Hamilton)

The same theme is picked up when Ammianus discusses the activities of the Praetorian Prefect of Illyricum, Anatolius, during the campaigns of Constantius II against the Limigantes on the frontiers of Pannonia.

> Under the rule of Anatolius, who was then praetorian prefect in Illyricum, supplies of all kinds had been collected even before they were needed and were pouring in without expense to anyone. It is an established fact that the northern provinces

have never to this day been so prosperous under any other prefect. Anatolius ... relieved the provincials from the enormous expense of the imperial post service, which had ruined countless homes, and from the hardships of taxation. In fact the inhabitants of those parts might well have lived thereafter happy and untroubled lives with all their grievances settled, but for the abominable refinements of taxation to which they were later exposed. (Ammianus 19.11, trans. Hamilton)

The imperial palace and administrative center at Trier, Augusta Treverorum, which had been the capital of the breakaway Gallic empire under Postumus in the 260s, was at the hub of Roman power in northwest Europe. The city covered an area of c.285 hectares with an estimated population of 80,000, by far the largest urban settlement north of the Alps. Construction in the city was on a comparably grand scale. The fortifications of the third century were completed by the Black Gate, whose four-storied towers with a great frontal facade of arcades and colonnades were built not for functional defense but to make a deliberate statement about imperial power. The central palace, adjoining a hippodrome, housed the tetrarch Maximianus and his Caesar Constantius. In 326 work began on a new religious core for the city: two large basilicas, the smaller already complete by 330, and a baptistery. This formed the north end of an enlarged palatial complex, including the finest imperial audience chamber to survive to modern times. Trier was a residence for Constans in the 340s, for Valentinian from 365–75, and for Gratian and the usurper Magnus Maximus in the 380s. It has been argued that Julian, who spent little time in Trier, deliberately avoided the city between 358 and 360 as he was building up his Gallic power base further south in Gallia Belgica, in preparation for this own bid for power in 360.[70] The city was also the headquarters of the Praetorian Prefect for Gaul. Trier was already notable for a very large bath house built in the second century AD. This was to be eclipsed by the so-called *Kaiserthermen*, the imperial baths (Plate 3.2). Work on these began before the middle of the fourth century, but they seem to have been converted for use as another palatial or administrative center under Valentinian. Large warehouses were also built near the river Mosel at this period, presumably to supply the imperial *comitatus*.

Trier was eclipsed as the empire's western capital at the end of the fourth century. Valentinian II was briefly based there in 389–90, but Honorius, who was raised to the rank of Augustus to succeed him in January 393, never ventured beyond the protective ring of the Alps. He was resident in Milan for almost a decade, but moved for greater security to Ravenna at the end of 402, marking a definitive change in the regime style of the western empire. At the same period the residence of the regional praetorian prefect was moved to Arles in Provence, at the southern end of the central Gallic highway. Arles had become a ruler's residence in the early fourth century, both for Maximianus between 307 and 310, and for Constantine between 314 and 316. A hippodrome built at this period incorporated an obelisk of Egyptian granite, a clear mark of a major imperial center.[71] Arles was famously described as *Gallula Roma Arelas*, a small Gallic version of Rome (Ausonius, *Ordo Urbium nobilium* 10). The success of its riverine harbor depended partly on its commercial role, but much of the activity which took place there has been related to the Roman *annona* system. This is shown in the brief account of Gaul by the mid-fourth-century author of the *Expositio Totius Mundi*, whose description focused on its two imperial cities:

> It is said that [the province of Gaul] has a very great city called Trier, where, it is said, the emperor lives; this is in the middle of the land. It also has another city which comes to the aid of Trier in all things, it is situated by the sea and is called Arles. It receives the merchandise of the whole world and sends it on to the previously mentioned city. (*Exp. Tot. Mundi* 58)

The fortunes of Arles were therefore intimately linked to those of the western empire.[72] The fortifications were rebuilt in late antiquity, probably during the fifth century as a defense against the Visigoths. The walls were evidently the result of local efforts at self help, and the size of the defended area of the city, around seventeen hectares, placed Arles among the smaller towns of Gaul, much reduced from the settlement in the first three centuries.[73]

This was part of a general pattern in fifth-century Gaul, a region whose economic resilience lay in the countryside. By the beginning of the sixth century the region between the Rhine and the Loire was controlled by the Frankish kingdom of the Merovingians. Franks had been a presence in the Rhineland during the third and fourth centuries, and clearly began to settle in numbers south and west of the Rhine as the frontier disintegrated at the beginning of the fifth century. Through the early fifth century their settlements spread until they became political masters of the region. The tomb of the first king of the dynasty, Childeric, who died around 481, was discovered at Tournai in the seventeenth century, and the grave goods, including imported coins from the east Roman kingdom, establish a benchmark for our grasp of the material culture of the Frankish nobility.

A recent survey of the evidence on the ground suggests that the evolution of a new Frankish polity in northern France was gradual not dramatic. Archaeology has conclusively refuted the traditional belief that the regional economy in late antiquity depended on large estates, owned by the wealthy few and worked by an increasingly depressed tenantry.[74] In contrast to the eastern empire, only one large landholding, comprising several rural settlements enclosed by a landwall, has been identified in northern Gaul, near Trier. The larger houses of the Roman elite, with evidence for reception rooms, galleries, bath-houses, and heating systems, are no longer found after 300, but peasant life continued uninterrupted. Dispersed villages, often in forested country and built from wood rather than stone, were the most important settlement type. It is difficult to distinguish settlements of the incoming Franks from those of the existing inhabitants, although the appearance of a new settlement type extending from the Rhine to Normandy and comprising groups of large rectilinear wooden longhouses, resembling cattle sheds in design, may be associated with the

Germanic peoples.[75] During the later fourth and through the fifth centuries the number of identifiable sites was reduced, and imports of fine pottery from the Mediterranean production centers of northern Italy, southern Gaul, and Spain were not resumed until the sixth and early seventh centuries, when some African and eastern products occur. However, the local pottery manufacturing centers of L'Argonne and Mayon continued until the end of the sixth or seventh centuries, implying that the trading economy did not collapse but was re-oriented around local consumers, who had replaced the Roman army as the main market. Trade and exchange at a local level certainly facilitated the mixture and fusion of former provincials and the incoming Franks. By 500 the decline in population had bottomed out and most of northern France established a sustainable, largely self-sufficient rural economy.

This was the social and economic underpinning of the Frankish kingdom. The Frankish kings dispersed their power by maintaining royal residences in some of the old centers, notably Metz, Trier, Soissons, and Paris, and these were to emerge again as significant centers in the later Merovingian period.[76] The evolution of Metz between the fourth and seventh century is the best illustration of this process. The walls of the Roman town enclosed a defended area of about seventy hectares. Bath houses and churches were being constructed up to the late fourth century, and Metz's prosperity is probably due to its links via the river Mosel and by road with Trier. However, excavations at different sites through the city all point to a break at the beginning of the fifth century, sometimes marked by fire damage, and this may be linked to a similar collapse of the rural villa system. The downturn is surely connected with the barbarian incursions after 407 and the imperial retreat from Trier. A low point in this process came in 451, when Metz was sacked by Attila's Huns, with only the cathedral of St Stephen being spared (Hydatius, *Chronicle* 100–1; Greg. Tur., *Hist.* 2.6). Halsall, in a recent study, argues that many of the inhabitants of the rump of Roman Metz lived outside the walls south of the former civic center, but the main church remained protected. The city did not revive until after 560. It was chosen as a royal capital by the Frankish kings, and their impact can be seen in energetic church building (some directly due to royal foundations), aristocratic burials, and the introduction of important ritual processions which were the occasions for competitive aristocratic display. By this period traders were again active (Greg. Tur., *Mir.* 4.29) and traffic along the Mosel with Trier had been resumed. The political evolution of the Frankish kingdom and the behavior of the Frankish aristocracy appear responsible for this economic upturn which continued into the seventh century and the later Merovingian period.[77]

To the north and beyond the English channel, the picture is less rosy. The Ardennes region of Belgium and the Hunsrück between Cologne and Trier, for instance, appear largely deserted at this period. In fifth- and sixth-century England agricultural settlement was significantly poorer, and the absence of wheel-made pottery suggests that a market economy hardly survived in the post-Roman period.[78]

The pattern in southern Gaul was different, particularly in the areas with ready access to Mediterranean ports and in regular contact with Italy. The countryside had been dominated by large landowners, closely linked by tradition, family ties, and shared culture to the senatorial aristocracy of Italy. By far the best-known representative of this class was Sidonius Apollinaris. The southern Gallic landowners were the first provincial group outside the imperial government that had to work out a *modus vivendi* with the barbarian kingdoms during the mid-fifth century. They ceded land, tax revenue, and important strong points, especially at Toulouse and in Aquitaine, to the Visigoths, and in the Rhone valley to the Burgundians, while attempting to retain their regional influence, economic purchase, and social position. Such men were not lacking in experience and a measure of military steel. After the virtual disappearance of Roman troops, they looked to their own defense, organized local militias, and manned the walls of the southern Gallic cities.

As the political structures of the western empire disintegrated, the major families built their hopes for survival on the church. Sidonius' career is emblematic, as he transformed himself from being a seigneurial landowner, and one of the last prominent representatives of western classical culture, to become bishop of the embattled town of Clermont-Ferrand, holding out against the pressures from the Burgundian and Visigothic courts.[79] A generation later Caesarius of Arles, now schooled in the Christian ascetic tradition rather than in classical literature, came from a similar landed Roman background to become bishop of Arles, the most powerful ecclesiastical position in southern Gaul.[80] Gradually in this transition great private estates evolved into church properties and monastic foundations.

Growing insecurity was certainly a factor which led to the decline of the larger villas, especially during the fifth century, but it seems likely that many of their inhabitants regrouped in the cities. The main towns remained viable centers both of local administration and of economic activity. Although their wall circuits were reduced and their the populations were significantly smaller than in the early empire, Geneva, Arles, Bordeaux, Vienne, and Lyon contained numerous churches and monastic establishments. The ruling elite, now in ecclesiastical garb, were able to commandeer the resources of the countryside and transform them into public buildings. Previously inhabited areas, however, were abandoned, while larger urban houses were overlain by smaller structures and sometimes replaced by intra-mural burial sites around the churches.[81]

The conspicuous exception to this pattern was Gaul's main Mediterranean harbor at Marseilles, which displays ample signs of economic vitality up till the seventh century.[82] Marseilles came into its own after the end of the fourth century. The occupied area of the city, unlike those of the other Gallic cities, seems to have grown substantially, and Christianization was very marked. The baptistery of the Episcopal church, built around 400, was over twice the size of any other baptistery in southern France and larger even than that of the imperial capital of Milan. Marseilles illustrates the rule that harbor cities had a much greater capacity for population growth than towns in the interior. Trade, commerce, and manufacture all flourished. Imports from the eastern Mediterranean and from Africa passed through the port and into the interior of France along the traditional riverine routes. As African trade with Italy may have declined during the Vandal period, the economic axis between Carthage and the north Mediterranean probably shifted west to Marseilles. Conversely, the port became the Frankish kingdom's outlet to the Mediterranean world.

The fall of the Roman Empire had a major economic impact on Gaul. After the end of the fourth century, as territory in the western provinces was surrendered to the Germanic kingdoms, the Roman tax base, deriving largely from landed income, shrunk. The northwestern provinces were thrown back on their own resources. The most vivid single illustration of this underlying trend relates not to Gaul but to Britain. In 410 the British *civitates* at first chose to govern themselves independently of the legitimate western emperor Honorius and the usurper Constantine and then, when they appealed to Honorius for troops to protect them from the Saxons, received the reply that they should look to their own defense (Zosimus 6.5.3, 10.2). The writing was also on the wall for their continental neighbors.

In Gaul, the transition to a post-Roman, early medieval world differed between the north and the south. In the north the withdrawal of permanent Roman garrisons and garrison towns along and near the Rhine frontier removed the raison d'être for the complex and sophisticated system of communications which had been created in the early empire, employing both river and road transport, and which had been the basis for most economic activity. The Franks, who soon fused with the existing settled population, put in place their own networks of exchange which were smaller scale, more self sufficient, and based on local markets. In the south civic traditions were stronger and the towns survived, although they were now transformed into smaller fortified centers, dominated by a new ecclesiastical hierarchy. Contacts and commercial exchange with the Mediterranean were still maintained, above all through the port of Marseilles. However, the driving forces of the economy were no longer the needs of the Roman state but the demands and aspirations of the Frankish kings and of the organized church, which through its monastic foundations, growing landholdings, and expanding network of churches, was the main stakeholder in the regional economy.

Italy

Italy's relative importance within the western empire increased during late antiquity. This was due both to the practical division of the empire itself after 395, and to the loss of territory in the west and in Africa to the barbarian kingdoms. A moment of major significance came when Honorius transferred the imperial capital of the western empire from Milan to Ravenna in 402. Ravenna had been important under the empire as the headquarters of the

Roman fleet in the Adriatic, and as such had been a center of shipbuilding and some commercial activity. The main harbor was at Classis, about four kilometers from the city, and the site had been chosen for defensive reasons. The marshes and canals of this coastal region provided a buffer against attack from the land, while the harbor guaranteed communications and enabled supplies to be brought in by sea. After 476 Ravenna continued to serve as the administrative center first of Odoacer's kingdom and then of Ostrogothic Italy, and in the 560s was transformed into a dependency of Byzantium, the Exarchate. The city is famous above all for its extraordinary monuments associated with the rulers who made their homes there: the Mausoleum of Galla Placidia, constructed around 450; the baptisteries respectively for the orthodox Catholic and Arian Gothic communities; the basilica churches of the first half of the sixth century, S. Apollinare Nuovo, S. Apollinare in Classe, and S. Vitale (Plate 5.6), which contain the finest surviving ecclesiastical mosaics of late antiquity; and the circular Mausoleum of Theoderic (Plate 6.1). The lavishness and quality of these buildings provides a corrective to the impression of political weakness that is implicit in all narratives of the final generations of the western empire. They bear witness to the vigor of the Ostrogothic court. Whereas the written sources, above all the *Variae* of Cassiodorus, portray Theoderic and his successors as rulers of Italy in the style of western emperors, operating in close concert with the Italian senatorial aristocracy, the art of Ravenna shows close links to the cultural world of the eastern empire and the court at Constantinople.

Ravenna depended on a northern Italian hinterland, which comprised the Po Valley to the west, and Istria, across the Adriatic, to the east. Cassiodorus described the latter as Ravenna's Campania, "the storeroom of the royal city, covered with olives, glorious for its corn, rich in vines, where all crops flow in desirable fertility, as though from three udders generous in their milk." The sea produced fish and shellfish, but also substantial tax revenues which were collected both in gold and in kind (Cassiodorus, *Var.* 12.22, trans. Barnish). Most of the produce which was consumed in Ravenna must have been brought in by sea through the port at Classis, and excavations here are an important index of Ravenna's rise and decline. There is no evidence for commercial activity after 700.[83]

The overall picture of Italian settlement in late antiquity suggests that rural settlements became fewer and more impoverished between the third and seventh centuries.[84] The evidence of several recent rural survey projects in central Italy suggests that the numbers of sites occupied around 500 were only 20 percent of the figures for the first century. Smaller sites in particular virtually vanish from the record.[85] By the seventh century the lack of coinage in circulation, especially in northern regions, suggests that the market economy had in large part collapsed.

On the other hand the population and economy of southern Italy appears to have held up. No comparable decline in settlement numbers is apparent in Apulia, Basilicata, and Lucania, and the cities of Lucania and Bruttium were still going concerns in the early sixth century.[86] This was due to the growing contribution made by south Italy to the needs of Rome itself. Rome's economic horizon had begun to close in during the fourth century, as Constantinople acquired the status of an imperial capital and received imports, especially from Egypt, that had previously been shipped to Italy. Under the Vandals the city no longer received tax grain from Africa. It drew instead on local resources and there was a huge traffic in food staples from the Italian countryside to Rome, whose population still approached half a million in the mid-fifth century. The implications of Rome's continuing food requirements and their impact on the economy especially of southern Italy has been explored in a remarkable study by Barnish. Legal sources, literature, and archaeological evidence can be combined to produce a picture of complex and vibrant economic activity with wide social ramifications. These factors help to explain why southern Italy remained prosperous when areas to the north were in sharp decline. The recent excavations of villa sites in Samnium and Lucania demonstrate that they were heavily involved in pig-rearing, unquestionably to supply the Roman market, where pork had been added to the grain ration of the early imperial period. During late antiquity wine production in southern Italy appears to have outstripped the output from Etruria, Latium, and Campania, which had traditionally supplied early imperial Rome. Amphoras of the type Keay LII, which occur in considerable quantities between the late fourth and late fifth centuries at Rome and Marseilles, as well as at other coastal sites of the western Mediterranean and the Adriatic, were produced in Calabria. They suggest large-scale wine exports.[87]

Between the fourth and sixth centuries these developments particularly benefited senatorial families, which had consolidated their wealth in great estates, particularly in the south and in Sicily. The influence of such families, and their importance to Italy's rulers, emperors and kings alike, is best illustrated by a famous letter, penned by Cassiodorus in the name of Theoderic, which asked the Senate to confirm the rank of *patricius* on his own father after he had served as governor of Sicily, the province that virtually adjoined the family's main estates in Bruttium. The letter refers to the achievements of the honorand's father and grandfather as well. His grandfather had defended Bruttium and Sicily against the Vandals around 440. His father had been a member of a delegation to Attila acting on behalf of Aetius, but had subsequently retired from public service to the family estates in Bruttium. Another branch of the family had distinguished itself in Constantinople in the later fifth century (Cassiodorus, *Var.* 1.4). Cassiodorus himself retired from service in 537, and transferred from Ravenna to Constantinople at the end of Belisarius' campaign in 540. He returned to Italy after the peace of 554 to his family estate at Squillace in Bruttium, now to create a monastic retreat amid a community of monks and a library of Christian literature. His retreat from the challenges of secular politics mirrors that of the emperor Justinian in his later years.

A serious down-turn in the villa economies only seems to set in after the first quarter of the sixth century. This was due to a complex interplay of factors, including the climatic disasters of the 530s and 540s, the declining population and market in Rome, and the impact of the Roman invasion of 536 and the Gothic wars, which devastated Italy for nearly twenty years up to the mid-550s (see below, chapter 11).[88]

Italy now became a frontier province of the east Roman Empire. The Longobards (Lombards) invaded Italy in 568 and began a lengthy struggle for control with the east Roman exarchate. Their impact may be compared with that of the Berbers in Africa at this period. Unlike the Ostrogoths, who had taken control of Italy with Roman blessing and exploited the Roman administrative framework, the Longobards had no stake in the Roman Empire or interest in perpetuating it in a modified form. Italy was divided into a patchwork of protectorates between the newcomers and the Romans. There are many indications of discontinuity on city sites, even when these continued to be occupied. Wood replaced stone as the main building material in many areas; imported pottery was entirely supplanted by local coarse wares; population levels certainly dropped. It is a matter for debate how far these indications should be seen as symptoms of absolute economic and social decline, or of a radically altered social system. It is hard to dispute that most identifiable traces of the political and economic structures of the ancient classical world had now disappeared.[89] But this is not quite the end of the story. The Latin language was not supplanted by a Germanic dialect, the Lombard aristocracy in the eighth century had tombstones carved that transparently mimicked Roman gravestones of the early imperial period, and Lombard leaders were buried in Roman-style sarcophagi.[90] They, like the Burgundians, continued to assert a claim to a form of Roman identity after Roman political power had collapsed.

The Danube region and the Balkans

The Balkans under late Roman rule was the least developed and least classical part of the Roman Empire. The mark left by Rome was nevertheless clear and took a familiar military form. Along the Danubian frontier itself there were legionary fortresses, smaller military installations, and a frontier road. There were bridges and other major engineering works along the Danube and its tributaries. The Black Sea fleet patrolled the Danube's lower reaches, and freight was transported along the river. The main east–west trunk road from Constantinople ran through Adrianople, Serdica, Naissus, Viminacium, Singidunum, Sirmium, Mursa, and Poetovia to Aquileia in northeast Italy. This route witnessed all the major troop movements and the engagements of the civil wars between Diocletian's victory over Carinus in 285 and Theodosius' defeat of Eugenius in 394. These wars were on a larger scale than any of the confrontations between Romans and barbarian groups in the region, and their regional impact was correspondingly very large.[91] The *via Egnatia*, from Constantinople to Thessalonica and across northern Greece to Dyrrhachium, which had been built in the second century BC, played a subsidiary role in imperial communications in the third and fourth centuries, but became more important in the fifth and sixth centuries, as the central Balkan region became insecure. These roads and military installations were the direct product of imperial policies, decisions, and initiatives.

Civic life, however, remained seriously underdeveloped away from the eastern Aegean, Propontic, and western Black Sea coasts. Between the first and third centuries there were no more than sixty-nine municipalities and colonies in all the Rhine and Danube frontier provinces between the North Sea and the Black Sea.[92] Local aristocracies only sporadically emerged to dominate provincial society through their continued control of landed wealth. There is little evidence for large landed estates, and the Balkans, with the marginal exception of Dalmatia on the Adriatic, produced few Roman senators.[93] Military officers and soldiers were the most powerful element in society, and it was not unusual for such men to serve as magistrates in local towns, many of which had grown up in the immediate neighborhood of military camps.[94]

The archaeological study of settlements in the Danube region is less developed than in Gaul or Italy. Most work has been done in the provinces of Valeria and Pannonia Prima (modern Hungary), where the late Roman remains, notably a series of rectangular, fortress-like enclosures of the later fourth century attest a general climate of insecurity. Their walls, strengthened by numerous round towers, protected stone-built granaries, churches, and slighter structures. They have been variously interpreted as fortified refuges for the local populations, an interior frontier line behind the Danube *limes*, or secure collection points for the imperial *annona*.[95]

In the later Roman Empire the two most important urban centers were Sirmium in the West and Thessalonica in the East, both of which were used as headquarters by the praetorian prefects of Illyricum. The defenses of Sirmium were improved by Petronius Probus during Sarmatian and Quadic attacks on Pannonia in 373. Ammianus' description indicates that the civic building of a theater was sacrificed to allow the town defenses to be improved:

> He cleared out the moats, which were choked with rubbish, and indulged his native taste for building by raising the greater part of the walls, which had been neglected and allowed to decay owing to the long peace. Even high towers with battlements were now erected, and the works were quickly finished, because he found that materials collected some time before to build a theater would suffice for his purpose. (Ammianus 29.6, trans. Hamilton)

Thessalonica, which was accessible by sea from Constantinople, proved a more secure base than Sirmium. Under the tetrarchy it became Galerius' capital, whose buildings included the surviving triumphal arch built to celebrate his victories over the Sassanians in 297, a rotunda intended as his mausoleum, and a palace with a hippodrome next to it. Thessalonica was the imperial base for Constantine's naval campaign against Licinius in 324 and for his campaigns on the Danube in the 330s, and became Theodosius' headquarters from 380 to 382 during his attempt to redress the disastrous situation after the battle of Adrianople. The city was a secure haven for Valentinian II and

Justina when they fled to Theodosius from Magnus Maximus. As well as high-level administrative personnel attached to the praetorian prefect of Illyricum there was always a substantial garrison. In the later 440s Thessalonica definitively replaced Sirmium, which had been sacked by the Huns, as the administrative center of Illyricum, and received lengthy fortifications, accompanied by new government buildings and major churches.[96] According to the seventh-century *Life of St Demetrius*, when Zeno showed signs of relinquishing imperial control over the city to Theoderic the Amal in the 470s, the inhabitants threw down imperial statues and besieged the palace of the prefect of Illyricum, seized the keys of the city gate from the prefect, and handed them over to the bishop of the city. St Demetrius' life also shows that in the early seventh century Thessalonica was the only safe haven against the barbarians, as the Balkans were lost to Roman control.[97] A large pilgrimage church was built around the hexagonal martyr's shrine of Demetrius (reconstruction and plan in *CAH* 14, 959, fig. 56).

The populations of the western Danubian provinces used Latin for official and administrative purposes, but this was replaced by Greek in the east. The dividing line ran diagonally northwest from the Adriatic to the Danube, with the cities of Dyrrhachium, Scupi, and Serdica, and the coastal settlements of the western Black Sea on the Greek side of the frontier. The Danube basin itself, even in the lower stretch of the river, remained Latin-speaking throughout, thanks to the influence of the army camps and veteran settlements.[98] Military careers provided many with access to a distinctive and militarized version of Roman culture. Here were the roots of the *Romanitas* of Diocletian and his colleagues in the tetrarchy, and of Justin and Justinian in the sixth century. It was the Latin linguistic experience of the Balkan regions, which ensured that Latin remained the language of government at Constantinople up to the time of Justinian.

These Balkan emperors did not lose touch with their roots. Diocletian, on retirement, returned to his place of origin on the Dalmatian Adriatic coast at Split; Galerius constructed a stately home for himself at Romuliana (Gamzigrad). That was named after his redoubtable (and pagan) mother Romula, whose own name, a female version of Romulus, also precisely advertised the family's Roman culture. Both Split and Gamzigrad were designed to be simultaneously fortresses and palaces.[99] It is significant that retirement in these cases did not mean moving to a Mediterranean city. Justin and Justinian showed similar local loyalty in creating the city of Justiniana Prima, equipped with massive fortifications and conspicuous churches, in the rural country south of Naissus where their families had grown up.[100]

Another fundamental feature both of the culture and of the settlement and economic pattern of the Danubian regions was the continual stream of immigration from north of the Danube. Larger movements and population displacements are mentioned in the historical narratives and occasionally in inscriptions, including the 100,000 *Transdanuviani* who were brought across the frontier into Moesia by Ti. Plautius Silvanus Aelianus to become tribute-paying subjects of Rome in the mid-first century (*ILS* 986). Many more large groups were to follow over the following centuries.[101] Barbarians were also continually being absorbed piecemeal, some finding their way as recruits to auxiliary military units, others simply crossing the river frontier as individuals or in family groups, to find land, work, and livelihoods. The pattern of immigration surely implies that there was land enough for all. The appearance of dark burnished wares in late fourth-century sites on the middle Danube has been linked to the growing predominance of barbarian *foederati* in the *limes* forts.[102]

The presence of well armed and organized barbarian groups under strong leadership had a huge impact on the Balkan regions. The fear that such groups aroused in the cities of the region is especially brought home by Zosimus' account, derived from Eunapius, of Alaric's attack on Greece in 396.

> They immediately fell to plundering the countryside and the utter destruction of the cities, killing the men of all ages and carrying off women and children in droves as well as all the wealth as booty. The whole of Boeotia and the other parts of Greece the barbarians passed through after they entered Greece at Thermopylae were so ravaged that they exhibit from that day to this the signs of their over-throw. Only Thebes escaped, partly because of the city's strength, and partly because Alaric was too impatient to lay siege in his haste to capture Athens. (Zosimus 5.5.5–7, trans. Ridley)

Athens was saved, according to the pagan historians, by dramatic apparitions of the goddess Athena on the city wall, and of Achilles at the head of the local militia, but other evidence suggests that the city was overrun.

Half a century later the most vivid literary testimony to the condition of the central Balkans is to be found in the historian Priscus' compelling eye-witness account of the Constantinopolitan embassy of 449 to Attila the Hun. The delegation reached Naissus, deserted by its inhabitants except for the sick who sought refuge in the ruins of its churches. The party made camp a little way outside the city some distance above the river valley, which was full of the bones of men who had fallen in the recent war with the Huns. The following day they reached the camp of *dux Illyrici*, Agintheus, who was obliged to hand over five escapees from the Huns, to be returned by the party to Attila and certain death. After spending a night there they reached the Danube, where they were ferried across the river on boats made from hollowed logs, built for the convenience of Attila when he chose to go hunting on Roman territory. These paragraphs offer a haunting picture of Roman impotence and the utter collapse of the former frontier. What city or what fort, Attila was later to claim in an incensed altercation with the embassy, had been able to hold out against him when he was bent on its capture? The narrative of Priscus documents the fall to the Huns of Sirmium, the greatest fortress city of the western Balkans, of Viminacium, the Moesian frontier city on the Danube, and Ratiaria. Almost all the major fortified cities between Aquileia at the head of the Adriatic to Constantia on the Black Sea were overrun during the period of Attila's hegemony.[103]

Another written source, the life of St Severinus, written by Eugippius around 511, throws light on the upper Danubian frontier region at the end of the fifth century, as the provinces of Pannonia and Noricum were being abandoned by the Romans. Noricum covered the northeast access to Italy from the Danube. By the early fifth century the neighboring regions of Raetia and Pannonia had been given up to barbarian control. Ammianus noted that even in the early 370s the great legionary fortress of Carnuntum of the early empire was a filthy and abandoned town (Ammianus 29.6). Noricum is one of the few areas of the Danube basin where archaeological survey can provide a range of data to match the literary record. This suggests that the local populations began to build fortified hilltop refuges, corresponding to the *castella* mentioned by the saint's life. Roman frontier positions along the upper Danube on either side of Vienna were maintained until the 480s. Severinus himself had moved into this region in the period shortly after Attila's death in 453, and combined the roles of a secular and ecclesiastical leader until the end of his life in 482. He founded a monastery at Favianis, on Vienna's western outskirts, and himself lived in a fortified tower, a *burgus*, where he was eventually buried.[104] His life reveals the precarious security of the region. The frontier was still held by small isolated groups of *limitanei*, including a group of barbarian *foederati* at the fort of Comagenis (*Life of Severinus* 1–2). Their situation is reminiscent of the pockets of Roman military populations that had survived along the Rhine, as northern Gaul was gradually engulfed by Franks and Alemanni. Barbarian raiders regularly crossed the river to round up livestock or raid for food and other booty; Roman troops mounted sorties to make reprisals (*Life* 4.1–5). Ammianus had observed similar conditions in Pannonia a century before (Ammianus 29.6.5). The region was largely self sufficient in agricultural produce – grain, wine, livestock – but there was some capacity for local trade. Severinus himself distributed olive oil, a notable luxury, brought from Italy. Foodstuffs were brought down the river Inn, on the western frontier with Raetia, to the Danube and thence to the Vienna region, when it was suffering from local shortage (*Life* 3.1–3).

Severinus maintained relations with the Rugians, the main barbarian group settled north of the Danube, but his death left the region more exposed to their attacks and his monastery was pillaged. Odoacar, now king of Italy, intervened and sent his brother Hunwulf (Onoulph) to reclaim the frontier, but this attempt ended in 488 with the evacuation of the remaining Romans and the body of Severinus himself from Noricum to Naples. The withdrawal claimed victims. A group of soldiers from the frontier fort at Batavis undertook to march to Italy to collect pay owing to them, but were ambushed and cut to pieces by barbarians on the journey (*Life* 20). Noricum was occupied in the early sixth century by the Rugi, followed in the middle of the century by the Baiovari, the Bavarians. Like the encroachment of the Franks in northern Gaul, this brought a definite end to Roman control.

Despite the pressures and the spread of barbarian settlements, the Romans never definitively abandoned the attempt to maintain control of the middle and eastern stretches of the Danube. According to the *Notitia Dignitatum* there were eight legions in these provinces around the beginning of the fifth century, that is 8,000 men, who may have been supported by more than 40,000 *limitanei* and comparable numbers from the mobile field armies of Illyricum and Thrace.[105] These hypothetical figures represent troop numbers on paper, which may have greatly exceeded the true strength on the ground. It is clear, however, that the east Roman emperors, and above all Justinian, made major efforts to secure the closest frontier region to Constantinople itself. Garrisons on the lower Danube were supplied by sea, as is shown by significant finds of late Roman amphora types 1 and 2, which were used between the fourth and sixth centuries to transport wine and olive oil as part of the military *annona* to this area.[106] Procopius provides an impressive account of the construction of fortifications throughout Illyricum (*Buildings* 4). This involved strengthening the key linear defenses at Thermopylae and the Isthmus of Corinth, to protect Greece, and the wall across the Thracian Chersonese and the Anastasian wall west of Constantinople, which served a similar strategic function in Thrace. Procopius claimed that Justinian also improved the city walls of Ulpiana (modern Ljubljana), Serdica, Naissus, and Pautalia, and refurbished the forts of the lower Danube. Events were to show that these measures were insufficient to restore security to the Balkans as a whole (see below, chapter 12).

Conclusions

It would be facile to attempt to draw detailed conclusions from this inevitably superficial regional survey of the later Roman Empire. However, a number of points emerge with reasonable clarity. Firstly, the great cities of the Roman world were critically important for its economic development. The infrastructure which was necessary for feeding the huge populations of Rome and Constantinople had a transforming effect on the provinces of the empire. The delivery of grain, oil, wine, bacon, and dried goods in the form of *annona* deliveries both to Rome and Constantinople was certainly the largest enterprise in the transport of foodstuffs from rural producers to urban consumers ever achieved in the pre-industrial world. The agricultural economies of Africa and southern Italy, and of Egypt and southern Asia Minor, were largely shaped by the demands of the capital cities. Major ports to handle the trade had already developed in the early empire, in particular Alexandria and Carthage, which grew in size and importance in late antiquity to become mammoth cities in their own right. The *annona* depended entirely on a secure and highly organized system of maritime transport, and shipping became the largest industry of the period. The effects of this are most obvious in the southern Asia Minor coastal region of Cilicia, which had always been an important timber-producing and shipbuilding region, but which now became one of the most highly developed and intensively urbanized parts of the empire, with its own major center at Corycus. The supply requirements of the city of Rome also had a transforming effect on the economy of southern Italy between the fourth and sixth centuries. It is fair to assume that much of the produce of southern Italy to Rome would also have been transported by sea.

Detailed analysis of commercial trading patterns suggests that they too were heavily influenced by the organization of the imperial *annona*. Ships that carried grain and other foodstuffs could carry additional cargoes of higher value for sale in urban markets. It is difficult otherwise to account for the domination of African fine pottery in the urban markets of the western Mediterranean. Egypt and Alexandria also became the main transit entrepôt for the imported luxuries of the East, including silks, gems, and spices, overtaking the overland routes through the Near East.

Meanwhile the most important overland lines of communication in the Roman Empire were interrupted or broken. The Roman roads that ran though the Balkans, which had held the eastern and western parts of the empire together until the late fourth century, became insecure and were for long periods simply given up to the control of the Goths, Huns, Avars, and other barbarian groups. Insecurity in fifth-century Gaul led Rome to lose control over the great north–south trunk road from Marseilles and Arles to the northern capital at Trier, which was abandoned as an administrative center. Thus the northwest provinces, which depended on secure overland communications, were also lost to the empire. The result of these developments was a Roman world which was much more strongly oriented towards the Mediterranean than it had been in the age of Augustus and the early empire. The key centers of Roman economic and political power were now its sea ports.[107] Constantinople, the new capital, was above all a maritime city.

Urban settlements, that is cities, were a central defining feature of the Roman Empire. The cities were the locations where large landowners, the members of the ruling elites, could concentrate and display their wealth. They thus became the inevitable foci of power at a regional or provincial level. From the perspective of the imperial authorities it was also important that tax collection was organized on a city-by-city basis, even though the majority of tax income was levied on landed property. Thus state and regional interest converged in the creation and maintenance of prosperous and sustainable civic institutions, which became the visible and material symbols of the empire itself. The viability of the empire may reasonably be measured by the presence or absence of city life. This criterion provides one of the most valuable distinctions that can be drawn between the western and eastern halves of the empire in late antiquity. In Britain, northern Gaul, and most of the Danubian provinces, urban settlements shrank in size or disappeared during the fifth century. There is no evidence for civic buildings, local governmental structures, or large-scale communal organization outside that of the church. The populations of these regions were barely linked to wider networks of commercial exchange. They now lived in villages or other small rural settlements, which exchanged goods and services within a localized regional economy, but had few connections to a wider network of exchange. Their links to the Roman Empire had effectively been broken in social and economic, as well as in political, terms.

This pattern of settlement contrasts acutely with the situation that can be observed in the eastern empire. Here cities continued to flourish at least until the middle of the sixth century, and in some regions much later. This was not at the expense of smaller rural settlements, but as a consequence of the age-old symbiosis of town and country, which was the bedrock of classical city-state existence. Thus regions with flourishing small cities, such as the harbor towns of Lycia in southwest Asia Minor, were supported by a correspondingly prosperous highland hinterland. The densely populated limestone massif of northern Syria, covered with villages large and small, had its exact counterpart in the huge cities of late Roman Syria, Cyrrhus, Apamea, and above all Antioch.

Global security was vitally important for sustaining civic life in the Roman provinces. The greatest single threat to growth and sustainable prosperity was not plague, blight, or famine due to natural causes, but warfare. The Roman Empire was sustained, in the last analysis, by its ability to deploy military force effectively to protect its communities. When the use or the threat of force failed to achieve this aim, as in fifth-century Gaul, in the central Balkans against Attila's Huns, or in Illyricum as a whole against the Avars and Sclaveni in the later sixth century, then the provinces slid from Rome's grasp and civic life collapsed. The extraordinarily high levels of urban prosperity and the large populations of the eastern empire were only threatened when the Roman state was no longer able to deploy its military force and diplomatic skills to protect them.

NOTES

1 For an excellent short discussion of the role of the Bedouin, see M. Whittow, *The Making of Byzantium 600–1025* (London, 1996), 32–6. At more length D. F. Graf, "Rome and the Saracens: Reassessing the nomadic menace," in T. Fahd (ed.), *L'Arabie préislamique et son environnement historiqure et culturel* (Leiden, 1989), 341–400.

2 H. C. Butler, *Early Churches in Syria. Fourth to Seventh Centuries* (Princeton, 1929, repr. Amsterdam, 1969), 17–19, Church of Umm idj-Djimal, AD 345; other dated churches of southern Syria in 366/7 and 368, pp. 25–6; earliest dated church at Fafirtin 372, pp. 33–4, northern Syria, church at Bankusa, c.350. For a recent survey of the epigraphic evidence see F. R. Trombley, "Christian demography in the *territorium* of Antioch (4th–5th c.): Observations on the epigraphy," in I. Sandwell and J. Huskinson (eds.), *Culture and Society in Later Roman Antioch* (Oxford, 2004), 59–85.

3 M. Whittow, *The Making of Byzantium 600–1025*, 63–8.

4 J.-P. Sodini, "Déhès (Syrie du Nord). Campagnes I–III (1976–8): recherches sur l'habitat rural," *Syrie* 57 (1980), 1–304.

5 K. Butcher, *Roman Syria* (London, 2003), 153–7.

6 K. A. Yener et al., "The Amuq valley regional project 1995–98," *AJA* 104 (2000), 163–220; J. Casana, "The archaeological landscape of late Roman Antioch," in I. Sandwell and J. Huskinson (eds.), *Culture and Society in Later Roman Antioch* (Oxford, 2004), 102–25.

7   The phrase was coined by a western pilgrim from Piacenza, who passed through the city at this period, J. Wilkinson, *Jerusalem Pilgrims* (Warminster, 1977), 89.

8   G. Foerster and Y. Tsafir, in A. Hoffmann and S. Kerner (eds.), *Gadara-Gerasa und die Dekapolis* (Antike Welt Sonderband, Mainz, 2002), 83–5; and "Urbanism at Scythopolis – Beth Shean, fourth to seventh centuries," *Dumbarton Oaks Papers* 51 (1997), 85–146.

9   W. Liebeschuetz, "Late late antiquity in the cities of the Roman Near East," *Mediterraneo Antico (economie società culture)* 3 (2000), 43–75 at 48–9.

10 A. Hoffmann and S. Kerner (eds.), *Gadara-Gerasa und die Dekapolis*; W. Liebeschuetz, *Mediterraneo Antico* 3 (2000), 55–6.

11 H. M. Cotton, W. E. H. Cockle, and F. G. B. Millar, "The papyrology of the Roman Near East: A survey," *JRS* 85 (1995), 214–35 list the Nessana papyri at 233–5.

12 Y. Hirschfeld, "Social aspects of the late-antique village of Shivta (Negev)," *JRA* 16 (2003), 395–408. See also Y. Hirschfeld, *The Palestinian Dwelling in the Roman-Byzantine Period* (Jerusalem, 1995), rev. M. Fischer et al., *JRA* 11 (1998), 670–8.

13 C. A. M. Glucker, *The City of Gaza in the Roman and Byzantine Periods* (Oxford, 1987).

14 B. Ward-Perkins, *CAH* 14, 371–4.

15 S. Mitchell, "Festivals, games and city life in Roman Asia Minor," *JRS* 80 (1990), 183–93.

16 S. Mitchell, *Anatolia* II (Oxford, 1993), 81–4.

17 G. Fowden, "Bishops and temples in the eastern empire," *JTS* 29 (1978), 53–78; J. Vaes, *Ancient Society* 15–17 (1984–6), 305–443.

18 C. Foss and P. Magdalino, *Rome and Byzantium* (London, 1977), 74–5; C. Foss, *Ephesus after Antiquity. A Late Antique, Byzantine and Turkish City* (Cambridge Mass., 1979).

19 Information from the unpublished PhD thesis of P. Talloen, *Cult in Pisidia. Religious Practice in Southwestern Asia Minor from the Hellenistic to the Early Byzantine Period* (2002).

20 R. Cormack, "The classical tradition in the Byzantine provincial city: The evidence of Thessalonike and Aphrodisias," *Byzantium and the Classical Tradition* (1981), 103–18; R. Cormack, "The temple as cathedral," in C. Roueché and K. Erim (eds.), *Aphrodisias Papers: Recent Work on Architecture and Sculpture* (Ann Arbor, 1990), 75–88.

21 See the comments of R. R. R. Smith, "Late antique portraits in a public context: Honorific statuary at Aphrodisias in Caria," *JRS* 89 (1999), 156–9.

22 L. Robert, *Epigrammes du Bas-Empire*, Hellenica IV (1948).

23 C. Roueché, *Performers and Partisans at Aphrodisias in the Roman and Late Roman Periods* (JRS Monograph no. 6, London, 1993).

24 S. Mitchell and M. Waelkens, *Pisidian Antioch. The Site and its Monuments* (Wales and London, 1998), 106–10.

25 C. Foss, "The Lycian coast in the Byzantine age," *Dumbarton Oaks Papers* 48 (1994), 1–52.

26 B. Leadbetter, "Diocletian and the purple mile of Aperlae," *Epigraphica Anatolica* 36 (2003), 127–36. The milestone is, alas, made from limestone, not porphyry.

27 C. Foss, "Cities and villages of Lycia in the *Life* of St Nicholas of Holy Zion," *Greek Orthodox Theological Review* 36 (1991), 303–39.

28 F. Trombley, "Korykos in Kilikia Trachis: The economy of a small coastal city in late antiquity (Saec. V–VI)," *The Ancient History Bulletin* 1 (1987), 16–23.

29 For the archaeology of this region see Guyer and Herzfeld, *MAMA* II, 90–194 (Korykos); J. Keil and A. Wilhelm, *MAMA* III (especially for the epigraphy). F. Hild and H. Hellenkemper, *Tabula Imperii Byzantini V. 1. Kilikien und Isaurien* (Vienna, 1990), 108–27 (economy), and 320–5 (Corycus).

30 S. Mitchell, "Olive cultivation in the economy of Roman Asia Minor," in S. Mitchell and C. Katsari (eds.), *Patterns in the Economy of Roman Asia Minor* (Wales, 2005), 83–113, especially 101–3.

31 M. Konrad, "Research on the Roman and early Byzantine frontier in North Syria," *JRA* 12 (1999), 392–410.

32 Fergus Millar, *The Roman Near East 31 BC–AD 337* (Harvard, 1993), 174–89; K. Butcher, *Roman Syria* (London, 2003), 417, fig. 191.

33 N. Pollard, *Soldiers, Cities and Civilians in Roman Syria* (Michigan, 2000), 72–9.

34 W. Liebeschuetz, "The defences of Syria in the sixth century," *Akten des 10. Internationalen Limeskongresses* (Cologne, 1977), 487–99.

35 G. Greatrex, *Rome and Persia at War 502–532* (Liverpool, 1998).

36 Argued by J. D. Howard-Johnson, "Procopius, Roman defences north of the Taurus and the new fortress of Citharizon," in D. H. French and C. S. Lightfoot, *The Eastern Frontier of the Roman Empire* I (Oxford, 1989), 203–29.

37 D. Braund, *Georgia in Antiquity* (Oxford, 1994), 290–4.

38 See B. Croke and J. Crow, "Procopius and Dara," *JRS* 63 (1983), 159.

39 See note 101.

40 M. Whittow, *The Making of Byzantium 600–1025* (London, 1996), 200.

41 E. K. Fowden, *The Barbarian Plain Saint Sergius between Rome and Iran* (Berkeley, 1999), 45–59.

42 Important details of the foundation of Dara are also found in the ecclesiastical history of Ps-Zachariah 7.6. See B. Croke and J. Crow, *JRS* 63 (1983), 143–59; Michael Whitby, "Procopius and the development of Roman defences in upper Mesopotamia," in P. Freeman and D. Kennedy, *The Defence of the Roman and Byzantine East* (Oxford, 1986), 717–35, and "Procopius' description of Dara (*Buildings* 2.1–3)," in *The Defence of the Roman and Byzantine East*, 737–83.

43 R. Bagnall, *Egypt in Late Antiquity* (Princeton, 1993), 321 n. 20.

44 See W. Liebeschuetz, *Decline and Fall of the Roman City* (Oxford, 2001), 170.

45 See the map in W. Liebeschuetz, *Decline and Fall of the Roman City*, 261, fig. 16.

46 A. K. Bowman, *The Town Councils of Roman Egypt* (Toronto, 1971); for the pre-history of municipal organization, see A. K. Bowman and D. Rathbone, "Cities and administration in Roman Egypt," *JRS* 82 (1992), 107–27.

47 A. K. Bowman, "Landholding in the Hermopolite nome in the fourth century AD," *JRS* 75 (1985), 137–63; R. Bagnall, "Landholding in late Roman Egypt: The distribution of wealth," *JRS* 82 (1992), 128–49 suggests that 25–30 percent of the landed property in the nome of Hermopolis was owned by city dwellers.

48 R. Bagnall, "Religious conversion and onomastic change," *Bulletin of the American Society of Papyrologists* 19 (1982), 105–24 (demographic evidence from papyri); R. Bagnall, *Egypt in Late Antiquity* (Princeton, 1993), 278–89; E. Wipsycka, "La christianisation de l'Égypte aux Iᵉ–Vᵉ siècles. Aspects sociaux et ethniques," *Aegyptus* 68 (1988), 117–65 (especially for the literary evidence).

49 R. Bagnall, *Egypt in Late Antiquity*, 310–25.

50 R. Alston, *The City in Roman and Byzantine Egypt* (London, 2002).

51 Alan Cameron, "Wandering poets: A literary movement in Byzantine Egypt," *Historia* 14 (1965), 470–509.

52 J. Banaji, *Agrarian Change in Late Antiquity. Gold, Labour and Aristocratic Dominance* (Oxford, 2001), 39–88.

53 W. Liebeschuetz, *The Decline and Fall of the Roman City* (Oxford, 2001), 169–202; J. Keenan, *CAH* XIV, 625–33.

54 For recent work on late antiquity in Africa see N. Duval, *Revue des Etudes Anciennes* 92 (1990), 349–87; 95 (1993), 583–640; D. J. Mattingly and R. Hitchner, "Roman Africa: An archaeological survey," *JRS* 85 (1995), 209–13.

55 J.-M. Lassère, *Ubique Populus. Peuplement et Mouvements de population dans l'Afrique Romaine de la chute de Cartahe à la fin de la dynastie des Sévères* (Paris, 1977); D. J. Mattingly and R. Hitchner, *JRS* 85 (1995), 171–4.

56 P. Salama, *Bornes milliaires de l'Afrique Proconsulaire. Un panorama historique du Bas Empire romain* (Paris, 1987); references at D. J. Mattingly and R. Hitchener, *JRS* 85 (1995), 179 n. 154.

57 C. Lepelley, *La cité de l'Afrique romaine au Bas-Empire* (2 vols, Paris, 1979–80).

58 D. J. Mattingly and R. Hitchner, *JRS* 85 (1995), 210.

59 *CJust.* 11.63.1; J. Percival, in B. Levick (ed.), *An Ancient Historian and his Materials (presented to C. E. Stevens)* (Farnborough, 1975), 213–27; D. Mattingly, "Olive cultivation and the Albertini tablets," in *L'Africa Romana* 6.1 (1989), 403–15.

60 A. Carandini, "Pottery and the African economy," in P. Garnsey et al. (eds.), *Trade in the Ancient Economy* (Cambridge, 1983), 145–62; C. Wickham, "Marx, Sherlock Holmes and late Roman commerce," *JRS* 78 (1988), 183–93 at 190–3. For olives see D. Mattingly, "Oil for export? A comparison of Libyan, Spanish and Tunisian olive oil production in the Roman empire," *JRA* 1 (1988), 33–56.

61 Y. Modéran, "L'établissment territorial des Vandales en Afrique," *Ant. Tard.* 10 (2002), 87–122 with map on p. 89.

62 D. Pringle, *The Defence of Byzantine Africa from Justinian to the Arab Conquest* (2 vols., Oxford, 1981); W. Liebeschuetz, *The City in Late Antiquity* (2002), 100–1.

63 J. Durliat, *Les dédicaces d'ouvrages de défence dans l'Afrique Byzantine* (Rome, 1981), 93–8.

64 See the excellent overview of Averil Cameron, *CAH* 14, 552–69.

65 W. Liebeschuetz, *The Decline and Fall of the Roman City* (Oxford, 2001), 377–8.

66 R. Agache, *La Somme préromaine et romaine d'après les prospections aériennes à basse altitude* (Amiens, 1978).

67 For Rheinzabern see E. Künzl, *Die Alamannenbeute aus dem Rhein bei Neupotz. Plünderungsgut aus dem römischen Gallien* (Monographien Römisch-Germanisches Zentralmuseum, 4 vols., Mainz, 1993).

68 H. Schöneberger, "The Roman frontier in Germany: An archaeological survey," *JRS* 59 (1969), 144–97 at 177–87.

69 N. Christie, "Towns and peoples on the middle Danube in late antiquity and the early Middle Ages," in N. Christie and S. T. Loseby (eds.), *Towns in Transition* (Aldershot, 1996), 71–98 at 77.

70 D. Potter, *The Roman Empire at Bay* (London, 2004), 502–3.

71 O. and C. Nicholson, "Lactantius, Hermes Trismegistus and Constantinian obelisks," *JHS* 109 (1989), 200.

72 S. Loseby, "Arles in late antiquity: Gallula Roma Arelate and Urbs Genesii," in N. Christie and S. T. Loseby, *Towns in Transition*, 45–70.

73 M. Meijmanns, "La topographie de la ville d'Arles durant l'antiquité tardive," *JRA* 12 (1999), 143–67; S. Loseby, "Arles in late antiquity: Gallula Roma Arelate and Urbs Genesii," in N. Christie and S. T. Loseby, *Towns in Transition*, 45–70; W. Liebeschuetz, *The Decline and Fall of the Roman City* (Oxford, 2001), 84.

74 P. van Ossel and P. Ouzoulias, "Rural settlement economy in Northern Gaul in the late empire: An overview and assessment," *JRA* 13 (2000), 151–3.

75 P. Van Ossel and P. Ouzoulias, *JRA* 13 (2000), 149–50.

76 W. Liebeschuetz, *The Decline and Fall of the Roman City*, 86; for Metz see B. S. Bachrach, "Fifth-century Metz. Late Roman Christian *urbs* or ghost town?" *Ant. Tard.* 10 (2002), 363–81, who argues that the town continued to flourish in the fifth century. The Franks built a large palace south of the cathedral in view of the amphitheater which was inside the defensive walls.

77 G. Halsall, "Towns, societies and ideas: The not-so-strange case of late Roman and early Carolingian Metz," in N. Christie and S. T. Loseby, *Towns in Transition*, 235–61.

78 C. Wickham, "Un pas vers le Moyen Âge. Permanences et mutations," in P. Ouzoulles et al., *Les campagnes de la Gaule à la fin de l'Antiquité* (Colloque Montpellier 1998, publ. Antibes, 2001), 555–67.

79 C. E. Stevens, *Sidonius Apollinaris and his Age* (Oxford, 1934); J. Harries, *Sidonius Apollinaris and the Fall of Rome* (Oxford, 1994).

80 W. Klingshirn, *Caesarius of Arles. The Making of a Christian Community in Late Antique Gaul* (Cambridge, 1993); see also W. Klingshirn, *Caesarius of Arles: Life, Testament, Letters* (Liverpool, 1994).

81 W. Liebeschuetz, *Decline and Fall of the Roman City*, 84–8; S. T. Loseby, "Marseilles: A late antique success story?" *JRS* 82 (1992), 169.

82 S. T. Loseby, "Marseilles: A late antique success story?" *JRS* 82 (1992), 165–85.

83 N. Christie, *The Lombards* (Oxford, 1995), 140.

84 B. Ward-Perkins, *CAH* 14, 355.

85 W. Liebeschuetz, *Decline and Fall of the Roman City*, 379–80, 388–90.

86 W. Liebeschuetz, *Decline and Fall of the Roman City*, 382.

87 P. Arthur, "Some observations on the economy of Bruttium under the later Roman empire," *JRA* 2 (1989), 133–42.

88 S. J. B. Barnish, "Pigs, plebeians and *potentes*: Rome's economic hinterland c.350–600 AD," *PBSR* 55 (1987), 157–85. P. Arthur, "Some observations on the economy of Bruttium under the later Roman empire," *JRA* 2 (1989), 133–42.

89 For the view that we should not draw excessively pessimistic conclusions from the archaeological evidence, see C. Wickham, *Early Medieval Italy. Central Power and Local Society 400–1000* (London, 1981), 99–118, contested by W. Liebeschuetz, *Decline and Fall of the Roman City*, 395–9.

90 N. Christie, *The Lombards*, 129–31, with figs. 21 and 22.

91 See B. D. Shaw, "War and violence," in G. W. Bowersock et al. (eds.), *Late Antiquity* (Cambridge Mass., 1999), 130–69.

92 J. Kolendo, "L'aristocratie municipale dans les provinces rhénanes et danubiennes à l'époque du Haut-Empire," *JRA* 4 (1991), 327–30, table on p. 329.

93 R. Syme, "Roman senators from Dalmatia," *Danubian Papers* (1971), 110–2.

94 H. Wolff, "Administrative Einheiten in den Nordprovinzen und ihre Beziehungen zu römischen Funktionsträgern," in W. Eck (ed.), *Lokale Autonomie und römische Ordnunugsmacht in den kaiserzeitlichen provinzen vom 1. bis 3. Jht* (Munich, 1999), 47–60.

95   N. Christie, "Towns and peoples on the middle Danube in late antiquity and the early Middle Ages," in N. Christie and S. T. Loseby, *Towns in Transition*, 71–98 at 75–7.

96   B. Croke, "Hormisdas and the late Roman walls of Thessalonica," *GRBS* 19 (1978), 251–8. Plan: *CAH* 14, 710, fig. 22.

97   W. Liebeschuetz, *Decline and Fall of the Roman City*, 284–5; see below p. 415.

98   Map in N. McLynn, *Ambrose of Milan*, 89.

99   J. J. Wilkes, *Diocletian's Palace, Split* (1996), *passim* and 66–70 for Gamzigrad.

100   See plans in *CAH* 14, 719, fig. 243, and 922, fig. 41.

101   G. E. M. de Ste Croix, *The Class Struggle in the Ancient Greek World* (London, 1983).

102   N. Christie, "Towns and peoples on the middle Danube in late antiquity and the early Middle Ages," in N. Christie and S. T. Loseby, *Towns in Transition*, 71–98 at 78.

103   Michael Whitby, *CAH* 14, 704–12.

104   The tomb and tower may even be identifiable with the excavated remains at Heligenstadt, see J. Haberl with Christopher Hawkes, "The last of Roman Noricum: St Severin on the Danube," in C. F. C. and S. Hawkes (eds.), *Greeks, Celts and Romans. Studies in Venture and Resistance* (Towota, 1973), 97–149 at 143–4.

105   W. Treadgold, *Byzantium and its Army 282–1081* (Stanford, 1995), 50–2; J. F. Haldon, *Byzantium in the Seventh Century* (Cambridge, 1997), 251.

106   O. Karagiorgiou, "LR2: A container for the military annona on the Danubian border?" in S. Kingsley and M. Decker, *Economy and Exchange* (Oxford, 2001), 129–66.

107   See below p. 386. Note also W. Liebeschuetz, *Decline and Fall of the Roman City*, 289, for the emergence of fortress cities at coastal sites in the sixth and seventh centuries.

11
The Challenges of the Later Sixth Century

| 250 | 300 | 350 | 400 | 450 | 500 | 550 | 600 | 650 |

The eight years between the recall of Belisarius after the capture of Ravenna in 540 and his second withdrawal from Italy in 548 saw Roman hopes wither in the West. The situation was to be recovered at a military level by the campaigns of Belisarius' successor, Narses, who eventually brought an end to the Gothic kingdom in the campaigns and battles of 552–3 (see below), but Italy itself, like Africa, was a wasteland in the middle years of the sixth century. All this was starkly apparent to Procopius, writing at the beginning of the 550s and expressed in his uncompromising judgments on the whole program of Justinianic reconquest. The decade of the 540s formed one of the major caesuras of Roman history. How should we assess the setbacks and disasters of these years?

The Bubonic Plague and Other Natural Catastrophes

In the last days of the year 2004 an undersea earthquake located off the coast of Indonesia caused a colossal tidal wave that engulfed the shorelines of the Indian Ocean and drowned approximately 300,000 people. By a remarkable coincidence a valuable study of the late Roman world, published a month before this natural disaster, was entitled "Ammianus and the great tsunami." At the end of his account of the revolt of the usurper Procopius in 365–6, Ammianus presented a complex and vivid description of a massive inundation of the east Mediterranean basin, which providentially matched and presaged the travails of the Roman Empire itself.[1]

Contemporary accounts of later Roman history pay an extraordinary amount of attention to natural disasters. Much of the immediacy of later Roman history derives precisely from the parallels that can be drawn between the crises faced by the empire and those that are felt in the modern world. It is not fanciful to suggest that many contemporary observers saw natural disasters as a reflection of mankind's precarious condition, which called into question the essential viability of the Roman Empire. In relation to the middle and later years of the sixth century arguments have been put forward that such events in nature may not merely have been a metaphor for crisis and decline, but literal causes of the empire's collapse.

The early years of Justinian's reign had been swept forward by a wave of irrepressible optimism. The anxieties that had gripped the empire in the years around 500, when many had expected the world to end (see above pp. 171–3 for the *Chronicle* of Ps-Joshua of Edessa), had evaporated with the passing of the years. The religious tension between the Monophysite sympathies of the aging emperor Anastasius and the largely Chalcedonian beliefs of his subjects in Constantinople was resolved with the accession of Justin. The succession of Justinian, who was already in effective charge of the state before his uncle's death, released an outburst of energy. The emperor was supported by a dynamic generation of officials and military men, and the self-confidence of his regime was crowned by military success. The challenge of the Sassanians was dissolved in the eternal peace of 532; Africa had been recovered in Belisarius' lightening campaign of 533; that triumph, celebrated in 534, was followed by the conquest of Sicily in 536; and the recovery of the western empire was now anticipated:

> By means of mighty wars God granted us the opportunity to make peace with the Persians, to abase the Vandals, Alans and Moors, to gain possession of the whole of Africa, and of Sicily in addition, and to have high hopes that God would grant us ruling power over the remaining territories which the Romans of old once conquered as far as the boundaries of the two oceans, but then cast away in their subsequent carelessness. (Justinian, *Nov.* 30.11.2 [536])

The only clouds to darken the horizon had gathered in the East. The hostilities with the Sassanians and their Saracen allies under the Lakhmid chieftain

Al-Mundhir had brought war to the Orontes Valley and up to the walls of Emesa and Apamea. Moreover, a series of earthquakes had inflicted heavy damage on the cities of Syria, principally Antioch, which was shattered in 526 by a quake which Procopius reported as killing 300,000 people (Procopius, *Bell. Pers.* 2.14.6; cf. Malalas 420, 6–7).

The pattern of natural catastrophes which occurred after the mid-530s is known to us only through the hindsight of the surviving sources. They retain virtually none of the optimism which radiated from the imperial pronouncements of the early part of the decade. The event above all which shaped this pessimistic outlook was the devastating onset of bubonic plague in 541/2. The first outbreak of plague in Constantinople, where it raged for four months in the first half of 542, is described in detail by Procopius (*Bell. Pers.* 2.22–23) and in an account by John of Ephesus, which was transmitted in the Syriac translation of his ecclesiastical history (*Chronicle of Ps-Dionysius of Tel-Mahre* Pt. III, 74–98). This recorded the effects both in the Palestinian countryside and in the capital.

> Day by day we too – like everybody – knocked at the gate of the tomb. If it was evening, we thought that death would come upon us in the night, and again if morning had broken, our face was turned the whole day towards the tomb.

Even more telling is a sentence from an edict of March 1, 542, issued by the emperor himself,

> That which has occurred in the present time requires no explanation, for the presence about us of death, which pervades every place, makes it necessary for no one to hear about that which each one of us has endured. (Justinian, *Edict* VIII)

Procopius established that the infection had arrived from the Egyptian port of Pelusium, and the church historian Evagrius may well be correct in claiming that it had originated in Ethiopia (Evagrius 4.29).[2] The plague probably manifested itself in three forms: buboes, the outbreak of infected boils in lymphatic nodes, especially the groin; septicemia, when the infection spread through the blood system; and infection of the lungs.[3] Transmission of the first two symptoms was due to fleas, whose bites spread the infection between rats and men, while the third could be passed from person to person through spittle. Septicemic infection of the plague was spectacularly virulent, often causing death within hours, as contemporary witnesses observed, although they were unable to establish its cause. The mortality rate in the capital accelerated rapidly from 5,000 to 10,000 deaths per day. John of Ephesus reported a maximum daily toll of 16,000 deaths, and observed that the official casualty count was halted when it reached 230,000 overall. Justinian ordered soldiers and a senior official (a *referendarius*) to take charge of the logistic horror of burial. The towers of the fortifications of Sycae, across the Golden Horn, were transformed into plague pits, and the stench of the rotting corpses was blown back over the city

(Procopius, *Bell. Pers.* 2.23.5–11). The casualty figures reported in the sources are unlikely in themselves to be more than approximations. A recent study argues that the victims may have amounted to one-third of a total population for the city of around 750,000.[4] In the *Secret History* Procopius alleged that half the inhabitants of the empire, having survived previous devastation by warfare, famine, earthquake, and flood, died from the plague (6.22 and 18.44).

Procopius and Evagrius indicate that the first outbreak, which lasted into 543, covered the entire world (Procopius, *Bell. Pers.* 2.22.3 and 6; Evagrius 4.29). The epidemic was carried in the first place by ship, striking harbor cities before it spread to the interior. Alexandria was engulfed before Constantinople itself. Inscriptions from Nessana in southern Palestine record premature deaths, doubtless from the plague, in October and November of 541, matched by gravestones from Gaza and elsewhere in the region.[5] The literary sources speak of whole settlements being abandoned, and of cattle and crops untended in the fields. Evagrius, who himself survived the first outbreak in 542 as a child of six, recorded the impact on his own family in Antioch. He observed another vital and catastrophic aspect of the epidemic, that it recurred at intervals, more or less in synchronism with the fifteen-year indiction cycle. By the time he was writing, in his fifty-eighth year, it had taken the lives of his wife, his only son and a daughter, other relatives, and numerous servants and dependants on their estates. Epidemiological studies of the closest historical parallel to the Justinianic plague, the Black Death, indicate that recurrences of bubonic plague could be expected, sometimes at no more than four-yearly intervals.[6] Sources of the later sixth century indicate that there were fresh outbreaks in the Roman Empire in 553/4, 555, 558 (for six months in Constantinople), 560/61 (in Antioch and Cilicia), 567/8, 572/3, 580/81, 585/6, 592, 598/9, 607, 615, and 639.[7] The epidemics continued until the later eighth century.

The overall impact of the plague on the society and economy of the Mediterranean world of the sixth and seventh centuries is disputed. There are some grounds for arguing that the ancient writers, by concentrating on the dramatic and terrifying outbreak of 541–3, have exaggerated its long-term consequences. Just as Europe recovered to its former level of population within a century of the Black Death, which may have killed between a third and a half of its inhabitants, so the effects of the Justinianic plague may have been reduced or annulled by the end of the sixth century.[8] The parallel with the Black Death indicates that some cities and rural areas would have suffered more seriously than others, although given the state of current knowledge it is hard to draw significant distinctions in its regional impact. No doubt the remoter, landlocked areas suffered less than densely populated coastal areas, and the death toll would have been highest in the teeming *metropoleis* of Constantinople, Antioch, and Alexandria. It is worth noting that rural Galatia, in the center of Asia Minor, had numerous thriving village communities at the end of the sixth century, even though we know for certain that it had been touched by the plague in 542.[9] However, the provisional assessment, which is all that our current evidence will allow, must be pessimistic rather than optimistic. Most commentators have argued for a population fall of between 20 and 50 percent between 542 and the death of Heraclius a century later.[10] The frequent recurrence of plague through the sixth and early seventh centuries surely pushed population levels down, especially in the cities. So did the fact that the Roman Empire as an entity relied heavily, in economic and military terms, on seaborne transport throughout the Mediterranean. This held its fabric together, but also made easy the spread of disease.[11]

Other disasters, natural and manmade, afflicted the empire. By far the most significant of these was a remarkable climatic episode which persisted through 535 and 536. Procopius observed that in the tenth year of Justinian's reign a most terrible portent occurred. "The sun's rays lacked any brightness, and for an entire year shone like the moon, just as though it were in eclipse, and from that time on men were beset by war, plague and anything else that portended death."[12] This observation is confirmed by other contemporary writers, including John of Ephesus:

> There was a sign from the sun, the like of which had never been seen and reported before. The sun became dark and its darkness lasted for eighteen months. Each day it shone for about four hours, and still this light was no more than a feeble shadow. Everyone declared that the sun would never recover its full light again. (John of Ephesus in *Chronicle of Ps-Dionysius* 65, copied by Michael the Syrian 9.26)

Cassiodorus in Italy observed that for almost a full year the light from the sun cast no shadows and the temperature even in the hottest season was feeble. Crops did not come to fruition and there was even a fear of frost at harvest time. His detailed description clearly implies that ordinary visibility was much reduced by dust. "The air, condensed from snow by excessive cold, is not thinned by the sun's fire; but it endures in the density that it has acquired, obstructs the heat of the sun, and cheats the gaze of human frailty. For things in space dominate our sight, and we can see through them only what the rarity of their substance allows" (*Var.* 12.25, trans. Barnish).

The most precisely dated information comes from the Monophysite historian, Ps-Zacharias of Mytilene, who wrote that "the sun began to be darkened by day and the moon by night, while the ocean was tumultuous with spray (?) from the 24th of March in this year till the 24th of June in the following year fifteen." The year-sequence is the indiction cycle that began in 522/3, and he refers to the period between March 24, 535 and June 24, 536. The year of darkness also coincided with the visit to Constantinople of the bishop of Rome, Agapetus. This is confirmed for the eastern empire by the chronicle of Marcellinus, which indicates that conflict over grazing grounds between the rival Saracen confederations of the Lakhmids and the Ghassanids became particularly acute in 536, in the wake of disastrous crop failures (Marcellinus, *Chron.* 2, 105), and by Procopius' note that the year of darkness coincided with the winter during which Belisarius was in Sicily and Solomon in Carthage, that is 535–6. One important imperial measure that should be connected with these circumstances is a major edict of 538/9 concerned with new regulations for the delivery of grain to Constantinople from Egypt (Justinian, *Edict* 13).

Cassiodorus' letter is associated with a batch of official correspondence relating to the difficulties of collecting tax in kind from the provinces of Italy. A general letter dating to September 537, the first year of the following indiction period, insisted on the necessity of landowners paying their dues (*Var.* 12.16). This was followed later in the autumn by a letter to the inhabitants of the province of Istria, insisting that they should pay in kind in full as travelers had reported that the region had produced its due crop of grain, wine, and olives that year (*Var.* 12.22). Instructions, however, were also sent to the local tribune to collect fish and salt from the coastal region around Venice, which would not have been affected by agricultural harvest failures (*Var.* 12.24). Another letter reported that wine, corn, and millet had all failed among the Veneti, and that requisitioned army supplies from Concordia, Aquileia, and Forum Iulii were to be restricted to meat, while wine could be obtained at market rates from the Istrians (*Var.* 12.26). Cassiodorus also passed on royal instructions from the Gothic king Theodahat to the bishop of Milan, to sell millet from the state granaries at Pavia and Dertona to a famished populace (*Var.* 12.27). The climatic disaster had effectively destroyed the harvests of 535 and 536. The correspondence of autumn 537 may imply some recovery, at least in Istria, but overall the situation remained desperate.

The evidence from Cassiodorus is confirmed by details of Procopius' description of Belisarius' war against the Goths. The narrative turns time and again to the theme of famine. During the year-long siege of Rome until the end of March 538 both sides were afflicted by acute food shortages. Famine was the even-handed enemy of the Roman garrison at Ariminum, which was relieved in late summer 538, and the Gothic forces at Auximum and Urbinum. Starvation brought the towns of Umbria and Picenum to their knees and wiped out entire rural populations in 539, where the inhabitants had been prevented from planting crops by the hostilities, thus compounding the plight of recurrent failed harvests. Procopius' eye-witness accounts of the famished inhabitants of central Italy during the Gothic War, where over 50,000 peasants starved to death in Picenum alone, help to place him among the great war historians:

> I shall now tell of the appearance which they came to have and in what manner they died, for I was an eye-witness. All of them first became lean and pale; for the flesh being ill supplied with nourishment, according to the old saying "laid hold upon itself," and the bile, having now the mastery of their bodies by reason of its excess, lent them almost its own appearance. And as the malady developed, all moisture left them, and the skin became very dry so that it resembled leather more than anything else, giving the appearance of having been fastened upon the bones. And as they changed from a livid to a black colour, they came to resemble torches thoroughly burned. And their faces always wore an expression of amazement, while they always had a dreadful sort of insane stare. . . . And no one ever laid them in the earth, for there was in fact not a man to concern himself about burying them; and yet they remained untouched by the numerous birds which

have the habit of feeding on dead bodies, for they offered nothing which the birds craved. For all the flesh, as I have previously stated, had already been consumed by starvation. Such was the manner in which famine visited the land. (Procopius, *Bell. Goth.* 6.20, extracts from 15–33, trans. Dewing)

Famine forced Naples to surrender to Totila in 544. Roman forces hovered on the verge of mutiny and relied in desperation on supplies shipped in to Ancona or the Campanian ports. The barbarian forces of Franks, Burgundians, Heruli, and Lombards that descended on northern Italy after 539 resembled a locust swarm, driven from place to place by the desperate search for food.

The cause of the major occlusion of the sun is a matter for conjecture, but by far the likeliest explanation is that the earth's upper atmosphere had become contaminated by the dust-cloud of a major volcanic eruption. That is the reasonable conclusion of David Keys in his ambitious investigation of world-wide evidence relating to a major environmental catastrophe during the 530s and 540s. It rests not only on texts from the classical world and the Far East, but on the evidence of dendrochronology and geological deposits in datable archaeological contexts. A composite graph of tree-ring growth throughout Europe shows that vegetation growth was strikingly depressed in the late 530s and the early 540s, with spectacular lows in 536, 539, and 540. These figures are confirmed by data from elsewhere in the world, indicating that the climatic aberration was universal. The effect of the dust clouds, if these are rightly thought to be responsible, continued for several years.[13] Agricultural activity almost came to a standstill. The fields of the Mediterranean world were bare, and the people starved. Only the wealthy survived as best they could.

An important passage of Procopius' *Secret History* blamed the chain of natural disasters which engulfed the empire up to the greatest catastrophe, the outbreak of the plague, on Justinian's own demonic powers (*Secret History* 18.36–45). Among the natural disasters Procopius identified disastrous flooding and numerous earthquakes. The state of anxiety in this period led to earth tremors being observed and chronicled with obsessive attention, irrespective of their seriousness.[14] In Constantinople itself the greatest damage and terror was caused by earthquakes in 542 and 557. The latter event led to the collapse of the precarious dome of St Sophia, and both earthquakes provoked a lasting religious response in the form of the introduction of annual processions to plead for God's mercy and protection from further disasters.[15] It is not irrelevant in this context to note a modern parallel and its consequences. In 1999 northwest Turkey, in particular the province of Izmit, ancient Nicomedia, was devastated by a major earthquake, which claimed over 18,000 lives. It was and is regarded as only a matter of time before a comparable disaster shatters the huge metropolitan area of Istanbul, home now to some twenty million people. The perception of imminent danger has reputedly already led as many as a million of the inhabitants to leave the city and make their homes on the Turkish south coast. Fear of earthquake is by far the largest constraint on planning and development in the city today.

Setbacks and Recovery in the Mid-Sixth Century

Contemporary observers focused on and doubtless often exaggerated the dramatic immediate impact of famine, earthquake, or plague. They have little to say about their long-term consequences, and indeed had no means of evaluating these. What then were the immediate consequences of natural disasters for the empire of the mid-sixth century? It is possible that they had a particularly dramatic impact on the capacity and activities of the emperor himself. Contemporaries noted that after 542 Justinian concerned himself to an extraordinary degree with religious matters, and neglected virtually all secular business. Procopius presents a famous image of Justinian, closeted with aged churchmen, discussing finer points of doctrinal theology and neglecting matters of state (Procopius, *Bell. Goth.* 7.35.11). In the *Secret History* Procopius depicted Justinian's religiosity, in particular the extreme fasting and vigils which he endured around the time of the Easter festival, in a highly negative light (*Secret History* 13.28–30), but it is evident that the emperor himself ensured that information about exactly this behavior was widely circulated. It was for this reason that Procopius included a virtually identical account of his fasting habits in the panegyric context of the *Buildings* (1.7.7–12). Insofar as Justinian presented himself to public view at all in his later years, it was in contexts of ostentatious piety. There is an extreme contrast between the secular military triumph which he celebrated in 534 after the reconquest of Africa, based on a re-invention of ancient Roman practice (see above, chapter 4), and the ceremonial, also described as a triumph, which followed the victory of Belisarius after the Kutrigurs broken through the Anastasian wall in 559. Justinian made one of his extremely rare journeys outside Constantinople, as far as Selymbria, to witness the repairs that had been made to the fortifications, and then returned with an entourage of senators in all solemnity to the city. At the climax of this *adventus* he made his way to the Church of the Holy Apostles, lit candles, and prayed to the memory of his wife Theodora, who had died eleven years earlier (Constantine Porphyrogennitus, *On Ceremonies*, appendix to book 1, 497–8). The pictorial representations of the emperor show a similar evolution from secular triumph to ostentatious religious piety. The Barberini ivory from the 530s, perhaps symbolizing the African conquest itself, showed the emperor as the archetypal Christian warrior. The mosaic panel illustrating the dedication of the Church of S. Vitale in Ravenna in 548 showed the bare-headed emperor, surrounded by clergymen, in the act of making a pious offering (see above, chapter 5).

Almost all of Justinian's recorded activity during the later 540s and 550s concerned doctrinal matters and church politics, especially his final attempts at the Council of Constantinople in 553 to lay down the law to the Monophysites. The legislative frenzy of his earlier years came to a standstill after 542, and only forty-six *Novellae* were issued for the entire remainder of his reign. Even treason did not stir him to react. Neither the conspiracy of a small clique of Armenian nobles, including a prominent general Artabanes, in 549 (Procopius, *Bell. Goth.* 7.31–2; for Artabanes see below p. 381), nor the more serious treason of a group of prominent political figures in 561 provoked more than virtual indifference, a passive response, which the sources characterize as due to the emperor's merciful nature.[16]

How should we explain the contrast between the early and later years of Justinian? One supposition might be that the emperor, having achieved his political aims, consciously chose to refrain from further innovation, just as he had ordered that no further interpretations or commentaries of Roman law should be admitted after the publication of the *Digest*. Another suggestion, supported by the religious overtones of the emperor's self-representation, was that he redefined the imperial role in starkly religious terms, bringing fundamentalist Christian considerations to bear on all forms of political activity and decision-making. Neither of these explanations, however, accounts convincingly for the extraordinary collapse of a powerful personality.

Little was seen of the emperor in the years after the first outbreak of the plague, from which he himself had suffered, and this gave rise to extraordinary rumors. Among them was Procopius' famous supposition that Justinian and Theodora were incarnate demons. Men reported that they were not in the presence of the emperor but of an evil spirit phantom:

> Some of those who were in the presence of the emperor, holding conference with him, I suppose, far into the night, obviously in the palace, men whose souls were pure, seemed to see a sort of phantom spirit unfamiliar to them in place of him. One of them asserted that Justinian would rise suddenly from the royal throne and wander off there (indeed he was never used to remaining seated for long periods); his head would disappear suddenly, but the rest of his body seemed to keep making these same long circuits, and the observer, as though his own organs of sight were in the poorest of health, stood there for the most part in distress, wondering what to do. But afterwards, when the head returned to the body, he thought that the gap that had been for a while inexplicably missing was now filled again. And another said that he stood beside Justinian when he was seated and suddenly saw that his face appeared to have become like featureless flesh; for neither eyebrows nor eyes were in their proper place, and showed no recognisable means of identification whatsoever; after a time, however, he saw the features of his face return. (*Secret History* 12.20–23)

We might simply dismiss this passage as feverish speculation, but Procopius' informants, the men of pure spirit, were presumably the senior elderly churchmen with whom Justinian convened in the later 540s, and they appear to have been trying to find words to describe what they had actually seen. A rationalist reading of this passage suggests that the emperor may have suffered a serious and irreversible breakdown of his mental health. His personality and behavior bore no relationship to those of his earlier years. At moments such as those that spooked his pious companions, he had, quite literally, become a zombie, a ghost of his former self.

However, the empire had always in the past been able to survive the incapacity of an individual emperor, and, whatever the reasons for Justinian's
disfunctionality, this was certainly true of the regime in Constantinople in the
mid-sixth century. One of the written works to survive from the period is the
three-book treatise *On Magistrates*, written in the 550s by the imperial bureaucrat John the Lydian, whose active career had begun under Anastasius. *On
Magistrates* is a disorganized compilation of information and opinion. In part
it is a historical treatise which traced the origins of Roman offices and officials
to the earliest period of Roman history. As such it is the best testament to the
sense of history and Roman antiquarianism that marked the early Justinianic
period, and which are also reflected in the prefaces to many of the emperor's
new laws. At the same time Lydus' work contains an unsystematic survey of
the way in which the imperial bureaucracy of the mid-sixth century functioned. However, its heart seems to be the virulent attack which John Lydus
directed against John the Cappadocian, praetorian prefect from 529–41, whose
career was briefly interrupted when he was removed after the Nika riot of 532
and replaced by John Lydus' own hero, Phocas. John the Cappadocian had
presided over an office that had administered the eastern Roman Empire, and
exacted taxation with more rigor and efficiency than any that had preceded it.
The papyrological evidence from Egypt in the east, and also documents from
the newly recovered western possessions, especially the exarchate of Ravenna,
shows that the Roman administrative machine continued to function through
the second half of the sixth century with impressive thoroughness.[17]

There was a substantial change in Roman foreign policy after 540, which
was as apparent to contemporaries as it is to modern historians. In their
histories Agathias (5.14.1–2) and Menander (fr. 5.1), public men who had
lived through the last part of Justinian's reign, contrasted the energy and
dynamism shown during the conquests of Africa and Italy with the lassitude
(*rathumia*) of Justinian's old age. They deduced this from the way that he dealt
with Rome's enemies. Whereas before he had eagerly undertaken wars against
them, now he preferred to play his enemies off against each other, or win them
over by gifts and subsidies. The tactics of sowing dissension among enemy
peoples and using Roman wealth to make new friends had an impeccable
pedigree and had long been demonstrably effective. In itself this change in
foreign policy constitutes no good argument for the emperor's incompetence.
Furthermore, the Romans showed no lack of determination in foreign wars,
although they no longer enjoyed the easy success of the first African campaign.
Roman forces continued to campaign in Africa, Italy, and Lazica for much of
the 550s. The abiding impression is of the government's implacable determination to retain and assert control over the reconquered territories of the West.

From 543 to 549 a succession of commanders tried to impose Roman
authority across the length of North Africa from Tripolitania to Mauretania.
The enemy were no longer the Vandals but the native Moorish peoples, aided
and reinforced by Roman deserters. After Roman reverses in 543 and 544, a
new command team was sent to Africa in 545 under the Armenian *magister*

militum Areobindus. A rebel officer murdered Areobindus, but fell victim to a counter-plot, masterminded by another Armenian Artabanes (Procopius, *Bell. Vand.* 4.25–27). Artabanes was rewarded with promotion to the rank of *magister militum prasentalis* at Constantinople, and replaced by John Troglites, who undertook four seasons of campaigning against the Moors to try to restore order to Africa (Procopius, *Bell. Vand.* 4.28.45–51). However, the overall outcome was far from happy either for the native inhabitants or for the Roman would-be rulers of reconquered Africa. Procopius ends his narrative of the Vandal Wars with words of cold comfort for the province's residents: "So it resulted that those of the Africans who had survived, few in number and thoroughly impoverished, finally and at great cost obtained some peace" (Procopius, *Bell. Vand.* 4.28.52). He offered an even bleaker assessment of the devastation of Africa in the *Secret History* (18.5–12).

The aftermath of the conquest of Italy was also a protracted war waged against the new occupiers. Vitigis was succeeded by an even more formidable Gothic leader, Totila, who established military superiority and won the support of the local population. The Goths had been established in northern Italy for more than fifty years. Justinian's forces were an occupying army of diverse ethnic contingents – Isaurians, Thracians, and Armenians – whose conduct since the fall of Ravenna had been marked by rank indiscipline. The inhabitants of the Po Valley had little reason to favor the incomers (Procopius, *Bell. Goth.* 7.5).

Totila took full advantage of the situation in 543, recovering most of southern Italy, including Naples (Procopius, *Bell. Goth.* 7.6–7) and proposed to the Roman Senate that they should throw their hand in with the Goths and restore the successful and peaceful days of Theoderic and Amalasuntha. At the end of 544, Justinian ordered Belisarius back to Italy (Procopius, *Bell. Goth.* 7.8–9), where he established a foothold on the Adriatic coast and sent two senior officers to stiffen the resolve of the besieged garrison at Rome (Procopius, *Bell. Goth.* 7.10–11). Another letter was sent to Constantinople, and this vividly described the demoralization and pitiful state of Roman forces. It urged the need for reinforcements, fresh armaments and mounts, and money enough to pay the mutinous Roman troops. Totila meanwhile accepted the surrender of more Italian cities as a prelude to his main objective, the recapture of Rome.

The second siege of Rome lasted through 546. The occupants of the city were reduced, after the grain supplies were consumed, to eating nettles. The Roman troops and their commander profiteered vigorously by selling at ever increasing prices the stocks of grain that they still controlled. Eventually there was no option but to let the civilian population escape as best it could, and the city fell on December 17, 546, when a group of Isaurians guided an assault party of Goths over the wall at the Asinaria gate. The streets of the city were almost deserted as Totila made his way across the Tiber to celebrate mass at St Peter's Basilica. Procopius used the siege to introduce his own reflections on the changes in human fortunes. A pitiful sight now was Rusticiana, daughter of the patrician Symmachus and widow of the famous philosopher Boethius, reduced to begging from door to door.

> The Romans in general, and particularly the members of the senate, found themselves reduced to such straits that they clothed themselves in the garments of slaves and rustics, and lived by begging bread or any other food from their enemies; a very notable example of this change of fortune being that of Rusticiana, the daughter of Symmachus, who had been wife of Boethius, a woman who was always lavishing her wealth on the needy. Indeed these wretches went about to all the houses and kept knocking at the doors and begging that they give them food, feeling no shame in doing so. (Procopius, *Bell. Goth.* 7.20.27–28)

Some of Totila's men were for putting her to death, as she had destroyed statues of the great Theoderic, who had executed her father and husband in 526 (Procopius, *Bell. Goth.* 7.20). This episode surely marks the demise of the senatorial class as a force to be reckoned with, and this was a crucial break in Italian history.[18] The Senate House itself no longer served as a meeting place and was converted for use as a church in the seventh century.

Totila sent peace proposals to Justinian, aimed at restoring the status quo of 535:

> We request that you take for yourself the benefits of peace and allow them to us. We have the finest memorials and examples of this in the persons of Anastasius and Theoderic, who have ruled as monarchs not long ago, and filled everything with peace and good things throughout their reigns. If this could be achieved in accordance with your wishes, you would properly be called my father, and you would have us as your allies to use against whoever you wish. (Procopius, *Bell. Goth.* 7.21.22–24)

Justinian brusquely dismissed the delegation and instructed Totila to make terms with his plenipotentiary Belisarius (Procopius, *Bell. Goth.* 7.15–21). But Belisarius was powerless to prevent the Goths taking control of Italy and was himself recalled to Constantinople in 548. In a passage of the *Gothic War* which he repeated almost word-for-word in the *Secret History* Procopius was scathing about his former hero:

> Belisarius, in Italy for the second time, departed thence in the most shameful circumstances. For during a five-year period he never succeeded in setting foot on land, as was explained by me in my previous account, except where there was some sort of fortress, but he kept navigating during this period going round the coastal regions. Totila was desperate to come to grips with him outside fortifications, but he never encountered him, since Belisarius and the whole Roman army were gripped by deep fear. For this reason he never recovered any of the places that had been lost, but even lost Rome as well and practically everything else. (Procopius, *Secret History* 5.1–3; cf. *Bell. Goth.* 7.35.1)

Procopius matches this bitter verdict with an equally bleak reading of the overall historical balance sheet. By the end of 548 the barbarians were undisputed masters of the West. The upshot of the Gothic War for the Romans was that

Italy had been lost at an enormous human and financial cost. Illyricum and Thrace were plundered and devastated by the barbarians who lived on their borders. Gaul as far as the Mediterranean and much of Transpadane Italy including the Veneto was in Frankish hands. Their kings controlled this region with Justinian's blessing, but declared their independence by minting gold coins without the emperor's head (Procopius, *Bell. Goth.* 7.33.2–7). Sirmium and the cities of Dacia, which the Romans had won back from the Ostrogoths in 536, were now held by the Gepids (Procopius, *Bell. Goth.* 7.33.8–9). The Lombards held most of Noricum and Pannonia, and plundered Dalmatia and Illyricum, making slaves of many of its inhabitants (Procopius, *Bell. Goth.* 7.33.10–12). The Heruls showed their contempt of Justinian by terrorizing Illyricum and Thrace (Procopius, *Bell. Goth.* 7.33.13–14). In 549 splinter groups of Lombards and Gepids pushed into northern Italy, threatening to join forces with the Ostrogoths (Procopius, *Bell. Goth.* 7.35.19–30).

Nevertheless, Roman foreign policy in the 550s was far from inert. The struggle to control Africa was problematic and unremitting, but Rome did not abandon the conquests of 533–4. Procopius' exaggeratedly negative verdict on the desolate state of Africa in the late 540s is offset by the fact that the Roman occupation continued in relative peace, secured by a network of new fortifications. In 551 Procopius himself acknowledged the success of John Troglites in winning over the allegiance of one of the Moorish rulers, Cutzinas, and subduing Antalas and Iaudas in Byzacena and Numidia respectively (Procopius, *Bell.* 8.17.20–22). He remained in control of a pacified Africa until the early 560s when his exploits were commemorated in a four-book verse epic by Corippus.[19]

Indeed there was a further chapter to the Roman *Drang nach Westen*. In 551 Athanagild, a relative of the Visigothic king Agila, appealed to Justinian to intervene in Spain. The circumstances are obscure and poorly documented. One objective was probably to protect the African provinces from attacks by the Visigoths in Spain, but it may be that the main motivation was to support the Catholic population against the Arian Goths. The Romans had already secured the Balearic islands, Cadiz, and the southern side of the Strait of Gibraltar during the initial campaign against the Vandal kingdom (*Bell. Vand.* 3.1.6, 4.5.6), and thus controlled the approaches to Spain by sea. Despite the advanced years of their general, Liberius, and conflict with their erstwhile ally Athanagild, the Romans swiftly established control in Andalusia as far as Cadiz including the major center of Cordoba (Jordanes, *Get.* 303; Greg. Tur., *Hist.* 4.8). The occupation was not merely a temporary matter. As late as 589 Comentiolus, a leading general of the emperor Maurice, held the post of *magister militum Spaniae* and was responsible for building a monumental fortified gate in the walls of Cartagena (New Carthage), carrying an inscription that read "thus let Spain for ever rejoice under such a governor, as long as the poles rotate and the sun circles round the earth" (*ILS* 835).

The Romans were even more determined to re-assert their domination in Italy after Totila's Gothic forces re-occupied Rome in 550 (Procopius, *Bell. Goth.* 7.36–37). A command was initially assigned to Justinian's nephew,

Germanus, who married the Gothic princess Matasuntha, Vitigis' widow, and attracted numerous barbarian recruits to the army, many paid for from his private fortune. On the eve of the expedition Germanus unexpectedly died (Procopius, *Bell. Goth.* 7.39–40), and was replaced by his son-in-law, John, and son, Justinian. As Totila's Gothic fleet launched naval raids on Corcyra and the islands off Epirus, with the objective of interrupting Roman supply lines (Procopius, *Bell.* 8.22.17–32), John launched a vital expedition to relieve the Roman garrison in the strategic harbor of Ancona, the critical bridgehead on Italy's Adriatic coast (Procopius, *Bell.* 8.23). His warships won a decisive battle at the anchorage of Sena Gallica, which confirmed the Romans' unchallenged mastery of the Adriatic and indeed the Mediterranean at large. This was critical to the subsequent campaign. In 552 the main command was transferred to a senior figure, the eunuch Narses. He led as large a coalition of forces as the treasury could afford: substantial new forces from Constantinople, Thrace, and Illyricum, the private army of Germanus which had passed on to his son-in-law John, 2,500 Lombards, 3,000 Herul cavalry, large numbers of Huns, 400 Gepids, and others. There was also money to cover arrears of pay owing to Roman troops that had defected to Totila (Procopius, *Bell.* 8.26.5–18). Narses led his forces on a remarkable *blitzkrieg*. They marched round the head of the Adriatic gulf to Venetia, added reinforcements at Ravenna, and overcame the resistance of the Gothic garrison of Ariminum, before setting out to cross the Apennines. Totila moved his own forces forward from Rome to Tadinae. The two armies fought a decisive battle at a place known to Procopius as the Funerary Pyre of the Gauls, Busta Gallorum. The outcome was a decisive victory for Narses' men. Six thousand Goths, including Roman deserters, perished on the battlefield and many more who surrendered were slain by their captors. Totila fled but died of his wounds at Caprae (Procopius, *Bell.* 8.29–32).

The Gothic War now entered its final phase. Narses rid himself of his Lombard allies, who in a frenzy of looting, arson, and rape provided a foretaste of the havoc they were to cause when they invaded Italy in 568. The Roman army advanced to Rome where the Gothic garrison vainly barricaded themselves between Hadrian's mausoleum (Castel San Angelo) and a stretch of the old Aurelianic wall. Thus in the autumn of 552 Rome fell to an enemy army for the fifth time in Justinian's reign (Procopius, *Bell.* 8.33). A further season of campaigning was needed to deal with Totila's successor, Teja. The Gothic strongholds were scattered throughout the peninsula and fell one by one to treachery or assault: Perugia, Taranto, Centumcellae, and finally Cumae in Campania, where the largest part of Totila's treasure had been deposited. Teja marched the length of Italy along the Adriatic coast before crossing to Campania to the area of Mount Vesuvius and the site of the final battle of the war, at Mount Lactarius above the Mediterranean resort of Amalfi. He was slain by a javelin and his head raised on a pole by the victors. The Goths who survived the battle disavowed further hostilities and were allowed safe passage out of Italy (Procopius, *Bell.* 8.34–35).

Narses now introduced a new regime for Italy, just twenty years after similar arrangements had been made for Africa. This was laid down in a major imperial ruling, the Pragmatic Sanction of 554 (*Corpus Iuris Civilis* [ed. R. Schöll and W. Kroll], *Novellae* app. VII [August 13, 554]). He himself remained the ruler of Roman Italy until he was dismissed in 568. The administrative structure of Italy was replaced by a new hierarchy of military and civilian offices, controlled by Narses in his capacity as *ex praeposito palati*, and was ultimately dependent on Constantinople. Details of these arrangements can be recovered from the correspondence of Pope Gregory the Great, dating to the 590s.[20] The essence of the new order was succinctly conveyed by an inscription from the end of Justinian's reign, which commemorated the construction of a bridge over the river Anio near Rome:

> When our master the most pious and eternally triumphant Justinian, father of the fatherland, Augustus, was emperor in his 39th year, after the victory over the Goths, when their kings themselves had been conquered and humbled in the public conflict with amazing speed, and liberty had been restored to the city of Rome and the whole of Italy, Narses, the most glorious man, commandant of the palace, former consularis and patrician, has restored the bridge on the Salarian road, which had been destroyed down to the water level by the most wicked tyrant Totila, after the river bed has been cleansed to a better state than it has ever been in. (*ILS* 832, dated between April and November 565)

It is inevitable that assessments of Justinian's reign, and especially of his wars of reconquest in the West, are colored by Procopius' judgment in his *Wars* and in the *Secret History*. As he drew his narratives to a close around 550, he came to a damning verdict concerning both Africa and Italy. Initial success had swiftly been followed by reverses and systematic failure. The wars had dragged on and brought little but suffering. The provinces of the former western empire were laid waste and impoverished. However, this conclusion appears premature in the light of subsequent events. The 540s had been a horrendous decade for the empire. The devastation of the plague was accompanied by severe famine throughout the empire. The Romans would have been faced by acute manpower shortages and dwindling tax revenues. The consequence in a military context was that Roman forces went for long periods without pay, often causing them to mutiny, and they were rarely reinforced from Constantinople. There was a fractious military stalemate both in Africa and in Italy. Roman forces were disheartened, ill-supplied, and barely a match for their barbarian enemies.

The turning-point was reached shortly after Procopius finished the first seven books of his *Wars* and the *Secret History*. Already the supplementary eighth book, which was completed around 554, had a more optimistic story to tell, above all in its account of Narses' successful invasion of Italy, which dealt with Totila's Gothic forces almost as swiftly as Belisarius had defeated Gelimer's Vandals twenty years before. The empire had taken heavy blows from natural catastrophes between 535 and 545. Justinian himself was a changed character, perhaps personally broken by the burdens and responsibilities that he had taken upon himself. The hammer blows of misfortune may have caused levels of public anxiety to rise and may explain a shift in religious behavior (see below, chapter 12). But the Roman Empire itself was resilient. Military and civilian affairs continued to be in the hands of men of high competence. The systems of government remained intact and effective. It would have occurred to no one that decline and fall were imminent, or that the overall balance sheet of Justinian's reign, at least in political and military terms, was not a positive one.

What Justinian achieved by the *riconquista* was to recover a considerable proportion of the former Roman Empire in the West, including all its resources of manpower and tax revenues, but on a substantially different basis from previously. The fundamental difference was that the Roman Empire, now ruled from Constantinople, had a maritime base. It relied on communication by sea and naval control, not on the roads and land-based armies that had underpinned earlier Roman successes. The keys to power were no longer the great road system and fortified cities of Illyricum, but major ports – Carthage, Cartagena, Marseilles, Genoa, the port of Rome, Naples, Lilybaeum, Syracuse, Otranto, Brundisium, Ancona, Ravenna, Venice, and Salona – that were critical for transport and supply, the movement of armies, officials, tax revenues, and food stuffs. These critical strategic bridgeheads enabled the Romans to reassert their rule in the western Mediterranean.

The transformed maritime empire had been created out of the extraordinary challenges of the mid-sixth century. It attests to what the Romans were still capable of achieving thanks to their wealth, military strength, tradition, organization, and political will. There is no significant evidence for decadence and collapse once morale had recovered from the dire setbacks of the 540s. The challenges that Rome's leaders and armies had to face came not from within but from beyond the borders of their empire.

The Challenge of the Sassanians

Rome's relations with Persia had worsened drastically since the beginning of the sixth century, culminating in the outright, although limited, confrontations of 502–7 and 527–32.[21] The two powers were well matched. The geographical scale of the Sassanian Empire corresponded closely with that of the Roman Empire of the East, although the large expanses of desert country in the center and southeast of Iran probably contributed relatively little to the state's overall resources. The Persian domain as a whole was predominantly a highland one, dominated by the two great chains of the Zagros and Elburz mountains, which came together in the knotted volcanic landscapes of Azerbaijan (Map 11.1). The main reservoir of agricultural wealth was in the flat lands of Mesopotamia and in the middle and lower reaches of the Euphrates and the Tigris rivers. A hydraulic civilization, based on labor-intensive irrigation, made this the Sassanian counterpart to the Nile Valley. Since the region's produce could not easily be exported, it was inevitable that the largest population centers and the imperial capital, Ctesiphon, should be located here. History had shown that the Mesopotamian base of Persian power was vulnerable to attack from the Roman side. The approaches from the north along the two river valleys were accordingly strongly defended by fortresses and fortified cities, which are well documented in the accounts of Julian's invasion of 363. The northern frontier of the Iranian Empire stretched to the steppes of central Asia, exposing the Sassanians, even more than the Romans, to attacks from the nomadic peoples of the Asiatic steppe. Throughout the fifth century the Huns north of the Caucasus, and the Hepthalites across the huge zone which extended from the Caspian to the Aral Sea, were an unabating threat, and this was the main factor that kept the Sassanians and Romans from going to war with one another in the fifth century. The defenses against the barbarians depended on Persian garrisons in the main trans-Caucasian passes, which were maintained partly with the aid of Roman subsidies, and by elaborate, multi-linear defensive walls, west and especially east of the Caspian. The latter defended one of Persia's wealthiest regions, the horse-breeding grasslands of the Gurgan plain, ancient Hyrcania, the recruiting ground for much of the Sassanian cavalry force.[22]

Despite its huge land area, geographical diversity and disparate ethnic populations, the Sassanian Empire had been forged into a unity by means which were broadly analogous to those of the Roman Empire. Power was focused on the kings and projected by visual propaganda: imposing buildings, elaborate symbolic reliefs, repeated ceremonials, coinage, and the distribution of prestige gifts, notably silverware decorated with traditional images of royal authority. Sassanian rulership was based on a warrior ethos, and until a serious defeat of the aged Khusro I in 576, the Sassanian kings usually led their forces in person.[23] The monarchic system was stable and effective, as is clear from the long reigns of many of the rulers, although there is ample evidence at various periods for challenges to individual kings, either headed by disaffected elements of the landed nobility or as a result of regional insurrection. Secular authority was consolidated by a centralized state religion, often misleadingly labeled Zoroastrianism, which was controlled by a cadre of high priests (*magi*) and based on fire-worship. The importance of this is underlined in the mid-sixth century by Agathias, writing about the originator of the Sassanian dynasty, Ardashir I:

> He was a devotee of the magian religion and a practitioner of its mysteries. Consequently the priestly cast of the *magi* rose to inordinate power and arrogance. It had indeed existed before, and its name was very ancient, but it had never before been elevated to such a position of privilege and immunity. . . . Nowadays . . . the *magi* are the object of extreme awe and veneration, all public business being conducted at their discretion and in accordance with their prognostications. In private affairs too they preside over and oversee the proceedings when anyone makes an agreement or conducts a suit, and nothing whatever is held to be lawful and right among the Persians unless it is ratified by a *magus*. (Agathias 2.26.3, trans. Fowden)

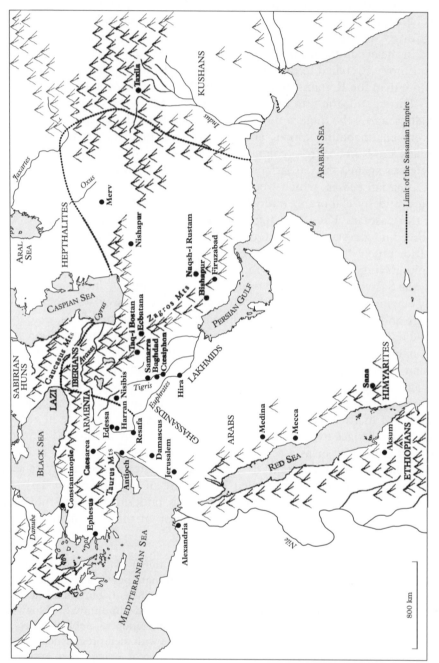

Map 11.1 The Roman Empire and the East in late antiquity

Fire altars were maintained throughout the empire. Eternal fire symbolized the ubiquitous and enduring presence of the supreme Iranian god, Ahura-Mazda, who was depicted in many of the great royal reliefs of the Sassanian kings at the moment of investiture, passing the ring or diadem of power to the new monarch.[24]

In assessing the military potential of the Sassanians, as with the Romans, a distinction should be made between regionally-based garrisons, especially along the northern frontiers, and the mobile armies, with a preponderance of cavalry, which were the main opponents of Rome to the west. The accounts of Roman–Persian warfare in the sixth and early seventh centuries imply that the two sides were closely matched. At full strength the Persian campaigns into Mesopotamia may have brought together field armies of up to 60,000 men.

It was an inevitable consequence of the comparisons that could be made between them, that the Roman and Sassanian empires conceived themselves as a complementary pair. This is implicit in the symbolism of world rulership found in Shapur I's great triumphal relief carved in a cliff beside his new city at Bishapur. At the center of the composition was the enthroned figure of the great king. To his right were the ranks of his own supporters and vassals; to his left were his defeated enemies, and among them the captured standards of Roman legions. But the rows of Romans and Persians were placed on a level with one another, with the implication that Shapur claimed merely to have subordinated his enemies, not humiliated them. In the fourth and fifth centuries, despite the military and political rivalry between the great powers, this imagery was developed and consolidated by generations of diplomacy (see above, chapter 4). In their diplomatic correspondence the respective titles of the rulers were carefully and ostentatiously weighed against each other. Metaphorically, the two empires became the two eyes or two lights of the world, language which acknowledged them as cultural as well as political equals, in contrast to the darkness of uncivilized barbarism which lay beyond their frontiers. The notion was most clearly expressed by Peter the Patrician, Justinian's long-serving master of offices, who had undertaken numerous diplomatic missions to Persia, and who put these words into the mouths of Persian negotiators in 298:

> It is apparent to all mankind, that the Roman and Persian empires match each other as though they were two lights, and it is necessary that like eyes they should be adorned by the light from their counterpart and should not treat each other as enemies with the aim of wiping each other out. (Petrus Patricius fr. 13)

The same conception was expressed in a letter sent by Khusro II to the emperor Maurice in 590 (Theophylact 4.11.2).

In the sixth century Persian power increased, above all thanks to the rulership of Justinian's near contemporary, Khusro I (Khusro Anurshivan, "immortal soul"), who ruled from 531 to 579. Procopius presented him as a Sassanian Justinian, "an extraordinary lover of revolutionary innovations" (*Bell. Pers.* 1.23–1), but the extremely complex middle Persian and Arabic sources indicate that he carried out a comprehensive reorganization of the land and poll tax, at the same time as reforming the structure of the army by creating a more centralized elite cavalry force from the nobility.[25]

The relationship between Rome and Persia from the mid-sixth to the early seventh centuries was dominated by three major acts of aggression, two from the Sassanian side by Khusro I in 540 and Khusro II in 603, and one, in 573, by Justin II. The "endless peace" of 532 between Rome and Persia lasted only until 539. Procopius placed the responsibility firmly on Khusro I.[26] An initial *casus belli* arose from a dispute between the Saracens under Al-Mundhir, who were linked to the Sassanians, and other bands under Al-Harith (Arethas), Rome's ally, concerning grazing rights along the frontier district of Syria known as the Strata. There was further friction in Armenia among the major landowning families, whose allegiances were split between Rome and Persia. The Persian faction, led by members of the Arsacid family, which was descended from the old pro-Persian Armenian monarchy (cf. Procopius, *Buildings* 3.1), brought their complaints to Khusro. The speech which Procopius ascribed to them is doubtless an invention, but it rehearsed in detail Persia's grievances with Rome. During the previous war Justinian had imposed Roman taxes on Persarmenia, subjugated the Tzani, turned Lazica into a client state whose king was subject to a Roman magistrate's authority, attached the Bosporan region to Constantinople, made a defensive alliance with the Ethiopians, and attached the Himyarites and the palm groves of that region to the Roman Empire. The conquests in Africa and Italy underlined the extent of the threat that Justinian posed. Now the final straw was his attempt to make further trouble by putting pressure on Al-Mundir, and supporting Hunnic incursions (Procopius, *Bell. Pers.* 2.3.39–47). This catalogue of charges encompassed the full geographical sweep of the common frontier of the two empires, from the Caucasus to the Horn of Africa. Khusro was swayed by these arguments. After exchanging diplomatic letters with Justinian in the winter of 539/40, Khusro invaded Roman territory in the following spring (Procopius, *Bell. Pers.* 2.4.13–26).

The Roman defenses were exposed as being hopelessly inadequate to deal with their opponents.[27] The war took the form of the Sassanian army attacking an uncoordinated group of city states. Khusro deployed tactics that were arbitrary, willful, and terrifying. Wholesale massacres and the destruction of cities were interspersed with casual and fleeting threats. The cities of Syria, usually under the leadership of their bishops, tried as best they could to defend themselves or to buy off trouble. The city of Sura was captured by a ruse, and most of its population was massacred (Procopius, *Bell. Pers.* 2.5). Nearby Sergioupolis, modern Resafa, was spared the same fate when Candidus, its bishop, agreed to pay two hundred pounds of gold as a price for ransoming 12,000 captives that Khusro had taken at Sura, and was given two years to find the money. When Khusro returned to collect the debt, he tortured Candidus until he handed over the church treasures of St Sergius, and even then besieged the city until he had to abandon the attempt due to lack of water.[28]

Justinian's commanders in the field and their pitifully small forces were powerless (Procopius, *Bell. Pers.* 2.6.3–8). Beroea was captured and most of the small garrison of Roman soldiers deserted to the Persians (Procopius, *Bell. Pers.* 2.7.14–18). Khusro agreed not to plunder the land around Hierapolis at a price to the city of 2,000 pounds of silver. Justinian's senior representatives had by now reached Antioch, but declined the terms which Khusro was prepared to offer. The city fell to the Persian assault, abandoned by the Roman troops that had been sent to protect it, and these escaped, unhindered by the Persians, to the suburb of Daphne (Procopius, *Bell. Pers.* 2.8.25–6). Antioch's inhabitants were treated as those of Sura had been. Many were killed, and others were herded back to Persian territory and resettled in a new city near Ctesiphon (Procopius, *Bell. Pers.* 2.14.1–4). The destruction of Antioch by the Persians, coming only fourteen years after the great earthquake of 526, was burned on the conscience of the Roman world.[29] Procopius wrote,

> I become bewildered as I write of such great suffering, and transmit it to the record for the future, and I am unable to understand why on earth it should be the will of God to exalt on high the fortunes of a man or of a place, and then to cast them down and destroy them for no cause which is apparent to us. For it is not rightful to say that with Him not everything occurs according to reason, even though He himself then experienced seeing Antioch, whose beauty and universal grandeur even now cannot altogether be made invisible, being razed to its foundations at the hands of a most impious man. (Procopius, *Bell. Pers.* 2.10.4–5, trans. Dewing)

The fate of Antioch was simply irreconcilable with belief in the providence of a righteous God.[30]

Khusro offered peace terms: an indemnity from the Romans of 5,000 pounds of gold, to be supplemented by an annual payment of 500 pounds. For this the Persians would maintain peace and security, garrison the Caspian Gates themselves, and raise no further complaints about Dara. The Romans protested that they would thus be seen as tributary subjects of Persia, but Khusro insisted that there was a distinction: The Romans would simply be paying the Persians as if they were hired mercenaries, just as they already made annual payments to the Huns and the Saracens, so that these would protect Roman territory from plundering (Procopius, *Bell. Pers.* 2.10.1–3). The system of securing peace by paying protection money, which had served Constantinople through much of the fifth century, was to continue.

As these conditions were transmitted to Justinian for ratification the Persians continued to turn the screw on the provinces of Syria and Mesopotamia, which were now at their mercy. Khusro undertook a victory parade and fund-raising tour around the remaining major cities of Syria, threatening and plundering at will. From the sea at Seleucia, where he bathed symbolically in the Mediterranean, he passed through Daphne, torching the Church of St Michael, and came to the great city of Apamea, whose inhabitants were spared massacre or deportation by a famous miracle of the Cross.[31] Famously, the Persian king ordered charioteers to stage a race in the hippodrome, and supported the Greens. This advertised his victory over Justinian, who had been a long standing backer of the Blues before he became emperor. Chalcis ad Belum and Edessa were spared from being besieged on payment of 2,000 pounds of gold (Procopius, *Bell. Pers.* 2.12). News now reached Khusro that Justinian had accepted his terms, at which he released the hostages he had taken and offered to sell back the prisoners of war taken in captivity from Antioch. The detailed local sources, which were clearly available to Procopius, indicated that the whole population of Edessa, including the prostitutes and humble peasants, contributed to the fund to buy them back, but were prevented from doing so by the Roman *magister militum* Bouzes. Khusro himself declined similar payments offered by the people of nearby Carrhae, on the grounds that as unbelievers (moon-worshippers) they should not be buying the freedom of Christians. Evidently the Sassanian king saw the inhabitants of pagan Carrhae as a potentially important fifth column in Roman Mesopotamia. Further payments were extracted from Constantina, but Roman troops commanded by Martinus staged successful resistance when Khusro attempted to besiege and storm Dara. This Persian attempt to take the city was construed by Justinian as a breach of the freshly negotiated agreement with Khusro (Procopius, *Bell. Pers.* 2.13).

In 541 Belisarius returned from Italy and finally took up his command on the Persian front. This signaled a decision by the belligerent emperor to fight back against the Sassanians at all costs rather than agree the terms that had been offered. The theater of war now extended to Lazica in the north. Justinian's troops and their commanders had alienated the local population, and the Lazi turned to Khusro for help.[32] The Sassanians moved virtually unopposed into Lazica and stormed the main stronghold at Petra. John Tzibous, the Roman commander, perished from an arrow shot and many of the Roman troops deserted (Procopius, *Bell. Pers.* 2.17). This news was brought to Belisarius when he reached the Syrian front and spurred a counterattack on Mesopotamia (Procopius, *Bell. Pers.* 2.15.14–35, 2.16). However, his forces took only the small stronghold of Sisara (Sisauranon). Their supposed allies, the lightly armed but highly mobile Saracen forces under Al-Harith, made off with the plunder, while Roman troops succumbed to fever in the blistering summer heat, and a third of them had to be invalided out on wagons. The force also returned to protect Roman territory exposed to raiding by the hostile Saracen tribes led by Al-Mundir (Procopius, *Bell. Pers.* 2.18–19).

In the spring of 542, Khusro weighed the prospect of making a rapid swoop across the desert via Palmyra to Palestine and Jerusalem. Meanwhile Belisarius opposed him with the combined, but inadequate Roman forces in Syria. At a parley with Khusro's legate, Belisarius attempted to cover his military weakness with a show of strength, a studiedly casual parade of six hundred troops, purposely picked from the full ethnic range – Thracians, Illyrians, Goths, Heruli, Vandals, and Moors – dressed in hunting gear. The Persians withdrew, pausing to take captive the peasant inhabitants of Callinicum. However, it is clear that they had not been deterred by the Romans but by a far more devastating enemy, the plague, from which neither the Persian nor the Roman Empire was spared (Procopius, *Bell. Pers.* 2.21.23–24).

Fear of the plague restricted campaigning in 543 to the northern highlands east of the Euphrates. The Romans sent large forces on a front which extended from Theodosioupolis (Erzurum) in the north, to Martyropolis in the south. From this broad front they converged eastwards against the city of Dubios (Dvin) in eastern Armenia, close to the old center of Artaxata, eight days journey east of Theodosioupolis. (Procopius, *Bell. Pers.* 2.25.1–4). The Persian commander Nabedes lured the Roman forces into an ambush and inflicted a major defeat on them, capturing most of their baggage train and weapons (Procopius, *Bell. Pers.* 2.25.5–35).

In 544 Khusro turned his attention again to Mesopotamia, setting his sights on Edessa, which had defied him in 541 (Procopius, *Bell. Pers.* 2.12.7–34). According to Procopius, this attack on a major Christian center was to be intended as an attack on the God worshipped by the Christians. The Persians were eventually obliged to withdraw, having extracted a payment of 500 pounds of gold (Procopius, *Bell. Pers.* 2.26–27). Justinian now sent ambassadors to discuss an armistice, seeking the return of Lazica and a lasting peace. Khusro agreed a five-year truce on these terms, provided that he also received 2,000 pounds of gold and the services of a Roman physician who had previously treated him successfully for an unspecified condition (Procopius, *Bell. Pers.* 2.28.1–11).

The truce which was established in 545 and renewed in 551 led to a cessation of hostilities on the Mesopotamian frontier. Meanwhile the main theater of war shifted to Persian-occupied Lazica, which had been expressly excluded from the terms of the armistice. Lazica, modern Georgia, was an extensive and fertile enclave at the east end of the Black Sea, providing a sharp environmental contrast to the mountain arena which formed most of the frontier lands between the two empires. Since the 460s its rulers, and probably most of the population, had been Christian. Although it was exposed to strong Persian political influence, most of the Lazi resented Sassanian attempts to rule them (Procopius, *Bell. Pers.* 2.28.25–26). Lazica became a focus of Roman attention as a result of the Roman thrust in the 520s to Christianize the Black Sea (see above, chapter 4). Major Roman fortifications were built at Petra and at the inland site of Nokalakevi/Archaeopolis. The region also controlled access from the west to the passes through the Caucasus, which were of particular concern to the Sassanians as they sought to defend themselves against the Huns.

Khusro had mixed reasons for his designs on the region. By imposing himself on Lazica he hoped to contain rebellious elements in neighboring Iberia, which was always regarded as part of the Persian Empire, to secure the Caucasus passes against the Huns, and, by gaining access to the Black Sea, to create the possibility of a direct seaborne attack on Constantinople. His ultimate ambition was to remove the pro-Roman king Goubazes, transplant the Lazi elsewhere in his empire, and replace them with more complaisant Persian settlers (Procopius, *Bell. Pers.* 2.28.18–30, 8.7.12). The focal point of the hostilities was Petra, whose impressive fortifications are still well preserved (see above, chapter 10). The historian Agathias noted that the emperor's determination to secure Lazica was motivated both by loyalty to Rome's friends, and by religion (Agathias 2.18.6). The mostly Christian inhabitants of the region had divided loyalties, but tended on balance to give more encouragement to Rome than to Persia. For several years control was divided, with Roman forces dominating north of the river Phasis, while the Persians held southern Lazica around Petra. In 551 the latter were driven from Petra by the Roman general Bessas, and forced back into the hinterland and the approaches to Iberia, thus relinquishing their foothold on the Black Sea coast. The conflict now shifted to the interior of the country, and continued until 557. Eventually the Sassanians gave up the struggle, defeated in the last analysis by logistic difficulties in sustaining a war so far from the centers of their empire (Agathias 4.30.7). Lazica was definitively ceded to Rome in the treaty of 562.[33]

The peace agreement between Rome and Persia, which was finally agreed by plenipotentiaries of the two rulers at a neutral location on the frontier near Dara in 562, is the fullest treaty document to have survived from the ancient world. The contents were checked word for word, guaranteed by the seals of a team of twelve interpreters, and recorded with equal scrupulousness by the historian Menander (fr. 6). It is not impossible that he personally had been one of the translators of the document. The treaty was to last for fifty years. Clauses dealt with the Caucasus passes, the role of the Arab tribes, the activities of Roman and Persian merchants and the points at which they could cross the frontier, the protection and privileges of official ambassadors and couriers, the return of refugees and fugitives to their state of origin, and the settling of civil disputes that arose between Romans and Persians. The recurring feud over Dara was put to rest by the Persians acknowledging that the Romans had a right to retain the fortress, provided that its garrison was no larger than appropriate to a city, and that it was not used as the headquarters of the Roman commander of Oriens. An elaborate article of the treaty set up a system of local judges, with channels of appeal to higher authorities, to deal with complaints of cities damaged by local cross-border feuding.[34]

The realpolitik was as important as the formal wording of the treaty. The atmosphere in which agreement was reached was tense and hostile. Justinian's *magister officiorum*, Peter the Patrician, delivered a speech in which he expressly warned the Persians to behave modestly in the presence of the Romans and not to boast of their achievement in sacking Antioch. The Persian response was a calculated insult. Khusro thought nothing of so commonplace an event as the capture of Antioch; leveling a Roman city was all in a day's work for Persian forces. The main territorial advantage for the Romans was to confirm their sovereignty in Lazica. The fact was not mentioned in the treaty. Another condition favorable to Rome was an agreement, not included in the formal treaty, that Christians in the Sassanian Empire should be allowed freedom of worship and to build churches, and not compelled to follow the religion of the *magi*, although they were not to proselytize. Nestorian Christianity had made significant headway and claimed converts at high levels of society (see above, chapter 4).

However, these gains came at a price and at a cost to Roman prestige. All the sixth-century agreements between Rome and Persia involved payments to the latter, which were a source of deep controversy. In 532 Justinian had secured the "eternal peace" with a single payment of 11,000 gold pounds, which was understood as Rome's contribution to the military costs of securing the Caucasus frontier (Procopius, *Bell. Pers.* 1.22.3). The five-year truce of 545 was obtained on payment of a further 2,000 gold pounds (*Bell. Pers.* 2.28.10). In 551 the cost of renewal was only fixed after protracted negotiation. The Persians demanded 2,000 pounds for the coming five years and 600 for the previous eighteen months since the beginning of 550, when payments had been interrupted. The emperor Justinian initially proposed paying 400 pounds annually, to ensure that the Persians adhered to the conditions of the truce, but then agreed to full payment for five years in advance, to avoid the appearance that the Romans were now annual tributaries of the Persian Empire. Precisely these matters were at issue in 562. The annual figure was set at 30,000 gold coins (*nomismata*), which historians of the seventh and eighth centuries judged to have been worth 500 gold pounds. However, at the usual equivalence of 72 *nomismata* to a gold pound, the cost per year would have been 416 pounds, virtually the same as in the previous agreements.[35] There was to be an immediate payment covering the first seven years, followed by one for three years, and annual payments thereafter. Theophylact, but not the contemporary Menander, interpreted the payments as covering the cost of the Caucasus garrisons (3.9.11). It is evident that their significance and purpose could be read in different ways. For the Persians, and for internal critics of Justinian, they would naturally be understood as a form of tribute. The Roman regime presented them as a cost-effective subsidy to a foreign nation which was undertaking defense duties on its behalf, although the fact that the Caucasus passes were largely irrelevant to Roman defenses made it increasingly difficult to sustain this argument.

The atmosphere in which the treaty of 562 had been concluded indicates that relations between Rome and Persia in the later sixth century were sour. This is confirmed on the Roman side by the hostile tone to be found in the authors of the period. Procopius provided a damning assessment of Khusro I, understandable from the viewpoint of a writer who had witnessed at first hand his lack of scruple and the conduct of his armies during the invasions of Syria and the sack of Antioch (Procopius, *Bell. Pers.* 2.9.8–18). Agathias painted an even more hostile picture of the Persians, as barbaric, perverse, and cruel.[36] This was to be expected at a period when the political outlook of the two great powers was polarized between the political and religious stance of two domineering rulers, Justinian and Khusro I, which sharpened the geopolitical conflict.

In 569 Justin II, Justinian's successor, agreed to the second, three-year installment of payments to the Sassanians, but the demand for annual payments from 572 was one of the *casus belli* which led to the outbreak of another Roman–Persian war. The Romans also found other reasons for complaint. The largely Christian population of eastern Armenia (Persarmenia) allegedly wished to be part of the Roman Empire (John of Ephesus, *Ecclesiastical History* 2.32), and assassinated their Persian governor (Evagrius 5.7); the Sassanians were interfering in the affairs of the Himyarites in the Yemen, claimed as part of the Roman protectorate since the 530s. Meanwhile Justin's agents were plotting to coordinate hostilities with the emergent power of the western Turks, who had replaced the Hepthalite Huns as a major threat to Persia from the steppes. A Persian embassy to Constantinople, led by an Armenian Christian, responded unprovocatively, merely requiring continuation of the promised annual subsidy, but it was repudiated by an emperor bent on war (Menander fr. 16). Justin sent his nephew, the *patricius* Marcian, with 3,000 inadequately equipped troops drawn from the local frontier garrisons, to begin a war in Arzanene, the Persian province north of the Tur Abdin and east of Martyropolis (Theophylact 3.10.1–3).[37] The attack provoked a crushing response from the Sassanians in 573. Khusro himself overwhelmed the Roman forces near Nisibis and after a six-month siege captured Dara. His general Adarmahan crossed the Euphrates at Circesium and reached the Orontes Valley, the heart of Roman Syria, ravaging the suburbs of Antioch and putting Apamea to the torch (Evagrius 5.9–10; John of Ephesus 6.5–6; Theophylact 3.10.4–11.4). The loss of Dara is said to have driven Justin II mad. His wife Sophia took a prominent role in agreeing terms with Khusro in spring 574, involving further Roman payments which secured peace in Mesopotamia but which left the Armenian question unresolved (Evagrius 5.11–12; Menander fr. 18, 37–8). Another consequence of the debacle was the adoption of Tiberius II to succeed Justin II, creating a virtual regency until the latter's death in 578 (Evagrius 5.13).

The uneasy truce was prolonged until 576 (Theophylact 3.12.10; Menander fr. 39–40, 50). Rome used the respite to rebuild military strength and discipline (Theophylact 3.12.7; Evagrius 5.14), and these were formative years for the future emperor Maurice, himself an author of a work on military tactics and one of Rome's great warrior rulers. In 576 the adversaries launched attacks on one another, the Romans attacking Armenia from the direction of Amida in Mesopotamia, while Khusro led his forces across the Euphrates against Caesarea in Cappadocia. On the return march he sacked Melitene, but his army was ambushed as it withdrew east across the river (Menander fr. 18.6; John of Ephesus 6.8–9; Evagrius 5.14), with the loss of men, booty, and the king's personal fire altar. Roman historians report that from this moment a law was introduced that Persian kings should no longer lead military expeditions. Khusro's personal prestige was seriously damaged by the debacle and he was threatened by mutinies,[38] while the events of these years show that properly equipped and trained Roman forces were more than a match for the Sassanians in the frontier areas. The initiative passed now to the rejuvenated Roman forces. An army invaded Azerbaijan, through the territory of Persarmenia and Iberia, where it found significant support from the Christian populations, and over wintered deep in Sassanian territory in 576/7 (Theophylact 3.15.1–2; John of Ephesus 6.10). This strategy was replicated exactly half a century later in the devastating counteroffensive staged by Heraclius against Khusro II. Fierce fighting continued in spring 578 with a Sassanian thrust into Mesopotamia, followed by a Roman counterattack against Arzanene and beyond the Tigris as far as Singara, led by Maurice (Evagrius 5.19; Theophylact 3.15.11–16.2; John of Ephesus 6.15).

Justin II died in October 578, followed by Khusro I in the following spring, during negotiations which aimed to return Dara to Roman control and sovereignty over Persarmenia and Iberia to the Sassanians. Khusro's successor Hormizd, however, broke off the diplomatic exchanges and initiated a further period of warfare on the Mesopotamian front. In 580 and 581 Maurice led attacks into Media and Mesopotamia respectively, in the second year at first aided but then betrayed by the Ghassanid leader Al-Mundhir. The following year he defeated a Sassanian force, which had counterattacked near Constantina in Mesopotamia, before returning to Constantinople where he became emperor in succession to Tiberius, who died in August 582 (Theophylact 3.17.5–18.3).

During the early years of Maurice's reign matters along the eastern frontier remained in the balance. Maurice sent his treacherous Arab allies, Al-Mundhir and his son Numan, into exile (Evagrius 6.2), while John the Thracian and Philippicus led Roman campaigns in Arzanene and the territory of Nisibis. Priscus replaced Philippicus late in 587, at a moment when financial pressures forced the emperor to reduce military pay. This provoked a serious mutiny, which erupted at Easter 588 in Mesopotamia. The troops elected Germanus, the military commander in Phoenice Libanensis, to supplant Priscus, and the emperor himself re-appointed Philippicus to the command in Mesopotamia. Germanus himself, aided by further promises of imperial money, calmed the mutineers and led a successful campaign against the Persians, who had taken advantage of the confusion to attack Constantina. Germanus won a significant victory at Martyropolis, and the booty taken from the Sassanian army went some way to meeting the soldiers demands (Theophylact 3.1.1–4.6; Evagrius 6.4–7, 9). Gregory, the bishop of Antioch, played a leading role in conciliating the army with its imperial commander, Philippicus. It appears from Evagrius' virtually contemporary account of these actions that Gregory was effectively the secular as well as the ecclesiastical leader of Antioch, and responsible among other things for recruitment and the provision of logistical supplies to the army (Evagrius 6.11–13).[39] However, 589 saw a further setback when Martyropolis was betrayed to the Persians. Philippicus, who was unable to recover the city, was again replaced by Comentiolus, and hostilities continued in Arzanene between Roman forces, who had seized the stronghold of Akbas, and the Persians, who maintained their bridgehead in Roman territory at Martyropolis (Evagrius 6.14–15; Theophylact 3.5.11–15).

Decisive developments came from a different quarter. The catalyst was the appearance of a major new force in the steppes east of the Caspian, the western Turkic tribes led by their Chagan.[40] The Turks demanded huge sums of protection money from the Sassanians to keep the peace along the northern frontier:

> The Turkish realm, then, had been made very rich by the Persians, and this particular nation had turned to great extravagance; for they hammered out gold couches, tables, goblets, thrones, pedestals horse-trappings, suits of armour and everything which has been devised by the inebriation of wealth. Subsequently when the Turks broke the treaty and demanded that they be given more than the customary money and that there should be a very heavy supplement, the Persians, intolerant of the burden of the imposed tribute, elected to make war. (Theophylact 3.6.11–12, trans. Whitby and Whitby)

The successful Sassanian reprisals were led by Bahram, who then proceeded to attack the western Caucasian kingdom of Suania, which was a perpetual source of dispute between Rome and Persia in the western Caucasus.[41] The Roman response was to send a force to Lazica, which advanced east into Albania and defeated Bahram's forces at a battle on the river Araxes (Theophylact 3.6.15–7.19). Bahram then defied the attempt of the Sassanian king Hormizd IV to dismiss him from his command, and led his mutinous forces as far as the river Zab (Theophylact 3.8.1–3, 10–12). This threat caused widespread further defections among Hormizd's followers, and the king was overthrown in a palace coup at Ctesiphon, were he was briefly succeeded by his son Khusro II (Theophylact 4.1.1–3.12). Bahram's army now moved southwards towards Ctesiphon and defeated Khusro, who was left with no option but to flee westward with his harem and a small entourage of followers to seek Roman protection. He was escorted from the frontier city of Circesium to Hierapolis where Comentiolus, commanding the Roman forces of the east, received him in March 590. As Bahram seized royal power in Persia, Khusro sent a delegation with a proposition for the emperor Maurice. If the Romans restored him to his throne, he would give back Martyropolis, Dara, and control over Armenia (Theophylact 4.13.24). The Armenian chronicle attributed to Sebeos preserves a similar narrative of these events but defines more precisely Khusro's territorial offer to Maurice: the region around Nisibis, control of Armenia as far as Mount Ararat, the city of Dvin and Lake Van, and territory in Georgia as far as Tiflis (*Armenian Chronicle Attributed to Sebeos* 76, 84). Rejecting the advice that Rome's interests were best served by leaving the Persian rivals to fight between themselves, Maurice decided to accept Khusro's proposal. This initiated an energetic and complicated campaign, much of it in Lake Urmia in Azerbaijan. Bahram's forces were eventually worsted at a battle near Ganzak, and the usurper fled to the east, seeking sanctuary among the Turks, but was murdered soon afterwards. These events marked a high point in Rome's struggle along the eastern frontier. Roman garrisons not only reclaimed Dara and Martyropolis, but also took charge of much of Persarmenia.

The events of 591 also sealed the relationship between the two great powers. Maurice's decision to support Khusro's legitimate claims against the usurper Bahram acknowledged the argument, expressed in Khusro's pleas for help, that the two empires gained more than they lost from having a stable counterpart on their frontier. It also showed a confidence in Roman strength, which was justified by the strategic gains of the campaigns of 590–1. What was not foreseen was that, less than a dozen years later, the favor shown to Khusro would be precisely reciprocated, as Maurice was in turn overthrown by the usurper Phocas, and a man who claimed to be his son, Theodosius, fled to safety under the protection of Khusro.

NOTES

1 Gavin Kelly, "Ammianus and the great tsunami," *JRS* 94 (2004), 141–67.
2 For the upper Nilotic regions of east Africa as a reservoir of plague-bearing fleas which transmitted the bubonic virus to the rodent population, crucially to the black rat, see D. Keys, *Catastrophe. An Investigation into the Origins of the Modern World* (London, 1999), 20–31.
3 K.-H. Leven, "Die 'justinianische' Pest," *Jahrbuch des Instituts für Geschichte der Medizin der Robert-Bosch-Stiftung* 6 (1987), 137–61.
4 C. Zuckerman, *Du village à l'empire. Autour du régistre fiuscale d'Aphroditô* (Paris, 2004), 189–212, basing his argument on figures for *annona* deliveries from Egypt during the early 540s.
5 H. D. Colt, *Excavations at Nessana* I (London, 1962), 168 no. 80, 179–81 nos. 112–14; C. E. M. Clucker, *The City of Gaza in the Roman and Byzantine Periods* (Oxford, 1987), 124–7 nos. 9–11; cf. *SEG* 28, 1393 (Oboda), and 38, 1602, 1607, and 1608 (Rehovot).
6 J.-N. Biraben and J. Le Goff, "La peste dans le Haut Moyen Age," *Annales* 24 (1969), 1484–1510 (English translation in R. Forster and O. Ranum, *Biology of Man in History* [Baltimore, 1975], 48–80).
7 M. Meier, *Das andere Zeitalter Justinians* (Göttingen, 2003), 327–8; D. Keys, *Catastrophe*, 16–19.
8 J. Durliat, "La peste du sixième siècle. Pour un nouvel examen des sources byzantines," *Hommes et richesses dans l'empire byzantin* I (Paris, 1989), 107–19, seeks to minimize the consequences, but his arguments are questioned by J.-N. Biraben, in the same volume, 121–5. M. Whittow, *The Making of Byzantium 600–1025* (London, 1996), 66–8, argues that the effects of the plague have been overestimated.
9 For the evidence of the *Life* of Theodore of Sykeon, see S. Mitchell, *Anatolia* II (Oxford, 1993), 122–34.
10 D. Stathakopoulos, "The Justinanic plague revisited," *Byzantine and Modern Greek Studies* 24 (2000), 256–76 (20–25%); P. Allen, "The 'Justinianic' plague," *Byzantion* 49 (1979), 5–20 (33%); J. A. S. Evans, *The Age of Justinian* (London and New York, 1996), 160, suggests a halving of the population of the empire between 500 and 600. All these figures are impressionistic.
11 See M. McCormick, "Bateaux de vie, bateaux de mort, maladie, commerce, transports annonaires et le passage économique du Bas-Empire au Moyen-Age," in *Morfologie sociali e culturali di Europa fra tarda antichità e alto medioevo* (Spoleto, 1998), 35–122. Further assessments of the plague by Michael Whitby, in Averil

Cameron (ed.), *The Byzantine and Early Islamic Near East III* (Princeton, 1995), 92–9; M. Meier, *Das andere Zeitalter Justinians* (Göttingen, 2003), 321–40, 373–87; L. Conrad, "Epidemic disease in central Syria in the late sixth century," *Byzantine and Modern Greek Studies* 18 (1994), 12–58.

12   Procopius, *Bell. Vand.* 4.14.5–6; cf. John Lydus, *de ostentis* 9.

13   D. Keys, *Catastrophe*, 343–57. Keys' book has been predictably criticized for attempting to explain too much (the origins of the modern world, no less). Many of his inferences are highly speculative, but the central points relating to the climatic catastrophe appear to be sound.

14   Full references for these and other catastrophes in M. Meier, *Das andere Zeitalter Justinians* (Göttingen, 2003), 656–70.

15   M. Meier, "Die Erdbeben der Jahre 542 und 554 in der byzantinischen Überlieferung," *ZPE* 130 (2000), 287–95.

16   M. Meier, *Das andere Zeitalter Justinians* (Göttingen, 2003), 261–73.

17   See the administrative documents from Ravenna published in *Papyri Italiae* dating between 552 and the second quarter of the seventh century.

18   S. J. B. Barnish, "Transformation and survival in the western senatorial aristocracy c. AD 400–700," *Papers of the British School at Rome* 56 (1988), 120–55.

19   Averil Cameron, *Corippus, Ioanni.* D. Pringle, *The Defences of Byzantine Africa from Justinian to the Arab Conquest* I (Oxford, 1981), 33ff. compares the evidence of Corippus and Procopius.

20   A. H. M. Jones, *Later Roman Empire* I (Oxford, 1964), 292 and 313.

21   G. Greatrex, *Rome and Persia at War 502–532* (Liverpool, 1998).

22   J. Howard-Johnston, "The two great powers in late antiquity," in Averil Cameron (ed.), *The Byzantine and Early Islamic Near East* III (Princeton, 1995), 180–203.

23   Michael Whitby, "The Persian king at war," in E. Dabrowa (ed.), *The Roman and Byzantine Army in the East* (Krakow, 1994), 227–63.

24   G. Fowden, *Empire to Commonwealth* (Princeton, 1993), 29–34.

25   Z. Rubin, "The reforms of Khusro Anushirwan," in Averil Cameron (ed.), *The Byzantine and Early Islamic Near East* III (Princeton, 1995), 227–97.

26   Averil Cameron, *Procopius* (London, 1985), 161–70, draws attention to the detailed local knowledge displayed by Procopius in the narrative of events in Mesopotamia and Syria from 540–2, and argues that the historian was present for much of them in person. There is a very brief summary in Evagrius 4.25.

27   W. Liebeschuetz, "The defences of Syria in the sixth century," in *Studien zu den Militärgrenzen Roms* II (Cologne, 1977), 487–99.

28   Procopius, *Bell. Pers.* 2.4, 20.1–16; E. K. Fowden, *The Barbarian Plain between Rome and Iran* (California, 1999), 133–4.

29   M. Meier, *Das andere Zeitalter Justinians* (Göttingen, 2003), 313–20.

30   A. Kaldellis, *Procopius of Caesarea* (Philadelphia, 2004), 205–9.

31   Procopius, *Bell. Pers.* 2.11; Evagrius 4.26 claims to have witnessed the miracle of the Cross as a small child attending school there.

32   Procopius, *Bell. Pers.* 2.15.1–13; cf. 2.28.27–28 for the dependence of the Lazi on the import of salt and other products. D. Braund, *Georgia in Antiquity* (Oxford, 1994), 292–5, suggests that Procopius exaggerates both the extent of Roman outrages and the behavior of their commander, John Tzibous, and the poverty of the region. But Lazica at this time may have been afflicted by the catastrophic crop failures of this period.

33   Full discussion in D. Braund, *Georgia in Antiquity* (Oxford, 1994), 268–314.

34 Details and discussion in E. Winter and B. Dignas, *Rom und das Persereich* (Berlin, 2002), 164–77.

35 Theophylact 3.9.10; Theophanes, *Chron.* for the year 664.

36 B. Isaac, "The army in the late Roman East," in Averil Cameron (ed.), *The Byzantine and Early Islamic Near East* III (Princeton, 1995), 125–55 at 127–9.

37 Michael Whitby, "Arzanene in the late Sixth Century," in S. Mitchell (ed.), *Armies and Frontiers in Roman and Byzantine Anatolia* (Oxford, 1983), 205–18.

38 Michael Whitby, "The Persian king at war," in E. Dabrowa (ed.), *The Roman and Byzantine Army in the East* (Krakow, 1994), 227–63.

39 Michael Whitby, "Recruitment in the Roman armies," in Averil Cameron (ed.), *The Byzantine and Early Islamic Near East* III (Princeton, 1995), 81–3.

40 For an account of the appearance of the Turks in this region see Theophylact 7.7.6–9.12.

41 D. Braund, *Georgia in Antiquity*, 311–14.

12

The Final Reckoning of the Eastern Empire

627	Heraclius resumes the offensive and reaches Ctesiphon; Khusro II is overthrown and the Cross restored to Jerusalem
628–33	Civil war in Persia
622–41	The first wave of Islamic conquests
622	Exile of Muhammad to Medina, the *hijra*
632	Death of Muhammad
636	The Arab followers of Muhammad defeat Roman forces at the Battle of the Yarmuk
638	Fall of Jerusalem
641	Capture of Alexandria, death of Heraclius
642	The Aras defeat the Sassanians at the battle of Nihavand
651	Assassination of the last Sassanian ruler, Yazdgird III

The Northern Barbarians in the Sixth Century

Avars, Slavs, and Lombards

Since the collapse of the Hunnic Empire in the middle of the fifth century, the entire area of the Balkans had become a dangerous no-man's land. Most of the major fortress cities south of the Danube, which had been devastated by Attila's armies, remained ruined and depopulated. Roman authority was maintained with difficulty along the lower Danube as this could be reached and supplied from Constantinople by sea, but the land routes running west from Constantinople and from the regional capital Thessalonica, north to Serdica, and northwest to Sirmium, were barely secure even for armed forces. In effect the limits of Roman power were the rapids of the middle Danube, around the Iron Gates, which marked the western limit of Rome's naval reach.

After the fall of the Huns, the regional power vacuum was filled by the Ostrogothic tribes, but these dispersed after Theoderic the Amal took his followers to Italy in 489, and this opened the door to incursions of new peoples, moving through the Ukraine across the river Dnieper to the Danube. Among these were the Turkic-speaking Bulgars (who were usually called Huns by Procopius), and the Sclaveni (Slavs), who began to mount successful incursions into Thrace, but were defeated by Justinian's troops in notable campaigns of 528–9.[1] Justinian consolidated Roman control of the eastern Balkans by rebuilding many of its fortresses, a major effort, which received detailed attention in Procopius, *Buildings*, book 4. The basic objective was to control crucial strategic positions (for instance the Danube crossing at Sirmium, or the passes into Greece at Thermopylae and the Isthmus) and to provide sufficient strongholds for the population to secure itself when danger threatened.[2] From 531 to 534 the *magister militum* in Thrace, Chilbudius, fought successfully against the Bulgars, Sclaveni, and Antae, but was killed in a fierce skirmish north of the

Danube. Procopius commented that thereafter the barbarians were able to cross the river and raid Roman territory at will (Procopius, *Bell. Goth.* 7.14.1–6). Justinian recovered Sirmium in 535 from the Ostrogoths, briefly arousing expectations that Roman authority might be reasserted across Illyricum as a whole, but within a year the city had fallen back into the hands of the Gepids, the German-speaking tribe that now occupied much of the Hungarian plain.

In 539 Procopius described a major incursion of Huns, by which he probably refers to a coalition of the new nomadic groups including the Bulgars and Kutrigurs, which extended from the Ionian Gulf to Constantinople. Greece was ravaged as far as the Isthmus of Corinth; thirty-two Illyrican fortresses and the city of Cassandria were overwhelmed; the invaders broke through the fortifications built to secure the Thracian Chersonese, and some even crossed the Hellespont into Asia. It is hard to dissociate these events from the famine conditions of the later 530s, which may have provoked this desperate onslaught (Procopius, *Bell. Pers.* 2.4.4–12; see above, chapter 11).[3] Other attacks on Illyricum occurred in 544 and 549, which Roman forces were powerless to prevent (Procopius, *Bell. Goth.* 7.11.15–16 and 29.1–3). The pressure both from the Sclaveni and the Kutrigur Huns intensified during the 550s, and Procopius has graphic descriptions of the former advancing towards the Hebrus river and the Thracian coast, overwhelming fortified towns by sheer force of numbers, slaughtering the men by impalement and immolation, and leading women and children off to slavery. Only the presence of the Roman army, which Germanus was assembling for the renewed campaign against the Goths in Italy, prevented them from falling on their main target, Thessalonica (Procopius, *Bell. Goth.* 7.38, 40.1–8).

Security in Illyricum was less dependent on fortifications along the Danube than on Roman ability to orchestrate an elaborate diplomatic dance among the barbarian peoples north of the frontier. In 551 the Gepids made a precarious peace with their Lombard neighbors (settled in former Roman Pannonia), but also called in the help of the Kutrigurs, not believing that the pact would hold. However, when their warlike new allies arrived, rather than set them against the Lombards, they escorted them across the river crossing at Sirmium, which they controlled, to plunder richer pickings from Roman territory. Justinian's response was to enlist the help of another steppic group, the Utrigurs, currently established east of the Sea of Azov, to attack the remaining Kutrigurs in the Ukraine (who were in any case receiving regular payments from Constantinople). The Utrigur intervention was doubly successful in that it enabled many thousands of Roman prisoners of the Kutrigurs to escape back to their homes, and also caused the Kutrigur warriors who had crossed the Danube at Sirmium to abandon their raids on Illyricum. However, one band of 2,000 Kutrigurs, led by a chieftain who had previously been part of Belisarius' expedition against the Vandals, successfully claimed asylum from Justinian, who settled them in Thrace on condition that they made themselves available for military service. Sandil, the king of the Utrigurs, was incensed. Why should his people, friends of the Romans, put themselves at risk on Justinian's behalf when their accursed enemies were thus allowed to enjoy the comfort and luxury of settling in the empire?

We eke out our existence in a deserted and thoroughly unproductive land, while the Kutrigurs are at liberty to consume grain at state expense, to nurse hangovers in city wine-bars, and to toy with all manner of luxurious titbits from the table. Presumably they get free access to bath houses and can swan around in gold ornaments, with no lack of fine clothing dyed in many colours and embroidered with gold. (Procopius, *Bell.* 8.19.16–17)

Envy and greed, as well as dire necessity, impelled the barbarian raids. Beyond the huts and tents that housed the Slavic and Turkic-speaking tribes around the northern confines of the Black Sea, loomed an image of the Roman Empire, wealthy beyond the dreams of avarice.

The last great Kutrigur attack on the empire came in 559 when Zabergan led a force of Kutrigurs and Sclaveni into Macedonia and Greece up to the gates of Thermopylae and across the plains of Thrace to overrun the long walls of Constantinople. In the crisis, Belisarius was called out from retirement to lead the defense (Agathias 5.11–25).

The next challenge along Rome's northeast frontier arrived two years after Justinian's death. The Avars, a warrior nomadic people which originated from Mongolia, had been moving inexorably westwards through the 540s and 550s, driven in the rear by the Turks, but lured on by tales of Roman wealth.[4] The Romans, as might be expected, initially used them as a foil to the Kutrigurs and Utrigurs. In 567 they made a pact with the Lombards against the Gepids, whose terms are recorded by Menander (fr. 9). As the Avar newcomers annihilated the Gepids, the Romans took advantage of the moment to re-occupy Sirmium, which had been in Gepid hands since 536, while the Lombards under King Audoin made the fateful decision to abandon their settlements in Pannonia and move south into Italy.

The Avars were now by far the strongest and most aggressive barbarian power along Rome's northern frontier and they dictated the shape of Roman policy in the Balkans for a generation. The tribal structure of the Avars broadly resembled that of the Huns,[5] and their leader, the Khagan, assumed the role that Attila had played in the 440s. From 572, probably after three years of plundering, the Avars began to receive an annual payment of 80,000 gold solidi from Rome as the price for leaving the Balkans unmolested. In 578 they renewed the offensive against Sirmium when the new Roman emperor Tiberius II refused payment and captured the city in 581, after a siege that had lasted for more than two years. The Romans were compelled to make good the deficient payments (Menander fr. 63–6; John of Ephesus 6.30–32). During this period the Sclaveni, evidently acting in concert with the Avars, had devastated Greece, Thessaly, and Thrace. In May 583 the Avar Khagan raised his demands from the new emperor Maurice, who succeeded Tiberius II in 582, to 100,000 solidi a year. When payment was not forthcoming he moved swiftly eastwards, capturing Singidunum, Augustae, Viminacium, and Anchialus on the Black Sea coast, where his harem enjoyed the luxury of hot baths. A high-level Roman embassy sent to discuss terms was humiliated, but returned the following year, when the Romans agreed to pay the full sum demanded by the Khagan (Theophylact 1.3.1–6.3). The agreement bought no respite from the Sclaveni, who in 585 attacked the long walls of Constantinople before they were driven from Thrace by a Roman victory at Adrianople (Theophylact 1.7.3–6; John of Ephesus 6.25). Athens and Corinth were sacked, perhaps in the same year, and in September 586 the Slavs briefly laid siege to Thessalonica. The city was saved, it was believed, by the miraculous intervention of its patron saint Demetrius.[6] The first permanent Slavic settlements in Greece are to be dated from this period. Moreover, the Khagan alleged that the Romans had provided refuge for a man who had slept with one of his harem, and used this as a pretext for attacking Roman cities in the lower Danubian provinces of Scythia and Moesia (Theophylact 1.8).

Through the later 580s the Avars held the initiative, as Roman troops were heavily committed in the war against the Sassanians on the eastern front, and they repeated their attack on Anchialus and the Long Walls in 588, abetted by the Slavs.[7] The tide turned in the Roman favor only after Maurice agreed the peace treaty with Persia in 591 and thus released manpower reserves that could be deployed in the Balkans. For most of the final decade of the sixth century, under the generalship of Priscus and Comentiolus, Roman forces applied effective tactics expounded in the *Strategikon*, the military manual which the emperor had written himself before coming to power. It was not until 598 that the Khagan achieved another major success, advancing through Moesia to Tomi, outmaneuvering the Roman generals, and forcing the emperor to lead troops in person to man the long walls. Negotiations led to a new agreement whereby the Avars withdrew to the north of the Danube, but the level of protection money demanded of the Romans was raised by a further 20,000 solidi (Theophylact 7.13.1–15.9). In the following years, however, Roman troops continued on the offensive, inflicting heavy losses on the Avars in a battle near Viminacium and campaigning across the Danube against Slav settlements.

As the desperate and dispiriting struggles of the later years of the sixth century unfolded, the Balkans were undergoing a decisive demographic transformation. The key people in this change were not the dominant Avars, who, like Attila's Huns in the fifth century, were to fade from prominence within two generations, but the Slavs. The Sclaveni are the least documented of Rome's barbarian neighbors in late antiquity. Their name, cognate with the word "slave," denotes that they were regarded as an underclass. The classical sources record virtually no named leaders. The Slavs were not, it seems, organized as large purposeful tribal groups, operating under warrior leadership, but comprised the inhabitants of lowland villages from across the river basins of the Dnieper and Dniester rivers, the former homelands of the precursors of the Goths. Their settlements were small clusters of pit dwellings, rounded huts with thatched roofs, earthed up around their low stone or timber walls, hardly visible above the level of the plain. Their economy was based on cattle raising and the cultivation of low-grade cereals, especially millet. Contact with the more developed economies of the Roman Empire led them to adapt and upgrade this lifestyle to wheat cultivation and horse-rearing.[8]

The infiltration of Slavic peoples into the Balkan provinces was at such a humble level of material culture that it is difficult to trace archaeologically. The most likely hypothesis is that they colonized the low-lying country, including marshlands, which were little favored by the settled populations of the Roman provinces, not least as this land had been so exposed to devastation by earlier barbarian movements. It is evident that the Slavs adapted readily to their new surroundings. The lowlands between the Haemus and Rhodope mountains of Moesia and Thrace provided an excellent environment for their settlements, which were inserted between the small towns and precariously held forts created by the Roman occupation. The first Slav incursions of the 520s heralded an undramatic but relentless demographic transformation, as these new peoples, introducing a new language, gradually extended into areas abandoned by earlier occupants. Growing acquaintance with their barbarian neighbors, including the Avars, and awareness of the wealth of the Roman Empire, helped to transform their society, especially in terms of military organization, and by the late sixth and early seventh centuries they were able to mount long-distance incursions against Roman cities. This paved the way for Slavic families and small communities to extend their colonization into Greece, as well as westwards across central Europe.[9] The movement of the Slavs into southeast Europe is comparable in many respects to the gradual spread of the Arabs across Syria throughout late antiquity, which was to prepare the way for the Islamic conquests in the seventh and eighth centuries.

The other major consequence of the Avar incursion of the 560s was the displacement of the Lombards (Longobardi, "Long-Beards") from Pannonia into Italy. King Audoin led his people back to the areas where they had campaigned with Narses against the Goths in 553. Supported by other German-speaking groups, they controlled most of Italy north of the Po, including the stronghold of Ticinum by 572. Lombards also occupied the fortress and region of Spoleto, thus cutting off Roman communications between Ravenna and Rome along the *via Flaminia*, and the area of Beneventum. These large enclaves were to evolve as independent duchies.[10] Roman control of Italy was thus badly fragmented. The Romans retained authority over the Ligurian coast around Genoa, a corridor of land across the Apennines through Perugia, which linked Ravenna and Rome, the important enclave of Naples and Salerno, the southern regions of Bruttium and Calabria, and the rich island of Sicily. The geographical division of Italy at the end of the sixth century between Romans and Lombards draws attention to the significance of Roman sea-power. All Roman territory focused on major ports and was thereby integrated into the empire as a whole. Even so, the bonds were loosening, and in 578 the emperor Tiberius II declined the offering of 3,000 gold solidi made by the Roman authorities of Italy at his accession, requesting instead that the money be used to pay for Lombard soldiers to join his Persian expedition. The decision in effect indicated that the Romans in Italy would henceforth be left to their own devices in dealing with local challenges. The regional government, which was reorganized as the Roman Exarchate of Italy under the emperor Maurice, did not have the resources or land-based military strength to dominate the whole of the peninsula. Thus in geopolitical terms Italy began to take the shape that it was to retain until the later Middle Ages, a patchwork of Roman territory interspersed by the Lombardic duchies.[11] For Constantinople, henceforth, ecclesiastical relations with the papacy were of greater consequence than those with the secular government of its western province.[12]

The Fall of Maurice

Roman warfare in the Balkans led to an unforeseen disaster. Maurice had re-established Roman supremacy on the eastern frontier and gained striking successes against the Avars and Sclaveni in the last decade of the sixth century. This had not been achieved without cost. Twice during the campaigns Maurice had been forced by financial stringency to reduce military pay (Theophylact 3.4.4, 7.1.8). We may infer that the empire's tax revenues were no longer sufficient to sustain the burden of frontier defense and aggressive campaigning, and in Thrace, in contrast to Mesopotamia, there was no prospect of supplementing revenue by any significant war spoils. In 602 the field army of Thrace was required to conduct a winter campaign against the Slavs, an operation which promised military success according to Maurice's own strategic theories but offered scant hope of booty and little prestige (Maurice, *Strategikon* 11.4.82ff.). The soldiers showed signs of growing rebelliousness, defied repeated orders from the emperor, and pressed initially for better conditions of service (John of Nikiu 102, 10–11). Fierce winter conditions were compounded by renewed orders from the emperor to attack the barbarians north of the Danube, without provisions from the commissariat, in the expectation that the troops would live off the land they were occupying. A delegation from the ranks pleaded that they should be allowed home for the winter (Theophylact 8.6.2–10). It is clear that Maurice's commanders in the field thought the imperial orders to be hopelessly misjudged, but had no option except to insist that the campaign continue. The troops assembled without their officers over two successive days and brought their protests to a head by raising one of their delegates, the centurion Phocas, on the shields of his fellow-soldiers in the ritual traditionally associated with the creation of a new emperor (Theophylact 8.7.1–7).

Theophylact's detailed account of the fall of Maurice forms the climax to his history and is likely to have been the seed from which his whole work was conceived. At some date, probably early in Heraclius' reign, he had been invited to deliver a eulogy of Maurice, which had moved his audience to tears (Theophylact 8.12.3–7). The narrative which survives in the history not only contains elements that were surely drawn from this panegyric, but also shows numerous traces of Theophylact's own careful enquiries into the course of events. This is the most revealing analysis of a major political event in Constantinople since the accounts of the Nika riot of 532. The crisis developed rapidly amid a complex interplay of forces: the emperor Maurice and the members of his family; the claims and political credibility of a wealthy rival, Germanus, whose daughter had married Maurice's son Theodosius; Phocas and his close-knit group of military officers, which had led the mutiny on the Danube; the urban mob at Constantinople; and the only organized groups in the city that could in any way represent or articulate the people's wishes, the circus factions. The Blues, and especially the Greens, were to play a larger role in the fall of Maurice than in any previously attested political context. It appears mistaken to argue that they were motivated by specific political allegiances or objectives. They were, nevertheless, a major force, and the events of the coup made it clear that the circus factions could be a potent political force in the cities of the empire at the beginning of the seventh century.[13]

As rumors of the mutiny spread rapidly among the population, Maurice's general Peter brought the news to the capital. Maurice attempted to reassure his subjects by staging chariot-races in the hippodrome, and used the opportunity to seek the support of the Greens and the Blues. The registered partisans, almost 2,000 in number, were dispatched to garrison the Theodosian Walls, while Phocas and his troops gathered outside the city. The mutineers began negotiations by approaching Maurice's son, Theodosius, and Theodosius' father-in-law Germanus, and offered loyalty if either of these would oust Maurice and take over the empire. The compromised Germanus was summoned before Maurice and ordered to take his own life, but fled first to his own house on the Mese and then, with his own armed followers, to the nearby church of the Virgin, built by Theodosius II's minister Cyrus. By nightfall Germanus and his men had moved to the sanctuary of St Sophia itself, where the rebellion came to a climax. Enormous crowds gathered outside the church and began to chant insults against the emperor, and the partisans of the factions abandoned their positions on the walls to join the mob. As the rioting people burnt down the grand house of Maurice's praetorian prefect of the East, Constantine Lardys, the emperor, disguised as a commoner, took flight with his wife, other family members, and the praetorian prefect to the church of St Autonomus on the south side of the sea of Marmara. His son, Theodosius, and Constantine were then instructed to escape from the empire and seek help from Khusro (Theophylact 8.7.8–9.12).

For a brief moment it was uncertain whether Germanus or Phocas would take charge after Maurice's departure, but the hostility of the Green faction to Germanus decided the issue, and a delegation from the Greens prevailed on Phocas to advance to the Hebdomon, at the seventh milestone from the city center, where he was inaugurated at the great church of John the Baptist, a traditional location for the proclamation of new emperors. Phocas entered the city on November 25, 602. Amid the chariot races which were staged in celebration, largesse was showered on the members of the circus factions and on Phocas' own military following. Two days later Maurice and his entourage were arrested and brought back to Chalcedon, but the rumor that he was still alive led to rioting in the hippodrome, during the coronation ceremony of Phocas' wife Leontia, between the Greens, who had been the main instruments of Phocas' coup, and the Blues. Another close associate of Phocas, Lilius, was ordered to do away with Maurice and his sons. Their bodies were thrown into the Bosporus before huge crowds of onlookers, while the head of Maurice was brought back and displayed to Phocas' troops at the Hebdomon outside the city. The only family member to avoid the immediate slaughter was the emperor's eldest son Theodosius who had escaped as far as Nicaea, but was then reported to have returned with Constantine Lardys to the Church of St Autonomus, where it was alleged that he had been killed by one of Phocas' leading officers, Alexander (Theophylact 8.9.13–12.12).

The Last Great War of Antiquity

After the fall of Maurice a rumor spread that Theodosius had managed to escape, as his father had hoped, and reached Colchis, from where he made his way to Khusro's court (Theophylact 8.13.1–6). When, five months later, Lilius presented Phocas' credentials to Khusro as the new Roman emperor, he was repudiated. Khusro II dismissed Phocas as a usurping tyrant, and declared war with the aim of restoring Theodosius to his father's kingdom. Eastern sources helped to spread the word that the son had escaped (Theophylact 8.13.5; *Armenian Chronicle Attributed to Sebeos* 106, 110).

> And so Chosroes exploited the tyranny as a pretext for war, and mobilized that world-destroying trumpet: for this became the undoing of the prosperity of Romans and Persians. For Chosroes feigned a pretence of upholding the pious memory of the emperor Maurice. And so in this way the Persian war was allotted its birth, and Lilius remained among the Persians in great hardship. In these days error came upon the inhabited world, and the Romans supposed that Theodosius was not dead. And this became an opportunity for great evils, and this false supposition contrived an abundance of slaughters. (Theophylact 8.15.7–8, trans. Whitby and Whitby)

The overthrow of Maurice was the first successful violent deposition of a Roman emperor in the East since Diocletian's coup d'état in 284. Phocas was widely perceived as an illegitimate ruler. Disaffection was aggravated by the religious dissidence of the Monophysite communities of Syria and Egypt, and by rivalry of the circus factions.[14]

Phocas depended on violent repression of opponents loyal to the old regime. Five of Maurice's sons had been murdered with their father at the time of the coup; his widow, previously confined to a monastery, and daughters were implicated in a broad-based plot and put to death in 605. The bald account in the *Chronicon Paschale* of the suppression of this supposed conspiracy is an indication of a new brutality which characterized the style of the regime:

In this year in the month of Daisius, June according to the Romans, on a Saturday, there were beheaded Theodore the praetorian prefect, John *antigrapheus*, Romanus *scholasticus*, Theodosius subadjutant of the *magister*, Patricius *illustris*, nephew of Domnitziolus who was curator of the palace of Hormisdas, John and Tzittas, *spatharii* and *candidati*, Athanasius *comes largitionum*, Andrew *illustris* who was also called Scombrus, and Elpidius *illustris*. Elpidius had his tongue cut out and his four extremities removed; he was paraded on a stretcher and carried down to the sea; when his eyes had been gouged out, he was thrown into a skiff and burnt. The other people aforementioned were beheaded, on the grounds that they were discovered plotting against the emperor Phocas. (*Chron. Pasch.* 605, trans. Whitby and Whitby)

There were serious external setbacks. The Lombards in Italy under King Agilulf forced Smaragdus, the exarch of Ravenna, to make major territorial concessions in a treaty of 604/5, and in the same year the Avars raised their tribute demands, after Phocas had been forced to move many of his Balkan troops to the eastern front. However, the decisive events which were to topple the regime came from renewed conflict with Persia. Promptly after Phocas' accession, Narses, the *magister militum* based in Mesopotamia, led a military rebellion in support of Theodosius. Khusro put the full weight of Sassanian power behind him and the eastern frontier crumbled. Dara fell after a siege in 604, the Roman commanders in Armenia offered support to Theodosius, and placed the key east Anatolian fortresses of Theodosiopolis and Citharizon under his and the Persians' control in 607. Mesopotamia and the whole of Asia Minor were thus exposed, and the strongholds soon toppled: Mardin, Amida, Rhesaina, and, in 609, Edessa.

Phocas' authority was fatally undermined by this huge loss of territory, and he faced another internal challenge. In 608 Heraclius, the exarch of Africa based in Carthage, sent a fleet commanded by his nephew Nicetas to seize Alexandria and cut off the Constantinopolitan grain supply. The island of Cyprus was taken, and in September 610 Heraclius' son, also called Heraclius, sailed with a fleet of warships from the sea of Marmara towards the capital. Preparations had been made in the city, and partisans of the Greens opened the harbors to the invaders. Supporters of the rebels already controlled most of the territory and resources of the Levant and Heraclius father and son had for two years issued gold, silver, and bronze coinage, which identified them with the insignia of consuls. This symbolism declared their own standing within the Roman state, while it implicitly denied the legitimacy of the usurper Phocas.[15] Phocas was killed on October 5, 610.

The reign of Heraclius, from 610 to 641, encompassed the last great struggle between the Roman and Sassanian empires, the surrender of Roman control in the Balkans, and the collapse of the empire in the Near East and Egypt. Both the Romans and the Sassanians were confronted and overwhelmed by the growing power of the Arabs united by the religion of Islam. The sources which document these events reflect the complexity of the events themselves. The accounts of this period represent the various regional perspectives in diverse linguistic and historical traditions, a daunting challenge to a classical historian.[16] The Roman perspective is represented by the *Chronicon Paschale* up to 629/ 30, which focuses on developments in the capital; the chronicle of Theophanes, compiled in the eighth century;[17] and the panegyric poems in praise of Heraclius, written by George of Pisidia.[18] Theophanes' account derives in part from the detailed accounts by which Heraclius reported on the progress of his campaigns of the 620s. John, bishop of Nikiu, wrote a world chronicle, originally in Greek and written from the viewpoint of an inhabitant of the Egyptian delta, which has reached us through a series of translations and provides an indispensable account of the conquest of Egypt by the Arabs.[19] Armenian history, including many observations on the coming of the Arabs, is provided by the work ascribed to Sebeos.[20] The Persian version of the collapse of the Sassanian Empire lingers only as transmuted into the epic tales of the *Shahname* of Ferdowsi and the great history, written in Arabic, of Tabari, a native of the Caspian region. The fragmentary west Syriac chronicles of the seventh century throw a patchy light on the early Arab conquests of the Levant.[21] More complex and difficult than any of these are the earliest Islamic accounts themselves, from a historio-graphical tradition that bore virtually no relation to classical predecessors.[22] Beside the bewildering diversity of the literary sources, there is evidence from archaeology, numismatics, and the documentary record in Egypt, but much work needs to be done in these fields too before a clear picture of the early seventh century is likely to emerge. What follows is intended as no more than a summary and an attempt to highlight the main issues.[23]

In 609/10 the Sassanian general Shahin invaded Cappadocia and besieged its capital, Caesarea. The city was handed over to the attackers in 611 by its Jewish inhabitants after the Christian population had fled. Meanwhile the main Persian offensive was sustained against Syria. Antioch and Apamea were taken in October 610, Emesa in 611, and Damascus in 613. A Roman counteroffensive led to the recapture of Cappadocian Caesarea in 612. The critical moment for Roman Syria came in 613, when the emperor Heraclius, who had broken with long tradition and led an expeditionary force in person, was defeated by Khusro's forces near Antioch. He withdrew north of the Cilician gates, leaving Cilicia and Syria at the mercy of the Persian general Shahrvaraz. Caesarea Maritima, the Roman administrative capital of the southern Levant, and, traumatically, Jerusalem, fell to the Persians in 614. While the Jews were accused of complicity with the Sassanians, huge numbers of Jerusalem's Christian population were slaughtered or resettled on Persian territory, and the relic of the Cross itself was removed as a trophy to Khusro's treasury at Ctesiphon.[24] The gateway to Egypt, Pelusium, was taken in 616 or 617, Alexandria surrendered after a siege in 619, and the Sassanians asserted control along the Nile Valley as far as Syene.[25] As was inevitable *annona* distributions had been suspended in Constantinople since 618 (*Chron. Pasch.* 618). Thus the whole of the Near East and Egypt was lost to Roman control.

The offensive in the Levant, commanded by Shahrvaraz, was matched by the campaigns of Shahin in Asia Minor, which was overrun from the east for the first time since the incursions of Shapur I in the mid-third century.[26] The old inner frontier which stretched from Trapezus through Satala to Melitene was already in Persian hands, and Anatolia could be raided virtually at will. In 615 a Sassanian force under the command of the general Shahin reached Chalcedon, across the waters of the Bosporus from Constantinople. When a desperate plea for peace was brought to Khusro by a high-level legation during the following winter, the ambassadors were simply interned and later put to death (*Chron. Pasch.* 615). In 617 Persian seaborne forces occupied Cyprus. It appears that most of the overland assaults on Asia Minor were directed, as might be expected, along the Roman road network north of the Taurus, while Roman resistance concentrated in the mountainous regions of the south. As the imperial mints in Cyzicus and Nicomedia ceased production in 616 and 619 respectively, Heraclius struck coins in Seleucian Isauria in 616–17 and in the fastness of Isaura itself in 618. Persian attention turned, as might be expected, to the richest cities, and Ancyra, Sardis, and Ephesus were sacked and plundered. While the immediate impact of warfare was dramatic, and is illustrated by archaeological evidence from these cities, it is less clear that the Sassanians, in the space of less than ten years, could have brought to an end the urban culture of late Roman Asia Minor.[27] A broad study of the impact of the Persians throughout the territories that they conquered in the Roman Near East argues that we should distinguish between the brutality and the devastation that they inflicted on centers of Roman resistance, and the much lighter touch with which compliant local populations were handled.[28]

Roman fortunes reached their lowest ebb in 622. A full-scale Sassanian attack coincided, surely by design, with an onslaught from the Balkans by the Avars. Heraclius, who had taken the field against the Persian army, returned in haste to Constantinople to begin negotiations with the Avars, who may have besieged Thessalonica during this period. In 623 the emperor ventured beyond the protection of the Thracian long walls to seal an agreement with the Avar Chagan, but was almost captured in an ambush, losing much of his entourage. In the crisis one of the emblems of the city's protection, the robe of the Virgin which was kept at the church at Blachernae, outside the Theodosian Walls, was hurried for safe-keeping to St Sophia.[29] Humiliating terms had to be agreed with the Avars. Ancyra, the greatest fortress of central Anatolia, was probably captured in 622. In 623, doubtless exploiting the opportunity provided by their new base in Egypt, the Sassanians seized the island of Rhodes and deported many of its inhabitants. Their hands were at the empire's throat.

Events were subject to an extraordinary reversal between 624 and 630.[30] Heraclius assembled a field army at Caesarea in Cappadocia, and then marched through northeast Asia Minor into Azerbaijan, through the regions with largely Christian populations which had been under Roman control after 591. Khusro's army, which had mustered at Ganzak, the location of Bahram's defeat in 591, withdrew across the Zagros. Heraclius chose to attack and destroy the fire-temple at Takht-e Suleiman, a formidable fortress which was the symbolic center of Sassanian power in the northwest of the empire, and over wintered

with his forces in the valley of the river Kur in Albania. In the following campaigning season he maintained the Roman presence along the southern side
of the Caucasus and occupied winter quarters near Lake Van. The Persian
riposte came in 626. The two Sassanian generals Shahrvaraz and Shahin led a
major counteroffensive, with Shahin advancing through Armenia and Shahrvaraz
through the Cilician Gates, both aiming for Constantinople. The plan was
coordinated with the Avars, and the Khagan simultaneously led an enormous
force against Constantinople from the West. Heraclius blunted the Persian
effort by defeating Shahin's forces in Anatolia, and Roman naval forces proved
strong enough to prevent Shahrvaraz, who was again encamped at Chalcedon,
from crossing the sea of Marmara and joining forces with the Khagan. The Avars,
aided by the Slavs, beleaguered Constantinople from the Thracian side in huge
numbers through late July and early August 626. The defenders, facing personal annihilation and fighting for the survival of the Roman Empire, forged
an unprecedented unity in face of the peril. The icon of their salvation was the
robe of the Virgin of Blachernae, and the accounts of the siege raised the cult
of the Virgin Mary, and the myth of her protective powers, to an unprecedented prominence.[31] The fullest account of the siege, in the *Chronicon Paschale*,
begins with an explicit acknowledgment of the Virgin's role:

> It is good to describe how now too the sole most merciful and compassionate
> God, by the welcome intercession of the undefiled Mother, who is in truth our
> Lady Mother of God and ever-Virgin Mary, with his mighty hand saved this
> humble city of his from the utterly godless enemies who encircled it in concert,
> and redeemed the people who were present within it from the imminent sword,
> captivity, and most bitter servitude. (*Chron. Pasch.* 626)

Heraclius participated in the thanksgivings at the capital over the winter of
626 before returning to the offensive in 627. He too made common cause with
an ally from the steppes, the western Turkic Khagan, and advanced through
Lazica and Iberia to meet these new allies outside the city of Tiflis, which was
placed under siege. While the Turks maintained the blockade, the Romans
moved south again into Azerbaijan. In December they crossed the Zagros and
confronted a large Sassanian army near Nineveh. Heraclius' victory opened
the path for the Romans to advance south on Ctesiphon itself. The presence of
a victorious and threatening enemy force on the river Zab achieved precisely
the same effect as Bahram's mutiny had done in 591. The Sassanian king
Khusro II was overthrown and murdered, to be replaced by his son Kavad
Siroe who negotiated an armistice and sued for peace. Heraclius returned to
Constantinople and a new treaty was struck with the Persians which restored
the boundary between the two empires along the frontier which had prevailed
before 591, running from Lazica through Theodosiopolis and Citharizon to
Dara in Mesopotamia.

Complications followed. Kavad Shiroe himself died in autumn 628 and was
succeeded by his young son Ardashir. Meanwhile, most of Syria, Palestine,

and Egypt remained in Sassanian hands under the control of Shahrvaraz, who was now based in Alexandria. He entered into negotiations with Heraclius to restore the Near East to Rome, provided that Rome supported his own bid to take power at Ctesiphon. He demanded that the northern frontier section of the empire should now also be shifted westwards to the line of the upper Euphrates. Heraclius, however, achieved a crucial prize, the restitution of the True Cross to Jerusalem. At the beginning of 630 Shahrvaraz entered Ctesiphon, and had Ardashir killed in April. Six weeks later he himself was dead and was succeeded in power by a daughter of Khusro II, who was forced by Heraclius to restore to Rome the Transcaucasian territory occupied between 591 and 602.

The Persian state now imploded into a civil war which saw six short-lived rulers succeed to the throne until the accession of Yazdgird III, the last Sassanian king who ruled between 633 and 651. Heraclius meanwhile celebrated his triumph by becoming the first Roman emperor to enter Jerusalem, where he presided over the ceremony of the restoration of the Cross.

Heraclius' success in the last great war with the Persian Empire depended on the Roman ability to transform the nature of their empire at a moment when it was on the verge of disintegration. This transformation took many forms. Heraclius' own route to power, from Africa via Alexandria to Constantinople, which took two years and involved the organization of the resources of Egypt and the Near East against the usurper Phocas, prepared the ground for a new style of rulership. Heraclius himself broke with a tradition more than two centuries old by opting to lead Roman forces on campaign in person. Just as his coup had illustrated the old secret of empire, that emperors might be created elsewhere than at the capital, so his brash campaigning showed that, in moments of extreme crisis, aggression in other critical areas paid greater dividends than relying on survival in fortress Constantinople. His personal style of leadership was linked to strategic adaptability. The emphasis on a cavalry strike force, which had been the hallmark of Roman armies since the fourth century, was reversed. Heraclius' wars were fought by troops in which infantry predominated, as was to be the case with later Byzantine forces. One reason for this may simply have been that it was less expensive and logistically less challenging to maintain infantry armies in the field.

Heraclius and his regime kept their nerve and drew on long experience during the years of crisis. Apart from maintaining a tactical and strategic initiative during the campaigns, they also played their diplomatic cards to good effect. The defense of the Balkans had to be abandoned. The Avars were held in check by tribute payments between 604 and 619, although they controlled all Illyricum west of Serdica and Naissus, which were both sacked around 614. The Sclaveni, whose diffused leadership was less amenable to diplomacy, were a continuous threat in Macedonia, Thessaly, and Greece. Thessalonica survived onslaughts in 604, 615, and 618 thanks to its mighty fortifications, stout local resistance, and the protection of St Demetrius. The Slavs created a primitive fleet of boats made from hollow tree trunks, with which they menaced the Aegean islands and the west coast of Asia Minor, and which almost succeeded in creating a bridge between the Persian and Avar forces at the siege of Constantinople in 626. After this failure the Avar–Slav coalition appears to have fractured, and although Slav colonization of the Balkans continued apace, the power of the Khagan ebbed away. Meanwhile on the eastern front, Rome struck critical new alliances with the Turkic tribes, who were now the most powerful force on the steppes. They were soon to show themselves to be a greater danger to the Sassanians than the Hepthalites had been in the fifth century.

Religious Transformations

One of the crucial achievements of the early seventh-century Roman Empire was to extract sufficient revenues from its dwindling territories to sustain the military effort against an enemy with greater resources at its disposal. Before the end of the sixth century Rome had left the exarchies of Africa and Italy to their own devices, and drew no more taxes or levies from the western Mediterranean. Throughout the 620s, moreover, the Sassanians appear to have been strengthening their own economic position by using the existing administrative structures in the territory that they had taken from Rome, especially in Egypt, to divert tax income and compulsory services to their own benefit.[32] Heraclius and his officials compensated, in part, by drawing on the wealth of the church. Church properties had increased substantially during the sixth century, especially since the reign of Justinian, and archaeological and textual evidence suggests that ecclesiastical silver was one of the most important areas of stored wealth in Syria and Asia Minor during the late sixth and seventh centuries.[33] The scale of this wealth is illustrated by the fact that the Persians seized 112,000 pounds of silver plate from Edessa in the 620s (Palmer, *West-Syrian Chronicles*, 133–4.). Despite Persian attacks on Asia Minor, the wealth of the Anatolian churches will have been relatively protected and available for the war effort. It seems probable that it was as much the demands of Heraclius as the depredations of the Sassanians that impoverished Asia Minor's cities from this period. They, more than any other communities of the Roman world, paid the price for the survival of the Byzantine Empire.

The church would only put its wealth at the state's disposal if its interests and those of the Roman rulers were aligned with one another. Since the accession of Justinian, Rome's ideology of rulership rested on the central proposition that the empire flourished as an explicit expression of God's will and providence. The religious beliefs that underpinned this concept had intensified as a consequence of the travails of the 540s and the example of piety and submission to the divine will that Justinian himself displayed in his later years. Justinian's example was closely followed by Justin II and his empress Sophia. Their religious devotion, especially to the cult of Mary, was emphasized at length in Corippus' panegyric written for Justin's inauguration (Corippus, *In Praise of Justin* I, 30–65). Heraclius had placed pictures of the Virgin on the mastheads of his ships when he had sailed to depose Phocas in 608. The

Marian cult and the reverence for her image and the talismanic icon of the Virgin's robe reached a high point during the siege of Constantinople in 626. Images of Mary were placed above the city gates, and the departure of the Avar host surely sealed the inhabitants' conviction that their survival was due to her protection.[34]

The Marian cult at Constantinople was one of the most conspicuous aspects of a religious transformation in the Roman Empire of the later sixth and seventh centuries. It was linked to two other phenomena, which are attested throughout the empire in this period. One was the increasing role and prominence of icons, which were identified as a source of protection, healing, or salvation for communities at times of danger or distress. Images of local saints and holy men, of the Virgin Mary, of the Holy Cross, and of Christ himself dominate many of the narratives of critical moments in the lives of communities, such as the celebrated stories of Apamea, protected in 540 by a wooden relic of the Cross; and Edessa, saved from the Persians in 544 by its famous image, "not made by human hand (*acheiropoetos*)," of the risen Christ. The popularity and efficacy of such talismans are illustrated by the traditions surrounding an image of Christ, also "not made by hand," which had come to light in the Cappadocian village of Kamulianai (Ps-Zachariah 12.4). According to different traditions this icon had been preserved in three separate locations before it was transported to Constantinople by Justin II.[35]

A parallel phenomenon to the reverence for images was the emergence of mass processions as the most powerful expression of community religious feeling, either to commemorate specific moments in the ritual calendar or as a spontaneous response to a crisis. Such processions had become more frequent and important in community life since the outbreak of the plague in Constantinople. They were promoted by the huge number of sixth-century church foundations, especially during the reign of Justinian, which created a new sacral topography in the cities of the empire, and especially in Constantinople. The processions articulated connections between the major centers of cult. Their function was to unite the entire community, rulers and subjects, in a common religious purpose, which was focused on a specific goal.[36] The *Life* of St Theodore of Sykeon, which provides a vivid panorama of life in early seventh-century Anatolia, demonstrates that such processions were not an exclusively urban or metropolitan phenomenon, but typical also of village life. When the saint conducted his major exorcisms, he would do so by leading a procession of the entire population between the village church and the source of religious defilement.[37]

In their attitudes to Christian icons and Christian rituals the rulers of the seventh-century Roman world were at one with their subjects and also with the perspective of the organized church. There was no conflict between sacred and secular aims. It is characteristic of the age of Heraclius that the main source of authority in Constantinople in the emperor's absence was the patriarch Sergius, who played a major role in organizing the defense of the city under attack and provided continuous political as well as religious and doctrinal leadership in support of the emperor. In this his contribution matched that of the bishops of the cities of Syria and Mesopotamia, who had long since been the leaders of their communities against the Sassanian threat. This sense of unified purpose enabled the emperor to conduct the struggle with Persia not as a fight for territory, or for prestige, but as a crusade, a holy war. In 625 Heraclius addressed his troops in a speech that foreshadows the rhetoric of modern fundamentalism:

> Be not disturbed, o my brothers, by the multitude of the enemy. For when God wills it, one man will rout a thousand. So let us sacrifice ourselves to God for the salvation of our brothers. May we win the crown of martyrdom that we may be praised in future and receive our recompense from God. (Theophanes, *Chron.* 442–43)

The fall of Jerusalem and the loss of the Cross, Christendom's holiest relic and icon, had spurred the Roman sense of purpose. The devastation of the fire-temple at Takht-e Suleyman should be seen as a reprisal. In these circumstances the church did not hesitate to place its wealth at the empire's disposal. After 615 the Roman state began to issue a series of heavy silver coins, hexagrams, which were used both as military pay and as a form of subsidy to the crucial allies that Rome needed to win the war in Transcaucasia (*Chron. Pasch.* 615). No doubt the bullion from which they were minted had been obtained by melting down church silver. These issues carried the Latin legend, *Deus adiuta Romanis*, "God, help the Romans!" Even more eloquent – since few of those who handled the coins would have understood the language – the reverse emblem was the Cross, standing on three steps, above a globe. World domination was a Roman right, guaranteed by God's power.[38] The Roman Empire of the early seventh century had been transformed by its rulers to confront challenges that could not have been imagined even a century earlier, but it remained, recognizably, the imperial power that had been forged six centuries before by Augustus.

The Coming of Islam

> At that time a certain man from among those same sons of Ishmael whose name was Mahmet, a merchant, as if by God's command appeared to them as a preacher and the path of truth. He taught them to recognize the God of Abraham, especially because he was learned and informed in the history of Moses. Now because the command was from on high, at a single order they all came together in unity of religion. Abandoning their vain cults, they turned to the living God who had appeared to their father Abraham. So Mahmet legislated for them: not to eat carrion, not to drink wine, not to speak falsely, and not to engage in fornication. He said: "With an oath God promised this land to Abraham and his seed after him for ever. And he brought about as he promised during that time while he loved Israel. But now you are the sons of Abraham, and God is

accomplishing his promise to Abraham and his seed for you. Love sincerely only the God of Abraham, and go and seize the land which God gave to your father Abraham. No one will be able to resist you in battle, because God is with you."
(*The Armenian History Attributed to Sebeos* 135, trans. R. W. Thompson)

The coming of Islam was a decisive moment. The last great conflict of the ancient world between Rome and Persia had brought both contestants to the verge of collapse. These events coincided with the kindling of Arab ambitions by the prophet Muhammad. From 622 until his death a decade later Muhammad led a rapidly growing coalition of Arab tribes on a campaign to overthrow the world order. In 636, four years after his death, the forces of Islam and Abu Bakr won the battle of Yarmuk to claim control of Syria, and two years later overwhelmed a Sassanian army at Qadisiya (near Hira), thus decisively establishing a new era in the history of the Near East.

It is beyond the scope of this book to analyze the origins of Islam and the rise of Arab power, but the bare facts are inescapable. In 622 Muhammad, the leader of the Hashemite branch of the Qurayshi tribe which controlled the area of western Arabia around Mecca, was exiled by his tribe and took refuge in Medina. This year of exile, *hijra*, became the era from which the Islamic calendar started. Over the following decade Muhammad constructed his power, which was based on twin foundations. Firstly, he relied on the warrior prowess of his followers, who began to enrich themselves at the expense of the trading caravans and the neighboring tribes. Secondly, and decisively, he presented himself as the prophet of a new monotheism. This doctrine drew both on pagan beliefs – the famous Black Stone of Mecca had been the focal point of a major local cult – and on Jewish and Biblical Christian traditions, which had been assimilated by many of the Arab peoples, but recast them into an extreme form of monotheism which recognized only Allah as God. This new creed was imposed on Muhammad's followers and on all those who chose to ally themselves with the new Arab power.

The Arab tribes had long since proved themselves as a military force to be reckoned with in the struggles between Rome and Persia. Many of the campaigns between the settled zones of Syria and the Euphrates had been conducted by the Lakhmids for the Sassanians and the Ghassanids for the Romans. These peoples had built up settlements in the previously thinly populated marginal regions around the desert, which complemented their traditional transhumant lifestyles. Moreover, the flourishing cities of Mesopotamia and the Near East, on either side of the imperial frontier, had attracted Arab settlers, bringing about a steady transformation in the demographic profile of the region. This Arabization of the Levant was a vital precursor to the military onslaught which was launched by Muhammad's followers. Before his death in 632 the prophet had taken over control of Medina, and his followers were the dominant force in western Arabia and the Hijaz as far north as the Gulf of Aqaba and the Wadi Rumm.[39] Religious and political leadership of the new movement passed to a series of caliphs (God's deputies), which began with Abu Bakr, and the early phase of Arab raiding was transformed into a holy war against non-believers. The cities of Transjordan were overwhelmed from 633 and Damascus fell to the Arabs in 635. In 636 the coalition of Muhammad's followers defeated the Roman field armies of Armenia and Oriens at the river Yarmuk in northern Jordan, on the route between Damascus and Jerash. This was the decisive battle.

> But the Greek king could raise no more troops to oppose them. So they divided their forces into three parts. One part went to Egypt and seized the country as far as Alexandria. One part was in the north, opposing the Greek empire. And in the twinkling of an eye they occupied the land from the edge of the sea as far as the bank of the great river Euphrates; and on the other side of the river they occupied Urha [Edessa] and all the cities of Mesopotamia. The third part went to the east, against the kingdom of Persia. (*The Armenian History Attributed to Sebeos* 137, trans. R. W. Thompson)

Jerusalem was captured in 638 after a lengthy siege, although on this occasion the city's holy Christian relics were rescued and taken to Constantinople. Caesarea Maritima fell two years later, and Alexandria, despite prolonged resistance, in 641. Although it was briefly recaptured, by the mid-640s Egypt was definitively in Arab hands.[40]

Neither Rome nor Persia had the military capacity to resist the Arab advance. The collapse of the Sassanian Empire was even more drastic. Two years after a Muslim force had first moved into southern Iraq, an Arab army defeated numerically superior Persian forces at the battle of Qadisiyya, close to the old Lakhmid stronghold of al-Hira. The Sassanians now abandoned their capital at Ctesiphon, known to the Arab sources as Al-Madain, and withdrew into the Zagros Mountains. They thus relinquished the economic powerhouse of Mesopotamia for their traditional highland homeland. In 642 the Arabs won the battle of Nihavand, and as a result gained control of the main strategic pass from central Mesopotamia to the northern Iranian plateau. The last Sassanian ruler, Yazdgird III, fled before the advancing army as Darius III had fled before Alexander. Like his Achaemenid predecessor, Yazdgird's life ended not on the battlefield but at the hands of an assassin, in the furthest northeast corner of his former kingdom, at Merv in 651. The Islamic conquerors had reached central Asia within twenty years of Muhammad's death.

They met sterner resistance from Rome. The cities of northern Syria and Mesopotamia, including Antioch, Edessa, and Dara, had fallen before the death of Heraclius in 641. Armenia as well as Azerbaijan, which Heraclius had ceded to Shahrvaraz, offered no significant resistance. An Arab raid even reached Chalcedon in 653. However, Roman resolution, bolstered by the new military organization which Heraclius had introduced, prevented the conquest of Asia Minor, and a new boundary was drawn along the line of the Taurus across Anatolia, from Seleucia in the southwest to Trapezus in the northeast on the Black Sea. This was now the eastern frontier of the Byzantine Empire with the Muslim-ruled world.

Historians have struggled to find explanations for the rapidity and decisiveness of the early Islamic conquests. Establishing a narrative for the early years is in itself problematic. The Muslim historical tradition, which formed about 150 years after the *hijra*, presented a received idea of Islamic origins which had emerged over six generations of oral transmission. Making sense of the conflicting strands that lay behind the later authorized version is a task of extraordinary difficulty.[41] For this reason, the modest quantity of information about the conquests that can be identified in non-Islamic sources is particularly important, in particular the evidence of the West Syrian chronicles of the mid-seventh century and of the Armenian history attributed to Sebeos, which has twice been cited above to provide a near contemporary view of the early impact of Islam. These external and relatively dispassionate observers provide evidence which must be integrated into any narrative with a claim to historical reliability.[42]

Two factors above all contributed to early Arab superiority over the Romans and Sassanians in the Levant. The Arabs developed a high level of military organization and a capacity for aggressive warfare which was comparable to that of the great steppic confederations of Huns, Avars, and Turks. As in those cases, the diverse Arab clans and small tribes were fused into large warrior nations which could mobilize sufficient forces to challenge the permanent empires of the classical world. The Arabs differed from the nomads of the steppes in that they were not primarily united by obedience to a dominant and charismatic individual leader, but by a compelling religious idea. The Islamic state was based on the notion of *umma*, the community of believers, which transformed Arab tribal society. The community was marked by its unconditional allegiance to the one God. The only intermediate authority that the *umma* recognized was that of his prophet Muhammad. He, and his followers the caliphs, thus established political leadership over the Islamic nation. The faith was both militant and exclusive. All followers of Muhammad were compelled to join the *umma*; leaving the alliance was treated as apostasy from God. The early Islamic nation thus achieved a complete fusion of political and religious loyalty, in a form that was completely independent of the monotheism of the Christian empire of Constantinople or the Mazdaean traditions of the Sassanians. Just as the intensification of Christian worship, and in particular the Marian cult, had strengthened Roman solidarity and the will to empire during Heraclius' wars, so the fusion of religious and political identities in Islam produced a new form of imperial power, in which conquest was to be seen as the purest expression of God's will for his chosen people. The holy war of the Christian empire was outmatched by a *jihad*.

The impact of the Arab conquests, like that of most wars, is told both in ancient and modern historiography from the point of view of the victors. In truth the Islamic warriors and their leaders had to develop the means of controlling a world of enormous cultural and religious complexity, as well as mastering a historical tradition that had been created by the Roman Empire. We may end with one glimpse of these complexities, as they are revealed by what may be the earliest mention by a Greek writer of the Arab invasions of southern Syria in a work known as the *Doctrina Jacobi* (*The Teachings of Jacob*), perhaps written in 634.[43] Even this first view contains the perception that the religious motive which drove the newcomers would realign the endemic conflicts between Christians and Jews and transform the religious landscape of the Near East and North Africa. The setting is the forced conversion of Jews to Christianity in the African capital of Carthage on the day of Pentecost 632. This itself was a reflection of Heraclius' aggressive Christian politics and the enduring power of the Roman Empire, which still reached to the exarchate of Africa. Among the converts was a Jewish trader from Palestine, Jacob, who after forcible baptism had come to see the truth of Christianity, and undertook the task of persuading fellow Jews to change their beliefs. The centerpiece of the work is a dialogue between Jacob and a recent arrival from Palestine, Justus. In the course of their discussion Justus quoted from a letter that he had received from his brother Abraham about the recent killing of a Roman commander by the Arabs.

> When the *candidatus* (Roman officer) was killed by the Saracens, I was at Caesarea and I set off by boat to Sykamina. People were saying "the officer has been killed," and we Jews were overjoyed. And they were saying that the prophet had appeared, coming with the Saracens, and that he was proclaiming the advent of the anointed one, the Christ who was to come. I, having arrived at Sykamina, stopped by a certain old man, well-versed in the scriptures, and I said to him: "What can you tell me about the prophet who has appeared with the Saracens?" He replied, groaning deeply: "He is false, for the prophets do not come armed with a sword. Truly there are works of anarchy being committed today and I fear that the first Christ to come, whom the Christians worship, was the one sent by God, and we instead are preparing to receive the Antichrist. Indeed Isaiah said that the Jews would retain a perverted and hardened heart until all the earth should be devastated. But you go, master Abraham, and find out about the prophet who has appeared." So I, Abraham, enquired and heard from those who had met him that there was no truth to be found in the so-called prophet, only the shedding of men's blood. He says also that he has the keys of paradise, which is incredible. (*Teachings of Jacob* V.16, 209, trans. Hoyland)

The message and the warning of Abraham seem as urgent and relevant in the contemporary world as they were when they were written in the seventh century.

NOTES

1   B. Croke, "Justinian's Bulgar victory celebration," *Byzantoslavica* 41 (1980), 188–95.
2   B. Bavant, in C. Morrisson (ed.), *Le monde byzantin* I (Paris, 2004), 341–3.
3   So also D. Keys, *Catastrophe. An Investigation into the Origin of the Modern World* (London, 1999), 44–6.

4 D. Keys, *Catastrophe*, 35–52, argues that conditions caused by the climatic disaster of 535–6 caused the Turks in Mongolia to oust the Avars from their grazing grounds and start their westward migration. This is beyond the bounds of current evidence, and in any case the Avar movement replicates those of the Huns earlier and of the Oguz Turks and Mongols at later times.

5 R. Pallas-Brown, "East Roman perceptions of the Avars in the mid- and late sixth centuries," in S. Mitchell and G. Greatrex, *Ethnicity and Culture in Late Antiquity* (Wales and London, 2000), 309–29.

6 P. Lemerle, *Les plus ancient miracles de S. Démétrius et la pénétration des Slaves dans les Balkans* (Paris, 1981), I, 13–15.

7 The chronology of the main account by Theophylact 5.16.1–6.6.1 is very confused; see the notes to the translation of Michael and Mary Whitby.

8 F. Curta, *The Making of the Slavs: History and Archaeology of the Lower Danube Region, ca. 500–700* (Cambridge, 2001).

9 B. Bavant, in C. Morrisson (ed.) *Le monde byzantin* I (Paris, 2004), 337–41.

10 N. Christie, *The Lombards* (Oxford, 1995).

11 M. Whittow, *The Making of Byzantium 600–1025* (London, 1996), 298–304, with excellent maps.

12 P. R. L. Brown, *The Rise of Western Christendom* (Oxford, 2003), 190–215.

13 Alan Cameron, *Circus Factions* (Oxford, 1976), 265–7, 280–2; W. Liebeschuetz, *Decline and Fall of the Roman City* (Oxford, 2001), 203–20, 249–57.

14 W. Liebeschuetz, *Decline and Fall of the Roman City* (Oxford, 2001), 269–75.

15 C. Morrisson, *Le monde byzantin* I (Paris, 2004), 40. The fullest ancient account of the revolt against Phocas is by John of Nikiu 107–9; see A. J. Butler, *The Arab Conquest of Egypt* (Oxford, 1978), 1–53.

16 See in general Averil Cameron and L. Conrad (eds.), *The Byzantine and Early Islamic Near East I. Problems in the Literary Source Material* (Princeton, 1992).

17 J. Howard-Johnston, "The official history of Heraclius' Persian campaigns," in E. Dabrowa (ed.), *The Roman and Byzantine Army in the East* (Krakow, 1994), 57–87.

18 Mary Whitby, "A new image for a new age: George of Pisidia on the emperor Heraclius," in E. Dabrowa (ed.), *The Roman and Byzantine Army in the East* (Krakow, 1994), 197–225.

19 This work survives in an Ethiopic translation of an Arabic version, which in turn derived from a Greek original. It focuses especially on events in Egypt. The English translation by R. H. Charles, *John, Bishop of Nikiu: Chronicle* (London, 1916) is available on-line at www.ccel.org/p/pearse/morefathers/nikiu1.

20 R. W. Thompson and J. D. Howard-Johnston, *The Armenian History Attributed to Sebeos* (2 vols., Liverpool, 1999).

21 A. Palmer, *The Seventh Century in West-Syrian Chronicles* (Liverpool, 1993).

22 Patricia Crone, *Slaves on Horses. The Evolution of the Islamic Polity* (Cambridge, 1980), 3–18.

23 For a lengthy recent account see W. E. Kaegi, *Heraclius, Emperor of Byzantium* (Cambridge, 2003). There is a crisp discussion by M. Whittow, *The Making of Byzantium 600–1025* (London, 1996), 69–82.

24 *Chron. Pasch.* 614; *The Armenian History Attributed to Sebeos*, ch. 34. The fullest account, by Antiochus Strategikos, preserved in a Georgian version of the Greek original, has been translated by F. C. Conybeare, *English Historical Review* 25 (1910), 502–17 (on-line at www.ccel.org/p/pearse/morefathers antiochus _strategos_capture.htm).

25 A. J. Butler, *The Arab Conquest of Egypt* (Oxford, 1978), 54–92.
26 C. Foss, "The Persians in Asia Minor and the end of antiquity," *English Historical Review* 90 (1975), 721–47.
27 J. Russell, "The Persian invasion of Syria/Palestine and Asia Minor in the reign of Heraclius: Archaeological, numismatic and epigraphic evidence," in E. Kountoura-Galake (ed.), *The Dark Centuries of Byzantium (7th–9th centuries)* (Athens, 2001), 41–71, argues that the impact of the Persian invasions was less dramatic than is suggested by Foss.
28 C. Foss, "The Persians in the Roman Near East," *Journal of the Royal Asiatic Society* 13 (2003), 149–70.
29 See *Chron. Pasch.* 623 with discussion of the date by Whitby and Whitby in appendix 4 of their translation; Averil Cameron, "The Virgin's robe: An episode in the history of early seventh-century Constantinople," *Byzantion* 49 (1979), 42–56.
30 J. Howard-Johnston, "Heraclius' Persian campaigns and the revival of the east Roman empire," *War in History* 6 (1999), 1–44, which is particularly important for the chronology and topography.
31 J. Howard-Johnston, "The siege of Constantinople in 626," in C. Mango and G. Dagron, *Constantinople and its Hinterland* (Aldershot, 1995), 131–42; Averil Cameron, "Elites and icons in Byzantium," *Past and Present* 84 (1979), 3–35, esp. 5–6, 20–4.
32 C. Foss, "The Persians in the Roman Near East," *Journal of the Royal Asiatic Society* 13 (2003), 156ff., 164ff.
33 M. Whittow, *The Making of Byzantium 600–1025* (London, 1996), 64–5.
34 Averil Cameron, "Images of Authority: Elites and icons in late sixth-century Byzantium," *Past and Present* 84 (1979), 3–35, is the fundamental study. See also Averil Cameron, "The Theotokos in sixth-century Constantinople," *Journal of Theological Studies* 39 (1978), 79–108. The themes are explored in detail by M. Meier, *Das andere Zeitalter Justinians* (Göttingen, 2003), 481–569.
35 M. Meier, *Das andere Zeitalter Justinians* (Göttingen, 2003), 532–8.
36 M. Meier, *Das andere Zeitalter Justinians* (Göttingen, 2003), 489–502. We may compare the development of the rogation rituals in the cities of Frankish Gaul.
37 S. Mitchell, *Anatolia* II (Oxford, 1993), 139–44.
38 J. Howard-Johnston, "Heraclius' Persian campaigns and the revival of the East Roman Empire, 622–30," *War in History* 6.1 (1999), 37.
39 F. M. Donner, *The Early Islamic Conquests* (Princeton, 1981), 101–11.
40 A. J. Butler, *The Arab Conquest of Egypt* (rev. edn. by P. M. Fraser, Oxford, 1978).
41 F. M. Donner, *Narratives of Islamic Origins. The Beginnings of Islamic Historical Writing* (Princeton, 1998) adopts a more optimistic view than Patricia Crone, *Slaves on Horses* (Cambridge, 1980), 3–18.
42 R. Hoyland, *Seeing Islam as Others Saw It. A Survey and Evaluation of Christian, Jewish and Zoroastrian Writings on Early Islam* (Princeton, 1997).
43 R. Hoyland, *Seeing Islam as Others Saw It* (Princeton, 1997), 55–61. G. Dagron and V. Deroche, "Juifs et chrétiens dans l'Orient du VIIe siècle," *Travaux et Mémoires* 11 (1991), 17–293 for a full edition and discussion of the *Doctrina Jacobi.*

Bibliography

This bibliography includes major studies under a series of thematic headings. It does not attempt to include all the specific items cited in the endnotes to this book.

GENERAL HISTORIES AND STUDIES

G. W. Bowersock, P. R. L. Brown, and O. Grabar (eds.), *Late Antiquity. A Guide to the Post-Classical World* (Cambridge Mass., 1999).

P. R. L. Brown, *The World of Late Antiquity from Marcus Aurelius to Muhammad* (London, 1971). See also "The World of Late Antiquity revisited," *Symbolae Osloenses* 72 (1997), 5–90.

P. R. L. Brown, *The Making of Late Antiquity* (Cambridge Mass., 1978).

J. B. Bury, *The Later Roman Empire from the Death of Theodosius I to the Death of Justinian (395–565)* (2 vols., 2nd edn., London, 1923).

Averil Cameron, *The Later Roman Empire* (London, 1993).

Averil Cameron, *The Mediterranean World in Late Antiquity AD 395–600* (London, 1993).

Averil Cameron, "The long late antiquity," in T. P. Wiseman (ed.), *Classics in Progress: Essays on Ancient Greece and Rome* (Oxford, 2002), 165–91.

Averil Cameron and P. Garnsey (eds.), *The Late Empire AD 337–425* (*CAH* XIII, 1998).

Averil Cameron, B. Ward-Perkins, and L. M. Whitby (eds.), *Late Antiquity: Empire and Successors AD 425–600* (*CAH* XIV, 2000).

R. M. Collins, *Early Medieval Europe* (New York, 1991).

A. Demandt, *Die Spätantike. Römische Geschichte von Diocletian bis Justinian 284–565 n. Chr.* (Berlin, 1989).

C. Foss and P. Magdalino, *Rome and Byzantium* (London, 1977).

P. Garnsey and C. Humphress, *The Evolution of the Late Antique World* (Cambridge, 2001).

E. Gibbon, *History of the Decline and Fall of the Roman Empire* (rev. edn. J. B. Bury, London, 1929).

E. Gibbon, *History of the Decline and Fall of the Roman Empire* (new edn. by D. Womersley, Harmondsworth, 1994).

P. Heather, *The Fall of the Roman Empire. A New History of Rome and the Barbarians* (Oxford, 2006).

A. H. M. Jones, *The Later Roman Empire 284–602. A Social, Economic and Administrative Survey* (Oxford, 1964).

A. H. M. Jones, *The Decline of the Ancient World* (London, 1966).

W. Liebeschuetz, *The Decline and Fall of the Roman City* (Oxford, 2001).

J. R. Martindale et al., *Prosopography of the Later Roman Empire* (3 vols., Cambridge, 1971–92).

C. Morrisson, *Le monde byzantin vol. I. L'Empire romain d'orient (330–641)* (Paris, 2004).

D. S. Potter, *The Roman Empire at Bay* AD *180–395* (London, 2004).

E. Stein, *Geschichte des spätrömischen Reiches I (284–476)* (Strasburg, 1928). French trans. by J.-R. Palanque, *Histoire du Bas-Empire I. De l'état romain à l'état byzantin.* 1 Texte and 2 Notes (Bruges, 1959).

E. Stein, *Histoire du Bas-Empire II. De la disparition de l'empire de l'occident à la mort de Justinien (476–565)* (Paris, 1949).

S. Swain and M. Edwards, *Approaching Late Antiquity. The Transformation from Early to Late Empire* (Oxford, 2004).

B. Ward-Perkins, *The Fall of Rome and the End of Civilization* (Oxford, 2005).

COLLECTED SOURCES IN TRANSLATION

P. R. Coleman-Norton, *Roman State and Christian Church. A Collection of Legal Documents to* AD *535* (3 vols., London, 1966).

B. Croke and J. Harries, *Religious Conflict in Fourth-Century Rome* (Sydney, 1982).

G. Greatrex and S. N. C. Lieu, *The Roman Eastern Frontier and the Persian Wars. Part II* AD *363–630. A Narrative Sourcebook* (London and New York, 2002).

A. D. Lee, *Pagans and Christians in Late Antiquity* (London and New York, 2000).

S. N. C. Lieu and D. Montserrat, *From Constantine to Julian. Pagan and Byzantine Views* (London and New York, 1996). This includes the anonymous *Origo Constantini Imperatoris (Anon. Val.)*, the *Latin Panegyric* VII (6) of 310, and Libanius, *Or.* 59.

M. Maas, *Readings in Late Antiquity: A Sourcebook* (London and New York, 2000).

R. W. Mathisen, *People, Personal Expression, and Social Relations in Late Antiquity* (2 vols., Ann Arbor, 2003).

J. Stevenson, *A New Eusebius. Documents Illustrating the History of the Church to* AD *337* (rev. edn. by W. Frend, London, 1987).

J. Stevenson, *Creeds, Councils and Controversies. Documents Illustrating the History of the Church* AD *337–461* (rev. edn. by W. Frend, London, 1989).

R. Valantasis, *Religions of Late Antiquity in Practice* (Princeton, 2000).

TRANSLATED TEXTS

In addition to the titles listed here, there is an invaluable bibliography of English translations of the Christian patristic literature of late antiquity in P. R. L. Brown, *The Rise of Western Christendom* (Oxford, 2003), 554–64.

The Library of the Nicene and Post-Nicene Fathers

This old series contains English translations of extensive selections from the works of the major church fathers, including Eusebius, Athanasius, Hilary of Poitiers, Basil, Gregory of Nysa, Gregory of Nazianzus, Ambrose, Jerome, Augustine, John Chrysostom, the church historians Rufinus, Socrates, Sozomen, and Theodoret, Leo the Great, and Gregory the Great. The publications are now available on-line at www.ccel.org/fathers. Further out-of-copyright translations of authors from late antiquity, including John of Ephesus, Zacharias of Mytilene, John of Nikiu, and other important texts, from several original languages, are at www.ccel.org/p/pearse/morefathers/home.html.

Liverpool Translated Texts for Historians

This invaluable and growing series of translations includes important introductions and commentaries.

Ambrose of Milan. Political Letters and Speeches (W. Liebeschuetz, 2005).
The Armenian History Attributed to Sebeos (R. W. Thompson and J. Howard-Johnston, 2 vols. 1999).
Aurelius Victor, De Caesaribus (H. W. Bird, 1994).
Avitus of Vienne: Letters and Selected Prose (D. Shanzer and I. Wood, 2002).
Caesarius of Arles: Life, Testament, Letters (W. Klingshirn, 1994).
Cassiodorus: Variae (S. J. B. Barnish, 1992).
The Chronicon Paschale 284–628 AD (Michael and Mary Whitby, 1989).
Constantine and Christendom (*The Oration to the Saints. Greek and Latin Accounts of the Discovery of the Cross; The Edict of Constantine to Pope Sylvester*) (M. Edwards, 2003).
Donatist Martyr Stories: The Church in Conflict in Roman North Africa (M. A. Tilley, 1996).
Evagrius Scholasticus, The Ecclesiastical History (Michael Whitby, 2000).
Eutropius, Breviarium (H. W. Bird, 1993).
The Goths in the Fourth Century (P. Heather and J. Matthews, 1991).
Iamblichus: On the Pythagorean Life (G. Clark, 1989).
The Emperor Julian. Polemic and Panegyric (Claudius Mamertinus, John Chrysostom, Ephraem the Syrian; S. Lieu, 1989).
Lactantius: Divine Institutes (A. Bowen and P. Garnsey, 2003).
Libanius: Antioch as a Centre of Hellenic Culture (A. F. Norman, 2000).
Libanius. Select Letters from the Age of Constantius and Julian (S. Bradbury, 2004).
Neoplatonic Saints. The Lives of Plotinus and Proclus by their Students (M. Edwards, 2000).
Optatus: Against the Donatists (M. Edwards, 1997).
Pacatus: Pangeyric to the Emperor Theodosius (C. E. V. Nixon, 1987).
Ps-Dionysius of Tel Mahre, Chronicle part 11 (W. Witowski, 1996).
Ps-Joshua the Stylite, Chronicle (J. Watt and F. Trombley, 2000).

Ruricius of Limoges and Friends. A Collection of Letters from Visigothic Gaul (R. W. Mathisen, 1999).
Themistius, Select Orations. Politics, Philosophy and Empire in the Fourth Century (P. Heather and D. Moncur, 2001).
Vegetius, Epitome of Military Science (N. P. Milner, 2nd edn. 1996).
Victor of Vita: History of the Vandal Persecution (J. Moorhead, 1992).
West-Syrian Chronicles for the Seventh Century (A. Palmer, 1993).

Loeb Classical Library (Original texts with English translations)

Ammianus Marcellinus, ed. J. C. Rolfe (3 vols., trans. J. C. Rolfe, 1935–40). Vol. 3 contains a translation of the anonymous *Origo Constantini Imperatoris (Anon. Val.)*.
Augustine, *City of God* (7 vols., G. E. McCracken and others, 1957–72), *Confessions* (2 vols., W. Watt, 1912), *Select Letters* (J. H. Baxter, 1930).
Ausonius, *Poems* (H. K. Evelyn-White, 1919–21).
Basil, *Letters* (4 vols., R. J. Deferrari, 1926–34).
Boethius, *Theological Tractates* and *On the Consolation of Philosophy* (H. F. Stewart and E. K. Rand, rev. by S. J. Tester, 1973).
Claudian (2 vols., M. Platnauer, 1922).
Eunapius, *Lives of the Philosophers and Sophists* (with Philostratus, W. C. Wright, 1921).
Eusebius, *Ecclesiastical History* (2 vols., K. Lake and J. Oulton, 1926–33).
Jerome, *Select Letters* (F. A. Wright, 1933).
Julian (3 vols., W. C. Wright, 1913–23).
Libanius, *Orations* (selection, 3 vols., trans. A. F. Norman, 1969–77), *Autobiography and Selected Letters* (A. F. Norman, 2 vols. 1992).
Procopius (8 vols., trans. H. B. Dewing, 1914–54).
Prudentius, *Poems* (H. J. Thompson, 1949–53).
Scriptores Historiae Augustae (3 vols., D. Magie, 1921–32).
Sidonius Apollinaris, *Letters and Poems* (2 vols., W. B. Anderson, 1936–65).

Penguin Classics

Ammianus Marcellinus. The Later Roman Empire (AD 354–378) (selection only, trans. W. Hamilton, 1986).
Eusebius, *History of the Church* (trans. G. A. Williamson, rev. edn. 1989).
Gregory of Tours, *History (History of the Franks)* (L. Thorpe, 1974).

Routledge Early Church Fathers

This series contains introductions to the writers and a selection of their works in translation with explanatory notes. The emphasis is on their theological contributions.

Ambrose (B. Ramsey, 1997), *Cyril of Alexandria* (N. Russell, 2000), *Gregory of Nyssa* (A. Meredith, 1999), *John Chrysostom* (W. Mayer and P. Allen, 2001), *Jerome* (S. Rebenich, 2002).

Other translations

Agathias, *The Histories* (Corpus Fontium Historiae Byzantinae, vol. 2a, J. D. Frendo, Berlin, 1975).

Augustine, *Confessions* (H. Chadwick, Oxford, 1991).

Augustine, *On Christian Teaching* (R. P. H. Green, Oxford, 1997).

Ausonius, *Works* (R. P. H. Green, Oxford, 1991).

Cyril of Scythopolis, *The Lives of the Monks of Palestine* (R. M. Price, Kalamazoo, 1991).

Eunapius, Olympiodorus, Priscus and Malchus, *The Fragmentary Classicizing Historians of the Fifth Century* (R. C. Blockley, 2 vols., Liverpool, 1983).

Eusebius, *Life of Constantine* (Averil Cameron and Stuart Hall, Oxford, 1999).

Eusebius, *In Praise of Constantine* and *Tricennial Orations* (H. Drake, Berkeley, 1976 and 1978).

Hydatius, *Chronicle* (R. W. Burgess, Oxford, 1993).

Jordanes, *Getica* (P. Mierow, Princeton, 1931).

(Ps.-) Joshua the Stylite, *Chronicle* (W. Wright, Cambridge, 1882).

Lactantius, *On the Deaths of the Persecutors* (J. L. Creed, Oxford, 1984).

The Latin Panegyrics: B. Rodgers and C. E. V. Nixon, *In Praise of Later Roman Emperors. The Panegyrici Latini* (California, 1994).

Malalas, *Chronicle* (E. Jeffreys, R. Scott, M. Jeffreys, Sydney, 1986).

Marcellinus, *Chronicle* (B. Croke, Oxford, 2001).

Menander the Guardsman, *History* (R. C. Blockley, Liverpool, 1985).

The Lives of Simeon Stylites (R. Doran, Kalamazoo, 1992).

Symmachus, *Relationes* (R. H. Barrow, *Symmachus Relationes, Prefect and Emperor. AD 384*, Oxford, 1973).

The Theodosian Code (C. Pharr, Princeton, 1952).

Theophanes Confessor, *Chronicle of Byzantine and Near Eastern History AD 284–813* (C. Mango and R. Scott, Oxford, 1997).

Theophylact Simocatta, *History* (Michael and Mary Whitby, Oxford, 1986).

Zacharias of Mytilene. Syriac text ed. by E. W. Brooks, *Corpus Scriptorum Christianorum Orientalium* 83/84 (1924). English trans. by E. J. Hamilton and E. W. Brooks (1899, available on-line).

Zosimus, text, French translation, and commentary by F. Paschoud (Paris, 1971–89, with a new, extensively revised edition of book 1, 2003); English trans. by R. T. Ridley (Sydney, 1982).

There are English translations of many of the important fragments of the fifth-century historians in C. D. Gordon, *The Age of Attila. Fifth-Century Byzantium and the Barbarians* (Michigan, 1960).

S. P. Scott, *The Civil Law* (17 vols., Cincinnati 1932), contains translations of the *Digest*, the *Codex Justininianus*, and the *Novellae* of Justinian, and is available on-line at www.constitution.org/sps/sps.htm.

HISTORIOGRAPHY AND SOURCES

P. Allen, *Evagrius Scholasticus, the Church Historian* (Louvain, 1981).

B. Baldwin, "Malchus of Philadelphia," *Dumbarton Oaks Papers* 32 (1978), 101–25.

B. Baldwin, "Olympiodorus of Thebes," *Antiquité Classique* 49 (1980), 212–31.

B. Baldwin, "Priscus of Panium," *Byzantion* 50 (1980), 18–61.

T. D. Barnes, "The lost *Kaisergeschichte* and the Latin historical tradition," *Bonner Historia Augusta Colloquium* (1968/9), 13–43.

T. D. Barnes, "The *epitome de Caesaribus* and its sources," *Classical Philology* 71 (1976), 258–68.

T. D. Barnes, *The Sources of the Historia Augusta* (Brussels, 1978).

T. D. Barnes, *Constantine and Eusebius* (Harvard, 1981).

T. D. Barnes, "Panegyric, history and hagiography in Eusebius' *Life of Constantine*" in R. Williams (ed.), *The Making of Orthodoxy: Essays in Honour of Henry Chadwick* (Cambridge, 1989), 94–123.

T. D. Barnes, *Ammianus Marcellinus and the Representation of Historical Reality* (Cornell, 1998).

Alan Cameron, "The Roman friends of Ammianus," *JRS* 54 (1964), 15–28.

Alan Cameron, *Claudian: Poetry and Propaganda at the Court of Honorius* (Oxford, 1970).

Alan and Averil Cameron, "Christianity and tradition in the historiography of the late empire," *CQ* 14 (1964), 312–28.

Averil Cameron, *Agathias* (Oxford, 1971).

Averil Cameron, *Procopius and the Sixth Century* (London, 1985).

G. Clarke et al. (ed.), *Reading the Past in Late Antiquity* (Rushcutters' Bay, 1990).

P. Cox, *Biography in Late Antiquity. A Quest for the Holy Man* (Berkeley, 1983).

B. Croke and A. M. Emmett (eds.), *History and Historians in Late Antiquity* (Sydney, 1983).

J. W. Drijvers and E. D. Hunt (eds.), *The Late Roman World and its Historian: Interpreting Ammianus Marcellinus* (London, 1999).

J. A. S. Evans, *Procopius* (New York, 1972).

W. Goffart, "Zosimus: The first historian of Rome's fall," *American Historical Review* 76 (1971), 412–41, reprinted in Goffart, *Rome's Fall and After* (London, 1989), 81–110.

W. Goffart, *The Narrators of Barbarian History* (Princeton, 1988).

G. Greatrex, "The date of Procopius' works," *Byzantine and Modern Greek Studies* 18 (1994), 101–14.

G. Greatrex, "Recent work on Procopius and the composition of *Wars* VIII," *Byzantine and Modern Greek Studies* 27 (2003), 45–67.

T. Hägg and P. Rousseau, *Greek Biography and Panegyric in Late Antiquity* (Berkeley, 2000).

J. Harries, *Sidonius Apollinaris and the Fall of Rome* (Oxford, 1994).

C. Holdsworth and T. P. Wiseman, *The Inheritance of Historiography 350–900* (Exeter, 1986).

W. E. Kaegi, *Byzantium and the Decline of Rome* (Princeton, 1968).

A. Kaldellis, "The historical and religious views of Agathias: A reinterpretation," *Byzantion* 69 (1999) 206–52.

A. Kaldellis, *Procopius of Caesarea. Tyranny, History, and Philosophy at the End of Antiquity* (Philadelphia, 2004).

G. Kelly, "Ammianus and the great tsunami," *JRS* 94 (2004), 141–67.

G. Marasco (ed.), *Greek and Roman Historiography in Late Antiquity, 4th–6th Century AD* (Leiden, 2003).

J. F. Matthews, "Olympiodorus of Thebes," *JRS* 63 (1973), 79–97; reprinted in *Political Life and Culture in Late Roman Society* (Variorum, 1985) III.

J. F. Matthews, *The Roman World of Ammianus Marcellinus* (London, 1989).

R. Rees, *Layers of Loyalty in Latin Panegyric* (Oxford, 2002).

W. Rohrbacher, *The Historians of Late Antiquity* (London and New York, 2002).

B. Rubin, *Prokopios von Kaisareia* (Stuttgart, 1954) = *RE* 23.1, 273–599 (publ. 1957).

C. E. Stevens, *Sidonius Apollinaris and his Age* (Oxford, 1933).

T. Urbainczyk, *Socrates of Constantinople* (Michigan, 1997).

T. Urbainczyk, "Observations on the differences between the church histories of Socrates and Sozomen," *Historia* 46 (1997), 355–73.

T. Urbainczyk, *Theodoret of Cyrrhus: The Bishop and the Holy Man* (Michigan, 2002).

P. van Nuffelen, *Un héritage de paix et piété. Étude sur les histoires ecclésiastiques de Socrate et Sozomène* (Leuven, 2005).

J. Vanderspoel, *Themistius and the Imperial Court. Oratory, Civic Duty and Paideia from Constantius to Theodosius* (Michigan, 1995).

Mary Whitby (ed.), *The Propaganda of Power. The Role of Panegyric in Late Antiquity* (Leiden, 1998).

Michael Whitby, "Greek historical writing after Procopius: Variety and vitality," in Averil Cameron and L. Conrad (eds.), *The Byzantine and Early Islamic Near East I: Problems in the Literary Source Material* (Princeton, 1992), 25–80.

G. Zecchini, "Teodosio II nella storiografia ecclesiastica," *Mediterraneo Antico* 5 (2002), 529–46.

THE HISTORICAL NARRATIVE

T. D. Barnes, *Constantine and Eusebius* (Cambridge Mass., 1981).

T. D. Barnes, *The New Empire of Diocletian and Constantine* (Cambridge Mass., 1982).

T. D. Barnes, "Constantine and the Christians of Persia," *JRS* 65 (1985), 126–36.

T. D. Barnes, *Athanasius and Constantius* (Cambridge Mass., 1993).

R. P. C. Blockley, *East Roman Foreign Policy: Formation and Conduct from Diocletian to Anastasius* (Leeds, 1992).

G. W. Bowersock, *Julian the Apostate* (London, 1978).

H. Brandt, *Geschichte der römischen Kaiserzeit von Diokletian bis zum Ende der konstantinischen Dynastie (284–363)* (Berlin, 1998).

J. B. Bury, "The Nika riot," *JHS* 17 (1897), 92–119.

Alan Cameron, "Theodosius the Great and the regency of Stilicho," *HSCP* 73 (1969), 247–80.

Alan Cameron, "The empress and the poet: Paganism and politics at the court of Theodosius II," *Yale Classical Studies* 27 (1982), 217–89.

Alan Cameron, J. Long, and L. Sherry, *Barbarians and Politics at the Court of Arcadius* (Berkeley, 1993).

Averil Cameron, "Constantinus Christianus" (review of Barnes, *Constantine and Eusebius*), *JRS* 73 (1983), 184–90.

P. J. Casey, *Carausius and Allectus: The British Usurpers* (London, 1994).

S. Corcoran, *The Empire of the Tetrarchs* (rev. edn. Oxford, 2000).

G. E. M. de Ste Croix, *The Class Struggle in the Ancient Greek World* (London, 1983).

P. S. Davies, "The origin and purpose of the persecution of AD 303," *JTS* 40 (1989), 66–94.

H. Elton, *Warfare in Roman Europe AD 350–425* (Oxford, 1996).

R. M. Errington, "The accession of Theodosius I," *Klio* 78 (1996), 438–53.

R. M. Errington, "Theodosius and the Goths," *Chiron* 26 (1996), 1–27.

M. Gleason, "Festive satire: Julian's *Misopogon* and the new year at Antioch," *JRS* 76 (1986), 106–19.

G. Greatrex, "The Nika riot: A reappraisal," *JHS* 117 (1997), 60–86.

K. Holum, *Theodosian Empresses. Women and Imperial Dominion in Late Antiquity* (Berkeley, 1982).

F. Kolb, *Diocletian und die Erste Tetrarchie* (Berlin, 1987).

A. D. Lee, *Information and Frontiers: Roman Foreign Relations in Late Antiquity* (Cambridge, 1993).

N. Lenski, *Failure of Empire: Valens and the Roman State in the Fourth Century AD* (Berkeley, 2002).

W. Liebeschuetz, *Barbarians and Bishops* (Oxford, 1990).

S. Lieu and D. Montserrat (eds.), *Constantine. History, Historiography and Legend* (London, 1998).

P. Maraval, *L'empéreur Justinien* (Paris, 1999).

J. F. Matthews, *Western Aristocracies and the Imperial Court AD 364–425* (rev. edn. Oxford, 1990).

M. Meier, *Justinian. Herrschaft, Reich und Religion* (Munich, 2004).

J. Moorhead, *Justinian* (London, 1994).

R. Rees, *Diocletian and the Tetrarchy* (Edinburgh, 2004).

S. Williams, *Diocletian and the Roman Recovery* (London and New York, 1985).

S. Williams and G. Friell, *Theodosius. The Empire at Bay* (London, 1994).

STATE AND SOCIETY

C. Ando, *Imperial Ideology and Provincial Loyalty in the Roman Empire* (Berkeley, 2000).

P. R. L. Brown, *Power and Persuasion in Late Antiquity. Towards a Christian Empire* (Wisconsin, 1992).

R. Browning, *Justinian and Theodora* (London, 1987).

Alan Cameron, *Porphyrius the Charioteer* (Oxford, 1973).

Alan Cameron, *Circus Factions. Blues and Greens and Rome and Byzantium* (Oxford, 1976).

G. E. M. de Ste Croix, *The Class Struggle in the Ancient Greek World from the Archaic Age to the Arab Conquests* (London, 1981).

H. Elton, *Warfare in Roman Europe AD 350–425* (Oxford, 1996).

J. A. S. Evans, *The Age of Justinian. The Circumstances of Imperial Power* (London and New York, 1996).

J. Harries, "The Roman imperial quaestor from Constantine to Theodosius II," *JRS* 78 (1988), 148–72.

Jill Harries, *Law and Empire in Late Antiquity* (Cambridge, 1999).

Jill Harries and Ian Wood (eds.), *The Theodosian Code: Studies in the Imperial Law of Late Antiquity* (London, 1993).

T. Honoré, *Emperors and Lawyers* (2nd edn. Oxford, 1994).

A. H. M. Jones, *The Roman Economy: Studies in Ancient Economic and Administrative History* (ed. P. A. Brunt, Oxford, 1974).

C. Kelly, *Ruling the Later Roman Empire* (Cambridge Mass., 2004).

F. Kolb, *Herrscherideologie in der Spätantike* (Berlin, 2001).

R. Kaster, *Guardians of Language: The Grammarian and Society in Late Antiquity* (Berkeley, 1988).

A. Laniado, *Recherches sur les notables municipaiux dans l'empire protobyzantine* (Paris, 2002).

W. Liebeschuetz, "The circus factions," *Convegno per Santo Mazzarino, Roma 9–11 Maggio 1991* (Saggi di storia antica 13, Rome, 2002), 163–85.

H. P. L'Orange, *Art Forms and Civic Life in the Later Roman Empire* (Princeton, 1965).

M. Maas, *John Lydus and the Roman Past. Antiquarianism and Politics in the Age of Justinian* (London and New York, 1992).

S. MacCormack, *Art and Ceremony in Late Antiquity* (Berkeley, 1981).

M. McCormick, *Eternal Victory. Triumphal Rulership in Late Antiquity, Byzantium and the Early Medieval West* (Cambridge, 1986).

R. MacMullen, *Corruption and the Decline of Rome* (New Haven, 1989).

R. MacMullen, "Cultural changes and political changes in the 4th and 5th centuries AD," *Historia* 52 (2003), 465–95.

J. F. Matthews, *Laying Down the Law. A Study of the Theodosian Code* (New Haven, 2000).

F. Millar, *Rome, the Greek World and the East, Volume 2. Government, Society, and Culture in the Roman Empire* (Chapel Hill, 2004).

F. Millar, *A Greek Roman Empire. Power, Belief and Reason under Theodosius II, 408–50* (Berkeley, 2006).

S. Mitchell and G. Greatrex, *Ethnicity and Culture in Late Antiquity* (Wales and London, 2000).

A. Momigliano, "Cassiodorus and the Italian culture of his time," *PBA* 41 (1955), 207–45.

M. J. Nicasie, *Twilight of Empire: The Roman Army from Diocletian until the Battle of Adrianople* (Amsterdam, 1998).

C. Roueché, *Performers and Partisans at Aphrodisias in the Roman and Late Roman Periods* (London, 1993).

A. Smith (ed.), *The Philosopher and Society in Late Antiquity* (Swansea, 2005).

R. R. R. Smith, "Late Roman philosopher portraits from Aphrodisias," *JRS* 80 (1990), 127–55.

R. R. R. Smith, "The public image of Licinius I: Portrait sculpture and imperial ideology in the early fourth century," *JRS* 87 (1997), 170–202.

R. R. R. Smith, "Late antique portraits in a public context: Honorific statuary at Aphrodisias in Caria," *JRS* 89 (1999), 155–89.

R. R. R. Smith, "The statue monument of Oecumenius: A new portrait of a late antique governor from Aphrodisias," *JRS* 92 (2002), 134–56.

W. Thiel, "Tetrakionia. Überlegungen zu einem Denkmaltypus tetrachischer Zeit im Osten des römischen Reiches," *Ant. Tard.* 60 (2002), 299–326.

W. Treadgold, *Byzantium and its Army* (Stanford, 1995).

Michael Whitby, "Recruitment in Roman armies from Justinian to Heraclius (ca. 565–615)," in Averil Cameron (ed.), *The Byzantine and Early Islamic Near East III. States, Resources and Armies* (Princeton, 1995), 61–124.

Michael Whitby, "The violence of the circus factions," in K. Hopwood (ed.), *Organised Crime in Antiquity* (Wales, 1998), 229–53.

Michael Whitby, "Emperors and armies AD 235–395," in S. Swain and M. Edwards (eds.), *Approaching Late Antiquity* (Oxford, 2004), 156–86.

BARBARIANS

P. Amory, "Names, ethnic identity and community in fifth and sixth century Burgundy," *Viator* 25 (1994), 1–30.

P. Amory, *People and Identity in Ostrogothic Italy* (Cambridge, 1997).

S. J. B. Barnish, "Taxation, land and barbarian settlement in the western empire," *PBSR* 54 (1986), 170–95.

T. S. Burns, *Barbarians Within the Gates of Rome. A Study of Roman Military Policy and the Barbarians c. 375–425 AD* (Indiana, 1984).

F. M. Clover, *The Late Roman West and the Vandals* (Variorum, 1993).

W. Goffart, *Romans and Barbarians AD 418–584. Techniques of Accommodation* (Princeton, 1980).

P. Heather, "Cassiodorus and the rise of the Amals: Genealogy and the Goths under Hun domination," *JRS* 79 (1989), 103–28.

P. Heather, *Goths and Romans 332–489* (Oxford, 1991).

P. Heather, "The emergence of the Visigothic kingdom," in J. Drinkwater and H. Elton (eds.), *Fifth-Century Gaul: A Crisis of Identity* (Cambridge, 1992), 84–92.

P. Heather, "The historical culture of Ostrogothic Italy," *Atti del XIII congresso internazionale di studi sull'Alto Medioevo* (Spoleto, 1993), 317–53.

P. Heather, "Theoderic king of the Goths," *Early Medieval Europe* 4 (1995), 145–73.

P. Heather, "The Huns and the end of the Roman Empire in the West," *EHR* (1995), 4–41.

P. Heather (ed.), *The Visigoths from the Migration Period to the Seventh Century: An Ethnographic Perspective* (Woodbridge, Suffolk, 1999).

P. Heather and J. F. Matthews, *The Goths in the Fourth Century* (Liverpool, 1991).

E. James, *The Franks* (Oxford, 1988).

W. Liebeschuetz, *Barbarians and Bishops* (Oxford, 1990).

W. Liebeschuetz, "Cities, taxes and the accommodation of the barbarians: The theories of Durliat and Goffart," in W. Pohl (ed.), *Kingdoms of the Empire: The Integration of Barbarians in Late Antiquity* (Leiden, 1997).

J. Man, *Attila. A Barbarian King and the Fall of Rome* (London, 2005).

J. Moorhead, *The Roman Empire Divided 400–700* (London, 2001).

W. Pohl (ed.), *Kingdoms of the Empire: The Integration of Barbarians in Late Antiquity* (Leiden, 1997).

W. Pohl and H. Reinitz (eds.), *Strategies of Distinction: The Construction of Ethnic Communities 300–800* (Leiden, 1998).

E. A. Thompson, *Romans and Barbarians: The Decline of the Western Empire* (Madison, 1982).

E. A. Thompson, *The Huns* (rev. edn. of *A History of Attila and the Huns* [Oxford, 1948] with afterword by P. Heather, Oxford, 1996).

H. Wolfram, *History of the Goths* (English trans. by T. Dunlap, California, 1988).

H. Wolfram, *The Roman Empire and its Germanic Peoples* (English trans. by T. Dunlap, California, 1997).

I. Wood, "Ethnicity and the ethnogenesis of the Burgundians," in H. Wolfram and W. Pohl, *Typen der Ethnogenese unter besonderer Berücksichtigung der Bayern* (Vienna, 1990), 53–69.

I. Wood, *The Merovingian Kingdoms 450–751* (London, 1994).

RELIGION

B. Ankarloo and S. Clark (eds.) *Witchcraft and Magic in Europe: Ancient Greece and Rome* (London and Pennsylvania, 1999).

P. Athanassiadi, *Julian. An Intellectual Biography* (London, 1992; first published as *Julian and Hellenism*, London, 1981).

P. Athanassiadi, *Damascius. The Philosophical History. Text, with Translation and Notes* (Athens, 1999).

P. Athanassiadi and M. Frede (eds.), *Pagan Monotheism in Late Antiquity* (Oxford, 1999).

T. D. Barnes, "Christians and Pagans under Constantius," *L'Église et l'Empire au IVe Siècle* (1989), 301–38.

T. D. Barnes, *Athanasius and Constantius. Theology and Politics in the Constantinian Empire* (Harvard, 1993).

R. Beck, "The mysteries of Mithras: A new account of their genesis," *JRS* 88 (1998), 115–28.

G. W. Bowersock, *Hellenism in Late Antiquity* (Ann Arbor, 1990).

P. R. L. Brown, *Religion and Society in the Age of Saint Augustine* (London, 1972).

P. R. L. Brown, *The Cult of the Saints. Its Rise and Function in Latin Christianity* (Chicago, 1981).

P. R. L. Brown, *Society and the Holy in Late Antiquity* (London, 1982).

P. R. L. Brown, *Poverty and Leadership in the Later Roman Empire* (Hanover, New England and London, 2002).

P. R. L. Brown, *The Rise of Western Christendom* (2nd edn. Oxford, 2003).

H. Chadwick, *The Early Church* (London, 1967).

A. Chaniotis, "The Jews of Aphrodisias: New evidence and old problems," *Studia Classica Israelica* 21 (2002), 209.

E. D. Digeser, *The Making of a Christian Empire. Lactantius and Rome* (Cornell, 2000).

J. W. Drijvers and J. W. Watt (eds.), *Portraits of Spiritual Authority in Late Antiquity. Religious Power in Early Christianity. Byzantium and the Christian Orient* (Leiden, 1999).

C. A. Faraone and D. Obbink (eds.), *Magika Hiera. Ancient Greek Magic and Religion* (Oxford, 1990).

G. Fowden, "Bishops and temples in the eastern empire," *JTS* 29 (1978), 53–78.

G. Fowden, "The pagan holy man in late antique society," *JHS* 102 (1982), 33–59.

G. Fowden, *From Empire to Commonwealth. Consequences of Monotheism in Late Antiquity* (Princeton, 1993).

W. H. C. Frend, *Martyrdom and Persecution in the Early Church* (Oxford, 1965).

W. H. C. Frend, *The Rise of the Monophysite Movement* (Cambridge, 1972).

W. H. C. Frend, *Religion Popular and Unpopular in the Early Christian Centuries* (London, 1976).

W. H. C. Frend, *The Rise of Christianity* (London, 1984).

W. H. C. Frend, *The Donatist Church: A Movement of Protest in Roman North Africa* (3rd edn. Oxford, 1985).

W. H. C. Frend, *Archaeology and History in the Study of Early Christianity* (London, 1988).

I. Gardner and S. N. C. Lieu, *Manichaean Texts from the Roman Empire* (Cambridge, 2004).

J. Geffcken, *The Last Days of Graeco-Roman Paganism* (English trans. by S. MacCormack, Amsterdam, London, New York, 1978).

J. Hahn, *Gewalt und Religiöser Konflikt. Studien zu den Auseinandersetzungen zwischen Christen, Heiden und Juden im Osten des römischen Reiches (von Konstantin bis Theodosius II)* (Berlin, 2004).

R. P. C. Hanson, *The Search for the Christian Doctrine of God. The Arian Controversy 318–381 AD* (Edinburgh, 1988).

J. D. Howard-Johnson and P. A. Hayward (eds.), *The Cult of Saints in Late Antiquity and the Early Middle Ages* (Oxford, 1999).

E. D. Hunt, "Christians and Christianity in Ammianus Marcellinus," *CQ* 35 (1985), 186–200.

W. Klingshirn, "Charity and power: Caesarius of Arles and the ransoming of prisoners in sub-Roman Gaul," *JRS* 75 (1985), 183–203.

R. Lane Fox, *Pagans and Christians* (London, 1985).

W. Liebeschuetz, *Continuity and Change in Roman Religion* (Oxford, 1972).

S. N. C. Lieu, *Manichaeism in the Later Roman Empire and in Medieval China* (2nd edn., Tübingen, 1992).

R. Lizzi, "Ambrose's contemporaries and the Christianization of northern Italy," *JRS* 80 (1990), 156–77.

N. McLynn, *Ambrose of Milan. Church and Court in a Christian Capital* (Berkeley, 1994).

R. MacMullen, *Paganism in the Roman Empire* (New Haven, 1981).

R. MacMullen, *Christianizing the Roman Empire AD 100–400* (New Haven, 1984).

R. MacMullen, *Christianity and Paganism in the Fourth to Eighth Centuries* (New Haven, 1997).

R. A. Markus, *The End of Ancient Christianity* (Cambridge, 1990).

F. Millar, "The Jews of the Graeco-Roman diaspora between paganism and Christianity AD 312–438," in J. Lieu, J. North, and T. Rajak (eds.), *The Jews among Pagans and Christians in the Roman Empire* (London, 1992), 97–123.

F. Millar, "Christian emperors, Christian church and the Jews of the Diaspora in the Greek East, CE 379–450," *Journal of Jewish Studies* 55 (2004), 1–24.

S. Mitchell, "Maximinus and the Christians in AD 312: A new Latin inscription," *JRS* 78 (1988), 105–24.

S. Mitchell, *Anatolia. Land, Men, and Gods in Asia Minor* II, *The Rise of the Church* (Oxford, 1993).

A. Momigliano (ed.), *The Conflict between Paganism and Christianity in the Fourth Century* (Oxford, 1963).

D. Ogden, *Magic, Witchcraft and Ghosts in the Greek and Roman Worlds. A Sourcebook* (Oxford, 2002).

J. B. Rives, "The decree of Decius and the religion of the empire," *JRS* 89 (1999), 135–54.

M. Salamon (ed.), *Paganism in the Later Roman Empire and in Byzantium* (Krakow, 1991).

M. R. Salzmann, *On Roman Time. The Codex-Calendar of 354 and the Rhythms of Urban Life in Late Antiquity* (Berkeley, 1990).

R. B. E. Smith, *Julian's Gods. Religion and Philosophy in the Thought and Action of Julian the Apostate* (London, 1995).

R. Tomlin, "Christianity and the late Roman army," in S. Lieu and D. Montserrat, *Constantine. History, Historiography and Legend* (London, 1998), 21–51.

F. R. Trombley, *Hellenic Religion and Christianization* (2 vols., Leiden, 1993–4).

R. van Dam, *Saints and their Miracles in Late Antique Gaul* (Princeton, 1993).

P. Weiss, "The vision of Constantine," *JRA* 16 (2003), 237–59.

R. L. Wilken, *John Chrysostom and the Jews. Rhetoric and Reality in the Late Fourth Century* (Berkeley, 1983).

R. Williams, *Arius. Heresy and Tradition* (2nd edn. London, 2001).

REGIONS AND ECONOMIES

S. J. B. Barnish, "'The transformation of classical cities and the Pirenne debate," *JRA* 2 (1989), 385–400.

M. O. H. Carver, *Arguments in Stone: Archaeological Research and the European Town in the First Millennium* (Oxford, 1993).

N. Christie and S. T. Loseby, *Towns in Transition. Urban Evolution in Late Antiquity and the Early Middle Ages* (Aldershot, 1996).

A. Giardino (ed.), *Società romana e impero tardoantico vol. 3. Le merci, le insediamenti* (Milan, 1986).

M. F. Hendy, *Studies in the Byzantine Monetary Economy c.300–1450* (Cambridge, 1985); cf. review by F. Millar, *JRS* 78 (1988), 198–202.

R. Hodges and D. Whitehouse, *Mohammed, Charlemagne and the Origins of Europe* (London, 1981).

Hommes et richesses dans l'empire byzantin I, IVᵉ–VIIᵉ siècle (Paris, 1989).

W. Liebeschuetz, *The Decline and Fall of the Roman City* (Oxford, 2001).

M. McCormick, *Origins of the European Economy. Communications and Commerce AD 300–900* (Cambridge, 2002).

J. Rich (ed.), *The City in Late Antiquity* (London, 1992).

C. Wickham, "Marx, Sherlock Holmes and late Roman commerce," *JRS* 78 (1988), 183–93.

Rome

J. Curran, *Pagan City and Christian Capital. Rome in the Fourth Century* (Oxford, 2000).

W. V. Harris (ed.), *The Transformation of Rome in Late Antiquity* (*JRA* Suppl. 33, 1999).

D. Kinney, "Rome," in G. W. Bowersock et al. (eds.), *Late Antiquity. A Guide to the Post-Classical World* (Cambridge Mass., 1999), 673–4.

R. Krautheimer, *Rome: Profile of a City 312–1308* (Princeton, 1980).

B. Lançon, *Rome in Late Antiquity* (Edinburgh, 2000).

C. Pietri, *Roma Christiana* (2 vols, Paris, 1976).

Roma. Dall'Antichità al Medioevo. Archeologia e Storia (Rome, 2001).

Constantinople

J. Bardill, "The great palace of the Byzantine emperors and the Walker Trust excavations," *JRA* 12 (1999), 217–30.

J. Crow, "Investigating the hinterland of Constantinople: Interim report on the Anastasian Long Wall," *JRA* 10 (1997), 235–62.

G. Dagron, *Naissance d'une capitale: Constantinople et ses institutions de 330 à 441* (Paris, 1974).

G. Downey, *Constantinople in the Age of Justinian* (Oklahoma, 1960).

C. Mango, *Le developpement urbain de Constantinople IVe–VIIe siècles* (Paris, 1991).

C. Mango and G. Dagron (eds.), *Constantinople and its Hinterland* (Aldershot, 1995).

A. Ricci, "Constantinople," in G. W. Bowersock et al. (eds.), *Late Antiquity. A Guide to the Post-Classical World* (Cambridge Mass., 1999), 391–2.

L. M. Whitby, "The long walls of Constantinople," *Byzantion* 55 (1985), 560–83.

Alexandria

C. Haas, *Alexandria in Late Antiquity. Topography and Social Conflict* (Baltimore, 1997).

C. Haas, "Alexandria," in G. W. Bowersock et al. (eds.), *Late Antiquity. A Guide to the Post-Classical World* (Cambridge Mass., 1999), 285–7.

J. Mackenzie, "Glimpsing Alexandria from archaeological evidence," *JRA* 16 (2003), 35–63.

J. Mackenzie, S. Gibson, and A. T. Reyes, "Reconstructing the Serapeum in Alexandria from archaeological evidence," *JRS* 94 (2004), 73–121.

Antioch

S. Campbell, *Mosaic Pavements of Antioch* (Toronto, 1988).

G. Dagron, "Un tarif des sportules à payer aux *curiosi* du port de Séleucie de Pisidie," *Travaux et Mémoires* 9 (1985), 435–55.

G. Downey, "The economic crisis at Antioch under Julian the apostate," *Studies in Honour of A. C. Johnson* (Princeton, 1951), 312–21.

G. Downey, *A History of Antioch in Syria from Seleucus to the Arab Conquest* (Princeton, 1961). Abbreviated edn. *Ancient Antioch* (Princeton, 1963).

A. J. Festugière, *Antioche paienne et chrétienne: Libanius, Chrysostome et les moines de Syrie* (Paris, 1959).

H. Kennedy, "Antioch: From Byzantine to Islam and back again," in J. Rich (ed.), *The City in Late Antiquity* (London, 1992), 181–98.

C. Kontoleon (ed.), *Antioch. The Last Ancient City* (Princeton, 2001).

J. Lassus, "Antioch on the Orontes," *Princeton Encyclopedia of Classical Sites* (Princeton, 1976), 61–3.

W. Liebeschuetz, *Antioch. City and Imperial Administration in the Later Roman Empire* (Oxford, 1972).

P. Petit, *Libanius et la vie municipale à Antioche au IVe siècle après J.-C.* (Paris, 1955), 305–22.

I. Sandwell and J. Huskinson (eds.), *Culture and Society in Later Roman Antioch* (Oxford, 2004).

L. M. Whitby, "Procopius and Antioch," in D. French and C. S. Lightfoot (eds.), *The Eastern Frontier of the Roman Empire* (2 vols., Oxford, 1989), 537–53.

The Near East

K. Butcher, *Roman Syria and the Near East* (London, 2003), 135–79.

H. C. Butler, *Early Churches in Syria. Fourth to Seventh Centuries* (Princeton, 1929, repr. Amsterdam, 1969).

M. O. H. Carver, "Transitions to Islam: Urban roles in the east and south Mediterranean, fifth to tenth centuries AD," in N. Christie and S. T. Loseby, *Towns in Transition. Urban Evolution in Late Antiquity and the Early Middle Ages* (Aldershot, 1996), 184–212.

P. Casey, "Justinian, the *limitanei*, and Arab-Byzantine relations in the sixth century," *JRA* 9 (1996), 214–22.

M. Decker, "Food for an empire: Wine and oil production in North Syria," in S. Kingsley and M. Decker (eds.), *Economy and Exchange in the East Mediterranean During Late Antiquity* (Oxford, 2001), 69–86.

C. Foss, "The near eastern countryside in late antiquity: A review article," in J. Humphreys (ed.), *The Roman and Byzantine Near East. Some Recent Archaeological Research* (Michigan, 1995), 213–34.

C. Foss, "Syria in transition AD 550–750. An archaeological approach," *Dumbarton Oaks Papers* 51 (1997), 189–269.

C. Foss, "Urban and rural housing in Syria," *JRA* 13 (2000), 796–800 (review rticle).

E. K. Fowden, *The Barbarian Plain. Saint Sergius between Rome and Iran* (Berkeley, 1999).

P.-L. Gatier, "Villages du Proche-Orient protobyzantin," in G. King and A. Cameron (eds.), *The Byzantine and Early Islamic Near East* (Princeton, 1994), 17–48.

C. A. M. Glucker, *The City of Gaza in the Roman and Byzantine Periods* (Oxford, 1987).

L. J. Hall, *Roman Berytus: Beirut in Late Antiquity* (London and New York, 2004).

Y. Hirschfeld, *The Palestinian Dwelling in the Roman-Byzantine Period* (Jerusalem, 1995).

Y. Hirschfeld, "Social aspects of the late-antique village of Shivta (Negev)," *JRA* 16 (2003), 395–408.

A. Hoffmann and S. Kerner (eds.), *Gadara-Gerasa und die Dekapolis* (Antike Welt Sonderband, Mainz, 2002).

H. Kennedy, "From polis to medina: Urban change in late antique and early Islamic Syria," *Past and Present* 106 (1985), 3–27.

H. Kennedy, "The last century of Byzantine Syria: A reinterpretation," *Byzantinische Forschungen* 10 (1985), 141–54.

H. Kennedy and W. Liebeschuetz, "Antioch and the villages of northern Syria in the fifth and sixth centuries: Trends and problems," *Nottingham Medieval Studies* 32 (1988), 65–90.

M. Konrad, "Research on the Roman and early Byzantine frontier in North Syria," *JRA* 12 (1999), 392–410.

W. Liebeschuetz, "Late late antiquity in the cities of the Roman Near East," *Mediterraneo Antico (economie società culture)* 3 (2000), 43–75.

P. Mayerson, *The Ancient Agricultural Systems of Nessana and the Central Negeb* (London, 1960).

I. Pena, *The Christian Art of Byzantine Syria* (Eng. trans. Reading, 1996).

C. Strube, *Die "toten Städte." Stadt und Land in Nordsyrien in der Spätantike* (Mainz, 1996).

G. Tate, *Les campagnes de Syrie du Nord* I (Paris, 1992).

G. Tchalenko, *Villages antiques de la Syrie du Nord* I–III (Paris, 1958).

F. Villeneuve, "L'économie rurale et la vie des campagnes dans le Hauran antique," in J. M. Dentzer (ed.), *Hauran* I (Paris, 1986), 63–129.

A. Walmsley, "Byzantine Palestine and Arabia: Urban prosperity in late antiquity," in N. Christie and S. T. Loseby, *Towns in Transition. Urban Evolution in Late Antiquity and the Early Middle Ages* (Aldershot, 1996), 126–58.

Asia Minor

R. Cormack, "The classical tradition in the Byzantine provincial city: The evidence of Thessalonike and Aphrodisias," *Byzantium and the Classical Tradition* (1981), 103–18.

R. Cormack, "The temple as cathedral," in C. Roueché and K. Erim (eds.), *Aphrodisias Papers: Recent Work on Architecture and Sculpture* (Ann Arbor, 1990), 75–88.

C. Foss, *Byzantine and Turkish Sardis* (Cambridge Mass., 1976).

C. Foss, "Late antique and Byzantine Ankara," *Dumbarton Oaks Papers* 31 (1977), 27–87.

C. Foss, *Ephesus after Antiquity. A Late Antique, Byzantine and Turkish City* (Cambridge Mass., 1979).

C. Foss, *History and Archaeology of Byzantine Asia Minor* (Aldershot, 1990).

C. Foss, "Cities and villages of Lycia in the Life of St Nicholas of Holy Zion," *Greek Orthodox Theological Review* 36 (1991), 303–39.

C. Foss, *Cities, Fortresses and Villages of Byzantine Asia Minor* (Aldershot, 1996).

S. Hill, *The Early Byzantine Churches of Cilicia and Isauria* (Birmingham Byzantine and Ottoman Monographs 1, Birmingham, 1996).

S. Mitchell, *Anatolia. Land, Men, and Gods in Asia Minor* II. *The Rise of the Church* (Oxford, 1993).

S. Mitchell, *Cremna in Pisidia. An Ancient City in Peace and in War* (Wales and London, 1995).

S. Mitchell and M. Waelkens, *Pisidian Antioch. The Site and its Monuments* (Wales and London, 1998).

C. Ratté, "New research on the urban development of Aphrodisias in late antiquity," in D. Parrish (ed.), *Urbanism in Western Asian Minor* (Rhode Island 2001), 117–47.

C. Roueché, *Aphrodisias in Late Antiquity* (*JRS* Monograph no. 5, London, 1989).

C. Roueché, *Performers and Partisans at Aphrodisias in the Roman and Late Roman Periods* (*JRS* Monograph no. 6, London, 1993).

Tabula Imperii Byzantini vols. 2, 4, 5, 7, 9 and 10, covering Cappadocia, Galatia, Lycaonia, Paphlagonia, Cilicia, Isauria, Phrygia, Pisidia, Pamphylia, and Lycia, by M. Restle, F. Hild, H. Hellenkemper, and K. Belke (Vienna, 1981–2004).

Michael Whitby, "Justinian's bridge over the Sangarius and the date of Procopius' *de aedificiis*," *JHS* 105 (1985), 129–48.

The eastern frontier

R. C. Blockley, "The division of Armenia between Rome and the Persians at the end of the fourth century," *Historia* 36 (1987), 222–34.

D. Braund, *Georgia in Antiquity. A History of Colchis and Transcaucasian Iberia 550 BC–AD 562* (Oxford, 1994).

B. Croke and J. Crow, "Procopius and Dara," *JRS* 63 (1983), 143–59.

E. K. Fowden, *The Barbarian Plain. Saint Sergius between Rome and Iran* (Berkeley, 1999).

D. H. French and C. S. Lightfoot, *The Eastern Frontier of the Roman Empire* (2 vols., Oxford, 1989).

G. Greatrex, *Rome and Persia at War 502–532* (Liverpool, 1998).

E. Gren, *Kleinasien und der Ostbalkan in der wirtschaftlichen Entwicklung der römischen Kaiserzeit* (Uppsala, 1942).

J. D. Howard-Johnson, "Procopius, Roman defences north of the Taurus and the new fortress of Citharizon," in D. H. French and C. S. Lightfoot, *The Eastern Frontier of the Roman Empire* I (Oxford, 1989), 203–29.

W. Liebeschuetz, "The defences of Syria in the sixth century," *Studien zu den Militärgrenzen Roms* II (Cologne, 1977), 487–99.

R. W. Thompson, "Armenia in the fifth and sixth century," *CAH* XIV, 662–77.

Michael Whitby, "Procopius and the development of Roman defences in upper Mesopotamia," in P. Freeman and D. Kennedy, *The Defence of the Roman and Byzantine East* (Oxford, 1986), 717–35.

E. Winter, "On the regulation of the eastern frontier of the Roman empire in 298," in D. H. French and C. S Lightfoot (eds.), *The Eastern Frontier of the Roman Empire* II (Oxford, 1989), 555–71.

Egypt

R. Alston, "Urban population in late Roman Egypt and the end of the ancient world," in W. Scheidel (ed.), *Debating Roman Demography* (Leiden, 2001).

R. Alston, *The City in Roman and Byzantine Egypt* (London, 2002).

R. S. Bagnall, *Egypt in Late Antiquity* (Princeton, 1993).

R. Bagnall and D. Rathbone (eds.), *Egypt from Alexander to the Copts. An Archaeological and Historical Guide* (London, 2004).

J. Banaji, *Agrarian Change in Late Antiquity: Gold, Labour, and Aristocratic Dominance* (Oxford, 2001).

A. K. Bowman, *Egypt after the Pharaohs 332 BC–AD 642. From Alexander to the Arab Conquest* (London, 1986).

J. Gascou, "L'Égypte byzantin (284–641)," in C. Morrisson (ed.), *Le monde byzantin* I (2004), 403–36.

D. Kehoe, "Aristocratic dominance in the late Roman agrarian economy and the question of economic growth," *JRA* 16 (2003), 711–19 (review of Banaji, *Agrarian Change in Late Antiquity*).

D. Rathbone, "Village, land and population in Graeco Roman Egypt," *PCPS* 36 (1990), 123–4.

Africa

Averil Cameron, "Byzantine Africa, the literary evidence," in J. Humphrey (ed.), *Excavations at Carthage 1978, conducted by the University of Michigan VII* (Ann Arbor, 1982), 26–92.

A. Carandini, "Pottery and the African economy," in P. Garnsey et al. (eds.), *Trade in the Ancient Economy* (Cambridge, 1983), 145–62.

C. Courtois, *Les Vandales et l'Afrique* (Paris, 1955).

N. Duval, "Quinze ans de recherches archéologiques sur l'antiquité tardive en Afrique du Nord 1975–90," *REA* 92 (1990), 349–87.

N. Duval, "Vingt ans de recherches archéologiques sur l'antiquité tardive en Afrique du Nord 1975–94," *REA* 95 (1993), 583–640.

W. H. C. Frend, *The Archaeology of Early Christianity. A History* (London, 1996).

C. Lepelley, *Les cités de l'Afrique romaine au bas-empire* (2 vols. Paris, 1979, 1981).

C. Lepelley, "The survival and fall of the classical city in late Roman Africa," in *Aspectes de l'Afrique romaine. Les cités, la vie rurale, et le christianisme* (Bari, 2001),

85–104 (originally in J. Rich [ed.], *The City in Late Antiquity* [London 1992], 50–76).

D. J. Mattingly, "Oil for export? A comparison of Libyan, Spanish and Tunisian olive oil production in the Roman empire," *JRA* 1 (1988), 33–56.

D. J. Mattingly, "Olive cultivation and the Albertini tablets," in *L'Africa Romana* 6. 1 (1989), 403–15.

D. J. Mattingly and R. Hitchner, "Roman Africa: An archaeological survey," *JRS* 85 (1995), 165–213.

A. H. Merrill, *Vandals, Romans and Berbers. New Perspectives on Late Antique North Africa* (Aldershot, 2004).

Y. Modéran, "L'établissment territorial des Vandales en Afrique," *Ant. Tard.* 10 (2002), 87–122.

D. Pringle, *The Defence of Byzantine Africa from Justinian to the Arab Conquest* (2 vols., Oxford, 1981).

P. Salama, *Bornes milliaires de l'Afrique Proconsulaire. Un panorama historique du Bas-Empire romain* (Paris, 1987).

B. D. Shaw, *Rulers, Nomads and Christians in Roman North Africa* (Aldershot, 1995).

B. H. Warmington, *The North African Provinces from Diocletian to the Vandal Conquest* (Cambridge, 1954).

Gaul

B. S. Bachrach, "Fifth-century Metz. Late Roman Christian *urbs* or ghost town?" *Ant. Tard.* 10 (2002), 363–81.

J. Drinkwater and H. Elton, *Fifth Century Gaul. A Crisis of Identity?* (Cambridge, 1992).

G. Halsall, *Settlement and Social Organisation. The Merovingian Region of Metz* (Cambridge, 1995).

G. Halsall, "Towns, societies and ideas: The not-so-strange case of late Roman and early Carolingian Metz," in N. Christie and S. T. Loseby, *Towns in Transition. Urban Evolution in Late Antiquity and the Early Middle Ages* (Aldershot, 1996), 235–61.

W. Klingshirn, *Caesarius of Arles. The Making of a Christian Community in Late Antique Gaul* (Cambridge, 1993).

S. Loseby, "Marseilles: A late antique success story?" *JRS* 82 (1992), 165–85.

S. Loseby, "Arles in late antiquity: Gallula Roma Arelate and Urbs Genesii," in N. Christie and S. T. Loseby, *Towns in Transition. Urban Evolution in Late Antiquity and the Early Middle Ages* (Aldershot, 1996), 45–70.

M. Meijmanns, "La topographie de la ville d'Arles durant l'antiquité tardive," *JRA* 12 (1999), 143–67.

H. von Petrikovitz, "Fortifications in the north-western Roman empire from the 3rd to the 5th century," *JRS* 61 (1971), 178–218.

W. Reusch, "Augusta Treverorum," *Princeton Encyclopedia of Classical Sites* (Princeton, 1976), 119–21.

H. Schöneberger, "The Roman frontier in Germany: An archaeological survey," *JRS* 59 (1969), 144–97.

R. Seager, "Roman policy on the Rhine and the Danube in Ammianus," *CQ* 49 (1999), 579–605.

C. Wickham, "Un pas vers le Moyen Âge. Permanences et mutations," in P. Ouzoulias et al., *Les campagnes de la Gaule à la fin de l'antiquité* (Colloque Montpellier 1998, publ. Antibes, 2001).

P. van Ossel and P. Ouzoulias, "Rural settlement economy in Northern Gaul in the late empire: An overview and assessment," *JRA* 13 (2000), 133–57.

Italy

P. Arthur, "Some observations on the economy of Bruttium under the later Roman empire," *JRA* 2 (1989), 133–42.
S. J. B. Barnish, "Pigs, plebeians and *potentes*: Rome's economic hinterland c.350–600 AD," *PBSR* 55 (1987), 157–85.
S. J. B. Barnish, "'Transformation and survival in the western senatorial aristocracy c. AD 400–700," *PBSR* 56 (1988), 120–55.
P. S. Barnwell, *Emperors, Prefects and Kings: The Roman West 395–565* (London, 1992).
N. Christie, "The Alps as a frontier (AD 168–774)," *JRA* 4 (1991), 410–30.
N. Christie, *The Lombards* (Oxford, 1995).
B. Ward-Perkins, *From Classical Antiquity to the Middle Ages. Public Building in Northern and Central Italy AD 300–850* (Oxford, 1984).
C. Wickham, *Early Medieval Italy. Central Power and Local Society 400–1000* (London, 1981).

The Danube Region

B. Bavant, "Illyricum," in C. Morrisson (ed.), *Le Monde Byzantin* I, 303–48.
N. Christie, "Towns and peoples on the middle Danube in late antiquity and the early Middle Ages," in N. Christie and S. T. Loseby, *Towns in Transition. Urban Evolution in Late Antiquity and the Early Middle Ages* (Aldershot, 1996), 71–98.
B. Croke, "Hormisdas and the late Roman walls of Thessalonica," *GRBS* 19 (1978), 251–8.
B. Croke, "Thessalonika's early Byzantine palaces," *Byzantion* 51 (1981), 475–83.
F. Curta, *The Making of the Slavs: History and Archaeology of the Lower Danube Region, ca. 500–700* (Cambridge 2001).
T. E. Gregory, "*Kastro* and *diateichisma* as responses to early Byzantine frontier collapse," *Byzantion* 62 (1992), 235–53.
J. Haberl with Christopher Hawkes, "The last of Roman Noricum: St Severin on the Danube," in C. F C. Hawkes and S. Hawkes (eds.), *Greeks, Celts and Romans. Studies in Venture and Resistance* (Towota, 1973), 97–149.
R. L. Hohlfelder (ed.), *City, Town, and Countryside in the Early Byzantine Era* (New York, 1982).
P. Lemerle, *Les plus anciens recueils des miracles de Saint Démétrius et la pénétration des Slaves dans les Balkans* (2 vols., Paris, 1981).
F. Lotter, *Severinus von Noricum. Legende und historische Wirklichkeit* (Stuttgart, 1976)
D. M. Metcalf, "Avar and Slav invasions into the Balkan peninsula (c.575–625): The nature of the numismatic evidence," *JRA* 4 (1991), 140–8.
V. Popovic, "La descente des Koutrigours, des Slaves et Avars vers la mer Égée: le témoignage de l'archéologie," *CRAI* 1978, 596–648.
V. Popovic, "Aux origines de la slavisation des Balkans: la constitution des premières sklavinies macédoniennes vers la fin du Vie siècle," *CRAI* 1980, 230–57.
J. M. Spieser, "Les inscriptions de Thessalonique," *Travaux et Mémoires* 5 (1973), 145–80.

J. M. Spieser, *Thessalonique et ses monuments du IVe au VIe siècles. Contribution à l'étude d'une ville paléochrétienne* (Paris, 1984).

Villes et peuplement dans l' Illyricum Protobyzantin (Collection Ecole Française de Rome 77, 1984).

J. J. Wilkes, *Diocletian's Palace, Split* (Sheffield, 1986).

The Sassanians

Averil Cameron, "Agathias on the Sassanians," *Dumbarton Oaks Papers* 23/4 (1969/ 70), 67–183.

G. Fowden, *Empire to Commonwealth. Consequences of Monotheism in Late Antiquity* (Princeton, 1993).

J. Howard-Johnston, "The two great powers of late antiquity: A comparison," in Averil Cameron (ed.), *The Byzantine and Early Islamic Near East III* (Princeton, 1995), 157–226.

Z. Rubin, "The reforms of Khusro Anushirwan," in Averil Cameron (ed.), *The Byzantine and Early Islamic Near East III* (Princeton, 1995), 227–97.

Michael Whitby, "The Persian king at war," in E. Dabrowa (ed.), *The Roman and Byzantine Army in the East* (Krakow, 1994), 227–63.

E. Winter and B. Dignas, *Rom und das Perserreich. Zwei Weltmächte zwischen Konfrontation und Koexistenz* (Berlin, 2002; English edition in preparation for Cambridge University Press).

THE LATER SIXTH CENTURY

P. Allen, "The Justinianic plague," *Byzantion* 49 (1979), 5–20.

Averil Cameron, "Images of authority: Elites and icons in late sixth century Byzantium," *Past and Present* 84 (1976), 3–35.

Averil Cameron, "The Theotokos in sixth century Constantinople," *JTS* 29 (1978), 79–108.

Averil Cameron (ed.), *The Byzantine and Early Islamic Near East III. States, Resources and Armies* (Princeton, 1995).

Averil Cameron and L. Conrad (eds.), *The Byzantine and Early Islamic Near East I. Problems in the Literary Source Material* (Princeton, 1992).

L. Conrad, "Epidemic disease in central Syria in the late sixth century," *Modern Greek and Byzantine Studies* 18 (1994), 12–58.

J. Durliat, "La peste du VIe siècle," *Hommes et richesses dans l'empire byzantin* (Paris, 1989), 107–19.

D. Keys, *Catastrophe. An Investigation into the Origin of the Modern World* (London, 1999).

M. McCormick, "Bateaux de vie, bateaux de mort, maladie, commerce, transports annonaires et le passage économique du Bas-Empire au Moyen-Age," *Morfologie sociali e culturali di Europa fra tarda antichità e alto medioevo* (Spoleto, 1998), 35–122.

M. Meier, *Das andere Zeitalter Justinians. Kontingenzerfahrung und Kontingenzbewältigung im 6. Jht. n. Chr.* (Göttingen, 2003).

H. Pirenne, *Mohammed and Charlemagne* (English trans. London, 1937).

D. Stathakopoulos, "The Justinianic plague revisited," *Byzantine and Modern Greek Studies* 24 (2000), 256–76.

M. Whittow, *The Making of Byzantium 600–1025* (London, 1996).

HERACLIUS AND THE FINAL WARS WITH PERSIA

Averil Cameron, "The Virgin's robe: An episode in the history of early seventh-century Constantinople," *Byzantion* 49 (1979), 42–56.

C. Foss, "The Persians in Asia Minor and the end of antiquity," *EHR* 90 (1975), 721–47.

C. Foss, "The Persians in the Roman Near East," *Journal of the Royal Asiatic Society* 13 (2003), 149–70.

J. Howard-Johnston, "The siege of Constantinople in 626," in C. Mango and G. Dagron (eds.), *Constantinople and its Hinterland* (Aldershot, 1985), 131–42.

J. Howard-Johnston, "The official history of Heraclius' Persian campaigns," in E. Dabrowa (ed.), *The Roman and Byzantine Army in the East* (Krakow, 1994), 57–87.

J. Howard-Johnston, "Heraclius' Persian campaigns and the revival of the East Roman Empire, 622–30," *War in History* 6. 1 (1999), 1–44.

W. E. Kaegi, *Heraclius, Emperor of Byzantium* (Cambridge, 2003).

G. J. Reinink and B. H. Stolte (eds.), *The Reign of Heraclius (610–41). Crisis and Confrontation* (Leiden, 2002).

J. Russell, "The Persian invasion of Syria/Palestine and Asia Minor in the reign of Heraclius: Archaeological and numismatic evidence," in E. Kountoura-Galake (ed.), *The Dark Centuries of Byzantium (7th–9th cent.)* (Athens, 2001), 41–71.

Mary Whitby, "A new image for a new age: George of Pisidia on the emperor Heraclius," in E. Dabrowa (ed.), *The Roman and Byzantine Army in the East* (Krakow, 1994), 197–225.

ISLAM

R. W. Bulliet, *The Camel and the Wheel* (Cambridge Mass., 1975).

A. J. Butler, *The Arab Conquest of Egypt and the Last Thirty Years of the Roman Dominion* (rev. edn. by P. M. Fraser, Oxford, 1978).

P. Crone, *Slaves on Horses. The Evolution of the Islamic Polity* (Cambridge, 1980).

F. M. Donner, *The Early Islamic Conquests* (Princeton, 1981).

F. M. Donner, *Narratives of Islamic Origins. The Beginnings of Islamic Historical Writing* (Princeton, 1998).

R. Hoyland, *Seeing Islam as Others Saw It. A Survey and Evaluation of Christian, Jewish and Zoroastrian Writings on Early Islam* (Princeton, 1997).

W. E. Kaegi, *Byzantium and the Early Islamic Conquests* (Cambridge, 1992).

Chronological List of Emperors and Other Rulers

Roman emperors (Augusti)

284–305	Diocletian		*Main usurpers*		
286–305	Maximian	289–93	Carausius		
305–6	Constantius I	293–6	Allectus		
305–11	Galerius				
306–7	Severus				
306–37	Constantine I	306–12	Maxentius		
308–24	Licinius	307–10	Maximian		
310–13	Maximinus				
337–40	Constantine II				
337–50	Constans	350–3	Magnentius		
337–61	Constantius II	350	Vetranio		
361–3	Julian				
363–4	Jovian				
364–75	Valentinian I	365–6	Procopius		
364–78	Valens				
367–83	Gratian				
375–92	Valentinian II	383–8	Magnus Maximus		
379–95	Theodosius I	392–4	Eugenius		
383–408	Arcadius (East)				
393–423	Honorius (West)	407–11	Constantine III		
408–50	Theodosius II (East)				
425–55	Valentinian III (West)				

Sassanian rulers (simplified)

224–40	Ardashir I
240–72	Shapur I
272–3	Hormizd I
273–6	Bahram I
276–93	Bahram II
293	Bahram III
293–302	Narses
302–9	Hormizd II
309–79	Shapur II
379–83	Ardashir II
383–8	Shapur III
388–99	Bahram IV
399–420	Yazdgird I
420–39	Bahram V (Gur)
439–57	Yazgird II

		Western emperors appointed from the East			
450–7	Marcian	455–6	Avitus	457–9	Hormizd III
		457–61	Majorian		
		461–5	Severus		
457–74	Leo I	467–72	Anthemius	459–84	Peroz
		472	Olybrius		
474–91	Zeno	473–5	Julius Nepos	484–8	Balash
		475–6	Romulus (Augustulus)	488–96	Kavad I
		Kings in Italy		496–8	Zamasp
491–518	Anastasius	476–93	Odoacar	499–531	Kavad I (resumed)
518–27	Justin I	493–526	Theoderic (Ostrogoth)	531–79	Khusro I (Anosirvan)
527–65	Justinian	526–34	Athalaric	579–90	Hormizd IV
		534–6	Theodahat	590–628	Khusro II
565–78	Justin II	536–40	Vitigis	628	Kavad Siroe
578–82	Tiberius II	540–1	Hildebad	628–30	Ardashir III
582–602	Maurice	540–52	Totila	630–1	Numerous usurpers
602–10	Phocas	552	Teja	631–3	Khusro IV
610–41	Heraclius			633–51	Yazdgird III

Index

Figures in *italic* refer to maps or photographic illustrations, diagrams or tables. For reasons of space, people and places are selectively indexed.

Mundus, commander in the E. 13, 138, 143
Mursa, battle in 353 49, 70, *71*, 358

Nag-Hammadi Gnostic library 238
Naissus, in Lower Moesia *50*, 62, *71*, *126*, 201, 265, 360–1
names, personal 179, 186; Aurelius 179; Flavius 179, 215
Naples *126*, *149*, 377; siege in 6C 143–4, 145
Narbonne, in Gaul *90*, 204, 205
Narses, military commander 138, 146, 185, 371, 384–5
naval warfare, navies: Adriatic fleet 356; Belisarius' expedition to Africa 141–2; Black Sea fleet 358; Danube fleet 199; expedition of Heraclius 411; expedition against Vandals in 468 116, 117; naval raids in Gothic War 384; of Theodosius II 112–13; *see also* transport, maritime; trade: by sea
Nebridius, friend of Augustine 271
Nedao River, in Pannonia, battle in 457 114
Negev region, in Palestine 334
Neoplatonism 22, 74, 131, 264, 268, 269, 270–1
Nessana, in Palestine 334, 374
Nestorius, bishop of Constantinople 108, 235, 290, 291
Nicaea, in Bithynia 51; council in 325 69, 236, 243, 248, 273, 278, 283–8
Nicomedia, in Bithynia *50*, 65–6, *90*, *126*, 264, 314
Nicopolis, in Moesia *133*, 195
Niebelunglied, saga of Burgundians 208
Nihavand, battle in 642 420
Nika riot in Constantinople 134–40, 380
Nile Valley 319, 412; *see also* Egypt
Nineveh, battle of in 627 414
Nisibis, in Mesopotamia 51, 53, 70, 78, *126*, *133*, *149*, *388*; frontier city 123–4, 133, 338; Roman defeat in 573 396
Nonnus, poet 229, 344
Noricum (province) *71*, 362

Notitia Dignitatum (catalogue of ranks) 36, 166, *182*, 363; of Constantinople 36, 314, 316; of Rome 36, 310
Nubel, king of Mauretania 82
Numerian (M. Aurelius Numerianus), emperor 47–8
Numidia 112, 113, 200, 280, 321

Odoacar, king of Italy 102, 116, 107, 119–20, 145, 197, 211, 215
offices and ranks: *assessor* (legal advisor) 26; in civil government *175*; *clarissimi* (lower-ranking senators) 183, 184; *coloni* (farmers) 86, *182*; *comes* (minister, count) 114, 116, 125, 157, *175*, 219; consuls 184, 308; *consulares* (former consuls) 183; *curiales*, *decuriones* (members of city councils) *182*, 183; *defensor civitatis* 324; denote social group 184; equestrian rank 183; *flamen* (imperial cult) 275; hereditary 183–4; *honorati 182*; *illustres 182*, 183–4; inflation of 183; *iudex* (provincial governor) *174*, 183; *magister officiorum* (master of offices) *175*; military 165, 167, *167*; *patricius* 119, 125, 210, 215, 359; *plebs, plebei* 159, *182*, 308; *praepositus sacro cubiculi 175*; praetor 157, 171, *174*; prefect 36, 157, 171, *175*, 177, 183, 262, 308, 317; proconsul 262; *quaestor* 157, *175*, 308; *rhetor* (public orator) 269; senator 183–4; *servus* (slave) *182*; social hierarchy *182*; *spectabiles 182*, 184; vicar (of diocese) 174
Olybrius, usurper 116
Olympiodorus of Thebes, historian 23, 24, 31–2, 93, 167, 198, 308
Olympius, *magister officiorum* 93, 94
Olympius, philosopher of Alexandria 250, 310
Onoulph, brother of Odoacar 119, 362
Optatus, Aurelius, prefect 60, 68, 260–1; *On the Schism of the Donatists* 280
oracles 25, 65, 233
Orbigo River, battle of in 456 205
Orestes, Pannonian officer 116, 119
Oriens (diocese) *90*, 330